To the Student: A Study Guide for this textbook is available through your college bookstore under the title Study Guide to accompany Legal Environment of Business 3rd edition by Michael P. Litka and James E. Inman. The Study Guide can help you with course material by acting as a tutorial, review, and study aid. If the Study Guide is not in stock, ask the bookstore manager to order a copy for you.

THE LEGAL ENVIRONMENT OF BUSINESS

public and private laws

Business Law Textbooks from John Wiley and Sons

THE LEGAL ENVIRONMENT OF BUSINESS

public and private laws

Michael P. Litka / James E. Inman

The University of Akron
College of Business Administration

3rd edition

John Wiley & Sons

New York / Chichester / Brisbane / Toronto / Singapore

cover art: THE BETTMANN ARCHIVE, INC.

Library of Congress Cataloging in Publication Data:

Litka, Michael P.
The legal environment of business.

Includes index.
1. Commercial law—United States—Cases.
I. Inman, James E. II. Title.
KF888.L58 1983 346.73'07 82-20226
ISBN 0-471-87455-8 347.3067

Printed in the United States of America

10 9 8 7 6 5 4 3 2 1

about the authors

Professor Litka received an undergraduate degree from Grinnell College and M.A. and J.D. degrees from the State University of Iowa. He has held teaching positions at the University of Missouri at Columbia, Southern Illinois University, and Notre Dame. Professor Litka presently is head of the Finance Department at the University of Akron. He is an active member of regional and national business law associations and is past president of the American Business Law Association. He has done considerable work in the area of academic due process. He has written *Business Law* with Marianne Jennings, *Real Estate Law* with William L. Atteberry and Karl G. Pearson, and *Contemporary Incidents in Real Estate* with Karl Shilliff.

Professor Inman received an undergraduate degree in business administration from Baldwin-Wallace College, an M.B.A. degree in finance from The Ohio State University, and a J.D. from the University of Akron. Professor Inman is currently the Director of Graduate Programs in Business at the University of Akron. He previously served for six years as Editor of the *Akron Business & Economic Review* and four years as a staff editor of the *American Business Law Journal.* He is a member of the Ohio Bar and the American Business Law Association. For over a decade, he has served as a labor arbitrator for the northeastern Ohio steel industry. He has written articles appearing in *Business Law Review, Atlanta Economic Review,* and *American Business Law Journal.* He is a frequent lecturer in management seminars in the field of government regulations and environmental affairs of business.

preface

The Legal Environment of Business: Public and Private Laws covers a wide field of legal topics that especially concern business persons and business institutions. This book encompasses those areas of the law that the reader should have a knowledge of in order to better understand the environment in which decisions are formulated that affect both individual rights and business transactions. We have stressed a conceptual view of the law, emphasizing the notion that law should be presented as a process and with concepts, rather than with a "rule" orientation. An additional purpose is to demonstrate that the different areas of law are interrelated and that the reader, in order to develop an understanding of any one of these areas, must necessarily acquire some knowledge about other areas.

It is not possible to present all the legal principles in depth. Therefore, a broad environmental approach is useful as an introduction to legal reasoning in those vast areas of law where there is not enough time for the principles approach. However, we are of the opinion that complete abandonment of traditional business law subjects in an environmental text is inadvisable because many business students are only exposed to a course in law once. Consequently, basic understanding of public policy positions in the substantive areas of business law is treated in a conceptual fashion; this text thus offers an alternative for those instructors who prefer coverage of traditional business law subjects in a conceptual approach.

The environmental approach of *The Legal Environment of Business* was prepared with three major pedagogical principles in mind. First, the text includes a sufficiently broad and descriptive coverage of the substantive, administrative, and institutional aspects of law to equip students with basic knowledge of the legal environment in which business must operate. Second, the student is not "spoon-fed" with "black-letter" rules. The extensive use of court opinions followed by questions that test the student's understanding requires student comprehension and analysis. Insights are thereby developed in legal reasoning. Student synthesis of a series of cases leads to identification of trends in the policy of the law. Student evaluation of public policy is also encouraged. These aspects of legal reasoning, trend identification, and policy evaluation are consistently utilized throughout. Finally, the text attempts to instill in the reader an appreciation for the dynamic qualities of law. Student appreciation of the dynamic quality of both the legal process and the government-business relationship is essential in the formulation of modern managerial philosophy. Executive leadership qualities are fostered through analytical and conceptual study of legal processes and trends, especially when coupled with the development of a value preference for sane and deliberate resolution of public policy in a free atmosphere of public debate of the issues.

The text is divided into four parts. Part One emphasizes materials that are designed to facilitate student understanding of the purposes of law and the legal process. Topics include legal philosophies, judicial and administrative processes, dynamic qualities of law, and constitutional provisions affecting business. These topics comprise all areas of business operations and are woven into the material in subsequent parts. The text tries to stress for the student the changing character of the law as it is influenced by technology, morality, and other social forces. The development of the law is illustrated by a series of chronological and "landmark" decisions that modify or overturn precedents. These decisions emphasize both the successful and frustrating aspects of working "within the system." Some students need to appreciate this orderly process of change if they are to employ it effectively, and others need such illustrations as reassurance of their faith in the American legal system.

In Part Two the various concepts of property and property rights are discussed and contrasted with other decisions that illustrate the evolving laws that restrict the use of private property to the detriment of society. This material is timely and of immense importance to the business community. Other chapters include the traditional business law subjects of contracts, sales, negotiable instruments, secured transactions, and agency and corporate law.

Part Three contains materials that relate the governmental efforts to preserve a competitive economic system. This part scans the historical development of antitrust laws and presents the various opposing viewpoints concerning appropriate antitrust policy. The basic substantive rules relating to the structure of industries and the conduct of firms are discussed.

Part Four concerns government regulation of business. Government regulation has so expanded in recent decades that it now has an enormous impact on business decision making. However, businesspersons and students alike are confused by the myriad of regulatory agencies and are perplexed to discover just what their individual and corporate relationships are to such administrative bodies. Accordingly, the text affords the student the opportunity to gain a basic understanding of the substantive regulations and institutional characteristics of the more important agencies in the legal environment of business.

Besides giving an understanding of laws, the judicial decisions selected for the text often illustrate analytical style. We were also very careful to select decisions that are interesting and enjoyable. The cases were edited to eliminate unnecessary confusion over legal procedures and procedural terminology, yet they still provide the reader with a "feel" for the law. The discipline of law has much intuitive appeal and pragmatic attractiveness. These characteristics are highlighted in the cases and create student interest, which invites additional learning. Students often request additional coursework in law as a direct result of having their intellectual appetites whetted through the use of this environmental approach.

This third edition of *The Legal Environment of Business* has been prepared so that the previous user will recognize the essential attributes of the earlier editions and also appreciate the improvements incorporated into this edition. For example, a chapter on the social responsibilities of business has been added that points out the ethical responsibilities of business that exceed the limited duties imposed by laws. Much international law has also been integrated throughout.

We have used the text in a four-hour semester course and we recommend that instructors select pertinent portions from each of the four parts if a shorter course is necessary. We believe the student should be exposed to each part, even if certain chapters or subchapters must be omitted. The textbook and courses of instruction may be supplemented with the accompanying student study guide that contains numerous questions to test the student's understanding of the text and expand applications of concepts and principles. The problems of the study guide have been carefully prepared and are closely keyed to chapter material. Together, the text and study guide provide unique materials that offer instructors wide flexibility in selecting coverage and in determining subject depth in the design of their courses.

We have been encouraged in our writing by many people and particularly would like to thank David Redle, Robert Shedlarz, and Bernie Winick, University of Akron; John Gray, Loyola College in Maryland; Jan Henkel, University of Georgia; Harold Hotelling, University of Kentucky; Paul Lansing, University of Iowa; Virginia Maurer, University of Florida; David Shaller, University of Missouri; George Spiro, University of Massachusetts–Amherst; William Volz, Wayne State University; and David Warner, Western Washington University.

It is hoped that *The Legal Environment of Business* will provide useful materials for those courses in law that follow the environmental approach. The emphasis is on the concepts of law and the book's contents reflect those areas that are of fundamental importance for every future business manager.

MICHAEL P. LITKA
JAMES E. INMAN

contents

chapter 7 BUSINESS TRANSACTIONS: CONTRACTS 177

chapter 8 BUSINESS ORGANIZATIONS 214

chapter 9 MARKETING TRANSACTIONS 258

part four GOVERNMENT REGULATIONS 457

chapter 16 CONSUMER PROTECTION LAWS 461

chapter 17 SECURITIES REGULATION: THE ISSUING OF SECURITIES 500

chapter 18 SECURITIES REGULATION: THE TRADING OF SECURITIES 528

chapter 19 LABOR-MANAGEMENT RELATIONS LAWS 553

chapter 20 FAIR AND SAFE EMPLOYMENT LAWS 586

chapter 21 ENVIRONMENTAL PROTECTION LAWS 622

table of cases

THE LEGAL ENVIRONMENT OF BUSINESS
public and private laws

part one
THE LEGAL ENVIRONMENT

Historically, each society has its own set of values reflected in the goals that its legal system promotes for the good of its citizens. The substance of the law is attained by recognizing certain interests and defining the legal limits in which they will be permitted to operate. These goals, priorities, and limitations must change as societies evolve and become more complex.

The role of law in American history has been unique. Its legal environment evolved over a period of approximately two centuries and has been fashioned by public policies of three basic eras. It began with English common law which was refined and adopted to meet the problems of a new nation. It was modified by the impact of the Industrial Revolution and its values on American society and faced radical adjustments in the modern era of social awareness and welfare consciousness.

Part One begins with a discussion of legal philosophies and the objectives of the U.S. legal system (Chapter 1). American ideals are explored in the context of the constitutional system of government, and the nature of international law is discussed in relation to legal philosophies.

Legal institutions are created to resolve conflicting priorities which will ultimately occur as individual citizens desire their interests to be promoted over those of other citizens. The availability of legal process ensures an orderly society in the resolution of disputes. Consequently, Part One includes discussions of both the judicial (Chapter 2) and administrative processes (Chapter 3), which provide arenas and procedures for resolving conflict.

The dynamic aspects of the legal process are discussed in Chapter 4. The changing nature of tort law and the judicial powers of interpretation are examined.

Chapter 5 explores the aspects of constitutional law that affect business. The regulatory powers of government are discussed and the protections of the Bill of Rights are reviewed as they relate to business interests.

In total, Part One builds an understanding of the foundations of the legal system in the United States. Its dynamic qualities are explored, and it is hoped that an appreciation for the difficult "balancing" between societal interests and those of the business firm is developed.

chapter 1

LEGAL PHILOSOPHIES

What is law? What are its origin and nature? Who creates or determines law? What are the objectives of a legal system, whether on a national or international level? These might be called jurisprudential or philosophical questions of law. They pose appropriate initial inquiries for the study of the legal environment of a politically organized society and, in some instances, of a society's interaction with other societies. In addition, discussions of legal philosophy provide foundations for better understanding the contemporary legal environment.

The readings in this chapter suggest explanations of the sources, objectives, and functions of law. Each reading represents a different time period, which implies that contemporary legal philosophy has evolved from numerous sources, societies, and scholars. The reader should achieve a broader understanding of the several philosophies of law that exist in American society and comprehend the basic objectives and structure of this legal system. In addition, there is an increasing need to comprehend the meaning of the international legal environment of business.

PHILOSOPHIES OF LAW

Studying jurisprudence or philosophies of law can be a valuable experience. The American judicial decision-making process, for example, devolves considerable discretion on justices as they resolve disputes brought before the courts. Their philosophical tendencies have an impact on their decisions. In other instances, political leaders often argue positions that are premised on a particular legal theory. Philosophical strengths and weaknesses of such political positions can be discerned by understanding more of legal philosophy itself.

Although there are a variety of legal philosophies, a particular few are most often discussed and widely known. An understanding of some of these basic philosophies will help the reader evaluate the impact of legal philosophies on the formulation of "rules" for a society.

LEGAL POSITIVISM: LAW AS THE EXPRESSION OF POLITICAL POWER

Legal positivists argue that law is the command of the highest political authority. To posit means to put, place, or impose something. Hence, legal positivists view law as that which is laid down or "posited" by the highest authority. The nineteenth-century English lawyer, John Austin, wrote, "The subject matter of jurisprudence is positive law . . . law set by political superiors to political inferiors."[1] Legal positivists assert that law is derived from some "basic norm" or superior lawful authority. For example, a judicial decision is lawful if it has been rendered in conformity with the Constitution. The legal positivists, therefore, believe that laws are the logical and consistent rules derived from the "basic norm." The philosophical writings of a positivist are either the logical analysis of a derived rule or the continuous searching for a basic norm on which to base the derived legal rule. The basic norm can take a variety of forms: a constitution, an assembly, a sovereign (king), or a mere acknowledgment of existing authority in some particular code or idea such as the Magna Carta. For example, Hans Kelsen has written the following.

> If we ask why the constitution is valid, perhaps we come upon an older constitution. Ultimately we reach some constitution that is the first historically and that was laid down by an individual usurper or by some kind of assembly. The validity of this first constitution is the last presupposition, the final postulate, upon which the validity of all the norms of our legal order depends.[2]

Legal positivists also believe ethical principles have no relevance to the study of law. Their concern is with the law "as it is" and not with law "as it should be."[3] They believe that value judgments have no place in the study of law.

NATURAL LAW: LAW AS HIGHEST HUMAN REASON OR DIVINE JUSTICE

Natural law theories have their origin in the political thought of the Greeks and its later incorporation into the Roman law. The Greeks conceptualized the *jus naturale,* which meant "the sum of those principles which ought to control human conduct, because founded in the very nature of man as a rational and social being."[4] This was largely synonymous with the Roman concept of law which consisted of those principles which were regarded "as so simple and reasonable that . . . they must be recognized everywhere and by everyone."[5]

Medieval lawyers and theologians added the concept that the law of nature was an expression of the Divine Will. They viewed the ultimate origin and final justification of the law to be God, since the law of nature is that part of God which is discoverable by human reason. They believed that natural law is not only that which is natural but also that which is known through connaturality (by being inborn). As such, natural law is dependent on divine reason and therefore "binds men in conscience, and is the prime foundation of human law[6]". The great English lawyer, Blackstone, reasoned, "The will of the Maker is called the Law of Nature . . . . This law, being . . . dictated by God himself, is obligatory upon all. No human laws are of any validity if contrary to this, as they derive their force and authority from this original."[7] The great Roman lawyer, Cicero, wrote:

> There is in fact a true law—namely, right reason—which is in accordance with nature, applies to all men, and is unchangeable and eternal. By its commands this law summons men to the performance of their duties; by its prohibitions it restrains them from doing wrong. Its commands and prohibitions always influence good men, but are without effect upon the bad. To invalidate this law by human legislation is never morally right, nor is it permissible ever to restrict its operation, and to annul it wholly is impossible. Neither the senate nor the people can absolve us from our obligation to obey this law, and it requires no . . . [great lawyer] to expound and interpret it. It will not lay down one rule at Rome and another at Athens, nor will it be one rule today and another tomorrow. But there will be one law, eternal and unchangeable, binding at all times upon all peoples; and there will be, as it were, one common master and ruler of men, namely God, who is the author of this law, its interpreter, and its sponsor.[8]

J. L. Brierly, in 1928, attempted to distinguish contemporary natural law from the notions expressed by Roman and medieval writers. His writing attempts to establish a variable content for the "absolutes" of natural law.

> When a modern lawyer asks what is reasonable, he looks only for an answer that is valid now and here, and not for one that is finally true; whereas a medieval writer might have said that if ultimate truth eludes our grasp, it is not because it is undiscoverable, but because our reasoning is imperfect. Some modern writers have expressed this difference by saying that what we have a right to believe in today is a law of nature with a *variable content*.[9]

The English lawyer, Sir Frederick Pollock, reasoned that "the law of nature . . . is a living embodiment of the collective reason of civilized mankind."[10] These modern-day natural law philosophers seem to agree with Jerome Hall (1958), who argued that "value is an essential element" in American jurisprudence.[11] Nevertheless, the more modern proponents of natural law reject the notion that the content of natural law is specific, permanent, and unchangeable.

THE HISTORICAL SCHOOL: LAW AS CUSTOM AND TRADITION

German jurists were among the first to state that law is not something that can be developed by a mind that understands and knows law (as in natural law theory) independent of experience. Likewise, to them a rule could not be put forth arbitrarily by a political authority (as in legal positivism). Law was to be understood only in terms of the history of a particular race. Such an approach was clearly a challenge to both the natural law theory and legal positivism. In England, Sir Henry Maine argued that law was formulated in different societies by following certain similar patterns while passing through certain stages.[12] It was the function of the historical school to observe various factors that contribute to the movement of or changes in the law from one stage of development to another. As the great American jurist, Oliver Wendell Holmes, expounded:

> The life of the law has not been logic; it has been experience. The felt necessities of the time, the prevelant moral and political theories, intuitions of public policy, avowed or unconscious, even the prejudices which judges share with their fellow men, have had a good deal more to do than the syllogism in determining the rules by which men should be governed. The law embodies the story of a nation's development through many centuries, and it cannot be dealt with as if it contained only the axioms and corollaries of a book of mathematics. In order to know what it is, we must know what it has been, and what it tends to become. We must alternately consult history and existing theories of legislation. But the most difficult labor will be to understand the combination of the two into new products at every stage. The substance of the law at any given time pretty nearly corresponds, so far as it goes, with what is then understood to be convenient; but its form and machinery, and the degree to which it is able to work out desired results, depend very much upon its past.[13]

INSTRUMENTALISM: LAW AS AN INSTRUMENT OF SOCIAL ORDER

The historical school of legal philosophy resulted in many derivative philosophies. One such derived philosophy could be labeled *instrumentalism.* A modern exponent of instrumentalism is Wolfgang Friedmann who wrote that "law is not a brooding omnipresence in the sky, but a flexible instrument of social order, dependent on the political values of the society which it purports to regulate." Moreover, he contends, "law must . . . respond to social change if it is to fulfill its function as a paramount instrument of social order."[14]

Besides being adaptable to new social conditions, the law, according to instrumentalists, must be understandable to the public so that it will be respected and followed. However, since much of today's law has become so complex and largely unknown to the public, it is the public's faith in the "ideals" of the law that cause them to continue to uphold and respect the law. If the citizens retain their faith that the law is rational and philosophically sound, law will remain an instrument of social order.

In addition, instrumentalists believe law is the pragmatic decision making of the processes that make or enact the law. Karl Llewellyn reasoned as follows:

> This doing of something about disputes, this doing of it reasonably, is the business of law. And the people who have the doing in charge, whether they be judges or sheriffs or clerks or jailers or lawyers, are officials of the law. What these officials do about disputes is, to my mind, the law itself.[15]

A pragmatist follows a trial-and-error methodology to develop an acceptable solution to a social problem. Legal pragmatists likewise use a trial-and-error technique to formulate the most appropriate law. Moreover, the pragmatist views law as a social instrument for the direction and control of individuals and group activities. Bently commented that, "The law at bottom can only be what the mass of people actually does and tends to some extent to make other people do by means of governmental agencies."[16]

Questions

1. How do you define law? Does your definition depend on your legal philosophy? Would the organized mass murders of the Nazi regime qualify as law to the positivist? To the theorist of natural law?
2. If you were the leader of a revolution against a tyrannical government, which legal philosophy would you probably declare to your followers?
3. Can you differentiate between law and justice?
4. Do natural law philosophers think all laws come from "highest reason" or God? What about a traffic law to drive on the right side of the road?
5. Karl Llewellyn's notion that law is created by officials' manipulation of rules is an expression similar to which basic philosophy?

THE OBJECTIVES OF A LEGAL SYSTEM

Although the obvious objective of law is justice, there may be a wide variety of views of what justice is. However, at any point in time, a prevailing social ideology or philosophy will dictate what *ought* to be. The fundamental principles underlying America's conceptions of justice have been derived largely from the preceding schools of legal philosophy.

Legal positivists have taught us that the objectives (what the law ought to achieve) are to be accepted as given by the sovereign political authority or basic law. Positivists will not inquire whether the objectives of the basic law were right or wrong because positivists do not accept the notion of ultimate or enduring values. Instead, they will merely seek consistency of rules with the basic norm. Accordingly, positivists have exerted considerable influence in American law by seeking proper consistency of the rules of government with basic constitutional principles (the basic norm).

On the other hand, constitutional principles have largely been derived from the concepts of natural law and the historical experiences of the English people, because of their respective emphasis on what ought to be and on evolutionary reform. Hence, the experiences of England in its search for "justice" and the values expressed by natural law proponents have had considerable impact on the objectives and purposes of our legal system.

PRESERVATION OF ORDER

Sir Frederick Pollock
The King's Peace

(from *Oxford Lectures and Other Discourses,* 1890)

"Against the peace of Our Lady the Queen, her crown and dignity." This formula was once the necessary conclusion, as it is still the accustomed one, of every indictment for a criminal offence preferred before the Queen's justices. Even to those who have nothing to do with assizes or quarter sessions the Queen's Peace is a familiar term. By the widely spread office of justice of the peace it is brought home to the remotest corners of England. And it seems to us a natural thing that throughout the realm peace should be kept—in other words that unlawful force should be prevented and punished—in the Queen's name and by officers armed with her authority. This does not look, on the face of it, like a fact requiring any special explanation. Our conception of an executive power, under whatever names and in whatever forms it is exercised, is that its first business is to preserve order. And that this power should be one and uniform in every part of a land ruled by the same laws appears to us so far from remarkable that anything contrary to it has the air of a puzzle and an anomaly. Such is our modern point of view, too obvious (one would think) to be worth stating. Yet it is so modern that there was demonstrably a time when it was an innovation. It belongs to the political theory of sovereignty which has superseded the feudal theory of autonomous personal allegiance. It assumes that the rights of private feud and war, rights exercised without contradiction far into the Middle Ages, are for us intolerable and impossible. It assumes, moreover, that a central authority has become strong enough to subdue local competition and jealousy. These conditions have been brought about in Western Christendom only by long processes of growth, strife, and decay. Perhaps examples might be assigned of lands and institutions where even yet they are not wholly fulfilled. The establishment of the king's peace is a portion, and in England no small one, of the historical transformation which has given us the modern in the place of the medieval State . . .

Questions

1. What is the "first business" of executive powers?
2. How far should the executive powers extend? What did the sovereign's power replace? What was necessary before this replacement occurred?
3. Can you identify any similar processes of replacement of local powers by stronger central powers in this country?
4. Will a similar transformation from national powers to a supranational government evolve?

GENERALITY, EQUALITY AND CERTAINTY

Sir Frederick Pollock

(from *A First Book of Jurisprudence,* 1929)

Let us pass on, then, to consider what are the normal and necessary marks, in a civilised commonwealth, of justice administered according to law. They seem capable of being reduced to Generality, Equality, and Certainty. First, as to generality, the rule of justice is a rule for citizens as such. It cannot be a rule merely for the individual; as the medieval glossators put it, there cannot be one law for Peter and another for John. Not that every rule must or can apply to all citizens; there are divers rules for divers conditions and classes of men. An unmarried man is not under the duties of a husband, nor a trader under those of a soldier. But every rule must at least have regard to a class of members of the State, and be binding upon or in respect of that class as determined by some definite position in the community. This will hold however small the class may be, and even if it consists for the time being of only one individual, as is the case with offices held by only one person at a time. Certain rules of law will be found, in almost every country, to apply only to the prince or titular ruler of the State, or to qualify the application of the general law to him. But these rules are not lacking in the quality of generality, for in every case they apply not to the individual person as such, but to the holder of the office for the time being. . . .

Next, the rule of generality cannot be fulfilled unless it is aided by the principle of equality. Rules of law being once declared, the rule must have the like application to all persons and facts coming within it. Respect of persons is incompatible with justice. Law which is the same for Peter and for John must be administered to John and to Peter evenly. The judge is not free to show favour to Peter and disfavour to John. As the maxim has it, equality is equity. So much is obvious and needs no further exposition. But it may be proper to point out that the rule of equality does not exclude judicial discretion. Oftentimes laws are purposely framed so as to give a considerable range of choice to judicial or executive officers as to the times, places, and manner of their application. It is quite commonly left to the judge to assign, up to a prescribed limit, the punishment of proved offences: indeed, the cases in which the court is deprived of discretion are exceptional in all modern systems. . . . Still, a judicial discretion, however wide, is to be exercised without favour and according to the best judgment which the person intrusted with the discretion can form on the merits of each case. Differences of personal character and local circumstances are often quite proper elements in the formation of such a judgment, but any introduction of mere personal favour is an abuse. We still aim at assigning equal results to equal conditions. Judicial discretion is not an exception to the principle of equality, but comes in aid of it where an inflexible rule, omitting to take account of conditions that cannot be defined beforehand, would really work inequality. This implies that only such conditions are counted as are material for the purposes of the rule to be applied. Of course no two persons or events can be fully alike. What rules of law have to do is to select those conditions which are to have consequences of certain kinds: which being done, it is the business of the courts to attend to all those conditions, and, saving judicial discretion where it exists, not to any others. . . . The law cannot make all men equal, but they are equal before the law in the sense that their rights are equally the subject of protection and their duties of enforcement.

Further, as the requirement of generality leads to that of equality, so does the requirement of equality lead to that of certainty. . . . We must administer a general rule, and administer it equally. There can be no law without generality; there can be no just operation of law without equality. But we cannot be sure of a rule being equally administered at different times and in the cases of different persons unless the rule is defined and recorded. Justice ought to be the same for all citizens, so far as the . . . conditions are the same. Now, to carry out this idea the dispenser of justice ought to be adequately furnished with two kinds of information. He should know what is accustomed to be done in like cases, and whenever new conditions occur he should know, or have the means of forming a judgment, which of them are material with a view of legal justice, and which are not. Moreover, there must be some means of securing an approximate uniformity of judgment; otherwise judges and magistrates of all degrees will make every one a law of his own for himself, and the principle of equality will not be satisfied. . . . Hence law becomes an artificial system which is always gathering new material. The controverted points of one generation become the settled rules of the next, and fresh work is built up on them in turn. Thus the law is in a constant process of approximation to an ideal certainty which, by the nature of the case, can never be perfectly attained at any given moment. Everyone who has studied the law knows that the approximation is apt to be a rough one, and is exposed to many disturbing causes. . . . For the practical purposes of a State governed according to law, that degree of certainty suffices which will satisfy the citizens that the law works on the whole justly and without favour . . . .

Questions

1. Pollock's principle of generality is that there "cannot be a rule merely for the individual. . . . But every rule must . . . have regard to a class of members . . . and be binding upon . . . that class." When Pollock says there cannot be one law for Peter and another for John, does he assume Peter and John are alike, that is, in the same class? In other words, may the law discriminate between (or classify) persons so that different laws might be applied to different classes? Could there be a law for Peter and another for John if Peter and John were not alike? Is this answered in Pollock's "divers rules for divers conditions and classes of men"?
2. Distinguish between "generality" and "equality".
3. To facilitate the concept of "equality" under the law, is there any need for judicial discretion?
4. To achieve "certainty" in the administration of law, how are subsequent judges to know what occurred in the past?

THE AMERICAN LEGAL SYSTEM

The philosophical underpinnings of the United States combine English and natural law ideals with American pragmatism and the desire to be ruled by the governed. The American legal system is effective not so much because of its power to levy penalties on those who interfere with the legal rights of others, but because Americans generally believe in the American ideals embodied in their legal system and its evolutionary processes of reform.

AMERICAN IDEALS

Declaration of Independence (1776)

We hold these truths to be self-evident, that all men are created equal; that they are endowed by their Creator with certain unalienable rights, that among these, are life, liberty, and the pursuit of happiness. That, to secure these rights, governments are instituted among men, deriving their just powers from the consent of the governed; that, whenever any form of government becomes destructive of these ends, it is the right of the people to alter or to abolish it, and to institute a new government, laying its foundation on such principles, and organizing its powers in such form, as to them shall seem most likely to effect their safety and happiness. Prudence, indeed, will dictate that goverments long established, should not be changed for light and transient causes; and, accordingly, all experience hath shown, that mankind are more disposed to suffer, while evils are sufferable, than to right themselves by abolishing the forms to which they are accustomed. But, when a long train of abuses and usurpations, pursuing invariably the same object, evinces a design to reduce them under absolute despotism, it is their right, it is their duty, to throw off such government, and to provide new guards for their future security. . . .

Wolfgang Friedmann

(from *Law in a Changing Society,* 1959)

A democratic ideal of justice must rest on the three foundations of equality, liberty and ultimate control of the government by the people. It is, however, far from easy to give these concepts a specific content.

. . . We can still not formulate the principle of equality in more specific terms than Aristotle who said that justice meant the equal treatment of those who are equal before the law. We can give to this apparent tautology a more concrete meaning by saying that a democratic ideal of justice demands that inequalities shall be inequalities of function and service but shall not be derived from distinctions based on race, religion, or other personal attributes . . . .

The meaning of "liberty" is hardly more easy to define. In terms of a democratic ideal of justice, liberty means certain rights of personal freedom which must be secure from interference by government. They include legal protection from arbitrary arrest, freedom of opinion and association, of contract, labour and many others. Briefly, they may be subsumed under the two broad categories of the freedom of the person and the freedom of the mind . . . .

Lastly, the principle of control by the people means that law must ultimately be the responsibility of the elected representatives of the people. This is, indeed, a vital principle but it can say little about the technique by which the modern legislator can discharge this function.

Questions

1. What are some of the basic American ideals expressed in these writings?
2. Is it an American ideal to "take up arms" against any government decree which violates one of the American beliefs?

U.S. CONSTITUTION

The Constitution of the United States is the supreme law of the land. One basic objective of this "supreme law" is to allocate governmental power. First, it attempts to allocate governing power between the federal and state governments, the results of which are referred to as *federalism.* Second, the Constitution attempts to allocate governing power between three separate federal departments, that is, the legislative, the executive, and the judicial. A third objective of the Constitution is to protect the civil rights of persons within the United States by designating specific limitations on the powers of government.

FEDERALISM

Many of the colonies had drawn up their own constitutions before the colonies declared war to achieve independence. The purpose of the state constitution was to establish the structure and power of the state government and to set forth limitations on that power. In contrast, the first national constitution (the Articles of Confederation) was in substance a document regulating a league or group of independent states which were joined together but not controlled by the union. Subsequent problems between the states on matters of boundaries and economic affairs led to the creation of a new national constitution which not only specified the structure and powers of the national government but also contained limitations and restrictions on the powers of the state governments. The new national constitution also took away certain powers from the states and gave them to the national government.

Under the Constitution all powers not delegated to the United States or prohibited by the Constitution are reserved to the states. This reservation merely confirms the fact that the states only surrendered to the national government those powers expressly delegated by the Constitution. The states retained the powers of policing, taxation, and eminent domain, as well as other powers that may be exercised by a sovereign. Perhaps the broadest power possessed by the states to control business affairs is the police power, which is defined as the power of the state to enact laws for the health, safety, morals, and general welfare of its citizens. In a general sense, this is the power to govern.

In contrast, the national government has enumerated, limited powers. It may act only on those powers that the Constitution grants to it. State governments, however, possess concurrent powers with the national government when the enumerated national powers are not made exclusively the domain of the national government. As long as a state law does not conflict with any national laws in these areas, the states may concurrently regulate the same subject area. However, when state laws attempt to regulate in an area exclusively delegated to the federal government or when their laws conflict with a federal government regulation in those areas in which concurrent regulation is allowed, state regulations become void. The differing factual issues that may concern the extent of national preemption in the area of concurrent powers often creates conflicting views as to the proper balance of power between the federal and state governments.

Under the Constitution the powers of the national legislative body (Congress) is based on the powers in Article I, Section 8 (see Appendix).

Any federal regulation in the United States raises the preliminary question of whether Congress has the power under its constitutional provisions to enact the legislation. Questions arose as to just how far and to what extent Congress may "regulate commerce . . . among the several states" or make "laws which shall be necessary and proper" for executing its powers. Almost from the outset of national existence, the courts were faced with these questions and in fashioning decisions played a vital role in defining the extent of congressional regulatory powers and, correspondingly, in defining the rules governing private economic affairs. Analysis of the courts' actual decisions on these questions is explored in Chapter 5. At this point, the second major allocation of government power must be reviewed.

SEPARATION OF POWERS

The separation of powers in the Constitution involves the creation of and the vesting of legislative (Article I), executive (Article II), and judicial (Article III) powers of government in three separate and independent branches. The purpose of the separation of powers, in the words of Justice Brandeis, is "not to promote efficiency but to preclude the exercise of arbitrary power. The purpose is, not to avoid frictions, but, by means of the inevitable friction incident to the distribution of the governmental power among the departments, to save the people from autocracy."[17]

Each branch is independent in that persons holding office in one branch do not owe their tenure to the will or preferences of persons in the other branches. Also, the Constitution makes clear that the office in one branch may not usurp or encroach on the powers vested in another branch. However, this constitutional prohibition does not limit the voluntary delegation by the legislature of some of its functions. Because statutes, of necessity, must be drafted in general terms, Congress leaves to the executive, the judiciary, or some administrative agencies the task of making detailed secondary rules to enforce the general mandate expressed in the statute. Also, Congress created courts, such as the Customs Court, and administrative agencies which embody judicial functions that are not within the judicial branch of government. These apparent violations of the separation of powers doctrine have been tolerated by the Supreme Court as a "quasi-judicial" function, different from a purely judicial task (see Chapter 3). These deviations illustrate that the separation of powers is a general constitutional principle or ideal that was never conceived or made operational as a rigid rule. Sometimes the pragmatic desire for efficiency overshadows the ideal constitutional separation of powers, especially where no sacrifice of independence is observed.

CONSTITUTIONAL LIMITATIONS

A third objective of the U.S. Constitution is to protect the civil rights of persons within the United States by designating specific limitations on the powers of government. These limitations protect individuals from arbitrary and unjust treatment by governmental officials. Besides the lesser known limitations contained in the Constitution, such as prohibitions against *ex post facto* laws and bills of attainder, the first 10 Amendments to the Constitution (Bill of Rights) contain the more generally known limitations on governmental powers. The First Amendment contains protections for speech, press, assembly, and religion. Other amendments protect the rights to bear arms and to have jury trials. The Fourth Amendment protects persons from unreasonable searches and seizures. Amendment Five requires the *federal* government to follow "due process of law" before any person's "life, liberty, or property" may be taken. Amendments Thirteen through Fifteen, added after the Civil War, eliminate slavery and require *state* governments, like the federal government, to grant persons "due process of law" before depriving them of life, liberty, or property. If any state officials deny due process of law to any person, the federal judiciary is available to correct the state officials.

JUDICIAL REVIEW

As previously mentioned, the laws of the federal government in those areas enumerated by the Constitution are supreme over conflicting state laws. This supremacy is explicitly stated in Article VI, Clause 2, of the Constitution. However, there is no clause in the Constitution granting supremacy of the judicial branch in determining whether or not an action by another branch (executive or legislative) is constitutional. Accordingly, there have been great debates since the earliest date of the union concerning the right of the judiciary to require the legislative and executive branches to conform to the judiciary's conceptions of constitutional requirements. The power of judicial review of the legislative branch was first asserted in the *Marbury* case.

Marbury v. Madison
5 U.S. (1 Cranch) 137 (1803)
Supreme Court of the United States

[William Marbury was named a Justice of the Peace for the District of Columbia at the close of the administration of President John Adams. The new Jefferson administration through Secretary of State, James Madison, decided against delivering the commission which was not delivered at the end of Adam's term. Marbury filed suit in the Supreme Court of the United States to command (mandamus) Madison to deliver the commission. Marbury's right to sue in the

Supreme Court was authorized by the Judiciary Act of 1789. The Court's decision determined whether this congressional legislation could confer additional judicial power on the Supreme Court when such power had not been granted by the written Constitution.]

Chief Justice Marshall

The [Judiciary] act to establish the judicial courts of the United States authorizes the Supreme Court "to issue writs of mandamus in cases warranted by the principles and usages of law, to any . . . persons holding office, under the authority of the United States."

The Secretary of State, being a person holding an office under the authority of the United States, is precisely within the letter of the description, and if this court is not authorized to issue a writ of mandamus to such an officer, it must be because the law is unconstitutional, and therefore absolutely incapable of conferring the authority, and assigning the duties which its words purport to confer and assign.

The constitution vests the whole judicial power of the United States in one Supreme Court, and such inferior courts as congress shall, from time to time, ordain and establish. This power is expressly extended to all cases arising under the laws of the United States. . . .

In the distribution of this power it is declared that "the Supreme Court shall have original jurisdiction in all cases affecting ambassadors, other public ministers and consuls, and those in which a state shall be a party. In all other cases, the Supreme Court shall have appellate jurisdiction."

* * *

When an instrument organizing fundamentally a judicial system, divides it into one supreme, and so many inferior courts as the legislature may ordain and establish; then enumerates its powers, and proceeds so far to distribute them, as to define the jurisdiction of the Supreme Court by declaring the cases in which it shall take original jurisdiction, and that in others it shall take appellate jurisdiction; the plain import of the words seems to be, that in one class of cases its jurisdiction is original, and not appellate; in the other it is appellate, and not original. . . .

To enable this court, then, to issue a mandamus, it must be shown to be an exercise of appellate jurisdiction, or to be necessary to enable them to exercise appellate jurisdiction.

* * *

It is the essential criterion of appellate jurisdiction, that it revises and corrects the proceedings in a cause already instituted, and does not create that cause. Although, therefore, a mandamus may be directed to courts, yet to issue such a writ to an officer for the delivery of a paper, is in effect the same as to sustain an original action for that paper, and, therefore, seems not to belong to appellate, but to original jurisdiction. . . .

The authority, therefore, given to the Supreme Court, by the act establishing the judicial courts of the United States, to issue writs of mandamus to public officers, appears not to be warranted by the constitution; and it becomes necessary to inquire whether a jurisdiction so conferred can be exercised.

* * *

. . . [T]he people have an original right to establish . . . their . . . government. . . . This original and supreme will organizes the government, and assigns to different departments their respective powers. It may either stop here, or establish certain limits not to be transcended by those departments.

The government of the United States is of the latter description. The powers of the legislature are defined and limited; and that those limits may not be mistaken, or forgotten, the constitution is written. To what purpose are powers limited, and to what purpose is that limitation committed to writing, if these limits may, at any time, be passed by those intended to be restrained? The distinction between a government with limited and unlimited powers is abolished, if those limits do not confine the persons on whom they are imposed. . . .

The constitution is either a superior paramount law, unchangeable by ordinary means, or it is on a level with ordinary legislative acts, and, like other acts, is alterable when the legislature shall please to alter it.

If the former part of the alternative be true, then a legislative act, contrary to the constitution, is not law: if the latter part be true, then written constitutions are absurd attempts on the part of the people, to limit a power, in its own nature, illimitable.

Certainly, all those who have framed written constitutions contemplate them as forming the fundamental and paramount law of the nation, and consequently, the theory of every such government must be that an act of the legislature, repugnant to the constitution, is void.

This theory is essentially attached to a written constitution, and is, consequently, to be considered, by this court, as one of the fundamental principles of our society. . . .

It is, emphatically, the province and duty of the judicial department to say what the law is. Those who apply the rule to particular cases, must of necessity expound and interpret that rule. If two laws conflict with each other, the courts must decide on the operation of each.

* * *

If then, the courts are to regard the constitution, and the constitution is superior to any ordinary act of the legislature, the constitution, and not such ordinary act, must govern the case to which they both apply. . . .

It is also not entirely unworthy of observation, that in declaring what shall be the *supreme* law of the land, the constitution itself is first mentioned; and not the laws of the United States generally, but those only which shall be made in *pursuance* of the constitution, have that rank.

Thus, the particular phraseology of the constitution of the United States confirms and strengthens the principle, supposed to be essential to all written constitutions, that a law repugnant to the constitution is void; and that courts, as well as other departments, are bound by that instrument. . . .

[The Court concluded that the judiciary act was unconstitutional and not to be enforced by the courts. By so ruling, the Court acknowledged itself as the sole and final interpreter of the U.S. Constitution.]

Questions

1. Does the Constitution vest the Supreme Court with original or appellate jurisdiction? Is the issuance of a mandamus order to a public official (which was the authority conferred on the Supreme Court by the judiciary act) an action of original or appellate power?
2. According to Chief Justice Marshall, why was the U.S. Constitution written?
3. Oliver Wendell Holmes in the *Common Law* reminds us of errors often made by students: "that of supposing, because an idea seems very familiar and natural to us, that it has always been so. Many things which we take for granted have had to be laboriously fought out or thought out in past times." Has the judiciary always had the power to declare acts of Congress unconstitutional? Do any precedents exist in England? The English Supreme Court is the House of Lords. Can the House of Lords declare acts of the House of Commons to be null and void because they are unconstitutional? Does England have a written constitution?

INTERNATIONAL LAW

Increasingly, business managers must be concerned with international law. The reality of global markets and foreign competitors forces management to become familiar with the international legal environment, which partly governs the international marketplace. In addition, the study of international law provides interesting opportunities to apply and contrast legal philosophies.

The task of defining what is meant by "international law" is a difficult one. Most of the definitions include a statement that international law is created by agreement between national states. Others conclude that international law is based on customs. One of the often-quoted definitions of international law comes from the case of the *S.S. Lotus* (1927).

> . . . International law governs relations between independent States. The rules of law binding upon States, therefore, emanate from their own free will as expressed in conventions or by usages generally accepted as expressing principles of law and established in order to regulate . . . [their] relations . . . with a view to the achievement of common aims. Restriction upon the independence of States cannot, therefore, be presumed.[18]

Chief Justice Marshall delineated the principal sources of the "laws" of nations when he wrote in *Thirty Hogsheads of Sugar* v. *Boyle* (9 Cranch 191, 197 [1815]).

The law of nations . . . derive[s] . . . rules, . . . which are recognized by all civilized and commercial states throughout Europe and America. This law is in part unwritten, and in part conventional. To ascertain that which is unwritten, we resort to the great principles of reason and justice; but, as these principles will be differently understood by different nations under different circumstances, we consider them as being, in some degree, fixed and rendered stable by a series of judicial decisions. The decisions of the courts of every country, so far as they are founded upon a law common to every country, will be received, not as authority, but with respect. The decisions of the courts of every country show how the law of nations, in the given case, is understood in that country, and will be considered in adopting the rule which is to prevail in . . . [any given case].

Questions

1. Is international law considered "law" by a legal positivist? Must law be enforceable by a political superior to be law?
2. Is international law consistent with the views held by natural law proponents?
3. Would the historical and instrumental schools of legal philosophy accept international law as "law"?
4. What are the sources of international law?

The Schooner Exchange v. M'Faddon

7 Cranch 116 (1812)
Supreme Court of the United States

[On the 24th of August, 1811, John M'Faddon and William Greetham, of the state of Maryland, filed their suit in the District Court of the United States, in Pennsylvania, against the Schooner Exchange, setting forth that they were her sole owners, on the 27th of October, 1809, when she sailed from Baltimore, bound to St. Sebastiana, Spain. That while lawfully and peaceably pursuing her voyage, she was, on the 30th of December, 1810, violently and forcibly taken by certain persons, acting under the decrees and orders of Napoleon, Emperor of France, in violation of the law of nations. That she had been brought into the port of Philadelphia, and was then within the jurisdiction of the court, and in possession of her captain Dennis M. Begon. Finally, they allege that no sentence or decree of condemnation had ever been pronounced against her by any court of competent jurisdiction; and, therefore, the property of the . . . (plaintiffs) in her remained unchanged and in full force.]

Chief Justice Marshall

This case involves the very delicate and important inquiry, whether an American citizen can assert, in an American court, a title to an armed national vessel, found within the waters of the United States.

In exploring an unbeaten path, with few, if any, aids from precedents or written law, the court has found it necessary to rely much on general principles. . . .

The jurisdiction of the nation within its own territory is necessarily exclusive and absolute. It is susceptible of no limitation not imposed by itself. Any restriction upon it, deriving validity from an external source, would imply a diminution of its sovereignty to the extent of the restriction. . . .

All exceptions, therefore, to the full and complete power of a nation within its own territories, must be traced up to the consent of the nation itself. They can flow from no other legitimate source.

This consent may be either express or implied. . . .

* * *

This full and absolute territorial jurisdiction . . . like the attribute of every sovereign . . . would not seem to contemplate foreign sovereigns nor their sovereign rights. . . . One sovereign being in no respect amenable to another; and being bound by obligations of the highest character not to degrade the dignity of his nation, by placing himself or its sovereign rights within the jurisdiction of another, can be supposed to enter a foreign territory only under an express license, or in the confidence that the immunities belonging to his independent sovereign station, though not expressly stipulated, are reserved by implication, and will be extended to him.

This perfect equality and absolute independence of sovereigns, and this common interest impelling them to mutual intercourse, and an interchange of good offices with each other, have given rise to a class of cases in which every sovereign is understood to waive the exercise of a part of that complete exclusive territorial jurisdiction, which has been stated to be the attribute of every nation.

One of these is admitted to be . . . the immunity which all civilized nations allow to foreign ministers . . . [which] is implied from the considerations that, without such exemption, every sovereign would hazard his own dignity by employing a public minister abroad. His minister would owe temporary and local allegiance to a foreign prince and would be less competent to the objects of his mission. A sovereign committing the interests of his nation with a foreign power, to the care of a person whom he has selected for that purpose, cannot intend to subject his minister in any degree to that power; and, therefore, a consent to receive him, implies a consent that he shall possess those privileges which his principal intended he should retain—privileges which are essential to the dignity of his sovereign, and to the duties he is bound to perform.

. . . If . . . [the minister's] crimes be such as to render him amenable to the local jurisdiction, it must be because they forfeit the privileges annexed to his character; and the minister, by violating the conditions under which he was received as the representative of a foreign sovereign, has surrendered the immunities granted on those conditions; or, according to the true meaning of the original assent, has ceased to be entitled to them.

* * *

[After discussion of a rule which prohibits the passage of an army through a foreign territory, the Court concludes that such rule] . . . does not appear to be equally applicable to ships of war entering the ports of a friendly power. The injury inseparable from the march of an army through an inhabited country, and the dangers often, indeed generally, attending it, do not ensue from admitting a ship of war, without special license, into a friendly port. A different rule therefore with respect to this species of military force has been generally adopted. If, for reasons of state, the ports of a nation generally, or any particular ports be closed against vessels of war generally, or the vessels of any particular nation, notice is usually given of such determination. If there be no prohibition, the ports of a friendly nation are considered as open to the public ships of all powers with whom it is at peace, and they are supposed to enter such ports and to remain in them while allowed to remain, under the protection of the government of the place.

* * *

When private individuals of one nation spread themselves through another as business or caprice may direct, mingling indiscriminately with the inhabitants of that other, or when merchant vessels enter for the purposes of trade, it would be obviously inconvenient and dangerous to society, and would subject the laws to continual infraction, and the government to degradation, if such individuals or merchants did not owe temporary and local allegiance, and were not amenable to the jurisdiction of the country. Nor can the foreign sovereign have any motive for wishing such exemption. His subjects thus passing into foreign countries, are not employed by him, nor are they engaged in national pursuits. Consequently, there are powerful motives for not exempting persons of this description from the jurisdiction of the country in which they are found, and no one motive for requiring it. The implied license, therefore, under which they enter can never be construed to grant such exemption.

Upon these principles, by the unanimous consent of nations, a foreigner is amenable to the laws of the place; but certainly in practice, nations have not yet asserted their jurisdiction over the public armed ships of a foreign sovereign entering a port open for their reception.

Without doubt, the sovereign of the place is capable of destroying this . . . [exception]. He may claim and exercise jurisdiction either by employing force, or by subjecting such vessels to the ordinary tribunals. But until such power be exerted in a manner not to be misunderstood, the sovereign cannot be considered as having imparted to the ordinary tribunals a jurisdiction which it would be a breach of faith to exercise.

The arguments in favor of this opinion . . . have been drawn from the general inability of the judicial power to enforce its decisions in cases of this description, from the consideration that the sovereign power of the nation is alone competent to avenge wrongs committed by a sovereign, that the questions to which such wrongs give birth, are rather questions of policy than of law, that they are for diplomatic, rather than legal discussion.

* * *

. . . [T]he Exchange, being a public armed ship, in the service of a foreign sovereign, with whom the government of the United States is at peace, and having entered an American port open for her reception, on the terms on which ships of war are generally permitted to enter the ports of a friendly power, must be considered as having come into the American territory under an implied promise, that while necessarily within it, and demeaning herself in a friendly manner, she should be exempt from the jurisdiction of the . . . [courts of this] country.

Questions

1. Define sovereignty. How are limitations on sovereign power created?
2. Identify some implied exemptions from a nation's jurisdiction.
3. Are American merchants in foreign lands exempt from foreign court jurisdiction?
4. If the legal process is closed to the plaintiff as in *Schooner Exchange,* what recourse is available for solution of problems like those revealed in *Schooner Exchange*?

CONCLUSION

The ultimate source of law varies with one's philosophy of law and determines one's agreement or disagreement with existing rules enforced by the political authority. Yet, beyond these philosophical beliefs of the nature or correctness of law, it can scarcely be doubted that law does serve as an instrument of social policy. It provides a mechanism for assigning priorities and resolving disputes between individuals and between individuals and the society as a whole.

The American system of law is largely the result of prior social experiences whereby legal precedents have been developed. Yet, the law involves a dynamic process by which rules are initially created, subsequently abandoned, or imaginatively adapted to fit new and unique situations of the modern era. Such knowledge and understanding of the nature of law is necessary for all educated persons but is particularly important for the business leaders of tomorrow in our complex regulated society.

CASE PROBLEMS

1. In the early 1970s, Texas had a statute making it a crime to obtain an abortion. In considering the constitutionality of this statute, the Supreme Court stated the following.

   We forthwith acknowledge our awareness of the sensitive and emotional nature of the abortion controversy, of the vigorous opposing views, even among physicians, and of the deep and seemingly absolute convictions that the subject inspires. One's philosophy, one's experiences, one's exposure to the raw edges of human existence, one's religious training, one's attitudes towards life and family and their values, and the moral standards one estalishes and seeks to observe, are all likely to influence and to color one's thinking and conclusions about abortion. . . .

Our task, of course, is to resolve the issue by constitutional measurement free of emotion and predilection.

The court's assertion could best be characterized as an expression of which legal philosophy?

2. Compare the following quotes. Can you identify the legal philosophy of the writer? Which of the systems would you prefer to live under (if either)?

... [T]here will not be different laws at Rome or at Athens, or different laws now and in the future. ... [O]ne eternal and unchangable law (shall) ... be valid for all nations at all times, and there will be one master and ruler, that is, God over us all, for He is the author of this law, its promulgator, and its enforcing judge. Whoever is disobedient is fleeing from himself and denying his human nature, and by reason of this very fact he will suffer the worst penalties, even if he escapes what is commonly considered punishment.

Law is the totality (a) of the rules of conduct, expressing the will of the dominant class and established in legal order, and (b) of customs and rules of community life sanctioned by state authority—their application being guaranteed by the compulsive force of the state in order to guard, secure, and develop social relationships and social orders advantageous and agreeable to the dominant class.

3. In *United States* v. *Nixon* (418 U.S. 683 [1974]) counsel for the president urged under the Separation of Powers Doctrine that the president of the United States should have absolute privileged communication, which precludes the courts from issuing a subpoena for presidential records that may reveal criminal activity. Do you agree?

4. In his book, *The Symbols of Government,* Judge Thurman Arnold wrote the following.

In the science of jurisprudence all of the various ideals which are significant to the man on the street must be given a place. It must prove that the law is certain and at the same time elastic; that it is just, yet benevolent; economically sound, yet morally logical. It must show that the law can be dignified and solemn, and at the same time efficient, universal and fundamental, and a set of particular directions. Jurisprudence must give a place to all of the economic, and also ethical, notions of important competing groups within our society, no matter how far apart these notions may be. In its method, it must make gestures of recognition to the techniques of each separate branch of learning which claims to have any relation with the conduct of individuals, no matter now different these techniques may be.

Such a task can only be accomplished by ceremony, and hence the writings of jurisprudence should be considered as ceremonial observances rather than as scientific observances. This is shown by the fact that the literature of jurisprudence performs its social task most effectively for those who encourage it, praise it, but do not read it. For those who study it today it is nothing but a troubling mass of conflicting ideas. However, it is not generally read, so that its troubles are known only to the few people who read it for the purpose or writing more of it. For most of those who reverence the law, the knowledge that there is a constant search going on for logical principles is sufficient.

> . . . There is comfort in such a literature, but there is no progress and no discovery.

To Arnold, what is the value of jurisprudential writings?

END NOTES

1. John Austin, *Lectures on Jurisprudence or the Philosophy of Positive Law,* rev. and ed. Robert Campbell, 2 vols., 5th ed. (London: John Murray, 1929), vol. 1, p. 86.
2. Hans Kelsen, *General Theory of Laws and State* (Cambridge, Mass.: Harvard University Press, 1945), p. 115.
3. J. J. Liefhafsky, *American Government and Business* (New York: Wiley, 1971), p. 33.
4. J. L. Brierly, *The Law of Nations* (London: Oxford University Press, 1928), p. 10.
5. Ibid.
6. Jacques Maritain, *The Range of Reason* (New York: Scribner's, 1952), p. 28.
7. Sir William Blackstone, *Commentaries on the Laws of England,* ed. William Hardcastle Browne (New York: L. K. Strouse, 1892), pp. 7–8.
8. Cicero, *On the Common Wealth,* trans. Sabine and Smith (Indianapolis, Ind.: Bobbs-Merrill, 1976), pp. 215–16.
9. Brierly, *Law of Nations,* pp. 14–15 (author's italics).
10. Frederick Pollock, "The Law of Reason," I *Mich. L. Rev.* 173 (1903).
11. Jerome Hall, *Studies in Jurisprudence and Criminal Theory* (New York: Oceana Pub., 1958), p. 14.
12. Sir Henry Maine, *Ancient Law: Its Connection with the Early History of Society and Its Relation to Modern Ideas,* with Sir Frederick Pollock's Notes (London: John Murray, 1906), chap. 2.
13. O. W. Holmes, *The Common Law* (Boston: Little, Brown & Co., 1881), pp. 1–2.
14. W. Friedmann, *Law in a Changing Society* (London: Stivens and Sons, and Berkeley: University of California Press, 1959), p. ix.
15. Karl Llewellyn, *The Bramble Bush* (New York: Oceana Pub., 1951), p. 91.
16. Arthur F. Bently, *The Process of Government* (Bloomington, Ind.: Principia Press, 1935), p. 276.
17. *Myers* v. *U.S.,* 272 U.S. 52 (1926), Justice Brandeis's dissent at p. 293.
18. *S.S. Lotus* (France v. Turkey), Per. Ct. Int. Jus., Judg. 9, Sept. 7, 1927, Ser. A, No. 10, p. 18.

chapter 2

THE JUDICIAL PROCESS

The judicial process is a system of regularized and institutionalized procedures for resolving public and private disputes. The basic elements of this process are the courts, the jury, the judge, the procedures, and the adversary system. The courthouse may be described as the arena provided by an organized society for resolving controversy. Each participant acts out his or her part in this arena. The function of the jurors is to determine the facts from which the controversy arose. Collectively, the jury must decide which of the opposing versions alleged and testified to is correct. Thus, the jury is the "finder" of the facts.

The judge is normally not allowed to interfere with the jury's fact-finding process. The judge is, however, the sole authority on the law which is to be applied to the facts as the jury found them. In addition, the judge directs the pace of the litigation and administers the rules of procedures. Procedural rules provide the guidelines for the orderly operation of the courts.

The adversary system activates the judicial process. The parties to the controversy, through their lawyers, have the obligation to investigate, initiate, and maintain the litigation. The court has no other means of obtaining the necessary information to resolve the controversy. The lawyers for each side must select the evidence essential to their cause. They attempt to present evidence which will convince the jury that their version of the facts is correct. The lawyers plan the sequence of the presentation of their witnesses, the questions that will be raised, and the evidence that will be needed to substantiate their claim. The theory of the adversary system is that the best decision will be rendered by the judge or jury if the parties presenting their views are real adversaries. If the parties have a real stake in the outcome of the case, they will present their case in a manner most favorable to their claim. Accordingly, the judge and jury can reach a better decision after having heard the best arguments on each side of the controversy.

The following materials emphasize the basic elements of the judicial process. These readings should assist the student in understanding the process of solving a legal controversy.

COURT SYSTEMS

A general familiarity with the court systems is necessary to understand the adjudicatory process. Initially, one should recognize that there is a distinction between a trial court and an appellate court. Trial courts, or courts of original jurisdiction, are courts where the cases are first heard and decided. It is in this arena that the opposing parties present their evidence and the jury determines its verdict. Ordinarily, a single judge presides over this hearing.

Although most cases go no further than the trial court, a party dissatisfied with the outcome of the trial may usually request an appellate court to review the process and decisions of the trial court. The appellate court ordinarily consists of a number of judges who read the record or transcript of the proceedings in the trial court and review the legal briefs filed by counsel outlining the supposed error that occurred in the trial court. The appellate court justices make their decisions from these written records and legal briefs. There are no new trials before the appellate courts. Rather, the appellate court will determine whether the lower court misinterpreted the law or committed some procedural error which necessitates a new trial in the lower court.

Each of the 50 states of the United States has its own court system. There are many differences in functions and labels given to the trial courts in the various states. Each state also has at least one appellate court. Some states provide intermediate appellate courts to relieve the highest appellate court of an excessive workload of appeal requests.

The federal court system is comparatively simple. The basic trial court at the

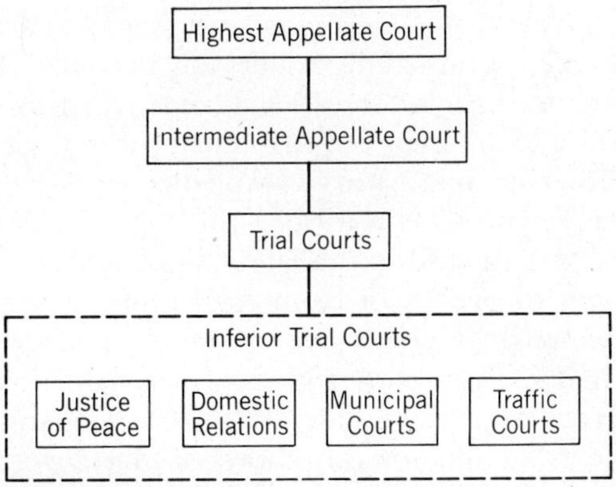

Figure 2-1. State court systems.

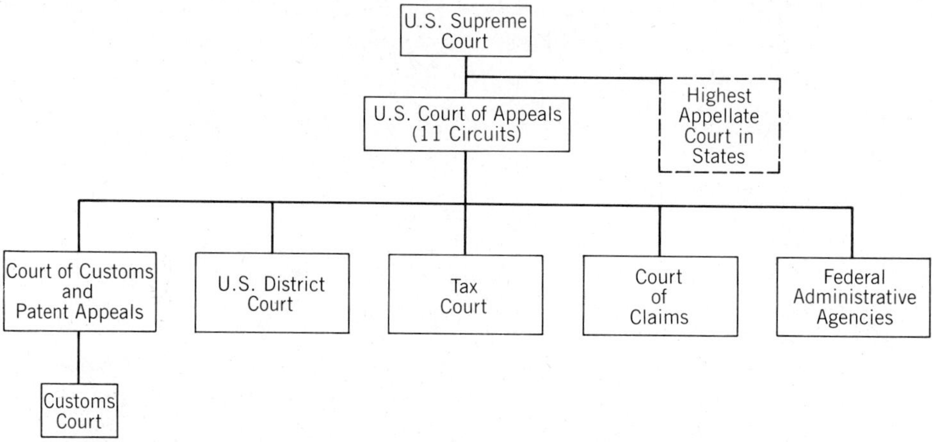

Figure 2-2. Federal court system.

federal level is the U.S. District Court. Appeals from these district courts are taken to the U.S. Court of Appeals which is divided into eleven circuits. Each circuit court hears appeals from decisions of district courts in its circuit. The highest appellate court in the federal system is the Supreme Court of the United States. Some cases can be appealed to the Supreme Court as a *right* granted in legislation. The Supreme Court may also select cases that it regards as of particular public importance for its determination by granting special permission through the *writ of certiorari*. Since legislative rights to appeal are infrequent, litigants cannot normally force the Supreme Court to hear their appeal.

PROCEDURAL DUE PROCESS

The states maintain courts in which individuals may seek appropriate legal remedies when their lawful rights have been violated. Each court is governed by procedural rules which seek to ensure that any party that properly comes before the court will be granted his or her "day in court." The rules of the court provide for a systematic resolution of legal controversies. The rules may vary from one court system to another, but they must comply with U.S. constitutional requirements. However, mandatory compliance with the U.S. Constitution has not always been required. Historically, the Bill of Rights and its protections for the individual were added to the U.S. Constitution to limit the power of the *federal* government to prevent it from exercising an oppressive power similar to the crown's exercise of power over its subjects in the colonies. Each of the states already had its own constitution, which afforded similar protections to state citizens from oppressive state action. Consequently, the Bill of Rights was not applicable as a limitation on powers of *state* government.

After the Civil War, however, the Fourteenth Amendment was added to the U.S. Constitution to limit the power of *state* governments and to ensure the power of the federal government to protect individuals in certain instances from state governments. This amendment's basic purpose was to provide federal protection to the freed slaves of the South from oppressive state governments. One protection afforded to individuals in the Fourteenth Amendment is the provision that no state shall deprive an individual of life, liberty, or property without following the requirements of "due process of law." This means, among other things, that the procedural rules used by state courts must conform to the requirements of due process of law as defined by the federal courts. Inevitably, this raises questions as to the proper definition of "due process."

Some have suggested that the Fourteenth Amendment "due process" clause embodies all the protections granted in the U.S. Bill of Rights and that the protections for individuals afforded in the Bill of Rights are, therefore, binding on the states as well as on federal authorities. The Supreme Court rejected this notion and, instead, adopted a selective approach in defining the substance of the Fourteenth Amendment's "due process."[1] This approach is called the "incorporation" or "absorption" theory, which means that the due process clause incorporates or absorbs, in whole or in part, various of the amendments in the Bill of Rights. In this manner, the incorporated amendment or portion thereof becomes applicable to the states also.

Those safeguards in the Bill of Rights that have only limited validity, such as the right of trial by a jury of 12 or immunity from prosecution unless initiated by a grand jury, are not so fundamental as to be implied or absorbed into the due process clause of the Fourteenth Amendment. However, freedom of the press, freedom of religion, and freedom from condemnation without a fair trial are rights that express those "fundamental principles of liberty and justice which lie at the base of all our civil and political institutions" and, therefore, are implied in the comprehensive concept of due process of law. Denial of these rights by federal or state authorities would be repugnant to the conscience of a free people. In this manner, the selective incorporation process has helped define the contours of due process.

Whether a criminal conviction deprives the defendant of due process of law is determined by the court reviewing "the whole course of proceedings in order to ascertain whether they offend those canons of decency and fairness which express the notions of justice of English speaking peoples."[2] Indeed, the safeguards of due process of law summarize the history of freedom of English-speaking peoples running back to the Magna Carta. As Justice Douglas has commented, "The history of American freedom is, in no small measure, the history of procedure."[3]

Shaughnessy v. United States

345 U.S. 206 (1953)
Supreme Court of the United States

Justice Black, dissenting

No society is free where government makes one person's liberty depend upon the arbitrary will of another. Dictatorships have done this since time immemorial. They do now. Russian laws of 1934 authorized the People's Commissariat to imprison, banish and exile Russian citizens as well as "foreign subjects who are socially dangerous." Hitler's secret police were given like powers. German courts were forbidden to make any inquiry whatever as to the information on which the police acted. Our Bill of Rights was written to prevent such oppressive practices. Under it this Nation has fostered and protected individual freedom. The Founders abhorred arbitrary one-man imprisonments. Their belief was—our constitutional principles are—that no person of any faith, rich or poor, high or low, native or foreigner, white or colored, can have his life, liberty or property taken "without due process of law." This means to me that neither the federal police nor federal prosecutors nor any other governmental official, whatever his title, can put or keep people in prison without accountability to courts of justice. It means that individual liberty is too highly prized in this country to allow executive officials to imprison and hold people on the basis of information kept secret from courts.

* * *

Procedural fairness, if not all that originally was meant by due process of law, is at least what it most uncompromisingly requires. . . .

Justice Jackson, concurs with dissent.

Procedural fairness and regularity are of the indispensable essence of liberty. Severe substantive laws can be endured if they are fairly and impartially applied. Indeed, if put to the choice, one might well prefer to live under Soviet substantive law applied in good faith by our common-law procedures than under our substantive law enforced by Soviet procedural practices. Let it not be overlooked that due process of law is not for the sole benefit of an accused. It is the best insurance for the Government itself against those blunders which leave lasting stains on a system of justice but which are bound to occur on *ex parte* consideration.

* * *

The most scrupulous observance of due process, including the right to know a charge, to be confronted with the accuser, to cross-examine informers and to produce evidence in one's behalf, is especially necessary where the occasion of detention is fear of future misconduct, rather than crimes committed. [P]roceeding[s] . . . [of] "preventive detention" are safeguarded with full rights to judicial hearings for the accused. On the contrary, the Nazi regime in Germany installed a system of "protective custody" by which the arrested could claim no judicial or other hearing process, and as a result the concentration camps were populated with victims of summary executive detention for secret reasons. That is what renders Communist justice such a travesty. There are other differences, to be sure, between authoritarian procedure and common law, but differences in the process of administration make all the difference between a reign of terror and one of law.

Questions

1. What does it mean that governmental officials are held accountable to courts of justice?
2. What specific rights of procedural due process are granted to a person detained by governmental authorities?
3. What test or standard does the court use to determine if the defendant received due process of law?
4. Technically, "procedural" due process refers to the regularity of the proceedings, that is, whether the court rules of procedure were properly and uniformly followed by the court. "Substantive" due process refers to the fairness of the procedure employed by the court, that is, assuming the rule is regularly and uniformly followed, whether that rule is fair or just. With these distinctions in mind, what kind of a violation of due process would it be to jail an unpopular political person without a trial? What if the jailing occurs after a regular trial which followed the court rule that defendants do not have the right to cross-examine the accusers?

JURISDICTION

Jurisdiction refers to the power of a court to hear and decide a particular controversy. A court has power to decide cases when it has jurisdiction over the subject matter of the case and jurisdiction over the parties to the case. A court's jurisdiction over the dispute or subject matter is usually determined by the Constitution or by some legislation. Either of these will specify the types of controversies that the particular court can resolve. State courts of general jurisdiction are normally empowered to hear all types of cases that are not specifically assigned to courts of limited or inferior jurisdiction. Inferior state courts (such as justice of the peace courts, mayor's courts, or municipal courts), hear cases involving limited periods of punishments and fines. However, even if the court possesses subject matter jurisdiction, it still may not resolve the controversy if it is unable to achieve jurisdiction over the parties.

Jurisdiction over the parties to the controversy must be obtained before the court has the power to render a judgment. Jurisdiction over the person of the plaintiff is easily obtained. The plaintiff's filing of the suit is a voluntary submission to the power of the court. However, jurisdiction over the person of the defendant may be obtained by a variety of means in which a summons is delivered to the defendant. The summons contains a copy of the complaint against the defendant. The "service of process" may be delivered by a private person or a deputy sheriff, or the defendant may voluntarily pick up the "service" at the courthouse. "Service" is more often accomplished by delivery of the summons through registered mail.

Historically, the U.S. Supreme Court ruled that service of process by state courts could not be delivered beyond the borders of the state. However, in the 1940s this concept of territorial restrictions on the issuance of the summons was modified. Many states enacted what have been called "long-arm" statutes which provide for service of process beyond the state boundaries.

Out-of-state service was challenged in the U.S. Supreme Court as a denial of due process of law under the Fourteenth Amendment in the case of *International Shoe Company* v. *Washington*, 326 U.S. 310 (1945). International Shoe contended that the company itself was not present in the state of Washington and that the notice sent by registered mail to the company was not a personal service that would have any force and effect outside the borders of the state of Washington. The Supreme Court denied the company's contention and said "due process requires only that in order to subject the defendant to a judgment *in personam*, if he is not present within the territory of the form, he have certain minimum contacts with it such that the maintenance of the suit does not offend traditional notions of fair play and substantial justice." Subsequent to the *International Shoe* decision, many states adopted statutes giving extraterritorial effect to their service of process. The following case illustrates the utilization of an Illinois long-arm statute in an attempt to compel an Indiana corporation to defend itself in an Illinois court.

Clements v. Barney's Sporting Goods Store

406 N.E. 2d 43 (1980)
Illinois Court of Appeals

This appeal raises the frequently litigated question of when has a foreign corporation submitted itself to the jurisdiction of our courts by the transaction of business within this State. Plaintiff, Thomas Clements, brought this action to recover damages for breach of warranty against defendant, Signa Corporation. According to plaintiff's complaint, he purchased a motor boat from Barney's Sporting Goods, an Illinois corporation, in 1974. The boat was manufactured by defendant, and defendant has allegedly breached its warranty of fitness for a particular purpose. Plaintiff further alleges that defendant, an Indiana corporation, is subject to the jurisdiction of Illinois courts under the "transaction of business" section of the Illinois Long-Arm Statute because of its sale of this boat to Barney's Sporting Goods in Illinois. Although defendant was served with summons, it failed to enter an appearance in this case. A default order was entered against defendant and, subsequently an *ex-parte* judgment of $6,220 was entered against defendant. Approximately one month later, defendant filed a special and limited appearance and affidavit contesting the jurisdiction of the trial court to enter a default judgment against defendant.

After a hearing on defendant's motion, the trial court ruled for . . . [plaintiff]. Defendant's subsequent motion for rehearing was denied by the trial court. Defendant now appeals.

Plaintiff seeks to sustain jurisdiction over defendant under the Illinois Long-Arm Statute. Section 17 provides in pertinent part:

> (1) Any person, whether or not a citizen or resident of this State, who in person or through an agent does any of the acts hereinafter enumerated, thereby submits such

person, and, if an individual, his personal representative, to the jurisdiction of the courts of this State as to any cause of action arising from the doing of any such acts:

(a) The transaction of any business within this State;

* * *

(3) Only causes of action arising from acts enumerated herein may be asserted against a defendant in an action in which jurisdiction over him is based upon this Section.

The purpose of section 17 is to exert *in personam* jurisdiction over non-resident defendants to the extent permitted by the due process clause of the Fourteenth Amendment to the United States Constitution. Due process requires the existence of sufficient "minimum contacts" between the forum state and the non-resident defendant so that the exercise of personal jurisdiction is consistent with traditional notions of fair play and substantial justice. This determination is to be made on the facts of each case and turns on an assessment of the quality and nature of defendant's activities. Thus, we must decide whether defendant has by some voluntary act or conduct purposely availed itself of the privilege of conducting business within Illinois and thereby invoked the benefits and protection of Illinois law. By displaying its boats and distributing literature at the Chicago Boat Show, advertising in magazines which have Illinois subscribers, and selling its boats to Illinois retailers, defendant has entered the Illinois marketplace and invoked the benefits and protection of Illinois law. Defendant's conduct constitutes direct solicitation of Illinois customers. Solicitation of business inside the State of Illinois has been found sufficient to sustain personal jurisdiction over a non-resident defendant. Additionally, defendant has indirectly entered the Illinois marketplace through the sale of its boat to the Illinois corporation, Barney's Sporting Goods Store. Although defendant was not a participant in the sale of this boat to the plaintiff, we believe defendant cannot insulate itself from the jurisdiction of our courts by using an intermediary or by professing ignorance of the ultimate destination of his goods. In *Gray* v. *American Radiator & Standard Sanitary Corp.* (1961), 22 Ill.2d 432, 176 N.E.2d 761, our supreme court said:

As a general proposition, if a corporation elects to sell its products for ultimate use in another State, it is not unjust to hold it answerable there for any damage caused by defects in those products. Advanced means of distribution and other commercial activity have made possible these modern methods of doing business, and have largely effaced the economic significance of State lines. By the same token, today's facilities for transportation and communication have removed much of the difficulty and inconvenience formerly encountered in defending lawsuits brought in other States.

Unless they are applied in recognition of the changes brought about by technological and economic progress, jurisdictional concepts which may have been reasonable enough in a simpler economy lose their relation to reality, and injustice rather than justice is promoted. Our unchanging principles of justice, whether procedural or substantive in nature, should be scrupulously observed by the courts. But the rules of law which grow and develop within those principles must do so in the light of the facts of economic life as it is lived today. . . .

Although the *Gray* court was applying the "commission of a tortious act" section of the Long-Arm Statute, we believe its analysis is equally applicable to the "transaction of business" section of that statute. Accordingly, we believe that defendant has transacted business as provided in section 17(1)(a) of the Civil Practice Act.

Section 17(3) of the Long-Arm Statute mandates that plaintiff's cause of action arose from the jurisdictional acts of defendant. A cause of action arises from a defendant's jurisdictional acts where it lies in the wake of defendant's commercial activities by which defendant submitted to the jurisdiction of the Illinois courts. We have previously held that "[w]here the jurisdictional activities consist of the solicitation of sales, a cause of action arising from the consequences of such a sale comes within the statutory definition of section 17(3)." In this case, plaintiff's purchase of the defective boat was, at least in part, a result of defendant's solicitation in Illinois. Therefore, we hold that defendant has submitted itself to the jurisdiction of our courts under section 17(1)(a) of the Illinois Long-Arm Statute. The order of the circuit court denying defendant's motion to reconsider is hereby affirmed.

Questions

1. What does due process require before a state can force an out-of-state defendant to answer a suit in the state? How was this requirement met in this instance?
2. What reasons did the court cite for extending the state's jurisdictional powers over nonresident defendants?
3. The Ilinois statute "mandates that the plaintiff's cause of action" must arise "from the jurisdictional acts of the defendant." What does this mean?
4. Another type of jurisdiction is called jurisdiction *in rem.* In the case of *Pennington* v. *Fourth National Bank*, 243 U.S. 269 (1917), the Supreme Court said:

   > The 14th Amendment did not, in guaranteeing due process of law, abridge the jurisdiction which a state possessed over property within its borders, regardless of the residence or presence of the owner. That jurisdiction extends alike to tangible and to intangible property. . . . The thing belonging to the absent defendant is seized and applied to the satisfaction of his obligation. The Federal Constitution presents no obstacle to the full exercise of this power.

   Why is jurisdiction *in rem* necessary?
5. The importance of possessing jurisdiction is that without it the state court's judgment is void, and with it the judgment is entitled to "full faith and credit" (i.e., enforcement) throughout the 50 states. A state court's judgment that possessed both subject matter and person jurisdiction is enforceable in all states because the U.S. Constitution requires all states to grant "full faith and credit" to the court judgments of the other states in the Union. Does the "full faith and credit" clause suggest a reason for the

out-of-state defendant to return and defend himself or herself in a state court from which a summons has been received?

6. Subject matter jurisdiction for federal courts falls into one of two categories: (1) cases involving "federal questions" (questions concerning a provision of the federal constitution, a federal statute, or an international treaty) and (2) cases involving "diversity of citizenship" (the respective parties are citizens of different states). All cases in the latter category could be tried in state courts. However, the apprehension of possible state court bias against the out-of-state party inspired the framers of the Constitution to allow such cases to be brought into federal courts. In addition to diversity of citizenship, the amount in controversy must exceed $10,000. Would overcrowding of federal courts with "diversity actions" suggest another reason why the Supreme Court upheld long-arm statutes as satisfying due process requirements?

THEORY OF PLEADINGS

The pleadings, or documents in a case, serve (1) to set the limits within which the litigation will operate and (2) to give notice of the plaintiff's claim to the defendant to gain personal jurisdiction over the defendant. In the written complaint filed with the clerk of the court, the plaintiff's attorney will present the client's version of what transpired and relate the particular relief the plaintiff is seeking from the defendant. In contesting the plaintiff's case, the defendant's attorney will file an answer with the court denying all or some of the plaintiff's allegations about what occurred. These documents isolate the issues of fact—that is, where the parties' version of the facts differ. This divergence of alleged events must be resolved by a trial.

Historically, the rules of pleading were burdened with intricacies and technicalities. The emphasis was on pleading "facts" which required elaborate documents with great detail. However, reform efforts brought about "notice" pleading and its corresponding "discovery" system.

Notice pleading requires the pleadings merely to give "notice" to the opposing parties of their respective claims. The "complaint" and "answer" in the following dispute of *Student* v. *Worker* illustrate the simplicity of notice pleading.

The "discovery" process allows the opposing parties to seek out further refinements or elaboration in the facts through the use of techniques separate from the pleading documents themselves. These privileges of discovery allow the parties to learn what sort of evidence the other party has that relates to the suit. Certain matters are not subject to discovery but, for the most part, any relevant matter may be ascertained. The techniques of discovery usually are written interrogatories, inspection of documents, physical examination of persons, and depositions. Such procedures allow for proper preparation for trials and aid pretrial settlements. They also eliminate most "surprises" at the trial, which might allow suits to be won or lost by tricks rather than on the merits of the case. The broadest discovery processes are available in civil suits. Many states allow a limited aspect of discovery in criminal suits also.

A "COMPLAINT"

A COMPLAINT

IN THE COURT OF COMMON PLEAS
SUMMIT COUNTY, OHIO

Ernest Student	)	
221 North Street	)	
Akron, Ohio 44304		
and	)	No. ____________
Dolly Student		
221 North Street	)	
Akron, Ohio 44304		
	)	
Plaintiffs		
v.	)	COMPLAINT
Herbert A. Worker	)	
2631 East Market Street		
Kent, Ohio 43204	)	
and		
Worldwide Flush, Inc.		
343 Industry Street		
Kent, Ohio 43204	)	
Defendants	)	

COUNT ONE

1. On May 6, 1982, plaintiff, Ernest Student, was driving an automobile, owned jointly by Ernest Student and his wife, plaintiff Dolly Student, southwardly in the left traffic lane of Exchange Street, a multilane public highway in Akron, Ohio.
2. At the same time defendant, Herbert Worker, was driving an automobile, leased by defendant Worldwide Flush, Inc., southwardly in the traffic lane of Exchange Street.
3. Negligently and without warning, defendant, Herbert Worker, shifted from the right traffic lane to the left traffic lane of Exchange Street immediately in front of plaintiff Ernest Student, thus causing plaintiff, Ernest Student, to strike the left rear of defendant, Herbert Worker's automobile.
4. At the time of the impact defendant, Herbert Worker, was the agent of defendant, Worldwide Flush, Inc., and was acting within the scope of his agency and authority.
5. As a direct result of the impact plaintiff, Ernest Student, has suffered a rib fracture, a contusion over the sternum, and a rupture of an intervertebral disk at L-5, S-1. To date, he has expended $767.58 in medical expenses and

has lost intermittently a total of 23 days of work. He has suffered great pain of body and mind and in the future will continue to do so and in the future will be compelled to expend additional sums for medical treatment and hospitalization and will suffer intermittently loss of wages. In addition, the automobile owned by plaintiffs, Ernest Student and Dolly Student, was damaged in the amount of $411.00. Being deprived of the use of the automobile for three weeks, plaintiff, Ernest Student, was required to expend $60.00 for public transportation.

WHEREFORE, plaintiffs demand judgment against defendant, Herbert Worker, or against Worldwide Flush, Inc., or against both of them as follows:

(a) In behalf of plaintiffs, Ernest Student and Dolly Student, for damage to their automobile in the sum of $411.00.

(b) In behalf of the plaintiff, Ernest Student in the sum of $15,000.00, together with the costs of this action.

COUNT TWO

1. For a second claim plaintiff, Dolly Student, restates all that is alleged in paragraphs 1 through 4 of Count One.
2. Plaintiff, Dolly Student, further states that she is the wife of Ernest Student and that as a direct result of the injuries suffered by Ernest Student as set forth in paragraph 5 of Count One, plaintiff, Dolly Student, has been and will be deprived of the consortium of her husband, Ernest Student.

WHEREFORE, plaintiff, Dolly Student, demands judgment against defendant, Herbert Worker, or against defendant, Worldwide Flush, Inc., or against both of them in the sum of $5,000.00 together with the costs of this action.

____

Chester Goodfellow, Attorney for Plaintiffs
Goodfellow, Nice & Easy, Attorneys at Law
221 West Market Street
Akron, Ohio 44304

TO THE CLERK:

Please issue summons, plus a copy of this complaint to the Sheriff of Summit County, Ohio, for personal service upon the defendants at their respective addresses, noted in the caption to this complaint, and make return of the same, according to law.

____

Chester Goodfellow, Attorney for Plaintiffs
Goodfellow, Nice & Easy, Attorneys at Law
221 West Market Street
Akron, Ohio 44304

AN ANSWER

AN ANSWER
IN THE COURT OF COMMON PLEAS
SUMMIT COUNTY, OHIO

Ernest Student)
221 North Street
Akron, Ohio 44304)) No. ____________
and
Dolly Student)
221 North Street
Akron, Ohio 44304)

Plaintiffs) ANSWER
v.)
Herbert A. Worker
2631 East Market Street)
Kent, Ohio 43204
and)
Worldwide Flush, Inc.
343 Industry Street)
Kent, Ohio 43204

Defendant Herbert A. Worker:

1. Admits the allegations contained in paragraphs 1 and 2 of Count One of the complaint, and admits these same paragraphs as incorporated by reference in Count Two of the complaint.
2. Denies the allegations contained in paragraph 3 of Count One of the complaint, and denies the same paragraph as incorporated by reference in Count Two of the complaint.
3. Alleges that he is without knowledge or information sufficient to form a belief as to the truth of the allegations contained in paragraphs 4 and 5 of Count One of the complaint, and alleges that he is without knowledge or information sufficient to form a belief as to the truth of the allegations contained in paragraph 4 as incorporated by reference in paragraph 1 of Count Two of the complaint, and further alleges that he is without knowledge or information sufficient to form a belief as to the truth of the allegations contained in paragraph 2 of Count Two of the complaint.

____
William Williams, Attorney for
Defendant, Herbert Worker
Williams, Jones & Smith, Attorneys
at Law
225 North High Street
Akron, Ohio 44304

CERTIFICATE OF SERVICE

A copy of this answer has been mailed, via ordinary U.S. mail, to the attorney for plaintiffs, Chester Goodfellow, Goodfellow, Nice & Easy, Attorneys at Law, 221 West Market Street, Akron, Ohio 44304, this ____________ day of ____________, 1982.

____

William Williams
Attorney for Defendant

Questions

1. What is the controversy in *Student* v. *Worker*? Which facts are admitted? Which "facts" are in dispute?
2. What additional "facts" might the parties want to discover? What discovery techniques might the parties utilize?

SUMMARY JUDGMENT

One of the recognized purposes of a summary judgment by the judge is to expedite the disposition of civil cases where no issue of material fact is presented to justify a trial. If the plaintiff's pleadings and other papers disclose no real defense and if the defendant fails to controvert such proof with evidence of the existence of a genuine defense, the court may find that no triable issue exists and grant summary judgment. With no genuine issues of fact, the court avoids the trial and thereby saves the plaintiff the time and expense of the trial while helping the court clear its congested calendar. On the other hand, if the plaintiff's claim or offer of proof is inadequate, the court can also grant a summary judgment (or nonsuit) in favor of the defendant.

CONDUCT OF THE TRIAL

The primary purpose of the trial is to resolve all controversy over questions of fact, that is, what events actually transpired. The pleadings serve to notify each party of the questions that each must be prepared to meet with the best evidence available. As the party that initiated the action, the plaintiff is obligated to proceed first in presenting his or her case. Following the plaintiff's presentation of evidence, the defendant will attempt with contra evidence to create doubt in the minds of the jurors concerning the plaintiff's version of the controversy. At the conclusion of the presentation of the evidence, the jury will return a verdict (finding of facts) in resolution of that portion of the legal controversy. In civil (noncriminal) cases, the plaintiff must present proofs to convince the jury by the preponderance of the evidence. This is a burden of proof that is much lower than the prosecutor's burden in a criminal case to convince the jury "beyond a reasonable doubt."

JURY SELECTION PROCESS

Prospective jurors are selected from a list of residents in the judicial district of the court. They are summoned to the courthouse and assigned to various trials. Prospective jurors are questioned concerning any possible connection with any of the participants in the trial or the possibility of some bias on the questions before the court. The opposing counsel may demand the exclusion of any prospective juror who demonstrates a specific cause for rejection. Moreover, opposing counsel have a limited number of "preemptory challenges" which allow prospective jurors to be dismissed without giving any reason. This privilege enables opposing counsel to exclude jurors who they feel may be hostile to their client's cause. Once the jury is empaneled, the lawyers present their opening statements. Then, the evidence is presented before the jury.

RULES OF EVIDENCE

Since the jurors are not expert factfinders, they may have considerable difficulty in determining the truth from the evidence. Because the jurors are laypersons, the rules of evidence have been shaped over time to protect the jury from irrelevant, misleading, and unreliable evidence. Repetitious evidence and evidence that may be in violation of certain confidential relationships are also excluded. These rules of evidence have been developed over the years and are too numerous and complex for full discussion here. Indeed, even judges themselves often commit error by introducing inappropriate evidence or failing to admit evidence that should have been presented to the jury. Some of the excerpts from the cases that follow illustrate the difficulties involved in selecting the proper evidence to be presented to the jury.

Batchoff v. Craney

172 P.2d 308 (1946)
Supreme Court of Montana

Plaintiff brought this action to recover damages for personal injuries sustained by him while riding as a guest in an automobile alleged to have been owned and controlled by defendant but which was being operated and driven by Bailey Stortz. . . .

The accident happened on November 2, 1940, near Big Timber as the automobile was being driven from Billings to Butte. . . .

Between 4 and 5 o'clock in the morning of that day [plaintiff] went to the Northern Pacific depot in Billings and was about to take the North Coast Limited to Butte after having purchased a ticket; there he met defendant. He said the following conversation ensued: "Well, I saw him come in with a car. He came in and asked me where I was going and I told him I was taking the train to Butte. Well, he said, 'Oh, hell, Jim, stay here and miss this train.' He said Senator Wheeler and Mrs. Wheeler and Bailey are coming off of this train and I got to ride back on the plane. He said, 'I am going to leave my automobile with Bailey to drive it back to Butte,'—that's Bailey Stortz—'and you can ride along with him. He said he is going to bring it back to Butte.' "

* * *

Pursuant to arrangements plaintiff met Stortz at the Grand Hotel in Billings about 3 p.m. that day and they started for Butte in the defendant's automobile with Bailey Stortz doing the driving. Plaintiff testified that Stortz drove the car from 70 to 75 miles per hour; that he, plaintiff, complained of the excessive speed but instead of slowing down the speed was increased to between 80 and 85 miles per hour; there were wet spots in the road; the car hit a wet spot, skidded around several times; the door of the car swung open and plaintiff was thrown from the car into a borrow pit and the car followed and struck him and ran over him causing the injuries complained of and rendering him unconscious.

Defendant produced witnesses who testified that he lent his car to Senator Wheeler for his use in and around Billings and that Stortz was acting as agent of Senator Wheeler in returning the car to Butte when the accident occurred. In other words, the evidence was in sharp conflict if it can be said that the testimony of plaintiff is worthy of belief. Whether his testimony was worthy of belief was for the jury to determine.

Thus in *Wallace* v. *Wallace*, 85 Mont. 492, 279 P. 374, 377, this court said:

> A jury may believe the testimony of one witness and disbelieve that of another, or any numbers of others, and the determination of the jury in this regard is final; having spoken, this court must assume that the facts are as stated by the witnesses believed by the jury, and claimed by the prevailing party. The preponderance of the evidence may be established by a single witness as against a greater number of witnesses who testify to the contrary.
>
> It follows that wherever there is a conflict in the evidence this court may only review the testimony for the purpose of determining whether or not there is any substantial evidence in the record to support the verdict of the jury, and must accept that evidence there found as true, unless that evidence is so inherently impossible or improbable as not to be entitled to belief; and, where a verdict is based upon substantial evidence which, from any point of view, could have been accepted by the jury as credible, it is binding upon this court, although it may appear inherently weak.

* * *

It should be noted that the statements made by plaintiff before the Industrial Accident Board and other declarations contrary to his testimony in this case may not be considered as substantive evidence in this case. . . . The only effect of declarations made by plaintiff at other times and places is to impeach him, leaving the question of his credibility for the jury.

Speaking of the effect of prior statements inconsistent with present testimony, this court in *State* v. *Peterson*, 102 Mont. 495, 59 P. 2d 61, 63, said:

These matters tend to discredit, but not destroy, the testimony of the [plaintiff]. 'A witness false in one part of his testimony is to be distrusted in others' and 'a witness may be impeached' by contradictory evidence that his general reputation for truth and integrity is bad, or that he has made at other times statements inconsistent with his present testimony; but while proof of falsity is one part of a witness' testimony, inconsistent statements at other times, contradictory evidence, and reputation may discredit the witness, such proof goes only to the credibility of the witness, of which the jury remains the sole judge, as well as the weight to be given thereto.

It follows that, although the jury may reject the false testimony and "assume, regarding the rest of it, an attitude of distrust," the jurors may render a verdict based upon the testimony of such witness if after examination they find it worthy of belief. And the extent to which impeaching evidence impaired the credibility of a witness assailed is a question exclusively for the jury.

* * *

Defendant contends that the damages are excessive. Dr. McMahon examined plaintiff about a week before the trial, which was in March, 1945. He explained in detail the injuries which plaintiff sustained, some of which he described as permanent. No useful purpose would be subserved in setting out all the injuries described by Dr. McMahon. Defendant does not contend that the verdict is excessive if plaintiff sustained the injuries described by Dr. McMahon. His contention is that Dr. McMahon enlarged upon the injuries and that we as well as the trial judge should accept the testimony of Dr. Shields as to the extent of the injuries. Our province is to ascertain whether the evidence viewed in the light most favorable to the prevailing party sustains the verdict. If it does we must sustain the action of the trial judge. It was the jury's province to pronounce between conflicting views contained in the evidence. There being substantial evidence to sustain the verdict, the court properly denied the motion for new trial.

We find nothing in the record to warrant us in saying that the court erred in not finding that the jury was actuated by passion and prejudice in fixing the amount of damages in the sum of $10,000.

The judgment is accordingly affirmed.

Questions

1. What is a "preponderance" of evidence? Does the side with the greatest number of witnesses win?
2. On review, must the appellate court always accept the verdict of the jury? Do appellate courts "second guess" the jury? If the evidence is conflicting, should the appeals court pick the version of facts it prefers or leave the selection to the jury? Why?
3. Does evidence of "prior inconsistent statements" destroy a witness' testimony?

ATTORNEY-CLIENT PRIVILEGE

Upjohn Co. v. United States
449 U.S. 383 (1981)
Supreme Court of the United States

Justice Rehnquist

We granted certiorari in this case to address important questions concerning the scope of the attorney-client privilege in the corporate context. . . .

Petitioner Upjohn manufactures and sells pharmaceuticals here and abroad. In January an audit of one of petitioner's foreign subsidiaries discovered that the subsidiary made payments to or for the benefit of foreign government officials in order to secure government business. The accountants so informed Mr. Gerard Thomas, petitioner's Vice-President, Secretary, and General Counsel. . . . He consulted with outside counsel and R. T. Parfet, Jr., petitioner's Chairman of the Board. It was decided that the company would conduct an internal investigation of what were termed "questionable payments." As part of this investigation the attorneys prepared a letter containing a questionnaire which was sent to "all foreign general and area managers" over the Chairman's signature. The letter began by noting recent disclosures that several American companies made "possibly illegal" payments to foreign government officials and emphasized that the management needed full information concerning any such payments made by Upjohn. The letter indicated that the Chairman had asked Thomas, identified as "the company's General Counsel," "to conduct an investigation for the purpose of determining the nature and magnitude of any payments made by the Upjohn Company or any of its subsidiaries to any employee or official of a foreign government." The questionnaire sought detailed information concerning such payments. Managers were instructed to treat the investigation as "highly confidential" and not to discuss it with anyone other than Upjohn employees who might be helpful in providing the requested information. Responses were to be sent directly to Thomas. Thomas and outside counsel also interviewed the recipients of the questionnaire and some 33 other Upjohn officers or employees as part of the investigation.

On March 26, 1976, the company voluntarily submitted a preliminary report to the Securities and Exchange Commission on Form 8-K disclosing certain questionable payments. A copy of the report was simultaneously submitted to the Internal Revenue Service, which immediately began an investigation to determine the tax consequences of the payments. Special agents conducting the investigation were given lists by Upjohn of all those interviewed and all who had responded to the questionnaire. On November 23, 1976, the Service issued a summons . . . demanding production of:

All files relative to the investigation conducted under the supervision of Gerard Thomas to identify payments to employees of foreign governments and any political contributions made by the Upjohn Company or any of its affiliates since January 1, 1971, and to determine whether any funds of the Upjohn Company had been improperly accounted for on the corporate books during the same period.

The records should include but not be limited to written questionnaires sent to managers of the Upjohn Company's foreign affiliates, and memoranda or notes of the interviews conducted in the United States and abroad with officers and employees of the Upjohn Company and its subsidiaries.

Federal Rule of Evidence 501 provides that "the privilege of a witness . . . shall be governed by the principles of the common law as they may be interpreted by the courts of the United States in light of reason and experience." The attorney-client privilege is the oldest of the privileges for confidential communications known to the common law. Its purpose is to encourage full and frank communication between attorneys and their clients and thereby promote broader public interests in the observance of law and administration of justice. The privilege recognizes that sound legal advice or advocacy serves public ends and that such advice or advocacy depends upon the lawyer being fully informed by the client. . . . [T]he privilege exists to protect not only the giving of professional advice to those who can act on it but also the giving of information to the lawyer to enable him to give sound and informed advice. The first step in the resolution of any legal problem is ascertaining the factual background and sifting through the facts with an eye to the legally relevant. . . .

In the case of the individual client the provider of information and the person who acts on the lawyer's advice are one and the same. In the corporate context, however, it will frequently be employees . . . who will possess the information needed by the corporation's lawyers. Middle-level—and indeed lower-level—employees can, by actions within the scope of their employment, embroil the corporation in serious legal difficulties, and it is only natural that these employees would have the relevant information needed by corporate counsel if he is adequately to advise the client with respect to such actual or potential difficulties. . . . But if the purpose of the attorney-client privilege is to be served, the attorney and client must be able to predict with some degree of certainty whether particular discussions will be protected. An uncertain privilege, or one which purports to be certain but results in widely varying applications by the courts, is little better than no privilege at all. . . .

The communications at issue were made by Upjohn acting as such, at the direction of corporate superiors in order to secure legal advice from counsel. As the magistrate found, "Mr. Thomas consulted with the Chairman of the Board and outside counsel and thereafter conducted a factual investigation to determine the nature and extent of the questionable payments *and to be in a position to give legal advice to the company with respect to the payments.*" Information, not available from upper-echelon management, was needed to supply a basis for legal advice concerning compliance with securities and tax laws, foreign laws, currency regulations, duties to shareholders, and potential litigation in each of these areas. The communications concerned matters within the scope of the employees' corporate duties, and the employees themselves were sufficiently aware that they were being questioned in order that the corporation could obtain legal advice. The questionnaire identified Thomas as "the company's General Counsel" and referred in its opening sentence to the possible illegality of payments such as the ones on which information was sought. A statement of policy accompanying the questionnaire clearly indicated the legal implications of the investigation. The policy statement was issued "in order that there be no uncertainty in the future as to the policy with respect to the practices which are the subject of this investigation." It began "Upjohn will comply with all laws and regulations," and stated that commissions or payments "will not be used as a subterfuge for bribes or illegal payments" and that all payments must be "proper and legal." Any future agreements with foreign distributors or agents were to be approved "by a company attorney" and any questions concerning the policy were to be referred "to the company's General Counsel." This statement was issued to Upjohn employees worldwide, so that even those interviewees not receiving a questionnaire were aware of the legal implications of the interviews. Pursuant to explicit instructions from the Chairman of the Board, the communications were considered "highly confidential" when made, and have been kept confidential by the company. Consistent with the underlying purposes of the attorney-client privilege, these communications must be protected against compelled disclosure.

. . . Application of the attorney-client privilege to communications such as those involved here, however, puts the adversary in no worse position than if the communications had never taken place. The privilege only protects disclosure of the underlying facts by those who communicated with the attorney:

> The protection of the privilege extends only to *communications* and not to facts. A fact is one thing and a communication concerning that fact is an entirely different thing. The client cannot be compelled to answer the question, "What did you say or write to the attorney?" but may not refuse to disclose any relevant fact within his knowledge merely because he incorporated a statement of such fact into his communication to his attorney.

Here the Government was free to question the employees who communicated with Thomas and outside counsel. Upjohn has provided the IRS with a list of such employees, and the IRS has already interviewed some 25 of them. While it would probably be more convenient for the Government to secure the results of petitioner's internal investigation by simply subpoenaing the questionnaires and notes taken by petitioner's attorneys, such considerations of convenience do not overcome the policies served by the attorney-client privilege. As Justice Jackson noted in his concurring opinion in *Hickman* v. *Taylor*, 329 U.S., at 516, "Discovery was hardly intended to enable a learned profession to perform its functions . . . on wits borrowed from the adversary."

Needless to say, we decide only the case before us, and do not undertake to draft a set of rules which should govern challenges to investigatory subpoenas. Any such approach . . . should be determined on a case-by-case basis. While such a "case-by-case" basis may to some slight extent undermine desirable certainty in the boundaries of the attorney-client privilege, it obeys the spirit of the Rules.

Questions

1. Courts and commentators have identified benefits arising out of the attorney-client privilege: benefits to the client, to society in general, and to the attorney. Can you explain these benefits?
2. Should the corporation be entitled to the attorney-client privilege? One commentator has answered: "It is generally assumed that corporations and other legal entities are entitled to the privilege just as much as individuals are. The idea seems to go unchallenged—perhaps because in law, as in life, many of the most deeply believed assumptions are unspoken." (Simon, "The Attorney-Client Privilege as Applied to Corporations," 65 *Yale L. J.* 953 [1956]).
3. What can the judge do about the conduct of an unruly defendant? The Supreme Court has provided some guidance in *Illinois* v. *Allen*, 397 U.S. 337 (1970).

> It is essential to the proper administration of criminal justice that dignity, order, and decorum be the hallmarks of all court proceedings in our country. The flagrant disregard in the courtroom of elementary standards of proper conduct should not and cannot be tolerated. We believe trial judges confronted with disruptive, contumacious, stubbornly defiant defendants must be given sufficient discretion to meet the circumstances of each case. No one formula for maintaining the appropriate courtroom atmosphere will be best in all situations. We think there are at least three constitutionally permissible ways for a trial judge to handle an obstreperous defendant like Allen: (1) bind and gag him, thereby keeping him present; (2) cite him for contempt; (3) take him out of the courtroom until he promises to conduct himself properly.

POST-TRIAL

After the jury renders its verdict, one of the parties is likely to be dissatisfied with the outcome. There are a number of alternatives available to test the correctness of the jury's verdict or the court's judgment. The judgment is the final decision of the court (judge) determined by applying the proper law to the facts as found by the jury. In civil cases, the losing party may ask the judge to rule against the jury's verdict because it is clearly contrary to the evidence (judgment *non obstante veredicto*). In addition, the losing party may seek a new trial if there was some irregularity in the trial proceedings. Also, the losing party may appeal to determine whether the law that was applied in the case was properly applied or whether the law itself is a proper law for contemporary conditions. After the case has been argued before the appeals court and it renders a judgment, the legal controversy is usually terminated. If no appeal is advanced, it is terminated at the conclusion of the proceedings in the trial court.

Appeals beyond the first apellate court are normally not available as a matter of "right." Rather, the highest courts usually determine at their own discretion which of the lower court decisions they wish to review. This procedure usually involves the filing of a petition by the party desiring an appeal with the highest court. The petition asks the high court to issue a writ of *certiorari* to the lower court. The writ of *certiorari* is an order by the high court to the lower court to certify a record of its proceedings for review by the high court. Of course, if the high court grants *certiorari*, this is not a determination of how the court will finally rule on the merits of the lower court decision. The decision on the merits will be decided only after a full hearing before the high court.

APPEAL FOR REVERSAL

State v. Liska
32 Ohio App. 2d 317 (1971)
Court of Appeals of Ohio

This action comes here from the Berea Municipal Court on appeal from the appellant's conviction and fine of One Hundred Dollars ($100) for an alleged violation of R. C. 2921.05, the so-called "flag desecration" statute. For the reasons stated below, the judgment of the trial court is reversed as being contrary to law.

The appellant, Liska, a student at Baldwin-Wallace College, was arrested and charged with unlawfully and willfully exposing a contemptuous representation of the American flag on the rear window of his automobile. The alleged contemptuous representation consisted of a decal composed of thirteen red and white stripes with a peace symbol appearing on a blue field.

There is nothing in the record to indicate that the appellant was in violation of any traffic laws, nor that he was behaving in a disorderly manner when arrested. The appellant described himself at trial as a conscientious objector to the Viet Nam War and a pacifist, and testified that his purpose in displaying the decal in question was to make a political statement of peace. The state's evidence consisted only of the testimony of the arresting officer and a photograph of the offending decal as it appeared on appellant's car.

Appellant assigned the following as error:

(1) The court erred in concluding that appellant's conduct was contemptuous as required by Section 2921.05 of the Revised Code of Ohio . . . .

Allowing the state's evidence its most favorable stance, it is apparent that the most this appellant has done is to display a decal composed of thirteen red and white stripes and a blue square upon which is superimposed a peace symbol. On the evidence in this case that configuration indicates only the appellant's aspiration for peace for his country. We hold that the symbolic indication indicated by the facts of this case, without more, was, as a matter of law, not a contemptuous act within the meaning of R.C. 2921.05.

The conviction is reversed and the appellant discharged.

Questions

1. Did the appellant challenge the facts? Does this explain why he asked for a reversal and not a new trial?
2. In seeking a reversal, what is the appellant asserting as error by the trial court?

RES JUDICATA

Commissioner of Internal Revenue v. Sunnen

333 U.S. 591 (1948)
Supreme Court of the United States

Justice Murphy

It is first necessary to understand something of the recognized meaning and scope of *res judicata*, a doctrine judicial in origin. The general rule of *res judicata* applies to repetitious suits involving the same cause of action. It rests upon considerations of economy of judicial time and public policy favoring the establishment of certainty in legal relations. The rule provides that when a court of competent jurisdiction has entered a final judgment on the merits of a cause of action, the parties to the suit and their privies are thereafter bound "not only as to every matter which was offered and received to sustain or defeat the claim or demand, but as to any other admissible matter which might have been offered for that purpose." *Cromwell* v. *County of Sac.* 94 U.S. 351, 352. The judgment puts an end to the cause of action, which cannot again be brought into litigation between the parties upon any ground whatever, absent fraud or some other factor invalidating the judgment.

Questions

1. What is *res judicata*? Does it apply to the same parties or to different parties?
2. Does *res judicata* prohibit an appeal?

CONCLUSION

The judicial process involves a series of interrelated actions that result in the resolution of legal controversies. The basic elements of the legal process are the pleading, trial, appeal, and ultimate decision (judgment). The pleadings and the trial collectively "determine" the facts, and the judgment of the trial judge is the application of the law to those facts so as to render a decision. Appellate courts determine whether the trial judge properly handled the case and attempt to ensure uniform interpretation of the laws.

The legal process can be a long and drawn-out process with numerous technicalities. However, the delays are often built into the process and technicalities often are designed to protect specific rights of the parties. It is precisely this due process of law that forms the basis of protecting the rights of a free people.

CASE PROBLEMS

1. Black and Blue were involved in an automobile accident which occurred in Wausaukee, Marinette County, Wisconsin, and Black was seriously injured. Black lives in South Bend, St. Joseph County, Indiana, and Blue lives in Iowa City, Johnson County, Iowa. Black wishes to bring suit against Blue to recover damages for his injuries in the amount of $4,500. Please advise him as to where to bring suit.

2. Roberts, as the representative of the deceased's estate sues Richards Aircraft Co. and Mohawk Airlines. The Richards company was operating the aircraft at the time of the fatal crash. The plane had been previously owned by the defendant, Mohawk Airlines, which is alleged to have sold it in defective condition. No specific acts by Mohawk in Oklahoma are alleged, but their commercials are seen on TV in Oklahoma. They have a telephone listing in Oklahoma City, and a travel agency in Oklahoma City sells tickets for Mohawk. The crash of the plane occurred in Colorado.

   Does the long-arm statute of Oklahoma provide jurisdiction against Richards? Against Mohawk?

3. In the pleadings, the defendant admitted liability for the deaths of the children. The sole remaining question in issue was the amount of damages suffered by the parents. In an action for wrongful death of minor children, the damages consist of the pecuniary loss to the parents in being deprived of the services, earning, society, comfort, and protection of the children. In measuring the damages, the judge allowed testimony of the manner in which the accident occurred, the force of the impact, and the defendant's intoxication. The defendant claims that the admission of this evidence was immaterial (not an issue) and prejudicial. He seeks a new trial. What decision on appeal?

4. Ted and his father both consulted an attorney to obtain professional advice. Each heard what the other said. In subsequent litigation between Ted and his father may either of them prevent the other from testifying as to the contents of that conversation on the grounds of privileged communication with the attorney?

END NOTES

1. *Malinski* v. *New York*, 324 U.S. 501 (1945).
2. Ibid.
3. Ibid.

chapter 3

THE ADMINISTRATIVE PROCESS

An administrative agency is any governmental authority other than courts and legislative bodies. Such an agency may be called a commission, bureau, authority, board, office, department, administration, division, or agency. The administrative process is the combination of methods and procedures used by administrative agencies in carrying out their tasks.

The average person is much more directly and more often affected by the administrative process than by the judicial process. A large proportion of our population goes through life without ever becoming a party to a lawsuit. However, the administrative process affects nearly everyone in many different ways almost every day. Administrative agencies protect people from numerous problems: air and water pollution; excessive prices for utility services or transportation rates; unwholesome meats; unfair labor practices by employers and unions; false advertising; and physically unsafe airplanes, bridges, and elevators. The list includes a wide range of items with which we have become so accustomed that we take them for granted.

Administrative agencies are as old as Congress itself. The first Congress conferred power on the president to establish an agency which provided military pensions for "invalids . . . wounded and disabled during the late war."[1] Such payments were to be made "under such regulations as the President of the United States may direct." Administrative law has been growing ever since. Such familiar acronyms as the ICC, the FTC, the EPA, the SEC, and the NLRB became part of America's vocabulary as the government increasingly sought to handle social and economic problems through the administrative process.

The rapid development and complexity of the American economy gave rise to a public concern for regulation of industry and trade to prevent abuses that might be detrimental to society. Initially, Congress attempted to legislate rules of proper conduct and have the attorney general's office enforce the laws. It soon became apparent, however, that this form of regulation was neither adequate nor effective, and in some instances, was impossible. The constant supervision and inspection necessary to ensure compliance with the rules of regulation could not be fulfilled by the legislature, the executive, or the judicial branches of government. Thus, there was a recognized need for a government body that was equipped for continuous supervision and that had the particular expertise required to cope with the technicalities of a dynamic economy. The complexity of the business environment, therefore, dictated the choice of the device of the administrative agency as a necessary instrument for the effective supervision and regulation of business activities.

LEGISLATIVE AND EXECUTIVE CONTROLS

The administrative agency is embodied with functions usually carried out by three separate branches of government. An administrative agency may exercise the legislative function by formulating rules to govern a particular trade or a specific business practice. The agency exercises an executive function when it investigates business activities and enforces its rules of proper conduct. Finally, the agency is empowered with the judicial function to hold a hearing and to determine if a particular defendant has violated any of the agency's rules.

A problem posed by the unique status of administrative agencies involves the nature of the powers that may be delegated to them. Final rulings are frequently contested on grounds that the work of the agency constituted an unconstitutional delegation of legislative power. In these cases the courts are concerned with whether sufficient limits and boundaries are placed on the powers and actions of the administrative agencies. The following case illustrates this problem.

LEGISLATIVE STANDARDS

South Terminal Corp. v. Environmental Protection Agency

501 F. 2d 646 (1974)

U.S. Court of Appeals (1st Cir.)

We are asked to review . . . the national primary and secondary ambient air quality standards prescribed by the Environmental Protection Agency (EPA) under authority of the Clean Air Act. In the Act, Congress has directed EPA, using latest scientific knowledge, to establish nationwide air-quality standards for each pollutant having an adverse effect upon the public health or welfare. It has further directed each state to have a plan to "implement" those standards—that is, to see that within the state the level of each such pollutant does not exceed limits prescribed in the national standards . . . .

Several petitioners have argued that the powers of EPA, as construed by us, constitute an unconstitutional delegation to an agency of legislative powers. We do not find the argument persuasive. The last time that a delegation of power to an administrative agency was upset occurred in *A.L.A. Schechter Poultry Corp.* v. *United States,* 295 U.S. 495, (1935), and the unique conditions of that case are not repeated here.

In *Schechter* Congress had delegated to the President the power to approve industry "codes" drawn up by local businessmen. Congress had not prescribed a purpose to be served by the codes, nor had it set boundaries on the provisions the codes could contain. The Court consequently characterized the delegation as utterly without standards and impermissible. Justice Cardozo, concurring, wrote that the legislation was unconstitutional because the power granted was "not canalized within banks that keep it from overflowing. It is unconfined and vagrant. . . . Here in effect is a roving commission to inquire into evils and upon discovery correct them."

The power granted to EPA is not "unconfined and vagrant." The Agency has been given a well defined task by Congress—to reduce pollution levels "requisite to protect the public health," in the case of primary standards. The Clean Air Act outlines the approach to be followed by the Agency and describes in detail many of its powers. Perhaps because the task is both unprecedented and of great complexity, and because appropriate controls cannot all be anticipated pending the Agency's collection of technical data in different regions, the Act leaves considerable flexibility to EPA in the choice of means. Yet there are many benchmarks to guide the Agency and the courts in determining whether or not the EPA is exceeding its powers, not the least of which is that the rationality of the means can be tested against goals capable of fairly precise definition in the language of science.

Administrative agencies are created by Congress because it is impossible for the Legislature to acquire sufficient information to manage each detail in the long process of extirpating the abuses identified by the legislation; the Agency must have flexibility to implement the congressional mandate. Therefore, although the delegation to EPA was a broad one, including the power to make essentially "local" rules and regulations when necessary to achieve the national goals, we have little difficulty concluding that the delegation was not excessive.

Questions

1. Since 1935 the Supreme Court has not invalidated a single legislative delegation to an administrative agency. Does this suggest that this matter is no longer of concern to the Court? According to the Supreme Court, what must the Congress do in order to make delegation of legislative power constitutional?
2. Does the standard in the EPA—"to protect the public health"—set

boundaries on the agency and prevent "a roving commission to inquire into evils and upon discovery correct them"?

3. In *State* v. *Marana Plantations, Inc.*, 252 P. 2d 87 (1953), the Arizona Board of Health was given the power to "formulate general policies affecting public health" and "to regulate sanitation and sanitary policies in the interests of public health." The Arizona Supreme Court said this was unconstitutional because it would allow the board to "flood the field with such sanitary laws as its unrestrained discretion may dictate." Could the same argument be made against the EPA?

CONGRESSIONAL CONTROLS

Other means of legislative control of administrative agencies have developed besides congressional design of the primary standard and boundaries.

Appropriations

The power of the purse has become a traditional method of legislative check on agency administration. In spite of the substantive declarations of Congress in many enactments, their enforcement and observance can be substantially weakened by refusal to appropriate funds for an adequate staff. Second, amendments to the original statutes creating agency powers can be added onto appropriation acts and thereby restrict future agency activities. Likewise, conditions attached to the spending of appropriated funds can modify the range of practical policy choices available to the agency.

Standing Committees

First, there exists the "subject matter" committees, one from each branch of Congress. These are charged with supervision of the content and substance of the relevant agency's assigned duties. The committee may act as a "watchdog" over the agency to determine whether additional legislation might be necessary to either expand or contract agency authority and influence. Second, a committee on Government Operations exists in both the House and Senate and is charged with the responsibility to ensure that the agencies operate with "economy and efficiency." When these committees are added to the appropriations committee, the result is that all agencies are answerable in certain contexts to at least six committees and maybe more.

EXECUTIVE CONTROLS

What is the extent of power of the executive, the president, to direct and supervise administrative action? The power to appoint the agency chief is the president's most effective weapon of control. Although this power is shared with the Senate, the president's nominees are most often accepted. Therefore, the president can be successful at changing the tempo and emphasis of the regulatory programs by the appointment process. Congress has often sought to diminish this presidential influence by providing certain statutory terms of office which require particular "cause" for removal from office. The question then arises: could the president ignore these constraints on the presidential leadership role?

In the early part of this century, Congress enacted a provision that postmasters were only to be removed with the Senate's consent. President Wilson removed Myers from his postmastership without asking for the Senate's approval. Myers sued for the salary he would have earned except for his "illegal" removal from office. The Supreme Court relied on Article II of the Constitution: "The executive power shall be vested in a President," and that the President "shall take care that the laws be faithfully executed." Then, the Court concluded that the president may properly supervise administrators "in order to secure that unitary and uniform execution of the laws which Article II of the Constitution evidently contemplated in vesting general executive power in the President alone. . . ." The president may remove any officer "on the ground that the discretion regularly entrusted to the officer by statute has not been on the whole intelligently or wisely executed." In this manner the president discharges the constitutional duty of seeing that the laws are "faithfully executed." Consequently, the Court ruled that the provision of the statute which restricted the president's power of removal was in violation of the Constitution and invalid.[2]

Humphrey's Executor v. United States
295 U.S. 602 (1935)
Supreme Court of the United States

[Humphrey, a Federal Trade Commissioner and a Republican, was removed from office by President Franklin D. Roosevelt who desired to staff the Commission with personnel of his own selection. Humphrey began suit for his salary, and after his death it was continued by his executor.]

Justice Sutherland

[The holding of the *Myers* case] goes far enough to include all purely executive officers, [but it does not] include an officer who occupies no place in the executive department and who exercises no part of the executive power vested by the Constitution in the President . . . . The Federal Trade Commission is an administrative body created by Congress to carry into effect legislative policies embodied in the statute in accordance with the legislative standard therein prescribed, and to perform other specified duties as a legislative or as a judicial aid. Such a body cannot in any proper sense be characterized as an arm or an eye of the executive. Its duties are performed without executive leave and, in the contemplation of the statute, must be free from executive control. In administering the provisions of the statute in respect of "unfair methods of competition"—that is to say in filling in and administering the details embodied by that general standard—the commission acts in part quasi-legislatively and in part quasi-judicially. . . .

We think it plain under the Constitution that illimitable power of removal is not possessed by the President in respect of officers of the character of those just named. The authority of Congress, in creating quasi-legislative or quasi-judicial agencies, to require them to act in discharge of their duties independently of executive control cannot well be doubted; and that authority includes, as an appropriate incident, power to fix the period during which they shall continue in office, and to forbid their removal except for cause in the meantime. For it is quite evident that one who holds his office only during the pleasure of another, cannot be depended upon to maintain an attitude of independence against the latter's will.

Questions

1. What is a "quasi-legislative" body? A "quasi-judicial" body?
2. Weiner, a war claims commissioner nominated by President Truman, was removed by President Eisenhower who desired personnel of his own selection. Wiener sued for his salary and the Supreme Court said, "Judging . . . the claim that the President could remove a member of an adjudicatory body like the War Claims Commission merely because he wanted his own appointees on such a commission, we are compelled to conclude that no such power is given to the President directly by the Constitution, and none is impliedly conferred upon him by statute simply because Congress said nothing about it. The philosophy of *Humphrey's Executor*, in its explicit language as well as its implications, precludes such a claim." *Wiener* v. *U.S.*, 357 U.S. 349 (1958). How is the fact that this was "an adjudicatory body" relevant and helpful in making the decision?
3. When are agencies independent of presidential control? Why could Myers be replaced in spite of congressional restraint on his removal and Humphrey could not?

INVESTIGATIVE PROCEDURES

The stages of administrative agency procedures are depicted in Figure 3-1. Since the executive powers of administrative agencies normally include the power to investigate, the preliminary procedural steps often begin with some pressure being exerted on the agency to investigate some problem. Individual members of the public or congressional representatives may complain or suggest to the administrative agency that they investigate a particular activity. Moreover, the administrative agency on its own initiative may begin an investigation.

The agency, in exercising its executive powers, may follow either of two approaches to investigating an alleged problem. It may proceed against an indi-

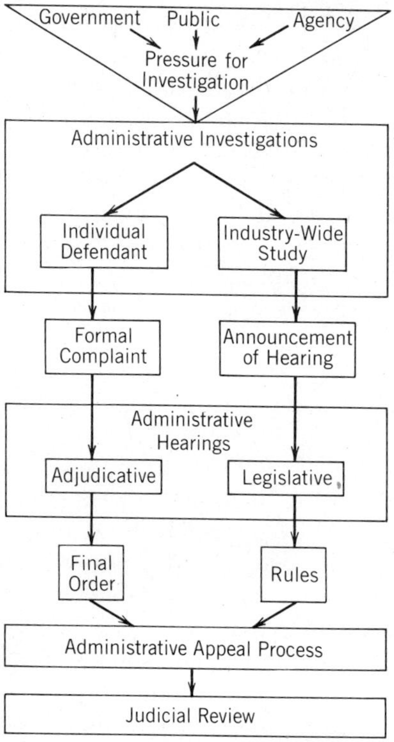

Figure 3-1. Stages of administrative agency procedures.

vidual defendant when it feels that the activity involved is peculiar to that defendant or it may proceed with an investigation of the entire industry if it believes the questionable practice is widespread. The Supreme Court affirmed this practice in *Moog Industries* v. *Federal Trade Commission*, 355 U.S. 414 (1958), when it said:

> . . . [A]lthough an allegedly illegal practice may appear to be operative throughout an industry, whether such appearances reflect fact and whether all firms in the industry should be dealt with in a single proceeding or should receive individualized treatment are questions that call for discretionary determination by the administrative agency. . . . Furthermore . . . the Commission alone is empowered to develop that enforcement policy best calculated to achieve the ends contemplated by Congress and to allocate its available funds and personnel in such a way as to execute its policy efficiently and economically.

Agencies normally possess a staff of attorneys, accountants, economists, or other appropriate specialists to aid in gathering the necessary information. In addition, to accomplish their purposes Congress conferred broad powers of investigation on the regulatory agencies. A set of judicially determined constitutional principles has been developed based on the idea that administrative power of investigation is a necessity for modern administrative government.

This clash between constitutional protections and broad investigative powers is illustrated in the following cases.

PROCEDURES FOR INVESTIGATIVE HEARINGS

Hannah v. Larche
363 U.S. 420 (1960)
Supreme Court of the United States

Chief Justice Warren

These cases involve the validity of certain Rules of Procedure adopted by the Commission on Civil Rights, which was established by Congress in 1957. They arise out of the Commission's investigation of alleged Negro voting deprivations in the State of Louisiana. . . . It was alleged, among other things, that the Commission's Rules of Procedure governing the conduct of its investigations were unconstitutional. . . .

The specific question which we must decide [is] . . . whether those procedures violate the Due Process Clause of the Fifth Amendment. . . .

Since the requirements of due process frequently vary with the type of proceeding involved, we think it is necessary at the outset to ascertain both the nature and function of this Commission. Section 104 of the Civil Rights Act of 1957 specifies the duties to be performed by the Commission. Those duties consist of (1) investigating written, sworn allegations that anyone has been discriminatorily deprived of his right to vote; (2) studying and collecting information "concerning legal developments constituting a denial of equal protection of the laws under the Constitution"; and (3) reporting to the President and Congress on its activities, findings, and recommendations. As is apparent from this brief sketch of the statutory duties imposed upon the Commission, its function is purely investigative and fact-finding. It does not adjudicate. It does not hold trials or determine anyone's civil or criminal liability. It does not issue orders. Nor does it indict, punish, or impose any legal sanctions. It does not make determinations depriving anyone of his life, liberty, or property. In short, the Commission does not and cannot take any affirmative action which will affect an individual's legal rights. The only purpose of its existence is to find facts which may subsequently be used as the basis for legislative or executive action.

The specific constitutional question, therefore, is whether persons whose conduct is under investigation by a governmental agency of this nature are entitled, by virtue of the Due Process Clause, to know the specific charges that are being investigated, as well as the identity of the complainants, and to have the right to cross-examine those complainants and other witnesses. . . .

"Due Process" is an elusive concept. Its exact boundaries are undefinable, and its content varies according to specific factual contexts. Thus, when governmental agencies adjudicate or make binding determinations which directly affect the legal rights of individuals, it is imperative that those agencies use the procedures which have traditionally been associated with the judicial process. On the other hand, when governmental action does not partake of an adjudication, as for example, when a general fact-finding investigation is being conducted, it is not necessary that the full panoply of judicial procedures be used. Therefore, as a generalization, it can be said that due process embodies the differing rules of fair play, which through the years, have become associated with differing types of proceedings. Whether the Constitution requires that a particular right obtain in a specific proceeding depends upon a complexity of factors. The nature of the alleged right involved, the nature of the proceeding, and the possible burden on that proceeding, are all considerations which must be taken into account. . . .

It is probably sufficient merely to indicate that the rights claimed by respondents are normally associated only with adjudicatory proceedings, and that since the Commission does not adjudicate it need not be bound by adjudicatory procedures. Yet, the respondents contend and the court below implied, that such procedures are required since the Commission's proceedings might irreparably harm those being investigated by subjecting them to public opprobrium and scorn, the distinct likelihood of losing their jobs, and the possibility of criminal prosecutions. That any of these consequences will result is purely conjectural. There is nothing in the record to indicate that . . . past Commission hearings have had any harmful effects upon witnesses appearing before the Commission. However, even if such collateral consequences were to flow from the Commission's investigations, they would not be the result of any affirmative determinations made by the Commission, and they would not affect the legitimacy of the Commission's investigative function.

On the other hand, the investigative process could be completely disrupted if investigative hearings were transformed into trial-like proceedings, and if persons who might be indirectly affected by an investigation were given an absolute right to cross-examine every witness called to testify. Fact-finding agencies without any power to adjudicate would be diverted from their legitimate duties and would be plagued by the injection of collateral issues that would make the investigation interminable. Even a person not called as a witness could demand the right to appear at the hearing, cross-examine any witness whose testimony or sworn affidavit allegedly defamed or incriminated him, and call an unlimited number of witnesses of his own selection. This type of proceeding would make a shambles of the investigation and stifle the agency in its gathering of facts.

In addition to these persuasive considerations, we think it is highly significant that the Commission's procedures are not historically foreign to other forms of investigation under our system. Far from being unique, the Rules of Procedure adopted by the Commission are similar to those which . . . have traditionally governed the proceedings of the vast majority of government investigating agencies.

A typical agency is the Federal Trade Commission. Its rules draw a clear distinction between adjudicative proceedings and investigative proceedings. Although the latter are frequently initiated by complaints from undisclosed informants, and although the Commission may use the information obtained during investigations to initiate adjudicative proceedings, nevertheless, persons summoned to appear before investigative proceedings are entitled only to a general notice of "the purpose and scope of the investigation," and while they may have the advice of counsel, "counsel may not, as a matter of right, otherwise participate in the investigation." The reason for these rules is obvious. The Federal Trade Commission could not conduct an efficient investigation if persons being investigated were permitted to convert the investigation into a trial. . . . [A]ny person investigated by the Federal Trade Commission will be accorded all the traditional judicial safeguards at a subsequent adjudicative proceeding, just as any person investigated by the Civil Rights Commission will have all of these safeguards, should some type of adjudicative proceeding subsequently be instituted. . . .

We think it is fairly clear from this survey of various phases of governmental investigation that witnesses appearing before investigating agencies . . . have generally not been accorded the rights of apprisal, confrontation, or cross-examination. . . .

Thus, the purely investigative nature of the Commission's proceedings, the burden that the claimed rights would place upon those proceedings, and the traditional procedure of investigating agencies in general, leads us to conclude that the Commission's Rules of Procedure comport with the requirements of due process.

Questions

1. What was the function or purpose of the hearing by the Commission on Civil Rights?
2. What rules of procedure did the witnesses desire? What reasons does the Court give for denying their claims?
3. Is the reader familiar with any legislative investigative hearings? Did they seem fair?
4. Can you distinguish between the two basic types of hearings that the Court discussed in *Hannah* v. *Larche*.

ADMINISTRATIVE SUBPOENA POWER

Many administrative investigations are accomplished voluntarily and without reliance on compulsory process. However, since the need for information is sometimes resisted, administrative agencies may enforce their request by seeking a subpoena from the appropriate court. The agency may call for a subpoena to seek the testimony of a person (*ad testificandum*) or to request records (*duces tecum*). A subpoena, if ignored, subjects the recipient to charges of "contempt of court." When the administrative agency is seeking judicial enforcement of its subpoena, the federal court may consider appropriate questions to determine whether the subpoena should be enforced. The Fourth Amendment protects "the people" from "unreasonable searches and seizures." It also prohibits court issuance of search warrants unless "probable cause" for the search is shown. If issued, the warrant must particularly describe the place to be searched and the person or things to be seized. Therefore, the court must determine whether the subpoena sought is overly broad and excessive in its request for information. Of course, the material sought also must be "subjects" that Congress has authorized the agency to investigate. Consider the attitude of the Court expressed in the following case.

Oklahoma Press Publishing Co. v. Walling

327 U.S. 186 (1946)
Supreme Court of the United States

Justice Rutledge

Petitioners . . . insist that the question of coverage must be adjudicated before the subpoenas may be enforced. . . .

It is claimed that enforcement would permit the Administrator to conduct general fishing expeditions into petitioners' books, records, and papers, in order to secure evidence that they have violated the Act, without a prior charge or complaint and simply to secure information upon which to base one, all allegedly in violation of the [4th] Amendment's search and seizure provision. . . .

Historically private corporations have been subject to broad visitorial power, both in England and in this country. And it long has been established that Congress may exercise wide investigative power over them, analogous to the visitorial power of the incorporating state, when their activities take place within or affect interstate commerce . . . .

Without attempt to summarize or accurately distinguish all of the cases, the fair distillation, in so far as they apply merely to the production of corporate records and papers in response to a subpoena or order authorized by law and safeguarded by judicial sanction, seems to be that . . . the Fourth . . . guards against abuse only by way of too much indefiniteness or breadth in the things required to be "particularly described," . . . [and] also the inquiry . . . [must be] one the demanding agency is authorized by law to make and the materials specified are relevant. The gist of the protection is in the requirement, expressed in terms, that the disclosure sought shall not be unreasonable.

. . . It is not necessary, as in the case of a warrant, that a specific charge or complaint of violation of law be pending or that the order be made pursuant to one. It is enough that the investigation be for a lawfully authorized purpose, within the power of Congress to command. This has been ruled most often perhaps in relation to grand jury investigations, but also frequently in respect to general or statistical investigations authorized by Congress. The requirement of "probable cause, supported by oath or affirmation," literally applicable in the case of a warrant, is satisfied in that of an order for production by the court's determination that the investigation is authorized by Congress, is for a purpose Congress can order, and the documents sought are relevant to the inquiry. Beyond this the requirement of reasonableness, including particularity in "describing the place to be searched, and the persons or things to be seized," also literally applicable to warrants, comes down to specification of the documents to be produced adequate, but not excessive, for the purposes of the relevant inquiry. Necessarily, as has been said, this cannot be reduced to formula; for relevancy and adequacy or excess in the breadth of the subpoena are matters variable in relation to the nature, purpose and scope of the inquiry.

When these principles are applied to the facts of the present cases, it is impossible to conceive how a violation of petitioners' rights could have been involved. . . . All the records sought were relevant to the authorized inquiry, the purpose of which was to determine two issues, whether petitioners were subject to the Act and, if so, whether they were violating it. . .

Petitioners stress that enforcement will subject them to inconvenience, expense and harassment. . . . There is no harassment when the subpoena is issued and enforced according to law. The Administrator is authorized to enter and inspect, but the Act makes his right to do so subject in all cases to judicial supervision. Persons from whom he seeks relevant information are not required to submit to his demand, if in any respect it is unreasonable or overreaches the authority Congress has given. To it they may make "appropriate defense" surrounded by every safeguard of judicial restraint.

Questions

1. Must a specific charge or complaint of violation of law be issued before a warrant or subpoena may be enforced?
2. When an administrative agency seeks enforcement of its subpoena, how does the court determine if "probable cause" to issue the subpoena is satisfied?
3. How does the court determine if the subpoena has sufficient "particularity" in describing the things sought by the agency?
4. May a subpoena be avoided on the grounds that it will subject the recipient to inconvenience and expense?
5. Moreover, in *United States* v. *Morton Salt Co.*, 338 U.S. 632 (1950) an agency sought court enforcement of an order requiring a "complete statement [of] prices, terms and conditions of sale" during a certain period of time. The defendants maintained that the agency was on a fishing expedition. The Court responded by saying, "We will assume for the argument that this is so. . . . We must not disguise the fact that sometimes, especially early in the history of the federal administrative tribunal, the courts were persuaded to engraft judicial limitations upon the administrative process. The courts could not go fishing, and so it followed neither could anyone else. . . . Even if one were to regard the request for information in this case as caused by nothing more than official curiosity, nevertheless law enforcing agencies have a legitimate right to satisfy themselves that corporate behavior is consistent with the law and the public interest."

Considering this language, what Fourth Amendment protection remains?

ADMINISTRATIVE HEARINGS

The Administrative Procedure Act (APA) contains provisions that pertain to the procedural aspects of activities by regulatory agencies. The APA prescribes procedures to be followed by administrative agencies in rule making and in adjudicatory proceedings. The cases in this section contrast the differences between rule making and adjudicatory hearings.

After preliminary investigations, an agency may begin an adjudicatory hearing by issuing a formal complaint against a particular defendant or defendants. The agency issues a complaint when it has "reason to believe" that the law has been violated in some manner. The defendants have a number of days in which to answer the complaint. Often the defendant may be interested in having the issue settled by the entry of a "consent order." The defendant is given an opportunity to negotiate an agreement with the agency which, if accepted, may become a consent order. In such consent orders, it is understood that the agreement is for purposes of settlement of the controversy and does not constitute an admission by the defendant of having violated the law. However, when a consent order is issued by the agency, it carries the force of law with respect to future behavior by the defendant. Any violations of such order by the defendant may result in civil penalties, such as a fine, for each violation. If the parties are not able to negotiate an agreement, an adjudicatory hearing is held to determine if a violation of the law as alleged in the complaint has, in fact, occurred.

NEED FOR ADJUDICATIVE HEARING

Often administrative officials act against a person without first affording the individual a hearing. Such instances are increasingly challenged as a denial of due process of law. For example, in 1961 it was held that due process requires notice and some opportunity for hearing before students at a tax-supported college could be expelled for misconduct.[3] Whether a hearing is required prior to administrative action depends on the circumstances and the interests of the parties involved. The students' "interest" was the right to remain at a public institution of higher learning without interruption of studies. On the other hand, the government's "interest" involved "no consideration of immediate danger to the public or of peril to the national security," which would prevent the school board from exercising at least the fundamental principle of fairness by giving the accused students an opportunity to be heard in their own defense. In effect, the Court ruled that the interest advanced by the students outweighed the interest of the state school system and, therefore, entitled the students to a hearing *prior* to administrative action.

In contrast, the Supreme Court held that a student dismissed for poor academic performance was not entitled to a hearing *prior* to dismissal.[4] The Court said that "there is a . . . significant difference between the failure of a student to meet academic standards and the violation by a student of valid rules of conduct. This difference calls for far less stringent procedural requirements in the case of an academic dismissal." The Court felt that the student had been awarded as much due process as was required because the school had fully informed the student of the faculty's dissatisfaction with her progress and the danger this posed to continued enrollment. The Court concluded:

> Academic evaluations of a student, in contrast to disciplinary determinations, bear little resemblance to the judicial and administrative factfinding proceedings to which we have traditionally attached a full hearing requirement.
>
> The decision to dismiss respondent . . . rested on the academic judgment of school officials that she did not have the necessary . . . ability to perform adequately . . . and was making insufficient progress toward the goal. Such a judgment is by its nature more subjective and evaluative than the typical factual questions presented in the average disciplinary decision. Like the decision of an individual professor as to the proper grade for a student in his course, the determination whether to dismiss a student for academic reasons requires an expert evaluation of cumulative information and is not readily adapted to the procedural tools of judicial or administrative decision-making.
>
> Under such circumstances, we decline to ignore the historic judgment of educators and thereby formalize the academic dismissal process by requiring a hearing.

In short, the Court was not convinced that this type of decision could be better handled in a formal hearing. Without sufficient benefits to be expected from the imposition of the hearing requirement and recognizing the burdens imposed on the educational institution by the hearing requirement, the Court ruled that the student's interest was sufficiently protected by the present process of warnings of possible academic dismissal.

Using the same "balancing" process in a business setting, the Court has ruled that in "extraordinary situations" it is necessary for administrative officials to seize business property or otherwise act immediately without an opportunity for a *prior* hearing. The Court has held that immediate administrative action is needed "to collect internal revenue of the United States, to meet the needs of the national war effort, to protect against economic disaster of a bank failure, and protect the public from misbranded drugs and contaminated food."[5] In each of these situations, the public's interest outweighs the private interest and justifies the summary action by the government. In most instances, a *subsequent* hearing is held to determine if the administrative official acted within his or her authority and reasonably in the circumstances. If not, the individual whose property was confiscated or whose interest was interfered with is entitled to compensation from the governmental official.

NEED FOR LEGISLATIVE HEARINGS

Pharmaceutical Manufacturers Association v. Finch
307 F. Supp. 858 (1970)
U.S. District Court (Del.)

In this action for declaratory and injunctive relief, the Pharmaceutical Manufacturers Association ("PMA"), on behalf of its members, seeks a preliminary injunction restraining the Secretary of Health, Education and Welfare [HEW] and the Commissioner of Food and Drugs from taking any action in reliance upon the regulations contained in the Commissioner's Order of September 19, 1969. The September regulations promulgated new standards of evidence necessary to demonstrate the effectiveness of drug products and applied those standards retroactively so as to place in jeopardy the continued marketing of thousands of drug products introduced before 1962 wih Food and Drug Administration ("FDA") approval and effectiveness of which FDA has not yet challenged. . . .

. . . PMA contends that the regulations are invalid because they were issued without notice and opportunity for comment in violation of the Administrative Procedure Act. . . .

. . . [T]he Administrative Procedure Act requires the rule-making by an agency be preceded by "general notice of proposed rule-making" in the Federal Register at least thirty days before the effective date of the proposed rule, and further requires that the agency afford interested persons "an opportunity to participate in the rule-making through submission of written data, views or arguments with or without opportunity for oral presentation." That procedure was not followed in this case. The September regulations were made effective by the Commissioner upon their publication in the Federal Register without prior notice or an opportunity for submission of comments by interested parties.

Exempt from the general requirements of notice and opportunity for comment are "interpretative rules, general statements of policy, or rules of agency organization, procedure, or practice." The Commissioner has characterized the September regulations as "procedural and interpretative" and thus contends that they fall within the exception to the notice and comment requirement. But the label placed on the September rules by the Commissioner does not determine whether the notice and comment provisions are applicable. As the Supreme Court has emphasized, in holding that a regulation of the Federal Communications Commission constituted an order subject to judicial review, "[T]he particular label placed upon it by the Commission is not necessarily conclusive, for it is the substance of what the Commission has purported to do and has done which is decisive."

. . . [T]hat determination must be made in the light of the basic purpose of those statutory requirements. The basic policy of Section 4 at least requires that when a proposed regulation of general applicability has a substantial impact on the regulated industry, or an important class of the members of the products of that industry, notice and opportunity for comment should first be provided. . . .

The all pervasive and substantial impact which the September regulations have upon the drug industry and in turn upon prescribing physicians and their patients, makes it imperative that the Commissioner comply with the notice and comment provisions of Section 4 before such regulations become effective.

Questions

1. The Administrative Procedure Act requires an agency to give notice and an opportunity to participate to those individuals affected by the creation of a new rule. However, the Administrative Procedure Act contains some exemptions. What exemptions did the secretary of HEW rely on to negate the necessity of providing notice and opportunity to participate? Why did the district court not agree with the secretary's determination on the status of this exemption?
2. Can a decision (rule) announced in an adjudicatory proceeding become a substitute process for announcing "rules"? The Supreme Court said the following:

   The rule-making provisions of . . . [the Administrative Procedure Act] . . . were designed to assure fairness and mature consideration of rules of general application. They may not be avoided by the process of making rules in the course of adjudicatory proceedings. There is no warrant in law for the Board to replace the statutory scheme with a rule-making procedure of its own invention. Apart from the fact that the device fashioned by the Board does not comply with statutory command, it obviously falls short of the substance of the requirements of the Administrative Procedure Act. The "rule" created in *Excelsior* was not published in the Federal Register which is the statutory and accepted means of giving notice of a rule as adopted; only selected organizations were given notice of the "hearing," whereas notice in the Federal Register would have been general in character; under the Administrative Procedure Act, the terms of substance of the rule would have to be stated in the notice of hearing, and all interested parties would have an opportunity to participate in the rule making. . . . Adjudicated cases may and do, of course, serve as vehicles for the formulation of agency policies, which are applied and announced therein. They generally provide a guide to action that the agency may be expected to take in future cases. Subject to the qualified role of *stare decisis* in the administrative process, they may serve as precedents. But this is far from saying . . . that commands, decisions, or policies announced in adjudication are "rules" in the sense that they must, without more, be obeyed by the affected public. *NLRB* v. *Wyman-Gordon Co.*, 394 U.S. 759 (1969).

PARTICIPATION IN HEARINGS

Administrative agencies are increasingly faced with the demand for a wider participation in the hearings. Various parties, often consumer groups, request the right to be heard in hearings usually reserved exclusively for the agency and party under the agency's jurisdiction. The following case illustrates the issues involved.

Hahn v. Gottlieb

430 F. 2d 1243 (1970)
United States Court of Appeals (1st Cir.)

In this appeal, we are asked to decide whether tenants in housing subsidized under the National Housing Act (NHA) have the right to an administrative hearing. . . .

Plaintiffs are members of a tenants' association at the Castle Square project in Boston (the project), a development of low- and middle-income housing financed under NHA. Defendants Gottlieb and Druker (the landlord) are the current owners of the project. Prior to the expiration of the plaintiffs' leases in July 1969, the landlord filed a proposed monthly rent increase of $28 per apartment with the Federal Housing Administration (FHA). Plaintiffs sought an opportunity to be heard on the proposed increase; and, when the FHA failed to satisfy their request, they brought suit in federal district court. . . .

. . . [T]he statute confers broad discretion on the Secretary of HUD. The Secretary is authorized to approve mortgagors and to supervise their operations "under a regulatory agreement or otherwise, as to rents, charges, and methods of operation, in such form and in such manner as in the opinion of the Secretary will effectuate the purposes of this section."

Implementing these broad grants of authority, the Secretary has promulgated regulations concerning priorities and income limits for occupancy in FHA projects. The Secretary also regulates the landlord's return on his investment by strictly supervising accounting practices, and, in the case of limited distribution mortgagors like defendants Gottlieb and Druker, by setting a six percent ceiling on return. Applications for rent increases must be submitted to the FHA, which takes into account the rental income necessary to maintain a project's economic soundness and "to provide a reasonable return on the investment consistent with providing reasonable rentals to the tenants." FHA's agreement with the landlord in this case further provides that rental increases will be approved if necessary to compensate for increases in expense "over which the owners have no effective control."

The regulations illustrate that the success of a FHA project requires a flexible exercise of administrative discretion. The ultimate goal of the program is housing for low- and middle-class families, but this goal is to be achieved by expanding the range of housing needs which can be met by private enterprise. To provide low-income housing maintaining a sound investment requires considerable adaptability. We think Congress recognized this need for adaptability when it authorized the Secretary to regulate mortgagors by individual agreement as well as by general rule. Of course, the need for administrative flexibility does not of itself preclude an agency hearing or judicial review, but we must take care lest we kill the goose in our solicitude for the eggs.

Plaintiffs' initial claim is that they are entitled to a formal hearing before the FHA prior to the approval of any rent increase. This contention finds no support in the text of the National Housing Act. Plaintiffs claim, however, that both the right to a hearing and its procedural characteristics can be derived from the Due Process Clause of the Fifth Amendment. . . .

The proceeding in which plaintiffs seek to assert their interest is basically an informal rate-making process. The landlord who seeks a rent increase submits documentation to the FHA showing his expenses, return on investment, and the like. The FHA staff then examines his proposal in the light of the terms of the regulatory agreement, the broad criteria of the regulations, and current economic conditions. Plaintiffs seek to encumber these negotiations with a formal hearing, the right to cross-examine adverse witnesses, and an impartial decision-maker, who must state the reasons for his decision and the evidence on which he relies. These procedural safeguards are characteristic of adjudicatory proceedings, where the outcome turns on accurate resolution of specific factual disputes. Such safeguards are not, however, essential in "legislative" proceedings, such as rate-making, where decision depends on broad familiarity with economic conditions. . . .

The distinction between "legislative" and "adjudicative" facts is particulary apt in this case, where it is the tenants rather than the landlord who seek a hearing. The tenants are unlikely to have special familiarity with their landlord's financial conditions, the intricacies of project management, or the state of the economy in the surrounding area. Hopefully, the FHA can check the accuracy of the landlord's documentation without their assistance. They may be aware of construction defects in their own living areas, but if, contrary to [law], a building has been approved which does not conform to applicable standards, there would seem to be limited utility in rehearsing old mistakes each time a rental increase is sought. Of course, tenant's complaints about maintenance and living conditions ought to be heard, but such grievances can be dealt with without requiring a trial-type hearing with each rent increase. Indeed, an effective grievance system should be operable at all times, not merely when the landlord seeks to raise his rents. Thus, the elaborate procedural safeguards which plaintiffs demand are unlikely to elicit essential information in the general run of cases.

These procedures would, however, place a significant burden on the relationship between the landlord and the FHA. At present, applications for rent increases are merely one aspect of an on-going relationship between insured and insurer. Plaintiffs would turn these applications into occasions for full-scale review of the relationship, as their conduct in the hearing they have already received illustrates. Such reconsideration may delay economically necessary rent increases and discourage private investors from entering the FHA program at all. Equally important the project in question contains some 500 tenants, each of whom has the same interest in low-rent housing.

Applying the constitutionally relevant test, therefore, it seems to us that the government interest in a summary procedure for approving rent increases outweighs the tenants' interest in greater procedural safeguards. The procedures demanded by plaintiffs would place substantial additional burdens on the insurer-insured relationship without necessarily improving the fundamental fairness of the proceedings. We, therefore, hold that tenants in housing financed under the National Housing Act are not constitutionally entitled to an administrative hearing on their landlord's proposals for increased rents.

Questions

1. What statutory authority does the FHA have over the owners of tenements in which the FHA has supplied funds? What factors does the FHA consider in determining the appropriate rental rates for FHA housing?
2. Why did the Court rule that the tenants were not entitled to a hearing when FHA is considering rental increases? Do you agree with the reasoning?
3. In *Hahn* the Court was faced with a hearing which was to establish "legislative" facts for the purpose of determining appropriate rental rates. Although it may be appropriate to deny tenants a hearing in regard to rate making, would the Court feel differently if the dispute concerned "adjudicative" facts? Consider *Escalera* v. *New York City Housing Authority*, 425 F. 2d 853 (2d. Cir., 1970) in which the housing authority terminated tenancies on the ground of nondesirability of the tenants. The procedural system to terminate included conversations between the project manager and the tenant, tenant hearings before the Tenant Review Board which allowed the tenant to summarize his or her position but not present any witness, a Review Board decision based on items in the tenant's file which may be unknown to the tenant, and no findings or reasons for the termination were released to the tenant. Would the Court consider this procedural system to be sufficient for the establishment of adjudicative facts with which to make a fair determination of the tenant's rights?

Despite the rationale of *Hahn*, the imbalance of consumer advocacy in administrative hearings that determine policy has been increasingly recognized in judicial decisions and legislative debates and proposals. In *United Church of Christ* v. *FCC*, 359 F. 2d 994 (D.C. Cir. 1966), an allegedly racist Mississippi radio station was applying for a renewal of its license before the Federal Communication Commission (FCC). The church petitioned for a right to intervene and present evidence and arguments in opposition to the relicensing. The FCC refused to hear the church on grounds that the listening public had not suffered an injury and that if the listeners had "standing to sue" in these cases, it would pose great administrative burdens on the agency. The court of appeals disagreed with the FCC and remanded the case back to the FCC with the provision that some "audience participation" be allowed in the new proceedings before the commission. The court determined that unless consumers could be heard, there might be no one to bring program deficiencies or offensive commercialization to the attention of the commission in an effective manner. As this case indicates, there is a growing body of case law in which the courts are requiring federal agencies to consider the consumer groups that are being affected by the agency's decisions.

The concept of intervention before regulatory bodies by state attorney generals is also growing. Since attorney generals are generally charged with the responsibility of representation before various bodies of state government, the attorney general may intervene to present various sides of an issue before a commission. It is not uncommon for two assistant attorney generals to appear on opposite sides on the same case before a commission.

Regulatory agencies that oversee public utilities are charged with protecting the public interest. Since the services and goods produced by these regulated industries are paid for by the consumer, the agencies seek to balance a "fair price" to the consumer for these services and products with a "fair return" to the supplier. Regulation seeks, like competition, to provide satisfactory services at rates that make efficient use of natural resources. However, historically the performance of regulatory agencies has not always been satisfactory from the consumer's point of view. The regulatory agencies usually set price levels on a cost-plus basis and interfere little in the development of standards of quality for service or products. Many feel this performance was the result of agencies being susceptible to great private pressures from the industries they regulate. To compensate for these industry pressures in the electric utility area, Congress enacted the Public Utility Regulatory Policies Act (PURPA) of 1978. PURPA entitles any consumer to intervene and participate as a matter of right in electric utility rate-making proceedings. PURPA also establishes alternative methods to compensate such consumer representatives if they substantially contribute to the approval of a rate incorporating their views.

ADMINISTRATIVE APPEALS

In larger administrative agencies adjudicatory hearings are often held before independent administrative law judges. These individuals are civil servants performing judicial duties on assignment to various agencies. The decision of the administrative law judge articulates the "findings of fact" and "interpretations of law," which are later reviewed by the top officials of the agency. This review by the agency commissioners or board members is an internal appeal process to correct or affirm the decisions of the hearing judge. Consequently, a final decision or order by the agency is not rendered until the entire process has been completed. Upon completion, the decision of the agency is subject to review by the courts which usually involves an appellate court because the agency served as the "trial court." To allow the agency to correct its own internal errors and avoid unnecessary court congestion, the courts generally review only the "final orders" of the agencies. Sometimes a party may attempt an earlier review by the courts. Such efforts are most often denied "on the long settled rule of judicial administration that no one is entitled to judicial relief for a supposed or threatened injury until the prescribed administrative remedy has been exhausted." *Myers* v. *Bethlehem Corp.,* 303 U.S. 41 (1938). This rule requiring exhaustion of the administrative remedy "cannot be circumvented by asserting that the charge on which the complaint rests is groundless" or "that the mere holding of the prescribed administrative hearing would result in irreparable damage." Trials are sometimes necessary to establish that the suit is groundless.

Questions

1. May a defendant obtain a court injunction to stop an administrative hearing which is outside the agency's statutory power?
2. What is the purpose of the rule requiring an exhaustion of administrative remedies prior to obtaining judicial review?

JUDICIAL REVIEW

Judicial review is employed as a control device over an administrative agency's actions upon completion of the administrative proceedings. The function of judicial review is not to examine the correctness of an administrative decision but rather to determine whether an agency has done the following:

1. Acted within its delegated authority.
2. Conducted a fair proceeding.
3. Made a reasonable choice supported by substantial evidence.

The function of judicial review may be restricted. The statute, for example, may provide that the agency's determination shall be final and not subject to judicial review. Congress, for example, has often established draft boards whose selection of young people for the armed forces is not subject to judicial review.

Also, there are practical limits on judicial review. Court review is expensive, it involves delay, and there is perhaps a fear of adverse publicity. Moreover, even if the court reverses the agency decision and remands the case, the agency can reach essentially the same decision again and merely correct its court-declared error.

STANDARDS FOR REVIEW

Citizens To Preserve Overton Park, Inc. v. Volpe

401 U.S. 412 (1971)
Supreme Court of the United States

Justice Marshall

A threshold question—whether petitioners are entitled to any judicial review—is easily answered. Section 701 of the Administrative Procedure Act, provides that the action of "each authority of the Government of the United States," which includes the Department of Transportation, is subject to judicial review except where there is a statutory prohibition on review or where "agency action is committed to agency discretion by law." In this case, there is no indication that Congress sought to prohibit judicial review and there is most certainly no "showing of 'clear and convincing evidence' of a . . . legislative intent" to restrict access to judicial review.

Similarly, the Secretary's decision here does not fall within the exception for action "committed to agency discretion." This is a very narrow exception. The legislative history of the Administrative Procedure Act indicates that it is applicable in those rare instances where "statutes are drawn in such broad terms that in a given case there is no law to apply."

Section 4(f) of the Department of Transportation Act and § 138 of the Federal-Aid Highway Act are clear and specific directives. Both the Department of Transportation Act and the Federal-Aid to Highway Act provide that the Secretary "shall not approve any program or project" that requires the use of any public parkland "unless (1) there is no feasible and prudent alternative to the use of such land, and (2) such program includes all possible planning to minimize harm to such park. . . ." This language is a plain and explicit bar to the use of federal funds for construction of highways through parks—only the most unusual situations are exempted. . . .

Plainly, there is "law to apply" and thus the exemption for action "committed to agency discretion" is inapplicable. But the existence of judicial review is only the start: the standard for review must also be determined. For that we must look to § 706 of the Administrative Procedure Act, which provides that a "reviewing court shall . . . hold unlawful and set aside agency action, findings, and conclusions found" not to meet six separate standards. In all cases agency action must be set aside if the action was "arbitrary, capricious, an abuse of discretion, or otherwise not in accordance with law" or if the action failed to meet statutory, procedural, or constitutional requirements. . . .

The court is first required to decide whether the Secretary acted within the scope of his authority. This determination naturally begins with a delineation of the scope of the Secretary's authority and discretion.

As has been shown, Congress has specified only a small range of choices that the Secretary can make. Also involved in this initial inquiry is a determination of whether on the facts the Secretary's decision can reasonably be said to be within that range. The reviewing court must consider whether the Secretary properly construed his authority to approve the use of parkland as limited to situations where there are no feasible alternative routes or where feasible alternative routes involve uniquely difficult problems. And the reviewing court must be able to find that the Secretary could have reasonably believed that in this case there are no feasible alternatives or that alternatives do involve unique problems.

Scrutiny of the facts does not end, however, with the determination that the Secretary has acted within the scope of his statutory authority. Section 706 (2) (A) requires a finding that the actual choice made was not "arbitrary, capricious, an abuse of discretion, or otherwise not in accordance with law." To make this finding the court must consider whether the decision was based on a consideration of the relevant factors and whether there has been a clear error of judgment.

Although this inquiry into the facts is to be searching and careful, the ultimate standard of review is a narrow one. The court is not empowered to substitute its judgment for that of the agency.

The final inquiry is whether the Secretary's action followed the necessary procedural requirements. Here the only procedural error alleged is the failure of the Secretary to make formal findings and state his reason for allowing the highway to be built through the park.

Undoubtedly, review of the Secretary's action is hampered by his failure to make such findings, but the absence of formal findings does not necessarily require that the case be remanded to the Secretary. Neither the Department of Transportation Act nor the Federal-Aid Highway Act requires such formal findings. Moreover, the Administrative Procedure Act requirements that there be formal findings in certain rule-making and adjudicatory proceedings do not apply to the Secretary's action here. And, although formal findings may be required in some cases in the absence of statutory directives when the nature of the agency action is ambiguous, those situations are rare. Plainly, there is no ambiguity here; the Secretary has approved the construction of I-40 through Overton Park and has approved a specific design for the project.

Thus it is necessary to remand this case to the District Court for plenary review of the Secretary's decision. That review is to be based on the full administrative record that was before the Secretary at the time he made his decision. But since the bare record may not disclose the factors that were considered or the Secretary's construction of the evidence it may be necessary for the District Court to require some explanation in order to determine if the Secretary acted within the scope of his authority and if the Secretary's action was justifiable under the applicable standard. The court may require the administrative officials who participated in the decision to give testimony explaining their action. Of course, such inquiry into the mental processes of administrative decisionmakers is usually to be avoided. But . . . it may be that the only way there can be effective judicial review is by examining the decisionmakers themselves.

The District Court is not, however, required to make such an inquiry. It may be that the Secretary can prepare formal findings that will provide an adequate explanation for his action. Such an explanation will, to some extent, be a "*post hoc* rationalization" and thus must be viewed critically. If the District Court decides that additional explanation is necessary, that court should consider which method will prove the most expeditious so that full review may be had as soon as possible.

Questions

1. The Administrative Procedure Act provides for judicial review except in two instances. What are those two exceptions to judicial review? Why did the Court think neither exception applied in this instance?
2. Having decided that the decision was subject to judicial review, the Court had to determine the appropriate standard for review. What standards are set in the Administrative Procedure Act?

3. What should the Court consider in deciding whether the secretary acted within the scope of his authority?
4. Assuming that the secretary did act within the scope of his statutory authority, the Court must determine whether the actual decision made by the secretary was not "arbitrary, capricious, an abuse of discretion, or otherwise not in accordance with law." How is the Court to determine whether the decision made by the secretary was arbitrary?
5. The Court on review can also determine whether the secretary followed any necessary procedural requirements. What procedural error was alleged to have been violated by the secretary? Did the Court conclude that this procedural requirement existed?

EXCEEDING AUTHORITY

SEC v. Sloan

436 U.S. 103 (1978)
Supreme Court of the United States

Justice Rehnquist

Under the Securities Exchange Act of 1934, the Securities and Exchange Commission has the authority "summarily to suspend trading in any security . . . for a period not exceeding ten days" if "in its opinion the public interest and the protection of investors so require." Acting pursuant to this authority the Commission issued a series of consecutive orders suspending trading in the common stock of Canadian Javelin, Ltd. (CJL), for over a year. . . .

. . . During this series of suspensions respondent Sloan, who owned 13 shares of CJL stock and had engaged in substantial purchases and short sales of shares of that stock, filed a petition in the United States Court of Appeals for the Second Circuit . . . [alleging] that the "tacking" of 10-day summary suspension orders for an indefinite period was . . . a deprivation of due process . . . [and] beyond the Commission's authority because the statute specifically authorized suspension "for a period not exceeding ten days. . . ."

[This] . . . is a case in which the Commission issued a series of summary suspension orders lasting over a year on the basis of evidence revealing a single, though likely sizable, manipulative scheme. Thus, the only question confronting us is whether, even upon a periodic redetermination of "necessity," the Commission is statutorily authorized to issue a series of summary suspension orders based upon a single set of events or circumstances which threaten an orderly market. This question must, in our opinion, be answered in the negative.

The first and most salient point leading us to this conclusion is the language of the statute. Section 12(k) authorizes the Commission "summarily to suspend trading in any security . . . *for a period not exceeding ten days* . . ." (emphasis added). The Commission would have us read the [italicized] phrase as a limitation only upon the duration of a single suspension order. So read, the Commission could indefinitely suspend trading in a security without any hearing or other procedural safeguards as long as it redetermined every 10 days that suspension was required by the public interest and for the protection of investors. While perhaps not an impossible reading of the statute, we are persuaded it is not the most natural or logical one. The duration limitation rather appears on its face to be just that—a maximum time period for which trading can be suspended for any single set of circumstances.

Apart from the language of the statute, which we find persuasive in and of itself, there are other reasons to adopt this construction of the statute. In the first place, the power to summarily suspend trading in a security even for 10 days, without any notice, opportunity to be heard, or findings based upon a record, is an awesome power with a potentially devastating impact on the issuer, its shareholders, and other investors. A clear mandate from Congress, such as that found in Section 12(k), is necessary to confer this power. No less clear a mandate can be expected from Congress to authorize the Commission to extend, virtually without limit, these periods of suspension. But we find no such unmistakable mandate in Section 12(k). Indeed, if anything, that section points in the opposite direction.

Other sections of the statute reinforce the conclusion that in this area Congress considered summary restrictions to be somewhat drastic and properly used only for very brief periods of time. When explicitly longer term, though perhaps temporary, measures are to be taken against some person, company, or security, Congress invariably requires the Commission to give some sort of notice and opportunity to be heard. For example, Section 12(j) of the Act authorizes the Commission, as it deems necessary for the protection of investors, to suspend the registration of a security for a period not exceeding 12 months if it makes certain findings "*on the record after notice and opportunity for hearing* . . ." (emphasis added). Another section of the Act empowers the Commission to suspend broker-dealer registration for a period not exceeding 12 months upon certain findings made only "*on the record after notice and opportunity for hearing*" (emphasis added). Former Section 15(b)(6), which dealt with the registration of broker-dealers, also lends support to the notion that as a general matter Congress meant to allow the Commission to take summary action only for the period specified in the statute when that action is based upon any single set of circumstances. That section allowed the Commission to summarily postpone the effective date of registration for 15 days, and then, *after appropriate notice and opportunity for hearing*, to continue that postponement pending final resolution of the matter. The section which replaced Section 15(b)(6) even further underscores this general pattern. It requires the Commission to take some action—either granting the registration or instituting proceedings to determine whether registration should be denied—within 45 days. In light of the explicit congressional recognition in other sections of the Act, both past and present, that any long-term sanctions or any continuation of summary restrictions must be accompanied by notice and an opportunity for a hearing, it is difficult to read the silence in Section 12(k) as an authorization for an extension of summary restrictions without such a hearing, as the Commission contends. The more plausible interpretation is that Congress did not intend the Commission to have the power to extend the length of suspensions under Section 12(k) at all, much less to repeatedly extend such suspensions without any hearing.

* * *

In sum, had Congress intended the Commission to have the power to summarily suspend trading virtually indefinitely we expect that it could and would have authorized it more clearly than it did in Section 12(k). The sweeping nature of that power supports this expectation. The absence of any truly persuasive legislative history to support the Commission's view, and the entire statutory scheme suggesting that in fact the Commission is not so empowered, reinforce our conclusion that the Court of Appeals was correct in concluding no such power exists.

Questions

1. What were the arguments of the SEC that it possessed the power to issue a series of summary suspension orders?
2. Why did the Supreme Court feel the SEC lacked such power?

DISCLOSING INFORMATION

Administrative agencies in their regulatory functions accumulate a great deal of information concerning individuals in business enterprises. The chief administrative agent, the president, has from the beginning of our nation asserted a constitutional right to withhold information. Presidents have withheld information from Congress and others under the doctrine of executive privilege. Issues concerning the extent of executive privilege are complex and continuing, but executive privilege unquestionably exists. The courts have jurisdiction to consider problems concerning the privilege and in determining its scope.

The Freedom of Information Act (FOIA) is a 1966 amendment of the Administrative Procedure Act. It requires disclosure of governmental records to anyone unless the governmental records are specifically exempted by the statute. District courts are given jurisdiction to enforce its provisions. The act requires that each agency shall make available to the public information in the following manner:

1. Substantive rules and general policies of general applicability adopted by the agency must be published in the *Federal Register*.
2. An agency must make available to the public its opinions, statements of policy, interpretations, staff manuals, and instructions.
3. Each agency on request shall make the records concerning facts compiled by the agency in the course of investigation or facts filed with the agency promptly available to any person.

These disclosures must be made regardless of motive, interest, or intent of the individual making the request. The request might include the right to inspect, copy, or suggest corrections in the records. The federal district court shall determine whether the record shall be disclosed or amended, with the burden of proof on the agency to justify its refusal to disclose or amend. Failure to obey district court orders would result in contempt of court citations for noncompliance against the administrative officials.

Strangely, the act did not mention executive privilege. Instead, the act made the following exemptions from disclosure for matters

(1) specifically required by Executive order to be kept secret in the interest of the national defense or foreign policy;
(2) related solely to the internal personnel rules and practices of an agency;
(3) specifically exempted from disclosure by statute;
(4) trade secrets and commercial or financial information obtained from a person and privileged or confidential;
(5) inter-agency or intra-agency memorandums or letters which would not be available by law to a party other than an agency in litigation with the agency;
(6) personnel and medical files and similar files the disclosure of which would constitute a clearly unwarranted invasion of personal privacy;
(7) investigatory files compiled for law enforcement purposes except to the extent available by law to a party other than an agency;
(8) contained in or related to examination, operating, or condition reports prepared by, on behalf of, or for the use of an agency responsible for the regulation or supervision of financial institutions; or
(9) geological and geophysical information and data, including maps, concerning wells.

The nine exemptions of the act are not the only law that protects against required disclosure. Administrative officers may be governed by other statutory law, by the common law, by executive privilege, by executive orders, and agency-made law in the form of regulations, orders, or instructions. Often legislation confers discretionary powers on agency officers to disclose or not disclose specified information. Consequently, the courts often have to balance the Information Act with other statutes that may apply to the situation. These confusing rules and contradictory enactments have caused many commentators to assert that Congress created a rather shabby product in the Information Act. They maintain that many deficiencies in the act result from congressional inattention and indifference. Perhaps, this is because Congress prepared this legislation rather than following the lead of the executive branch of government. Legislation originated and promoted through Congress by the executive branch appears more coherent and internally consistent. Although the principle of open government with citizenry access to governmental information is vital to a free system of government, it is unfortunate that Congress was not able to achieve these goals in a more satisfactory fashion. However, the first steps in any new frontier are usually small.

INFORMATIONAL PIRACY

Chrysler Corp. v. Brown
441 U.S. 369 (1979)
Supreme Court of the United States

Justice Rehnquist

The expanding range of federal regulatory activity and growth in the Government sector of the economy have increased federal agencies' demand for information about the activities of private individuals and corporations. These developments have paralleled a related concern about secrecy in Government and abuse of power. The Freedom of Information Act (hereinafter "FOIA") was a response to this concern, but it has also had a largely unforeseen tendency to exacerbate the uneasiness of those who comply with governmental demands for information. For under the FOIA third parties have been able to obtain Government files containing information submitted by corporations and individuals who thought the information would be held in confidence.

This case belongs to a class that has been popularly denominated "reverse-FOIA" suits, The Chrysler Corporation seeks to enjoin agency disclosure on the grounds that it is inconsistent wih the FOIA. . . .

As a party to numerous Government contracts, Chrysler is required to comply with Executive Orders 11246 and 11375, which charge the Secretary of Labor with ensuring that corporations who benefit from Government contracts provide equal employment opportunity regardless of race or sex. The U.S. Department of Labor's Office of Federal Contract Compliance Programs (OFCCP) has promulgated regulations which require Government contractors to furnish reports and other information about their affirmative action programs and the general composition of their work forces.

* * *

Regulations promulgated by the Secretary of Labor provide for public disclosure of information from records of the OFCCP and its compliance agencies. Those regulations state that notwithstanding exemption from mandatory disclosure under the Freedom of Information Act,

> records obtained or generated pursuant to Executive Order 11246 [as amended] . . . shall be made available for inspection and copying if it is determined that the requested inspection or copying furthers the public interest and does not impede any of the functions of the OFCC[P] or the Compliance Agencies except in the case of records disclosure of which is prohibited by law.

It is the voluntary disclosure contemplated by this regulation, over and above that mandated by the FOIA, which is the gravamen of Chrysler's complaint in this case.

* * *

We have decided a number of FOIA cases in the last few years. . . . We have, moreover, consistently recognized that the basic objective of the Act is disclosure.

In contending that the FOIA bars disclosure of the requested equal employment opportunity information, Chrysler relies on the Act's nine exemptions and argues that they require an agency to withhold exempted material. In this case it relies specifically on Exemption 4:

> (b) [FOIA] does not apply to matters that are—
> (4) trade secrets and commercial or financial information obtained from a person and privileged or confidential. . . .

Chrysler contends that the nine exemptions in general, and Exemption 4 in particular, reflect a sensitivity to the privacy interests of private individuals and nongovernmental entities. That contention may be conceded without inexorably requiring the conclusion that the exemptions impose affirmative duties on an agency to withhold information sought. In fact, that conclusion is not supported by the language, logic, or history of the Act.

The organization of the Act is straightforward. Subsection (a) places a general obligation on the agency to make information available to the public and sets out specific modes of disclosure for certain classes of information. Subsection (b), which lists the exemptions, simply states that the specified material is not subject to the disclosure obligations set out in subsection (a). By its terms, subsection (b) demarcates the limits of the agency's obligation to disclose; it does not foreclose disclosure.

That the FOIA is exclusively a disclosure statute is, perhaps, demonstrated most convincingly by examining its provision for judicial relief. Subsection (a)(4)(b) gives federal district courts "jurisdiction to enjoin the agency from withholding agency records and to order the production of any agency records improperly withheld from the complainant." That provision does not give the authority to bar disclosure, and thus fortifies our belief that Chrysler, and courts which have shared its view, have incorrectly interpreted the exemption provisions to the FOIA. The Act is an attempt to meet the demand for open government while preserving workable confidentiality in governmental decisionmaking. Congress appreciated that with the expanding sphere of governmental regulation and enterprise, much of the information within Government files has been submitted by private entities seeking Government contracts or responding to unconditional reporting obligations imposed by law. There was sentiment that Government agencies should have the latitude, in certain circumstances, to afford the confidentiality desired by these submitters. But the congressional concern was with the agency's need or preference for confidentiality; the FOIA by itself protects the submitter's interest in confidentiality only to the extent that this interest is endorsed by the agency collecting the information.

Enlarged access to governmental information undoubtedly cuts against the privacy concerns of nongovernmental entities, and as a matter of policy some balancing and accommodation may well be desirable. We simply hold here that Congress did not design the FOIA exemptions to be mandatory bars to disclosure.

This conclusion is further supported by the legislative history. The FOIA was enacted out of dissatisfaction with Section 3 of the Administrative Procedure

Act, which had not resulted in as much disclosure by the agencies as Congress later thought desirable. Statements in both the Senate and House Reports on the effect of the exemptions support the interpretation that the exemptions were only meant to permit the agency to withhold certain information, and were not meant to mandate nondisclosure. . . .

We therefore conclude that Congress did not limit an agency's discretion to disclose information when it enacted the FOIA. It necessarily folows that the Act does not afford Chrysler any right to enjoin agency disclosure.

Questions

1. What reason might Chrysler have for desiring to keep its submitted information private?
2. Is the agency empowered to label the information received from Chrysler as "confidential" and therefore exempt from disclosure?
3. Is Chrysler able to force the agency not to disclose the company's submitted information?

According to some authors, the FOIA has implanted "uncertainty in the minds of business about government's willingness and ability to protect against the privacy of proprietary information."[6] Although Congress believed the major beneficiaries of the FOIA would be journalists, scholars, and public interest groups seeking to scrutinize government behavior and remedy public injustices, researchers have found that over two thirds of all requests for government information have come from corporations or their law firms. The FOIA has become a vehicle for business firms to survey, at the public's expense, the private affairs and activities of business competitors. A small industry of FOIA middlemen now exists in the greater Washington, D.C., area. Such companies, for a fee, will make a freedom of information request on a client's behalf, thus masking the client's identity. Although this effect was unintended by Congress, the FOIA has become a means to abrogate some of the rights of business privacy. This result and uncertainty about the government's future policies in this regard have created an economic disincentive for firms to spend funds on studies that ultimately will be shared with business competitors. Some authors have come to the following conclusion:

> Should business be unable to limit diffusion or to command a price for [productivity studies], marginal projects will either be abandoned or will be developed by overseas firms operating under a different government environment thereby promoting foreign, rather than U.S., productivity.[7]

CONCLUSION

During the twentieth century, and particularly since the 1930s, detailed regulations of business affairs have mushroomed. Congress has sought to solve or prevent various business-social problems through the use of regulatory agencies.

Consequently, administrative law and procedure have become increasingly important as government attempts to carry out its policies and programs through regulatory agencies. The Administrative Procedures Act has established the basic guidelines for agency behavior and provided the people with opportunities to comment on proposed regulations. Moreover, the act assists individuals who seek to force agencies to meet their legal responsibilities or challenge the agency when they exceed their authority.

Ever-expanding regulation-related litigation has brought forth numerous suggestions for change of the regulatory system. One recommendation is for more specialized courts or special technical assistants for judges. However, the greatest regulatory relief comes from the process of deregulation itself. The advocates for greater reliance on the market system have been heeded by Congress in recent years. For example, Congress has legislated the gradual deregulation of the airline and trucking industries and limited the regulatory powers of the Federal Trade Commission in certain areas. Congress has even enacted the Regulatory Flexibility Act, which is designed to reduce the regulatory burden on small businesses. The balance between regulatory and market processes is difficult to achieve and continually evolving.

CASE PROBLEMS

1. The Amalgamated Meat Cutters seek to require the major meat packing companies to perform their obligations, under their 1970 collective bargaining agreements with the union, to grant a general wage increase of 25 cents an hour effective 6 September 1971. The employers respond that the implementation of the wage increase obligation would violate Executive Order 11615, promulgated by President Nixon on 15 August 1971, which establishes a 90-day price-wage freeze. The union's position is that this defense is insufficient as a matter of law because the act authorizing the freeze is unconstitutional and the executive order is invalid because the act unconstitutionally delegates legislative power to the president, in violation of the general constitutional principle of the separation of powers, and in contravention of Article I, Section I of the Constitution, which provides that "All legislative Powers herein granted shall be vested in a Congress of the United States."

   The union's position is that the act's broad authority to the president "to issue such orders and regulations as he may deem appropriate to stabilize prices, rents, wages and salaries" vests "unbridled legislative power in the President," a naked grant of authority to determine whether they "will be controlled, and the scope, manner and timing of those controls." Evaluate the union's assertion and decide.

2. James Gould, the operator of a sole proprietorship (B.A.C.A.) refused to allow access by the Interstate Commerce Commission to his transportation-related records. The ICC petitioned the district court to enforce its demand.

   Gould contends that his operations are not within ICC jurisdiction and that he need not respond to the ICC's demands unless it demonstrates probable cause for a belief that he has violated federal law or he has been adjudicated to be subject to ICC jurisdiction.

The ICC claims that it has the authority to determine its own jurisdiction by summary inspection procedures.

What are the ICC's powers?

3. Gould also resists the ICC's demands with an assertion of the Fifth Amendment privilege against self-incrimination, because his personal records are inextricably entwined with B.A.C.A.'s business records. The ICC agents would require Gould to point out, segregate, assemble, and turn over certain documents for examination on his premises.

   Will Gould prevail?

4. A dispute heard by an administrative law judge for the FCC involved an application by two attorneys named Johnson for a permit to establish a radio station. Opposition from an existing station (Faulkner) raised issues regarding the truth of representations made by the applicants to the commission. The applicants made counterallegations that the existing station was attempting merely to delay the entry of a competitor. In deciding the facts, the administrative law judge commented:

   > It may be said, finally, that there is nothing more precious and vital to a practicing lawyer than his "good name"; that the Johnsons evidently are attorneys of some distinction in Carrolton, Georgia; and that the Commission, thus, has at least a presumptive basis for preferring the veracity of Mr. Hollis Johnson's testimony over Mr. Thorburn's [representative of Faulkner], absent a persuasive justification to the contrary.

   The commission accepted the findings of the judge and not only granted the Johnsons a permit but also denied the existing station's application for renewal, partly because the administrative law judge had decided that it had made serious misrepresentations in the matter with the Johnsons.

   On appeal from the denial of its renewal application, Faulkner contends that the findings of the administrative law judge were tainted because he favored the Johnsons' testimony merely because they were lawyers. The commission urges the established rule that, on appeal, a court must accept the facts as found initially by the commission.

   Are the findings of the commission final?

END NOTES

1. K. C. Davis, *Administrative Law and Government* (St. Paul, Minn.: West Publishing Co., 1960), p. 25.
2. *Myers* v. *U.S.*, 272 U.S. 52 (1926).
3. *Dixon* v. *Alabama State Board of Education*, 294 F. 2d 150 (5th Cir., 1961).
4. *University of Missouri* v. *Horowitz*, 98 S.Ct. 948 (1978).
5. *Fuentes* v. *Shevin*, 407 U.S. 67 (1972).
6. William L. Casey, Jr., John E. Marthinsen, and Laurence S. Moss, "Business Move to Get Low-Cost Government Information about Competitors," *Collegiate Forum* (Dow Jones and Co., Inc.), Fall 1980, p. 3.
7. Ibid.

chapter 4

THE DYNAMICS OF LEGAL CHANGE

Today's laws have evolved on the basis of past experience and legal precedents set by expanding scientific knowledge and a changing society. The legal system in the United States contains a dynamic process by which laws are constantly being created, altered, and adapted to contemporary society. Indeed, for the legal system to be effective in a free society, laws must be kept relevant to the "felt necessities" of society's members. The usual method of changing laws is enacting legislation. However, another method of change and adaptation in the legal system is judicial modification of rules. Judges "make law" when they interpret a statute or a constitutional provision. They also make law when they create a new rule because no previous legislative rule or case precedent is directly applicable. Judge-made law is traditionally referred to as "common law"—a name first given to the rules fashioned by royal judges who rode throughout England fashioning rules which were to be common for all Englanders.

Judicial laws are largely formulated in appellate courts. Appellate courts attempt to obtain uniformity in law by resolving conflicting lower court opinions which differ on the interpretation of law. This process necessitates a written opinion by the court to explain exactly what legal questions the court is resolving, on what facts, and what reasons are given for the decision. The result of these appellate decisions is to clarify the court's conception of the current state of the law or to declare new law as modern social conditions warrant.

At various times the appellate courts will be faced with fact situations that are presented for the "first" time. In such a case, new law will have to be established. It will be necessary for the court in reaching its decision to develop a judicial standard to guide lower courts in deciding future cases. In addition, members of society rely on appellate decisions as guides for their future actions. However, before appellate decisions are subsequently employed as "precedent" to determine the outcome of similar future cases, subsequent courts must feel that the rule has continuing usefulness as proper public policy in contemporary circumstances. Once a legal standard is accepted and cited as precedent, it is continually tested and refined by later courts in light of any changes that may have occurred in technology, social conditions, economic policy, or concepts of morality.

In dealing with the variety of cases cited and argued to the courts as "precedent," the court will distinguish between the cases, accepting similar cases and pointing out the differences in others. The application of precedent to a present controversy is commonly referred to as *stare decisis et non quieta movere* (to adhere to precedent and not unsettle things that are settled). This process of *stare decisis* makes judicial decisions have a prospective effect as law for subsequent similar cases.

In the following materials, this dynamic character of the judicial process is explored. First, the field of tort law and its evolutionary qualities are presented. Then, a series of cases illustrate the enlargement of a legal standard because technological change affected its application. Additional cases show how the courts modify or change legal standards to fit current social conditions. Finally, some of the forces of resistance to change in legal standards by the courts and court attitudes on adhering to precedent in spite of changing conditions are explored.

DEVELOPING A RULE OF LAW

A body of law commonly called *torts* is primarily judge-made law and is concerned with compensating victims who are injured because of the "fault" of someone else. The Latin word *tortus* means twisted, implying that someone's conduct is twisted away from society's norm of acceptable behavior. This "unreasonable" conduct causes the individual to be labeled at fault and, as such, he or she must pay compensatory money damages to any victim injured as a result of this wrongful behavior.

A tort is not the same as a crime, though the same action by a person may constitute both a tort and a crime. The crime is an offense against the public at large which is prosecuted by the state. The purpose of such proceedings is to protect and vindicate the interest of the public by punishing violators, by eliminating them from society, by reforming their behavior, or by deterring others from imitating their actions. The only role of the victim of criminal behavior is to serve as an accuser and witness in the criminal prosecution. In contrast, the victim of a tort brings a civil action against the tort-feasor to gain compensation for sufferings caused by the tort. The court will aid the successful litigant in the collection of any monies awarded for his or her sufferings.

Liability for tortuous behavior has been imposed by judges on the following three fundamental grounds or legal theories:

1. *Intent* of the defendant to interfere with legally protected interests of the plaintiff.
2. *Negligence* of the defendant that causes harm to the plaintiff.
3. *Strict liability* (without "fault"), which is the imposition of liability for policy reasons, despite the absence of wrongful intent or negligence.

Under the common law, almost all torts have been categorized under some legal theory and given a name. However, some torts may not have a name and, of course, initially all of today's torts were without names. Observe the following language employed by a judge in an 1896 case:

> While no precedent is cited for such action, it does not follow that there is no remedy for the wrong, because every form of action, when brought for the first time, must have been without a precedent to support it. Courts sometimes of necessity abandon their search for precedents, and yet sustain a recovery upon legal principles clearly applicable to the new state of facts, although there was no direct precedent for it, because there had never been an occasion to make one. . . . For instance, the action for enticing away a man's wife, now well established, was at first earnestly resisted upon the ground that no such action had ever been brought. . . . As we recently said by this court in an action then without precedent, "If the most that can be said is that the case is novel, and is not brought plainly within the limits of some adjudged case, we think such fact not enough to call for a reversal of the judgment." The question therefore is not whether there is any precedent for the action, but whether the defendant inflicted such a wrong upon the plaintiff as resulted in lawful damages. (*Kujek* v. *Goldman et al.,* 150 N.Y. 176).

INTENTIONAL TORTS

Tortious intent is the desire to bring about physical results or consequences which are disapproved by law. By voluntarily (intentionally) contracting muscles in his or her body, the actor "intends" a result. If the desire of the muscular contraction is to bring about an invasion of the legally protected interest of another, the actor's intent is tortious whether the actual consequences were intended or not. For example, pulling a chair out from under a person about to be seated is intentionally desiring the consequence of physical impact of the person with the ground. As such, the defendant's assertions of intending no more than a practical joke or not intending to injure the plaintiff would not be acceptable as defenses because they describe the defendant's "motive" (inspiration for the act), rather than the "intent." The voluntary act (pulling away the chair) and the desire of particular results which invades another's personal interest (defendant's hitting the ground) is the relevant "intent" in determination of intentional torts.

Litigation involving the interests of persons to have their physical self and property free of intentional invasion by others has created a number of specifically named torts. Some intentional torts are described as follows:

Battery

The intentional and offensive contact with another person without consent is a battery. It is clear that persons are to be protected from indecent and hostile contact, but other relatively trivial contacts made without consent can be a battery also. An unappreciated kiss, joke, or physical assistance can be a battery. Since a certain amount of personal contact is inevitable in a crowded world, consent to ordinary contacts is assumed. Time, place, and circumstances of the touching will affect its characterization as being reasonable or unpermitted.

Assault

The intentional act to arouse apprehension of immediate harmful or offensive contact in the mind of another is an assault. No actual contact is necessary; rather the individual is to be compensated for purely mental disturbance caused by the defendant's actions. It is an assault on another to raise a fist to strike, to aim a weapon, or to corner with a display of force. Because menacing actions are necessary to create the fear of "immediate" contact, mere words or threats are usually not assaults because no reasonable apprehension of immediate contact results.

Mental Distress

The law has been slow to accept the notion that peace of mind is entitled to legal protection. However, in recent years the intentional infliction of mental distress by extreme or outrageous conduct has been recognized as a tort. The actions necessary to establish this tort must be especially calculated to cause serious mental distress. Spreading false rumors that the plaintiff's son had hung himself, or wrapping up a gory dead rat in place of a loaf of bread for the plaintiff to open are examples of the kind of outrageous conduct that forms this kind of action. Moreover, prolonged and extreme measures to collect debts, evict tenants, or adjust insurance claims can be defined as this type of tortious conduct.

False Imprisonment

A false imprisonment, or false arrest, is an intentional restraint on the free movement of another. "Imprisonment" doesn't mean only iron bars and the like; restraint on freedom of movement may suffice. Free movement could be constrained by locking the plaintiff in a room or out of a room, by refusing him or her the right to exit from an automobile or a store, or by compelling the plaintiff to accompany the defendant. The imprisonment need not last more than an appreciable amount of time. It is essential that the restraint be imposed against the plaintiff's will, though he or she need not resist to the point of physical violence. Under the common law, a storekeeper's detention of a suspected shoplifter who was ultimately found innocent can amount to a false arrest and subject the storekeeper to liability. However, most states have enacted legislation that protects the storekeeper from liability if the detention is reasonable and in good faith.

Trespass

Intentional trespass to land may be committed by entry upon the land, by casting objects upon it, or by remaining on the land after a right to entry has terminated. A similar trespass may be committed to personal properties also.

Conversion

A major interference with the personal property of another may be so serious as to justify the court, at the plaintiff's request, to order the intruder to buy the property from the plaintiff. The extent of interference is determined by many relevant factors, namely, the extent and duration of the interference, the defendant's intent, the harm done to the property, the degree of interference to the plaintiff, and the expense and inconvenience caused the plaintiff. The conversion occurs when the defendant intends to exercise control over another's personal property which is inconsistent with the owner's property rights and such exercise of control is determined to be a substantial interference.

Defamation

Defamation is the intentional publication to a third person of defamatory information which causes injury to the plaintiff's reputation. Defamatory information is any communication that tends to diminish the esteem, respect, and goodwill in which the plaintiff is held. Language that causes contempt, derogatory, or unpleasant feelings against the plaintiff is likewise defamatory. It is generally true that if the defendant can establish the truthfulness of his or her remarks, no liability attaches to the words. In addition, certain defamatory communications are qualifiedly privileged and immune from prosecution, such as publications fairly made by a person in the discharge of some public or private duty, as an employee remark to a superior to protect the employer from the believed criminal behavior of another employee.

Privacy

Interferences with the right of the plaintiff "to be let alone" can amount to the tort of privacy. This tort is a creation of this century. Four kinds of invasions of plaintiff's right to privacy are embodied in this tort. The four invasions are (1) intrusion upon the plaintiff's physical and mental solitude or seclusion (such as placing secret recording devices in plaintiff's bedroom); (2) public disclosure of private facts (such as publicly exhibiting films of a caesarean operation); (3) publicity which places the plaintiff in a false light in the public eye (such as using the face of an honest cab driver in a story about cheating propensities of taxi drivers); (4) appropriation, for the defendant's advantage, of the plaintiff's name or likeness (such as using plaintiff's name or picture without consent in an advertisement).

NEGLIGENCE

An unavoidable accident is an event that was not intended, and that, under the circumstances, could not have been foreseen or prevented by exercise of reasonable precautions. There is no liability in such a case because there is no wrongful intent or failure to exercise proper care. However, if the event could have been prevented by the exercise of reasonable care, then the defendant's failure to be careful causes him or her to be liable under the tort of negligence.

Negligence, as a cause of action, is established by the plaintiff when four elements are proven:

1. A duty of care was owed by the defendant to those foreseeable individuals who would be exposed to unreasonable risk if the defendant didn't exercise due care in whatever he or she was doing. When the risk of injury to others is greater than the burden to take adequate precautions, the defendant is under the lawful duty to take those precautions.
2. The failure of the defendant to exercise reasonable care as a reasonable person would have done under similar circumstances.
3. There was a reasonably close causal connection between the defendant's failure to exercise due care and the plaintiff's injury. This is commonly known as "proximate cause."
4. Actual injury or damage to the plaintiff occurred. Such injury to the plaintiff may include property damage, medical bills, loss of wages, and pain and suffering.

Although many courts prefer not to attempt to define different degrees of negligence, various statutes often require such definitions. The distinctions usually made are as follows: slight negligence is the failure to exercise the great care that persons of extraordinary prudence and foresight are accustomed to use, and gross negligence is the failure to exercise even scant care. Courts have difficulty in drawing a distinction between gross negligence and "reckless" conduct which is willful conduct in disregard of a known and probable risk.

Two usual defenses to a charge of negligence are contributory negligence and assumption of risk. Contributory negligence is negligence by the plaintiff that contributed to his or her own injuries. In the eyes of the law, both plaintiff and defendant are at "fault," and consequently, the plaintiff is unable to recover from the defendant. A few states require the courts by statute to compare the negligence of each party, and if the defendant's negligence outweighs the plaintiff's, the plaintiff is allowed to recover losses minus an amount attributed to his or her own negligence. This process of comparative negligence, in effect, apportions the loss between the unequally negligent parties.

The assumption of risk defense means the plaintiff, with knowledge of the risk, voluntarily entered some activity or relation agreeing to take his or her own chances. The legal result is that the defendant is not under a duty to the plaintiff as to those known and assumed risks.

STRICT LIABILITY

The last hundred years have witnessed the overthrow of the doctrine of "no liability without fault." As one writer put it, there is "a strong and growing tendency, where there is blame on neither side, to ask, in view of the exigencies of social justice, who can best bear the loss and hence to shift the loss by creating liability where there has been no fault."[1] The courts are weighing various factors in our complex and dangerous civilization to determine, as a matter of social policy, which party is best able to shoulder the loss. The defendant is held liable on the court's conclusion that the responsibility *should* be the defendant's, as a matter of social adjustment of losses. This approach by the courts is a far cry from the common law determination of individual fault on the basis of intent or failure to exercise proper care. Rather, the normal basis of strict liability is the creation of undue risk of harm to other members of the community while personally exercising ordinary care and intending no harm. For example, keeping a pet bear creates undue risk of harm to others if the bear escapes. Though intending no harm and taking care to prevent escape, the owner would, nevertheless, be held strictly liable for any damages resulting from the bear's escape. It is usually said that legal liability for "ultrahazardous activities" by the defendant which necessarily involve a risk of serious harm cannot be eliminated by the exercise of utmost care. The liability normally extends to the limits of the risk on society imposed by that dangerous activity. However, the plaintiff's assumption of risk will normally relieve the defendant of strict liability.

Strict liability theory has been extended into many fields of law. Sellers of goods have found increasing court propensities to find them strictly liable for defective goods which cause harm to the purchasers. Carriers and innkeepers are strictly liable for goods entrusted to their care unless statutes have modified such responsibility. However, strict liability theory is employed more often in legislation. Workers' compensation, pure foods acts, child labor statutes, and numerous other enactments utilize strict liability theory. Likewise, no-fault auto insurance schemes ignore the determination of whose fault the accident was.

EXPANDING ROLE OF PUBLIC POLICY

As a primary arena for the fair adjustment of conflicting claims by litigating parties, the law of torts is a continuous battleground of social theory with increasing realization that the interests of society are necessary ingredients in the resolution of private disputes. The notion of public policy in private cases is not new to tort law but is certainly a more important variable in today's cases. Consequently, the courts are making more conscientious efforts to direct the law along lines that will achieve desirable social results. The tort process may be a slow, confusing, and often painful progress toward achieving the best rule for society, but ultimately the rules formulated must coincide with public opinion or the continuing processes of evolution in legal theory will be pushed at a faster pace.

Numerous cases in this and other chapters contain illustrations of how public policy is granted an expanding influence in the determination of the court's decision.

EXTENDING A RULE OF LAW

In this section a series of tort cases from the courts of New York is presented to illustrate the flexibility of the common law and its evolving content over time.

The tort of defamation was previously defined as the injury to one's reputation caused by the tort feasor's intentional publication to a third person of defamatory information. The injured person may recover damages for the injury to his or her reputation caused by the defamatory material. If the defamatory information is spoken to a third person, the tort is subcategorized as slander. If the defamatory information is written, it is called libel. Because the writing is permanent and, therefore, capable of more injury to the victim, the courts allow recovery for libel whether the victim can prove actual monetary damages to his or her reputation. In slander, since the words once said are then forever gone and potential injury thereby diminished, the victim must prove special monetary damages to be able to recover. There is one exception to this rule of special damages and that involves statements considered "slanderous per se." Statements considered slanderous per se include accusations of having committed serious crimes, of having contracted loathsome diseases, of lack of chastity, and of incompetence in professional or occupational capacity. Each of these are considered so evil in themselves that special damages need not be proven, even if the statements are orally declared.

The cases that follow deal with the tort of defamation and the rule that special damages must be proven if the information published was merely slanderous. The reader should note the extension of the definition of libel and how the judges have reacted to the technological developments which expand people's ability to harm one another through defamatory remarks.

DICTATION TO STENOGRAPHER—LIBEL?

Ostrowe v. Lee
175 N.E. 505 (1931)
Court of Appeals of New York

The complaint . . . charges that the defendant composed a letter accusing the plaintiff of the crime of larceny; that he dictated this letter to his stenographer; that the stenographer, in obedience to his orders, read the notes and transcribed them; and that the letter so transcribed was received by the plaintiff through the mails. . . . The question is whether [this] . . . states the publication of a libel. . . .

. . . A defamatory writing is not published if it is read by no one but the one defamed. Published it is, however, as soon as read by any one else. . . . The legal consequence is not altered where the symbols reproduced or interpreted are the notes of a stenographer. Publication there still is as result of the dictation, at least where the notes have been examined or transcribed.

Enough that a writing defamatory in content has been read and understood at the behest of the defamer.

The argument is made that the wrong in such a case is slander and not libel.

Very often a stenographer does not grasp the meaning of dictated words till the dictation is over and the symbols have been read. This is particularly likely to be the case where a defamatory charge is made equivocally or with evasive innuendoes. The author who directs his copyist to read, has displayed the writing to the reader as truly and effectively as if he had copied it himself.

To hold otherwise is to lose sight of history and origins. The schism in the law of defamation between the older wrong of slander and the newer one of libel is not the product of mere accident. . . . It has its genesis in evils which the years have not erased. Many things that are defamatory may be said with impunity through the medium of speech. Not so, however, when speech is caught upon the wing and transmuted into print. What gives the sting to the writing is its permanence of form. The spoken word dissolves, but the written one abides and "perpetuates the scandal." When one speaks of a writing in this connection, one does not limit oneself to writings in manuscripts or books. Any symbol suffices—pictures, hieroglyphics, shorthand notes—if only what is written is intelligible to him who reads. . . . There is publication of a libel if a stenographer reads the notes that have been taken by another. Neither the evil nor the result is different when the notes that he reads have been taken by himself.

Questions

1. When one *orally* dictates one's message to a stenographer, why aren't the defamatory remarks labeled slander?
2. Would it be a libel if the stenographer understood the defamation as dictated but never transcribed the notes?

MOTION PICTURE—LIBEL?

Brown v. Paramount Publix Corporations
270 N.Y.S. 545 (1934)
Supreme Court, Third Dept., New York

The defendant . . . produced for sale or distribution to and exhibition by moving picture houses throughout the country, a talking motion picture production under the title of "An American Tragedy," in which it has caused to be portrayed, by actors, scenes, characteristics, and otherwise what purports to be a reproduction of the lives of Chester Gillette, Grace Brown, and their families by the similarity of the characters, locations, scenes and incidents so closely associated with the actual incidents of the life of said Chester Gillette and Grace Brown as to induce the public to believe that the same portrayed the conditions surrounding the lives of said characters. The defendant caused these films to be sent generally throughout the state of New York and especially in the locality where the plaintiff resides. After setting forth the plaintiff's good character as well as that of her husband, their respectability, and the proper rearing and education of their daughter, the complaint then alleges: "But that disregarding the character, appearance, reputation and good name of the plaintiff, the defendant willfully, wrongfully and maliciously, through the manufacture, use, lease and exhibition of said films and pictures, purporting of and concerning the plaintiff, the following false, untrue, slanderous, libelous and defamatory matter, to wit: that the plaintiff was an illiterate, unkempt, slovenly, neglectful and low-grade person; that she was the wife of a mean, illiterate, unkempt, lazy, low-type or degenerate person; that she had neglected her daughter, the said Grace Brown, both educationally and morally, or had compelled her, through lack of care, to seek her own livelihood as a mere child; that she had permitted her said daughter, Grace Brown, to carry on clandestine relations with Chester Gillette, or others, and so depicted the plaintiff, by the manner of said pictures and films, as to render the plaintiff an object of contempt and ridicule among her friends, neighbors, and those who knew her or knew of her; and that the references and allusions to the plaintiff were understood by her acquaintances and friends, and by the public generally, to apply to her; that by such allusions, innuendo and intimation, plaintiff was made therein to appear as poor-white-trash, and a disreputable, untidy product of the hills, without decent care for her daughter and as contributing to the condition in which her daughter found herself. . . .

. . . We are met here, however, with a novel and different situation. This is a comparatively new form of libel. It is not accomplished by the printed word, but by the somewhat recent invention of the talking motion picture. The exhibition is made to the public by means of projecting from a film onto a screen a series of a large number of still pictures so rapidly that the objects there displayed present the illusion of moving and acting as in everyday life. Accompanying these projected pictures are sounds mechanically reproduced and so synchronized that they appear to emanate from the objects on the screen. We are told that many of the scenes which upon the screen appear to be real are produced artificially and by illusion. Such a production may be libelous. . . . In the hands of a wrongdoer these devices have untold possibilities toward producing an effective libel. . . . We must base our decision on the allegations of the complaint alone. The production is defamatory of the plaintiff.

RADIO—LIBEL?

Hartmann v. Winchell
73 N.E. 2d 30 (1947)
Court of Appeals of New York

Does the utterance of defamatory remarks, read from a script into a radio microphone and broadcast, constitute publication of libel? . . .

In *Snyder* v. *Andrews,* 1849, it was held that reading a defamatory letter in the presence of a stranger was a sufficient publication to sustain an action for libel. . . .

We accept *Synder* v. *Andrews,* as a correct statement of the rule which still prevails in this State but it is said that this rule can have no application to radio broadcasting because the persons who hear the broadcast do not know that the spoken words are being read from a writing.

Unless in the case of broadcasting we are prepared to do what Mansfield, C.J., in 1812 declared he could not do in *Thorley* v. *Kerry,* namely abolish the distinction between oral and written defamation, we must hold to the reason for the distinction so well expressed in a single phrase in *Ostrowe* v. *Lee,* 256, N.Y. 36, 39, . . . "What gives the sting to the writing is its permanence of form." This is true whether or not the writing is seen. Visibility of the writing is without significance and we hold that the defendant's defamatory utterance was libel, not slander. We do not reach the question, which has been much discussed, whether broadcasting defamatory matter which has not been reduced to writing should be held to be libellous because of the potentially harmful and widespread effects of such defamation. . . .

Questions

1. Why are defamations through a motion picture held to be libel?
2. Why did the court say the defamation *spoken* through the radio was libel?
3. What question did the court in *Winchell* avoid answering?

Judge Fuld wrote a concurring opinion to the *Winchell* case. As such, he voted with the majority justices that the defendant's broadcast was libel, but for a different reason. Since his reasons are not those of the majority, they cannot be cited as precedent. However, his views may be persuasive to future justices considering this type of case.

Judge Fuld (concurring)

Though I concur in the conclusion reached—that defendant's utterance over the radio is actionable per se, without allegation or proof of special damage—I cannot agree with the court's rationale. It impresses me as unreal to have liability turn upon the circumstances that defendant read from a script when, so far as appears from the complaint before us, none of his listeners saw that script or, indeed, was even aware of its existence. As I see it, liability cannot be determined here without first facing and deciding the basic question whether defamation by radio, either with or without a script, should be held actionable per se because of the likelihood of aggravated injury inherent in such broadcasting.

Traditionally, the distinguished characteristics of a libel has been its expression in "some *permanent and visible* form, such as writing, printing, pictures, or effigies," whereas a slanderous statement "is made in spoken words. . . ."

Where, as here, the contents of a defamatory writing reach a third person only in the form of spoken words, of "speech . . . upon the wing" (*Ostrowe* v. *Lee*, 256 N.Y. 36, 39), and with no hint of the existence of a writing, there is a publication of words, not of writing, which, *considered apart from the distinctive features of radio broadcasting,* would, by traditional standards, constitute slander rather than libel.

Our attention is directed to the decision of the English Court of Appeal in *Forrester* v. *Tyrrell* (1893), and to American cases in accord, that the reading aloud of a libelous document in the hearing and presence of a third person amounts to the publication of a libel. . . .

There might, perhaps, be some basis for urging that where such a third person actually *witnesses* the reading of a written defamation, the extent of the consequent damage to reputation in the hearer's estimation is the same as if he had himself read the document. But, certainly, where he does not know, and is not made aware of the existence of a writing, and the scandalous matter reaches him only in the form of spoken words, the resultant injury is essentially the same as if the defamatory words had been uttered without any writing. . . . The writing in such circumstances can have no "sting." See *Ostrowe* v. *Lee*.

If the base of liability for defamation is to be broadened in the case of radio broadcasting, justification should be sought not in the fiction that reading from a paper *ipso facto* constitutes a publication by writing, but in a frank recognition that sound policy requires such a result. . . .

Abolition of the line between libel and slander would, I agree, be too extreme a break with the past to be achieved without legislation. . . . It is, however, the function of the courts, when called upon to determine which of two competing standards of liability shall be applied in a novel situation, to re-examine and reapply the old rules and to give them new content in the light of underlying vital principles.

The common-law action on the case for slander, in its sixteenth-century origin, embraced written as well as oral defamation, and the same rules were applicable to both. . . . All other defamation was actionable only upon allegation and proof of special damage. The newer tort of libel—adapted by the common-law judges in the latter part of the seventeenth century . . . made the writing itself presumptive proof of damage.

This emphasis on the form of publication was apparently designed to cope with the new conditions created by the development of the printing press.

Another development, another invention—here the radio—invites a similar reappraisal of the old rules. . . .

The primary reason assigned by the courts from time to time to justify the imposition of broader liability for libel than for slander has been the greater capacity for harm that a writing is assumed to have because of the wide range of dissemination consequent upon its permanence in form. . . . When account is taken of the vast and far-flung audience reached by the radio today—often far greater in number than the readers of the largest metropolitan newspaper . . . it is evident that the broadest of scandalous utterances is in general as potentially harmful to the defamed person's reputation as a publication by writing. That defamation by radio, in the absence of a script or transcription, lacks the measure of durability possessed by written libel, in nowise lessens its capacity for harm. Since the element of damage is, historically, the basis of the common-law action for defamation . . . and since it is as reasonable to presume damage from the nature of the medium employed when a slander is broadcast by radio as when published by writing, both logic and policy point to the conclusion that defamation by radio should be actionable *per se.*

Questions

1. Was Judge Fuld concerned about the presence or absence of the script?
2. To Judge Fuld, what reasons justified the extension of the definition of libel?
3. How would Judge Fuld label a defamation uttered through a megaphone? Through an amplifier attached to a moving sound truck?

TELEVISION—LIBEL?

Shor v. Billingsley
158 N.Y.S. 2d 476 (1956)
Supreme Court, N.Y. County, New York

Defendants move to dismiss each of the [three] causes of action for insufficiency. The complaint is based upon a telecast of "The Stork Club Show" over a nationwide network of stations and facilities. . . . Defendant Stork operates "The Stork Club," defendant Mayfair prepared and produced "The Stork Club Show," defendant American Broadcasting telecast the show, and defendant Billingsley acted as a performer and master of ceremonies on the show.

Plaintiff earns his livelihood as the operator and manager of "The Toots Shor Restaurant," with which The Stork Club competes.

During the show, the following conversation was telecast between Billingsley and one Brisson, a guest on the program, and plaintiff's picture was telecast in connection therewith:

Mr. Billingsley: I see, I would like to show you a few pictures taken here lately. The first—now, how did this picture get in here?

Mr. Brisson: That is Toots Shor and a man I don't know.

Mr. Billingsley: You want to know something?

Mr. Brisson: Want to know something? I saw Toots Shor, he's a good-looking fellow, isn't he?

Mr. Billingsley: Yes, he is. Want to know something? I wish I had as much money as he owes.

Mr. Brisson: Owes you or somebody else?

Mr. Billingsley: Everybody—oh, a lot of people.

Mr. Brisson: He doesn't owe me anything, but he is a good-looking fellow just the same. A little (indicating)—you know.

Mr. Billingsley: I wish I could agree with you.

Three causes of action for defamation are pleaded. All allege that the statements so telecast and the innuendoes necessarily implicit therein were false, which defendants knew or should have known, that they were uttered with malice and for the express purpose of injuring plaintiff in his business. The second cause of action adds the allegation that the statements were read by Billingsley from a prepared script or notes. The third adds the allegation that a permanent sound and motion picture film recording was made of the telecast, which recording was exhibited at various times to various individuals.

Defendants contend that there is nothing defamatory in the portion of the dialogue complained of. Their argument runs: "Such a statement can hardly be considered defamatory or even inconsistent with our economic society which is fundamentally based upon credit. There is hardly an individual today who does not temporarily owe money and usually, the more solvent an individual, the greater is his or her capacity for credit. It would be no idle remark to wish that one had as much money as some of our 20th century financial wizards would owe on any given date."

Defendants may be able to convince a jury that their language should be given such an innocuous connotation. But I will not hold as a matter of law that the jury must reach such conclusion. Accordingly, the motion is denied as to the second cause of action, *Hartmann* v. *Winchell,* 296 N.Y. 296, and as to the third cause of action, *Brown* v. *Paramount-Publix Corp.,* 270 N.Y.S. 544. That leaves for consideration the real problem in the case—whether the first cause of action based upon a telecast not read from a prepared script sounds in libel or in slander.

This precise question has not been passed upon by our appellate courts, nor apparently in any other jurisdiction. *Hartmann* v. *Winchell* held that the "utterance of defamatory remarks, *read from a script* into a radio microphone and broadcast, constitute(s) publication of libel" (italics supplied). It expressly did not reach the question "whether broadcasting defamatory matter which has not been reduced to writing should be held to be libellous because of the potentially harmful and widespread effects of such defamation." Fuld, J., concurring, held that it should "because of the likelihood of aggravated injury inherent in such broadcasting."

"Permanence of form" was the factor which justified such an extension; it is not necessarily a prerequisite to a libel. "That defamation by radio . . . lacks the measure of durability possessed by written libel, in nowise lessens its capacity for harm" (Fuld, J., concurring in *Hartmann* v. *Winchell*).

Cardozo himself was the first to recognize the duty of the courts to extend an established principle of law to a new technological development to which the logic of the principle applied, even though it was not covered by the literal language of the previous decisions. "Precedents drawn from the days of travel by stagecoach do not fit the conditions of travel today. The principle that the danger must be imminent does not change, but the things subject to the principle do change. They are whatever the needs of life in a developing civilization require them to be." Defendants argue that the application of the law of libel to broadcasting or telecasting without a script must be made (if at all) by the legislature rather than the courts. Such legislation has been enacted in England. . . . However, I do not agree that such a change must await legislative action.

Our own courts experience no difficulty in applying the law of libel to the new instrumentality of the motion picture because "in the hands of a wrongdoer these devices have untold possibilities toward producing an effective libel." *Brown* v. *Paramount-Publix Corp.*, 270 N.Y.S. 544, sustained a complaint for libel. . . .

Accordingly, the motion to dismiss is denied as to the first three causes of action.

Questions

1. On what authority or theory of recovery did the court accept the second and third causes of action?
2. What reasons are advanced for accepting the first cause of action?
3. Why were the plaintiffs interested in extending the definition of libel from writings to motion pictures, radio, and/or television?
4. What new standard for determination of libel is emerging from these cases?

While the states, like New York, were expanding the coverage of the laws of libel, the Supreme Court began another trend of decisions restricting the power of states to protect individual reputations through libel laws. In so doing, the Court has abolished several of the old common law rules of libel on the grounds that the danger posed to free speech outweighs the states' need for such rules to protect reputation of their citizens. For example, the Court has abolished the common law rule that if a publication is found by the court to be defamatory per se, the plaintiff need not prove that he or she had been damaged. The Court has held that damages must always be proven (*Gertz* v. *Robert Welch, Inc.*, 418 U.S. 323 [1974]). The Court has also abolished the rule that truth is a defense only when published with good motives and to a justifiable end. Truth is now an absolute defense to a libel suit, even when published for malicious purposes (*Time, Inc.* v. *Hill*, 385 U.S. 374 [1967]). Finally, the plaintiff must show that the publisher was at least negligent in failing to discover that the publication was false.

The result of these decisions by the Court has been to greatly curtail, if not altogether eliminate, the use of libel laws to protect reputations. Instead, the new tort of privacy is growing as a substitute means of individual protection.

PRIVACY—MODERN SUBSTITUTE FOR LIBEL?

Spahn v. Julian Messner, Inc.
274 N.Y.S. 2d 877 (1966)
Court of Appeals of New York

To the knowing and the novice alike, the name Warren Spahn brings to mind one of professional baseball's great left-handed pitchers. . . .

The size of the audience attracted to each game, whether in person or by transmission, is the profession's bread and butter. The individual player's income will frequently be a direct reflection of his popularity and ability to attract an audience. Professional privacy is thus the very antithesis of the player's need and goal.

With this background, the plaintiff, Warren Spahn, seeks an injunction and damages for the defendants' unauthorized publication of a fictitious biography of his life.

The action is predicated on section 51 of the Civil Rights Law, which authorizes the double remedy where a person's "name, portrait or picture is used within this state for advertising or for the purposes of trade" without that person's written consent. Its enactment may be traced directly to this court's opinion in *Roberson* v. *Rochester Folding Box Co.,* 171 N.Y. 538, wherein we denied the existence of a legal right to privacy in New York but said that "The legislative body could very well interfere and arbitrarily provide that no one should be permitted for his own selfish purpose to use the picture or the name of another for advertising purposes without his consent." . . .

Over the years since the statute's enactment in 1903, its social desirability and remedial nature have led to its being given a liberal construction consonant with its over-all purpose. But at the same time, ever mindful that the written word or picture is involved, courts have engrafted exceptions and restrictions onto the statute to avoid any conflict with the free dissemination of thoughts, ideas, newsworthy events, and matters of public interest.

One of the clearest exceptions to the statutory prohibition is the rule that a public figure, whether he be such by choice or involuntarily, is subject to the often searching beam of publicity and that, in balance with the legitimate public interest, the law affords his privacy little protection.

But it is erroneous to confuse privacy with "personality" or to assume that privacy, though lost for a certain time or in a certain context, goes forever unprotected. Thus it may be appropriate to say that the plaintiff here, Warren Spahn, is a public personality and that, insofar as his professional career is involved, he is substantially without a right to privacy. That is not to say, however, that his "personality" may be fictionalized and that, as fictionalized, it may be exploited for the defendants' commercial benefit through the medium of an unauthorized biography.

The factual reporting of newsworthy persons and events is in the public interest and is protected. The fictitious is not. This is the heart of the cases in point.

The plaintiff's status as a public figure makes him newsworthy and thus places his biography outside the protection afforded by the statute. But the plaintiff does not seek an injunction and damages for the unauthorized publication of his biography. He seeks only to restrain the publication of that which purports to be his biography.

In the present case, the findings of fact go far beyond the establishment of minor errors in an otherwise accurate biography. They establish "dramatization, imagined dialogue, manipulated chronologies, and fictionalization of events." In the language of Justice Markowitz, who presided at the trial, "the record unequivocally establishes that the book publicizes areas of Warren Spahn's personal and private life, albeit inaccurate and distorted, and consists of a host, a preponderant percentage, of factual errors, distortions and fanciful passages." A sufficient number of specific instances of falsification are set forth in that opinion to make repetition here unnecessary.

It is urged upon us that application of the statute to the publication of a substantially fictitious biography will run afoul of the freedoms of speech and the press guaranteed by the First and Fourteenth Amendments to the Federal Constitution. . . .

. . . The free speech which is encouraged and essential to the operation of a healthy government is something quite different from an individual's attempt to enjoin the publication of a fictitious biography of him. No public interest is served by protecting the dissemination of the latter. We perceive no constitutional infirmities in this respect.

We thus conclude that the defendants' publication of a fictitious biography of the plaintiff constitutes an unauthorized exploitation of his personality for purposes of trade and that it is proscribed by section 51 of the Civil Rights Law.

Questions

1. How was the law of privacy created in New York?
2. What is a "public figure"? Could a public figure prohibit the publication of an unauthorized factual biography? A fictitious biography?

Nader v. General Motors Corporation

255 N.E. 2d 765 (1970)
Court of Appeals of New York

Chief Judge Fuld

The complaint, in this action by Ralph Nader, pleads four causes of action against General Motors Corporation (GMC), and three other defendants allegedly acting as its agents. The first two causes of action charge an invasion of privacy. . . .

The plaintiff, an author and lecturer on automotive safety, has, for some years, been an articulate and severe critic of General Motors' products from the standpoint of safety and design. According to the complaint—which, for present purposes, we must assume to be true—[GMC], having learned of the imminent publication of the plaintiff's book "Unsafe at Any Speed," decided to conduct a campaign of intimidation against him in order to "suppress plaintiff's criticism of and prevent his disclosure of information" about its products. To that end, [GMC] authorized and directed the other defendants to engage in a series of activities which, the plaintiff claims . . . violated his right to privacy.

Specifically, the plaintiff alleges that the GMC agents (1) conducted a series of interviews with acquaintances of the plaintiff, "questioning them about, and casting aspersions upon [his] political, social, . . . racial, and religious views . . . ; his integrity; his sexual proclivities and inclinations; and his personal habits"; (2) kept him under surveillance in public places for an unreasonable length of time; (3) caused him to be accosted by girls for the purpose of entrapping him into illicit relationships; (4) made threatening, harassing and obnoxious telephone calls to him; (5) tapped his telephone and eavesdropped, by means of mechanical and electronic equipment, on his private conversations with others; and (6) conducted a "continuing" and harassing investigation of him. In point of fact, the parties have agreed—at least for purposes of this motion—that the sufficiency of these allegations is to be determined under the law of the District of Columbia. The District is the jurisdiction in which most of the acts are alleged to have occurred, and it was there, too, that the plaintiff lived and suffered the impact of those acts. It is, in short, the place which has the most significant relationship with the subject matter of the tort charged.

* * *

Turning, then, to the law of the District of Columbia, it appears that its courts have not only recognized a common-law action for invasion of privacy but have broadened the scope of that tort beyond its traditional limits. Thus, in the most recent of its cases on the subject, *Pearson* v. *Dodd* 133 U.S. App.D.C. 279, the Federal Court of Appeals for the District of Columbia declared:

> We approve the extension of the tort of invasion of privacy to instances of intrusion, whether by physical trespass or not, into spheres from which an ordinary man in a plaintiff's position could reasonably expect that the particular defendant should be excluded.

Quite obviously, some intrusions into one's private sphere are inevitable concomitants of life in an industrial and densely populated society, which in law does not seek to proscribe even if it were possible to do so. "The law does not provide a remedy for every annoyance that occurs in everyday life." However, the District of Columbia courts have held that the law should and does protect against certain types of intrusive conduct, and we must, therefore, determine whether the plaintiff's allegations are actionable as violations of the right to privacy under the law of that jurisdiction. . . .

It should be emphasized that the mere gathering of information about a particular individual does not give rise to a cause of action under this theory. Privacy is invaded only if the information sought is of a confidential nature and the defendant's conduct was unreasonably intrusive. Just as a common-law copyright is lost when material is published, so, too, there can be no invasion of privacy where the information sought is open to public view or has been voluntarily revealed to others. In order to sustain a cause of action for invasion of privacy, therefore, the plaintiff must show that the appellant's conduct was truly "intrusive" and that it was designed to elicit information which would not be available through normal inquiry or observation.

* * *

Turning, then, to the particular acts charged in the complaint, we cannot find any basis for a claim of invasion of privacy, under District of Columbia law, in the allegations that the [defendant], through its agents or employees, interviewed many persons who knew the plaintiff, asking questions about him and casting aspersions on his character. Although those inquiries may have uncovered information of a personal nature, it is difficult to see how they may be said to have invaded the plaintiff's privacy. Information about the plaintiff which was already known to others could hardly be regarded as private to the plaintiff. Presumably, the plaintiff had previously revealed the information to such other persons, and he would necessarily assume the risk that a friend or acquaintance in whom he had confided might breach the confidence. If, as alleged, the question tended to disparage the plaintiff's character, his remedy would seem to be by way of an action for defamation, not for breach of his right to privacy.

Nor can we find any actionable invasion of privacy in the allegations that the [defendant] caused the plaintiff to be accosted by girls with illicit proposals, or that it was responsible for the making of a large number of threatening and harassing telephone calls to the plaintiff's home at odd hours. Neither of these activities, howsoever offensive and disturbing, involved intrusion for the purpose of gathering information of a private and confidential nature.

* * *

Apart, however, from the foregoing allegations which we find inadequate to spell out a cause of action for invasion of privacy under District of Columbia law, the complaint contains allegations concerning other activities by [GMC] or its agents which do satisfy the requirements for such a cause of action. The one which most clearly meets those requirements is the charge that [GMC] and its codefendants engaged in unauthorized wiretapping and eavesdropping by mechanical and electronic means. In point of fact, the [defendant] does not dispute this, acknowledging that, to the extent the two challenged counts charge it with wiretapping and eavesdropping, an actionable invasion of privacy has been stated.

There are additional allegations that the [defendant] hired people to shadow the plaintiff and keep him under surveillance. In particular, he claims that, on one occasion, one of its agents followed him into a bank, getting sufficiently close to him to see the denomination of the bills he was withdrawing from his account.

From what we have already said, it is manifest that the mere observation of the plaintiff in a public place does not amount to an invasion of his privacy. But, under certain circumstances, surveillance may be so "overzealous" as to render it actionable. Whether or not surveillance in the present case falls into this latter category will depend on the nature of the proof. A person does not automatically make public everything he does merely by being in a public place, and the mere fact that Nader was in a bank did not give anyone the right to try to discover the amount of money he was withdrawing. On the other hand, if the plaintiff acted in such a way as to reveal that fact to any casual observer, then, it may not be said that the [defendant] intruded into his private sphere. In any event, though, it is enough for present purposes to say that the surveillance allegation is not insufficient as a matter of law.

Questions

1. How did the legal right of privacy develop? The source of the district's common-law action for invasion of privacy is the classic article by Warren and Brandeis ("The Right to Privacy," 4 *Harv. L. Rev.* 192). It was premised, to a large extent, on principles originally developed in the field of copyright law. The authors based their thesis on a right granted by the common law to "each individual . . . of determining, ordinarily, to what extent his thoughts, sentiments, and emotions shall be communicated to others." Their principal concern appeared to be not with a broad "right to be let alone" but, rather, with the right to protect oneself from having one's private affairs known to others and to keep secret or intimate facts about oneself from the prying eyes or ears of others.
2. What activities did the court feel were actionable "intrusions" to privacy? Which activities were not actionable? What criteria did the court use to decide?

CHANGING A RULE OF LAW

Cases tell us a great deal about the customs, habits, traditions, and moral standards of people at the time of their decisions. The facts of each case and the attitude of the courts in explaining their result reflect the changing environment. Thus, as social, political, economic, and technological changes take place in our society, legal standards are modified and changed. The following cases dramatize situations in which the law has been kept contemporary by the courts. The courts make new laws by interpreting either the common law, the enactments of the legislatures, or the constitutions of the states and of the United States.

In the last half of the twentieth century with its advances in medical science, the debate concerning the rights of unborn children has increased. These debates have flourished in legislative halls and in executive and administrative processes. The following cases indicate that the courts have not been spared these controversies either. The courts have been utilized as an instrument to settle controversies over the rights of the unborn in certain instances. One's philosophy, religious training, and moral standards influence one's conclusions concerning these difficult issues. Decisions by the courts on questions involving moral issues do not bring universal public agreement.

WRONGFUL INJURY

Woods v. Lancet
303 N.Y. 349 (1951)
Supreme Court, Appellate Div., New York

The complaint served on behalf of this infant plaintiff alleges that, while the infant was in his mother's womb during the ninth month of her pregnancy, he sustained, through the negligence of defendant, such serious injuries that he came into this world permanently maimed and disabled. Defendant moved to dismiss the complaint as not stating a cause of action, thus taking the position that its allegations, though true, gave the infant no right to recover damages in the courts of New York. The Special Term granted the motion and dismissed the suit, citing *Drobner* v. *Peters,* 232 N.Y. 220. . . .

. . . The precise question for us on this appeal is: shall we follow *Drobner* v. *Peters,* or shall we bring the common law of this State, on this question, into accord with justice? I think, as New York State's court of last resort, we should make the law conform to right.

. . . *Drobner* v. *Peters* must be examined against a background of history and of the legal thought of its time and of the thirty years that have passed since it was handed down. Early British and American common law gives no definite answer to our questions, so it is not profitable to go back farther than *Dietrich* v. *Inhabitants of Northampton,* 138 Mass. 14, decided in 1884, with an opinion by Justice Holmes, and, apparently the first American case. . . .

The principal ground asserted by the Massachusetts Supreme Court, for a denial of recovery was that "the unborn child was a part of the mother at the time of the injury" and that "any damage to it which was not too remote to be recovered for at all was recoverable by her" (the mother). . . .

There were, in the early years of this century, rejections of such suits by other courts, with various fact situations involving before-birth traumas . . . and quite recently, Massachusetts has reaffirmed the Dietrich rule. . . . Thus, when *Drobner* v. *Peters* came to this court in 1921, there had been no decisions upholding such suits. . . .

In *Drobner* v. *Peters,* this court, finding no precedent for maintaining the suit, adopted the general theory of *Dietrich* v. *Inhabitants of Northampton,* taking into account, besides the lack of authority to support the suit, the practical difficulties of proof in such cases, and the theoretical lack of separate human existence of an infant *in utero*. It is not unfair to say that the basic reason for *Drobner* v. *Peters* was absence of precedent. However, since 1921, numerous and impressive affirmative precedents have been developed. . . .

What, then, stands in the way of a reversal here? Surely, as an original proposition, we would, today, be hard put to it to find a sound reason for the old rule. Following *Drobner* v. *Peters* would call for an affirmance but the chief basis for that holding (lack of precedent) no longer exists. And it is not a very strong reason, anyhow, in a case like this. . . . Negligence law is common law, and the common law had been molded and changed and brought up-to-date in many another case. Our court said, long ago, that it had not only the right, but the duty to re-examine a question where justice demands it. . . . That opinion notes that Chancellor Kent, more than a century ago, had stated . . . that decisions which seem contrary to reason "ought to be examined without fear, and revised without reluctance, rather than to have the character of our law impaired, and the beauty and harmony of the system destroyed, by the perpetuity of error." . . . We act in the finest common-law tradition when we adapt and alter decisional law to produce common-sense justice.

The other objection to recovery here is the purely theoretical one that a foetus *in utero* has no existence of its own separate from that of its mother, that is, that it is not "a being *in esse*." . . .

To hold, as matter of law, that no viable foetus has any separate existence which the law will recognize is for the law to deny a simple and easily demonstrable fact. This child, when injured, was in fact, alive and capable of being delivered and of remaining alive, separate from its mother. We agree with the dissenting Justice below that "To deny the infant relief in this case is not only a harsh result, but its effect is to do reverence to an outmoded, timeworn fiction not founded on fact and within common knowledge untrue and unjustified."

The judgments should be reversed.

Judge Lewis (dissenting)

I agree with the view of a majority of the court that prenatal injury to a child should not go unrequited by the one at fault. If, however, an unborn child is to be endowed with the right to enforce such requital by an action at law, I think that right should not be created by a judicial decision on the facts in a single case. Better, I believe, that the right should be the product of legislative action taken after hearings at which the Legislature can be advised, by the aid of medical science and research, not only as to the stage of gestation at which a foetus is considered viable, but also as to appropriate means—by time limitation for suit and otherwise—for avoiding abuses which might result from the difficulty of tracing causation from prenatal injury to postnatal deformity. When, in England, the right—unknown to the common law—was created which permitted suit to recover damages for negligently causing the death of a human being, it was accomplished by legislative action. In our own jurisdiction a similar right of action—carefully limited as to time and by other measures to prevent abuse—has long been the subject of statute law adopted by the process incident to statutory enactment. That same process, in my opinion, is peculiarly appropriate for the solution of the problem now before us where unknown factors abound.

Accordingly, I dissent and vote for affirmance.

Questions

1. What technological change required a modification of the law in *Woods*? What "difficulties of proof" exist in a case like *Woods*? Do these "difficulties" suggest reasons for the old rule denying recovery to the infant?
2. Should the lack of precedent preclude the formation of the new law? Should a previous legal fiction (infant has no existence separate from its mother) preclude a new ruling enlightened by medical science?
3. Why did the dissenting judge want to follow the precedent of *Drobner* v. *Peters*?

WRONGFUL PREGNANCY

Troppi v. Scarf

187 N.W. 2d 511 (1971)
Court of Appeals of Michigan

In August 1964, plaintiffs were the parents of seven children, ranging in age from six to sixteen years of age. John Troppi was 43 years old, his wife 37.

While pregnant with an eighth child, Mrs. Troppi suffered a miscarriage. She and her husband consulted with their physician and decided to limit the size of their family. The physician prescribed an oral contraceptive, Norinyl, as the most desirable means of insuring that Mrs. Troppi would bear no more children. He telephoned the prescription to defendant, Frank H. Scarf, a licensed pharmacist. Instead of filling the prescription, Scarf negligently supplied Mrs. Troppi with a drug called Nardil, a mild tranquilizer.

Believing that the pills she had purchased were contraceptives, Mrs. Troppi took them on a daily basis. In December 1964, Mrs. Troppi became pregnant. She delivered a well-born son on August 12, 1965.

Plaintiff's complaint alleges four separate items of damage: (1) Mrs. Troppi's lost wages; (2) medical and hospital expenses; (3) the pain and anxiety of pregnancy and childbirth, and (4) the economic cost of rearing the eighth child. . . .

We begin by noting that the fundamental conditions of tort liability are present here. The defendant's conduct constituted a clear breach of duty. A pharmacist is held to a very high standard of care in filling prescriptions. When he negligently supplied a drug other than the drug requested, he is liable for resulting harm to the purchaser.

We assume, for the purpose of appraising the correctness of the ruling dismissing the complaint, that the defendant's negligence was a cause in fact of Mrs. Troppi's pregnancy. The possibility that she might become pregnant was certainly a foreseeable consequence of the defendant's failure to fill a prescription for birth control pills; we therefore could not say that it was not a proximate cause of the birth of the child.

Setting aside, for the moment, the subtleties of the damage question, it is at least clear that the plaintiffs have expended significant sums of money as a direct and proximate result of the defendant's negligence. The medical and hospital expenses of Mrs. Troppi's confinement and her loss of wages arose from the defendant's failure to fill the prescription properly. Pain and suffering, like that accompanying childbirth, have long been recognized as compensable injuries.

This review of the elements of tort liability points up the extraordinary nature of the trial court's holding that the plaintiffs were entitled to no recovery as a matter of law. We have here a negligent, wrongful act by the defendant, which act directly and proximately caused injury to the plaintiffs. . . .

In *Shaheen* v. *Knight* (1957), a Pennsylvania court ruled that a physician who violated his promise to perform an elective sterilization operation was not liable for the consequences of his breach of contract. . . .

Underlying the *Shaheen* opinion are two principal ideas. The first is that the birth of a healthy child confers such an undoubted benefit upon the plaintiff as to outweigh, as a matter of law, the expenses of delivering and rearing the child. The second is that if the child is really unwanted, plaintiff has a duty to place him for adoption, in effect to mitigate damages. . . .

Our review has been conducted to determine whether the defendant in this case should be exempted from the consequences of his negligence. We conclude that there is no valid reason why the trier of the fact should not be free to assess damages as it would in any other negligence case. . . .

Overriding Benefit. It is arguable that the birth of a healthy child confers so substantial a benefit as to outweigh the expenses of his birth and support. In the great majority of cases, this is no doubt true, else, presumably, people would not choose to multiply so freely. But can we say, as a matter of law, that a healthy child always confers such an overriding benefit?

Thus, if the defendant's tortious conduct conferred a benefit to the same interest which was harmed by his conduct, the dollar value of the benefit is to be subtracted from the dollar value of the injury in arriving at the amount of damages properly awardable.

Since pregnancy and its attendant anxiety, incapacity, pain and suffering are inextricably related to child bearing, we do not think it would be sound to attempt to separate those segments of damage from the economic costs of an unplanned child in applying the "same interest" rule. Accordingly, the benefits of the unplanned child may be weighed against all the elements of claimed damage.

The trial court evidently believes, as did the court in *Shaheen* v. *Knight,* that application of the benefits rule prevents any recovery for the expenses of rearing an unwanted child. This is unsound. Such a rule would be equivalent to declaring that in every case, as a matter of law, the services and companionship of a child have a dollar equivalent greater than the economic costs of his support, to say nothing of the inhibitions, the restrictions, and the pain and suffering caused by pregnancy and the obligation to rear the child.

There is a growing recognition that the financial "services" which parents can expect from their offspring are largely illusory. As to companionship, cases decided when "loss of companionship" was a compensable item of damage for the wrongful death of a child reveal no tendency on the part of juries to value companionship so highly as to outweigh expenses in every foreseeable case. . . .

What must be appreciated is the diversity of purposes and circumstances of the women who use oral contraceptives. Unmarried women who seek the pleasures of sexual intercourse without the perils of unwed motherhood, married women who wish to delay slightly the start of a family in order to retain the career flexibility which many young couples treasure, married women for whom the birth of another child would pose a threat to their own health or the financial security of their families, all are likely users of oral contraceptives. Yet it is clear that in each case the consequences arising from negligent interference with their use will vary widely. A rational legal system must award damages that correspond with these differing injuries. The benefits rule will serve to accomplish this objective.

Consider, for example, the case of the unwed college student who becomes pregnant due to a pharmacist's failure to fill properly her prescription for oral contraceptives. Is it not likely that she has suffered far greater damage than the young newlywed who, although her pregnancy arose from the same sort of negligence, had planned the use of contraceptives only temporarily, say, while she and her husband took an extended honeymoon trip? Without the benefits rule, both plaintiffs would be entitled to recover substantially the same damages.

Application of the benefits rule permits a trier of fact to find that the birth of a child has materially benefitted the newly wed couple, notwithstanding the inconvenience of an interrupted honeymoon, and to reduce the net damage award accordingly. Presumably a trier of fact would find that the "family interests" of the unmarried coed have been enhanced very little.

The essential point, of course, is that the trier must have the power to evaluate the benefit according to all the circumstances of the case presented. Family size, family income, age of the parents, and marital status are some, but not all, the factors which the trier must consider in determining the extent to which the birth of a particular child represents a benefit to his parents. That the benefits so conferred and calculated will vary widely from case to case is inevitable.

Mitigating Damages. It has been suggested that parents who seek to recover for the birth of an unwanted child are under a duty to mitigate damages by placing the child for adoption. If the child is "unwanted," why should they object to placing him for adoption, thereby reducing the financial burden on defendant for his maintenance?

However, to impose such as duty upon the injured plaintiff is to ignore the very real difference which our law recognizes between the avoidance of conception and the disposition of the human organism after conception. . . . At the moment of conception, an entirely different set of legal obligations is imposed upon the parents. A living child almost universally gives rise to emotional and spiritual bonds which few parents can bring themselves to break.

Once a child is born he obviously should be treated with love regardless of whether he was wanted when he was conceived. Many, perhaps most, persons living today are conceptional accidents in the sense that their parents did not desire that a child result from the particular intercourse in which the person was conceived. Nevertheless, when the child is born, most parents accept him with love. That the plaintiffs accepted their eighth child does not change the fact that the birth of another child, seven years younger than the youngest of their previously born children, unbalanced their life style and was not desired by them.

The doctrine which requires a plaintiff to take measures to minimize the financial consequences of a defendant's negligence requires only that reasonable measures be taken. . . .

In determining reasonableness, the best interests of the child must be considered. The law has long recognized the desirability of permitting a child to be reared by his natural parents. The plaintiffs may have believed that the hazards of adoption would damage the child.

A child will not be taken from his mother without her consent. . . . The mother's right to keep the child is not dependent on whether she desired the conception of the child.

As a matter of personal conscience and choice parents may wish to keep an unwanted child. Indeed, parents have been known to keep children that many think should be institutionalized, e.g., mentally retarded children, not because of any anticipated joy or happiness that the child will bring to them but out of a sense of obligation. So, too, the parents of an unplanned, healthy child may feel, and properly so, that whether they wanted the child or not is beside the point once the child is born and that they have an obligation to rear the child as best they can rather than subject him to rearing by unknown persons.

Further, even though the parents may not want to rear the child they may conclude that the psychological impact on them of rejecting the child and placing him for adoption, never seeing him again, would be such that, making the best of a bad situation, it is better to rear the child than to place him for adoption.

Many women confronted with an unwanted pregnancy will abort the fetus, legally or illegally. Some will bear the child and place him for adoption. Many will bear the child, keep and rear him. The defendant does not have the right to insist that the victim of his negligence have the emotional and mental makeup of a woman who is willing to abort or place a child for adoption. If the negligence of a tortfeasor results in conception of a child by a woman whose emotional and mental makeup is inconsistent with aborting or placing the child for adoption, then, under the principle that the tortfeasor takes the injured party as he finds him, the tortfeasor cannot complain that the damages that will be assessed against him are greater than those that would be determined if he had negligently caused the conception of a child by a woman who was willing to abort or place the child for adoption.

While the reasonableness of a plaintiff's efforts to mitigate is ordinarily to be decided by the trier of fact, we are persuaded to rule, as a matter of law, that no mother, wed or unwed, can reasonably be required to abort (even if legal) or place her child for adoption. The plaintiffs are entitled to have the jurors instructed that if they find that negligence of the defendant was a cause in fact of the plaintiff's injury, they may not, in computing the amount, if any, of the plaintiff's damages, take into consideration the fact that the plaintiffs might have aborted the child or placed the child into adoption.

Uncertainty of Damages. Of the four items of damage claimed by plaintiffs, each is capable of reasonable ascertainment. The medical and hospital expenses and Mrs. Troppi's lost wages may be computed with some exactitude. Plaintiff's claimed pain and anxiety, if not capable of precise determination, is a component of damage which triers of fact traditionally have been entrusted to ascertain. As to the costs of rearing the child until his majority, this is a computation which is routinely performed in countless cases.

It should be clear that ascertainment of *gross* damages is a routine task. Whatever uncertainty attends the final award arises from application of the benefits rule, which requires that the trier of fact compute the dollar value of the companionship and services of an unwanted child. Placing a dollar value on these segments may well be more difficult than assessing damages for, say, Mrs. Troppi's lost wages. But difficulty in determining the amount to be subtracted from the gross damages does not justify throwing up our hands and denying recovery altogether.

The assessment of damages in this case is properly within the competence of the trier of fact. The element of uncertainty in the net recovery does not render the damages unduly speculative.

Reversed and remanded for trial.

Questions

1. Did the analogous area of a physician's liability for failure of a nontherapeutic sterilization operation resulting in the birth of an unwanted child provide relevant precedent?
2. What actual loss or injury resulted in *Troppi*?
3. In *Shaheen* v. *Knight* (1957) the court concluded that "we are of the opinion that to allow damages for the normal birth of a normal child is foreign to the universal public sentiment of the people." Do sentiments change?
4. Mitigation of damages involves the responsibility of the injured party to take reasonable steps to avoid or minimize further loss. In order to mitigate their damages, must the plaintiff place her unwanted newborn child for adoption?
5. The court concluded that although the benefits of having the child are to be deducted from the gross damages, such benefits do not as a matter of law override the damages suffered. Can you give any examples?
6. Would the awarding of damages to the parents for "wrongful conception" cause the child to feel unwanted and emotionally like a "bastard"?

The first case to expressly reject [this] . . . argument and to hold that the parents of an unplanned normal child could recover all damages proximately caused by a negligently performed sterilization operation was *Custodio* v. *Bauer,* 251 Cal. App. 2d 303 (1967).

Rejecting the argument that an award of damages could reduce the child to an emotional bastard, the court found that the possibility of psychological harm was no greater than in any other case where a child learns that his existence is the result of his parents' ineptitude at birth control. Most persuasively, the court observed that modern attitudes with respect to family establishment and the use of contraceptives had changed, and further insinuated that the birth of an unplanned child may now be viewed by some as something less than a "blessed event."

Sherlock v. *Stillwater Clinic,* 260 N.W. 2d 169 (Minn., 1977).

WRONGFUL DEATH

Roe v. Wade

410 U.S. 113 (1973)
Supreme Court of the United States

Justice Blackmun

The Texas statutes under attack here are typical of those that have been in effect in many States for approximately a century. . . . These make it a crime to "procure an abortion," as therein defined, or to attempt one, except with respect to "an abortion procured or attempted by medical advice for the purpose of saving the life of the mother." Similar statutes are in existence in a majority of the States.

It perhaps is not generally appreciated that the restrictive criminal abortion laws in effect in a majority of states today are of relatively recent vintage. Those laws, generally proscribing abortion or its attempt at any time during pregnancy except when necessary to preserve the pregnant woman's life, are not of ancient or even of common law origin. Instead, they derive from statutory changes effected, for the most part, in the latter half of the nineteenth century. . . .

The Common Law. It is undisputed that at the common law, abortion performed *before* "quickening"—the first recognizable movement of the fetus *in utero,* appearing usually from the 16th to the 18th week of pregnancy—was not an indictable offense. . . .

It is thus apparent that at common law, at the time of the adoption of our Constitution, and throughout the major portion of the 19th century, abortion was viewed with less disfavor than under most American statutes currently in effect. Phrasing it another way, a woman enjoyed a substantially broader right to terminate a pregnancy than she does in most States today. At least with respect to the early stage of pregnancy, and very possibly without such a limitation the opportunity to make this choice was present in this country well into the nineteenth century. Even later, the law continued for some time to treat less punitively an abortion procured in early pregnancy. . . .

Three reasons have been advanced to explain historically the enactment of criminal abortion laws in the nineteenth century and to justify their continued existence.

It has been argued occasionally that these laws were the product of a Victorian social concern to discourage illicit sexual conduct. Texas, however, does not advance this justification in the present case, and it appears that no court or commentator has taken the argument seriously. . . .

A second reason is concerned with abortion as a medical procedure. When most criminal abortion laws were first enacted, the procedure was a hazardous one for the woman. . . . Thus it has been argued that a State's real concern in enacting a criminal abortion law was to protect the pregnant woman, that is, to restrain her from submitting to a procedure that placed her life in serious jeopardy.

Modern medical techniques have altered this situation. Appellants . . . refer to medical data indicating that abortion in early pregnancy, that is, prior to the end of the first trimester, although not without its risk, is now relatively safe. Mortality rates for women undergoing early abortions, where the procedure is legal, appear to be as low or lower than the rates for normal childbirth. Consequently, any interest of the State in protecting the woman from an inherently hazardous procedure, except when it would be equally dangerous for her to forgo it, has largely disappeared. Of course, important State interests in the area of health and medical standards do remain. The State has a legitimate interest in seeing to it that abortion, like any other medical procedure, is performed under circumstances that insure maximum safety for the patient. This interest obviously extends at least to the performing physician and his staff, to the facilities involved, to the availability of after-care, and to adequate provision for any complication or emergency that might arise. The prevalence of high mortality rates at illegal "abortion mills" strengthens, rather than weakens, the State's interest in regulating the conditions under which abortions are performed. Moreover, the risk to the woman increases as her pregnancy continues. Thus the State retains a definite interest in protecting the woman's own health and safety when an abortion is proposed at a late stage of pregnancy.

The third reason is the State's interest—some phrase it in terms of duty—in protecting prenatal life. Some of the argument for this justification rests on the theory that a new human life is present from the moment of conception. The State's interest and general obligation to protect life then extends, it is argued, to prenatal life. Only when the life of the pregnant mother herself is at stake, balanced against the life she carries within her, should the interest of the embryo or fetus not prevail. Logically, of course, a legitimate state interest in this area need not stand or fall on acceptance of the belief that the life begins at conception or at some other point prior to live birth. In assessing the State's interest, recognition may be given to the less rigid claim that as long as at least *potential* life is involved, the State may assert interests beyond the protection of the pregnant woman alone. . . .

It is with these interests, and the weight to be attached to them, that this case is concerned.

The Constitution does not explicitly mention any right of privacy. In a line of decisions, however . . . the court has recognized that a right of personal privacy, or a guarantee of certain areas or zones of privacy, does exist under the Constitution. . . . They also make it clear that the right has some extension to activities relating to marriage, procreation, contraception, and child rearing and education. . . .

This right of privacy, whether it be founded in the Fourteenth Amendment's concept of personal liberty and restrictions upon state action, as we feel it is, or, as the District court determined, in the Ninth Amendment's reservation of rights to the people, is broad enough to encompass a woman's decision whether or not to terminate her pregnancy. The detriment that the State would impose upon the pregnant woman by denying this choice altogether is apparent. Specific and direct harm medically diagnosable even in early pregnancy may be involved. Maternity, or additional offspring, may force upon the woman a distressful life and future. Psychological harm may be imminent. Mental and physical health may be taxed by child care. There is also the distress, for all concerned, associated with the unwanted child, and there is the problem of bringing a child into a family already unable, psychologically and otherwise, to care for it. In other cases, as in this one, the additional difficulties and continuing stigma of unwed motherhood may be involved. All these are factors the woman and her responsible physician necessarily will consider in consultation.

On the basis of elements such as these, appellants . . . argue that the woman's right is absolute and that she is entitled to terminate her pregnancy at whatever time, in whatever way, and for whatever reason she alone chooses. With this we do not agree. Appellant's arguments that Texas either has no valid interest at all in regulating the abortion decision, or no interest strong enough to support any limitation upon the woman's sole determination, is unpersuasive. The Court's decisions recognizing a right of privacy also acknowledge that some state regulation in areas protected by that right is appropriate. As noted above, a state may properly assert important interests in safeguarding health, in maintaining medical standards, and in protecting potential life. At some point in pregnancy, these respective interests become sufficiently compelling to sustain regulation of the factors that govern the abortion decision. The privacy right involved, therefore, cannot be said to be absolute. In fact, it is not clear to us that the claim asserted . . . that one has an unlimited right to do with one's body as one pleases bears a close relationship to the right of privacy previously articulated in the Court's decisions. The Court has refused to recognize an unlimited right of this kind in the past.

We therefore conclude that the right of personal privacy includes the abortion decision, but that this right is not unqualified and must be considered against important state interests in regulation. . . .

Where certain "fundamental rights" are involved, the Court has held that regulation limiting these rights may be justified only by a "compelling state interest," and that legislative enactments must be narrowly drawn to express only the legitimate state interests at stake. . . .

Texas urges that, apart from the Fourteenth Amendment, life begins at conception and is present throughout pregnancy, and that, therefore, the State has a compelling interest in protecting that life from and after conception. We need not resolve the difficult question of when life begins. When those trained in the respective disciplines of medicine, philosophy, and theology are unable to arrive at any consensus, the judiciary, at this point in the development of man's knowledge, is not in a position to speculate as to the answer. . . .

In view of all this, we do not agree that, by adopting one theory of life, Texas may override the rights of the pregnant woman that are at stake. We repeat, however, that the State does have an important and legitimate interest in preserving and protecting the health of the pregnant woman, whether she be a resident of the State or a non-resident who seeks medical consultation and treatment there, and that it has still *another* important and legitimate interest in protecting the potentiality of human life. These interests are separate and distinct. Each grows in substantiality as the woman approaches term and, at a point during pregnancy, each becomes "compelling."

With respect to the State's important and legitimate interest in the health of the mother, the "compelling" point, in the light of present medical knowledge, is at approximately the end of the first trimester. This is so because of the now established medical fact . . . that until the end of the first trimester mortality in abortion is less than mortality in normal childbirth. It follows that, from and after this point, a State may regulate the abortion procedure to the extent that the regulation reasonably relates to the preservation and protection of maternal health. Examples of permissible state regulation in this area are requirements as to the qualifications of the person who is to perform the abortion; as to the licensure of that person; as to the facility in which the procedure is to be performed, that is, whether it must be a hospital or may be a clinic or some other place of less-than-hospital status; as to the licensing of the facility; and the like.

This means, on the other hand, that, for the period of pregnancy prior to this "compelling" point, the attending physician, in consultation with his patient, is free to determine, without regulation by the State, that in his medical judgment the patient's pregnancy should be terminated. If that decision is reached, the judgment may be effectuated by an abortion free of interference by the States.

With respect to the State's important and legitimate interest in potential life, the "compelling" point is at viability. This is so because the fetus then presumably has the capability of meaningful life outside the mother's womb. State regulation protective of fetal life after viability thus has both logical and biological justifications. If the State is interested in protecting fetal life after viability, it may go so far as to proscribe abortion during that period except when it is necessary to preserve the life or health of the mother.

Measured against these standards, the Texas Penal Code, in restricting legal abortions to those "procured or attempted by medical advice for the purpose of saving the life of the mother," sweeps too broadly. The statute makes no distinction between abortions performed early in pregnancy and those performed later, and it limits to a single reason, "saving" the mother's life, the legal justification for the procedure. The statute, therefore, cannot survive the constitutional attack made upon it here. . . .

This holding we feel, is consistent with the relative weights of the respective interests involved, with the lessons and examples of medical and legal history, with the lenity of the common law and with the demands of the profound problems of the present day. The decision leaves the State free to place increasing restrictions on abortion as the period of pregnancy lengthens, so long as those restrictions are tailored to the recognized state interests. The decision vindicates the right of the physician to administer medical treatment according to his professional judgment up to the point where important state interests provide compelling justifications for intervention. Up to those points the abortion decision in all its aspects is inherently, and primarily, a medical decision, and basic responsibility for it must rest with the physician. If an individual practitioner abuses the privilege of exercising proper medical judgment, the usual remedies, judicial and intra-professional, are available.

Questions

1. What "law" was the Court "interpreting" in *Roe*?
2. For the stage of pregnancy prior to the end of first trimester, the abortion decision and its effectuation must be left to whom?
3. What may the state do during the second trimester?
4. After the fetus has reached "viability," may the state proscribe abortion?
5. May the state proscribe an abortion which is necessary for the preservation of the life or health of the mother?

ADHERING TO PRECEDENT

In our legal system, the mandate of the courts has been to apply and interpret settled law as well as to modify law to new social conditions. Often when adhering to legal precedent and refusing to alter existing law, the courts have decided to leave any change in the law to the decision processes of the legislature. This deference to the legislative process is illustrated in the following cases.

DEFERENCE TO LEGISLATURE

The Constitution of the United States made the central government one of limited powers. Article I, Section 8, of the U.S. Constitution details the legislative power of the U.S. Congress. Any attempt by the Congress to legislate in an area not specifically delegated by the Constitution is unconstitutional and of no legal effect. One of the powers granted to Congress is to regulate interstate commerce. Historically, the court interpreted this to mean that Congress could not regulate business activities that were not interstate commerce but rather involved *intra*state commerce only. The following 1921 case dealt with whether baseball was interstate or intrastate commerce. If intrastate, the federal legislation, the Sherman Act, was inapplicable to baseball.

Federal Baseball Club of Baltimore v. National League
259 U.S. 200 (1921)
Supreme Court of the United States
Justice Holmes

This is a suit for threefold damages brought by the plaintiff under the Anti-Trust Acts of . . . 1890 [Sherman Act]. . . . The defendants are the National League of Professional Baseball Clubs and the American League of Professional Baseball Clubs, unincorporated associations, composed respectively of groups of eight incorporated baseball clubs, joined by defendants . . . and three other persons having powers in the Federal League of Professional Baseball Clubs. . . . It is alleged that these defendants conspired to monopolize the baseball business. . . .

The plaintiff is a baseball club incorporated in Maryland, and with seven other corporations was a member of the Federal League of Professional Baseball Players, a corporation under the laws of Indiana, that attempted to compete with the combined defendants. It alleges that the defendants destroyed the Federal League by buying up some of the constituent clubs and in one way or another inducing all those clubs except the plaintiff to leave their League, and that the three persons connected with the Federal league and named as defendants, one of them being the President of the League, took part in the conspiracy. Great damage to the plaintiff is alleged. The plaintiff obtained a verdict for $80,000 in the [trial] Court and a judgment for treble the amount was entered, but the Court of Appeals, after an elaborate discussion, held that the defendants were not within the Sherman Act. . . .

. . . The clubs composing the Leagues are in different cities and for the most part in different States. The end of the elaborate organizations and sub-organizations that are described in the pleadings and evidence is that these clubs shall play against one another in public exhibitions for money, one or the other club crossing a state line in order to make the meeting possible. . . . Of course the scheme requires constantly repeated traveling on the part of the clubs, which is provided for, controlled and disciplined by the organizations, and this it is said means commerce among the States. But we are of opinion that the Court of Appeals was right. The business is giving exhibitions of baseball, which are purely state affairs. It is true that in order to attain for these exhibitions the great popularity that they have achieved, competitions must be arranged between clubs from different cities and States. But the fact that in order to give the exhibitions the Leagues must induce free persons to cross state lines and must arrange and pay for their doing so is not enough to change the character of the business. According to the distinction insisted upon in *Hooper* v. *California,* 155 U.S. 648, 655, the transport is a mere incident, not the essential thing. That to which it is incident, the exhibition, although made for money would not be called trade or commerce in the commonly accepted use of those words. As it is put by the defendant, personal effort, not related to production, is not a subject of commerce. That which in its consummation is not commerce does not become commerce among the States because the transportation that we have mentioned takes place. To repeat the illustrations given by the Court below, a firm of lawyers sending out a member to argue a case, or the Chautauqua lecture bureau sending out lecturers, does not engage in such commerce because the lawyer or lecturer goes to another State.

If we are right, the plaintiff's business is to be described in the same way and the restrictions by contract that prevented the plaintiff from getting players to break their bargains and the other conduct charged against the defendants were not an interference with commerce among the States.

Questions

1. What reasons did the Court cite for baseball not being in interstate commerce?
2. Did the Court also conclude that a lawyer's services, though he or she may cross state lines, are not interstate commerce?

Toolson v. New York Yankees

346 U.S. 356 (1953)
Supreme Court of the United States

Per Curiam

In *Federal Baseball Club of Baltimore* v. *National League,* this Court held that the business of providing public baseball games for profit between clubs of professional baseball players was not within the scope of the federal antitrust laws. Congress has had the ruling under consideration but has not seen fit to bring such business under these laws by legislation having prospective effect. The business has thus been left for thirty years to develop, on the understanding that it was not subject to existing antitrust legislation. The present cases ask us to overrule the prior decision and, with retrospective effect, hold the legislation applicable. We think that if there are evils in this field which now warrant application to it of the antitrust laws it should be by legislation. Without re-examination of the underlying issues, the judgments below are affirmed on the authority of *Federal Baseball Club of Baltimore* v. *National League* so far as that decision determines that Congress had no intention of including the business of baseball within the scope of the federal antitrust laws.

Justice Burton (dissenting)

Whatever may have been the situation when the *Federal Baseball Club* case was decided in 1922, I am not able to join today's decision which, in effect, announces that organized baseball, in 1953, still is not engaged in interstate trade or commerce. In the light of organized baseball's well-known and widely distributed capital investments used in conducting competitions between teams constantly traveling between states, its receipts and expenditures of large sums transmitted between states, its numerous purchases of materials in interstate commerce, the attendance at its local exhibitions of large audiences often traveling across state lines, its radio and television activities which expand its audiences beyond state lines, its sponsorship of interstate advertising, and its highly organized "farm system" of minor league baseball clubs, coupled with restrictive contracts and understandings between individuals and among clubs or leagues playing for profit throughout the United States, and even in Canada, Mexico and Cuba, it is a contradiction in terms to say that the defendants in the cases before us are not now engaged in interstate trade or commerce as those terms are used in the Constitution of the United States and in the Sherman Act.

Questions

1. Does the Court's statement, "Without re-examination of the underlying issues . . ." suggest the Court doesn't want to consider those issues because they recognize the growth of the baseball business undermines the previous reasons for the rule?
2. What reason did the court give for not exercising its power of reversal when, as in this case, the reason for the original rule had disappeared?
3. Consider the following excerpt from *Flood* v. *Kuhn* 407 U.S. 258 (1972):

> We continue to be loath, 50 years after *Federal Baseball* and almost two decades after *Toolson,* to overturn those cases judicially when Congress, by its positive inaction has allowed those decisions to stand for so long and, far beyond mere inference and implication, has clearly evinced a desire not to disapprove them legislatively.
>
> Accordingly, we adhere once again to *Federal Baseball* and *Toolson* and to their application to professional baseball. We adhere also to *International Boxing* and *Radovich* and to their respective applications (of the antitrust laws) to professional boxing and professional football. If there is any inconsistency or illogic in all this, it is an inconsistency and illogic of long standing that is to be remedied by the Congress and not by this Court. If we were to act otherwise, we would be withdrawing from the conclusion as to congressional intent made in *Toolson* and from the concerns as to retrospectivity therein expressed. Under these circumstances, there is merit in consistency even though some might claim that beneath that consistency is a layer of inconsistency.

Why allow antitrust laws in boxing and football, but not baseball? What consistency is the Court talking about?

INADEQUATE KNOWLEDGE

Powell v. Texas

392 U.S. 514 (1967)
Supreme Court of the United States

Justice Marshall

In late December, 1966, appellant was arrested and charged with being found in a state of intoxication in a public place, in violation of Texas Penal Code. . . . His counsel urged that appellant was "afflicted with the disease of chronic alcoholism," "that his appearance in public [while drunk was] . . . not of his own volition," and therefore that to punish him criminally for that conduct would be cruel and unusual, in violation of the Eighth and Fourteenth Amendments to the United States Constitution.

The principal testimony was that of Dr. Davis Wade, a Fellow of the American Medical Association, duly certificated in psychiatry. . . . Dr. Wade sketched the outlines of the "disease" concept of alcoholism; noted that there is no generally accepted definition of "alcoholism"; alluded to the ongoing debate within the medical profession over whether alcohol is actually physically "addicting" or merely psychologically "habituating"; and concluded that in either case a "chronic alcoholic" is an "involuntary drinker," who is "powerless not to drink," and who "loses his self-control over his drinking." He testified that he had examined appellant, and that appellant is a "chronic alcoholic," who "by the time he has reached [the state of intoxication] . . . is not able to control his behavior, and [who] . . . has reached this point because he has an uncontrollable compulsion to drink." Dr. Wade also responded in the negative to the question whether appellant has "the willpower to resist the constant excessive consumption of alcohol." He added that in his opinion jailing appellant without medical attention would operate neither to rehabilitate him nor to lessen his desire for alcohol. . . .

Appellant testified concerning the history of his drinking problem. He reviewed his many arrests for drunkenness; testified that he was unable to stop drinking; stated that when he was intoxicated he had no control over his actions and could not remember them later, but that he did not become violent; and admitted that he did not remember his arrest on the occasion for which he was being tried. On cross-examination, appellant admitted that he had had one drink on the morning of the trial and had been able to discontinue drinking. . . . The State made no effort to obtain expert psychiatric testimony of its own, or even to explore with appellant's witness the question of appellant's power to control the frequency, timing, and location of his drinking bouts, or the substantial disagreement within the medical profession concerning the nature of the disease, the efficacy of treatment and the prerequisites for effective treatment. . . . Instead, the State contented itself with a brief argument that appellant had no defense to the charge because he "is legally sane and knows the difference between right and wrong."

Following this abbreviated exposition of the problem before it, the trial court indicated its intention to disallow appellant's claimed defense of "chronic alcoholism." . . .

In the first place, the record in this case is utterly inadequate to permit the sort of informed and responsible adjudication which alone can support the announcement of an important and wideranging new constitutional principle. We know very little about the circumstances surrounding the drinking bout which resulted in this conviction, or about Leroy Powell's drinking problem, or indeed about alcoholism itself. . . .

. . . Debate rages within the medical profession as to whether "alcoholism" is a separate "disease" in any meaningful biochemical, physiological or psychological sense, or whether it represents one peculiar manifestation in some individuals of underlying psychiatric disorders. . . .

It is one thing to say that if a man is deprived of alcohol his hands will begin to shake, he will suffer agonizing pains and ultimately he will have hallucinations; it is quite another to say that a man has a "compulsion" to take a drink, but that he also retains a certain amount of "free will" with which to resist. It is simply impossible, in the present state of our knowledge, to ascribe a useful meaning to the latter statement. This definitional confusion reflects, of course, not merely the undeveloped state of the psychiatric art but also the conceptual difficulties inevitably attendant upon the importation of scientific and medical models into a legal system generally predicated upon a different set of assumptions.

Despite the comparatively primitive state of our knowledge on the subject, it cannot be denied that the destructive use of alcoholic beverages is one of our principal social and public health problems. . . .

There is as yet no known generally effective method for treating the vast number of alcoholics in our society. . . . Most psychiatrists are apparently of the opinion that alcoholism is far more difficult to treat than other forms of behavioral disorders, and some believe it is impossible to cure by means of psychotherapy; indeed, the medical profession as a whole, and psychiatrists in particular, have been severely criticised for the prevailing reluctance to undertake the treatment of drinking problems. Thus it is entirely possible that, even were the manpower and facilities available for a full-scale attack upon chronic alcoholism we would find ourselves unable to help the vast bulk of our "visible"—let alone our "invisible"—alcoholic population.

However, facilities for the attempted treatment of indigent alcoholics are woefully lacking throughout the country. It would be tragic to return large numbers of helpless, sometimes dangerous and frequently unsanitary inebriates to the streets of our cities without even the opportunity to sober up adequately which a brief jail term provides. . . . Yet the medical profession cannot, and does not, tell us with any assurance that, even if the buildings, equipment and trained personnel were made available, it could provide anything more than slightly higher-class jails for our indigent habitual inebriates. Thus we run the grave risk that nothing will be accomplished beyond the hanging of a new sign—reading "hospital"—over one wing of the jailhouse. . . .

Faced with this unpleasant reality, we are unable to assert that the use of the criminal process as a means of dealing with the public aspects of problem drinking can never be defended as rational. The picture of the penniless drunk propelled aimlessly and endlessly through the law's "revolving door" of arrest, incarceration, release and rearrest is not a pretty one. But before we condemn the present practice across the board, perhaps we ought to be able to point to some clear promise of a better world for these unfortunate people. Unfortunately, no such promise has yet been forthcoming. If, in addition to the absence of a coherent approach to the problem of treatment, we consider that almost complete absence of facilities and manpower for the implementation of a rehabilitation program, it is difficult to say in the present context that the criminal process is utterly lacking in social value. This court has never held that anything in the Constitution requires that penal sanctions be designed solely to achieve therapeutic or rehabilitative effects, and it can hardly be said with assurance that incarceration serves such purposes any better for the general run of criminals than it does for public drunks.

Ignorance likewise impedes our assessment of the deterrent effect of criminal sanctions for public drunkenness. The fact that a high percentage of American alcoholics conceal their drinking problems, not merely by avoiding public displays of intoxication, but also by shunning all forms of treatment, is indicative that some powerful deterrent operates to inhibit the public revelation of the existence of alcoholism. Quite probably this deterrent effect can be largely attributed to the harsh moral attitude which our society has traditionally taken toward intoxication and the shame which we have associated with alcoholism. Criminal conviction represents the degrading public revelation of what Anglo-American society has long condemned as a moral defect, and the existence of criminal sanctions may serve to reinforce this cultural taboo, just as we presume they serve to reinforce other, stronger feelings against murder, rape, theft, and other forms of antisocial conduct. . . .

It is not difficult to imagine a case involving psychiatric testimony to the effect that an individual suffers from some aggressive neurosis which he is able to control when sober; that very little alcohol suffices to remove the inhibitions which normally contain these aggressions, with the result that the individual engages in assaultive behavior without becoming actually intoxicated; and that the individual suffers from a very strong desire to drink, which is an "exceedingly strong influence" but "not completely overpowering." Without being untrue to the rationale of this case, should the principles advanced in dissent be accepted here, the Court could not avoid holding such an individual constitutionally unaccountable for his assaultive behavior.

Traditional common law concepts of personal accountability and essential considerations of federalism lead us to disagree with appellant. We are unable to conclude, on the state of this record or on the current state of medical knowledge, that chronic alcoholics in general, and Leroy Powell in particular, suffer from such an irresistible compulsion to drink and to get drunk in public that they are utterly unable to control their performance of either or both of these acts and thus cannot be deterred at all from public intoxication. . . .

It is simply not yet the time to write into the Constitution formulas cast in terms whose meaning, let alone relevance, are not yet clear either to doctors or to lawyers.

Questions

1. In *Robinson* v. *California,* 370 U.S. 660 (1962), the state made it a crime to "be addicted to the use of narcotics." The court held that "a state statute which imprisons the person thus inflicted [with narcotics addiction] as a criminal, even though he has never touched any narcotic drug within the state or been guilty of any irregular behavior there, inflicts a cruel and unusual punishment. . . ." In effect, California was making a particular status (narcotic addiction) a crime. The court ruled that California could not make such status a crime any more than it could make the status of being mentally ill or a leper a crime. Would this case form an argument for Leroy Powell?

2. Was Powell convicted of being a chronic alcoholic (status) or for being in public while drunk (behavior)? Could California make it a crime to *use* an unprescribed narcotic?
3. Why was the court not willing to allow chronic alcoholism as a defense like mental illness is a defense in other crimes? Could a defendant like Powell resist intoxication and prevent himself or herself from appearing in public places?

CONCLUSION

The legal system attempts to resolve controversies. It involves an analysis of the relevant facts in the case, selecting past cases for guidance, evaluating alternative solutions, and reaching a conclusion with articulated reasoning. Understanding this process of legal analysis begins with an appreciation for the dynamic quality of the case-law method—how changing factual situations bring about different legal conclusions and how a new rule is formulated when the reasons for the rule become outdated or no longer serve societal needs. The better the student can fully appreciate how a legal dispute is resolved, the better such a student will understand the dynamics of law. Consequently, the application of the rules of law to various factual situations have been reviewed to gain understanding of the framework for legal analysis and the changing nature of law.

CASE PROBLEMS

1. The plaintiff was in the process of moving her furniture out of her apartment when the landlord appeared with a pistol. He threatened her and told her not to move anything out of the apartment since he had a lien on the goods because of the unpaid rent. The gun was unloaded, but the plaintiff didn't know that. The plaintiff sued for assault. If the defendant meant no actual harm and the gun was unloaded, would this be an assault?

2. Roberts took his Oldsmobile into Breisig's for repairs. Roberts asked when the car would be ready. Breisig said he hoped the repairs would be completed by the end of the day and that he would park the car in the parking lot of his shop so Roberts could pick it up that evening.

   Breisig finished the work and parked the car in the lot, leaving the keys in the car. Soon thereafter two teenage boys stole the car and, while driving, negligently struck George, the plaintiff, who suffered serious injuries.

   George brought an action against Breisig, claiming that the keys in the unattended automobile constituted an act of negligence. Breisig denied that his conduct constituted negligence, contending that his action was not the proximate cause of plaintiff's injuries. Decide.

3. Jacques entered a Sears store in New York to purchase business supplies. He picked up 19 reflectorized letters and numbers worth 10 cents apiece and put them in his pocket. He also selected a mailbox and had two extra keys made. He paid for the mailbox and keys, but left the store without paying for the letters and numbers. At the time he had over $600 in cash and a $400 check in his wallet.

   A Sears' security officer observed Jacques putting the items in his pocket and leaving the store without paying for them. As Jacques approached his car in the store parking lot, the officer stopped him and told him that he was under arrest. He took Jacques back to a security office, where Jacques admitted having taken the letters without paying for them. He said he wished to pay for the letters, that he was "sorry about the whole thing," and that he "would never do anything like this again."

   Sears' security officers called the New York police, who took Jacques to police headquarters, booked him, and later released him on bail.

   Jacques brought this action for damages against Sears, alleging false imprisonment and false arrest. Sears contended that its detention of Jacques was "reasonable." Decide.

4. Mrs. Garner went into a drug store to buy some soap. Her father, who was ill, remained in her car in the parking lot in front of the store. She found the bar of soap, took it to the cashier, paid for it, and received a sales ticket. The cashier put the soap in a small bag. Mrs. Garner's sister was with her and had not finished shopping. Mrs. Garner said that she was going out to the car to see if their father was all right. She walked out of the store, but before she got to her car, the manager of the store yelled at her, telling her to stop, and accused her of stealing the bar of soap. She denied it, but he told her she would have to go back into the store with him to prove that she hadn't stolen the soap. There were a number of people in the parking lot who heard the manager's loud and rude accusations. When the manager and Mrs. Garner got back to the store, the cashier verified that Mrs. Garner had paid for the soap. Mrs. Garner was then released. Is the store liable to the plaintiff for slander and false imprisonment?

END NOTE

1. Ezra Pound, "The End of Law as Developed in Legal Rules and Doctrines," 27 *Harv. L. Rev.* 195 (1914): 233.

chapter 5

THE CONSTITUTION AND BUSINESS

This chapter concentrates on constitutional law that affects business. In particular, Supreme Court rulings about the rights of business are explored. Since the Court has clearly reversed itself on major constitutional issues over the years, the reader should be exposed to historical interpretation as well as to modern decisions in order to gain a broader perspective of the impact of constitutional law on business.

The process of amending the Constitution has been only sparingly used in its almost 200-year history. However, the first 10 amendments (the Bill of Rights) were added almost immediately. The first session of Congress by a two-thirds vote approved the Bill of Rights, and the necessary consent of three fourths of the state legislatures followed within the time period specified by Congress. Although 26 amendments have been added to the Constitution in this manner, this number is relatively small when compared to the duration of the Constitution itself. One reason for the paucity of amendments has been the Supreme Court's interpretative powers over the general terms of the Constitution. Some would say more cynically that the Constitution is "amended" every time the Supreme Court renders a new interpretation.

CONSTITUTIONAL BASIS OF REGULATION

From the earliest history of the United States, American business has placed a firm faith in the workings of a free-market economy. Protection against those who might exploit or abuse society in the production and distribution of the nation's goods and services was to be effectuated through the forces of competition. Consequently, substantial government interference with economic activities is of fairly recent origin. Of course, the decisions concerning a change in the role of government and the variety of methods to be employed in economic regulation have not been accomplished without opposition. At the outset, debate centered on the nature of the "power" of the government to legislate and regulate economic activity. Of course, the Supreme Court decided the constitutional extent of governmental powers.

Initially, the U.S. Supreme Court was committed to the ideology of *laissez-faire*. Hence, the Court utilized its power of judicial review to protect the American capitalistic system from the legislative or executive branches of government that attempted to interfere with the fundamental basis of American capitalism, that is, private property and the liberty to contract. The Supreme Court utilized general clauses of the Constitution to restrict both state and federal legislative bodies to a *laissez-faire* policy.

JUDICIAL RESTRICTIONS ON STATE LEGISLATURES

Efforts of the state legislatures to regulate their economic affairs is founded on the state's police power which empowers the state to protect the health, safety, morals, or general welfare of the state citizenry. However, the Supreme Court has utilized constitutional interpretation to limit state legislation over economic affairs. Since the commerce clause of the U.S. Constitution grants to the federal government the power to regulate interstate commerce, by implication the states were denied this power. The purpose of inserting the commerce clause in the Constitution was to prevent the states from imposing tariffs or duties on imports into their state or otherwise discriminating against interstate merchants transporting goods into the state. The commerce clause was intended to create a free market throughout the states of the Union. Consequently, the Supreme Court could utilize the clause to prohibit state governments from regulating certain aspects of commerce which the Court deemed to be interstate, and beyond the reach of state governments. The Supreme Court has stated that whenever the subject of economic regulation requires a national or uniform plan, Congress possesses *exclusive* power for legislative solution. And even if no uniformity of regulation is required, the Court has held that state regulations may not discriminate against interstate commerce or substantially and unduly burden interstate commerce. Only if the economic affair was not one requiring uniformity and the state law did not discriminate against or unduly burden interstate commerce was the state free of this judicial trap which restricted state legislative efforts to regulate economic activity.

A second judicial constraint was imposed on the state governments in their efforts to regulate economic affairs. Originally, the Bill of Rights and its protections for the individual were added to the U.S. Constitution to limit the power of the *federal* government and prevent its becoming an oppressive central government exercising its power as the crown did over its subjects in the colonies. Each of the states already had its own constitution, which afforded similar protection to state citizens from oppressive state actions. Consequently, the Bill of Rights was not applicable as a limitation on powers of *state* government. After the Civil War, however, the Fourteenth Amendment was added to the U.S. Constitution as a limitation on the power of *state* government and as a source of power to the federal government to protect individuals in certain instances from unwarranted state actions. This Amendment's basic purpose was to provide federal protection to the freed slaves of the South from oppressive state governments.

One protection afforded to individuals in the Fourteenth Amendment is that no state could deprive an individual of life, liberty, or property without following the requirements of "due process of law." Initially, *process* was a synonym for *procedure,* and "due process of law" meant that appropriate procedures of law must be followed in depriving an individual of life, liberty, or property. Legislative due process would require that state legislative bodies follow their respective constitutional and statutory procedures before and during the enactment of law. However, the Supreme Court extended the power of the due process clause of the Fourteenth Amendment from a procedural constraint to a substantive restraint on legislators. "Substantive" due process involves the Court's declaration of unconstitutionality of those state regulatory statutes which the Court determines to be unreasonable interferences with liberty or property. In this sense, the due process clause was utilized to eliminate state regulations whenever the Court was convinced the statute was unreasonable or did not conform to the justices' concept of *laissez-faire* philosophy. The Supreme Court, in effect, had the last word or veto power over state legislatures by virtue of substantive due process interpretation.

Substantive due process restrictions on state legislatures began with the Supreme Court decision that adopted the common law tradition that the prices charged in certain industries and trades were properly subject to public (state) regulation.

In *Munn* v. *Illinois,* 94 U.S. 113 (1876), the Supreme Court declared the following:

. . . [I]t has been customary in England from time immemorial, and in this country from its first colonization, to regulate ferries, common carriers, hackmen, bakers, millers, wharfingers, innkeepers, . . . and in so doing to fix a maximum of charge to be made for services rendered, accommodations furnished, and articles sold. . . .

From this it is apparent that, down to the time of the adoption of the Fourteenth Amendment, it was not supposed that statutes regulating the use, or even the price of the use, of private property necessarily deprived an owner of his property without due process of law. Under some circumstances they may, but not under all. The amendment does not change the law in this particular: it simply prevents the States from doing that which will operate as such a deprivation.

This brings us to inquire as to the principles upon which this power of regulation rests, in order that we may determine what is within and what without its operative effect. Looking then, to the common law, from whence came the right which the Constitution protects, we find that when private property is "affected with a public interest, it ceases to be *juris privati* only." This was said by Lord Chief Justice Hale more than two hundred years ago . . . and has been accepted without objection as an essential element in the law of property ever since. Property does become clothed with a public interest when used in a manner to make it of public consequence, and affect the community at large.

According to the reasoning of *Munn* v. *Illinois,* the states were freed of the constitutional barrier of due process and permitted to regulate those industries that were "affected with the public interest." Other industries not so affected with the public interest remained beyond the authority of the state government to impose public regulations.

There were two categories of industry considered to be affected with the public interest and, hence, subject to state regulation. First, as was indicated in *Munn* v. *Illinois,* it included those industries where buyers or sellers were apt to be caught in a "distress position" which subjected them to extreme price exploitation. Examples include the grain elevators in *Munn* v. *Illinois* or stockyards, hotels, and docks. Second, there are the "natural monopolies," where the economies of large-scale operation necessitated concentration of the industry into a single business entity in order to produce units at lowest average cost. Obvious examples of these industries include light and gas companies, telephone companies, and urban transit.

Within these two categories of industries, the legislatures of the states were empowered to regulate industry prices. However, the Court did not fully retreat from its activist policy of protecting *laissez-faire* economic philosophy. Instead, the Court undertook to protect the regulated companies from a regulated price level that was so low as to constitute a deprivation of the utility's property rights.[1] The Court determined that rates must allow a "fair return" on the invested value of property in such organizations. In these instances, the Court acted as a superlegislature and reviewed the reasonableness of the rates in any regulated industry.

In those industries not affected with the public interest, the Court adopted a policy of protection from "unreasonable" regulations. In *Allgeyer* v. *Louisiana,* 165 U.S. 578 [1897], the Court invalidated state statutes which prohibited their citizens from contracting with companies outside the state. In the field of labor relations, numerous state statutes designed to aid workers were held to be unreasonable interferences with liberty and, consequently, in violation of the due process clause. In *Lochner* v. *New York,* 198 U.S. 45 (1905), the Court held a New York statute unconstitutional because it limited the hours of work by those employed in bakeries. The Court opinion was as follows:

In every case that comes before this court, therefore, where legislation of this character is concerned, and where the protection of the Federal Constitution is sought, the question necessarily arises: Is this a fair, reasonable, and appropriate exercise of the police power of the state, or is it an unreasonable, unnecessary, arbitrary interference with the right of the individual to his personal liberty, or to enter into those contracts in relation to labor which may seem to him appropriate or necessary for the support of himself and his family . . . ?

We think the limit of the police power has been reached and passed in this case. There is, in our judgment, no reasonable foundation for holding this to be necessary and appropriate as a health law to safeguard the public health or the health of individuals who are following the trade of baker.

Justice Holmes dissented from the *Lochner* decision and began an attack on substantive due process:

This case is decided upon an economic theory which a large part of the country does not entertain. If it were a question whether I agreed with that theory, I should desire to study it further and long before making up my mind. But I do not conceive that to be my duty, because I strongly believe that my agreement or disagreement has nothing to do with the right of a majority to embody their opinions in law. . . . [A] constitution is not intended to embody a particular legal theory, whether of paternalism and the organic relation of the citizen to the state or of *laissez-faire*. It is made for people of fundamentally different views, and the accident of our finding certain opinions natural and familiar, or novel, and even shocking, ought not to conclude our judgment upon the question whether statutes embodying them conflict with the Constitution of the United States.

In spite of Holmes's dissent, the Supreme Court continued to use substantive due process to void many state statutes which attempted to regulate economic affairs. Thus, many statutory economic controls that the state legislatures desired were held to be unconstitutional during the era from 1890 to 1937.

JUDICIAL RESTRICTIONS ON THE FEDERAL LEGISLATURE

In the early history of the federal government there were only limited efforts in economic regulation. Federal economic regulation actually began as a result of the Supreme Court decision invalidating state regulation of the railroads. The Court held that the interstate nature of the railroads required *uniform* regulations, which states could not supply. Therefore, the federal Congress found it necessary to pass the Interstate Commerce Commission (ICC) Act of 1887 to deal with growing monopolistic abuses in the railroad industry. The Supreme Court upheld the ICC Act because railroads were involved in interstate commerce. The Supreme Court upheld other federal regulations of interstate trade which involved questions of immorality or "harmful products." For example, the Court allowed Congress to prohibit interstate lotteries, interstate shipment of adulterated food or drugs, interstate transport of prostitutes, or interstate transportation of stolen motor vehicles.

However, there were other Supreme Court interpretations of the commerce clause which were calculated to restrict the power of the federal government to regulate economic activities. For example, the Court restricted the meaning of interstate commerce to *transportation* of goods from one state to another. The effect of this interpretation was to limit the commerce clause to those activities surrounding transportation. Consequently, any federal legislation designed to deal with a particular subject area other than transportation was held to be beyond the powers of Congress. Insurance was held not to be "commerce" and not subject to federal regulation. The Sherman Antitrust Act was initially held not to apply to local manufacturing activities.

The field of labor relations was among those areas most greatly affected by the Supreme Court's narrow interpretation of the commerce clause. In the famous case of *Hammer* v. *Dagenhart,* 247 U.S. 251 (1918) the Court held the Federal Child Labor Act to be unconstitutional. The act attempted to prohibit the shipment in interstate commerce of articles manufactured in factories in which children under 14 years of age were employed in production. The Court concluded that this manufacturing was beyond the reach of the "interstate commerce" power. Moreover, since the manufactured articles were not "harmful," the Court reasoned that Congress was really attempting to regulate social problems (child labor abuses), not commerce. Hence, the Court concluded that these social problems were not part of the federal government's constitutional powers.

During the economic depression of the 1930s, despite public demands for increased federal action, the Supreme Court struck down the National Industrial Recovery Act as extending beyond the constitutional power conferred under the commerce clause. The Supreme Court also invalidated the Railroad Retirement Act of 1934 because the statute was said to deal with purely social ends without any "direct" relation to interstate commerce. The Bituminous Coal Conservation Act of 1935, which set minimum wages and maximum hours for miners whose coal production was subsequently shipped in interstate commerce, was held unconstitutional. Mining was said to precede commerce and to have only an indirect effect on interstate commerce; consequently, it was beyond the control of federal powers.

The Supreme Court frustrated both state and federal legislative attempts to deal with perceived economic problems, based on the Court's belief that its conception of economic theory and policy was best suited for America. The Court used its powers of judicial review in an effort to preserve a governmental policy (*laissez-faire*) which the state and federal legislatures felt was no longer appropriate to the era.

NEW ERA OF LEGISLATIVE ECONOMIC POLICY

The Court declined to use substantive due process to veto state economic legislation and thereby abandoned its policy of promoting *laissez-faire* economic philosophy in the 1930s. The change in policy was announced in the 1934 case of *Nebbia* v. *New York,* 291 U.S. 502, in which the Court admitted the following:

> The phrase "affected with the public interest" can, in the nature of things, mean no more than that an industry, for adequate reasons, is subject to control for the public good. In several of the decisions of this Court wherein the expression "affected with the public interest," [has] been brought forward as the criteri[on] of the validity of price control, it has been admitted that [it is] not susceptible of definition and form[s] an unsatisfactory test of the constitutionality of legislation directed at business practices or prices.

Since the Court rejected the "affected with the public interest" criterion for determining the power of the states to impose regulation, a new test for violation of "due process" was needed. Therefore, the Court asserted that

> Neither property rights nor contract rights are absolute; for government cannot exist if the citizen may at will use his property to the detriment of his fellows, or exercise his freedom of contract to work them harm. Equally fundamental with the private right is that of the public to regulate it in the common interest.
>
> So far as the requirement of due process is concerned . . . a state is free to adopt whatever economic policy may reasonably be deemed to promote public welfare, and to enforce that policy by legislation adapted to its purpose. The courts are without authority either to declare such policy, or, when it is declared by the legislative arm, to override it. If the laws passed are seen to have a reasonable relation to a proper legislative purpose, and are neither arbitrary nor discriminatory, the requirements of due process are satisfied . . . . With the wisdom of the policy adopted, with the adequacy or practicability of the law enacted to follow it, the courts are both incompetent and unauthorized to deal.

In 1941 the Supreme Court wrote:

> We are not concerned, however, with the wisdom, need, nor appropriateness of the legislation. Differences of opinion on that score suggest a choice which "should be left where . . . it was left by the Constitution—to the states and to Congress."[2]

Later, the Court revised its ruling.

> This court . . . has consciously returned closer and closer to the earlier Constitutional principle that states have power to legislate against what are found to be injurious practices in their internal commercial and business affairs, so long as their laws do not run afoul of some specific federal constitutional prohibition, or of some valid federal law. . . . Under this doctrine the Due Process Clause is no longer to be so broadly construed that the Congress and the state legislatures are put in a strait-jacket when they attempt to suppress business and industrial conditions which they regard as offensive to the public welfare.[3]

By 1955, the Supreme Court was of the following opinion:

> The day is gone when this Court uses the Due Process Clause of the Fourteenth Amendment to strike down state laws, regulatory of business and industrial conditions, because they may be unwise, improvident, or out of harmony with a particular school of thought.[4]

Consequently, the constitutional door was open for state legislatures to regulate all forms of business activity. The only constitutional restraints remaining are the requirements that the law have a "reasonable relation to a proper legislative purpose" and be neither "arbitrary nor discriminatory." In effect, the states have broad regulatory powers over all industries.

In 1937, another series of Supreme Court decisions began which broadly interpreted the commerce clause and thereby expanded the federal congressional power to deal with economic affairs. In the *National Labor Relations Board*

v. *Jones & Laughlin Steel Corp.*, 301 U.S. 1 (1937), the Supreme Court upheld the National Labor Relations Act and its application in a *manufacturing* setting. In effect, the Supreme Court was abandoning its restrictive interpretation of "interstate commerce" as dealing with transportation only. In *U.S.* v. *Darby Lumber*, 312 U.S. 100 (1941), the Supreme Court upheld the legislative exercise of the "commerce" power in the Fair Labor Standards Act of 1938 and applied its provisions to an *intrastate* merchant who paid less than the federal minimum wage. In that case, the Supreme Court concluded that the "commerce" power may be utilized to exclude any article from interstate commerce whether the product itself is harmful or not. This conclusion permits Congress to regulate social problems, such as child labor abuses, which were previously considered beyond congressional reach. As a consequence of *Darby Lumber*, Congress was empowered to eliminate from commerce items manufactured without payment of the minimum federal wage or, alternatively, to impose a fine on those who violated the federal minimum wage law. Additional comprehensive federal regulation of a purely local commercial activity was proposed in the Agricultural Adjustment Act of 1938, which was challenged in the following case.

Wickard v. Filburn

317 U.S. 111 (1942)
Supreme Court of the United States

Justice Jackson

It is urged that under the Commerce Clause of the Constitution, Congress does not possess the power . . . [to fix a wheat] quota that the farmer may harvest for sale or for his own farm needs, and [to] . . . declare that wheat produced on excess acreage may neither be disposed of nor used except upon payment of [a] . . . penalty . . . .

Defendant says that this is a regulation of production and consumption of wheat. Such activities are, he urges, beyond the reach of Congressional power under the Commerce Clause, since they are local in character, and their efforts upon interstate commerce are at most "indirect." In answer the Government argues it is sustainable as a "necessary and proper" implementation of the power of Congress over interstate commerce.

* * *

The Court's recognition of the relevance of the economic effects in the application of the Commerce Clause . . . has made the mechanical application of legal formulas no longer feasible. Once an economic measure of the reach of the power granted to Congress in the Commerce Clause is accepted, questions of federal power cannot be decided simply by finding the activity in question to be "production," nor can consideration of its economic effects be foreclosed by calling them "indirect." The present Chief Justice has said in summary of the present state of the law: "The commerce power is not confined in its exercise to the regulation of commerce among the states. . . . The power of Congress over interstate commerce is plenary and complete in itself, may be exercised to its utmost extent, and acknowledges no limitations other than are prescribed in the Constitution. . . . It follows that no form of state activity can constitutionally thwart the regulatory power granted by the commerce clause to Congress. Hence the reach of that power extends to those intrastate activities which in a substantial way interfere with or obstruct the exercise of the granted power."

Whether the subject of the regulation in question was "production," "consumption," or "marketing" is, therefore, not material for purposes of deciding the question of federal power before us. That an activity is of local character may help in a doubtful case to determine whether Congress intended to reach it. The same consideration might help in determining whether in the absence of Congressional action it would be permissible for the state to exert its power on the subject matter, even though in so doing it to some degree affected interstate commerce. But even if [defendant's] activity be local and though it may not be regarded as commerce, it may still, whatever its nature, be reached by Congress if it exerts a substantial economic effect on interstate commerce, and this irrespective of whether such effect is what might at some earlier time have been defined as "direct" or "indirect."

The effect of consumption of home-grown wheat on interstate commerce is due to the fact that it constitutes the most variable factor in the disappearance of the wheat crop. Consumption on the farm where grown appears to vary in an amount greater than 20 per cent of average production. The total amount of wheat consumed as food varies but relatively little, and use as seed is relatively constant.

The maintenance by government regulation of a price for wheat undoubtedly can be accomplished as effectively by sustaining or increasing the demand as by limiting the supply. The effect of the statute before us is to restrict the amount which may be produced for market and the extent as well as to which one may forestall resort to the market by producing to meet his own needs. That defendant's own contribution to the demand for wheat may be trivial by itself is not enough to remove him from the scope of federal regulation where, as here, his contribution, taken together with that of many others similarly situated, is far from trivial.

It is well established by decisions of this Court that the power to regulate commerce includes the power to regulate the prices at which commodities in that commerce are dealt in and practices affecting such prices. One of the primary purposes of the Act in question was to increase the market price of wheat, and to that end to limit the volume thereof that could affect the market. It can hardly be denied that a factor of such volume and variability as home-consumed wheat would have a substantial influence on price and market conditions. This may arise because being in marketable condition such wheat overhangs the market and, if induced by rising prices, tends to flow into the market and check price increases. But if we assume that it is never marketed, it supplies a need of the man who grew it which would otherwise be reflected by purchases in the open market. Home-grown wheat in this sense competes with wheat in commerce. The stimulation of commerce is a use of the regulatory function quite as definitely as prohibitions or restrictions thereon. This record leaves us in no doubt that Congress may properly have considered that wheat consumed on the farm where grown, if wholly outside the scheme of regulation, would have a substantial effect in defeating and obstructing its purpose to stimulate trade therein at increased prices.

It is said, however, that this Act, forcing some farmers into the market to buy what they could provide for themselves, is an unfair promotion of the market and prices of specializing wheat growers. It is of the essence of regulation that it lays a restraining hand on the self-interest of the regulated and that advantage from the regulation commonly falls to others. The conflicts of economic interest between the regulated and those who advantage by it are wisely left under our system to resolution by the Congress under its more flexible and responsible legislative process. Such conflicts rarely lend themselves to judicial determination. And with the wisdom, workability, or fairness of the plan of regulation we have nothing to do.

Questions

1. Under the Interstate Commerce Clause, may the federal government regulate marketing? Production?
2. How far does the interstate commerce power extend into the states?
3. May the Supreme Court inquire into congressional purposes for passing legislation in order to determine if Congress is regulating "economic affairs" and not some "social or moral" problem? *In the Heart of Atlanta Motel, Inc.* v. *U.S.*, 379 U.S. 241 (1964), the Supreme Court made the following ruling:

> . . . In framing [the Civil Rights Act of 1964] . . . Congress was also dealing with what is considered a moral problem. But that fact does not detract from the overwhelming evidence of the disruptive effect that racial discrimination has had on commercial intercourse. It was this burden which empowered Congress to enact appropriate legislation, and, given this basis for the exercise of its power, Congress was not restricted by the fact that the particular obstruction to interstate commerce with which it was dealing was also deemed a moral and social wrong. It is said that the operation of the motel here is of a purely local character. But, assuming this to be true, "(i)f it is interstate commerce that feels the pinch, it does not matter how local the operation which applies the squeeze." *United States* v. *Women's Sportswear Mfrs. Assn.*, 336 U.S. 460, 464 (1949). . . . Thus the power of Congress to promote interstate commerce also includes the power to regulate the local incidents thereof, including local activities in both the States of origin and destination, which might have a substantial and harmful effect upon that commerce. One need only examine the evidence . . . to see that Congress may—as it has—prohibit racial discrimination by motels serving travelers, however "local" their operations may appear. Nor does the Act deprive appellant of liberty or property under the Fifth Amendment. The commerce power invoked here by the Congress is a specific and plenary one authorized by the Constitution itself. The only questions are (1) whether Congress had a rational basis for finding that racial discrimination by motels affected commerce, and (2) if it had such a basis,

whether the means it selected to eliminate that evil are reasonable and appropriate. If they are, appellant has no "right" to select its guests as it sees fit, free from governmental regulation.

JUDICIAL ABDICATION

Society's commitment to a *laissez-faire* philosophy of government has come to an end. Though at a slower pace, the Supreme Court's ideological commitment to *laissez-faire* through a narrow interpretation of the commerce clause and through the use of the 14th Amendment's substantive due process interpretations has likewise met its demise. The Supreme Court has abdicated its commitment to *laissez-faire* philosophy and, instead, has expanded the reach of legislative powers. The Court, through expansive definitions of interstate commerce, has created a federal legislative preeminence in the fashioning of national economic policy. Indeed, the new ideological commitment of the Court in the modern age appears to be one of governmental imperative in economic affairs. Justices, like members of society, may differ as to the kinds and degree of governmental action, but by far the majority of individuals and justices consider governmental action to be a necessity. However, the policy choices of governmental action will largely remain a legislative function. The Court has removed itself from the role of second guessing legislative economic policies. Its function will be restricted mostly to statutory interpretation.

CONSTITUTIONAL RIGHTS

Often the courts are faced with difficult questions involving constitutionally protected rights. Moreover, the courts feel a special responsibility to safeguard these rights. Therefore, the resolution of conflict between society's desire to regulate and the businessperson's right to freedom involves many controversial decisions.

THE TAXING POWER

The Constitution gives Congress the power to tax. Besides raising revenue, taxation may be used as a tool of regulation. For example, a tax may be coupled with a requirement to keep detailed records which provide a means for government supervision of trading in goods, such as firearms, drugs, and liquors.

Historically, the Supreme Court overturned congressional taxing schemes which attempted to use the tax to regulate some activities that the Court considered beyond the constitutional power of Congress to regulate. However, in 1937 the Court retreated from this position with the following statement:

> Inquiry into the hidden motives which may move Congress to exercise a power constitutionally conferred upon it is beyond the competency of the Court. . . . We are not free to speculate as to the motives which move Congress to impose it, or as to the extent to which it may operate to restrict the activities taxed. As it is not attended by offensive regulation, and since it operates as a tax, it is within the taxing power.[5]

Congress possesses a broad taxing authority, but the states are prohibited from interference with interstate commerce through their taxing powers. The Court has noted that "a State 'cannot impose taxes on persons passing through the state or coming into it merely for a temporary purpose' such as itinerant drummers. . . . Moreover, it is beyond dispute that a State may not lay a tax on a 'privilege' of engaging in interstate commerce. . . . Nor may a State impose a tax which discriminates against interstate commerce either by providing a direct commercial advantage to local business . . . or by subjecting interstate commerce to the burden of 'multiple taxation' "[6] For example, in 1981, the Supreme Court refused to allow the state of Louisiana to tax natural gas that passed through the state for sale in other states.[7]

In contrast, the state may apply a tax to that portion of income "reasonably attributable" to business conducted within the state. Iowa taxed the income resulting from about 20 percent of the gross sales of an Illinois business that sold about 20 percent of its products in Iowa. The Supreme Court upheld the tax scheme and said that unless the business firm could show that the method of calculation resulted in a gross distortion in taxes, the Courts would not invalidate the tax scheme. Absent any actual discriminatory effect on interstate commerce, such state taxation of the profits obtained from interstate commerce is permissible.

Just as with interstate commerce, the Constitution gives Congress power to regulate international trade. Consequently, states may not interfere with international commerce in its taxing scheme. For example, the Supreme Court invalidated a tax imposed by California on shipping containers owned by Japanese companies that were used in international commerce on Japanese ships. California attempted to tax these containers while they were in the state during loading and unloading. The Supreme Court held that states are precluded from taxing foreign commerce and that only the federal government may regulate and tax foreign trade.

POLITICAL SPEECH

The First Amendment of the U.S. Constitution provides that "Congress shall make no law . . . abridging the freedom of speech. . . . " The First Amendment prohibits congressional encroachment on freedom of speech. However, the Supreme Court has ruled that the First Amendment freedoms are among those fundamental rights and liberties protected by the due process clause of the Fourteenth Amendment as well. In effect, the Court has absorbed the First

Amendment freedoms into the 14th Amendment's due process clause as a limitation on *state* action also.

The Supreme Court has never considered the First Amendment guarantee of freedom of speech to be absolute. The Court has recognized that "free speech will not protect a man in falsely shouting fire in a theatre and causing panic."[8] Consequently, the Court has had to define which speech is protected and which speech is subject to governmental regulations.

First National Bank of Boston v. Bellotti

435 U.S. 765 (1978)
Supreme Court of the United States

Justice Powell

In sustaining a state criminal statute that forbids certain expenditures by banks and business corporations for the purpose of influencing the vote on referendum proposals, the Massachusett's Supreme Judicial Court held that the First Amendment rights of a corporation are limited to issues that materially affect its business, property, or assets.

The statute at issue, Mass. Gen. Laws Ann., Ch. 55, Section 8, prohibits [plaintiffs], two national banking associations and three business corporations, from making contributions or expenditures "for the purpose of . . . influencing or affecting the vote on any question submitted to the voters, other than one materially affecting any of the property, business, or assets of the corporation." The statute further specifies that "[n]o question submitted to the voters solely concerning the taxation of the income, property or transactions of individuals shall be deemed materially to affect the property, business, or assets of the corporation."

[Plaintiffs] wanted to spend money to publicize their views on a proposed constitutional amendment that was to be submitted to the voters as a ballot question at a general election on November 2, 1976. The amendment would have permitted the legislature to impose a graduated tax on the income of individuals. After [defendant], the Attorney General of Massachusetts, informed [plaintiffs] that he intended to enforce Section 8 against them, they brought this action seeking to have the statute declared unconstitutional.

* * *

[Plaintiffs] argued that Section 8 violates the First Amendment, the Due Process and Equal Protection Clauses of the Fourteenth Amendment. . . . They prayed that the statute be declared unconstitutional on its face and as it would be applied to their proposed expenditures. . . .

The court below framed the principal question in this case as whether and to what extent corporations have First Amendment rights. We believe that the court posed the wrong question. The Constitution often protects interests broader than those of the party seeking their vindication. The First Amendment, in particular, serves significant societal interests. The proper question, therefore, is not whether corporations "have" First Amendment rights and, if so, whether they are coextensive with those of natural persons. Instead, the question must be whether Section 8 abridges expression that the First Amendment was meant to protect.

The speech proposed by [plaintiffs] is at the heart of the First Amendment's protection.

> The freedom of speech and of the press guaranteed by the Constitution embraces at the least the liberty to discuss publicly and truthfully all matters of public concern without previous restraint or fear of subsequent punishment. . . . Freedom of discussion, if it would fulfill its historic function in this nation, must embrace all issues about which information is needed or appropriate to enable the members of society to cope with the exigencies of their period. *Thornhill* v. *Alabama,* 310 U.S. 88, 101–102 (1940).

The referendum issue that [plaintiffs] wish to address falls squarely within this description. . . . The question in this case, simply put, is whether the corporate identity of the speaker deprives this proposed speech of what otherwise would be its clear entitlement to protection. We turn now to that question.

> In a series of decisions beginning with *Gitlow* v. *New York,* 268 U.S. 652, (1925), this Court held that the liberty of speech and of the press which the First Amendment guarantees against abridgment by the federal government is within the liberty safeguarded by the Due Process Clause of the Fourteenth Amendment from invasion by state action. That principle has been followed and reaffirmed to the present day.

Freedom of speech and the other freedoms encompassed by the First Amendment always have been viewed as fundamental components of the liberty safeguarded by the Due Process Clause, and the Court has not identified a separate source for the right when it has been asserted by corporations. . . . [T]he Court's decisions involving corporations in the business of communication or entertainment are based not only on the role of the First Amendment in fostering individual self-expression but also on its role in affording the public access to discussion, debate, and the dissemination of information and ideas. Even decisions seemingly based exclusively on the individual's right to express himself acknowledge that the expression may contribute to society's edification.

* * *

We thus find no support in the First or Fourteenth Amendment, or in the decisions of this Court, for the proposition that speech that otherwise would be within the protection of the First Amendment loses that protection simply because its source is a corporation that cannot prove, to the satisfaction of a court, a material effect on its business or property. The "materially affecting" requirement is not an identification of the boundaries of corporate speech etched by the Constitution itself. Rather, it amounts to an impermissible legislative prohibition of speech based on the identity of the interests that spokesmen may represent and a requirement that the speaker have a sufficiently great interest in the subject to justify communication.

In the realm of protected speech, the legislature is constitutionally disqualified from dictating the subjects about which persons may speak and the speakers who may address a public issue. If a legislature may direct business corporations to "stick to business," it also may limit other corporations—religious, charitable, or civic—to their respective "business" when addressing the public. Such power in government to channel the expression of views is unacceptable under the First Amendment. Especially where, as here, the legislature's suppression of speech suggests an attempt to give one side of a debatable public question an advantage in expressing its views to the people, the First Amendment is plainly offended. Yet the State contends that its action is necessitated by governmental interests of the highest order. We next consider these asserted interests. The constitutionality of Section 8's prohibition of the "exposition of ideas" by corporations turns on whether it can survive the exacting scrutiny necessitated by a state-imposed restriction of freedom of speech. Especially where, as here, a prohibition is directed at speech itself, and the speech is intimately related to the process of governing, "The State may prevail only upon showing a subordinating interest which is compelling," "and the burden is on the Goverment to show the existence of such an interest." Even then, the State must employ means "closely drawn to avoid unnecessary abridgment. . . ."

Preserving the integrity of the electoral process, preventing corruption, and "sustain[ing] the active, alert responsibility of the individual citizen in a democracy for the wise conduct of the government" are interests of the highest importance. Preservation of the individual citizen's confidence in government is equally important.

[Defendant] advances a number of arguments in support of his view that these interests are endangered by corporate participation in discussion of a referendum issue. They hinge upon the assumption that such participants would exert an undue influence on the outcome of a referendum vote, and—in the end—destroy the confidence of the people in the democratic process and the integrity of government. According to [defendant], corporations are wealthy and powerful and their views may drown out other points of view. If [defendant's] arguments were supported by record or legislative findings that corporate advocacy threatened imminently to undermine democratic processes, thereby denigrating rather than serving First Amendment interests, these arguments would merit our consideration. But there has been no showing that the relative voice of corporations has been overwhelming or even significant in influencing referenda in Massachusetts, or that there has been any threat to the confidence of the citizenry in government. Nor are [defendant's] arguments inherently persuasive or supported by the precedents of this Court. Referenda are held on issues, not candidates for public office. The risk of corruption perceived in cases involving candidate elections, simply is not present in a popular vote on a public issue. To be sure, corporate advertising may influence the outcome of the vote; this would be its purpose. But the fact that advocacy may persuade the electorate is hardly a reason to suppress it: The Constitution "protects expression which is eloquent no less than that which is unconvincing." We noted only recently that "the concept that government may restrict the speech of some elements of our society in order to enhance the relative voice of others is wholly foreign to the First Amendment. . . ." Moreover, the people in our democracy are entrusted with the responsibility for judging and evaluating the relative merits of conflicting arguments. They may consider, in making their judgment, the source and credibility of the advocate. But if there be any danger that the people cannot evaluate the information and arguments advanced by [plaintiffs], it is a danger contemplated by the Framers of the First Amendment. In sum, "[a] restriction so destructive of the right of public discussion [as Section 8], without greater or more imminent danger to the public interest than existed in this case, is incompatible with the freedom secured by the First Amendment.

* * *

Because that portion of Section 8 challenged by [plaintiffs] prohibits protected speech in a manner unjustified by a compelling state interest, it must be invalidated.

Questions

1. Is the free speech privilege solely designed to protect the speaker? Or is society's interest in hearing the speaker also protected by the First Amendment?
2. Is the question in *Bellotti* whether the corporation has First Amendment rights equal to those of natural persons? Or, is the question whether the state can abridge expression which the First Amendment protects?
3. Does the fact that the speaker is a corporation deprive the "speech" of its First Amendment protection?
4. The state may prohibit speech when that speech interferes with some "compelling" state interest. Identify some "compelling state interests." Did plaintiff's speech threaten these state interests?

COMMERCIAL SPEECH

In 1942, the Supreme Court decided that commercial speech was not entitled to First Amendment protection.[9] However, in 1964, the Court limited its commercial speech doctrine by protecting paid political advertisements.[10] In 1975, the Court held abortion advertisements were protected by the Constitution.[11] Then, in 1976, the Court concluded that even if the advertiser's motivation was purely economic, this did not necessarily disqualify the advertisement from constitutional protection.[12] The Court's constitutional analysis utilized in commercial speech cases is illustrated by the following case.

Central Hudson Gas & Electric Corporation v. Public Service Commission of New York

447 U.S. 557 (1980)
Supreme Court of the United States

Justice Powell

* * *

In December 1973, the Commission ordered electric utilities in New York State to cease all advertising that "promot[es] the use of electricity."

* * *

The Commission declared all promotional advertising contrary to the national policy of conserving energy. It acknowledged that the ban is not a perfect vehicle for conserving energy. For example, the Commission's order prohibits promotional advertising to develop consumption during periods when demand for electricity is low. By limiting growth in "off peak" consumption, the ban limits the "beneficial side effects" of such growth in terms of more efficient use of existing power plants.

* * *

The Commission's order explicitly permitted "informational" advertising designed to encourage "*shifts* of consumption" from peak demand times to periods of low electricity demands. Informational advertising would not seek to increase aggregate consumption, but would invite a leveling of demand throughout any given 24-hour period. The agency offered to review "specific proposals by the companies for specifically described [advertising] programs that meet these criteria."

* * *

The Commission's order restricts only commercial speech, that is, expression related solely to the economic interests of the speaker and its audience. . . . The First Amendment, as applied to the States through the Fourteenth Amendment, protects commercial speech from unwarranted governmental regulation. Commercial expression not only serves the economic interest of the speaker, but also assists consumers and furthers the societal interest in the fullest possible dissemination of information. In applying the First Amendment to this area, we have rejected the "highly paternalistic" view that government has complete power to suppress or regulate commercial speech. "[P]eople will perceive their own best interest if only they are well enough informed and . . . the best means to that end is to open the channels of communication, rather than to close them . . . ." Even when advertising communicates only an incomplete version of the relevant facts, the First Amendment presumes that some accurate information is better than no information at all.

Nevertheless, our decisions have recognized "the common-sense" distinction between speech proposing a commercial transaction, which occurs in an area traditionally subject to government regulation and other varieties of speech." . . . The Constitution therefore accords a lesser protection to commercial speech than to other constitutionally guaranteed expression. The protection available for particular commercial expression turns on the nature both of the expression and of the governmental interests served by its regulation.

The First Amendment's concern for commercial speech is based on the information function of advertising. Consequently, there can be no constitutional objection to the suppression of commercial messages that do not accurately inform the public about lawful activity. The government may ban forms of communication more likely to deceive the public than to inform it, or commercial speech related to illegal activity.

If the communication is neither misleading nor related to unlawful activity, the government's power is more circumscribed. The state must assert a substantial interest to be achieved by restrictions on commercial speech. Moreover, the regulatory technique must be in proportion to that interest. The limitation on expression must be designed carefully to achieve the State's goal. . . .

* * *

In commercial speech cases, . . . a four-part analysis has developed. At the outset, we must determine whether the expression is protected by the First Amendment. For commercial speech to come within that provision, it at least must concern lawful activity and not be misleading. Next, we ask whether the asserted governmental interest is substantial. If both inquiries yield positive answers, we must determine whether the regulation directly advances the governmental interest asserted, and whether it is not more extensive than is necessary to serve that interest.

We now apply this four-step analysis for commercial speech to the Commission's arguments in support of its ban on promotional advertising.

The Commission does not claim that the expression at issue either is inaccurate or relates to unlawful activity. Yet the New York Court of Appeals questioned whether Central Hudson's advertising is protected commercial speech. Because plaintiff holds a monopoly over the sale of electricity in its service area, the state court suggested that the Commission's order restricts no commercial speech of any worth. The court stated that advertising in a "noncompetitive market" could not improve the decisionmaking of consumers. The court saw no constitutional problem with barring commercial speech that it viewed as conveying little useful information.

This reasoning falls short of establishing that [plaintiff's] advertising is not commercial speech protected by the First Amendment.

* * *

Even in monopoly markets, the suppression of advertising reduces the information available for consumer decisions and thereby defeats the purpose of the First Amendment. The New York court's argument appears to assume that the providers of a monopoly service or product are willing to pay for wholly ineffective advertising. Most businesses—even regulated monopolies—are unlikely to underwrite promotional advertising that is of no interest or use to consumers. Indeed, a monopoly enterprise legitimately may wish to inform the public that it has developed new services or terms of doing business. A consumer may need information to aid his decision whether or not to use the monopoly service at all, or how much of the service he should purchase. In the absence of factors that would distort the decision to advertise, we may assume that the willingness of a business to promote its products reflects a belief that consumers are interested in the advertising. Since no such extraordinary conditions have been identified in this case, [plaintiff's] monopoly position does not alter the First Amendment's protection for its commercial speech.

The Commission offers . . . [energy conservation] . . . as justification for the ban on promotional advertising. . . . Any increase in demand for electricity—during peak or offpeak periods—means greater consumption of energy. The Commission argues, and the New York court agreed, that the State's interest in conserving energy is sufficient to support suppression of advertising designed to increase consumption of electricity. In view of our country's dependence on energy resources beyond our control, no one can doubt the importance of energy conservation. Plainly, therefore, the state interest asserted is substantial.

. . . There is an immediate connection between advertising and demand for electricity. Central Hudson would not contest the advertising ban unless it believed that promotion would increase its sales. Thus, we find a direct link between the state interest in conservation and the Commission's order.

We come finally to the critical inquiry in this case: whether the Commission's complete suppression of speech ordinarily protected by the First Amendment is no more extensive than necessary to further the State's interest in energy conservation. The Commission's order reaches all promotional advertising, regardless of the impact of the touted service on overall energy use. But the energy conservation rationale, as important as it is, cannot justify suppressing information about electric devices or services that would cause no net increase in total energy use. In addition, no showing has been made that a more limited restriction on the content of promotional advertising would not serve adequately the State's interests.

* * *

The Commission's order prevents [plaintiffs] from promoting electric services that would reduce energy use by diverting demand from less efficient sources, or that would consume roughly the same amount of energy as do alternative sources. In neither situation would the utility's advertising endanger conservation or mislead the public. To the extent that the Commission's order suppresses speech that in no way impairs the State's interest in energy conservation, the Commission's order violates the First and Fourteenth Amendments and must be invalidated.

The Commission also has not demonstrated that its interest in conservation cannot be protected adequately by more limited regulation of [plaintiff's] commercial expression.

* * *

Our decision today in no way disparages the national interest in energy conservation. We accept without reservation the argument that conservation, as well as the development of alternate energy sources, is an imperative national goal. Administrative bodies empowered to regulate electric utilities have the authority—and indeed the duty—to take appropriate action to further this goal. When, however, such action involves the suppression of speech, the First and Fourteenth Amendments require that the restriction be no more extensive than is necessary to serve the state interest. In this case, the record before us fails to show that the total ban on promotional advertising meets this requirement.

Accordingly, the judgment of the New York Court of Appeals is reversed.

Questions

1. Why is commercial speech afforded less protection under the First Amendment than other constitutionally protected expressions?
2. The protection of commercial speech depends on the "nature both of the expression and of the governmental interests served by its regulation."

What is the First Amendment's concern for commercial speech—its positive nature? What governmental interests are argued to be served by the ban on promotional advertising? How did the court weigh these interests?
3. Is misleading commercial speech protected by the First Amendment?
4. Was the ban on promotional advertising "more extensive than is necessary to serve" the government's interests?

UNREASONABLE SEARCH

The Fourth Amendment provides that "the right of the people to be secure in their persons, houses, papers, and effects, against unreasonable searches and seizures, shall not be violated, and no Warrants shall issue, but upon probable cause. . . ." Although most cases involving this amendment are concerned with the proper method of search of suspected criminals or of seizure of criminal evidence, recent cases also question the search methods used by regulatory agencies operating under the civil law. The following is a case involving a governmental inspector showing up at a business and asking to inspect the premises. Must the business permit entry?

Marshall v. Barlow's, Inc.
436 U.S. 307 (1978)
Supreme Court of the United States

Justice White

Section 8(a) of the Occupational Safety and Health Act of 1970 (OSHA or Act) empowers agents of the Secretary of Labor (Secretary) to search the work area of any employment facility within the Act's jurisdiction. The purpose of the search is to inspect for safety hazards and violations of OSHA regulations. No search warrant or other process is expressly required under the Act.

On the morning of September 11, 1975, an OSHA inspector entered the customer service area of Barlow's, Inc., an electrical and plumbing installation business located in Pocatello, Idaho. The president and general manager, Ferrol G. "Bill" Barlow, was on hand; and the OSHA inspector, after showing his credentials, informed Mr. Barlow that he wished to conduct a search of the working areas of the business. Mr. Barlow inquired whether any complaint had been received about his company. The inspector answered no, but that Barlow's, Inc., had simply turned up in the agency's selection process. The inspector again asked to enter the nonpublic area of the business; Mr. Barlow's response was to inquire whether the inspector had a search warrant. The inspector had none. Thereupon, Mr. Barlow refused the inspector admission to the employee area of his business. He said he was relying on his rights as guaranteed by the Fourth Amendment of the United States Constitution.

Three months later, the Secretary petitioned the United States District Court for the District of Idaho to issue an order compelling Mr. Barlow to admit the inspector. The requested order was issued . . . and was presented to Mr.

Barlow . . . . Mr. Barlow again refused admission, and he sought his own injunctive relief against the warrantless searches assertedly permitted by OSHA. A three-judge court was convened. . . . [I]t ruled in Mr. Barlow's favor. Concluding that *Camara* v. *Municipal Court,* 387 U.S. 523 (1967), controlled this case, the court held that the Fourth Amendment required a warrant for the type of search involved here and that the statutory authorization for warrantless inspections was unconstitutional. An injunction against searches or inspections pursuant to Section 8(a) was entered. The Secretary appealed, challenging the judgment.

The Warrant Clause of the Fourth Amendment protects commercial buildings as well as private homes. To hold otherwise would belie the origin of that Amendment, and the American colonial experience. . . . The general warrant was a recurring point of contention in the Colonies immediately preceding the Revolution. The particular offensiveness it engendered was acutely felt by the merchants and businessmen whose premises and products were inspected for compliance with the several parliamentary revenue measures that most irritated the colonists. . . . Against this background, it is untenable that the ban on warrantless searches was not intended to shield places of business as well as of residence.

This court has already held that warrantless searches are generally unreasonable, and that this rule applies to commercial premises as well as homes. . . .

These same cases also held that the Fourth Amendment prohibition against unreasonable searches protects against warrantless intrusions during civil as well as criminal investigations. . . . If the government intrudes on a person's property, the privacy interest suffers whether the government's motivation is to investigate violations of criminal laws or breaches of other statutory or regulatory standards. It therefore appears that unless some recognized exception to the warrant requirement applies, *See* v. *City of Seattle* would require a warrant to conduct the inspection sought in this case.

The Secretary urges that an exception from the search warrant requirement has been recognized for "pervasively regulated business[es]," and for "closely regulated" industries "long subject to close supervision and inspection." These cases are indeed exceptions, but they represent responses to relatively unique circumstances. Certain industries have such a history of government oversight that no reasonable expectation of privacy could exist for a proprietor over the stock of such an enterprise. Liquor and firearms are industries of this type; when an entrepreneur embarks upon such a business, he has voluntarily chosen to subject himself to a full arsenal of governmental regulation.

* * *

Whether the Secretary proceeds to secure a warrant or other process, with or without prior notice, his entitlement to inspect will not depend on his demonstrating probable cause to believe that conditions in violation of OSHA exist on the premises. Probable cause in the criminal law sense is not required. For the purposes of an administrative search such as this, probable cause justifying the issuance of a warrant may be based not only on specific evidence of an existing violation but also on a showing that "reasonable legislative or administrative standards for conducting an . . . inspection are satisfied with respect to a particular [establishment]."

* * *

Nor do we agree that the incremental protections afforded the employer's privacy by a warrant are so marginal that they fail to justify the administrative burdens that may be entailed. The authority to make warrantless searches devolves almost unbridled discretion upon executive and administrative officers, particularly those in the field, as to when to search and whom to search. A warrant, by contrast, would provide assurances from a neutral officer that the inspection is reasonable under the Constitution, is authorized by statute, and is pursuant to an administrative plan containing specific neutral criteria. Also, a warrant would then and there advise the owner of the scope and objects of the search, beyond which limits the inspector is not expected to proceed. These are important functions which underlie the Court's prior decisions that the Warrant Clause applies to inspections for compliance with regulatory statutes. We conclude that the concerns expressed by the Secretary do not suffice to justify warrantless inspections under OSHA or vitiate the general constitutional requirement that for a search to be reasonable a warrant must be obtained.

We hold that Barlow's was entitled to a declaratory judgment that the Act is unconstitutional insofar as it purports to authorize inspections without warrant or its equivalent and to an injunction enjoining the Act's enforcement to that extent.

Questions

1. What industries are identified as subject to warrantless searches? Why?
2. What must OSHA administrators show to a court to obtain a warrant?
3. What advantages are achieved by a system of issuing warrants only on a court's approval?

COMPELLED SELF-INCRIMINATION

The Fifth Amendment protects individuals from being compelled to testify against themselves. This right protects not only compelled oral testimony, but one's possession of documents, records, or other objects that might be incriminating in nature. The following case illustrates some of the limitations on the Fifth Amendment rights in relation to business operations.

United States v. White

322 U.S. 694 (1944)
Supreme Court of the United States

Justice Murphy

* * *

Respondent contends that an officer of an unincorporated labor union possesses a constitutional right to refuse to produce, in compliance with a subpoena *duces tecum,* records of the union which are in his custody and which might tend to incriminate him. He relies upon the . . . explicit guarantee of the Fifth Amendment that no person shall be compelled in any criminal case to be a witness against himself. . . .

The Constitutional privilege against self-incrimination is essentially a personal one, applying only to natural individuals. It grows out of the high sentiment and regard of our jurisprudence for conducting criminal trials and investigatory proceedings upon a plane of dignity, humanity and impartiality. It is designed to prevent the use of legal process to force from the lips of the accused individual the evidence necessary to convict him or to force him to produce and authenticate any personal documents or effects that might incriminate him . . . .

Since the privilege against self-incrimination is a purely personal one, it cannot be utilized by or on behalf of any organization, such as a corporation. . . . Moreover, the papers and effects which the privilege protects must be the private property of the person claiming the privilege, or at least in his possession in a purely personal capacity. But individuals, when acting as representatives of a collective group, cannot be said to be exercising their personal rights and duties nor to be entitled to their purely personal privileges. Rather they assume the rights, duties, and privileges of the artificial entity or association of which they are agents or officers and they are bound by its obligations. In their official capacity, therefore, they have no privilege against self-incrimination. And the official records and documents of the organization that are held by them in a representative rather than in a personal capacity cannot be the subject of the personal privilege against self-incrimination, even though production of the papers might tend to incriminate them personally. . . .

Such records and papers are not the private records of the individual members or officers of the organization. Usually, if not always, they are open to inspection by the members and this right may be enforced on appropriate occasions by available legal procedures. They therefore embody no element of personal privacy and carry with them no claim of personal privilege.

* * *

Basically, the power to compel the production of the records of any organization, whether it be incorporated or not, arises out of the inherent and necessary power of the federal and state governments to enforce their laws, with the privilege against self-incrimination being limited to its historic function of protecting only the natural individual from compulsory incrimination through his own testimony or personal records.

It follows that labor unions, as well as their officers and agents acting in their official capacity, cannot invoke this personal privilege. This conclusion is not reached by any mechanical comparison of unions with corporations or with other entities nor by any determination of whether unions technically may be regarded as legal personalities for any or all purposes. The test, rather, is whether one can fairly say under all the circumstances that a particular type of organization has a character so impersonal in the scope of its membership and activities that it cannot be said to embody or represent the purely private or personal interests of its constituents, but rather to embody their common or group interests only. If so, the privilege cannot be invoked on behalf of the organization or its representatives in their official capacity. Labor unions—national or local, incorporated or unincorporated—clearly meet the test. . . .

These various considerations compel the conclusion that respondent could not claim the personal privilege against self-incrimination under these circumstances. The subpoena *duces tecum* was directed to the union and demanded the production only of its official documents and records. Respondent could not claim the privilege on behalf of the union because the union did not itself possess such a privilege. Moreover, the privilege is personal to the individual called as a witness, making it impossible for him to set up the privilege of a third person as an excuse for a refusal to answer or to produce documents. . . . Nor could respondent claim the privilege on behalf of himself as an officer of the union or as an individual. The documents he sought to place under the protective shield of the privilege were official union documents held by him in his capacity as a representative of the union. No valid claim was made that any part of them constituted his own private papers. He thus could not object that the union's books and records might incriminate him as an officer or as an individual.

Questions

1. The Court indicated that the protection of the Fifth Amendment is personal. What does the Court mean by an essentially *personal* privilege against self-incrimination?
2. What basic reason did the Court use for restricting the constitutional protection of the Fifth Amendment to individuals?
3. Are the records of all "collective groups" subject to administrative investigative powers? May an administrative agency gain information from a corporation? From a nonincorporated entity? From a religious organization? From a communist organization? From the National Association of Colored People?

PUBLIC RECORDS

The privilege against self-incrimination does not apply to records required to be kept by statute or some valid regulation. In *Shapiro* v. *United States,* 335 U.S. 1 (1948), the Supreme Court held that all business records, if required to be kept, are "public" and therefore subject to agency investigation and utilization in criminal prosecutions. The Court declared that "the Privilege which exists as to private papers cannot be maintained in relation to 'records required by law to be kept in order that there may be suitable information of transactions which are the appropriate subjects of governmental regulation and the enforcement of restrictions validly established.' " Moreover, in *California* v. *Byers,* 402 U.S. 424 (1971) the Court ruled that the privilege against self-incrimination cannot be invoked to prevent compelled disclosures unless the disclosures involve "substantial hazards of self-incrimination." Since the defendant had been charged with failure to stop and identify himself at the scene of an auto accident as required by law, the Court had to determine whether such disclosures with respect to automobile accidents entailed a risk of self-incrimination. The Court answered in the negative and emphasized that the statutory purpose was noncriminal and that self-reporting was indispensable to the fulfillment of the statute. The Court said, "A name, linked with a motor vehicle, is no more incriminating than the tax return linked with the disclosure of income. It identifies but does not by itself implicate anyone in criminal conduct."

IMMUNITY STATUTES

The privilege against self-incrimination has been limited by congressional enactment of "immunity" statutes. These statutes compel testimony and production of records even when the privilege of the Fifth Amendment applies. However, the statute confers immunity from prosecution for any offense disclosed in such testimony and records. The Compulsory Testimony Act of 1892 provides the following:

> No person shall be excused from . . . testifying or from producing . . . papers . . . before the [administrative agency], or in obedience to the subpoena of the [agency] . . . on the ground . . . that the . . . evidence . . . may tend to incriminate him . . . but no person shall be prosecuted or subject to any penalty or forfeiture for or on account of any transactions, matter or thing, concerning which he may testify, or produce evidence, documentary or otherwise, before said [agency], or in obedience to its subpoena.

In 1970 an amendment was added to this statute which requires that anyone who refuses to testify or to produce records may be fined or imprisoned. All major regulatory agencies have a similar provision to aid in the enforcement of their regulatory powers. The Supreme Court has ruled that such statutes are constitutional because prosecution for crimes revealed by such testimony may not be maintained. Other penalties, such as loss of job, expulsion from organizations, requirement of state registration, or passport ineligibility, do not affect the constitutionality of the statute.

CONCLUSION

Although the Supreme Court has opened wide the governmental powers to regulate business, it has also interpreted the Constitution and the Bill of Rights to provide many protections for the private enterprise system. The Court's interpretations of the First Amendment right to free speech has assured business corporations of the right to participate in the formulation of public policies. Moreover, the Court has afforded protection to strictly commercial speech from overly extensive governmental regulations. The procedural safeguards of "due process of law" secure these constitutional rights and provide protections for business firms from politically motivated harassment, such as searches instigated because of failure to contribute to political campaign coffers. Other constitutional protections, such as freedom from government impairment of contract, will be discussed in subsequent chapters in reference to the subject matter then under discussion. But this review of the Constitution reveals it to be a dynamic instrument with varying interpretations of its terms over time.

CASE PROBLEMS

1. Hughes holds a Texas license to operate a commercial minnow business near Wichita Falls, Texas. An Oklahoma game ranger arrested him on a charge of violating Section 4-115(b) by transporting from Oklahoma to Wichita Falls a load of minnows purchased from a minnow dealer licensed to do business in Oklahoma. Hughes's defense that Section 4-115(b) was unconstitutional because it was repugnant to the commerce clause was rejected, and he was convicted and fined. What is the result on appeal?

2. ABC Company ships its goods from southern Pennsylvania to Kentucky for sale. The goods pass along Ohio highways on the way to Kentucky. Ohio has imposed *ad valorem* tax on such goods. Is this tax permissible?

3. In December 1973, the Public Service Commission of New York ordered electric utilities in New York State to cease all advertising that promotes the use of electricity because the intraconnected utility system in New York did not have a sufficient supply to furnish all customers' demands for the 1973–74 winter. After the fuel shortage had ceased in 1977, the prohibition was extended for "promotional" advertising (that intended to stimulate the purchase of electrical services) as being contrary to the national policy of conserving energy.

   Con Edison contends this prohibition of promotional advertising is a violation of its First Amendment rights of free speech in that the "prohibition" is more extensive than necessary to serve the state's interest in conserving energy. Decide.

4. A leaflet stating "Independence is still a goal, and nuclear power is needed to win the battle" was included in one mailing of Con Edison's billing envelope. The leaflet stated Con Edison's view that the benefits of nuclear power outweighed any potential risk, that nuclear power plants are safe, economical, and clean, and that the use of nuclear power would further U.S. independence from foreign energy sources.

   Immediately, the Natural Resources Defense Council (NRDC) requested Con Edison to enclose in the next billing envelopes a rebuttal leaflet prepared by NRDC. Con Edison refused. Therefore, NRDC asked the Public Service Commission of New York to order Con Edison's billing envelopes to be opened for contrasting views on controversial issues of public importance.

   The Public Service Commission refused NRDC's request, but prohibited "utilities from using billing inserts to discuss political matters, including the desirability of future development in nuclear power." The commission supported its order with the argument that bill recipients are a "captive audience" of diverse views and that Con Edison should not be able to force its views on this "captive audience." The commission did not prohibit inserts "not discussing controversial issues of public policy."

Con Edison appealed the commission's prohibition. Decide.

END NOTES

1. *Smyth* v. *Ames,* 169 U.S. 466 (1898).
2. *Olsen* v. *Nebraska,* 313 U.S. 236, 246–247 (1941).
3. *Lincoln Federal Labor Union* v. *Northwestern Iron & Metal Co.,* 335 U.S. 325, 536–537 (1949).
4. *Williamson* v. *Lee Optical of Oklahoma,* 348 U.S. 483, 487–488 (1955).
5. *Sonzinsky* v. *U.S.,* 300 U.S. 506 (1937).
6. *Northwestern States Portland Cement Co.* v. *Minnesota,* 358 U.S. 450 (1959).
7. *Arkansas & Louisiana Gas Co.* v. *Hall,* 101 S. Ct. 2925 (1981).
8. *Schenck* v. *U.S.,* 249 U.S. 47 (1919).
9. *Valentine* v. *Chrestensen,* 316 U.S. 52 (1942).
10. *New York Times* v. *Sullivan,* 376 U.S. 255 (1964).
11. *Bigelow* v. *Virginia,* 421 U.S. 809 (1975).
12. *Virginia Pharmacy Board* v. *Virginia Citizens Commerce Council,* 425 U.S. 746 (1976).

part two

CONCEPTS OF BUSINESS LAW

Organized society in an industrial democracy is the source of all sanctions in the field of business operations. Private business management receives its sanction through the right of private property. This is basically the right to hold, control, and use property in the personal interests of individuals or groups with due regard for the public interests. Private property is the basis for decentralization of political and economic power and a secure foundation for individual freedoms. The free enterprise system is founded on the right of private property and the decentralization of control over national economic resources.

Society has delegated to individuals the right to own and use physical property for the production and distribution of goods and services to the public. The owners of this property, to maintain a "free" system, are obliged to provide goods and services in the quality and quantity needed by society. The right to profit—that is, to increase one's holdings of private property—is dependent upon the ability of business organizations to discharge their service responsibilities to the public. To the extent that business is able to comply with this responsibility, it is not necessary for organized society to modify the rights and privileges of private property and of private management of economic resources.

Some modification of the rights of private property becomes necessary as industrial economies become more complex. Increased modification of private property rights are necessary when the liberties granted by society are abused. When individuals or business leaders misuse their authority to the detriment of the public interest, it seems necessary to increase the regulation of business activity. Each governmental regulation is a modification of the right of private property and contributes to a further breakdown of the free enterprise system.

Basic business law is formulated as an expression of the public policy at a given period of time. Initially, public policy favored the rights of private property and free contractual relations. Governmental policy was restricted to enforcing contractual rights and otherwise protecting the rights of private property. However, public policy is dynamic and its directions vary with the current needs of society. Consequently, a business contract found valid in one age may be unacceptable in another. Unbridled use of land in frontier times cannot be tolerated in today's crowded cities. The historical public preference for sole proprietorships gave way to the corporate device as an instrument of capitalistic expansion and organizational efficiency. The evolving content of public policy and its impact on the basic tenets of private property, contracts, financial transactions, and business organizations are presented in Part Two.

Chapter 6 includes a study of property concepts and their application in business affairs. The materials in Chapter 7 present an overview of the principles of contract law and the protection of contractual rights. Chapter 8 discusses the legal aspects of sales contracts and the marketing of goods. Legal limitations on "unfair" marketing tactics are also explained. Chapter 9 contains a discussion of the legal aspects of financial transactions, including the laws of negotiable instruments and secured transactions. Chapter 10 deals with the organization of businesses, including concepts of agency, partnerships, and corporations.

chapter six

PROPERTY

One of the fundamental principles of society in the United States is that of private property. Inherent in private property is the right of the owner to obtain governmental assistance in maintaining exclusive use and enjoyment of the property. This was not always the situation, however. Prior to the formation of an organized society to grant and protect the rights of private property, the concept of property was not known. Every person could take possession of as much land or movable objects as was unappropriated and as necessity dictated. Use of these possessions was dependent on the ability to maintain exclusive occupancy and control.

As nomadic tribes of hunters and fishers began to group themselves into societies for defense, it became apparent that rules and group enforcement of those rules would be needed to protect an individual's possessions. In some instances, the inhabitants of these primitive societies attempted to solve their problem by drawing lines on the ground throughout the settlement and agreeing among themselves that within these "landmarks" the respective landholders alone had a possessory right during their period of occupancy. Later, as societies became more permanent, this possessory theory evolved into a "lawful" claim of ownership protected by society. The legal theory of "ownership" affords protection to property holders whether or not the owners have actual possession. Hence, the legal process is essential to the concept of ownership. One author wrote, "Property and law are born together, and die together. Before laws were made there was no property; take away laws, and property ceases."[1]

After the fall of the Roman Empire and its protection of property rights, alliances between communities again became a necessity to provide common protection and defense. These alliances evolved into kingdoms with ownership of the unappropriated lands passing to the sovereign. As one early English lawyer, Blackstone, wrote, "the King is esteemed in the eyes of the law as the original proprietor of all the lands in the kingdom." Others acquired ownership rights, at first, as the king allowed and, subsequently, as the people demanded. As society evolved, so the legal concepts of property changed.

In America, with the prospect of developing the vast natural resources available and with enterprising individuals eager for the task, substantial changes were needed in the restrictive English property laws. English landholding involved the obligations of rent or service to the crown. In contrast, America created a "free" system of landholding. Land was free to be bought and sold like other properties without any obligation owed to the government. In fact, the self-sufficiency afforded to citizens through private property rights formed the basis on which the U.S. economic and political systems were organized. American land-law was conceived as the means to secure and to protect both personal liberties and property rights. As John Adams exclaimed, "Property must be secure, or liberty cannot exist." Another author argued as follows:

> What maintains liberty . . . more than any other thing is the great mass of people who are independent because they have, as Aristotle said, "a moderate and sufficient property." They resist the absolute state. An official, a teacher, a scholar, a minister, a journalist, all those whose business it is to make articulate and to lead opinion, will act the part of free men if they can resign or be discharged without subjecting their wives, their children, and themselves to misery and squalor.[2]

In the early nineteenth century, American concern for expansion and economic development of the continent dictated the use of property rights as the tool for expansion. Homestead laws and land grants fostered the development of farming, railroads, and educational institutions in the West. However, by the end of the nineteenth century and with the rise of financial and industrial "empires," large concentrations of power and wealth developed. As a result, America became increasingly concerned for the personal rights of poor individuals whose "rights" were not secured by property holdings. Government, therefore, assumed a positive duty to promote the welfare of society, even at the expense of the rights of private property.

In the twentieth century, land-law has evolved toward increasing limitations on the freedom of land use. Wasteful use of property was restrained by laws providing for proper utilization of soil and the conservation of natural resources. The doctrine of reasonable use of land has been eroded by zoning and city planning. More recently, society has further restricted property rights in its concern for a good quality natural environment.

Presently, it would seem that a *societal* theory of land use prevails over that of individual determination of property use. The traditional absolute freedom of private decision in regard to property use, which initially was thought incapable of restriction without subverting the very foundations of all liberties, is now within the purview of governmental control.

PROPERTY RIGHTS AND LIMITATIONS

In its most technical legal sense, property is an intangible concept signifying the rights, privileges, and powers that the law recognizes as vested in an individual in relation to others as to certain things tangible or intangible. It includes every interest anyone may have in anything that may be the subject of ownership, including the right to freely possess, use, enjoy, and dispose of the same. The sum of these proprietory rights is designated as "title" to property.

Property rights are classified in law according to the nature of the object concerning which rights are claimed. Immovable property—land and those things permanently attached to it—is considered real property, whereas movable items, or chattels, are designated as personal property. Land can be possessed and controlled: however, personal property is not only possessed and controlled, it may also be handled, manually transferred, altered, and destroyed with relative ease.

Proprietory rights are exclusive rights of the individual owner and are protected against infringement by others. In the final analysis, these rights represent a relationship between the owner and other individuals with respect to objects that can be owned. Part of those rights includes the relationship between owners of private property and the government's power to regulate or take that property interest. The following materials emphasize the changing relationship between the power of the state and individual property rights.

EMINENT DOMAIN

In Re Forsstrom
38 P. 2d 878 (1934)
Supreme Court of Arizona

[The City of Tulsa believed a railroad-street crossing to be a hazard to public travel. Consequently, the City determined to construct an underpass below the tracks. In agreement with the State of Arizona the City by eminent domain condemned the property required for construction of the underpass and paid "just compensation" to acquire it. The underpass also deprived the plaintiff, an adjacent property holder, of entry and exit onto the street. He maintains that such deprivation was a "taking" of an "appurtenant" to his property which is entitled to compensation.]

Eminent domain is the right and power of a sovereign state to appropriate private property to particular uses, and it embraces all cases whereby under the authority of the state the property of the individual is appropriated permanently without his consent, for the purpose of being devoted to some particular use for the public good. This right is an inherent one which pertains to sovereignty as a necessary, constant, and unextinguishable attribute, and constitutional provisions in regard to it do not create or grant the power, but are limitations thereon. But the right has always carried with it, even in the absence of constitutional limitations, the principle that in some manner and to some extent compensation must be made for its exercise.

In order that we may understand the better what is meant by a "taking" of property, we should have a clear knowledge of what property really is. The word is used at different times to express many varying ideas. Sometimes it is taken in common parlance to denote a physical object, as where one says an automobile or a horse is his property. On careful consideration, however, it is plain that "property" in the true and legal sense does not mean a physical object itself, but certain rights over the object. A piece of land in an unexplored and uninhabited region which belongs to no one does not necessarily undergo any physical change merely by reason of its later becoming the property of any person. A wild animal may be exactly the same physically before and after it is captured, but, when it is running free in the forest, no one would speak of it as property. We must therefore look beyond the physical object itself for the true definition of property. Many courts and writers have attempted to define it, using different words, but meaning in essence the same thing. One of the great writers on jurisprudence says:

> Property is entirely the creature of the law. . . . There is no form, or color, or visible trace, by which it is possible to express the relation which constitutes property. It belongs not to physics, but to metaphysics; it is altogether a creature of the mind. *Bentham Works* (Ed. 1843) vol. 1, p. 308.

We think that "property" may well be defined as the right to the possession, use, and disposition of things in such manner as is not inconsistent with law.

When real property is considered, a man has not only rights of use, of possession and disposition in a particular area of land, but he has at times other rights over contiguous and surrounding areas affecting the use of the particular area, and these are as much his property as the right to the use of the area he possesses. Such, for instance, are the right to the support of soil, to light and air, to access, the right to be undisturbed by nuisances on the adjoining property, and similar matters. Of course, these rights vary greatly in accordance with circumstances, but, whenever they do exist, and to the extent to which they are secured by law, they are truly property as much as the right to use the land to which they appertain. It would follow from these definitions and explanations of the meaning of the term "property" that since it consists, not in tangible things themselves, but in certain rights in and appurtenant to them, it would logically follow that, when a person is deprived of any of these rights, he is to that extent deprived of his property, and that it is taken in the true sense, although his title and possession of the physical object remains undisturbed. Any substantial interference, therefore, with rights over a physical object which destroys or lessens its value, or by which the use and enjoyment thereof by its owner is in any substantial degree abridged or destroyed, is both in law and in fact a "taking" of property. . . .

We are satisfied that the word "taking," when used in constitutions or statutes in regard to property, and particularly realty, includes the permanent taking or diminishing of any of the rights which one has by reason of and appurtenant to his ownership of the realty in question, as well as a deprivation of the title to the physical object. . . . The very purpose of establishing streets in a city is to afford access, light, and air to the property through which they pass, and it is therefore generally held that all lots abutting upon a street have these easements appurtenant thereto. This right of access extends to the use of the street as an outlet from the abutting property by any mode of travel or conveyance appropriate to the highway in such manner as is customary or reasonable. . . . [I]t certainly could not be abolished or narrowed by the . . . [government] without compensation therefor.

Questions

1. What is eminent domain? What is its source?
2. What is property? What are the "rights" of property?
3. Besides the appurtenant of entry and exit, what other appurtenant rights exist for real property?
4. The court mentioned "the right to be undisturbed by nuisances." How would you define a nuisance? Would it depend on the circumstances? Can you think of any example? Just as one has the right to be free of nuisances, so does one's neighbor. Consequently, the rights of private property are restricted in the sense that property use may not be a nuisance to the neighbors.

POLICE POWER

Fred F. French Investment Co., Inc. v. City of New York

350 N.E. 2d 381 (1976)
Court of Appeals of New York

The issue is whether the rezoning of buildable private parks exclusively as parks open to the public, thereby prohibiting all reasonable income productive or other private use of property, constitutes a deprivation of property rights without due process of law in violation of constitutional limitations. . . .

The power of the State over private property extends from the regulation of its use under the police power to the actual taking of an easement or all or part of the fee under the eminent domain power. The distinction, although definable, between a compensable taking and a noncompensable regulation is not always susceptible of precise demarcation. Generally, as the court stated in *Lutheran Church in Amer.* v. *City of New York,* 316 N.E.2d 305, 310: "[G]overnment interference [with the use of private property] is based on one of two concepts—either the government is acting in its enterprise capacity, where it takes unto itself private resources in use for the common good, or in its arbitral capacity, where it intervenes to straighten out situations in which the citizenry is in conflict over land use or where one person's use of his land is injurious to others. Where government acts in its enterprise capacity, as where it takes land to widen a road, there is a compensable taking. Where government acts in its arbitral capacity, as where it legislates zoning or provides the machinery to enjoin noxious use there is simply noncompensable regulation." . . .

In the present case, while there was a significant diminution in the value of the property, there was no actual appropriation or taking of the parks by title or governmental occupation. . . . There was no physical invasion of the owner's property; nor was there an assumption by the city of the control or management of the parks. Indeed, the parks served the same function as before the amendment, except that they were now also open to the public. Absent factors of governmental displacement of private ownership, occupation or management, there was no "taking" within the meaning of constitutional limitations. There was, therefore, no right to compensation as for a taking in eminent domain.

Since there was no taking within the meaning of constitutional limitations, it is necessary to determine whether the zoning amendment was a valid exercise of the police power under the due process clauses of the State and Federal Constitutions.

The broad police power of the State to regulate the use of private property is not unlimited. Every enactment under the police power must be reasonable. An exercise of the police power to regulate private property by zoning which is unreasonable constitutes a deprivation of property without due process of law.

What is an "unreasonable" exercise of the police power depends upon the relevant converging factors. Hence, the facts of each case must be evaluated in order to determine the private and social balance of convenience before the exercise of the power may be condemned as unreasonable. A zoning ordinance is unreasonable, under traditional police power and due process analysis, if it encroaches on the exercise of private property rights without substantial relation to a legitimate governmental purpose. A legitimate governmental purpose is, of course, one which furthers the public health, safety, morals or general welfare. Moreover, a zoning ordinance, on similar police power analysis, is unreasonable if it is arbitrary, that is, if there is no reasonable relation between the end sought to be achieved by the regulation and the means used to achieve that end.

Finally, and it is at this point that the confusion between the police power and the exercise of eminent domain most often occurs, a zoning ordinance is unreasonable if it frustrates the owner in the use of his property, that is, if it renders the property unsuitable for any reasonable income productive or other private use for which it is adapted and thus destroys its economic value, or all but a bare residue of its value.

The ultimate evil of a deprivation of property, or better, a frustration of property rights, under the guise of an exercise of the police power is that it forces the owner to assume the cost of providing a benefit to the public without recoupment. There is no attempt to share the cost of the benefit among those benefited, that is, society at large. Instead, the accident of ownership determines who shall bear the cost initially. Of course, as further consequence, the ultimate economic cost of providing the benefit is hidden from those who in a democratic society are given the power of deciding whether or not they wish to obtain the benefit despite the ultimate economic cost, however initially distributed. In other words, the removal from productive use of private property has an ultimate social cost more easily concealed by imposing the cost on the owner alone. When successfully concealed, the public is not likely to have any objection to the "cost-free" benefit.

In this case, the zoning amendment is unreasonable and, therefore, unconstitutional because, without due process of law, it deprives the owner of all his property rights, except the bare title and a dubious future reversion of full use. The amendment renders the park property unsuitable for any reasonable income productive or other private use for which it is adapted and thus destroys its economic value. . . .

It is recognized that the "value" of property is not a concrete or tangible attribute but an abstraction derived from the economic uses to which the property may be put. Thus, the development rights are an essential component of the value of the underlying property because they constitute some of the economic uses to which the property may be put. As such, they are a potentially valuable and even a transferable commodity and may not be disregarded in determining whether the ordinance has destroyed the economic value of the underlying property.

Solutions must be reached for the problems of modern zoning, urban and rural conservation, and last but not least landmark preservations, whether by particular buildings or historical districts. Unfortunately, the land planners are now only at the beginning of the path to solution. In the process of traversing that path further, new ideas and new standards of constitutional tolerance must and will evolve. It is enough to say that the loose-ended transferable development rights in this case fall short of achieving a fair allocation of economic burden. . . .

The legislative and administrative efforts to solve the zoning and landmark problem in modern society demonstrate the presence of ingenuity. That ingenuity further pursued will in all likelihood achieve the goals without placing an impossible or unsuitable burden on the individual property owner, the public fisc, or the general taxpayer. These efforts are entitled to and will undoubtedly receive every encouragement. The task is difficult but not beyond management. The end is essential but the means must nevertheless conform to constitutional standards.

Questions

1. Why did the court conclude in *French Inv. Co.* that there was no "taking" of plaintiff's property?
2. How did the court determine if the exercise of police power was reasonable?
3. What is the "evil" of frustrating private property rights under the guise of an exercise of the police power?

4. What is the extent of the police power? Consider the words of the U.S. Supreme Court:

> . . . We deal, in other words, with what traditionally has been known as the police power. An attempt to define its reach or trace its outer limits is fruitless, for each case must turn on its own facts. The definition is essentially the product of legislative determinations addressed to the purpose of government, purposes neither abstractly nor historically capable of complete definition. Subject to specific constitutional limitations, when the legislature has spoken, the public interest has been declared in terms well-nigh conclusive. In such cases the legislature, not the industry, is the main guardian of the public needs to be served by social legislation. . . .
>
> Public safety, public health, morality, peace and quiet, law and order—these are some of the more conspicuous examples of the traditional application of the police power to municipal affairs. Yet they merely illustrate the scope of the power and do not delimit it. . . . The concept of the public welfare is broad and exclusive. The values it represents are spiritual as well as physical, aesthetic as well as monetary. It is within the power of the legislature to determine that the community should be beautiful as well as healthy, spacious as well as clean, well-balanced as well as carefully patrolled. . . .
>
> If those who govern the [City] . . . decide that [it] . . . should be beautiful as well as sanitary, there is nothing in the Fifth Amendment that stands in the way. *Berman* v. *Parker* 348 U.S. 26 (1954).

CONSTITUTIONAL LIMITS TO USE

PruneYard Shopping Center v. Robins
100 U.S. 74 (1980)
Supreme Court of the United States

Justice Rehnquist

PruneYard is a privately owned shopping center in the city of Campbell, California. It covers approximately 21 acres—five devoted to parking and 16 occupied by walkways, plazas, sidewalks, and buildings that contain more than 65 specialty shops, 10 restaurants, and a movie theater. The PruneYard is open to the public for the purpose of encouraging the patronizing of its commercial establishments. It has a policy not to permit any visitor or tenant to engage in any publicly expressive activity, including the circulation of petitions, that is not directly related to its commercial purposes. This policy has been strictly enforced in a nondiscriminatory fashion.

[Plaintiffs] are high school students who sought to solicit support for their opposition to a United Nations resolution against "Zionism." On a Saturday afternoon they set up a card table in a corner of PruneYard's central courtyard. They distributed pamphlets and asked passersby to sign petitions, which were to be sent to the President and Members of Congress. Their activity was peaceful and orderly, and, so far as the record indicates, was not objected to by PruneYard's patrons.

Soon after [plaintiffs] had begun soliciting signatures, a security guard informed them that they would have to leave because their activity violated PruneYard regulations. The guard suggested that they move to the public sidewalk at the PruneYard's perimeter. [Plaintiffs] immediately left the premises and later filed this lawsuit in the California Superior Court of Santa Clara County. They sought to enjoin [defendants] from denying them access to the PruneYard for the purpose of circulating their petitions.

The Superior Court held that [plaintiffs] were not entitled under either the Federal or California Constitution to exercise their asserted rights on the shopping center property. It concluded that there were "adequate, effective channels of communication for [plaintiffs] other than soliciting on the private property of the [PruneYard]."

The California Supreme Court reversed, holding that the California Constitution protects "speech and petitioning, reasonably exercised, in shopping centers even when the centers are privately owned." It concluded that [plaintiffs] are entitled to conduct their activity on PruneYard property . . . .

* * *

[Defendants] contend that a right to exclude others underlies the Fifth Amendment guarantee against the taking of property without just compensation. . . .

It is true that one of the essential sticks in the bundle of property rights is the right to exclude others. And here there has literally been a "taking" of that right to the extent that the California Supreme Court has interpreted the state constitution to entitle its citizens to exercise free expression and petition right on shopping center property. But it is well-established that "not every destruction or injury to property by governmental action has been held to be a 'taking' in the constitutional sense." Rather, the determination whether a state law unlawfully infringes a landowner's property in violation of the Taking Clause requires an examination of whether the restriction on private property "forc[es] some people alone to bear public burdens which, in all fairness and justice, should be borne by the public as a whole." This examination entails inquiry into such factors as the character of the governmental actions, its economic impact, and its interference with reasonable investment backed expectation. When "regulation goes too far, it will be recognized as a taking."

Here the requirement that [defendants] permit [plaintiffs] to exercise state-protected rights of free expression and petition on shopping center property clearly does not amount to an unconstitutional infringement of [defendants'] property rights under the Taking Clause. There is nothing to suggest that preventing [defendants] from prohibiting this sort of activity will unreasonably impair the value or use of their property as a shopping center. The PruneYard is a large commercial complex that covers several city blocks, contains numerous separate business establishments, and is open to the public at large. The decision of the California Supreme Court makes it clear that the PruneYard may restrict expressive activity by adopting time, place, and manner regulations that will minimize any interference with its commercial functions. [Plaintiffs] were orderly, and they limited their activity to the common areas of the shopping center.

In these circumstances, the fact that they may have "physically invaded" [defendants'] property cannot be viewed as determinative.

* * *

A state is, of course, bound by the Just Compensation Clause of the Fifth Amendment, but here [defendants] have failed to demonstrate that the "right to exclude others" is so essential to the use or economic value of their property that the State-authorized limitation of it amounted to a "taking."

* * *

[Defendants] finally contend that a private property owner has a First Amendment right not to be forced by the State to use his property as a forum for the speech of others. [However] . . . the shopping center by choice of its owner is not limited to the personal use of [defendants]. It is instead a business establishment that is open to the public to come and go as they please. The views expressed by members of the public in passing out pamphlets or seeking signatures for a petition thus will not likely be identified with those of the owner. Second, no specific message is dictated by the State to be displayed on [defendants'] property. There consequently is no danger of governmental discrimination for or against a particular message. Finally, as far as appears here [defendants] can expressly disavow any connection with the message by simply posting signs in the area where the speakers or handbillers stand. Such signs, for example, could disclaim any sponsorship of the message and could explain that the persons are communicating their own messages by virtue of state law.

We conclude that neither [defendants'] federally recognized property rights nor their First Amendment rights have been infringed by the California Supreme Court's decision recognizing a right of [plaintiffs] to exercise state protected rights of expression and petition on [defendants'] property. The judgment of the Supreme Court of California is therefore affirmed.

Questions

1. Why did the Court in *PruneYard* feel there was no "taking" of the property right to *exclusive* use?
2. The owners of a private pond invested substantial amounts of money in dredging the pond, developing it into an exclusive marina, and building a surrounding marina community. The marina was open only to fee-paying members, and the fees were paid in part "to maintain the privacy and security of the pond." The federal government sought to compel free public use of the private marina on the ground that the marina became subject to the federal navigational servitude because the owners had dredged a channel connecting it to "navigable water." The Court ruled the government's attempt to create a public right of access to the improved pond interfered with the owner's "reasonable investment backed expectations." It held that it went "so far beyond ordinary regulation or improvement for navigation as to amount to a taking . . ." *Kaiser Aetna* v. *United States,* 100 S. Ct. 383 (1979). Why is this decision different from that of *PruneYard*?

OWNERSHIP AND POSSESSION

The terms *ownership* and *possession* are not synonymous. They refer to two separate rights to property—rights that need not be held by the same person. The owner has title to the things owned: he or she has a series of rights in the property which are protected by law. Possession, on the other hand, is simply the right to control a physical object. It may be had by right of ownership or may be had temporarily by one who is not the owner. For example, if A rents his house to B, A retains ownership but B takes possession.

Possession may be actual or constructive. Actual possession indicates physical control over an object. Constructive possession indicates that although the possessor's legal rights to the article still exist, the article is not under his or her physical control. For example, an individual has actual possession of anything carried on his or her person, such as a watch or a wallet; the person would have only constructive possession of these same items had they been left at home.

Property in land is traditionally dealt with in terms of estates. The extent to which an owner may enjoy ownership of real property is described as his or her estate. The quality, nature, and extent of an interest in real property will depend on the type of estate held. From this arises the interchangeable use of the terms *real property* and *real estate.* Although, technically, the former refers to the land itself and the latter to an interest in the land, the distinction is seldom observed. Some estates include the right of possession whereas others do not.

ESTATES

The description of an estate details the rights and privileges of the estate holder in relation to others. The most substantial estate is the *fee simple absolute.* This estate has a potentially infinite duration in that the owner's rights, if not conveyed away during the owner's lifetime or by will at death, are statutorily inherited by his or her heirs. One wishing to convey a fee simple absolute to, say, John Doe traditionally uses the language "to John Doe and his heirs." This does not mean that any interest is thereby conveyed to Doe's heirs. They inherit nothing if John conveys his fee simple absolute to another by deed or will. The reference to heirs describes Doe's estate rather than designating the heirs of John Doe as co-owners.

However, in the overwhelming majority of states today, any form of expression of intention to convey a fee simple absolute is given effect whether the words "and his heirs" are used or not. This result is usually based on a statute.

Some land ownership interests are defeasible, that is, capable of being undone or annulled with the ownership interest returning to the previous owner. For example, a "fee simple subject to a condition subsequent" is a transfer of ownership subject to some limitation which, if broken, causes the property to return to the previous grantor. If the grantor, John Doe, was to grant Blackacre to the community church on the condition that the land be used only for housing of religious services, any deviation from this delineated activity could cause Blackacre to be returned to John Doe.

The creation of a "life estate" is a split of the fee simple absolute estate into a possessory estate (life estate) and a nonpossessory estate (remainder). A life estate is an estate the duration of which is specifically described in terms of the life or lives of one or more human beings and which is not terminable at any fixed or computable period of time. For example, land may be conveyed by A to "B for her life." B has the right to possess and enjoy the land during her life. During this time, A has a nonpossessory right to the "remainder." At B's death, the grantor's remainder rights allow him to reclaim the land and reestablish his fee simple absolute estate.

CONCURRENT OWNERSHIP

Several persons may have simultaneous interest of a *different* nature in the same thing (that is, one has a fee simple determinable and another the possibility of reverter), but they may also have simultaneous interests of an *identical* nature in the same property (that is, they both own the same type of estate). Simultaneous or concurrent ownership comprehends the situation in which two or more persons share ownership in the same subject. In law, concurrent ownership is synonymous with "cotenancy" which means the two or more owners simultaneously share equal rights in possession and use of the property subject. There are basically two types of cotenancy—joint tenancy and tenancy in common. Tenancy in common is easily defined as the type of co-ownership that exists if the co-ownership is not a joint tenancy. Joint tenancy requires special attention to be created.

Four unities are said to be necessary to create a joint tenancy: unities of interest, title, time, and possession. Unity of interest means the parties must equally share identical estates (both share a fee simple absolute or both share a life estate). Unity of title and time means the parties must claim their interest through the same instrument or deed which granted them their rights at the same time. Unity of possession means each party has the right to share possession of the property subject. Consequently, any deed that grants two or more persons equal interests in the same estate and grants equal rights to possession has created the four unities prerequisite for a joint tenancy. However, the additional language of "survivorship" or the word "jointly" is necessary to form a joint tenancy. Under the "right of survivorship," the surviving cotenant becomes the sole owner of the property on the demise of the other cotenant. The heirs of the deceased cotenant get no interest in the property. In contrast, the fractional interest of a tenant-in-common passes to the tenant's heirs. Finally, it should be noted that a transfer of the fractional interest by a joint tenant causes a severance of the unities and thereby terminates the joint tenancy. The new tenant receiving the transfer of ownership becomes a tenant-in-common with the remaining tenant (the former joint tenant).

DEEDS

A deed is a written instrument in which the grantor expresses an intention to pass an interest in real property to the grantee. Deeds differ in the kind of interest they convey: (1) a *quit claim* deed conveys the interest of the grantor, if any, without specifying the interest, and makes no warranties; (2) a *general warranty* deed transfers a specified interest and obligates the grantor on certain warranties.

A *general warranty* deed ordinarily contains the following warranties: (1) a covenant of seisen, (2) a covenant of the right to convey, (3) a covenant against incumbrances, (4) a covenant for quiet enjoyment, and (5) a covenant for further assurances.

A *covenant of seisen* is a guaranty that the grantor owns the exact estate that he or she intends to convey to the grantee. It is a covenant to the effect that the grantor has and conveys the title described in the conveyance. In a quit claim deed, the grantor purports to convey his or her interest, if any, to the grantee; and in the absence of fraud, if the grantor had nothing, the grantee gets nothing.

A *covenant of right to convey* is a guaranty that the grantor has the right to make the conveyance.

A *covenant against incumbrances* is an undertaking by the grantor that no lien or burden not described in the conveyance is outstanding against the property. In other words, the grantor warrants that the property is free from any incumbrances such as mortgages, tax liens, mechanic's liens, or judgment liens, except those, if any, detailed in the deed.

A *covenant for quiet enjoyment* is a general warranty that the grantee will not be disturbed by posssessory or title claims not already disclosed, and, if such are established and are settled by the grantee, that the grantor will reimburse him or her for the sums expended. Actually, the grantor agrees to defend the title to the property against all who claim to have a superior title.

A *covenant for further assurance* is a promise by the grantor to execute any additional document that may be required to perfect the title of the grantee.

The warranties in a deed give some protection to the buyer that the purchase is clear and free of claims by other persons against the property. However, the seller may die or become financially insolvent, in which case the claim of the buyer against the seller will be barren. Accordingly, other measures of protection of the buyer's investment should be taken. Although the methods differ in the various states, every state makes some provision for the recording of deeds and other documents that affect title to real property. Every purchaser should search the public records for determination that the seller possesses a "clear title." Public records give priority to those documents first recorded over rival claimants to the same property. An attorney skilled in the task of searching the public records should be employed for such tasks.

A careful investigation of the public record may disclose many monetary claims against the property. All unpaid taxes, mortgages, or other restrictions against the property can be noted through a search of the public records. However, the buyer is subject to possible errors in indexing, to errors in the examination process, and to claims of those whose rights would not be revealed in the public records. The records would not reveal forged deeds or wills, invalid or undisclosed wills, undisclosed errors, or deeds by persons supposedly single but secretly married. A host of other possible hidden defects in the title may exist. Detection against these risks can be obtained only by purchasing title insurance. Title insurance is a contract to indemnify the buyer against losses through defects in title to real property. The insurance company guarantees the buyer against loss due to any defects in title and to pay all expenses in defense of any lawsuits attacking the title.

Boehringer v. Montalto

254 N.Y.S. 276 (1931)
Supreme Court, Westchester County, New York

[Plaintiff] sues . . . for breach of covenant against incumbrances.

The [defendant] conveyed the property to the [plaintiff] by [a general warranty] . . . deed . . . and . . . the property conveyed was warranted free from incumbrances.

It now develops that the Bronx Valley sewer commission had procured . . . the right to construct and maintain the Bronx Valley sewer through the premises, and that the sewer has been constructed across the property at a depth of 150 feet . . . [and] provided no right of access from the surface of the property.

At a time when nobody foresaw the use to which the air above the land might be put, a maxim appears in the law to the effect that he who owns the soil owns everything above and below, from heaven to hell. . . .

In *Smith* v. *New England Aircraft Co.,* 270 Mass. 511, the Supreme Judicial Court of Massachusetts stated that it would assume that private ownership extends to all reasonable heights above the underlying land; that the experience of mankind, although not necessarily a limitation upon rights, is the basis upon which air space must be regarded.

The Massachusetts court held in that case that the statutory regulation of 500 feet as the minimum altitude flight by aircraft was a permissible exercise of the police power, although the experience of mankind indicates many structures exceeding 500 feet in height.

It therefore appears that the old theory that the title of an owner of real property extends indefinitely upward and downward is no longer an accepted principle of law in its entirety. Title above the surface of the ground is now limited to the extent to which the owner of the soil may reasonably make use thereof.

By analogy, the title of an owner of the soil will not be extended to a depth below ground which the owner may not reasonably make use thereof.

It is concluded that the depth at which the Bronx Valley sewer exists is beyond the point to which the owner can conceivably make use of the property, and is therefore not an incumbrance.

Questions

1. What is the meaning of the old legal maxim that the owner of land owned everything "from heaven to hell"?
2. Why was there no breach of the deed warranty against incumbrances?

TYPES OF PERSONAL PROPERTY

Personal property is classified as *chattels real* and *chattels personal.* Chattels real are temporary interests in land; a prime example is a lease for a specified period of time. All other personal property is chattels personal.

Personal property may be further subdivided into tangible or intangible property. Tangible personal property includes all movable property, even large items such as animals, cars, and standing trees that have been sold and are to be removed from the land. Intangible property includes things to which one does not have a right of possession but to which legal rights in the subject matter are granted. For example, A may purchase a copy of a book copyrighted by B; A owns and enjoys the exclusive possession of the tangible book, but B owns the intangible property right to republish additional copies of the book. This intangible property right of B will receive court protection. Additional examples of intangible property are evidenced in pieces of paper; such as negotiable instruments, bank accounts, insurance policies, and stock certificates. The following cases are illustrative of intangible property and the variety of rules associated with the various forms of personal property.

GOODWILL

Mohawk Maintenance Co., Inc., v. Kessler
437 N.Y.S. 2d 646 (1981)
Court of Appeals of New York

The instant litigation arises out of the October 10, 1972, sale of defendant Kessler's controlling shareholder's interest in Mohawk Maintenance Co. to plaintiff for the sum of $2,000,000. Since its incorporation in 1952, Mohawk had been engaged in the business of providing building maintenance services in the tri-State area encompassing New York, New Jersey and Connecticut and had developed an impressive list of customers largely through the efforts of defendant Kessler, the firm's president and principal shareholder. In connection with the sale of the business, Kessler agreed that he would not "either as owner, partner, officer, employee, agent, consultant manager, lessee or lessor or in any other capacity, directly or indirectly . . . carry on or engage . . . in any business competitive with any business carried on by Mohawk" for a period of five years after the closing date of the sale. The geographical scope of the restriction of Kessler's business activities was confined to New York, Connecticut and any other State where Mohawk was actively doing business on the date of contract closing. Additionally, it was agreed between the parties that Kessler would continue to work for Mohawk as an employee for a period of three years and that the provisions of his employment contract would continue in force if he elected to remain with the company after his initial term of employment ended. The employment agreement also contained an anticompetition clause which precluded Kessler from engaging in any rival business "for a period of 24 months after the termination of this agreement."

Kessler remained in Mohawk's employ until August of 1978, when he voluntarily resigned his position. Shortly thereafter, he formed a new corporation, Sure-Way Maintenance Services, and began once again to engage in the business of providing building maintenance services. It is not seriously disputed that Kessler's new business was competitive in certain respects with the business carried on by Mohawk. Indeed, the affidavits submitted indicate that Kessler may have approached at least one of his former customers in an effort to lure its patronage away from Mohawk.

On January 23, 1979, Mohawk commenced the instant action seeking damages and a permanent injunction to prevent Kessler and Sure-Way from competing with it until August of 1980, the date that Mohawk claimed would mark the expiration of the anticompetition clause in defendant Kessler's employment agreement. Additionally, Mohawk sought an order permanently restraining defendants from soliciting the patronage of Kessler's former Mohawk customers.

When a business is sold, the purchaser acquires no legal right to expect that the seller will refrain from engaging in a competing enterprise. Indeed, the seller remains free to pursue his own economic interests without restraint unless the purchaser has managed to extract from him an express promise to refrain from competing.

At one time in the early history of the common law, such promises were routinely held to be unenforceable, since they were deemed to be violative of the strong public policy in favor of encouraging free trade and discouraging monopolies. Later, however, the inflexible approach of the judiciary to such agreements was relaxed to some extent as the courts came to realize that a blanket prohibition against agreements purporting to restrain trade was contrary to the equally strong public policy in favor of allowing individuals to dispose of their property freely and to enter into binding contracts. Ultimately, agreements restricting the parties' right to compete were recognized by the courts and were held fully enforceable if the restrictions were found to be "reasonable" in geographic scope and duration. Indeed, the modern trend in the case law seems to be in favor of according such convenants full effect when they are not unduly burdensome, particularly in cases where the agreement in question is made in connection with the sale of a business and its accompanying "good will." Nevertheless, as defendants correctly point out, the requirement that such covenants be "reasonable" in scope has never been completely abandoned and remains an important part of our case law.

We see no sound reason, however, to extend the test of durational "reasonableness" to cases such as this which involve only the so-called "implied covenant" to refrain from soliciting former customers following the sale of the "good will" of a business. This "implied covenant" restricts the economic freedom of the seller only insofar as it precludes him from approaching his former customers and attempting to regain their patronage after he has purported to transfer their "good will" to his purchaser. As such, the "implied covenant" imposes a much narrower duty than do express covenants purporting to restrict the seller's right to compete in a particular geographical area or field of endeavor. Accordingly, this "implied covenant" might well be regarded as inherently "reasonable," notwithstanding its indefinite duration.

More important, the right acquired by the purchase of the "good will" of a business by virtue of this "implied covenant" must logically be regarded as a permanent one that is not subject to divestiture upon the passage of a reasonable period of time. Indeed, it may be somewhat misleading to describe the duty of the seller to refrain from soliciting his former customers as one emanating from an "implied covenant," since the duty is, in reality, one imposed by law in order to prevent the seller from taking back that which he has purported to sell. When the intangible asset of good will is sold along with the tangible assets of a business, the purchaser acquires the right to expect that the firm's established customers will continue to patronize the business. The essence of the transaction is, in effect, an attempt to transfer the loyalties of the business' customers from the seller, who cultivated and created them, to the new proprietor. Of course, the attempted transfer may not be entirely successful, in that some of the firm's customers may choose to take their business elsewhere as a consequence of the change in ownership. Indeed, the occurrence of a certain amount of attrition is one of the risks that the purchaser must assume when he acquires an established business.

It is quite another matter, however, when the seller actively interferes with the purchaser's relationship with his newly acquired customers by capitalizing upon their personal loyalties to him in an effort to recapture their patronage. When the seller conducts himself in such a manner, he is, in effect, directly impairing the very asset which he has purported to transfer—the "good will" of his former business.

It is to prevent such an eventuality that the law imposes upon the seller a specific duty to refrain from soliciting his former customers after he has sold his business and the accompanying "good will" to another.

* * *

In light of the rationale underlying the rule prohibiting the seller from soliciting the patronage of his former customers, it would make little sense for us to hold that the prohibition should be lifted after a "reasonable" time has passed following the transfer. A purchaser who acquires the "good will" of a business pays good and valuable consideration for the seller's implied promise to do everything within his power to transfer the loyalties of his customers to the new proprietor. At the very least the purchaser obtains the exclusive right, as between himself and the seller, to exploit the established loyalties of the firm's customers for the benefit of his newly acquired business. The expectation in the purchaser that arises as a result of the transaction is clearly a vested property right of indefinite duration. It would make no more sense to hold that the seller may attempt to defeat this right by soliciting his former customers after the passage of a "reasonable" period of time than it would to hold that the seller of a business may re-enter and attempt to retake the premises and tangible assets of the firm after a "reasonable" time has expired.

In the present case, there can be little doubt that a transfer of "good will" was intended, even though the contract of sale did not expressly provide as much. The circumstances surrounding the sale, particularly the size of the purchase price and the existence of express convenants barring competition by the seller, provide persuasive proof that defendant Kessler did indeed intend to part with Mohawk's "good will" along with its tangible assets when he sold the business to plaintiff's predecessor. Inasmuch as defendants have failed to produce any concrete evidence to the contrary upon the present motion for summary judgment, the issue must be resolved against them.

Since there is no doubt that the "good will" of Mohawk passed to the purchaser when the business was sold, it follows from our holding that plaintiff is entitled to enjoy the use of this intangible asset indefinitely without interference by defendants. Although defendants may accept the patronage of those customers who were actively dealing with Mohawk on the date of the sale if such customers choose to leave Mohawk without prompting from defendants, the defendants remain under a positive and permanent duty to refrain from interfering with the rights acquired by plaintiff as a result of its acquisition of Mohawk's "good will." Accordingly, defendants were properly enjoined from soliciting the business of defendant Kessler's former customers, and the fact that the injunction establishes a permanent restraint does not provide an adequate ground for challenging the order of the court below.

Questions

1. What is the "goodwill" of a business? Sale of the property rights of goodwill implies a "specific duty" on the seller. What is the content of that duty? What is the duration of the duty?
2. Express promises "not to compete" contained in a sale-of-business contract must be "reasonable" in *time* and *area* to be enforceable. What would be a reasonable time and area in this case?

TRADE SECRETS

Black, Sicalls & Bryson, Inc., v. Keystone Steel Fab.

584 F. 2d 946 (1978)
United States Court of Appeals (10 Cir.)

At great expense, plaintiff Black, Sivalls & Bryson, Inc. (BS&B) . . . developed a market for a device designed to uniformly heat certain industrial fluids. . . . When defendant Smalling, the former head of BS&B's heater sales group, left BS&B and immediately began to underbid his former employer in the industrial fluid heater market, BS&B became suspicious that Smalling may have stepped over that unfathomable line between the use of personal experience and the employment of trade secrets.

BS&B's discovery enabled it to offer proof at trial that Smalling's quick and successful market entry was accomplished with no prior experience in heater design except that gained with BS&B. BS&B was also able to present evidence that: (1) when originally introduced, BS&B's heater was "unique" and few heaters could achieve generally uniform temperatures around the heater tubes; (2) there was functional equivalency and some design similarity between the two heaters; (3) Smalling's first successful underbidding was confidently accomplished without building or testing a prototype of the proposed unit; (4) Smalling commenced his design calculations for tube wall dimensions with a certain critical mathematical number which had been identified by BS&B after much experimentation and which was employed as an "outside heat transfer coefficient" to calculate the proper tube wall thickness (this coefficient will be denominated "Ø" to preserve its claimed trade secret status); (5) Smalling's only explanation for commencing calculations with the coefficient instead of deriving it through trial and error was that he had pulled the number "out of the air"; (6) Smalling had BS&B's design manual, several design reports, and BS&B pricing information in his possession when he left BS&B . . . .

The trial court . . . [considered] the questions of whether relevant trade secrets existed and whether Smalling had illegally appropriated them . . . [and then] granted defendants' . . . motion for a directed verdict and entered judgment for defendants. . . . The standard for reviewing the propriety of directed verdicts is whether there is a genuine issue of material fact to be resolved by the trier of the fact. Stated positively, a verdict should "be directed where both the facts and the inferences to be drawn from the facts point so strongly in favor of one party that the court believes that reasonable men could not come to a different conclusion." In applying the directed verdict standard we must view the evidence in the light most favorable to the party against whom the motion for a directed verdict was addressed and give such party the benefit of all inferences which the evidence fairly supports, even though contrary inferences could reasonably be drawn.

Plaintiff argues on appeal that the evidence showed the following to be trade secrets: (1) the identity and application of the coefficient Ø; (2) the volute design; (3) the burner design; (4) the control panel; (5) pricing information which estimated the man-hours and materials necessary to build a heater and was useful in calculating the bid price of plaintiff's heaters; and (6) information regarding customers of plaintiff. We are satisfied from our examination of the record and the application of proper standards of review that BS&B presented enough evidence to raise a jury issue as to claimed secrets (1) and (5) but not as to the other four.

A trade secret is a formula, pattern, device or compilation of information which is used in one's business and which gives him an opportunity to gain an economic advantage over competitors who do not know or use it. A trade secret must have a substantial element of secrecy. While it need not be patentable it must contain elements which are unique, and not generally known or used in the trade. To prevail in its claim that defendants wrongfully appropriated its trade secrets, plaintiff must establish that: (1) a trade secret existed, (2) defendants acquired the trade secret through a confidential relationship, and (3) defendants used the trade secret without authorization from plaintiff.

The record indicates that several of plaintiff's claimed trade secrets may be discovered through an examination of plaintiff's heaters. In addition, some had been revealed in information which had been published or otherwise disseminated. As such, they cannot qualify as trade secrets for purposes of this litigation.

Based on the evidence, a jury could reasonably infer that Ø was helpful to Smalling as a starting point for his calculations and that without it he could not have been able to develop his heater as confidently and quickly as he did. A jury could also infer that Smalling would have been unable to successfully bid on a job without building a prototype were it not for his having that verified starting point. If nothing else, a jury could find that Smalling did not have to experiment with the broad range of disclosed coefficients to determine the proper starting point. Furthermore, based on the evidence regarding Smalling's familiarity with the coefficient through his employment with plaintiff and the fact that Smalling did not present evidence of an independent source of that coefficient, a jury could view with incredulity Smalling's statement that he pulled the number Ø "out of the air."

Confidential data regarding operating and pricing policies can also qualify as trade secrets. It is apparent that the ability to predict a competitor's bid with reasonable accuracy would give a distinct advantage to the possessor of that information. While it may be argued that plaintiff's 1961 pricing information was too out-of-date to give Smalling confidence in its use, it may also reasonably be inferred, since the uncontradicted evidence shows that Smalling possessed that information, that Smalling's immediate success in bidding against plaintiff may have been due at least partially to the use of plaintiff's pricing information. Viewing the evidence in the light most favorable, it may be reasonable to infer that one could compensate for inflation and use plaintiff's pricing information to approximate plaintiff's bid on a particular heater.

Smalling argues that, in designing his heaters, he merely used knowledge gained through experience. It is difficult in a case such as this to draw distinctions between the skills acquired by an employee in his work and the trade secrets, if any, of his employer. . . . [T]he former may be used by the employee in subsequent employment while the latter may not. Against this background it seems clear that trade secret status should be accorded the fruits of research carried out by the plaintiff, compiled by plaintiff in the form of charts, graphs, tables and the like for its day-to-day use, and carefully guarded by plaintiff as confidential information. Notwithstanding the difficulty of distinguishing between normally acquired skills and trade secret information, where there is circumstantial evidence from which a jury reasonably could infer trade secret use, the question is for a jury to decide.

Although the evidence of trade secret misappropriation is not strong, "in our view, the facts and circumstances, when viewed in their totality, do permit the inference that there was such misappropriation." Assuming Ø and the pricing information to constitute trade secrets, the fact that such information or part of it could have been subsequently procured by Smalling through independent research or experience did not justify Smalling's conduct. Few others in the field of heater development and manufacturing had obtained plaintiff's result with industrial fluid heaters. Therefore, the jury could assume that had Smalling worked for other heater manufacturers he would have not acquired the knowledge he now asserts the right to use. We are satisfied that there is sufficient circumstantial evidence to take this case to a jury. In reaching this conclusion we do not hold that plaintiff does in fact have trade secrets which were misappropriated by defendants. The evidence "does not point in one direction and different inferences might reasonably be drawn from it. There was, however, sufficient evidence to go to the jury and it is the jury which 'weighs the contradictory evidence and inferences' and draws 'the ultimate conclusion as to the facts.' "

The trial court's judgment . . . based on the verdict directed for defendants . . . is reversed and that case is remanded for a new trial with reference to the two claimed trade secrets improperly withdrawn from jury consideration.

Questions

1. What is a trade secret? May competitors "reverse engineer" products to learn trade secrets and use the revealed secret?
2. When is a competitor precluded from using trade secrets? What must the plaintiff-owner of trade secrets prove to obtain court assistance in preserving trade secrets?
3. Why did the appellate court order a trial?

BAILMENTS

Weinberg v. Wayco Petroleum Company
402 S.W. 2d 597 (1966)
St. Louis Court of Appeals

There is only one issue presented in this appeal and that is to determine whether the relationship between the parties was, as plaintiff contends, that of bailee and bailor.

With respect to cases involving automobiles and the contents thereof when loss occurs after the automobile is left in a parking lot, the relationship between the parties is usually one of bailment or license, and whether it is one or the other depends upon the circumstances of the particular case and especially upon the manner in which the parking lot in question is being operated and with whom control of the allegedly bailed article or articles is vested. The obligations of the parties flow from the relationship (bailment or license) once it is established.

A "bailment" in its ordinary legal sense imports the delivery of personal property by the bailor to the bailee who keeps the property in trust for a specific purpose, with a contract, express or implied, that the trust shall be faithfully executed, and the property returned or duly accounted for when the special purpose is accomplished or that the property shall be kept until the bailor reclaims it. This court has said that ". . . the term 'bailment' . . . signifies a contract resulting from the delivery of goods by bailor to bailee on condition that they be restored to the bailor, according to his directions, so soon as the purposes for which they were bailed are answered." We need not examine all the elements of bailment to determine whether or not the relationship exists in the instant case. In *Suits* v. *Electric Park Amusement Co.*, it was held ". . . there must be a delivery to the bailee, either actual or constructive. . . . It has been held that such a full delivery of the property must be made to the bailee as will entitle him to exclude for the period of the bailment the possession thereof, even of the owner. . . ."

In *National Fire Ins. Co.* v. *Commodore Hotel* (1961), 107 N.W. 2d 708, the plaintiff was a guest at a luncheon held at the defendant's hotel. She hung her mink jacket in an unattended cloakroom on the main floor across from the lobby desk. After the luncheon the plaintiff went to the cloakroom to retrieve her jacket and discovered it was gone. The court held that no negligence had been established against the defendant and stated:

> . . . [W]e do not feel that it is incumbent upon a hotel or restaurant owner to keep an attendant in charge of a free cloakroom for luncheon or dinner guests or otherwise face liability for loss of articles placed therein. The maintenance of such rooms without attendants is a common practice, and where the proprietor has not accepted control and custody of articles placed therein, no duty rests upon him to exercise any special degree of care with respect thereto.
>
> Likewise, failure to post a warning disclaiming responsibility would not seem to constitute negligence when, as here, a guest is aware that a cloakroom is unattended, adjacent to the lobby, and accessible to anyone; and has used it under similar circumstances on many prior occasions. The absence of such warning signs does not appear to have been material in a number of decisions absolving proprietors from liability although when posted they appear to be regarded as an added factor in establishing such nonliability.

It is obvious from the facts in the instant case that there was no delivery to Wayco sufficient to create the relationship of bailee and bailor between the parties here involved. Cases of the nature here involved are to be distinguished from those where the parking operation is such that the attendants collect a fee and assume authority or control of the automobile by parking it and/or retaining the keys so that the car can be moved about to permit the entrance or exit of other automobiles and where the tickets that are given to the owner of the automobile are issued for the purpose of identifying the automobile for redelivery. In such instances a bailment relationship is almost invariably held to exist.

In the instant case Wayco never secured control or authority over the plaintiff's automobile. No agent or employee of Wayco parked it or kept the keys to it or issued any ticket whereby the automobile could be identified by comparison of a portion of the ticket left with the automobile when it was parked. The plaintiff parked his own automobile, locked it, and took the keys with him. Certainly Wayco, the alleged bailee, did not have the right under these circumstances to exclude the purposes of the owner or even anyone else who might have had the keys. In the instant case the plaintiff never made a delivery, actual or constructive, of the automobile to Wayco under circumstances leading to the creation of a bailee-bailor relationship between them. Other jurisdictions where the factual situation present have been similar to the instant case have ruled that no bailment was created.

Of course, if Wayco was not a bailee of the plaintiff's automobile, it was not a bailee of the contents.

Questions

1. What is a bailment? Why did the court rule in *Weinberg* that no bailment existed?
2. What is the duty of the bailee to the bailor in relation to the bailed property? What is the duty of a lessor of parking space to the lessee's auto?
3. May a bailee by contract relieve himself or herself of the duty of care over the bailed property? Might this practice be unfair to the bailor in certain circumstances? Should the court protect against such efforts of the bailee to avoid responsibility?

LOST OR MISPLACED PROPERTY

Schley v. Couch
284 S.W. 2d 333 (1955)
Supreme Court of Texas

[Defendant] was the owner of a tract of land near Hamilton, Texas, upon which was situated a dwelling house with an attached garage and storeroom. At the time [defendant] moved upon the premises there was a concrete floor covering only the front half of the garage, and the remaining half was a dirt floor. . . . [Defendant] employed a Mr. Tomlinson and his crew of workmen—among whom was [plaintiff]—to put a concrete floor in the rear half of the garage. . . .

. . . While digging in this soil, [plaintiff's] pick struck a hard object and [plaintiff] found the $1,000 sued for buried in the ground. The money was in currency. The owner of the money is unknown.

. . . [Plaintiff] sued [defendant] for the money. . . . The trial court submitted the case to the jury upon two special issues. One inquired if the money were "lost" property, and the other inquired if the money were "mislaid" property. The jury answered the money was "mislaid" property, and upon that verdict the trial court rendered judgment in favor of the defendant as bailee for the true owner. Upon appeal the Court of Civil Appeals reversed the trial court's judgment and rendered judgment for the [plaintiff] against the defendant for the money. The Court of Civil Appeals held that the money constituted neither "lost" nor "mislaid" property, but fell into yet a third category known in some jurisdictions as "treasure trove." It accordingly held the right of possession to be in the finder [plaintiff].

Neither party claims to be the true owner of the money, but each claims the right to have possession of the money for the benefit of the true owner, should he ever appear and establish his claim. Title to the money is not involved, but only the right of possession thereof.

This is a case of first impression in Texas. If the money constitutes treasure trove the decision of the Court of Civil Appeals is correct and in accordance with the decided cases from other jurisdictions. However, we have decided not to recognize the "treasure trove" doctrine as the law in Texas, but that this case should be governed by the rules of law applicable to lost and mislaid property. There is no statutory law in Texas regarding the disposition of such property, or provisions defining the respective rights of various claimants. The rule of treasure trove is of ancient origin and arose by virtue of the concealment in the ground and other hiding places of coin, bullion, and plate of the Roman conquerors when they were driven from the British Isles. These Romans expected to return at a later date and reclaim their buried and hidden treasures. For a time laws were in effect which gave all this treasure trove which might be discovered to the sovereign, but it was later held to belong to the finder, and this regardless of whether he was in ownership or possession of the land where the treasure was found. The doctrine only applied to "money or coin, gold, silver, plate, or bullion found hidden in the earth or other private places, the owner thereof being unknown." Such doctrine has never been officially recognized in Texas, although it has been recognized and applied under the common law in many states of the American Union. We can see no good reason at the present time and under present conditions in our nation, to adopt such a doctrine. Therefore, we treat the money involved herein as no different from other personal property and will adjudicate the possession thereof in accordance with the rules governing personal property generally. . . .

Lost property may be retained by the finder as against the owner or possessor of the premises where it is found.

On the other hand, "mislaid property is to be distinguished from lost property in that the former is property which the owner intentionally places where he can again resort to it, and then forgets. Mislaid property is presumed to be left in custody of the owner or occupier of the premises upon which it is found, and it is generally held that the right of possession to mislaid property as against all except the owner is in the owner or occupant of such premises."

The facts of this case show that the bills were carefully placed in the jar and then buried in the ground and further show that the owner did not part with them inadvertently, involuntarily, carelessly or through neglect. Rather it shows a deliberate, conscious and voluntary act of the owner desiring to hide his money in a place where he thought it was safe and secure, and with the intention of returning to claim it at some future date. All the evidence indicates that the money must have been buried in the garage after the garage had been built. That was only a scant four years prior to the finding of the money. . . .

The facts in this case show, as a matter of law, that the property is not to be classed in the category of lost property. Conceivably, there may be cases in which the issue as to whether the property is lost or mislaid property would be for determination by a jury under appropriate instructions by the court. The trial judge submitted the matter to a jury in the present case. There were no objections raised by either party to the definitions of "lost" and "mislaid" property as contained in the charge. The jury upon consideration of all the facts found that the property was mislaid rather than lost property.

Property which is found embedded in the soil under circumstances repelling the idea that it has been lost is held to have the characteristics of mislaid property. The finder acquires no rights thereto, for the presumption is that possession of the article found is in the owner and, accordingly, it is held that the right to possession of such property is in the landowner. . . .

[Plaintiff] relies strongly upon the case of *Danielson* v. *Roberts* to sustain his right to recover the money from [defendant]. In that case the money was found in an old rusty half-gallon tin can containing a number of musty and partially deteriorated tobacco sacks. This demonstrated the money had been buried for some considerable period of time, and the court said: "The circumstances under which it was discovered, the condition of the vessel in which it was contained, and the place of deposit (in an old hen house) . . . all tend . . . to indicate that it had been buried for some considerable time, and that the owner was probably dead or unknown." In all the other cases relied upon by [plaintiff] the property was held to be either lost property or treasure trove, and belonged to the finder. That is recognized as the correct rule of law in such cases, but we have held, under the facts of this case, the property herein not to be lost property, but to be mislaid property, and the well recognized rules of law award the possession to the owner of the premises upon which the property is found. This being mislaid property, the right to possession thereof is in the owner of the premises where it was found.

The judgment of the Court of Civil Appeals is reversed and the judgment of the trial court is affirmed.

Justice Calvert (concurring)

I can agree to the judgment rendered herein but there is much in the majority opinion to which I cannot agree. I suggest that in an effort to simplify the law of found property, as applied in other common law jurisdictions, by declining to approve and adopt the law of "treasure trove" in this state, the majority opinion has only succeeded in confusing it.

The majority opinion declares, as a matter of law, that the property involved in this case is not to be classed as "lost" property because the facts show conclusively it was not "involuntarily parted with through neglect, carelessness or inadvertence." It then declares the property to be "mislaid property."

In none of the cases analyzed did the courts treat the property involved as mislaid property. In no case cited to this court or found by us has it been held that property found imbedded in the soil fell in the category of mislaid property, or had the characteristics of mislaid property.

The majority opinion fails to recognize a fourth category of found property . . . that is, the category of personal property found imbedded in the soil. The majority opinion has adopted the rule applicable to this category of property but has defined it as mislaid property. There is no need for this departure from the common-law rules. The rule as stated in American Jurisprudence is as follows: "Where property, not treasure trove, is found imbedded in the soil under circumstances repelling the idea that it has been lost, the finder acquires no title thereto. . . ." All we need do in order to achieve our objective of rejecting the law of treasure trove is to eliminate from the foregoing rule the words "not treasure trove," thus adopting the rule that all personal property or chattels found imbedded in the soil under circumstances repelling the idea that it has been lost will be held to be rightfully in the possession of the owner of the soil as against all the world except the true owner.

If we are to disavow the doctrine of treasure trove—and I doubt the wisdom of doing so—I would not undertake to narrow the classifications of found property to "lost" and "mislaid" property. I certainly would not hold that the classification of property found imbedded in the soil was a jury question, and I would not hold that the length of the period for which it had been buried had any effect in determining whether it was lost or mislaid property. I would simply hold that all property found imbedded in the soil, including that known as treasure trove in England and other jurisdictions, was, as a matter of law, to be held in the possession of the landowner as bailee or trustee for the true owner.

Questions

1. In *Schley* v. *Couch,* the court cited the case of *Danielson* v. *Roberts* in which some boys found money buried in the soil beneath a henhouse. The court awarded the money to the boys. How did the majority opinion in *Schley* rationalize the *Danielson* case with the rule they accepted as law in *Schley*?
2. The concurring opinion in *Schley* suggests three types of property that can be found and, therefore, three rules as to who gets possession of the found property. What are the three types of property? The three rules?
3. In *Erickson* v. *Sinykin,* 223 Minn. 232, the court approved the trial court's finding that money discovered under a hotel room carpet had been "abandoned," though the only evidence of abandonment was the likelihood, in view of its age, that the money had been undisturbed for over 15 years. Why label it "abandoned"? Who would get the money under the regular rules of misplaced or lost property?

CONCLUSION

One of the fundamental principles of a free society is the concept of private property. Inherent in this concept is the right of the owner, protected by legal mechanisms, to maintain an exclusive use and enjoyment of the property. However, the rights of private property have evolved to meet the changing social and economic needs of society.

At the outset, property rights were a tool of economic and geographical expansions; hence, an absolute freedom of property rights was the policy of the day. The importance of property rights in America can be observed in the Constitution. The Fifth Amendment provides that "No person shall be . . . deprived of life, liberty, or property, without due process of law." As with life and liberty, property was granted the constitutional guarantee of "due process of law." However, property rights must sometimes yield to other constitutional guarantees, such as the right to free speech.

As the opportunities for further expansion were reduced and conditions became more crowded, government became concerned for the welfare of society and initiated regulations of private property. Absolute freedoms in the use of private property were reduced to "reasonable use." Waste in resources was restrained by laws providing for proper use of resources. Concern for the environment has further restricted private property rights. The government, through legislation and the courts, seeks to balance the sometimes conflicting interest of private property rights with other interests of social welfare. Nevertheless, the rights of private property remain as the essential foundation of the economic and political system of America.

CASE PROBLEMS

1. The community of Youngtown was founded in 1954, just off Grand Avenue, about 14 or 15 miles west of Phoenix. Farming operations had been conducted in the area since 1911, and Spur started a feedlot about 2½ miles south of Youngtown in 1956. By 1959 there were 25 cattle feeding or dairy operations in the area. In 1959 Del Webb began planning the development of a large retirement community, Sun City, south of Grand Avenue and directly east of Youngtown. One year later, 450 homes were completed or under construction. The units just south of Grand Avenue sold well, but sales resistance increased as the location of the homes got closer and closer to the feedlots. By 1962 Spur expanded its operation from 35 to 114 acres. By 1963 Del Webb found it impossible to sell any homes in the southwestern portion of Sun City. By 1967 the properties were within 500 feet of each other at one point, and Spur was feeding between 20,000 and 30,000 head of cattle on its lots, producing over a million pounds of wet manure per day. Del Webb sued to enjoin Spur as a public nuisance, due to the flies and odor. Decide.

2. Richard Cook purchased 62 acres of farmland from Otto Beermann. When Cook inspected the property he observed an irrigation well complete with pump and motor. The pump was positioned in the well. The motor, which was supplied with fuel by an underground natural gas line running from the house, was bolted to a concrete pad directly adjacent to the well. The irrigation pipe and sprinkler system were unassembled and stacked behind the

house. Cook informed Beermann that he would have no use for the pipe or sprinkler system.

The sales agreement, signed by the purchaser, provided that the sale included "all fixtures and equipment permanently attached to said premises." The space provided for listing personal property included in the sale was left blank. Also in the agreement was a typewritten provision that had been added to the printed form, which stated, "The irrigation equipment is not included in this sale."

Before the purchasers took possession of the property, Beermann notified them that the pump and motor did not go with the real estate. The purchasers disagreed, claiming that the exclusion of "irrigation equipment" referred only to the pipe and sprinkler system, not to the pump and motor. Beermann sold the pump and motor to a third party. Cook sued Beermann for the value of the pump and motor. Decide.

3. Laczko was an employee under contract to BBF Group. The contract required him to turn over to BBF the title to and all supporting documents concerning any improvements on certain plastic molding devices he developed while working for BBF. Laczko developed certain improvements while in BBF's employ, and during that time he also organized the defendant company, Kontrols, Inc. Laczko quit BBF and marketed the improvements through this new company. BBF sued Laczko and Kontrols, Inc. for misappropriating trade secrets. Decide.

4. The plaintiff, Bernice Paset, a safety deposit box subscriber at the Old Orchard Bank found $6,325 on the seat of a chair in an examination booth in the safety deposit vault. The chair was partially under a table. The plaintiff notified officers of the bank and turned the money over to them. She was told by bank officials that the bank would try to locate the owner, and that she could have the money if the owner was not located within one year.

   The bank contacted everyone who had been in the safety deposit vault area either on the day of, or on the day preceding, the discovery. No one reported the loss of currency, and the money remained unclaimed a year after it had been found. However, when the plaintiff requested the money, the bank refused to deliver it to her, explaining that it was obligated to hold the currency for the owner. Decide.

END NOTES

1. Jeremy Bentham, *Theory of Legislation Principles of the Civil Code,* Part I, 113, Dumont, ed.; Hildreth, trans. (London: Trübner, 1864).
2. Walter Lippman, *The Method of Freedom* (New York: Macmillan Co., 1934), p. 102.

chapter 7

BUSINESS TRANSACTIONS: CONTRACTS

When the feudal practice of self-sufficiency began to decline and society proceeded to develop the rudimentary economic concepts of division of labor, specialization, and exchange of surpluses, there developed also the need to safeguard the exchange process. As the new capitalistic system developed, so the common law traditions transformed the "contract" from elementary judicial concepts into a practical tool of merchants for protecting their bargains. In effect, the contract brought rationality and order to the exchange process by court enforcement of merchants' promises. The contract concept requires that the reasonable expectations arising from promises receive protection of law. With such knowledge, most merchants will carry out their bargains as promised, and those who breach promises are ordered by the courts to compensate the aggrieved party.

It is no accident that the contract concept is especially adaptable to the free enterprise system. The contract is the inevitable counterpart of free enterprise. The legal system, responsive to society's needs, modified the contract to accommodate the business community. Since the courts could not anticipate every type of business transaction required by merchants, the courts, by delegation of authority to individuals, permitted the parties to draw up their own set of rules and embody them in their agreements. Merchants, therefore, are free to contract as the business situation dictates, and this freedom of contract, as accorded by the courts, is an integral part of the *free enterprise* system. Indeed, much of the legal history of contracts reflects the concepts of free enterprise. Rugged individualism is mirrored in the rule that the party must protect himself or herself in the bargaining over contract terms. It is not the court's duty to protect the individual from foolish bargains. Moreover, the business community coupled with court enforcement of contracts was theorized as being efficiently regulated by competition without necessity of further governmental involvement. Therefore, *laissez-faire* flourished as the concept explaining the role of government in the free enterprise system. Indeed, free enterprise, as we know it, is inseparable from the contract concept.

Early American contract law reflected society's concern for individual freedom of decision. The fundamental natural rights expounded by our ancestors included the right to freely and voluntarily enter into contracts. The Constitution included a contract clause that prohibited state governments from impairing the obligations of contracts. They sought to prevent local governments from interfering with the individual in the exercise of free will. However, since natural justice meant living up to the bargain, it became the positive duty of courts to maintain and enforce contracts. Together with the rights of private property, the freedom to contract has formed the basis of the free enterprise system, which developed the natural resources of the American continent.

Contract law expanded during the Industrial Revolution. To facilitate commercial dealings, judges fashioned new relationships and new rules. The freedoms of contract law and the evolutionary qualities of the legal system provided the business community with the legal instruments needed to foster the expansion of the industrial society.

However, with the coming of the twentieth century and the concentration of wealth and power in large economic units, contracts with freely negotiated terms were often replaced by the contract that offered a take-it-or-leave-it bargain. Consequently, the attitudes of the courts began to change. Judges sometimes refused to enforce contracts which they considered unequal or unfair bargains. The social unrest and change in this century resulted in the belief that society should provide fairer standards of work and living for its citizens. The more recent aspects of "social justice" have caused contracts to be "regulated" on the basis of reasonableness and judged on the basis of equality of bargaining power. In short, government regulation of contractual terms has flourished in this modern era, obviously reducing the freedoms of contract law.

CONTRACT ESSENTIALS

Today, to accommodate the business community, the ceremony necessary to create a contract must be reduced to the absolute minimum. As such, the bargains can be made quickly and performed with efficiency. The legal requirements to form a contract are as follows:

1. A genuine agreement (normally, an offer and acceptance).
2. Consideration (mutuality of legal inducement).

3. Legal capacity or competency of the parties.
4. Lawful purpose (i.e., not declared illegal by statute or judicial decision).

OFFER AND ACCEPTANCE

Trimount v. Chittenden Trust
379 A. 2d 1266 (1977)
Supreme Court of New Hampshire

This case concerns the existence of contracts to refinance the business of a third party allegedly created through the exchange of correspondence among the parties.

All three parties in this case were creditors of Paquette Paving, Inc. In March 1972, Paquette owed the plaintiff (Trimount) nearly $30,000 for materials purchased on credit for its business operations and a much larger sum to the bank. Munson first became a creditor when it advanced money to Paquette, which at the time was a subcontractor on a Munson job. Munson thereafter made further advances. In order to avoid bankruptcy, Paquette entered into negotiations with its creditors. Plaintiff characterizes these negotiations as having culminated in a moratorium agreement, which its letter of April 12, 1972, to Paquette accepted. The letter reads:

> This is to certify that there is a balance of $29,924.41 due us from [Paquette] and we agree to forego immediate legal action on the basis that you make prompt evidence to us of bank financing.
>
> If the financing discloses an indication that you will be in a position to carryon [sic] a profitable business we will agree to accept payment of the $29,924.41 balance on the basis of 20% each year over a five year period starting October 15, 1972. This arrangement to be guaranteed by a 6% interest bearing note.

Chittenden's letter to Trimount was dated May 11, 1972. It reads:

> Please be advised that satisfactory refinancing of the existing loans of the . . . [Paquette Paving] corporation to this Bank have been arranged over four and five-year terms. It is our understanding that additional financial assistance has also been obtained from the Munson Earth Moving Corporation.
>
> I trust the above information will be helpful to you.

Munson's letter to Trimount on May 18, 1972, "confirmed" that adequate financing would be provided:

> It is our pleasure to confirm that adequate financing for the Paquette Paving, Inc., of Ashland, New Hampshire, will be provided by this Corporation and from the Chittenden Trust Company of Burlington, Vermont, from whom a letter of confirmation may also be obtained.
>
> This financing will be adequate to satisfy whatever requirements are necessary to maintain the business in a healthy condition for whatever time period shall be necessary, initially set for a five year period.

Your cooperation has been generous and is recognized by this firm. It is cooperation like yours that will help pull these men through.

Both defendants [Chittenden Trust and Munson] did in fact extend further financing to Paquette, and Munson obtained a controlling interest in Paquette for security. However, it never utilized the power that interest provided to assume actual control of Paquette's operations. Until late summer of 1974, Paquette made regular payments on all current accounts of Trimount and reduced the old account to $11,955. Then Paquette requested additional credit from Chittenden, which was granted only after Munson agreed to guarantee Paquette's indebtedness. Paquette failed to make payments and Chittenden called in Munson's note. Without notifying the other creditors, Munson in turn exercised its control to take over Paquette and forced it into bankruptcy.

Immediately before its default, Paquette completed a job in Laconia for which it purchased $13,915 of materials from Trimount on credit. At the time of bankruptcy, Paquette owed Trimount $25,871.19 on all its outstanding accounts.

The problems of offer and acceptance have long ceased to be the sole cutting edge of contract law. The principles for interpreting a course of negotiations are relatively well settled. Plaintiff's first contention is that its letter of April 12 constituted an acceptance of a prior moratorium agreement, thus creating binding obligations, similar to those arising in business subscriptions between itself and any parties theretofore committed. Admittedly, a binding contract does arise from a parol (oral) agreement unless the parties did not intend to be bound until the agreement was reduced to writing. Nonetheless, we cannot know from the record whether a contract did in fact result from the course of negotiations among the parties before the April 12 letter or if its terms were sufficiently definite to enforce. Since the party claiming to rely on the preliminary oral contract has not borne its burden of proving it, the master correctly refused to find such a contract.

If the alleged contracts that form the substance of this litigation arose at all, they must have been created expressly through the exchange of letters themselves or impliedly by the conduct of the parties from which a mutual understanding can be inferred. Trimount's April 12 letter is susceptible to interpretation as an offer. It promises to refrain from legal action against Paquette if the latter can obtain financing sufficient to conduct a profitable business and agrees to pay its outstanding debt according to a stated schedule. By accepting this offer in a later letter, Paquette's rights and obligations were sufficiently well defined to enable a court to determine performance and measure damages. But the offer is addressed only to Paquette and there is no indication that Chittenden or Munson ever received copies. Only the offeree can accept an offer. Nevertheless, the preliminary discussions among the parties indicate that the defendants either requested or at least expected that such an offer would be made. Even if they did not have actual knowledge of this specific offer, they must have known that Trimount was extending credit to Paquette and refraining from suing because of their promises. "Preliminary actions and communications, even though not in themselves legally operative as an offer . . . may nevertheless be highly important in determining whether a contract has subsequently been consummated and what are its terms." Hence, we find Trimount's letter to be an offer or sufficient evidence of an offer.

The bank advised Trimount that it had satisfactorily refinanced Paquette's loans. Whether this was an acceptance of Trimount's offer or a counteroffer which Trimount then accepted by its subsequent performance need not be belabored. In any event, the bank bound itself to no more than providing satisfactory refinancing. Its letter indicates that it had executed its promise. Its later extension of credit was not part of the agreement and had to be secured by Munson before granted. We agree . . . that the bank fully performed its contract.

Munson's letter was more detailed. It agreed to provide financing for whatever requirements are necessary for at least five years. Again, we need not worry about the status of this letter as acceptance or counteroffer. The parties obviously intended to enter into a contract; they have behaved as though they were so bound. This court will not rely on overly technical legal logic to defeat the intentions of the parties, but will attempt to interpret the ambiguities of the agreement to conform to those intentions.

Plaintiff relies heavily on the terms "whatever requirements" and "healthy condition." It claims that Munson never placed Paquette in a healthy position or that because Paquette was forced into bankruptcy, Munson did not provide adequate financing. The record refutes the first contention as a matter of fact. Partially as a result of Munson's financing, Paquette was able to operate on at least a break-even level for two years. During that time, it substantially reduced its outstanding debt to Trimount and remained current on all its new accounts with the plaintiff. The evidence indicates that Paquette's ultimate demise resulted from gross mismanagement by its president, over whom Munson did not in fact exercise control and not from inadequate financing.

Our final inquiry confronts us with the meaning of the phrase "whatever requirements." The plaintiff argues that even if Paquette were put in a healthy condition, Munson obligated itself to do more. However, this reads the letter too liberally. Munson agreed to provide whatever financing was necessary for the business. Had Paquette's president not diverted a substantial segment of its funds from the company's concerns, it might well have survived. We do not read more into the letter than a good faith effort to maintain the business as a going concern. Munson made that effort. It is a relatively small company with an annual gross of $1,500,000; yet it provided credit and guaranteed loans of over $650,000 for Paquette during a three-year period. This shows a substantial commitment by Munson.

Because we hold there is no liability on the contracts, we need not consider plaintiff's remaining contentions.

Questions

1. May a binding contract be formed by an oral agreement without being committed to writing?

2. Can a contract be implied from the conduct of the parties?
3. Can the exchange of letters result in a contract? Was the letter of April 12 an offer? To whom? Who can accept the offer?
4. Was either letter from Chittenden Trust or Munson to Trimount an acceptance of the April 12 letter? Or was it a counteroffer? If a counteroffer, did Trimount accept? How?
5. Was there a contract in *Trimount*? If so, what were its terms? Had Chittenden Trust and Munson adequately performed?

OBJECTIVE INTENT

Lucy v. Zehmer
84 S.E. 2d 516 (1954)
Supreme Court of Appeals of Virginia

This suit was instituted by W. O. Lucy and J. C. Lucy, against A. H. Zehmer and Ida S. Zehmer, his wife, defendants, to have specific performance of a contract by which it was alleged the Zehmers had sold to W. O. Lucy a tract of land known as the Ferguson farm, for $50,000. . . .

The instrument sought to be enforced was written by A. H. Zehmer on December 20, 1952, in these words: "We hereby agree to sell to W. O. Lucy the Ferguson Farm complete for $50,000, title satisfactory to buyer," and signed by the defendants, A. H. Zehmer and Ida S. Zehmer.

A. H. Zehmer admitted that at the time mentioned W. O. Lucy offered him $50,000 cash for the farm, but that he, Zehmer, considered that the offer was made in jest; that so thinking . . . he wrote out "the memorandum" quoted above and induced his wife to sign it; that he did not deliver the memorandum to Lucy, but that Lucy picked it up, read it, put it in his pocket, attempted to offer Zehmer $5 to bind the bargain, which Zehmer refused to accept, and realizing for the first time that Lucy was serious, Zehmer assured him that he had no intention of selling the farm and that the whole matter was a joke. Lucy left the premises insisting that he had purchased the farm. . . .

The defendants insist that the evidence was ample to support their contention that the writing sought to be enforced was prepared as a bluff or dare to force Lucy to admit that he did not have $50,000; that the whole matter was a joke; that the writing was not delivered to Lucy and no binding contract was ever made between the parties.

It is an unusual, if not bizarre, defense. When made to the writing admittedly prepared by one of the defendants and signed by both, clear evidence is required to sustain it. . . .

If it be assumed, contrary to what we think the evidence shows, that Zehmer was jesting about selling his farm to Lucy and that the transaction was intended by him to be a joke, nevertheless the evidence shows that Lucy did not so understand it but considered it to be a serious business transaction and the contract to be binding on the Zehmers as well as on himself. The very next day he arranged with his brother to put up half the money and take a half interest in the land. The day after that he employed an attorney to examine the title. The next night, Tuesday, he was back at Zehmer's place and there Zehmer told him for the first time, Lucy said, that he wasn't going to sell and he told Zehmer, "You know you sold that place fair and square." After receiving the report from his attorney that the title was good he wrote to Zehmer that he was ready to close the deal.

Not only did Lucy actually believe, but the evidence shows he was warranted in believing, that the contract represented a serious business transaction and a good faith sale and purchase of the farm.

In the field of contracts, as generally elsewhere, "We must look to the outward expression of a person as manifesting his intention rather than to his secret and unexpressed intention. 'The law imputes to a person an intention corresponding to the reasonable meaning of his words and acts.'"

At no time prior to the execution of the contract had Zehmer indicated to Lucy by word or act that he was not in earnest about selling the farm. They had argued about it and discussed its terms, as Zehmer admitted, for a long time. Lucy testified that if there was any jesting it was about paying $50,000 that night. The contract and the evidence show that he was not expected to pay the money that night. Zehmer said that after the writing was signed he laid it down on the counter in front of Lucy. Lucy said Zehmer handed it to him. In any event there had been what appeared to be a good faith offer and a good faith acceptance, followed by the execution and apparent delivery of a written contract. Both said that Lucy put the writing in his pocket and then offered Zehmer $5 to seal the bargain. Not until then, even under the defendants' evidence, was anything said or done to indicate that the matter was a joke. Both of the Zehmers testified that when Zehmer asked his wife to sign he whispered that it was a joke so Lucy wouldn't hear and that it was not intended that he should hear.

The mental assent of the parties is not requisite for the formation of a contract. If the words or other acts of one of the parties have but one reasonable meaning, his undisclosed intention is immaterial except when an unreasonable meaning which he attaches to his manifestations is known to the other party. . . .

An agreement or mutual assent is of course essential to a valid contract but the law imputes to a person an intention corresponding to the reasonable meaning of his words, and acts. If his words and acts, judged by a reasonable standard, manifest an intention to agree, it is immaterial what may be the real but unexpressed state of his mind.

So a person cannot set up that he was merely jesting when his conduct and words could warrant a reasonable person in believing that he intended a real agreement.

Whether the writing signed by the defendants and now sought to be enforced by the complainants was the result of a serious offer by Lucy and a serious acceptance by the defendants, or was a serious offer by Lucy and an acceptance in secret jest by the defendants, in either event it constituted a binding contract of sale between the parties.

The [plaintiffs] are entitled to have specific performance of the contract.

Questions

1. What is meant by "objective intent" to form a contract? Can you contrast it with "subjective intent?" Which intent is relevant for determination of serious intent to contract?
2. The usual remedy for breach of contract is a money payment to compensate for any damages caused by the breach. However, if the remedy of money payment is inadequate to accomplish justice, the courts will decree "specific performance" (that is, order the party who breached to specifically perform as he or she promised). Historically, the money-payment (or "damages") remedy has been generally held inadequate when there is failure to deliver a "unique" performance. Thus, if a seller refused to deliver his antique 1918 Ford that he had contracted to sell, the court would order its delivery since a money-payment remedy would be inadequate to compensate the injured buyer. Had the Ford been a modern and a more readily available model, the specific performance remedy would be denied and the buyer's remedy would have to be "damages" (the *extra* amount of money over the contract price necessary to buy the modern Ford elsewhere). In *Lucy* why was the court willing to grant the remedy of specific performance?
3. A contract is formed and based upon a "meeting of minds" or agreement by the parties. Sometimes there are disputes as to whether an "offer" had been extended or whether the communication was merely an *invitation* to another to enter into negotiations.

> The commonest example of offers meant to open negotiations and to call forth offers in the technical sense are advertisements, circulars and trade letters sent out by business houses. While it is possible that the offers made by such means may be in such form as to become contracts, they are often merely expressions of a willingness to negotiate.
>
> Business advertisements published in newspapers and circulars sent out by mail or distributed by hand stating that the advertiser has a certain quantity or quality of goods which he wants to dispose of at certain prices, are not offers which may become contracts as soon as any person to whose notice they may come signifies his acceptance by notifying the other that he will take a certain quantity of them. They are merely invitations to all persons who may read them that the advertiser is ready to receive offers for the goods at the price stated. *Craft* v. *Elder & Johnson Co.,* 38 N.E. 2d 416 (1941).

Can you think of any reason why an advertisement should not be held to be an "offer"? What if you advertise your auto in the newspaper and four people arrive and accept your advertised "offer." Are you now in breach of three contracts?

MUTUAL MISTAKE

Oswald v. Allen
417 F. 2d 43 (1969)
United States Court of Appeals (2d Cir.)

Dr. Oswald, a coin collector from Switzerland, was interested in Mrs. Allen's collection of Swiss coins. In April of 1964 Dr. Oswald was in the United States and arranged to see Mrs. Allen's coins. The parties drove to the Newburgh Savings Bank of Newburgh, New York, where two of her collections referred to as the Swiss Coin Collection and the Rarity Coin Collection were located in separate vault boxes. After examining and taking notes on the coins in the Swiss Coin Collection, Dr. Oswald was shown several valuable Swiss coins from the Rarity Coin Collection. He also took notes on these coins and later testified that he did not know that they were in a separate "collection." The evidence showed that each collection had a different key number and was housed in labeled cigar boxes.

On the return to New York City, Dr. Oswald sat in the front seat of the car while Mrs. Allen sat in the back with Dr. Oswald's brother, Mr. Victor Oswald, and Mr. Cantarella of the Chase Manhattan Bank's Money Museum, who had helped arrange the meeting and served as Dr. Oswald's agent. Dr. Oswald could speak practically no English and so depended on his brother to conduct the transaction. After some negotiation a price of $50,000 was agreed upon. Apparently the parties never realized that the references to "Swiss coins" and "Swiss Coin Collection" were ambiguous. The trial judge found that Dr. Oswald thought the offer he had authorized his brother to make was for all of the Swiss coins, while Mrs. Allen thought she was selling only the Swiss Coin Collection and not the Swiss coins in the Rarity Coin Collection. . . .

Appellant attacks the conclusion of the Court below that a contract did not exist since the minds of the parties had not met. The opinion below states:

> . . . plaintiff believed that he had offered to buy all Swiss coins owned by the defendant while the defendant reasonably understood the offer which she accepted to relate to those of her Swiss coins as had been segregated in the particular collection denominated by her as the 'Swiss Coin Collection.'

The trial judge based his decision upon his evaluation of the credibility of the witnesses, the records of the defendant, the values of the coins involved, the circumstances of the transaction and the reasonable probabilities. Such findings of fact are not to be set aside unless "clearly erroneous." There was ample evidence upon which the trial judge could rely in reaching this decision.

In such a factual situation the law is settled that no contract exists. The Restatement of Contracts in section 71(a) adopts the rule of *Raffles* v. *Wichelhaus*, 159 Eng. Rep. 375 (Ex. 1864). Professor Young states that rule as follows:

> When any of the terms used to express an agreement is ambivalent, and the parties understand it in different ways, there cannot be a contract unless one of them should

have been aware of the other's understanding. Young, "Equivocation in Agreements," 64 *Colum. L. Rev.* 619, 621 (1964).

Even though the mental assent of the parties is not requisite for the formation of a contract, the facts found by the trial judge clearly place this case within the small group of exceptional cases in which there is "no sensible basis for choosing between conflicting understandings." The rule of *Raffles* v. *Wichelhaus* is applicable here.

Questions

1. Generally, for a contract to be rescindable for a mistake, the mutual mistake of the parties must go "to the whole substance of the agreement." What determines whether a mistake goes to the "substance" of the contract? There are generally two types of mutual mistakes which involve "the whole substance of the agreement." First, as in *Oswald,* each party was thinking, and reasonably so, of different subject matters (the Swiss Coin Collection, versus *all* Swiss coins). This kind of mutual mistake involves the identification of differing subject matters by each party and goes to the entire "substance of the agreement." The second kind of mutual mistake is illustrated by the case of the "barren cow." The buyer and the seller had made a contract for the sale of a barren cow, both thinking she was incapable of breeding. Later, the seller refused to deliver the cow for the $80 purchase price because she was with calf. The court ruled as follows:

   > the mistake or misapprehension of the parties went to the whole substance of the agreement. If the cow was a breeder, she was worth at least $750; if barren, she was worth not over $80. The parties would not have made the contract of sale except upon the understanding and belief that she was incapable of breeding, and of no use as a cow. It is true she is now the identical animal that they thought her to be when the contract was made; there is no mistake as to the identity of the creature. Yet the mistake was not of the mere quality of the animal, but went to the very nature of the thing. A barren cow is substantially a different creature than a breeding one. . . . If the mutual mistake had simply related to the fact whether she was with calf or not for one season, then it might have been a good sale, but the mistake affected the character of the animal for all time, and for its present and ultimate use. She was not in fact the animal, or the kind of animal, the defendants intended to sell or the plaintiff to buy. She was not a barren cow, and, if this fact had been known, there would have been no contract. The mistake affected the substance of the whole consideration, and it must be considered that there was no contract to sell . . . the cow as she actually was. The thing sold and bought had in fact no existence. *Sherwood* v. *Walker,* 66 Mich. 568 (1887).

   This kind of mutual mistake is usually referred to as a mistake as to the existence of the subject matter.
2. The cases make a distinction between a statement of fact and a statement of opinion. A misstatement of fact may be grounds for rescission of the

contract, whereas an honest statement of opinion may not. If A expresses an opinion in order to induce B to enter into a bargain and B relies on that statement of opinion in deciding to enter into the contract, why should B not be allowed to rescind if it is proven that A was mistaken?

3. It is important to note that the duty of the court is to enforce the contract or bargain of the parties and not to rewrite the contract. The concept of freedom to contract, in effect, includes the right to make foolish as well as sharp bargains. The court's duty is not to protect every fool. If actual fraud or duress is perpetrated on one of the parties, the court will afford a remedy just as in the case of mutual mistakes. But, otherwise, the court enforces contracts as drawn by the parties. What advice do these rules provide for the negotiator of contractual terms?

CONSIDERATION

Contract law is commonly supposed to exist for the enforcement of promises. But not all promises are to receive legal enforcement. Friends who fail to show up for a promised engagement are not subject to legal suits for damages. Nor is a promise to make a gift enforceable. The question naturally arises, how do you determine which promises are legally enforceable? The courts have drawn certain lines and limitations that are largely the product of English and American history. Other countries have other methods to determine which promises are enforceable. But in the United States, the test of legally enforceable promises is the doctrine of "consideration." The idea of consideration is the idea of a bargain. The promise given is conditioned on the receiving of an agreed exchange. The promisor is to receive a benefit in exchange for his or her promise or the promisee is to experience some detriment at the promisor's request. Having received what he or she bargained for, the promisor is now held to that promise. But failure to receive consideration means the promisor need not keep the promise. Nevertheless, the application of the doctrine of consideration in particular situations is not always easy, as the following cases illustrate.

Hamer v. Sidway

27 N.E. 256 (1891)
Court of Appeals of New York

[William E. Story promised to pay $5,000 to his nephew, William E. Story, 2d, if he would "refrain from drinking liquor, using tobacco, swearing, or playing cards or billiards for money until he should become 21 years of age." The nephew refrained from this conduct until his 21st birthday and now is suing on the contract for the $5,000 payment. The uncle's executor denies the existence of a contract, citing the absence of consideration because the uncle received no benefit from the bargain.]

The exchequer chamber in 1875 defined "consideration" as follows: "A valuable consideration, in the sense of the law, may consist either in some right, interest, profit, or benefit accruing to the one party, or some forbearance, detriment, loss, or responsibility given, suffered, or undertaken by the other." Courts "will not ask whether the thing which forms the consideration does in fact benefit the promisee or a third party, or is of any substantial value to any one. It is enough that something is promised, done, forborne, or suffered by the party to whom the promise is made as consideration for the promise made to him." Anson, Cont. 63. "In general a waiver of any legal right at the request of another party is a sufficient consideration for a promise." Pars. Cont. *444. Pollock in his work on Contracts . . . says: " 'Consideration' means not so much that one party is profiting as that the other abandons some legal right in the present, or limits his legal freedom of action in the future, as an inducement for the promise of the first." Now, applying this rule to the facts before us, the promisee used tobacco occasionally, drank liquor, and he had a legal right to do so. That right he abandoned for a period of years upon the strength of the promise of the testator that for such forbearance he would give him $5,000. We need not speculate on the effort which may have been required to give up the use of those stimulants. It is sufficient that he restricted this lawful freedom of action within certain prescribed limits upon the faith of his uncle's agreement, and now, having fully performed the conditions imposed, it is of no moment whether such performance actually proved a benefit to the promisor, and the court will not inquire into it; but, were it a proper subject of inquiry, we see nothing in this record that would permit a determination that the uncle was not benefited in a legal sense. Few cases have been found which may be said to be precisely in point, but such as have been, support the position we have taken.

Questions

1. Would the result in *Hamer* have been different if the uncle had merely promised to pay his nephew $5,000 on his 21st birthday? How is this promise different from the promise made in *Hamer*?
2. To be consistent with the concept of freedom to contract, should the court determine if the value of the two considerations are approximately equal (that is, a fair bargain)? Or should the court not inquire whether the consideration is adequate as long as the court finds some consideration from each side?

Laclede Gas Company v. Amoco Oil Company

522 F. 2d 33 (1975)
U.S. Court of Appeals (8th Cir.)

On September 21, 1970, Midwest Missouri Gas Company (now Laclede), and American Oil Company (now Amoco), the predecessors of the parties to this litigation, entered into a written agreement which was designed to provide central propane gas distribution systems to various residential developments in

Jefferson County, Missouri, until such time as natural gas mains were extended into these areas. The agreement contemplated that as individual developments were planned the owners or developers would apply to Laclede for central propane gas systems. If Laclede determined that such a system was appropriate in any given development, it could request Amoco to supply the propane to that specific development. This request was made in the form of a supplemental form letter, as provided in the September 21 agreement; and if Amoco decided to supply the propane, it bound itself to do so by signing this supplemental form.

Once this supplemental form was signed the agreement placed certain duties on both Laclede and Amoco. Basically, Amoco was to "[i]nstall, own, maintain and operate . . . storage and vaporization facilities and any other facilities necessary to provide [it] with the capability of delivering to [Laclede] commercial propane gas suitable . . . for delivery by [Laclede] to its customers' facilities." Amoco's facilities were to be "adequate to provide a continuous supply of commercial propane gas at such times and in volumes commensurate with [Laclede's] requirements for meeting the demands reasonably to be anticipated in each Development while this Agreement is in force." Amoco was deemed to be "the supplier," while Laclede was "the distributing utility."

Since it was contemplated that the individual propane systems would eventually be converted to natural gas, one paragraph of the agreement provided that Laclede should give Amoco 30 days written notice of this event, after which the agreement would no longer be binding for the converted development.

Another paragraph gave Laclede the right to cancel the agreement. However, this right was expressed in the following language:

> This Agreement shall remain in effect for one (1) year following the first delivery of gas by [Amoco] to [Laclede] hereunder. Subject to termination as provided in Paragraph 11 hereof [dealing with conversions to natural gas], this Agreement shall automatically continue in effect for additional periods of one (1) year each unless [Laclede] shall, not less than 30 days prior to the expiration of the initial one (1) year period or any subsequent one (1) year period, give [Amoco] written notice of termination.

There was no provision under which Amoco could cancel the agreement.

A bilateral contract is not rendered invalid and unenforceable merely because one party has the right to cancellation while the other does not. There is no necessity "that for each stipulation in a contract binding the one party there must be a corresponding stipulation binding the other."

The important question in the instant case is whether Laclede's right of cancellation rendered all its other promises in the agreement illusory so that there was a complete *failure* of consideration. This would be the result had Laclede retained the right of immediate cancellation at any time for any reason. Professor Corbin agrees and states simply that when one party has the power to cancel by notice given for some stated period of time, "the contract should never be held to be rendered invalid thereby for lack of consideration." The law of Missouri appears to be in conformity with this general contract rule that a cancellation clause will invalidate a contract only if its exercise is *unrestricted*.

Here Laclede's right to terminate was neither arbitrary nor unrestricted. It was limited by the agreement in at least three ways. First, Laclede could not cancel until one year had passed after the first delivery of propane by Amoco. Second, any cancellations could be effective only on the anniversary date of the first delivery under the agreement. Third, Laclede had to give Amoco 30 days written notice of termination. These restrictions on Laclede's power to cancel clearly bring this case within the rule.

A more difficult issue in this case is whether or not the contract fails for lack of "mutuality of consideration" because Laclede did not expressly bind itself to order all of its propane requirements for the Jefferson County subdivisions from Amoco.

While there is much confusion over the meaning of the terms "mutuality" or "mutuality of obligation" as used by the courts in describing contracts, our use of this concept here is best described by Professor Williston:

> Sometimes the question involved where mutuality is discussed is whether one party to the transaction can by fair implication be regarded as making any promise; but this is simply an inquiry whether there is consideration for the other party's promise.

As stated by the Missouri Supreme Court:

> Mutuality of contract means that an obligation rests upon each party to do or permit to be done *something* in *consideration* of the other; that is, neither party is bound unless both are bound.

We are satisfied that, while Laclede did not expressly promise to purchase all the propane requirements for the subdivisions from Amoco, a practical reading of the contract provisions reveals that this was clearly the intent of the parties. In making this determination we are mindful of three pertinent rules of contract law. First, the contract herein consisted of both the September 21, 1970, agreement and the supplemental letter agreements, for a contract may be made up of several documents. Second, "the consideration for a contract will not be held uncertain if by the application of the usual tests of construction, the court can reasonably discover to what the parties agreed." Finally, "[w]here an agreement is susceptible of two constructions, one of which renders the contract invalid and the other sustains its validity, the latter construction is preferred."

Once Amoco had signed the supplemental letter agreement, thereby making the September 21 agreement applicable to any given Jefferson County development, it was bound to be the propane supplier for that subdivision and to provide a continuous supply of the gas sufficient to meet Laclede's reasonably anticipated needs for that development. It was to perform these duties until the agreement was cancelled by Laclede or until natural gas distribution was extended to the development.

For its part, Laclede bound itself to purchase all the propane required by the particular development from Amoco. This commitment was not expressly written out, but it necessarily follows from an intelligent, practical reading of the agreement.

When analyzed in this manner, it can be seen that the contract herein is simply a so-called "requirements contract." Such contracts are routinely enforced by the courts where, as here, the needs of the purchaser are reasonably foreseeable and the time of performance is reasonably limited.

We conclude that there is mutuality of consideration within the terms of the agreement and hold that there is a valid, binding contract between the parties as to each of the developments for which supplemental letter agreements have been signed.

Questions

1. A unilateral contract is formed when one party offers a promise requesting some action and the second party performs the requested action. For example, a reward offer is accepted by performing the action requested by the reward, that is, finding a missing wallet or supplying information to catch a thief. In contrast, a bilateral contract is a contract in which each party has made a promise to the other. Can a bilateral contract be formed if one of the alleged promises is an illusion, such as I promise to buy your car if I decide to buy it? Was Laclede's promise to buy propane unless it canceled the contract a valid promise or an illusionary promise?
2. What is meant by "mutuality of consideration"? What was Laclede "bound" to do under the contract? Was its duty expressly stated or implied from the writings?

Lampley v. Celebrity Homes, Inc.
594 P. 2d 605 (1979)
Colorado Court of Appeals

Lampley began to work for Celebrity on May 13, 1975. On July 29, 1975, Celebrity announced the initiation of a profit sharing plan. The plan was effective retroactively to April 1, 1975, for all salaried employees as of June 30, 1975. Distributions under the plan were to be made in cash to the employees between May 15 and June 15 of 1976 for the company's fiscal year ending March 31, 1976. Lampley continued her employment with Celebrity until she was terminated on January 13, 1976. A distribution under the profit sharing plan was made for the 1975–76 fiscal year, and Lampley brought this action to recover her proportionate share.

Celebrity contends that the profit sharing plan was offered as gratuity and that, therefore, it had not legally obligated itself to pay the bonus. In *Fontius Shoe Co.* v. *Lamberton,* 78 Colo. 250, (1925), the profit sharing plan was held to be an offer of a mere gratuity and not a contract. However, the *Fontius* plan specifically provided that all bonuses thereunder were gratuitous. In the present case, there is no such provision. Rather, the plan expressly provides that if the company's profit goals are attained, the employee will receive a share in the profits determined according to a formula set out in the plan. Accordingly, Celebrity's profit sharing plan is not gratuitous in its nature, but, in this respect, was a covenant by Celebrity, conditioned only upon the attainment of the specified profit.

In further support of its claim that the plan is not a binding contract, Celebrity contends that there was no consideration. Benefit to the promisor or detriment to the promisee, however slight, can constitute consideration. The plan states as its objective:

> Our goal is . . . to produce added employee benefits gained through a higher quality of operation. Through teamwork in our day to day operation, we can achieve not only higher levels of profits, but also better performance for our customers, a better quality in design of products, fair treatment of customers, subcontractors and suppliers.

This language indicates that the plan was established as an inducement to Celebrity's employees to remain in its employ and to perform more efficient and faithful service. Such result would be of obvious benefit to Celebrity, and thus consideration was present.

Relative to its claim of lack of consideration, Celebrity also argues that the distribution of benefits under the plan is discretionary with the company. We disagree. Courts will not torture words and phrases to import ambiguity where their ordinary meaning leaves no room for ambiguity. The plan expressly states that if company goals are attained, the employees will share in the profits. Nowhere in the plan is there a provision stating that a distribution is discretionary with the company. In addition, the plan establishes a definite time when the distributions will be made. These terms indicate that the profit payments were not discretionary.

Lampley, who was employed for an indefinite term, was not obligated to remain until 1976, and it can be inferred from the evidence in the record that she was induced to do so, in part at least, by the profit sharing offer made to her by Celebrity. The memorandum of the profit sharing plan was an offer to add additional terms to the original employment for a contract and Lampley's continued employment with Celebrity was an acceptance of the offer and the consideration for the contract.

Once the announced plan became a binding contract, i.e., on July 29, 1975, Lampley's rights under the plan immediately vested. The time of payment under the plan is irrelevant to the time of vesting of Lampley's rights.

Finally, Celebrity argues that even if the plan were a contract, the employee must be employed with the company at the time of distribution. While Celebrity's plan specified a time of distribution, it is silent as to whether an employee must be working for the company at the time of distribution.

Where the payment of a profit sharing plan is a contract, rather than a gratuity, the obligation to pay profits to an employee may not be defeated by discharging the employee before the distribution is made. Celebrity disputes the trial court's finding that Lampley was wrongfully discharged. However, since sufficient evidence exists to support the trial court's finding, it is binding on review, and thus Lampley is entitled to a share of the profits for the fiscal year 1975.

Questions

1. What "consideration" flowed from Lampley to Celebrity? Was it valuable? Was it bargained for? Was it in exchange for Celebrity's promise?
2. Contrast the results obtained from a gratuitous profit sharing plan and from a contractual profit sharing plan.
3. The [husband] had assaulted his wife, who took refuge in [a neighbor's] house. The next day the husband gained access to the house and began another assault upon his wife. The wife knocked [the husband] down with an axe, and was on the point of cutting his head open or decapitating him while he was [lying] on the floor, and the plaintiff [neighbor] intervened, caught the axe as it was descending, and the blow intended for [the husband] fell upon [the neighbor's] hand, mutilating it badly, but saving [the husband's] life. Subsequently, [the husband] orally promised to pay the plaintiff [neighbor] her damages; but . . . failed to pay anything. . . .

   The question presented is whether there was a consideration recognized by our law as sufficient to support the promise. The Court is of the opinion that, however much the [husband] should be impelled by common gratitude to alleviate the plaintiff's misfortune, a humanitarian act of this kind, voluntarily performed, is not such consideration as would entitle her to recover at law. *Harrington* v. *Taylor* 35 SE 2d 227 (N. Carolina, 1945).

   Why, under the doctrine of consideration, is there no recovery in these circumstances? Was the consideration (hand in front of the axe) given in response to a bargain?

PROMISSORY ESTOPPEL

Because the doctrine of consideration has not been completely satisfactory in all situations, another rule has been developed which substitutes for consideration and yet binds the promisor to his or her promise. The rule is called "promissory estoppel" and is defined in the *Restatement, Contracts* 390 (1932) as follows:

> A promise which the promisor should reasonably expect to induce action or forbearance of a definite and substantial character on the part of the promisee and which does induce such action or forbearance is binding if injustice can be avoided only by enforcement of the promise.

In one case, the court, in discussing this doctrine, stated,

> We think the promissory estoppel doctrine . . . extends to commercial transactions. . . . "To hold a defendant liable under this doctrine there must be a promise which reasonably leads the promisee to rely on it to his detriment, with injustice otherwise not being

avoidable. If the [statement made] . . . for any reason is not a promise affirmatively to do something, then the plaintiff cannot recover. Likewise if there is no reasonably foreseeable likelihood of reliance by the person receiving the offer or promise, the doctrine does not permit recovery. And the reliance must be justifiable. . . . Finally, there must be some substantial detriment due to the reliance." *N. Litterio & Co.* v. *Glassman Construction Co.*, 319 F. 2d 736 (D.C. Cir, 1963).

Question

1. Can you think of any instances in which promissory estoppel would require the enforcement of a promise unsupported by consideration?

PAROL EVIDENCE RULE

Keleher v. La Salle College

147 A. 2d 835 (1959)
Supreme Court of Pennsylvania

On March 2, 1953, Brother E. Stanislaus . . . defendant's President, wrote plaintiff to the effect that defendant could not offer him a new contract upon the expiration of the 1952–1953 contract, assigning as the reason therefor the necessity that defendant curtail its expenditures because of rising costs and diminishing enrollment. On March 7, 1953 the plaintiff wrote Brother Stanislaus questioning his authority to revoke "academic tenure" which plaintiff stated had been given him in June 1951 by Brother Paul (the defendant's former President). . . .

On September 18, 1953, plaintiff instituted an . . . action against defendant for an alleged breach of an *oral* contract of employment. In this action plaintiff alleged that in June of 1951, Brother Paul, defendant's President, entered into an *oral* contract with plaintiff increasing his salary to $4,160, . . . giving him "tenure of academic employment," and that the revocation without cause, of his tenure and employment by defendant, violated and breached this oral contract. Defendant's answer denied the existence of any oral contract and averred that plaintiff's employment arose solely under the two written contracts of June 15, 1951, and June 15, 1952.

When the matter came for trial . . . defendant's counsel offered in evidence the written contract of June 15, 1952, and, in response to a question addressed to him by defendant's counsel, plaintiff acknowledged that the signature on this written contract was his signature. After plaintiff's counsel had placed in evidence the March and April 1953 correspondence between plaintiff and Brother Stanislaus, the trial court granted "a motion for a nonsuit . . . ."

. . . [T]he fundamental issue is whether, in view of the written undertaking of June 15, 1952, between the parties, the plaintiff should be permitted to prove by parol evidence the terms of the alleged oral contract of June 1951.

Walker v. *Saricks,* 63 A. 2d 9, 10, well states the Pennsylvania Parol Evidence Rule: "Where parties, without any fraud or mistake, have deliberately put their engagements in writing, the law declares the writing to be not only the best, but the only, evidence of their agreement.

All preliminary negotiations, conversations and verbal agreements are merged in and superseded by the subsequent written contract . . . and unless fraud, accident, or mistake be averred, the writing constitutes the agreement between the parties, and its terms cannot be added to nor subtracted from by parol evidence. . . ."

The written contract of June 15, 1952, is clear and free of any ambiguity. It purports to encompass all the terms and conditions of the relationship between plaintiff and defendant concerning the former's employment as a teacher during the academic year 1952–1953. Plaintiff now seeks to prove an oral agreement which would clearly alter and vary the terms of this written contract in a most material instance, to wit, the length of plaintiff's employment. The written contract distinctly and unambiguously sets forth that plaintiff is employed for the academic year 1952–1953. What plaintiff wants to prove is that, as the result of an oral contract, he acquired "academic tenure" by which we understand permanent tenure. That plaintiff's oral contract would vary and alter the written contract is clear beyond any peradventure of doubt.

Plaintiff neither alleges nor does he seek to prove any fraud, accident or mistake, but simply contends that the parol evidence rule is inapplicable because the written contract did not constitute an integration of the alleged oral contract and that both the oral and the written contract are co-existent. A comparison of the subject-matter of the written contract with that of the alleged oral contract clearly indicates an integration of the latter by the former. To allow plaintiff to prove an oral contract under these circumstances would violate the parol evidence rule, a rule to which this Court requires rigid adherence. Both the spirit and the letter of the parol evidence rule . . . and a host of . . . decisions, compel the rejection of evidence as to any alleged oral contract in June 1951 between all parties.

For the reasons stated, judgment is directed to be entered for the defendant.

Questions

1. What type of exceptions to the parol evidence rule were alluded to in *Keleher* v. *LaSalle*?
2. People usually put their contracts in writing, not necessarily because the law requires it, but because the writing serves as evidence of the existence of the contract. Does the parol evidence rule suggest another reason for putting contracts in writing?
3. When the language used in an agreement might be interpreted two or more ways, extrinsic (outside the writing) evidence may be considered not to vary or modify the terms of the written agreement but to aid the court in ascertaining the true intent of the parties. Suppose the written contract called for the delivery of "300 chickens." Could one of the parties introduce extrinsic evidence of the "trade" meaning of the word "chicken"?

4. The parol evidence rule is not a bar to admission of testimony if the parties do not intend the writing to be the repository of all of the terms of their agreement. The terms not incorporated in the writing are still a part of the binding contract even though they are provable only by parol testimony. What the intention of the parties was is a question of fact. Did the parties in *Keleher* v. *La Salle* intend the writing to be the full "repository of all terms of their agreement"?

CAPACITY TO CONTRACT

Kiefer v. Fred Howe Motors, Inc.
158 N.W. 2d 288 (1968)
Supreme Court of Wisconsin

The law governing agreements made during infancy reaches back over many centuries. The general rule is that ". . . the contract of a minor, other than for necessaries, is either void or voidable at his option." . . .

The underpinnings of the general rule allowing the minor to disaffirm his contracts were undoubtedly the protection of the minor. It was thought that the minor was immature in both mind and experience and that, therefore, he should be protected from his own bad judgments as well as from adults who would take advantage of him. The doctrine of the voidability of minors' contracts often seems commendable and just. If the beans that the young naive Jack purchased from the crafty old man in the fairy tale "Jack and the Bean Stalk" had been worthless rather than magical, it would have been only fair to allow Jack to disaffirm the bargain and reclaim his cow. However, in today's modern and sophisticated society the "infancy doctrine" seems to lose some of its gloss.

Paradoxically, we declare the infant mature enough to . . . be responsible for his torts and crimes, but not mature enough to assume the burden of his own contractual indiscretions. In Wisconsin, the infant is deemed mature enough to use a dangerous instrumentality—a motor vehicle—at sixteen, but not mature enough to purchase it without protection until he is twenty-one.

No one really questions that a line as to age must be drawn somewhere below which a legally defined minor must be able to disaffirm his contract for non-necessities. The law over the centuries has considered this age to be twenty-one. . . .

Undoubtedly, the infancy doctrine is an obstacle when a major purchase is involved. However, we believe that the reasons for allowing that obstacle to remain viable at this point outweigh those for casting it aside. Minors require some protection from the pitfalls of the market place. Reasonable minds will always differ on the extent of the protection that should be afforded. . . .

Disaffirmance

The [dealer] questions whether there has been an effective disaffirmance of the contract in this case.

Williston, while discussing how a minor may disaffirm a contract, states:

> Any act which clearly shows an intent to disaffirm a contract or sale is sufficient for the purpose. Thus a notice by the infant of his purpose to disaffirm . . . a tender or even an offer to return the consideration or its proceeds to the vendor, . . . is sufficient.

The testimony of Steven Kiefer and the letter from his attorney to the dealer clearly establish that there was an effective disaffirmance of the contract.

Misrepresentation

[The dealer's] last argument is that the [minor] should be held liable in tort for damages because he misrepresented his age. Dealer would use these damages as a set-off against the contract price sought to be reclaimed by [the minor].

The nineteenth-century view was that a minor's lying about his age was inconsequential because a fraudulent representation of capacity was not the equivalent of actual capacity. This rule has been altered by time. There appear to be two possible methods that now can be employed to bind the defrauding minor: he may be estopped from denying his alleged majority, in which case the contract will be enforced or contract damages will be allowed; or he may be allowed to disaffirm his contract but be liable in tort for damages. Wisconsin follows the latter approach.

In *Wisconsin Loan & Finance Corp.* v. *Goodnough,* Mr. Chief Justice Rosenberry said:

> . . . In this case, if there is an estoppel which operates to prevent the defendant from repudiating the contract and he is liable upon it, the damages will be the full amount of the note plus interest and a reasonable attorney's fee. If he is held liable, on the other hand, in deceit, he will be liable only for the damages which the plaintiff sustained in this case, the amount of money the plaintiff parted with, which was $352 less the $25 repaid. There seems to be sound reason in the position of the English courts that to hold the contract enforceable by way of estoppel is to go contrary to the clearly declared policy of the law . . . . The contract [should not be] . . . enforced, he is held liable [instead] for deceit as he is for other torts such as slander . . . and trespass. . . .

Having established that there is a remedy against the defrauding minor, the question becomes whether the requisites for a tort action in misrepresentation are present in this case.

The trial produced conflicting testimony regarding whether Steven Kiefer had been asked his age or had replied that he was "twenty-one." Steven and his wife, Jacqueline, said "No," and Frank McHalsky, [the dealer's] salesman, said "Yes." Confronted with this conflict, the question of credibility was for the trial court to decide, which it did by holding that Steven did not orally represent that he was "twenty-one." This finding is not contrary to the great weight and clear preponderance of the evidence and must be affirmed.

Even accepting the trial court's conclusion that Steven Kiefer had not orally represented his age to be over twenty-one, the [dealer] argues that there was still a misrepresentation. The "motor vehicle purchase contract" signed by Steven Kiefer contained the following language just above the purchaser's signature:

> I represent that I am 21 years of age or over and recognize that the dealer sells the above vehicle upon this representation.

Whether the inclusion of this sentence constitutes a misrepresentation depends on whether elements of the tort have been satisfied. They were not. In *First Nat. Bank in Oshkosh* v. *Scieszinski* it is said:

> To be actionable the false representation must consist, first of a statement of fact which is untrue; second, that it was made with the intent to defraud and for the purpose of inducing the other party to act upon it; third, that he did in fact rely on it and was induced thereby to act, to his injury or damage.

No evidence was adduced to show that the plaintiff had an intent to defraud the dealer. To the contrary, it is at least arguable that the majority of minors are, as the plaintiff here might well have been, unaware of the legal consequences of their acts.

Without the elements of scienter being satisfied, the plaintiff is not susceptible to an action in misrepresentation. Furthermore, the reliance . . . must be . . . "justifiable reliance." We fail to see how the dealer could be justified in the mere reliance on the fact that the plaintiff signed a contract containing a sentence that said he was twenty-one or over. The trial court observed that the plaintiff was sufficiently immature looking to arouse suspicion. The [dealer] never took any affirmative steps to determine whether the plaintiff was in fact over twenty-one. It never asked to see a draft card, identification card, or the most logical indicium of age under the circumstances, a driver's license. Therefore, because there was no intent to deceive, and no justifiable reliance, the [dealer's] action for misrepresentation must fail.

Chief Justice Hallows (dissenting)

My . . . ground . . . [for] dissent is that an automobile to this plaintiff was a necessity and therefore the contract could not be disaffirmed. Here, we have a minor, aged 20 years and 7 months, the father of a child, and working. While the record shows there is some public transportation to his present place of work, it also shows he borrowed his mother's car to go to and from work. Automobiles for parents under 21 years of age to go to and from work in our current society may well be a necessity and I think in this case the record shows it is. An automobile as a means of transportation to earn a living should not be considered a non-necessity because the owner is 5 months too young. I would reverse.

Questions

1. Why protect minors by giving them an escape from the contract?
2. What must a minor do to disaffirm?

3. In Wisconsin, a minor may be held liable for the tort of fraud or misrepresentation. What elements must be proven to establish the tort of fraud? Which elements were not proven in *Kiefer*?
4. Minors are held liable for contractual consumption of "necessaries" and the dissenting justice in *Kiefer* felt the auto was a necessity. Why do you think the majority of the court did not think an auto was a necessity?
5. How drunk does one have to be to lose the legal capacity to contract?

> Mere drunkenness is not sufficient to release a party from his contracts. To render a transaction voidable on account of the drunkenness of a party to it, the drunkenness must have been such as to have drowned reason, memory, and judgment, and to have impaired the mental facilities to such an extent as to render the party non compos mentis (not of sound mind) for the time being. . . . Though the mind of a person may be to some extent impaired by age or disease, still if he has the capacity to comprehend and act rationally in the transaction in which he is engaged—if he can understand the nature of his business and the effect of what he is doing, and can exercise his will with reference thereto—his acts will be valid. *Martin* v. *Harsh, et al.*, 83 N.E. 164 (1907).

CONDITIONS

Lach v. Cahill

85 A. 2d 481 (1951)
Supreme Court of Errors of Connecticut

The plaintiff sues to recover a deposit he made with one of the defendants upon a written agreement to purchase a house belonging to the other. The trial court concluded that the agreement never came into existence because it was subject to a condition which had not been fulfilled. It rendered judgment for the plaintiff for the return of the deposit and the defendants appealed.

The finding . . . discloses the following facts: On November 10, 1949, the plaintiff signed an agreement with the defendant Cahill, acting through his agent, the defendant Rabbett, to purchase Cahill's house in Windsor Locks for $18,000 and paid a deposit of $1,000. A few days later Cahill also signed the agreement and accepted the deposit. The contract contained the following provision: "This agreement is contingent upon buyer being able to obtain mortgage in the sum of $12,000 on the premises, and have immediate occupancy of the premises." The conveyance was to be made by warranty deed within thirty days after acceptance of the agreement by the seller.

The plaintiff had been a practicing attorney for a little more than one year, was married and the father of three small children. Rabbett knew the financial position of the plaintiff and that he contemplated a bank mortgage payable in installments over a reasonable period of time. On November 14, the plaintiff applied to the First National Bank of Windsor Locks for $12,000 mortgage, which was denied. Thereafter, in the period up to November 21, he unsuccessfully applied for a mortgage loan at five different banks and loaning institutions. He was informed that the banks in Hartford were not interested in placing loans on outlying property. He conferred with the federal housing administration examiners, who advised him that although he was a veteran his income did not meet the requirements for an F.H.A. guaranteed loan. Rabbett informed the plaintiff not later than November 18 that Cahill was definitely not interested in a purchase mortgage. On December 1, the plaintiff wrote to Cahill that he was unable to secure a mortgage in the amount of $12,000 and requested the return of the deposit. . . .

The decisive issues in the case are whether the ability of the plaintiff to secure a $12,000 mortgage was a condition precedent to his duty to perform his promise to purchase and whether he made a reasonable effort to secure the mortgage. Unless both questions are answered in the affirmative the plaintiff cannot recover. A condition precedent is a fact or event which the parties intend must exist or take place before there is a right to performance. . . . A condition is distinguished from a promise in that it creates no right or duty in and of itself but is merely a limiting or modifying factor. . . . If the condition is not fulfilled, the right to enforce the contract does not come into existence. . . . Whether a provision in a contract is a condition the nonfulfillment of which excuses performance depends upon the intent of the parties, to be ascertained from a fair and reasonable construction of the language used in the light of all the surrounding circumstances when they executed the contract.

The plaintiff was a young man of limited means, just starting in his profession and under the necessity of finding a home for his wife and their three small children. He required a mortgage payment in reasonable instalments over a period of time if he was to complete the prospective purchase of Cahill's house. The court properly concluded that the language used, read in the light of the situation of the parties, expressed an intention that the plaintiff should not be held to an agreement to purchase unless he could secure a mortgage for $12,000 on reasonable terms as to the amount and time of instalment payments.

The condition in the contract implied a promise by the plaintiff that he would make reasonable efforts to secure a suitable mortgage. . . . The performance or nonperformance of this implied promise was a matter for the determination of the trial court. The conclusion reached upon the facts was proper.

Question

1. Generally, the problems arising under contract law involve either (1) a dispute concerning whether the contract exists or (2) a dispute in which the parties admit the contract but disagree concerning their rights under the contract. Which type of dispute existed in *Lach*?

Notes

1. As in *Lach,* the condition is said to be "precedent" when some event must occur before the party becomes bound to complete his or her performance or duty. Failure of that event to occur obviously relieves the party from any duty under the contract.

   On the other hand, when the party has already become bound to complete performance but will be relieved from such responsibility by the happening of some event, the condition is "subsequent." A condition subsequent can be illustrated by conditions commonly contained in insurance policies. After an auto accident (condition precedent), the insurance company is bound by the contract to pay the insured for his or her loss. But if the insured fails to notify the insurance company within a stipulated time period, as stated in the policy (the condition subsequent), the insurance company is relieved from its duty to indemnify the insured.

2. There are also what are called "conditions concurrent" though this term is more of a misnomer. Its real meaning is that when the performance of the parties is to occur concurrently, then it is a condition precedent to a suit by either party that such a party do something to put the other in default. The something that must be done will vary according to the circumstances, but it is generally called making a "tender" of performance (that is, offering his or her half of the bargain and if the second party refuses or cannot concurrently perform, then that party is in default). In effect, the "concurrent conditions" concept requires tender of performance as a condition that must occur before the other party is bound to perform, failing which puts him or her in breach.

CERTAINTY OF DAMAGES

Evergreen Amusement Corporation v. Milstead

112 A. 2d 901 (1955)
Court of Appeals of Maryland

The appellant, by counterclaim, sought recovery of lost profits for the period of delay. The court held the amount claimed to have been so lost to be too uncertain and speculative, and refused evidence proffered to support appellant's theory. . . .

The real reliance of the Evergreen Amusement Corporation is on the slowness of the contractor in completing the work. It says that the resulting delay in the opening of the theater from June first to the middle of August cost it twelve thousand five hundred dollars in profits. It proffered a witness to testify that he had built and operated a majority of the drive-in theaters in the area, that he is in the theater equipment business and familiar with the profits that drive-in theaters make in the area, that a market survey was made in the area before the site of the theater was selected, and that it had shown the need for such a theater in the neighborhood. It was said he would testify as to the reasonably anticipated profits during the months in question by comparing the months in its second year of operation with those in which it could not operate the year before, and would say that the profits would have been the same. His further testimony would be, it was claimed, that weather conditions, the population, and competition were all approximately the same in the year the theater opened and the following year. . . .

We think the court did not err in refusing the proffered evidence. Under the great weight of authority, the general rule clearly is that loss of profit is a definite element of damages in an action for breach of contract or in an action for harming an established business which has been operating for a sufficient length of time to afford a basis of estimation with some degree of certainty as to the probable loss of profits, but that, on the other hand, loss of profits from a business which has not gone into operation may not be recovered because they are merely speculative and incapable of being ascertained with the requisite degree of certainty. *Restatement, Contracts,* Sec. 331, states the law to be that damages are recoverable for profits prevented by breach of contract "only to the extent that the evidence affords a sufficient basis for estimating the amount of money with reasonable certainty," and that where the evidence does not afford a sufficient basis, "damages may be measured by the rental value of the property." Comment "d" says this: "If the defendant's breach has prevented the plaintiff from carrying on *a well-established business,* the amount of profits thereby prevented is often capable of proof with reasonable certainty. On the basis of its past history, a reasonable prediction can be made as to its future." That damages for profits anticipated from a business which has not started may not be recovered, is laid down in 25 C.J.S., Damages, §42.

See also "The Requirement of Certainty for Proof of Lost Profits," 64 *Harvard L. Rev.* 317. The article discusses the difficulties of proving with sufficient certainty the profits which were lost, and then says: "These difficulties have given rise to a rule in some states that no new business can recover for its lost profits." While this Court has not laid down a flat rule (and does not hereby do so), nevertheless, no case has permitted recovery of lost profits under comparable circumstances. . . .

It would seem that a new theater would not for some time be well enough known to attract the same number of patrons it would draw after a period of operation. We think the court was right in basing the damages for delay in the completion of the site on fair rental value. . . .

LIQUIDATED DAMAGES

As in *Evergreen Amusement Corporation,* it is often difficult to estimate with any degree of certainty the amount of actual damage that will result from a breach of contract. Often contracts provide that if the party has not completed his or her performance by a specified time, he or she must pay a certain amount of money per day until performance is completed. These "damages" are referred to as liquidated damages, and the injured party has a right to claim the amount specified as the measure of damages. For liquidated damages to be recovered, the amount stipulated must be reasonable and bear some relationship to the probable damages incurred by the injured party. Furthermore, the amount of damages stipulated must be intended as compensation for possible breach and not as a penalty to force performance. Liquidated damages will be interpreted as a penalty when the amount stipulated is out of proportion to the possible loss. However, once the court decides that the amount is reasonable, that amount will be awarded without inquiry to the actual damages sustained by the injured party. Although a liquidated damage provision is involved in the following case, the central issue is the determination of whether "consequential damages" may be recovered.

CONSEQUENTIAL DAMAGES

Krauss v. Greenbarg
137 F. 2d 569 (1943)
United States Court of Appeals (3d Cir.)

On July 30, 1940, the defendants who used the business name of King Kard Overall Company, received an award and contract from the War Department of the United States to supply 698,084 pairs of leggings. The contract called for deliveries of certain quantities of leggings at stated intervals and provided for a sum as liquidated damages for each day of delay. By a memorandum of the same date the defendants (Greenbarg) placed an order with the plaintiff (Krauss), whose business was carried on under the name of American Cord and Webbing Company, for the webbing to be used in making the leggings. The order provided for certain quantities of webbing to be delivered at given dates. On March 11, 1941, the webbing company (Krauss) started suit in the Eastern District of Pennsylvania to recover $15,326.13 for the webbing sold and delivered to the overall company (Greenbarg) pursuant to the latter's order. The buyers (Greenbarg) admitted nonpayment but filed a counterclaim for $22,740.99. The jury returned a verdict in favor of the overall company for the counterclaim and judgment was entered for the difference. . . . The webbing company filed this appeal.

The issues raised on this appeal concern the counterclaim. The theory of the counterclaim is that the webbing company did not maintain the scheduled deliveries of the webbing and as a result thereof the overall company could not meet its schedule with the Government. Because of this it incurred the per diem penalty provided for in the government contract for each day's delay in deliveries which amounted to $22,740.99. These special damages it seeks to charge to the webbing company. The latter admits that it failed to deliver the webbing as per schedule. It denies, however, liability on its part for the special damages sought. . . .

The rule governing special damages in contract cases applied in the Pennsylvania decisions has been laid down in the leading English case of *Hadley* v. *Baxendale,* 9 EX. 341 (1854). It is that special damages for breach of contract are not recoverable unless they can fairly and reasonably be considered as arising naturally from the breach or as being within the contemplation of the parties, at the time the contract was made, as the probable result of the breach.

Where the consequential damages claimed were within the comtemplation of the parties at the time of the contracting as the probable result of the breach, their recovery has been allowed. The question stressed as ultimately determinative in all these cases is whether at the time of making the contract the party who broke his promise knew that his breach would probably result in the kind of special damages claimed and thus could be said to have foreseen them. If he did, then he was liable for the consequential damages.

On the question in the case at bar we have a special finding by the jury. At the trial of the case the court submitted three questions to the jury. One asked whether Krauss (the webbing company) knew, at the time he made his contract with Greenbarg (the overall company), that the latter's contract with the Government provided that delay in delivery would subject it to penalty. The jury answered yes. This finding, which is unassailed, establishes definitely that the webbing, which it undertook to furnish, was not delivered as scheduled in the contract and as a result the leggings could not be delivered on time, the overall company would incur the special damages it now claims.

Questions

1. In *Krauss,* who must have foreseen the loss for the court to allow recovery for consequential damages? When must the loss have been foreseen? Why?
2. What type of reactions (specifically) might a business manager have to the greater risk associated with a breach of the contract when he or she is told of a potential consequential damage?
3. Although contract law seeks to compensate the aggrieved contracting party, do *Evergreen* and *Krauss* suggest some realistic protection for the breacher also? From what type of risks?

ILLEGALITY

Historically, the common law courts have refused to enforce illegal bargains. An agreement is considered illegal if its formation or performance is a crime or tort, or otherwise opposed to public policy. The parties to such agreement are not entitled to the aid of courts. Agreements for bribery, fraud, wagers, usery, and agreements obstructing legal process (such as the suppression of evidence) are clearly obnoxious to society. Besides these relatively few judicially declared illegal agreements, the law of contracts was oriented to private agreements between private individuals as they freely determine their bargain. Freedom to contract was overwhelming public policy. However, the Supreme Court made it clear in 1911 that the freedom to contract was not an absolute right. In the opinion of the court,

freedom of contract is a qualified and not an absolute right. There is no absolute freedom to do as one wills or to contract as one chooses. The guaranty of liberty does not withdraw from legislative supervision that wide department of activity which consists of the making of contracts, or deny to government the power to provide restrictive safeguards. Liberty implies the absence of arbitrary restraint, not immunity from reasonable regulations and prohibitions imposed in the interests of the community. *Chicago B & O.R.* v. *Maguire,* 219 U.S. 549 (1911).

Nevertheless, in the early twentieth century the Supreme Court held numerous governmental intrusions into the freedom of contract as unconstitutional. They ruled against the initial congressional efforts in the field of minimum wage and child labor laws, finding such legislation to be an unconstitutional interference with the liberty of contract. In the 1930s, however, the Supreme Court changed its point of view and upheld congressional intrusion into the freedom of contract because the consequences of substandard wages and of child labor abuses were too harmful to the welfare of individuals and society. Consequently, in the modern era numerous legislative attempts to define contractual terms have been upheld and represent a general move to make modern law more "just."

Courts have recognized that contracts presented before the court are no longer a single instrument drafted for those particular parties. Instead, contracts of insurance, contracts of purchase of goods, or contracts for a bank loan are all prepared in a uniform fashion with an industry-wide pattern. Such contracts often require that the consumers conform to the industry terms, or do without that industry's goods. The appreciation that such contractual terms result from unequal bargaining power has resulted in judicial and congressional modification and regulation of contract. The Supreme Court has said that

when a widely diffused public interest has become enmeshed in a network of multitudinous private arrangements, the authority of the state "to safeguard the vital interests of its people" . . . is not to be gainsaid by abstracting one such arrangement from its public context and treating it as though it were an isolated private contract constitutionally immune from impairment. *East New York Savings Bank* v. *Hahn,* 326 U.S. 230, 232 (1945).

As a result, local, state, and national laws have been created which statutorally regulate contractual terms. For example, the terms of insurance policies are regulated by statutes, credit terms and consumer loans are often dictated by statutes, and contracts in the marketing of goods may run afoul of statutes or court decisions which condemn certain practices as unfair methods of competition.

These statutory and judicial restrictions on the freedom of contract have had an important impact on commercial activities. It reduces the freedom to contract from the theoretical absolute privilege of selecting contractual terms to a governmentally modified privilege. Such modifications have gone so far as in certain instances to even regulate with whom one contracts (gender, race, and so forth). Becoming familiar with these numerous substantive governmental "regulations" in the formulation of contracts is of fundamental importance in understanding the concept of illegality and in recognizing such intrusion as a continuing technique of government to rectify perceived inequities in bargaining power and to achieve social justice. However, as the following case illustrates, legislative regulations may go too far to be constitutionally permissible.

IMPAIRMENT OF CONTRACT

Allied Structural Steel Co. v. Spannaus
438 U.S. 234 (1978)
Supreme Court of the United States

Justice Stewart

The issue in this case is whether the application of Minnesota's Private Pension Benefits Protection Act to the Allied Structural Steel Co. violates the Contract Clause of the United States Constitution.

In 1974 Allied Structural Steel Co. (company), a corporation with its principal place of business in Illinois, maintained an office in Minnesota with 30 employees. Under the company's general pension plan, adopted in 1963 and qualified as a single-employer plan under § 401 of the Internal Revenue Code, [a] salaried employee . . . who did not die, did not quit, and was not discharged before meeting one of the requirements of the plan would receive a fixed pension at age 65 if the company remained in business and elected to continue the pension plan in essentially its existing form.

On April 9, 1974, Minnesota enacted the law here in question, the Private Pension Benefits Protection Act. Under the Act, a private employer of 100 employees or more—at least one of whom was a Minnesota resident—who provided pension benefits under a plan meeting the qualifications of § 401 of the Internal Revenue Code, was subject to a "pension funding charge" if he either terminated the plan or closed a Minnesota office.

During the summer of 1974 the company began closing its Minnesota office. On July 31, it discharged 11 of its 30 Minnesota employees, and the following month it notified the Minnesota Commissioner of Labor and Industry, as required by the Act, that it was terminating an office in the State. At least nine of the discharged employees did not have any vested pension rights under the company's plan, but had worked for the company for 10 years or more and thus qualified as pension obligees of the company under the law that Minnesota had enacted a few months earlier. On August 18, the State notified the company that it owed a pension funding charge of approximately $185,000 under the provisions of the Private Pension Benefits Protection Act.

There can be no question of the impact of the Minnesota Private Pension Benefits Protection Act upon the company's contractual relationships with its employees. The Act substantially altered those relationships by superimposing pension obligations upon the company conspicuously beyond those that it had voluntarily agreed to undertake. But it does not inexorably follow that the Act, as applied to the company, violates the Contract Clause of the Constitution.

The language of the Contract Clause appears unambiguously absolute: "No State shall . . . pass any . . . Law impairing the Obligation of Contracts." U.S.

Const., Art. I, § 10. The Clause is not, however, the Draconian provision that its words might seem to imply. As the Court has recognized, "literalism in the construction of the contract clause . . . would make it destructive of the public interest by depriving the State of its prerogative of self-protection."

* * *

First of all, it is to be accepted as a commonplace that the Contract Clause does not operate to obliterate the police power of the States. "It is the settled law of this court that the interdiction of statutes impairing the obligation of contracts does not prevent the State from exercising such powers as are vested in it for the promotion of the common weal, or are necessary for the general good of the public, though contracts previously entered into between individuals may thereby be affected. This power, which, in its various ramifications, is known as the police power, is an exercise of the sovereign right of the Government to protect the lives, health, morals, comfort and general welfare of the people, and is paramount to any rights under contracts between individuals."

If the Contract Clause is to retain any meaning at all, however, it must be understood to impose *some* limits upon the power of a State to abridge existing contractual relationships, even in the exercise of its otherwise legitimate police power. The existence and nature of those limits were clearly indicated in a series of cases in this Court arising from the efforts of the States to deal with the unprecedented emergencies brought on by the severe economic depression of the early 1930s.

In *Home Building & Loan Assn.* v. *Blaisdell,* 290 U.S. 398, the Court upheld against a Contract Clause attack a mortgage moratorium law that Minnesota had enacted to provide relief for homeowners threatened with foreclosure. Although the legislation conflicted directly with lenders' contractual foreclosure rights, the Court there acknowledged that, despite the Contract Clause, the States retain residual authority to enact laws "to safeguard the vital interests of [their] people." In upholding the state mortgage moratorium law, the Court found five factors significant. First, the state legislature had declared in the Act itself that an emergency need for the protection of homeowners existed. Second, the state law was enacted to protect a basic societal interest, not a favored group. Third, the relief was appropriately tailored to the emergency that it was designed to meet. Fourth, the imposed conditions were reasonable. And, finally, the legislation was limited to the duration of the emergency.

The *Blaisdell* opinion thus clearly implied that if the Minnesota moratorium legislation had not possessed the characteristics attributed to it by the Court, it would have been invalid under the Contract Clause of the Constitution.

* * *

In applying these principles to the present case, the first inquiry must be whether the state law has, in fact, operated as a substantial impairment of a contractual relationship. The severity of the impairment measures the height of the hurdle the state legislation must clear. Minimal alteration of contractual obligations may end the inquiry at its first stage. Severe impairment, on the other hand, will push the inquiry to a careful examination of the nature and purpose of the state legislation.

The severity of an impairment of contractual obligations can be measured by the factors that reflect the high value the Framers placed on the protection of private contracts. Contracts enable individuals to order their personal and business affairs according to their particular needs and interests. Once arranged, those rights and obligations are binding under the law, and the parties are entitled to rely on them.

Here, the company's contracts of employment with its employees included as a fringe benefit or additional form of compensation, the pension plan. The company's maximum obligation was to set aside each year an amount based on the plan's requirements for vesting. The plan satisfied the current federal income tax code and was subject to no other legislative requirements. And, of course, the company was free to amend or terminate the pension plan at any time. The company thus had no reason to anticipate that its employees' pension rights could become vested except in accordance with the terms of the plan. It relied heavily, and reasonably, on this legitimate contractual expectation in calculating its annual contributions to the pension fund.

Thus, the statute in question here nullifies express terms of the company's contractual obligations and imposes a completely unexpected liability in potentially disabling amounts. There is not even any provision for gradual applicability or grace periods. Yet there is no showing in the record before us that this severe disruption of contractual expectations was necessary to meet an important general social problem. . . .

. . . [Moreover], the legislation . . . clearly has an extremely narrow focus. It applies only to private employers who have at least 100 employees, at least one of whom works in Minnesota, and who have established voluntary private pension plans, qualified under Section 401 of the Internal Revenue Code. And it applies only when such an employer closes his Minnesota office or terminates his pension plan. Thus, this law can hardly be characterized, like the law at issue in the *Blaisdell* case, as one enacted to protect a broad societal interest rather than a narrow class.

This legislation, imposing a sudden, totally unanticipated, and substantial retroactive obligation upon the company to its employees, was not enacted to deal with a situation remotely approaching the broad and desperate emergency economic conditions of the early 1930s-conditions of which the Court in *Blaisdell* took judicial notice.

Entering a field it had never before sought to regulate, the Minnesota Legislature grossly distorted the company's existing contractual relationships with its employees by superimposing retroactive obligations upon the company substantially beyond the terms of its employment contracts. And that burden was imposed upon the company only because it closed its office in the State.

This Minnesota law simply does not possess the attributes of those state laws that in the past have survived challenge under the Contract Clause of the Constitution. The law was not even purportedly enacted to deal with a broad, generalized economic or social problem. It did not operate in an area already subject to state regulation at the time the company's contractual obligations were originally undertaken, but invaded an area never before subject to regulation by the

State. It did not effect simply a temporary alteration of the contractual relationships of those within its coverage, but worked a severe, permanent, and immediate change in those relationships—irrevocably and retroactively. And its narrow aim was leveled, not at every Minnesota employer, not even at every Minnesota employer who left the State, but only at those who had in the past been sufficiently enlightened as voluntarily to agree to establish pension plans for their employees.

* * *

[Accordingly] . . . we . . . hold that if the Contract Clause means anything at all, it means that Minnesota could not constitutionally do what it tried to do to the company in this case.

Questions

1. Does the contract clause's prohibition of governmental impairment of contracts prevent all state governmental exercise of police power regulations to modify existing contracts? Does it prohibit the state from insisting that future contracts contain certain terms?
2. Under what conditions may a state impair contractual obligations? Which of these conditions was absent in *Allied Structural Steel*?

TORTIOUS INTERFERENCE WITH CONTRACTS

Interference with contracts is a tort that began in England by permitting a master to sue one who had forcibly taken away his servants. Subsequently, courts allowed suits where a servant was enticed away without violence and, ultimately, to situations not involving a master-servant relationship. The elements of the tort require proof of intentional (not negligent) interference by the defendant with the contract of the plaintiff with another. The defendant's interference must have been the "proximate cause" of the breach of the plaintiff's contract. When the interference of the defendant involved tortious behavior, such as violence, coercion, or fraud, the courts have uniformly found the defendant liable. However, there is no such unanimity of judicial opinion where the defendant uses means that arc lawful in and of themselves. The majority of the courts hold that the action is still maintainable in the absence of justification. Justification (or privilege) for the defendant often includes action by the defendant to protect an equal or superior interest, such as a right to protect personal property or contract interest. Also, the defendant may refuse to enter into contracts, even though this results in an interference with the plaintiff's contract. If the interference results from the defendant's performing his or her legal duties, no cause of action will arise. Finally, the defendant's conduct may be justifiable on the grounds of some socially desirable objective. For example, in *Brimelow* v. *Casson,*[1] the defendant's purpose for preventing prostitution was held sufficient justification for his interference with the plaintiff's contracts.

Imperial Ice Co. v. Rossier et al.
112 P. 2d 631 (1941)
Supreme Court of California

The California Consumers Company purchased from S. L. Coker an ice distributing business, inclusive of good will, located in . . . Santa Monica. . . . In the purchase agreement Coker contracted . . . [to] "not engage in the business of selling and/or distributing ice . . . in [Santa Monica] so long as the purchasers, or anyone deriving title to the good will of said business from said purchasers, shall be engaged in a like business therein." Plaintiff, the Imperial Ice Company, acquired . . . the California Consumers Company full title to this ice distributing business including the right to enforce the covenant not to compete. Coker subsequently began selling in [Santa Monica] in violation of the contract ice supplied to him by a company owned by W. Rossier, J. A. Matheson, and Fred Matheson. Plaintiff thereupon brought this action in the superior court for an injunction to restrain Coker from violating the contract and to restrain Rossier and the Mathesons from inducing Coker to violate the contract. The complaint alleges that Rossier and the Mathesons induced Coker to violate his contract so that they might sell ice to him at a profit. The trial court . . . gave judgment for those defendants. Plaintiff has appealed from the judgment on the sole ground that the complaint stated a cause of action against the defendants Rossier and the Mathesons for inducing the breach of contract.

The question thus presented to this court is under what circumstances may an action be maintained against a defendant who has induced a third party to violate a contract with the plaintiff.

It is universally recognized that an action will lie for inducing breach of contract by a resort to means in themselves unlawful such as libel, slander, fraud, physical violence, or threats of such action. Most jurisdictions also held that an action will lie for inducing a breach of contract by the use of moral, social, or economic pressures, in themselves lawful, unless there is sufficient justification for such inducement.

Such justification exists when a person induces a breach of contract to protect an interest which has greater social value than insuring the stability of the contract. Thus, a person is justified in inducing the breach of a contract the enforcement of which would be injurious to health, safety, or good morals. The interest of labor in improving working conditions is of sufficient social importance to justify peaceful labor tactics otherwise lawful, though they have the effect of inducing breaches of contracts between employer and employee or employer and customer. In numerous other situations, justification exists depending upon the importance of the interest protected. The presence or absence of ill-will, sometimes referred to as "malice," is immaterial, except as it indicates whether or not an interest is actually being protected.

It is well established, however, that a person is not justified in inducing a breach of contract simply because he is in competition with one of the parties to the contract and seeks to further his own economic advantage at the expense of the other. Whatever interest society has in encouraging free and open competition by means not in themselves unlawful, contractual stability is generally accepted as of greater importance than competitive freedom. Competitive freedom, however, is of sufficient importance to justify one competitor in inducing a third party to forsake another competitor if no contractual relationship exists between the latter two. A person is likewise free to carry on his business, including reduction of prices, advertising, and solicitation in the usual lawful manner although some third party may be induced thereby to breach his contract with a competitor in favor of dealing with the advertiser. Again, if two parties have separate contracts with a third, each may resort to any legitimate means at his disposal to secure performance of his contract even though the necessary result will be to cause a breach of the other contract. A party may not, however, under the guise of competition actively and affirmatively induce the breach of a competitor's contract in order to secure an economic advantage over that competitor. The act of inducing the breach must be an intentional one. If the actor had no knowledge of the existence of the contract or his actions were not intended to induce a breach, he cannot be held liable though an actual breach results from his lawful and proper acts.

* * *

The complaint in the present case alleges that defendants actively induced Coker to violate his contract with plaintiffs so that they might sell ice to him.

The contract gave to plaintiff the right to sell ice in the stated territory free from the competition of Coker. The defendants, by virtue of their interest in the sale of ice in that territory, were in effect competing with plaintiff. By inducing Coker to violate his contract, as alleged in the complaint, they sought to further their own economic advantage at plaintiff's expense. Such conduct is not justified. Had defendants merely sold ice to Coker without actively inducing him to violate his contract, his distribution of the ice in the forbidden territory in violation of his contract would not then have rendered defendants liable. They may carry on their business of selling ice as usual without incurring liability for breaches of contract by their customers. It is necessary to prove that they intentionally and actively induced the breach. Since the complaint alleges that they did so and asks for an injunction on the grounds that damages would be inadequate, it states a cause of action. . . .

The judgment is reversed.

Questions

1. May an individual induce a breach of contract by unlawful means, such as libel, fraud, or threats of violence?
2. May an individual induce a breach of contract by lawful means, such as moral, social, or economic pressures?
3. When is a person "justified" in inducing a breach of contract? Is competition a justification?
4. Can a person be liable for inducing a breach of contract if he or she had no knowledge of the existence of the contract?

CONCLUSION

The American free enterprise economy is founded on the market system. The market system involves a host of contractual transactions between buyers and sellers. Each day, innumerable legal transactions are entered into by individuals and business firms seeking to satisfy particular needs and wants. One may contract for the transportation of goods, for the hiring of labor, for the leasing of space, for the purchase of real estate, or for the borrowing of money, or other similar business transactions. Reliance on the contractual relationship and the performance of contractual duties requires a firm knowledge of the principles of laws that govern the formation of contracts and the legal remedies available for breach of a contractual relationship. In short, the legal system supports the private economic system. It protects the economic expectations of contracting parties by urging performance of contractual duties or providing compensatory remedies.

CASE PROBLEMS

1. Shave signed a contract to sell real estate to Sherwin for $50,000 cash. Sherwin then signed the same contract, but above his signature he added the condition that he first obtain a loan of $35,000 on specified terms. Shave learned of the "conditional acceptance" and her broker told her it was not necessary to initial the changes although she found them acceptable. Sherwin then told Shave's broker he wished to withdraw his conditional acceptance. The broker had Shave initial the altered contract and obtained approval of a loan for Sherwin but later that day received a written confirmation of Sherwin's withdrawal of the "conditional acceptance."

   The broker claims that a contract had been made and wants his commission. Decide.

2. Marie, a 25-year employee at the time of her retirement in 1954 claims that in 1944 Mr. V, then president of the V Company told her that she would receive her salary of $375 a month for the rest of her life. In 1954, just before her retirement, Marie was told by Mr. G, who succeeded V as president after V's death, that the company would pay her full salary for the rest of her life. Marie than retired to care for a son who was ill. Marie received $375 a month from V Company until 1957, but then the company reduced it by half since she was eligible for social security. In 1961 the payments stopped. If it were not for her son's illness and the assurances of Messrs. V and G, Marie says she would still be working, and she sues V Company for breach of contract. V Company says that it received no consideration for the $375-a-month payments.

   Does Marie have an enforceable agreement?

3. While the age of majority was 21, a husband and wife both 19 years of age purchased a house trailer as their home, by executing a promissory note to the seller. At the time of the purchase both were employed and were living with the parents of the husband. The seller sued the couple for payment on the note, and the couple thereupon disaffirmed the contract on the basis that they were minors. The seller countered that despite their youth, the couple would be liable for payment for a house trailer, since lodging is a necessity.

   Would the couple be held to their contract? Was the house trailer a necessity for them?

4. Hannigan became a distributor of metal outdoor storage buildings manufactured by Fabricated. In 1958, Hannigan conceived of a new idea for outdoor storage cabinets. After negotiations, Hannigan and Fabricated entered into an agreement whereby Fabricated contracted to manufacture these cabinets exclusively for Hannigan; in consideration thereof Hannigan agreed to purchase all such outdoor storage cabinets from Fabricated. The contract placed no limitations on Fabricated's right to manufacture and sell its metal outdoor storage buildings, and Fabricated continued to manufacture and sell such storage buildings to various customers, including Sears.

   Hannigan sold the Fabricated manufactured outdoor cabinets to his various customers, which included Sears. Sears became Hannigan's customer in early 1959 and almost immediately attempted by letter to persuade Fabricated's sales manager to sell the lawn cabinets directly to Sears, notwithstanding its exclusive contractual commitment to Hannigan. Sears's avowed purpose for inviting Fabricated into a direct purchasing relationship was to avoid and eliminate the profit of the intermediary, Hannigan.

   Sears's buyer attempted to persuade Fabricated to sell cabinets directly to Sears or it would go elsewhere for steel storage buildings. At this time Fabricated was in large measure economically dependent on Sears because 60 percent of Fabricated's "business was devoted to Sears as a customer." After Fabricated agreed to Sears's proposal, Hannigan sued Sears. What is the result?

END NOTE

1. *Brimelow* v. *Casson* (1924) LR 1 Ch Div. 302, (1923) All Eng. 40.

chapter 8

BUSINESS ORGANIZATIONS

Each society selects the methods of organization best suited for allocating resources and products in the design of its economic system. The United States has placed its primary emphasis in economic organization on private ownership of productive property and the freedom of contractual relations as the means to distribute products and incomes. In America's early development, the freedom of "private" enterprise was as sacred as political liberty and, indeed, it was of critical importance in preserving political liberties. This emphasis on a "free" economic system was partly a reaction to the English mercantilist system which favored some merchants over others. Americans believed that political restrictions on disfavored merchants discouraged their initiative to the detriment of society. The American economic system was to be open for all participants willing to entertain the risks of a free market.

During the American colonial period, most business enterprises were organized as sole proprietorships or partnerships. The corporate form of business organization was not popular in America, despite the fact that English mercantile trading companies and a small number of native business corporations were already carrying on business activities here. The "free market" writings of Adam Smith, who was against incorporated enterprises, were widely circulated in America. The English mercantile companies were politically protected monopolies. America wanted no part of these large, exclusive, and monopolistic companies, nor were Americans interested in creating their own companies.

What few corporations were created had to be formed under a special enactment of the state legislature. No more than 250 corporate bodies were begun during the first decade after the Constitution. The impact of the Industrial

Revolution and episodes of corruption and bribery of state legislators to create particular corporations initiated the need for reform in the processes of creating incorporated bodies. The industrialization process requires large amounts of capital and the corporate form of organization provides a most successful vehicle to raise capital funds. The increasing pressures for incorporation led nearly all states to enact general incorporation statutes which allow persons to form corporations without special legislative favor.

As long as business corporations remained local, the states theoretically retained full control over corporate activities. However, when the Supreme Court held that a state could not exclude the interstate commercial activities of a foreign (chartered in another state) corporation, business organizations that intended to engage in interstate activity sought out those states for incorporation which provided a "liberal" corporate law favoring the interests of the incorporators. Initially, New Jersey became the most favored state of incorporation, and Delaware soon followed. Governor Woodrow Wilson, however, took New Jersey out of the "corporation home" competition with his tough reforms in 1913.

Corporations have grown steadily and have acquired increasing power within society. With theoretical perpetual existence and minimal state regulation or oversight, corporations have become self-perpetuating and largely autonomous. As a result, it has often been argued that federal control over the formation of corporations that do business in interstate commerce should be instigated. However, federal intervention in corporate affairs has mainly taken the form of superimposed regulatory legislation and the rejection of any federal incorporation law. In the modern era state legislation has attempted to balance more fairly the interest of shareholders, management, employees, and the public interest in corporate affairs. Moreover, judicial decisions have attempted to enhance business morality in corporate affairs by increasingly recognizing fiduciary duties on the part of directors, officers, and controlling stockholders.

Any study of American business organizations must begin with the important laws of agency. Agency law governs the power of an agent or employee of a business organization in relation to outsiders. In addition, agency law articulates basic principles concerning the legal relationships within the business firm itself.

AGENCY

Agency is a legal relationship based on consent of the parties that one party, the agent, will represent another, the principal, in contractual matters with third persons. Since a principal may appoint an agent to arrange most any transaction that he or she may legally conduct, an obvious purpose of an agency is to expand the principal's business interest by operating through agents. The agency relationship usually arises out of a contractual agreement between the parties, but it is possible to form an agency from mere consent without a contract. The crux of the agency status is that the agent acts for the benefit of the principal and is therefore subject to the principal's control.

By definition, an agent acts for the principal on contractual matters. In contrast, an employee acts for the employer (principal) on physical things and in service to the employer without power to make contracts for the employer. However, the employee is subject to the employer's direction and control.

An independent contractor is one who is not subject to direction or control by an employer (principal). Instead, the contractor is hired to accomplish the contractual result or end product through the exercise of skill and management. As such, an independent contractor is neither an agent nor an employee because he or she is not subject to the right of control by the principal.

RESPONDEAT SUPERIOR

Whereas agency is a voluntarily assumed status, the relationship is largely governed by a body of law that defines the respective rights and liabilities of the principal and agent to each other and to third persons. That body of law has been developed through the common law traditions in England and the United States over hundreds of years. One rule that has been settled for more than 250 years is still strange to many. That rule is *respondeat superior;* that is, let the master (principal) respond by paying compensatory damage awards to others who are tortiously injured by the acts of the agent-employee. The master-principal must bear liability for the servant-agent's torts, if such torts were committed in the "course of the agent's employment." Mr. Justice Holmes wrote the following:

> I assume that common sense is opposed to making one man pay for another man's wrong, unless he actually has brought the wrong to pass according to the ordinary canons of legal responsibility. . . . I therefore assume that common sense is opposed to the fundamental theory of agency.[1]

Although the initial reaction of common sense may be opposed to *respondeat superior,* many theorists have approved of the doctrine. Its long survival and present vigor indicate the rule must satisfy some instinct of public policy. Justifications advanced for the rule tend to be based on concepts of morality or economics.

In a moral sense, it is argued that since the principal has the power of control, the principal should take the responsibility for the agent's acts, or that since he or she gets the benefits of the agent's acts, he or she should bear the burden of the agent's misconduct. Moreover, although it is true that the principal is innocent, so is the person injured, and between the two, the person (principal) who initiated the activity (set the agent into action) should bear the loss.

Economically, it is argued that making the principal liable will induce him or her to exercise greater care in employing and supervising agents. The public will thereby benefit from less agent misconduct. Also, since injuries should be compensated, the public is better served if the master, who is likely to have greater financial responsibility, is held liable. This latter theory is called the "deep-pocket principle." Finally, the entrepreneur theory argues that the compensation of victims should be treated like any other cost of doing business. Ultimately, such costs will be covered, like any business expense, through the fees paid by consumers for the business service. Imposing liability on the principal thereby provides a means of fair and reasonable allocation of loss throughout society. Spreading the loss in this manner provides social justice for both the victims and the innocent principal.

No matter the justification chosen, *respondeat superior* is a viable and expanding legal principle as the following case illustrates.

Texaco, Inc. v. Layton
395 P. 2d 393 (1964)
Supreme Court of Oklahoma

This wrongful death action was brought by plaintiff Daniel Layton, Jr., as administrator of the estate of Jimmy Alexander, who, with two others, was burned to death in a fire in a filling station in Oklahoma City. Plaintiff did not sue the operator of the filling station, but elected to prosecute his action against Texaco, Inc., only.

There is no dispute as to the events surrounding the fire. The operator of the station was Bob Anderson, who leased it from Texaco, Inc., the defendant in the trial court. Anderson also had a "Gasoline Consignment Agreement" with Texaco. On the night of the fire, Anderson was not at the filling station but had left it in charge of Clarence Little, his employee. A truck driver and regular customer named Mauldin drove into the station for some gasoline, and told Little that he must first have some water cleaned out of his "saddle tank." He then drove the truck into the washroom for that purpose. Jimmy Alexander, plaintiff's decedent, had driven into the station with his father for some gasoline, and they entered the wash room to wait while the work on Mauldin's gas tank was being done. In the wash room were two gas appliances with pilot lights, a hot water heater and an overhead "space heater." Little opened the drain plug on the gas tank and drained the gas into two open containers which he set to one side. He "blew out the lines" with a compressed air hose and then applied the compressed air hose to the tank itself. At this time there was an explosion and fire which caused the deaths of Jimmy Alexander, his father, and Clarence Little.

Verdict and judgment were for plaintiff and against Texaco, and Texaco appeals.

The argument on appeal chiefly concerns the contractual relationship between Texaco and Anderson. In general, Texaco argues that the relationship was that of bailor and bailee, or principal and commission factor; and that the doctrine of *respondeat superior* does not arise from the existence of such relationships merely, but arises only where, in addition to the contractual relationship, it is shown that the superior (or principal, or bailor) had the right to control, or actually did control, the subordinate (or bailee, or commission factor) in the manner of the doing of the thing which resulted in the injury.

Plaintiff agrees generally with this statement of the law, but argues that the right to control is to be found in the contracts themselves, and that "The record in this case is replete with instances of actual control exercised by Texaco over the physical movements of Anderson and the other employees at this Texaco station." . . .

Winkelstein et al. v. *Solitare,* 129 N.J.L. 38, is particularly enlightening in this connection. The agreed facts in that case were that defendant Solitare went to the home of a friend to pick up his wife and take her home. He offered a ride to other guests who were present. He was in the driver's seat of the automobile; his wife got in beside him; and his sister-in-law, Ann Solitare, was to his wife's right. Defendant said "Ann, it is cold in here; close the door." The sister-in-law thereupon closed the door of the car upon the finger of the female plaintiff, who had grasped the door frame for support while entering the back seat of the car.

Defendant's motion for directed verdict upon the ground that "the negligence of Ann, the sister-in-law, was the act of an independent third party and not the act of the defendant's agent, servant or employee, so that if she were guilty of negligence, that negligence could not be imputed or attributed to the defendant as the master or principal" was sustained. The Supreme Court of New Jersey reversed the judgment and granted a new trial saying:

> . . . The closing of the door was at defendant's express direction, and in his presence; and thus the wrongful act in the execution of the command was his own. . . .
>
> . . . The actor was the agent or servant of defendant so as to render him liable for her wrongful act in the performance of the service thus undertaken at his request. . . . [T]o constitute that relation as to third persons, it is not requisite that 'any actual contract should subsist between the parties, or that compensation should be expected by the servant. . . .' The real test as to third persons . . . is whether the act is done by one for another, however trivial, with the knowledge of the person sought to be charged as master, or with his assent, express or implied. . . .

The points illustrated by the New Jersey case are (1) it is not necessary, in *respondeat superior* cases, to show the existence of a master-servant, or "superior-subordinate," relationship "in its full sense"; and (2) it *is* necessary to show such a relationship in respect to the transaction out of which the injury arose.

It also illustrates the fact that the doctrine of *respondeat superior* is not limited to instances in which the superior has the *right* to control the transaction out of which the injury arose, but extends also to instances in which the superior *actually exercises control,* regardless of any inherent or contractual right to do so. . . .

In summary, it may be said that the basic inquiry in any *respondeat superior* case in which the specific act of negligence by the subordinate is admitted (as it is in this case) is whether the superior had the right to control, or actually did control in some measure, the actions of the subordinate in respect to the transaction out of which the injury arose.

With that principle in mind, we now examine the record before us to see if the doctrine of *respondeat superior* is applicable in this case. We agree at the outset that plaintiff has pointed out many instances in which, under the two written contracts between Texaco and Anderson, Texaco retains the right to a substantial degree of control over Anderson. These "controls" concern such things as the retail price of gasoline to be collected by Anderson; the keeping and examination of records and taking of inventories; the prohibition of the sale of other brands under the Texaco trademark; the amount of Anderson's commission; the term of the lease and the related gasoline consignment agreement; and Anderson's credit policy. Without setting out in further detail the contents of the two instruments, it is sufficient to say that we do not find in either of them a "right" on the part of Texaco to control Anderson in the transaction out of which the injury arose. The remaining inquiry is whether, aside from the rights of Texaco under its contracts with Anderson, it actually did through Anderson control Little, in some measure, in the act which he admittedly performed negligently.

In this connection, there was evidence that Texaco inspectors visited the Anderson station about twice each month. On these visits they filled out inspection report forms entitled "Texaco Dealer's Registered Rest Room-Sparkle Report" and "Service Station Inspection Report." Anderson testified that on some occasions the inspectors would give him a copy of the report and at other times they did not. The sparkle report is apparently prepared in triplicate for the information of the Zone Manager, the State Manager, and the Division Office.

There was testimony from former employees that the station was inspected for cleanliness "and to see if it was run right," that the inspectors talked to Mr. Anderson and "told him how they wanted it run," that they would "tell us what we were doing wrong," that the inspectors were present when gasoline in open containers was being used in the washroom and grease room, and must have seen it; that on several occasions the inspectors spent some time in the role of filling station attendant, showing them "how to perform" their work; that they were never instructed not to drain gas tanks in the washroom. Most of former employees' testimony was denied by the inspectors.

Inspectors testified that their activities were for purely instructional and advisory purposes, and that their recommendations and suggestions were not binding upon Mr. Anderson; that he on occasion did not follow their suggestions; and that their purpose was merely to increase Anderson's volume of business, and his profits. They agreed that in increasing Anderson's profits, they also increased the profits to Texaco.

Anderson testified that the filling station attendants were his employees and not Texaco's; that he prescribed their working hours and wages, and that they took their instructions from him. He also testified that Texaco furnished him with no written set of rules and regulations to follow. . . .

As heretofore noted there is testimony in this case to the effect that the inspections were made to "see if it (the station) was run right," and inspectors told Mr. Anderson "how they wanted it run," and would tell us "what we were doing wrong." In view of all the facts and circumstances appearing from the record, and the ease with which Texaco was authorized to cancel their consignment agreement upon five days notice, without cause if it so elected, we are unable to determine as a matter of law the extent of the control which Texaco exercised upon Anderson and his employees in the operation of the station. . . .

As we have seen, insofar as the applicability of the doctrine of *respondeat superior* under the particular facts in this case is concerned, the written contracts between the parties did not justify a pre-emptory instruction by the court that Anderson was Texaco's agent for the purpose of the sale of gasoline only, since the contracts do not show on their face that Texaco retained the *right* to control Anderson or his employees in respect to the transaction out of which the injury arose.

Since the evidence with respect to whether Texaco *actually exercised control* in that respect is in conflict, it created at the most a question of fact for the jury, and not a question of law for the court, on this point. It is reversible error for the court, in its instructions, to invade the province of the jury, assume a controverted fact as proved or treat it as a question of law, and withhold the same from the determination of the jury.

Questions

1. Texaco could have been liable under the doctrine of *respondeat superior* if Texaco had the "right to control" the service station manager's activities in regard to the transaction out of which the injury arose. What right of control was retained by Texaco in its *contractual* dealings with the service manager?
2. Texaco could be liable under the doctrine of *respondeat superior* if it "actually exercised control" over the service station manager in relation to the activity in which the injury arose. Did Texaco "actually exercise control" over the service station manager in relation to the transaction out of which the injury arose? How was that determined?

THE AGENT'S AUTHORITY

Agents possess authority (power to make contracts for the principal) when the principal consents to such authority. This authority may arise by the principal manifesting consent to the agent's authority either expressly in words or impliedly by the principal's conduct. The authority granted to conduct a transaction includes the authority to do acts that are incidental to such authority or are reasonably necessary to accomplish the purpose of the authority conferred. The agent has the authority to follow usual business customs of the trade in carrying out his or her authority. In emergency situations, the agent's authority extends to additional acts reasonably believed necessary to protect the principal. Therefore, whether expressed in words, implied from conduct, or incidental or necessary to accomplish the agency purpose, the principal's consent is given and the agent possesses *actual* authority. In such situations, third parties dealing through the agent may make binding contracts between themselves and the principal. The agent is not bound on the contract but is merely the instrumentality through which the principal has contracted. Simply stated, the principal is bound on all contracts negotiated by the agent if such contracts were within the actual authority of the agent as conferred by the principal.

Dealing with a person who claims to be an agent but who possesses no actual authority conferred by the principal will not bind the principal to the bargain made by the unauthorized agent. Consequently, it is advisable for a third party to take additional steps to determine the extent of the authority which has been conferred by the principal. Although the principal may not be bound by an unauthorized agency, the agent who so respresents himself or herself may be liable to the third party for breach of implied warranty that he or she had authority as an agent.

Sometimes agents are placed in positions by a principal, but secret instructions limiting the agent's actual authority are given by the principal. May the principal escape liability to a third party on a contract made by such agent in which the agent violated the secret limitation and exceeded actual authority, but which to the third party appeared to be within the agent's authority as revealed by his or her position? The following case provides an answer.

Industrial Molded Plastic v. J. Gross & Son
398 A. 2d 695 (1979)
Superior Court of Pennsylvania

This is a breach of contract action brought by Industrial Molded Plastic Products, Inc. (Industrial) against J. Gross & Son, Inc. (Gross). Gross has denied liability, contending that the salesman who signed the contract lacked the authority to bind the corporate entity.

Industrial is in the business of manufacturing custom injection molded plastics by specification for various manufacturers. Industrial also manufactures various "fill-in" items during slack periods, such as electronic parts, industrial components, mirror clips, and plastic clothing clips. Industrial manufactured plastic clothing clips only for its house accounts of H. Daroff & Sons and Joseph H. Cohen & Sons. Gross is a wholesaler to the retail clothing industry, selling mostly sewing thread, but also other items such as zippers, snaps, and clips. Gross sold only a small amount of plastic clothing clips, never having more than \$100–\$200 worth of clips in inventory at any one time.

Sometime in the Fall of 1970, Mr. Stanley Waxman (Gross' President and sole stockholder) and his son Peter (a 22 year old salesman for Gross) appeared at the offices of Industrial's President, Mr. Judson T. Ulansey. They suggested to him that they might be able to market Industrial's plastic clothing clips in the retail clothing industry, in which they had an established sales force. At this initial meeting, there was no discussion of Peter Waxman's authority or lack thereof in the company. After this meeting, Stanley authorized Peter to purchase a "trial" amount of clips (not further specified) to test the market, but neither this authorization nor its limitation was communicated to Ulansey. All subsequent negotiations were between Ulansey and Peter Waxman only. Deceiving both his father and Ulansey, Peter held himself out as Vice-President of Gross, and on December 10, 1970, signed an agreement obligating Gross to purchase from Industrial five million plastic clothing clips during the calendar year of 1971, at a price of $7.50 per thousand units, delivery at Industrial's plant in Blooming Glen, Pennsylvania. Gross was granted an exclusive distributorship in the clips for the same time, excepting Industrial's two house accounts mentioned above. Before the execution of this agreement, Ulansey telephoned Stanley Waxman, who told Ulansey that Peter could act on behalf of Gross. There was no discussion of the specific terms of the agreement, such as the quantity purchased.

Industrial immediately began production of the five million clips during "fill-in" time. As they were manufactured, they were warehoused in Industrial's plant as per the contract. In February 1971, Peter Waxman picked up and paid for 772,000 clips. Stanley Waxman, who had to sign Gross' check for payment, thought that this was the "trial amount" he had authorized Peter to buy. These were the only clips which Gross ever took into its possession. On numerous occasions during the year Ulansey urged Peter to pick up more of the clips, which were taking up more and more storage space at Industrial's plant as they were being manufactured. Peter told Ulansey that he was having difficulty selling the clips and that Gross had no warehousing capacity for the inventory that was being accumulated. At no time, however, did Peter repudiate the contract or request Industrial to halt production. By the end of 1971, production was completed and Industrial was warehousing 4,228,000 clips at its plant.

On January 19, 1972, Industrial sent Gross an invoice for the remaining clips of $31,710, less credit of $203.55, for a balance due of $31,506.45. However, Gross did not honor the invoice or pick up any more of the clips. Ulansey wrote to Stanley Waxman on February 7, 1972, threatening legal action if shipping instructions were not received by March 1, 1972. Finally, on March 30, 1972, Peter Waxman responded with a letter to Ulansey, which stated that Gross' failure to move the clips was due to a substantial decline in the clothing industry in 1971 and competition with new lower-cost methods of hanging and shipping clothes. The letter asked for Industrial's patience and predicted that it would take at least the rest of the year to market the clips successfully. At this point, Industrial initiated legal action. Stanley Waxman learned of the five million clip contract for the first time when informed by his lawyer of the impending law suit. Industrial filed its complaint in August of 1972, and at the same time Peter began an extended (four years) leave of absence from Gross.

Gross contends that it was not bound by the agreement to purchase the clips because Peter Waxman had no authority to sign the contract for Gross. However, Peter was an agent of Gross and did have express authority to purchase for Gross, as its President instructed him to purchase a "trial amount" of clips. A principal's limitation of his agent's authority in amount only, not communicated to the third party with whom the agent deals, does not so limit the principal's liability. Although the agent violates his instructions or exceeds the limits set to his authority, he will yet bind his principal to such third persons, if his acts are within the scope of the authority which the principal has caused or permitted him to possess.

An admitted agent is presumed to be acting within the scope of his authority where the act is legal and the third party has no notice of the agent's limitation.

The third person must use reasonable diligence to ascertain the authority of the agent, but he is also entitled to rely upon the apparent authority of the agent when this is a reasonable interpretation of the manifestations of the principal.

Here, the limitation of Peter's authority was not communicated to Industrial. As Stanley Waxman brought Peter into the initial meeting soliciting business from Industrial, Ulansey could reasonably presume his authority to act for Gross in consummating the deal. Gross complains that Ulansey was not diligent in ascertaining Peter's authority, but in fact Ulansey telephoned Stanley Waxman precisely for the purpose of verifying Peter's authority. As Stanley said that Peter was authorized to act on behalf of Gross, the principal thus completed clothing the agent in apparent authority to bind the corporate entity on the agreement. If anybody was lacking in diligence, it was Stanley Waxman in not inquiring as to the amount of the contract Peter proposed to sign. Thus, we affirm the conclusion of the court below that Gross was bound by the agreement to purchase the clips.

Questions

1. Did Peter Waxman have the actual or expressed authority to contract for Gross? Did Peter have the expressed authority to contract for the amount that he purchased?
2. Can the principal's limitation on the authority of the agent be binding on third parties with whom the agent deals if the limitation of the principal's liability is unknown to the third party? What is apparent authority?

DUTIES BETWEEN AGENT AND PRINCIPAL

When the agent has completed his or her performance and the services were not intended gratuitous, the principal has the duty to compensate the agent. If not previously agreed on, the reasonable value of the agent's services is due the agent. Likewise, if the agent incurs expenses in carrying out the principal's task, the principal has the duty to reimburse the agent. Also, should the agent incur liability to a third person through no fault of the agent but for carrying out the instructions of the principal, the principal must indemnify the agent against the loss.

The agent has the duty to obey the principal's instructions. Failure to follow orders will make the agent liable to the principal for any resulting damage. The agent must exercise care and skill in carrying out the principal's affairs. Negligence or incompetence in professed skills will render the agent liable. Also, it is the duty of the agent to keep the principal's account and not to mingle his or her own property with that of the principal. The agent will lose his or her property if mingling results in inability to identify his or her portion. The agent also must inform the principal of any notices given to him or her for the principal.

All of these duties are important, but the highest duty of the agent is that of loyalty and good faith. The agent is a fiduciary (person in position of trust) to the principal and must not violate that trust by self-enrichment at the expense of the principal.

FIDUCIARY RESPONSIBILITIES

General Automotive Manufacturing Co. v. Singer
120 N.W. 2d 659 (1963)
Supreme Court of Wisconsin

Study of the record discloses that Singer was engaged as general manager of Automotive's operations. Among his duties was solicitation and procurement of machine shop work for Automotive. Because of Singer's high reputation in the trade he was highly successful in attracting orders. . . .

As time went on a large volume of business attracted by Singer was offered to Automotive but which Singer decided could not be done by Automotive at all, for lack of suitable equipment, or which Automotive could not do at a competitive price. When Singer determined that such orders were unsuitable for Automotive he neither informed Automotive of these facts nor sent the orders back to the customer. Instead, he made the customer a price, then dealt with another machine shop to do the work at a lesser price, and retained the difference between the price quoted to the customer and the price for which the work was done. Singer was actually behaving as a broker for his own profit in a field where by contract he had engaged to work only for Automotive. We concur in the decision of the trial court that this was inconsistent with the obligations of a faithful agent or employee.

Singer finally set up a business of his own, calling himself a manufacturer's agent and consultant, in which he brokered orders for products of the sort manufactured by Automotive—this while he was still Automotive's employee and without informing Automotive of it. Singer had broad powers of management and conducted the business activities of Automotive. In this capacity he was Automotive's agent and owed a fiduciary duty to it. . . . Under his fiduciary duty to Automotive Singer was bound to the exercise of the utmost good faith and loyalty so that he did not act adversely to the interests of Automotive by serving or acquiring any private interest of his own. . . . He was also bound to act for the furtherance and advancement of the interest of Automotive. . . .

If Singer violated his duty to Automotive by engaging in certain business activities in which he received a secret profit he must account to Automotive for the amounts he illegally received. . . .

The present controversy centers around the question whether the operation of Singer's side line business was a violation of his fiduciary duty to Automotive. . . .

The trial court found that Singer's side line business, the profits of which were $64,088.08, was in direct competition with Automotive. However, Singer argues that in this business he was a manufacturer's agent or consultant, whereas Automotive was a small manufacturer of automotive parts. The title of an activity does not determine the question whether it was competitive but an examination of the nature of the business must be made. In the present case the conflict of interest between Singer's business and his position with Automotive arises from the fact that Singer received orders, principally from a third party called Husco, for the manufacture of parts. As a manufacturer's consultant he had to see that these orders were filled as inexpensively as possible, but as Automotive's general manager he could not act adversely to the corporation and serve his own interests. On this issue Singer argues that when Automotive had the shop capacity to fill an order he would award Automotive the job, but he contends that it was in the exercise of his duty as general manager of Automotive to refuse orders which in his opinion Automotive could not or should not fill and in that case he was free to treat the order as his own property. However, this argument ignores, as the trial court said, "defendant's agency with plaintiff and the fiduciary duties of good faith and loyalty arising therefrom."

Rather than to resolve the conflict of interest between his side line business and Automotive's business in favor of serving and advancing his own personal interests, Singer had the duty to exercise good faith by disclosing to Automotive all the facts regarding this matter. . . . Upon disclosure to Automotive it was in the latter's discretion to refuse to accept the orders from Husco or to fill them if possible or to sub-job them to other concerns with the consent of Husco if necessary, and the profit, if any, would belong to Automotive. Automotive would then be able also to decide whether to expand its operations, install suitable equipment, or to make further arrangements with Singer or Husco. By failing to dislose all the facts relating to the orders from Husco and by receiving secret profits from these orders, Singer violated his fiduciary duty to act solely for the benefit of Automotive. Therefore he is liable for the amount of the profits he earned in his side line business. . . .

Questions

1. Why was Singer found liable to Automotive? What should Singer have done to avoid this liability?
2. What is a fiduciary?

SOLE PROPRIETORSHIP AND PARTNERSHIP

The form of organization selected for a particular business firm is dependent on a number of factors. The type of business, capital requirements, tax considerations, degree of delegated responsibilities, governmental regulations, and the individual's desire to exercise control are all relevant factors in the final choice. The most appropriate form of business organization for any particular business can be selected only after a full appreciation of all the facts involved and a careful consideration of tax and other aspects. Sometimes different forms of organization recommend themselves at different stages of the business life.

The individual or sole proprietorship is the oldest, simplest, and most prevalent form of business organization. It can be organized in an informal fashion and is subject to minimal governmental regulation. The sole proprietor retains full control in management of the organization and is entitled to all profits or losses. The sole proprietorship ends on the proprietor's death or retirement, but the business normally is freely transferable to others. A sole proprietorship is taxed as an individual. Smaller enterprises and new entrants into the business environment often utilize a sole proprietorship form of organization.

Partnerships are also more numerous than business corporations. A partnership is an association of two or more persons to operate a business for profit as co-owners. A partnership can be formed with little formality, although it is a sound practice to define the relationships among the partners in written detail. Sometimes statutes require the public filing of the partnership name. Most partnership law is governed by the Uniform Partnership Act (UPA). However, the partners in their written agreement often may vary from the statutory pattern imposed by the UPA.

The partnership requires no minimum capital contribution except as the partners agree. Partners may contribute cash, property, or personal services to the partnership. Partners may lend money or property to the partnership, and provision for interest on such contributions should be made in the written agreement. The written agreement should also deal with matters concerning the withdrawal of the capital contributed by each party.

Unless the partners agree otherwise in their written partnership agreement, each partner has an equal voice in the management and control of the partnership. Ordinarily matters will be determined by a majority vote; however, extraordinary matters, such as the sale of the business itself, require unanimous approval.

Because a partnership is a co-agency, the acts of either partner within the apparent scope of the partnership business bind the partnership for any liability arising therefrom. Each partner has authority to bind the partnership to contracts of both good and bad bargains. Likewise, all partners are subject to the further potential liability arising from the torts committed by a partner while acting within the scope of the partnership business. This liability of the partners, as with sole proprietors, is not limited to their capital contribution, but extends to their personal resources as well. Under the doctrine of marshalling of assets, the partnership creditors must first proceed against partnership assets before proceeding against the partners individually. A creditor of an individual partner must first proceed against the latter's personal property before attempting to attach the partnership interest.

A retiring partner remains personally liable for partnership debts incurred while he or she was a partner. The retiring partner will also be liable for new debts to persons who had previously extended credit to the partnership and who have not received actual notice of the retirement. Hence, retirement requires notification to all creditors and "publication" of a notice to all other potential creditors so that they cannot claim any right against the retiring partner. The retiring partner cannot sell his or her interest in the partnership without the consent of all the other partners.

A dissolution of the partnership can occur at the end of the specified term of the partnership existence, on death of a partner, bankruptcy of the partnership, withdrawal of the partner, or expulsion of a general partner by virtue of the contractual agreement or by court order. Unless the contractual agreement provides otherwise, dissolution is followed by winding up and termination of the partnership. In winding up, the assets of the general partnership are distributed in the following priority: (*a*) claims of creditors, (*b*) a debt obligation to a partner, (*c*) capital contributions of partners, and (*d*) partners' claims in respect to profits.

Unless there is an agreement to the contrary, profits are to be shared equally by the partners regardless of any differences in the amounts of their capital contributions. Losses are shared in the same proportions as profit. Any contractual provisions for the sharing of losses are effective among the partners but do not affect the partners' liability to partnership creditors.

A limited partnership may not be created unless there is a statute authorizing limited partnerships. Four fifths of the states have enacted the Uniform Limited Partnership Act. Most of the principles applicable to general partnerships apply in limited partnerships. However, a limited partnership can be created only in accordance with the formalities prescribed by the statute, which includes the filing and possible publication of a limited partnership certificate. Often the name of the limited partnership must include the word "limited" or its abbreviation, Ltd. Ordinarily, the name of the limited partners cannot be included in the name of the limited partnership. A limited partner can contribute cash or other property to the limited partnership but may not contribute services or otherwise take part in the control of the business. As such, the limited partner is immune from liability beyond his or her contribution. Limited partnerships are created for the purpose of attracting additional capital to the partnership venture.

CORPORATIONS

The corporation, in terms of business volume and capital assets, is the most important form of business enterprise. Innumerable variations are possible in setting up a corporation. Corporations range in size from a one-shareholder corporation to the more than two million shareholders of American Telephone & Telegraph Company. The term "incorporate" literally means to form into a body. By definition, therefore, an incorporation is an entity and is so regarded for most legal purposes. As an entity, it is solely responsible for its legal obligations. The shareholders' liability is limited to their contribution for shares.

CORPORATE FORMATION

Each state has general incorporation statutes that define the purposes for which corporations may be formed and detail the steps to be taken for incorporation. In applying for corporate recognition by the state, it is usually necessary to list the following:

1. The name and address of each incorporator.
2. The purpose or purposes for which the corporation is being organized.
3. The name of the corporation.
4. The kind of stock it intends to issue, the number of shares authorized, and other relevant stock information.
5. The period of corporate existence, which may be perpetual.

The application, signed by all the incorporators, and sometimes acknowledged by a notary public, is forwarded to a state official, usually the secretary of state. The secretary issues a charter which, together with the general incorporation statute, sets forth the powers, rights, and privileges of the corporation. Often, the charter must be filed in the proper recording office in the county in which the principal office of the business is to be located. Normally, corporate life begins when the charter has been issued. Additional requirements of law call for the subscription and payment to the corporation of, at least, the minimum amount of capital stock, for stockholder approval of corporate bylaws which govern internal relations, and for stockholder election of directors who appoint corporate officers.

Promoter's Contracts

A promoter is one who does the preliminary work necessary to bring a corporation into existence. The promoter often conceives the business or negotiates its purchase and performs any task necessary for the proposed venture to begin operations. In this function, however, the promoter cannot act as an agent of the corporation since the corporation is not legally in existence. He or she cannot be an agent for a nonexisting principal. The corporation, once it comes into existence, cannot automatically be held liable on contracts made in its behalf by the promoter. However, once corporate life begins, the corporation is free to adopt or reject the contracts made by the promoter. For the corporation to adopt the promoter's contracts, the contracts must be valid and within the legal authority of the corporation. In addition, the corporation must adopt the contracts in their entirety. However, unless a provision of the contract specifically exempts them from personal liability, promoters themselves normally continue to be liable on preincorporation contracts and are not relieved from liability by the corporation's adoption of the contract. However, the courts have developed numerous rules in resolving promoter's liability on contracts negotiated for the benefit of a proposed corporation.

Robertson v. Levy
197 A. 2d 443 (1964)
U.S. Court of Appeals (D.C. Cir.)

On December 22, 1961, Martin G. Robertson and Eugene M. Levy entered into an agreement whereby Levy was to form a corporation, Penn Ave. Record Shack, Inc., which was to purchase Robertson's business. Levy submitted articles of incorporation to the Superintendent of Corporations on December 27, 1961, but no certificate of incorporation was issued at this time. Pursuant to the contract an assignment of lease was entered into on December 31, 1961, between Robertson and Levy, the latter acting as president of Penn Ave. Record Shack, Inc. On January 2, 1962, the articles of incorporation were rejected by the Superintendent of Corporations but on the same day Levy began to operate the business under the name Penn Ave. Record Shack, Inc. Robertson executed a bill of sale to Penn Ave. Record Shack, Inc. on January 8, 1962, disposing of the assets of his business to that "corporation" and receiving in return a note providing for installment payments signed "Penn Ave. Record Shack, Inc. by Eugene M. Levy, President." The certificate of incorporation was issued on January 17, 1962. One payment was made on the note. The exact date when the payment was made cannot be clearly determined from the record, but presumably it was made after the certificate of incorporation was issued. Penn Ave. Record Shack, Inc. ceased doing business in June 1962 and is presently without assets. Robertson sued Levy for the balance due on the note as well as for additional expenses incurred in settling the lease arrangement with the original lessor.

The case presents the following issues on appeal: Whether the president of an "association" which filed its articles of incorporation, which were first rejected but later accepted, can be held personally liable on an obligation entered into by the "association" before the certificate of incorporation has been issued, or whether the creditor is "estopped" from denying the existence of the "corporation" because, after the certificate of incorporation was issued, he accepted the first installment payment on the note.

The Business Corporation Act of the District of Columbia, Code 1961, Title 29, is patterned after the Model Business Corporation Act which is largely based on the Illinois Business Corporation Act of 1933. On this appeal, we are concerned with an interpretation of Sections 29-921c and 29-950 of our act. Several states have substantially enacted the Model Act, but only a few have enacted both sections similar to those under consideration. . . .

For a full understanding of the problems raised, some historical grounding is not only illuminative but necessary. In early common law times private corporations were looked upon with distrust and disfavor. This distrust of the corporate form for private enterprise was eventually overcome by the enactment of statutes which set forth certain prerequisites before the status of corporation was achieved, and by court decisions which eliminated other stumbling blocks. Problems soon arose, however, where there was substantial compliance with the prerequisites of the statute, but not complete formal compliance. Thus the concept of *de jure* corporations, *de facto* corporations, and of "corporations by estoppel" came into being.

Taking each of these in turn, a *de jure* corporation results when there has been conformity with the mandatory conditions precedent (as opposed to merely directive conditions) established by statute. A *de jure* corporation is not subject to direct or collateral attack either by the state in a *quo warranto* proceeding or by any other person.

A *de facto* corporation is one which has been defectively incorporated and thus is not *de jure.* The Supreme Court has stated that the requisites for a corporation *de facto* are: (1) A valid law under which such a corporation can be lawfully organized; (2) An attempt to organize thereunder; (3) Actual user of the corporate franchise. Good faith in claiming to be and in doing business as a corporation is often added as a further condition. A *de facto* corporation is recognized for all purposes except where there is a direct attack by the state in a *quo warranto* proceeding. The concept of *de facto* corporation has been roundly criticized.

Cases continued to arise, however, where the corporation was not *de jure,* where it was not *de facto* because of failure to comply with one of the four requirements above, but where the courts, lacking some clear standard or guideline, were willing to decide on the equities of the case. Thus another concept arose, the so-called "corporation by estoppel." This term was a complete misnomer. There was no corporation, the acts of the associates having failed even to colorably fulfill the statutory requirements; there was no estoppel in the pure sense of the word because generally there was no holding out followed by reliance on the part of the other party. Apparently estoppel can arise whether or not a *de facto* corporation has come into existence. Estoppel problems arose where the certificate of incorporation had been issued as well as where it had not been issued, and under the following general conditions: where the "association" sues a third party and the third party is estopped from denying that the plaintiff is a corporation; where a third party sues the "association" as a corporation and the "association" is precluded from denying that it was a corporation; where a third party sues the "association" and the members of that association cannot deny its existence as a corporation where they participated in holding it out as a corporation; where a third party sues the individuals behind the "association" but is estopped from denying the existence of the "corporation"; where either a third party, or the "association" is estopped from denying the corporate existence because of prior pleadings.

One of the reasons for enacting modern corporation statutes was to eliminate problems inherent in the *de jure, de facto* and estopped concepts. Thus Sections 29-921c and 950 were enacted as follows:

§29-921c. Effect of issuance of incorporation.
Upon the issuance of the certificate of incorporation the corporate existence shall begin, and such certificate of incorporation shall be conclusive evidence that all conditions precedent required to be performed by the incorporators have been complied with and that the

corporation has been incorporated under this chapter, except as against the District of Columbia in a proceeding to cancel or revoke the certificate of incorporation.

§29-950. Unauthorized assumption of corporate powers.

All persons who assume to act as a corporation without authority so to do shall be jointly and severally liable for all debts and liabilities incurred or arising as a result thereof.

. . . No longer must the courts inquire into the equities of a case to determine whether there has been "colorable compliance" with the statute. The corporation comes into existence only when the certificate has been issued. Before the certificate issues, there is no corporation *de jure, de facto* or by estoppel. After the certificate is issued under Section 921c, the *de jure* corporate existence commences. Only after such existence has begun can the corporation commence business through compliance with Section 29-921d, by paying into the corporation the minimum capital, and with Section 921a(f), which requires that the capitalization be no less than $1,000. These latter two sections are given further force and effect by Section 29-918(a)(2) which declares that directors of a corporation are jointly and severally liable for any assets distributed or any dividends paid to shareholders which renders the corporation insolvent or reduces its net assets below its stated capital. . . .

The portion of § 29-921c which states that the certificate of incorporation will be "conclusive evidence" that all conditions precedent have been performed eliminates the problems of estoppel and *de facto* corporations once the certificate has been issued. The existence of the corporation is conclusive evidence against all who deal with it. Under § 29-950, if an individual or group of individuals assumes to act as a corporation before the certificate of incorporation has been issued, joint and several liability attaches. We hold, therefore, that the impact of these sections, when considered together, is to eliminate the concepts of estoppel and *de facto* corporateness under the Business Corporation Act of the District of Columbia. It is immaterial whether the third person believed he was dealing with a corporation or whether he intended to deal with a corporation. The certificate of incorporation provides the cut off point; before it is issued, the individuals, and not the corporation, are liable.

Turning to the facts of this case, Penn Ave. Record Shack, Inc. was not a corporation when the original agreement was entered into, when the lease was assigned, when Levy took over Robertson's business, when operations began under the Penn Ave. Record Shack, Inc. name, or when the bill of sale was executed. Only on January 17 did Penn Ave. Record Shack, Inc. become a corporation. Levy is subject to personal liability because, before this date, he assumed to act as a corporation without any authority so to do. Nor is Robertson estopped from denying the existence of the corporation because after the certificate was issued he accepted one payment on the note. An individual who incurs statutory liability on an obligation under Section 29-950 because he has acted without authority, is not relieved of that liability where, at a later time, the corporation does come into existence by complying with Section 29-921c. Subsequent partial payment by the corporation does not remove this liability.

The judgment appealed from is reversed with instructions to enter judgment against [Levy] on the note and for damages proved to have been incurred by [Robertson] for breach of the lease.

Questions

1. What is a corporation *de jure*? A corporation *de facto*? A corporation by estoppel? Why did these various conceptions become necessary? Who would win the case in *Robertson* if these common law rules were followed?
2. How did the Model Business Corporation Act attempt to solve and eliminate any issues of corporate existence?
3. The Model Act requires that, before a corporation begins to do business with the public, the minimum capital of the corporation be paid into the corporation. Which type of liability exists and on whom if this provision is not followed?

Stock Issuance

Before a corporation can begin to conduct business, it must obtain money to finance its operations. Initial funds are secured by the sale of equity securities, usually common stock. The authorization to sell equity securities is contained in the corporate charter (articles of incorporation). Unless authorized, any sale of stock would be void.

Purchasers of the stock become owners of the corporation. The money proceeds from the sale of stock become the corporation's stated capital. The corporation is not legally required to return any funds from the sale of equities to the shareholders, absence liquidation of the enterprise. In effect, shares have no maturity date and become a fund within the corporation which remains available to meet the corporate obligations to any creditors.

Most states authorize the issuance of more than one class of corporate stock, usually common stock or preferred stock. Owners of common stock assume the most risk in the corporate venture. However, common shareholders are given a voice in the election of corporate directors, who collectively appoint management. Each share usually entitles its owner to one vote per share. Preferred stock usually grants special rights and preferences when corporate distributions are made. Such preferences reduce the risk for preferred stock shareholders. Hence, preferred shareholders are usually given less voice in the formulation of corporate policy; they have voting rights only if preferred dividends are not paid for successive years.

Questions

1. Preferred stock is to have a preference in liquidation. Explain your understanding of the extent of the preference in distribution of the assets.
2. When are stockholders entitled to dividends?

   It is a well-recognized principle of law that the directors of a corporation, and they alone, have the power to declare a dividend of the earnings of the corporation and to determine its amount. . . . Courts . . . will not interfere in the management of the directors unless it is clearly made to appear that they are guilty of fraud or misappropriation of the corporate funds, or refuse to declare a dividend when the corporation has a surplus of net profits which it can, without detriment to its business, divide among its stockholders, and when a refusal to do so would amount to such an abuse of discretion as would constitute a fraud, or breach of that good faith which they are bound to exercise towards the stockholders. *Hunter* v. *Robers, Throp & Co.*, 47 N.W. 131, 134 (1890).

3. It is well-settled law that a shareholder of a corporation who sells his or her stock to the corporation while it is insolvent is liable to an injured creditor of the corporation for the amount paid to the shareholder for the stock. This liability is based on the adverse effect of the transaction on creditors, and not on the guilt or innocence of the shareholder, who is held liable even though there is no evidence of fraud. Why should the shareholder be liable? Is the shareholder ever permitted to sell his or her shares back to the corporation without incurring liability?

Stock Subscriptions

A stock subscription is an agreement between the corporation and a subscriber or prospective shareholder whereby the corporation agrees to issue shares and the subscriber agrees to pay for them. Stock subscriptions may be executed either before or after incorporation. The states vary in legal theory; however, a subscriber normally will be liable for payment for the shares if the subscriber obtains shareholder status.

Little Switzerland Brew. Co. v. Little Switzerland Brew. Co.
197 S.E. 2d 301 (1973)
Supreme Court of Appeals of West Virginia

Little Switzerland Brewing Company was incorporated and a charter was issued by the Secretary of State on January 28, 1968. The company had authorized capital stock of $200,000 consisting of 2,000,000 shares at the par value of ten cents a share. On February 18, 1968, Fred Ellison and Charles E. Oxley were made directors of the company after they purchased 5,000 shares at $5 per share. . . .

Little Switzerland contends that 275 citizens throughout the State of West Virginia subscribed for shares in the company prior to September 22, 1968. On September 25, 1968, Charles E. Oxley and Fred J. Ellison signed stock subscription agreements to purchase 5,000 shares of stock at $10 a share. . . . The "Note" that accompanied the stock subscription agreement was titled "Noninterest Bearing-Nonobligatory Note" and merely stated that Oxley and Ellison would pay "at their discretion" $50,000 to Little Switzerland Brewing Company. . . .

On March 24, 1970, eight of the ten directors of the company met and passed a resolution 7 to 1 to cancel the stock subscription agreements of Ellison . . . and Oxley. . . . On March 26, 1970, an involuntary petition for bankruptcy was filed against Little Switzerland Brewing Company. . . .

This action was instituted for the benefit of the creditors of the Little Switzerland Brewing Company pursuant to an order of the bankruptcy court in order to collect the defendant's money for their stock subscriptions. The authority for such action is contained in Code, 31-1-35, in the following language:

> Every stockholder of every corporation of this State shall be liable for the benefit of the creditors of such corporation for the amount of his subscription to the stock of such corporation, less the amount which he shall already have paid thereon, until he shall have paid such subscription in full, according to the terms thereof, . . . and, in the event of the insolvency of the corporation, all such liabilities of the stockholders shall be considered assets of the corporation and may be enforced by the receiver, trustee or other person winding up the affairs of the corporation, notwithstanding any release, agreement or arrangement, short of actual payment, which may have been made between the corporation and such stockholders. . . .

It should be noted that the defendants in the instant case were not only stockholders but were also directors of the company and it is their contention that the stock subscription agreements were only options to buy stock. However, the agreements were used to assure the Commissioner of Securities that the public offering had been fully subscribed and to free the other stock of the Little Switzerland Brewing Company for over-the-counter trading. The contention of the defendants would appear to be that the subscription agreements in question were merely fictitious or colorable subscriptions; but if this were done to induce others to subscribe and there was an understanding that there was to be no liability on the part of the defendants, the subscriptions are nevertheless just as binding on the subscribers as if they were made in good faith. . . .

It has been held that a corporation has no authority to accept subscriptions to its capital stock upon special terms, where the terms are such as to constitute a fraud upon other subscribers, or upon persons who become creditors of the corporation, and the invalidity of such terms or conditions will not release the subscriber from liability upon his subscription. . . .

The Supreme Court of the United States has consistently held since the case of *Sawyer* v. *Hoag,* that the capital stock of an insolvent corporation is a trust fund for the payment of its debts; that the law implies a promise by the subscribers of stock who did not pay for it to make such payment when demanded by the creditors of the corporation; and that any extrinsic agreement limiting the subscriber's liability therefor is void against creditors. . . .

It has been repeatedly held by this Court that the officers and directors of an insolvent corporation are trustees for the creditors.

It is clear from the authorities that the defendants in the instant case are liable for their stock subscriptions.

The answer to the second question involved in the case presented here is that the directors of the corporation did not have the authority in any event to release the defendants from liability on their stock subscription agreements. In the first place the directors of a solvent corporation have no authority to release any stockholder from liability on stock subscription agreements unless authorized by the stockholders of the corporation. Then, too, where a corporation is insolvent such action by the corporation is prohibited by statute. This statute not only provides that the defendants, as stockholders of the Little Switzerland Brewing Company, shall be liable for the benefit of the creditors of Little Switzerland for the amount of their stock subscriptions, but also that in the event of insolvency of Little Switzerland all such liability of the stockholders shall be considered as assets of the corporation and may be enforced by the proper person notwithstanding any release agreement or arrangement which may have been made between the corporation and the stockholders.

Questions

1. The defendants contend the stock subscription and agreement was merely an option to buy stock. On what grounds did the court reject this contention?
2. Why were the directors powerless to release the defendants from liability on their stock subscription agreement?

Illegal Issuance of Stock

United Steel Industries, Inc. v. Manhart
405 S.W. 2d 231 (1966)
Court of Civil Appeals of Texas

Plaintiffs Manhart filed this suit individually and as major stockholders against defendants United Steel Industries, Inc., Hurt, and Griffitts, alleging the corporation had issued Hurt 5000 shares of its stock in consideration of Hurt agreeing to perform CPA and bookkeeping services for the corporation for one year in the future; and had issued Griffitts 4000 shares of its stock in consideration for the promised conveyance of a 5 acre tract of land to the Corporation, which land was never conveyed to the Corporation. Plaintiffs assert the 9000 shares of stock were issued in violation of Article 2.16 Business Corporation Act, and prayed that such stock be declared void and cancelled. . . .

Article 12, Section 6, Texas Constitution . . . provides: "No corporation shall issue stock . . . except for money paid, labor done, or property actually received . . . ." And Article 2.16 Texas Business Corporation Act provides:

Payment for Shares.

A. The consideration paid for the issuance of shares shall consist of money paid, labor done, or property actually received. Shares may not be issued until the full amount of the consideration, fixed as provided by law, has been paid. . . .

B. Neither promissory notes nor the promise of future services shall constitute payment or part payment for shares of a corporation.

C. In the absence of fraud in the transaction, the judgement of the board of directors . . . as to the value of the consideration received for shares shall be conclusive.

The Fifth Circuit in *Champion* v. *CIR,* 303 F. 2d 887, construing the foregoing constitutional provision and Article 2.16 of the Business Corporation Act, held:

> Where it is provided that stock can be issued for labor done, as in Texas . . . , the requirement is not met where the consideration for the stock is work or services to be performed in the future. . . .

The 5000 shares were issued before the future services were rendered. Such stock was illegally issued and void.

Griffitts was issued 10,000 shares partly in consideration for legal services to the Corporation and partly in exchange for the 5 acres of land. The stock was valued at $1 per share and the land had an agreed value of $4000. The trial court found (upon ample evidence) that the 4000 shares of stock issued to Griffitts was in consideration of his promise to convey the land to the Corporation; that Griffitts never conveyed the land; and the issuance of the stock was illegal and void.

The judgement of the board of directors "as to the value of consideration received for shares" is conclusive, but such does not authorize the board to issue shares contrary to the Constitution, for services to be performed in the future (as in the case of Hurt), or for property not received (as in the case of Griffitts).

Questions

1. The Texas Constitution provides for the issuance of stock on three grounds. What are the three bases on which stock may be issued?
2. Why was the stock issued to Hurt to be canceled? What reasons were given for canceling Griffitts's stock?

SHAREHOLDERS' RIGHTS

Shareholders' control over corporate operations is indirect. Their influence is generally limited to voting during the shareholders' meetings. Such meetings are usually confined to selecting the corporate directors and approving certain extraordinary transactions. In effect, shareholders are precluded from directly controlling business policies. If the shareholders are unhappy with managerial policies, they may elect new directors. Nevertheless, stockholders possess other rights which are designed to protect their investments in the corporation.

A *direct* suit by a shareholder or shareholders by a class action involves situations where the injury is primarily to the shareholder. Consequently, the shareholder brings a legal action on his or her own behalf. For example, a shareholder may bring an action (1) to enforce the right to vote, (2) to enforce the right to inspect corporate books and records, (3) to protect preemptive rights, or (4) to compel the payment of lawfully declared dividends.

Preemptive Rights

Stokes v. Continental Trust Co.
78 N.E. 1090 (1906)
Court of Appeals of New York

What is the nature of the right acquired by a stockholder through the ownership of shares of stock? What rights can he assert against the will of a majority of the stockholders and all the officers and directors? While he does not own and can not dispose of any specific property of the corporation, yet he and his associates own the corporation itself, its charter, franchises and all rights conferred thereby, including the right to increase the stock. He has an inherent right to his proportionate share of any dividend declared, or of any surplus arising upon dissolution, and he can prevent waste or misappropriation of the property of the corporation by those in control. Finally, he has the right to vote for directors and upon all propositions subject by law to the control of the stockholders and this is his supreme right and main protection. Stockholders have no direct voice in transacting the corporate business, but through their right to vote they can select those to whom the law intrusts the power of management and control.

. . . The power to manage . . . [corporate] affairs resides in the directors, who are its agents, but the power to elect directors resides in the stockholders. This right to vote for directors and upon propositions to increase the stock . . . is about all the power the stockholder has. So long as the management is honest, within the corporate powers and involves no waste, the stockholders can not interfere, even if the administration is feeble and unsatisfactory, but must correct such evils through their power to elect other directors. Hence, the power of the individual stockholder to vote in proportion to the number of his shares, is vital and can not be cut off or curtailed by the action of all the other stockholders even with the cooperation of the directors and officers. . . .

We are thus led to lay down the rule that a stockholder has an inherent right to a proportionate share of new stock issued for money only and not to purchase property for the purposes of the corporation or to effect a consolidation, and while he can waive that right, he can not be deprived of it without his consent except when the stock is issued at a fixed price not less than par and he is given the right to take at that price in proportion to his holding.

Questions

1. What are the stockholders' preemptive rights? At least three rights were mentioned in *Stokes*.
2. The conclusion in *Stokes* is that the stockholder has the preemptive right in the issuance of new stock. Does this suggest that the stockholder has no preemptive rights in the reissuance of treasury stock?
3. The court also ruled that preemptive rights exist for stock issued for "money only" and not stock issued "to purchase property" or issued "to

effect a consolidation." Are these additional limitations on stockholders' preemptive rights?

4. Statutory enactments concerning preemptive rights are becoming increasingly frequent. The majority of jurisdictions expressly authorize the articles of incorporation to deny or limit preemptive rights and other jurisdictions would presumably follow the same result by implication. Are preemptive rights necessary in corporations of large size and with wide dispersal of their shares?

Voting Rights

General Inv. Co. v. Bethlehem Steel Corp.

100 A. 347 (1917)
Court of Chancery of New Jersey

This is an application for a temporary injunction to restrain Bethlehem Steel Corporation from increasing its capital stock. . . . The stock is to have all the characteristics of common, except that it will have no vote. . . .

The question is . . . whether a stockholder is entitled to require that any new stock issued should be vested with the privilege of voting. . . .

Turning to the statute:

> Every corporation organized under this act shall have power to create two or more kinds of stock, of such classes, with such designations, preferences and voting powers or restrictions or qualifications thereof as shall be stated and expressed in the certificate of incorporation or any certificate of amendment thereof.

No broader language could have been used, and, unless the usual meaning of these words is to be restricted by reason of the existence of some public policy, it is inconceivable to me that a corporation may not issue this class of common stock, or call it what you will. I have failed to find the existence of any such public policy. The matter is one for the stockholders to determine by their contract. If the public does not want to buy it, it does not have to. The legal rights of the present stockholders are not affected; they contracted at the time they went in that they would have the advice, consultation with, and action by (or rather the opportunity of securing such advice, consultation, and action) of the then existing stock (and this subject to its reduction in accordance with law): but there was no contract that the corporation would, if it created further stock, give that further stock the voting privilege, so that the present stockholders might have the opportunity of securing advice by and consultation with and action by the new stockholders.

The essential elements of common stock are that the holders have an opportunity to make profit if there is any and participate in the assets after all other claims are paid, and beat the loss if there be such. . . .

That the purpose of the plan is to retain control in the present stockholders does not vitiate it. The question is one of good faith. There is no charge of bad faith in the present case.

There are many cases in other states not necessary to cite holding that it is within the power of stockholders to combine for the purpose of maintaining a management in control, and if done in good faith there is no legal objection to it. The mere fact that one of the results of the plan may be to perpetuate the control in the hands of its present stockholders does not vitiate the plan. The stockholders were entitled to vote as their selfish interest dictated.

Questions

1. Voting rights, depending upon the jurisdiction involved, may be (*a*) straight, (*b*) cumulative, (*c*) class, (*d*) contingent, (*e*) disproportionate, or (*f*) nonvoting. In straight voting, each share carries one vote for each matter to be voted on. Cumulative voting gives each share as many votes as there are directors to be elected, with the shareholder being permitted to cumulate all his or her votes for one director or distribute them as desired. Cumulative voting is designed to assure minority representation on the board of directors. Class voting involves separate voting by classes of stock for separate classes of directors or for certain other matters. Contingent voting rights are dependent on a named contingency, often the default of specified dividends and the return of the original status when the contingency is over. Disproportionate voting rights involve fractional or multiple votes per share of certain classes of stock. Nonvoting stock is self-explanatory. Of course, each of these differing types of voting rights are dependent on the statute enacted in each of the states. Which kind of voting rights were to be granted by Bethlehem Steel Corporation?
2. The New York Stock Exchange, since 1926, has barred the listing of nonvoting common stock. Since 1940 it has barred the listing of nonvoting preferred stock which does not have the right as a class to elect at least two directors when six quarterly dividends, consecutive or nonconsecutive, are in default. Is the desire to be listed on the New York Stock Exchange strong enough to force large companies to grant voting rights?
3. May shareholders form a contractual agreement to vote as required by the contract? The leading case answering this question was *Manson* v. *Curtis,* 223 N.Y. 313, 119 N.E. 559 (1918), in which the court said:

   > An ordinary agreement, among a minority in number, but a majority in shares, for the purpose of obtaining control of the corporation by the election of particular persons as directors is not illegal. Shareholders have the right to combine their interests and voting powers to secure such control of the corporation in the adoption of and adhesion by it to a specific policy and course of business. Agreements upon a sufficient consideration between them, of such intendment and effect, are valid and binding, if they do not contravene any express charter or statutory provisions or comtemplate any fraud, oppression or wrong against other stockholders or other illegal object.

4. May a stockholder sell his or her right? The rule is stated in Fletcher, *Cyclopedia,* Corporations (Rev. Ed., 1967), Section 2066:

> [A]ny agreement by a stockholder to sell his vote or to vote in a certain way, or a consideration personal to himself is contrary to public policy and void.

5. Most states provide that the shareholders are entitled to vote by proxy. The proxy holder is the shareholder's agent for voting purposes at the meeting. In larger corporations, management's control of the proxy machinery tends to perpetuate management in office. Corporate funds may be used by management to solicit proxies and obtain a quorum at shareholder meetings. Often the Securities and Exchange Commission has the power to regulate proxies under the federal law. The SEC may utilize the courts to gain compliance of its rules and, in addition, private persons have been entitled to seek court enforcement of SEC proxy rules.

Right to Inspect Corporate Records

State Ex Rel. Pillsbury v. Honeywell, Inc.
191 N.W. 2d 406 (1971)
Supreme Court of Minnesota

Petitioner appeals from an order . . . denying . . . a petition for writs of mandamus to compel respondent, Honeywell, Inc., (Honeywell) to produce its original shareholder ledger, current shareholder ledger, and all corporate records dealing with weapons and munitions manufacture. . . .

Petitioner attended a meeting on July 3, 1969, of a group involved in what was known as the "Honeywell Project." Participants in the project believed that American involvement in Vietnam was wrong, that a substantial portion of Honeywell's production consisted of munitions used in that war, and that Honeywell should stop this production of munitions. . . .

On July 14, 1969, petitioner ordered his fiscal agent to purchase 100 shares of Honeywell. He admits that the sole purpose of the purchase was to give himself a voice in Honeywell's affairs so he could persuade Honeywell to cease producing munitions. . . .

This court has had several occasions to rule on the propriety of shareholders' demands for inspection of corporate books and records. . . .

While inspection will not be permitted for purposes of curiosity, speculation, or vexation, adverseness to management and a desire to gain control of the corporation for economic benefit does not indicate an improper purpose.

Several courts agree with petitioner's contention that a mere desire to communicate with other shareholders is, *per se,* a proper purpose. This would seem to confer an almost absolute right to inspection. We believe that a better rule would allow inspections only if the shareholder has a proper purpose for such communication. . . .

The act of inspecting a corporation's shareholder ledger and business records must be viewed in its proper perspective. In terms of the corporate norm, inspection is merely the act of the concerned owner checking on what is in part his property. In the context of the large firm, inspection can be more akin to a weapon in corporate warfare. The effectiveness of the weapon is considerable:

> Considering the huge size of many modern corporations and the necessarily complicated nature of their bookkeeping, it is plain that to permit their thousands of stockholders to roam at will through their records would render impossible not only any attempt to keep their records efficiently, but the proper carrying on of their business. *Cooke* v. *Outland*, 265 N.C. 601 (1965).

Because the power to inspect may be the power to destroy, it is important that only those with a bona fide interest in the corporation enjoy that power.

That one must have proper standing to demand inspection has been recognized by statutes in several jurisdictions. Courts have also balked at compelling inspection by a shareholder holding an insignificant amount of stock in the corporation.

Petitioner's standing as a shareholder is quite tenuous. He only owns one share in his own name, bought for the purposes of this suit. He had previously ordered his agent to buy 100 shares, but there is no showing of investment intent. While his agent had a cash balance in the $400,000 portfolio, petitioner made no attempt to determine whether Honeywell was a good investment or whether more profitable shares would have to be sold to finance the Honeywell purchase. . . .

Petitioner had utterly no interest in the affairs of Honeywell before he learned of Honeywell's production of fragmentation bombs. Immediately after obtaining this knowledge, he purchased stock in Honeywell for the sole purpose of asserting ownership privileges in an effort to force Honeywell to cease such production. . . .

But for his opposition to Honeywell's policy, petitioner probably would not have bought Honeywell stock, would not be interested in Honeywell's profits and would not desire to communicate with Honeywell's shareholders. His avowed purpose in buying Honeywell stock was to place himself in a position to try to impress his opinions favoring a reordering of priorities upon Honeywell management and its other shareholders. Such a motivation can hardly be deemed a proper purpose germane to his economic interest as a shareholder. . . .

We do not mean to imply that a shareholder with a bona fide investment interest could not bring this suit if motivated by concern with the long- or short-term economic effects on Honeywell resulting from the production of war munitions. Similarly, this suit might be appropriate when a shareholder has a bona fide concern about the adverse effects of abstention from profitable war contracts on his investment in Honeywell.

In the instant case, however, the trial court, in effect, has found from all the facts that petitioner was not interested in even the long-term well-being of Honeywell or the enhancement of the value of his shares. His sole purpose was to persuade the company to adopt his social and political concerns, irrespective of any economic benefit to himself or Honeywell. This purpose on the part of one buying into the corporation does not entitle the petitioner to inspect Honeywell's books and records.

Petitioner argues that he wishes to inspect the stockholder ledger in order that he may correspond with other shareholders with the hope of electing to the board one or more directors who represent his particular viewpoint. . . . While a plan to elect one or more directors is specific and the election of directors normally would be a proper purpose, here the purpose was not germane to petitioner's or Honeywell's economic interest. Instead, the plan was designed to further petitioner's political and social beliefs. Since the requisite propriety of purpose germane to his or Honeywell's economic interest is not present, the allegation that petitioner seeks to elect a new board of directors is insufficient to compel inspection.

Questions

1. Why did the court rule that petitioner's "proper purpose" to inspect was absent?
2. Did the petitioner have "proper standing" to demand inspection?
3. Statutes of the various states often modify the shareholder's right of inspection for proper purpose. Under SEC Proxy rules corporate management has an additional option in dealing with a security holder who wishes to communicate with stockholders. When the security holder demands a list of other stockholders from a corporation, the corporation may elect not to disclose the list, but to handle the mailing for him or her.

Derivative Suits

When the injury to the shareholders' investment results from a wrong committed against the corporation other than a wrong directed against the shareholder, the shareholder's injury is less direct. In this instance, the shareholder may bring a *derivative action* on behalf of the corporation to enforce a right belonging to the corporation. Any monetary judgment recovered from the suit goes into the corporate treasury rather than to the litigating shareholder. Such suits are brought by shareholders only where the corporation, through its directors, has failed to enforce such corporate claims.

If the directors, officers, or agents are acting outside the scope of their authority, are guilty of negligent conduct, or are engaging, or about to engage, in fraudulent activities with other shareholders that would be injurious to the corporation, a shareholder may bring a "derivative" suit. Because the shareholder has no individual rights against these persons for neglect in mismanagement resulting in damages to the corporation, he or she must bring the suit as a corporate cause of action. The corporate officials, for various reasons, may decide not to initiate this corporate action. In such case, the shareholder may derivatively bring the action if he or she properly follows the requirements of the state laws. Mere dissatisfaction with corporate management, however, will not normally justify a "derivative" suit.

A shareholder derivative suit is an effort to enforce a corporate right against insiders or outsiders, when those in control of the corporation refuse to enforce such corporate right. The derivative suit may provide protection for the whole community of corporate interests—creditors and shareholders. Although the derivative suit serves a useful social purpose, it is susceptible to abuse by what are called "strike suits." These suits involve shareholders with small holdings of stock and their attorneys seeking a private settlement of the claim and their own self-enrichment. Abuses of the derivative remedy have led many jurisdictions to place restrictions by statute or judicial interpretations on shareholders seeking to sue derivatively.

One of the restrictions imposed on shareholders in derivative suits is the requirement that the shareholder must own shares contemporaneously with the wrong that occurred to the corporation. This requirement prevents individuals from "shopping around" for alleged corporate injuries and then buying stock in such corporations to support a derivative suit. Numerous states have also required that dismissal or compromise of any derivative suit must first be approved by the court. Additional states have created provisions that permit the corporation to require the plaintiff-shareholder to post some bond or security for corporate expenses should the litigation be decided against the plaintiff. Such provisions normally apply to shareholders with small holdings in the corporation.

Many states require the shareholder to exhaust all efforts to achieve an intracorporate remedy before proceeding in court. Exhaustion of an intracorporate remedy usually involves a demand on the board of directors or shareholders or both, that they rectify the wrong against the corporation.

CORPORATE MANAGEMENT

Corporate management involves the functions of three groups within the corporation: shareholders, directors, and officers. Their roles are defined and limited by the corporation's charter, its bylaws, and the state's incorporation statutes. General management of the corporate business—making and implementing policy decisions—is delegated almost exclusively to the board of directors. However, the power to amend the corporate charter, sell all corporate assets, change the makeup of the corporation, and terminate corporate power remains with the shareholders. Making bylaws is also a shareholder function, unless this power is modified by statute.

The shareholders' principal control over the actions of the directors is through their voting power. The state incorporation statutes give the shareholders their voting power. The state incorporation statutes give the shareholders the right to remove a director with or without cause, and to elect a new director or board of directors. In large corporations, exercise of this right is hampered by the large number of shareholders and by management's control over proxy solicitation.

Because of the complexities of the modern corporation, the board of directors does not handle the daily activities of corporate business, delegating instead much of its authority to the officers of the company. The board retains a measure of control through its power of removal; it may remove an officer whenever it feels inclined to make a change.

Corporations are organized under an applicable state incorporation statute, nevertheless, most of the rules of management duties imposed on directors are the product of court decision rather than statutory implementation. The various duties of directors are owed directly to the corporation as an entity. Generally speaking, the duties of management are threefold: (*a*) obedience, (*b*) diligence, and (*c*) loyalty.

The duty of obedience requires the directors to act *intra vires* (within authority) as related to both the corporate charter and the bylaws, as well as statutory constraints. Willful or negligent disobedience will result in director liability to the corporation.

The duty of diligence contemplates the exercise of due care by directors in the conduct of their office. Although the standard of care varies in different jurisdictions, the general scheme is described as the care which ordinarily prudent persons would exercise under similar circumstances in like positions. When this duty of diligence is breached, the director is liable to the corporation for damages caused by his or her negligence.

The duty of loyalty contemplates the fiduciary principles of good faith and fair dealing. The director must refrain from any personal activities that injure or take advantage of the corporation. Any such disloyalty by a director to his or her profit will result in a disgorging of that profit to be returned to the corporation.

Under the "business judgment" rule, a court will not intefere with the internal management of a corporation and substitute its judgment for that of the directors as long as the directors exercise their judgment consistent with their duties of obedience, diligence, and loyalty. Having arrived at a decision, within the corporate powers and their authority, for which there is a reasonable basis, and acting in good faith, the "business judgment" rule will protect or immunize the directors from liability for a poor business judgment.

Prevention of "Waste" of Corporate Assets

Shlensky v. Wrigley
95 Ill. App. 2d 173 (1968)
Appellate Court of Illinois

This is an appeal from a dismissal of plaintiff's amended complaint on motion of the defendants. The action was a stockholders' derivative suit against the directors for negligence and mismanagement. . . . Plaintiff sought damages and an order that defendants cause the installation of lights in Wrigley Field and the scheduling of night baseball games.

Plaintiff is a minority stockholder of defendant corporation, Chicago National League Ball Club (Inc.), a Delaware corporation with its principal place of business in Chicago, Illinois. Defendant corporation owns and operates the major league professional baseball team known as the Chicago Cubs. The corporation also engages in the operation of Wrigley Field, the Cubs' home park, the concessionaire sales during Cubs' home games, television and radio broadcasts of Cubs' home games, the leasing of the field for football games and other events and receives its share, as visiting team, of admission moneys from games played in other National League stadia. The individual defendants are directors of the Cubs and have served for varying periods of years. Defendant Philip K. Wrigley is also president of the corporation and owner of approximately 80% of the stock therein.

Plaintiff alleges that since night baseball was first played in 1935 nineteen of the twenty major league teams have scheduled night games. In 1966, out of a total of 1620 games in the major leagues, 932 were played at night. Plaintiff alleges that every member of the major leagues, other than the Cubs, scheduled substantially all of its home games in 1966 at night, exclusive of opening days, Saturdays, Sundays, holidays and days prohibited by league rules. Allegedly this has been done for the specific purpose of maximizing attendance and thereby maximizing revenue and income.

The Cubs, in the years 1961–65, sustained operating losses from its direct baseball operations. Plaintiff attributes those losses to inadequate attendance at Cubs' home games. He concludes that if the directors continue to refuse to install lights at Wrigley Field and schedule night baseball games, the Cubs will continue to sustain comparable losses and its financial condition will continue to deteriorate.

Plaintiff further alleges that defendant Wrigley has refused to install lights, not because of interest in the welfare of the corporation but because of his personal opinions "that baseball is a 'daytime sport' and that the installation of lights and night baseball games will have a deteriorating effect upon the surrounding neighborhood." It is alleged that he has admitted that he is not interested in whether the Cubs would benefit financially from such action because of his concern for the neighborhood, and that he would be willing for the team to play night games if a new stadium were built in Chicago.

Plaintiff alleges that the other defendant directors, with full knowledge of the foregoing matters, have acquiesced in the policy laid down by Wrigley and have permitted him to dominate the board of directors in matters involving the installation of lights and scheduling of night games, even though they know he was not motivated by a good faith concern as to the best interests of defendant corporation, but solely by his personal view set forth above. It is charged that the directors are acting for a reason or reasons contrary and wholly unrelated to the business interests of the corporation; that such arbitrary and capricious acts constitute mismanagement and waste of corporate assets, and that the directors have been negligent in failing to exercise reasonable care and prudence in the management of the corporate affairs.

The question on appeal is whether plaintiff's amended complaint states a cause of action. It is plaintiff's position that fraud, illegality and conflict of interest are not the only bases for a stockholder's derivative action against the directors. Contrariwise, defendants argue that the courts will not step in and interfere with honest business judgment of the directors unless there is a showing of fraud, illegality or conflict of interest.

The cases in this area are numerous and each differs from the others on a factual basis. However, the courts have pronounced certain ground rules which appear in all cases and which are then applied to the given factual situation. The court in *Wheeler* v. *Pullman Iron and Steel Company,* 143 Ill. 197, 207, said:

> It is, however, fundamental in the law of corporations, that the majority of its stockholders shall control the policy of the corporation, and regulate and govern the lawful exercise of its franchise and business.
>
> . . . Every one purchasing or subscribing for stock in a corporation impliedly agrees that he will be bound by the acts and proceedings done or sanctioned by a majority of the shareholders, or by the agents of the corporation duly chosen by such majority, within the scope of the powers conferred by the charter, and courts of equity will not undertake to control the policy or business methods of a corporation, although it may be seen that a wiser policy might be adopted and the business more successful if other methods were pursued. The majority of shares of its stock, or the agents by the holders thereof lawfully chosen, must be permitted to control the business of the corporation in their discretion, when not in violation of its charter or some public law, or corruptly and fraudulently subversive of the rights and interests of the corporation or of a shareholder.

The standards set in Delaware are also clearly stated in the cases. In *Davis* v. *Louisville Gas & Electric Co.,* 16 Del. Ch. 157, 142 A. 654, a minority shareholder sought to have the directors enjoined from amending the certificate of incorporation. The court said on page 659:

> We have then a conflict in view between the responsible managers of a corporation and an overwhelming majority of its stockholders on the one hand and a dissenting minority on the other—a conflict touching matters of business policy, such as has occasioned innumerable applications to courts to intervene and determine which of the two conflicting views should prevail. The response which courts make to such applications is that it is not their function to resolve for corporations questions of policy and business management. The directors are chosen to pass upon such questions and their judgment unless shown to be tainted with fraud is accepted as final. The judgment of the directors of corporations enjoys the benefit of a presumption that it was formed in good faith and was designed to promote the best interests of the corporation they serve.

Plaintiff in the instant case argues that the directors are acting for reasons unrelated to the financial interest and welfare of the Cubs. However, we are not satisfied that the motives assigned to Philip K. Wrigley, and through him to the other directors, are contrary to the best interests of the corporation and the stockholders. For example, it appears to us that the effect on the surrounding neighborhood might well be considered by a director who was considering the patrons who would or would not attend the games if the park were in a poor neighborhood. Furthermore, the long run interest of the corporation in its property value at Wrigley Field might demand all efforts to keep the neighborhood from deteriorating. By these thoughts we do not mean to say that we have decided that the decision of the directors was a correct one. That is beyond our jurisdiction and ability. We are merely saying that the decision is one properly before directors and the motives alleged in the amended complaint showed no fraud. We feel that plaintiff's amended complaint was also defective in failing to allege damage to the corporation.

There is no allegation that the night games played by the other nineteen teams enhanced their financial position or that the profits, if any, of those teams were directly related to the number of night games scheduled. There is an allegation that the installation of lights and scheduling of night games in Wrigley Field would have resulted in large amounts of additional revenues and incomes from increased attendance and related sources of income. Further, the cost of installation of lights, funds for which are allegedly readily available by financing, would be more than offset and recaptured by increased revenues. However, no allegation is made that there will be a net benefit to the corporation from such action, considering all increased costs.

Plaintiff claims that the losses of defendant corporation are due to poor attendance at home games. However, it appears from the amended complaint, taken as a whole, that factors other than attendance affect the net earnings or losses. For example, in 1962, attendance at home and road games decreased appreciably as compared with 1961, and yet the loss from direct baseball operation and of the whole corporation was considerably less.

The record shows that plaintiff did not feel he could allege that the increased revenues would be sufficient to cure the corporate deficit. The only cost plaintiff was at all concerned with was that of installation of lights. No mention was made of operation and maintenance of the lights or other possible increases in operating costs of night games and we cannot speculate as to what other factors might influence the increase or decrease of profits if the Cubs were to play night home games.

Finally, we do not agree with plaintiff's contention that failure to follow the example of the other major league clubs in scheduling night games constituted negligence. Plaintiff made no allegation that these teams' night schedules were profitable or that the purpose for which night baseball had been undertaken was fulfilled. Furthermore, it cannot be said that directors, even those of corporations that are losing money, must follow the lead of the other corporations in the field. Directors are elected for their business capabilities and judgment and the courts cannot require them to forego their judgment because of the decisions of directors of other companies. Courts may not decide these questions in the absence of a clear showing of dereliction of duty on the part of the specific directors and mere failure to "follow the crowd" is not such a dereliction.

For the foregoing reasons the order of dismissal entered by the trial court is affirmed.

Miller v. American Telephone & Telegraph Company

507 F. 2d 759 (1974)

U.S. Court of Appeals (3d Cir.)

Plaintiffs, stockholders in American Telephone and Telegraph Company ("AT&T"), brought a stockholders' derivative action in the Eastern District of Pennsylvania against AT&T and all but one of its directors. The suit centered upon the failure of AT&T to collect an outstanding debt of some $1.5 million owed to the company by the Democratic National Committee ("DNC") for communications services provided by AT&T during the 1968 Democratic national convention. . . .

Plaintiffs' complaint alleged that "neither the officers or directors of AT&T have taken any action to recover the amount owed" from on or about August 20, 1968, when the debt was incurred, until May 31, 1972, the date plaintiffs' amended complaint was filed. The failure to collect was alleged to have involved a breach of the defendant directors' duty to exercise diligence in handling the affairs of the corporation, to have resulted in affording a preference to the DNC in collection procedures in violation of §202(a) of the Communications Act of 1934 . . . and to have amounted to AT&T's making a "contribution" to the DNC in violation of a federal prohibition on corporate campaign spending, 18 U.S.C. §610 (1970).

Plaintiffs sought permanent relief in the form of an injunction requiring AT&T to collect the debt, an injunction against providing further services to the DNC until the debt was paid in full, and a surcharge for the benefit of the corporation against the defendant directors in the amount of the debt plus interest from the due date. A request for a preliminary injunction against the provision of services to the 1972 Democratic convention was denied by the district court after an evidentiary hearing.

On motion of the defendants, the district court dismissed the complaint for failure to state a claim upon which relief could be granted. . . . The court stated that collection procedures were properly within the discretion of the directors whose determination would not be overturned by the court in the absence of an allegation that the conduct of the directors was "plainly illegal, unreasonable, or in breach of a fiduciary duty. . . ." Plaintiffs appeal from dismissal of their complaint.

The sound business judgment rule, the basis of the district court's dismissal of plaintiffs' complaint, expresses the unanimous decision of American courts to eschew intervention in corporate decision-making if the judgment of directors and officers is uninfluenced by personal considerations and is exercised in good faith. . . . Underlying the rule is the assumption that reasonable diligence has been used in reaching the decision which the rule is invoked to justify. . . .

Had plaintiffs' complaint alleged only failure to pursue a corporate claim, application of the sound business judgment rule would support the district court's ruling that a shareholder could not attack the directors' decision. . . . Where, however, the decision not to collect a debt owed the corporation is itself alleged to have been an illegal act, different rules apply. When New York law regarding such acts by directors is considered in conjunction with the underlying purposes of the particular statute involved here, we are convinced that the business judgment rule cannot insulate the defendant directors from liability if they did in fact breach 18 U.S.C. §610 as plaintiffs have charged.

* * *

The alleged violation of the federal prohibition against corporate political contributions not only involves the corporation in criminal activity but similarly contravenes a policy of Congress clearly enunciated in 18 U.S.C. §610. That statute and its predecessor reflect congressional efforts: (1) to destroy the influence of corporations over elections through financial contributions and (2) to check the practice of using corporate funds to benefit political parties without the consent of the stockholders. . . .

The fact that shareholders are within the class for whose protection the statute was enacted gives force to the argument that the alleged breach of that statute should give rise to a cause of action in those shareholders to force the return to the corporation of illegally contributed funds. Since political contributions by corporations can be checked and shareholder control over the political use of general corporate funds effectuated only if directors are restrained from causing the corporation to violate the statute, such a violation seems a particularly appropriate basis for finding breach of the defendant directors' fiduciary duty to the corporation. Under such circumstances, the directors cannot be insulated from liability on the ground that the contribution was made in the exercise of sound business judgment.

Since plaintiffs have alleged actual damage to the corporation from the transaction in the form of the loss of a $1.5 million increment to AT&T's treasury, we conclude that the complaint does state a claim upon which relief can be granted sufficient to withstand a motion to dismiss.

Questions

1. What is a derivative suit? What must a shareholder do before bringing such an action?
2. Explain the sound business judgment rule. Contrast its application in *Miller* v. *AT&T* with that in *Shlensky* v. *Wrigley.*

Corporate Officers

The officers of a corporation are its agents. As such, their powers are controlled by the laws of agency, subject to limitations imposed by the charter and bylaws or by the instructions of the board of directors. Management positions usually carry broad authority to act on behalf of the corporation. Delegation to the officers involves two concepts: (1) basic policy implementation and (2) ordinary policy implementation. Basic policy involves those matters which require board approval, whereas ordinary policies may be acted on by the chief executive officer alone.

Generally, the president is the presiding officer of the corporation. The treasurer, or controller, keeps corporate records and receives and disburses corporate funds. The secretary keeps the minutes of corporate meetings.

Where the officer performs solely an internal function, there are generally no incidental or inherent powers. The problems relating to the authority of the officers arises in transactions with persons outside the corporation. This usually involves the chief executive officer who is presumed to be able to do all things within the everyday business activity of the company. However, the third person must be aware of the usual limits of the authority of the officer with whom he or she is dealing and is responsible for his or her knowledge of the internal practices of the corporation and the customs of the trade.

The relationship of the officers to the corporation, like that of the directors, is fiduciary. For this reason, the officers are liable for any secret profits made in connection with the business of the corporation. They are liable for willful or negligent acts resulting in damage to the corporation. On the other hand, they are not liable for mere errors in judgment committed while exercising their discretionary powers, provided they have acted with reasonable prudence and skill.

Goldenberg v. Bartell Broadcasting Corporation
262 N.Y.S. 2d 274 (1965)
Supreme Court, New York

The plaintiff seek[s] recovery of damages for an alleged breach of a written contract of employment. The . . . cause of action is against the defendant Bartell Broadcasting Corporation, an entity incorporated under the laws of the State of Delaware. It is alleged in substance that on or about March 16, 1961, the plaintiff and the defendant Bartell Broadcasting Corporation entered into a written contract wherein the plaintiff was engaged as an Assistant to Gerald A. Bartell, the president of the defendant Bartell Broadcasting Corporation. The plaintiff's primary duties were to engage in corporate development in the field of pay television. The contract, which was for a period of three years, provided for (1) the payment to the plaintiff of $1,933.00 per month; and (2) for the delivery to plaintiff of 12,000 shares of "Free Registered" stock of defendant Bartell Broadcasting Corporation, which stock was payable in three installments of 4,000 shares in the months of January 1962, 1963 and 1964; and (3) the payment of plaintiff's traveling and living expenses in connection with his services to the employer; and (4) that defendant Bartell Broadcasting Corporation would provide the plaintiff with a private office and proper office facilities; and (5) that the agreement would be binding on any successor corporation or any corporation with which defendant Bartell Broadcasting Corporation would merge.

This written contract was signed by the plaintiff and by Gerald A. Bartell, in his capacity as the president of Bartell Broadcasting Corporation. It is further claimed that on or about May 1961, this contract was amended to increase plaintiff's monthly compensation from $1,933.00 to $2,400.00. It is further contended that the plaintiff was not paid his monthly compensation commencing with the month of November 1961; that the defendant Bartell Broadcasting Corporation failed to deliver the 4,000 shares of stock allegedly due in January 1962; and that in July 1962, the defendant Bartell Broadcasting Corporation denied the validity of plaintiff's employment contract. . . .

A corporation can only act through its directors, officers and employees. They are the conduit by and through which the corporation is given being and from which its power to act and reason springs. Therefore in every action in which a person sues a corporation on a contract executed on behalf of the corporation by one of its officers, one of the issues to be determined is whether the officer had the express, implied or apparent authority to execute the contract in question. . . .

The authority of an officer to act on behalf of a corporation may be express, implied or apparent. There has been no proof offered in this case indicating that Gerald A. Bartell, as president of the defendant Bartell Broadcasting Corporation, had express authority to enter into the agreement, dated March 16, 1961. . . .

Did Gerald A. Bartell then have either *implied* or *apparent authority* to execute the contract?

Implied authority is a species of actual authority, which gives an officer the power to do the necessary acts within the scope of his usual duties. Generally, the president of the corporation has the implied authority to hire and fire corporate employees and to fix their compensation. However the president of a corporation does *not* have the implied power to execute "unusual or extraordinary" contracts of employment. . . .

The agreement of March 16, 1961, not only provides for the payment of a substantial monthly compensation, but also requires the delivery of 12,000 shares of "free registered" stock of the defendant Bartell Broadcasting Corporation. While the payment of the monthly compensation would not make the contract of March 16, 1961, *"unusual or extraordinary,"* the Court is of the opinion that the inclusion in the contract of the provision requiring the delivery to plaintiff of 12,000 shares of "free registered stock," does bring the agreement within the category of being an *"unusual and extraordinary"* contract.

In *Gumpert* v. *Bon Ami Company,* 251 F. 2d 735, the plaintiff there sued on a one year employment contract under which he was to be paid $25,000 in cash and $25,000 in defendant's corporate stock. The contract was signed on behalf of the corporation's executive committee. . . . The Federal court . . . wrote:

> *Even if Rosenberg was chief executive officer . . . it is doubtful that he would possess power to make such an arrangement as a normal incident of his position. . . .*

In *Noyes* v. *Irving Trust Company,* 294 N.Y.S. 2, the plaintiff there sued on an employment contract under which he was to be paid $400 per month together with a bonus based upon the net profits. The contract was signed on behalf of the defendant corporation by its sales manager. The court . . . wrote:

> It is well settled that a contract of this character is not the usual and ordinary contract which one authorized to employ agents and servants may make. *It would require express authority. . . .*

The reason for the rule enunciated in the cases just cited is easily discernible. Corporate stock is the sinew, muscle and bone upon which the financial structure of a corporation is constructed. Corporate stock is sold, traded or disposed of in exchange for money, labor, services or other property. Thus in this manner a corporation acquires the necessary assets needed for the fulfillment of the corporate purposes. . . .

To permit the president of a corporation, without the express authority and approval of the corporation's Board of Directors, to barter or contract away the corporation's unissued (free) stock, would not only be an express violation of the statutes, but would also make possible the denudation of a corporation's assets, and the dilution of the value of the stock already issued to the detriment and disadvantage of the corporate stockholders. It should be noted here that in the case at bar, the stock of both defendant corporations is publicly owned and traded.

Apparent authority is the authority which the principal permits the agent to represent that he possesses. Generally, persons dealing with officers of a corporation are bound to take notice that the powers of an officer are derived from statutes, by-laws and usages which more or less define the extent of the officer's authority. In a doubtful case one must at his peril acquaint himself with the exact extent of the officer's authority. . . . The right of a third party to rely on the apparent authority of a corporate officer is subject to the condition that such third person has no notice or knowledge of a limitation in such authority. . . . Although it is true that secret instructions or limitations upon the apparent general authority of an officer of a corporation will not affect one who deals with the officer in the general line of his authority, and knows nothing of such limitations; however, this rule is not applicable to any limitations which are provided for in statutes. Those who contract with a corporation do so with knowledge of the statutory conditions pertaining to a corporation. . . .

The plaintiff is not a naive person, uninitiated in the business world, nor is he without knowledge of corporate financing or business practices. By his own testimony he is and was a stockholder, officer and director of several corporations. There is testimony that the plaintiff has engaged in the sale of securities to the general public. . . .

With the varied and broad business experience acquired by the plaintiff in his wide business associations as evidenced by his own career resume furnished to the defendants . . . and by plaintiff's own testimony, it can be truly said that he not only presumed to have knowledge of the statutory provisions of the law pertaining to corporations, but that he apparently also had actual knowledge of such laws. It is reasonable to infer that the plaintiff was aware, or at the least, had reason to be aware, that the authority for the issuance of corporate stock rests solely within the powers of the Board of Directors of the corporation, and that in the absence of express authority, the president of a corporation does not have the implied or apparent authority to enter into an employment contract which provides for the issuance of corporate stock as compensation. . . .

Questions

1. In what ways may a corporation be bound on a contract negotiated by its agent?
2. What documents would you want to observe to determine a corporate agent's express authority?

3. In *Employers Liability Assurance Corp.* v. *Hudson River Trust Co.,* 250 App. Div. 159, the court said:

   In the case of an officer or agent of a private corporation dealing with its funds the authority of such officer or agent is not known to all but depends upon the authority conferred upon him by the corporation which he represents. In such class of cases a bank knowingly receiving corporate funds for deposit in the individual account of such officer or agent is held to be under the duty of making inquiry to ascertain the extent of his authority in the transaction.

   Explain.

4. Are corporate officers and directors who take no steps to terminate their status as such, but simply abandon the corporation by ceasing to attend meetings and ceasing to perform the duties of their office, for whom no successors are elected, liable under the statute when the corporation subsequently is in default?

   The answer must be yes. A position of corporate trust, like a marriage, is not terminated merely by leaving the tent. Adequate protection of the myriad rights and interests involved in the sophisticated world of modern commerce requires something more than an Arabian directness and simplicity. It is to protect such interests that the statute exists. To ensure orderliness, as well as to locate corporate responsibility with certainty, a corporate officer or director retains his office until properly replaced by his successor (barring, perhaps, some particular by-law peculiarly bearing on the problem). Among the responsibilities of corporate offices, is the duty to see that the office is properly transferred into other hands. *Eberts Cadillac Co.* v. *Miller,* 159 N.W. 2d 217 (1968).

Business Strategy and Policy Formulation

Strategy formulation in the modern corporation is concerned with the determination of the organization's long-range goals and with the way to achieve them, considering the nature of the environment, potential opportunities, available skills and resources, and degrees of risk. Strategy decisions determine such things as product lines, target customers, pricing, and sales promotion. Planning of strategies provides all the employees with clear goals and directions to the future of the organization. Likewise, making the right decisions about the future and detecting and adapting to change affect the profitability, growth, and survival of the firm.

Occasionally a corporation will embark on a multinational course of business. Strategic decisions will have to be formulated on whether or not a product should be manufactured locally or imported, or whether the operation should be a wholly owned subsidiary, a joint venture, or a licensing operation. Strategy is needed to determine which country or countries offer the greatest long-run potential for the organization.

As with its domestic operations, each unit of a multinational enterprise faces a series of business risks. Some of these risks are associated with the macroeconomic environment of the particular country, while others involve its micro-

Exhibit 8-1
DOMESTIC AND MULTINATIONAL OPERATIONS

Factor	*Domestic*	*Multinational*
Language	English almost universal	Local language in many situations
Culture	Relatively homogeneous	Quite diverse, both between countries and within a country
Politics	Stable and relatively unimportant	Often volatile and important
Economy	Relatively uniform	Variations among countries; between regions within countries
Government interference	Minimal and reasonably predictable	Extensive and subject to rapid change
Labor	Skilled labor available	Skilled labor scarce, need training or redesign of production methods
Financing	Well-developed financial markets	Poorly developed financial markets. Capital flows subject to governmental control.
Market research	Data easy to collect	Data difficult and expensive to collect
Advertising	Many media and few restrictions	Media limited; many restrictions; low literacy rates may rule out print media
Money	U.S. dollar	Must convert currency; exchange rates and government restrictions are problems
Transportation/ communication	Among the best in the world	Often inadequate
Contracts	Are binding on both parties	Subject to being voided and renegotiated if one party becomes dissatisfied
Labor relations	Collective bargaining; can lay off workers easily	Often cannot lay off workers; may have mandatory worker participation in management
Trade barriers	Nonexistent	Extensive and very important

economic environment (see Exhibit 8-1). To be successful, the multinational enterprise must develop a conceptual framework for managing risk that seeks to maximize the financial return for an entire system, not just for the parent or for a single subsidiary. The following are items that must be considered in multinational strategy formulation.

1. Structuring of the organization and operational policies.
2. Tax implications of the operation.
3. The foreign exchange risk.
4. Shipping problems.
5. Import and export restrictions.
6. Inflation in the host country.
7. Expropriation and nationalization inclinations.
8. Political risks.

The board of directors and top corporate officers are primarily responsible for developing corporate strategies that will shape the long-term character of the corporation. Thereafter, corporate strategies are implemented through management adoption of policies that guide lower level corporate decision makers in their effort to achieve corporate strategies. Middle management is expected to supervise the daily operations of business by following the announced policies of top management. However, such organizational complexity often makes implementation of business policies in the operational aspects of business a difficult task which continually challenges top management.

CONCLUSION

Although sole proprietorship is the most common form of business organization, corporations hold most of the business assets utilized in America. The popularity of the corporate form is largely explained by the limited liability status obtained by corporate shareholders. The corporate form, therefore, is able to attract substantial investment funds for business use. Moreover, the corporation's relative permanence as a legal entity enables the business to continue uninterrupted with a transfer of ownership of shares or on the death of any of the shareholders. These advantages are not available generally to the sole proprietor or partnership form of organization.

A corporation is a legal entity created by the consent of the government and endowed with certain powers which enable it to engage in business enterprise. As a legal being, it is separate from the people who create, own, and manage it. Yet, it may own, control, and convey property, make contracts, sue or be sued, and generally carry on business transactions in its state of incorporation, in other states, or even in other countries.

The corporate form of business organization has become so utilized that the complex industrial society of America today relies on corporations to organize the conversion of most of our limited resources into desired goods and services. At the same time, the corporation strives to make prudent policy decisions which ensure a return on the investment of shareholders. Profitability is a prerequisite for the corporation to continue to attract funds from the shareholders.

As the corporation seeks to shape its image and character, management must also realize that the corporation functions within a complex environment; its influence is substantial. The modern corporation influences people and the types of goods they buy, the services they use, and the type of culture they enjoy. These organizations can provide the initiative for improving and adapting the flow of goods and services into new wants and desires. However, the threat of certain businesses to the well-being of the ecology, the consumer, or the investor increases the pressure for government regulation.

Since corporate strategy can easily be rendered obsolete by technological developments, changes in consumer behavior patterns, or social trends, corporate executives must come to understand not only the myriad relationships that exist within the organization, but also must learn to appreciate external factors that feel the impact of their decisions. Only then can corporations attempt to appropriately balance the sometimes conflicting social and economic interests that cry out for different corporate decisions.

CASE PROBLEMS

1. Lynch and Beane undertook to form a corporation. All the steps required by the statute for the creation of a corporation were taken except that the articles of incorporation were not filed with the county recorder. The corporation entered on the performance of its duties in the business of constructing houses and other buildings. At the end of six months the corporation was forced into bankruptcy. One of its creditors sued Lynch and Beane, as though they were partners, on the theory that the corporation had never been formed because not filing the articles with the county recorder constituted a substantial failure to comply with the statutes. Decide.

2. French, appointed receiver of Manufacturing Company in an action to establish its insolvency and force stockholders to pay for unpaid stock, sued Harding on the ground that his shares had never been fully paid. Harding shows that he is not an original subscriber, having bought the stock on the market through a broker. He states further that he did not know it was unpaid. Decide.

3. John Weigel held a controlling interest in the Weigel Broadcasting Company, which operated TV Station WCIU in Chicago. Then, J. W. O'Connor and Howard Shapiro acquired control by buying stock from Weigel. After Weigel lost controlling interest, he continued to be concerned about the workings of the corporation because he had induced many personal friends and business associates to purchase its common stock. In 1974, Weigel suspected that kick-

backs were being used to divert corporate profits for personal use by the corporate officers. Weigel questioned Shapiro and O'Connor about kickbacks at the annual shareholders' meeting but received an inadequate response. Thereafter, he made a formal demand to inspect corporate books and records which was denied by the corporation. May Weigel obtain a court order for inspection?

4. The Marengo State Bank was the only bank in town. Robert Poe, vice-president, director, and a stockholder of the bank received a visit from Ronald Sablick, owner of a bank in a neighboring town. Sablick wanted to know whether a majority of the Marengo bank's stock might be for sale. He offered $90 a share. Poe brought Sablick's proposal to S. J. Hawkins, the Marengo bank's president and one of its directors. Hawkins called the other directors and all shareholders that he and Poe could think of who had in the past expressed a wish to sell their stock. Soon Hawkins was able to deliver 5,266 shares, a majority of the bank's 10,000. After the sale, Sablick sent a letter to its remaining shareholders, offering to buy their shares for $60 per share. Many of them accepted this offer. But some who did also brought suit against the bank's officers and directors for failure to notify them of the initial $90 offer. Decide.

END NOTE

1. Oliver W. Holmes, "The History of Agency," 5 *Harv. L. Rev.* 1, 14 (1892).

chapter 9

MARKETING TRANSACTIONS

The basic activity of the business corporation is the development and manufacture of products that can be marketed at a profit. This process begins with the buying of space, equipment, and materials of the right qualities, in the right quantities, at the right time, and on a continuing basis. Firms must identify their needs, locate and select suppliers, negotiate contracts, and follow up to ensure performance of their purchase contracts.

Once the raw materials have been procured and transformed into finished products, they must be marketed to buyers. The marketing process involves such legal activities as negotiating contracts for warehousing, advertising, and transporting the finished goods. Contractual terms of sale and warranty must be determined also.

Historically, merchants have sought distinctive treatment for their business transactions. In early medieval times, disputes among merchants were settled in their own courts by elder merchants who primarily resolved the controversies by applying rules developed through business customs. The courts of the "law merchant" were swift in operation for the benefit of traveling merchants, and, in applying business customs as rules, the merchants came to know the law and developed it to fit their particular needs.

Later, many of the rules of the law merchant were incorporated into the common law courts of England and eventually brought to the courts of the colonies. The law developed by the various states of the union, however, followed different paths, and this diversity of rules was not conducive to the business community with its mass production and expanding markets. Therefore, efforts were begun to make the law of merchants uniform among the several states. The result was a series of uniform laws, such as the Uniform Sales Act. Much of the Uniform Sales Act was later made part of the Uniform Commercial Code (UCC), which covers not only sales law but other laws of the mercantile system as well. The UCC has been adopted in some manner by all the states of the Union.

SALES LAW

The word *sales* has a particular legal meaning. In general, a sale is a contract or a transfer of legal title of tangible personal property from seller to buyer for a monetary consideration. Personal property is all property that is not "real" property (land and things permanently attached thereto). Examples of tangible personal property would be desks, shoes, candy, or other tangible items not attached to real estate. Intangible personal property is evidenced in stocks, bonds, copyrights, or patent rights. Thus, "sales" law is the body of law covering and applicable only to transfers of tangible personal property for a price; it does not apply to intangible property or to contracts for services.

Article 2 of the UCC embodies the law of sales. Article 2 employs several new and unique concepts in an effort to reform sales law to conform better to the customs and practices of merchants. The UCC defines a *merchant* as a professional who deals in goods and who has a peculiar skill or knowledge of the goods he or she is purporting to deal with in the transaction. Merchants may be categorized as one of the following:

1. Buyers and sellers of goods who engage in buying and selling on more than an episodic basis.
2. Professionals who may not do the actual buying and selling but who are sufficiently familiar with the goods.
3. Anyone who, though not a merchant, hires one to do his or her work.

The UCC defines *good faith* for the nonmerchant as "honesty in fact in the conduct or transaction concerned." For the merchant, the Code requires "honesty in fact," plus the observance of "reasonable commercial standards of fair dealing in the trade." A person has "notice" of a fact, when he or she has actual knowledge of it, has received a notice of it, or, from all the facts, has *reason to know* that it exists.

The UCC defines the basic obligations of the sales relationship. These obligations of buyer and seller arise in two situations. The first is the contract. In accordance with the contract, the seller *agrees* to sell goods for a price, and the buyer *agrees* to buy it for a price. How the contract is formed, what it means, and the degree to which it may have been modified are subject to the UCC rules on contract formation, interpretation, and modification. As a result, such factors as usage of trade, or course of dealing, help to shape the contractual obligation. Hence, the sales contract that the parties end up with may be different from what they expected. Avoidance of this problem requires special knowledge of the rules of contract formation adopted by Article 2 of the UCC and skill in negotiating and drafting the contract language in light of previous dealings and trade customs.

BATTLE OF THE FORMS

Perhaps the most drastic of all things that can go wrong for merchants is to assume that they have a binding contract only to discover that they do not. Under contract principles, the acceptance of a contract offer must be unequivocal, that is, exact terms of the offer must be accepted without alteration or addition of different terms. This is sometimes called the "mirror-image" rule because the terms of the acceptance must be the mirror-image of the terms of the offer. Prior to the UCC, the parties, both using their respective forms provided by their individual attorneys and drawn with terms to their own individual advantage, would correspond with one another and believe they had formed a contract. However, if a dispute occurred, the parties would find the law saying that they had not formed a contract because the terms on the buyer's offer (order form) and the terms on the seller's acceptance (acknowledgment) did not conform. Since there was no mirror-image acceptance, there was no binding contract. In effect, one party was winning the suit for the wrong reason. In terms of respect for the law, this is as bad as the wrong party winning—which, of course, might also occur since the court was not really reaching the merits of the dispute.

The UCC attempted to deal with this problem which has been called the "battle of the forms." The Code attempts to solve the "battle of the forms" controversy through Section 2-207, which allows the formation of the contract even though the writings of the parties do not agree. The seller's acknowledgment form can contain new terms (not the mirror-image) and still form a contract. The policy of 2-207 is to form the contract as the parties intended and then determine the terms of their bargain. Merchants often form their agreements without establishing all the terms to the contract. The Code recognizes this reality and molds the law to fit the practice of merchants. Another section of the Code (2-204[3]) provides that "Even though one or more terms are left open a contract for sale does not fail for indefiniteness if the parties have intended to make a contract and there is a reasonably certain basis for giving an appropriate remedy." The court can normally fashion an appropriate remedy because the Code has what might be called "filler" provisions which normally establish "reasonable" terms whenever the merchants fail to establish their own exact terms. In this way, the contract is found to exist, and the court can get to the merits of the controversy and thus more probably determine justice between the parties.

C. Itoh & Co., Inc. v. Jordan International
552 F. 2d 1228 (1977)
U.S. Court of Appeals (7th Cir.)

The pertinent facts may be briefly restated. Itoh sent its purchase order for steel coils to Jordan which contained no provision for arbitration. Subsequently, Jordan sent Itoh its acknowledgment form which included . . . a broad arbitration term on the reverse side of the form. On the front of Jordan's form, the following statement also appears:

> Seller's acceptance is . . . expressly conditional on Buyer's assent to the additional or different terms and conditions set forth below and printed on the reverse side. If these terms and conditions are not acceptable, Buyer should notify Seller at once.

After the exchange of documents, Jordan delivered and Itoh paid for the steel coils. Itoh never expressly assented or objected to the additional arbitration term in Jordan's form. . . .

The instant case, therefore, involves the classic "battle of the forms," and Section 2-207 furnishes the rules for resolving such a controversy. Hence, it is to Section 2-207 that we must look to determine whether a contract has been formed by the exchange of forms between Jordan and Itoh and, if so, whether the additional arbitration term in Jordan's form is to be included in that contract. . . .

Under Section 2-207 it is necessary to first determine whether a contract has been formed under Section 2-207(1) as a result of the *exchange of forms* between Jordan and Itoh.

At common law, "an acceptance . . . which contained terms additional to . . . those of the offer . . . constituted a rejection of the offer . . . and thus became a counter-offer." Thus, the mere presence of the additional arbitration term in Jordan's acknowledgment form would, at common law, have prevented the exchange of documents between Jordan and Itoh from creating a contract, and Jordan's form would have automatically become a counter-offer.

Section 2-207(1) was intended to alter this inflexible common law approach to offer and acceptance:

> This section of the Code recognizes that in current commercial transactions, the terms of the offer and those of the acceptance will seldom be identical. Rather, under the current "battle of the forms," each party typically has a printed form drafted by his attorney and containing as many terms as could be envisioned to favor that party in his sales transactions. Whereas under common law the disparity between the fine-print terms in the parties' forms would have prevented the consummation of a contract when these forms are exchanged, Section 2-207 recognizes that in many, but not all, cases the parties do not impart such significance to the terms on the printed forms. . . . Thus, under Subsection (1), a contract . . . [may be] recognized notwithstanding the fact that an acceptance . . . contains terms additional to . . . those of the offer. . . .

And it is now well-settled that the *mere presence* of an additional term, such as a provision for arbitration, in one of the parties' forms will not prevent the formation of a contract under Section 2-207(1).

However, while Section 2-207(1) constitutes a sharp departure from the common law "mirror image" rule, there remain situations where the inclusion of an additional term in one of the forms exchanged by the parties will prevent the consummation of a contract *under that section.* Section 2-207(1) contains a proviso which operates to prevent an exchange of forms from creating a contract where "acceptance is expressly made conditional on assent to the additional . . . terms." In the instant case, Jordan's acknowledgment form contained the following statement:

> Seller's acceptance is . . . *expressly conditional* on Buyer's *assent* to the additional or different terms and conditions set forth below and printed on the reverse side. If these terms and conditions are not acceptable, Buyer should notify Seller at once.

The arbitration provision at issue on this appeal is printed on the reverse side of Jordan's acknowledgment, and there is no dispute that Itoh never expressly assented to the challenged arbitration term.

The Court of Appeals for the Sixth Circuit has held that the proviso must be construed narrowly. . . .

. . . [H]owever, it is clear that the statement contained in Jordan's acknowledgment form comes within the section 2-207(1) proviso.

Hence, the exchange of forms between Jordan and Itoh did not result in the formation of a contract under Section 2-207(1), and Jordan's form became a counteroffer. "[T]he consequence of a clause conditioning acceptance on assent to the additional or different terms is that *as of the exchanged writings, there is no contract.* Either party may at this point in their dealings walk away from the transaction." However, neither Jordan nor Itoh elected to follow that course; instead, both parties proceeded to performance—Jordan by delivering and Itoh by paying for the steel coils.

At common law, the "terms of the counter-offer were said to have been accepted by the original offeror when he proceeded to perform under the contract without objecting to the counter-offer." Thus, under pre-Code law, Itoh's performance (*i.e.*, payment for the steel coils) probably constituted acceptance of the Jordan counter-offer, including its provision for arbitration. However, a different approach is required under the Code.

Section 2-207(3) of the Code first provides that "[c]onduct by both parties which recognizes the existence of a contract is sufficient to establish a contract for sale although the writings of the parties do not otherwise establish a contract." As the court noted in *Dorton,* at 1166:

> [W]hen no contract is recognized under Subsection 2-207(1) . . . the entire transaction aborts at this point. If, however, the subsequent conduct of the parties—particularly, performance by both parties under what they apparently believe to be a contract—recognizes the existence of a contract, under Subsection 2-207(3) such conduct by both

parties is sufficient to establish a contract, notwithstanding the fact that no contract would have been recognized on the basis of their writings alone.

Thus, "[s]ince . . . [Itoh's] purchase order and . . . [Jordan's] counter-offer did not in themselves create a contract, Section 2-207(3) would operate to create one because the subsequent performance by both parties constituted 'conduct by both parties which recognizes the existence of a contract.' "

What are the terms of a contract created by conduct under Section 2-207(3) rather than by an exchange of forms under Section 2-207(1)? As noted above, at common law the terms of the contract between Jordan and Itoh would be the terms of the Jordan counter-offer. However, the Code has effectuated a radical departure from the common law rule. The second sentence of Section 2-207(3) provides that where, as here, a contract has been consummated by the conduct of the parties, "the terms of the particular contract consist of those terms on which the writings of the parties agree, together with any supplementary terms incorporated under any other provisions of this Act." Since it is clear that the Jordan and Itoh forms do not "agree" on arbitration, the only question which remains *under the Code* is whether arbitration may be considered a supplementary term incorporated under some other provision of the Code. . . .

Since provision for arbitration is not a necessary or missing term which would be supplied by one of the Code's "gap-filler" provisions unless agreed upon by the contracting parties, there is no arbitration term in the Section 2-207(3) contract which was created by the conduct of Jordan and Itoh in proceeding to perform even though no contract had been established by their exchange of writings.

We are convinced that this conclusion does not result in any unfair prejudice to a seller who elects to insert in his standard sales acknowledgment form the statement that acceptance is expressly conditional on buyer's assent to additional terms contained therein. Such a seller obtains a substantial benefit *under Section 2-207(1)* through the inclusion of an "expressly conditional" clause. If he decides after the exchange of forms that the particular transaction is not in his best interest, Subsection (1) permits him to walk away from the transaction without incurring any liability so long as the buyer has not in the interim expressly assented to the additional terms. Moreover, whether or not a seller will be disadvantaged *under Subsection (3)* as a consequence of inserting an "expressly conditional" clause in his standard form is within his control. If the seller in fact does not intend to close a particular deal unless the additional terms are assented to, he can protect himself by not delivering the goods until such assent is forthcoming. If the seller does intend to close a deal irrespective of whether or not the buyer assents to the additional terms, he can hardly complain when the contract formed under Subsection (3) as a result of the parties' conduct is held not to include those terms. Although a seller who employs such an "expressly conditional" clause in his acknowledgment form would undoubtedly appreciate the dual advantage of not being bound to a contract under Subsection (1) if he elects not to perform and of having his additional terms imposed on the buyer under Subsection (3) in the event that performance is in his best interest, we do not believe such a result is contemplated by Section 2-207. Rather, while a seller may take advantage of an "expressly conditional" clause under Subsection (1) when he elects not to perform, he must accept the potential risk under Subsection (3) of not getting his additional terms when he elects to proceed with performance without first obtaining buyer's assent to those terms. Since the seller injected ambiguity into the transaction by inserting the "expressly conditional" clause in his form, he, and not the buyer, should bear the consequence of that ambiguity under Subsection (3).

Questions

1. What is meant by the "battle of the forms"? What is the "mirror-image" rule?
2. Under 2-207(1), how does one differentiate between an acceptance and a counteroffer?
3. Did the parties form a contract by their writings?
4. Under the common law, Itoh's performance (that is, payment for the steel coils) probably constituted acceptance of the Jordan counteroffer, including its provision for arbitration. How does Section 2-207(3) of the Code change this result?

STATUTE OF FRAUDS

Certain types of contracts, although they fulfill the requirements of a valid contract, are not enforceable unless they are reduced to writing. The written contract has been a requisite for legal enforceability for certain types of agreements since the passage by the English Parliament in 1677 of the Statute of Frauds. Its theory involved the requirement that contracts be in writing to prevent the perpetration of frauds. Consequently, even if the plaintiff can prove with reasonable certainty the terms of the oral contract, the court will not enforce the contract when the defendant claims the protection of the statute. In essence, when a contract is the type that is required to be written by the statute, oral evidence is not allowed. The success of the Statute of Frauds in prevention of frauds has been minimal, but its viability as law has endured.

The Statute of Frauds applies only to the enforcement of executory contracts. If both parties have fully performed their obligations under an agreement, the courts treat the bargain as binding and allow it to stand. Although the law may vary somewhat from state to state, the more important kinds of agreements generally required by the statute to be put in writing are as follows:

1. Contracts to guarantee the debts or obligations of another.
2. Contracts that cannot be completed within one year from the date in which the agreement is made.
3. Contracts for the transfer of an interest in real property.
4. Contracts for the sale of tangible personal property valued at $500 or more.

The courts have not always been hospitable to the Statute of Frauds. Consequently, many judicial exceptions to the statute have been created. For example, A's promise to work for B for ten years must be in writing to be enforceable because it is not capable of being performed in less than a year. However, if A's promise is to work for his entire life for B, the courts do not require a writing because such promise is capable of being completely performed in less than a year (B could die in less than a year).

When a written contract is required, the writing, or connected writings, must contain all the essential terms of the contract. The written memoranda should contain the following information:

1. Essential terms of the contract.
2. Names and identities of the parties to the contract.
3. Signature of the party to be charged.

The written evidence of an agreement is enforceable only against the party or parties who have signed it. The party's signature denies him or her the right to assert the protection of the statute. However, Article 2 of the UCC has made an important change in this theory concerning signatures as the following case illustrates.

Cook Grains, Inc. v. Fallis

395 S.W. 2d 555 (1965)
Supreme Court of Arkansas

Plaintiff, Cook Grains, Inc., filed this suit alleging that it entered into a valid contract with defendant, Paul Fallis, whereby Fallis sold and agreed to deliver to Cook 5,000 bushels of soybeans at $2.54 per bushel. It is alleged that Fallis breached the alleged contract by failing to deliver the beans, and that as a result thereof Cook has been damaged in the sum of $1,287.50. There was a judgement for Fallis. The grain company has appealed.

Plaintiff introduced evidence to the effect that its agent, Lester Horton, entered into a verbal agreement with defendant whereby defendant sold and agreed to deliver to plaintiff grain company 5,000 bushels of beans; that delivery was to be made in September, October, and November, 1963. Fallis denied entering into such a contract. He contends that although a sale was discussed, no agreement was reached. He also contends that [the written confirmation of the oral understanding sent by Cook Grains to Fallis as] the alleged contract is barred [from court enforcement] by the statute of frauds.

The plaintiff grain company concedes that ordinarily the alleged cause of action would be barred by the statute of frauds, but contends that here the alleged sale is taken out of the statute of frauds by the Uniform Commercial Code. It is as follows:

§ 2-201 Formal requirements—Statute of frauds.—(1) Except as otherwise provided in this section a contract for the sale of goods for the price of $500 or more is not enforceable by way of action or defense unless there is some writing sufficient to indicate that a contract for sale has been made between the parties and signed by the party against whom enforcement is sought or by his authorized agent or broker.

(2) Between merchants if within a reasonable time a writing in confirmation of the contract and sufficient against the sender is received and the party receiving it has reason to know its contents, it satisfies the requirements of subsection (1) against such party unless written notice of objection to its contents is given within ten (10) days after it is received. . . .

Thus, it will be seen that under the statute, if defendant is a merchant he would be liable on the alleged contract because he did not, within ten days, give written notice that he rejected it.

The solution of the case turns on the point of whether the defendant Fallis is a "merchant" within the meaning of the statute. § 852104 provides:

'Merchant' means a person who deals in goods of the kind or otherwise by his occupation holds himself out as having knowledge or skill peculiar to the practices or goods involved in the transaction or to whom such knowledge or skill may be attributed by his employment of an agent or broker or other intermediary who by his occupation holds himself out as having such knowledge or skill. . . .

There is not a scintilla of evidence in the record, or proffered as evidence, that defendant is a dealer in goods of the kind or by his occupation holds himself out as having knowledge or skill peculiar to the practices of dealers in goods involved in the transaction, and no such knowledge or skill can be attributed to him.

The evidence in this case is that defendant is a farmer and nothing else. He farms about 550 acres and there is no showing that he has any other occupation. Our attention has been called to no case, and we have found none holding that the word farmer may be construed to mean merchant.

. . . There is nothing whatever in the statute indicating that the word "merchant" should apply to a farmer when he is acting in the capacity of a farmer, and he comes within that category when he is merely trying to sell the commodities he has raised.

Notes 1 and 2 under § 2-104 (Uniform Commercial Code) defining merchant indicate that this provision of the statute is meant to apply to professional traders. In Note 1 it is stated: "This section lays the foundation of this policy defining those who are to be regarded as professionals or 'merchants,' . . ." It is said in Note 2: "The term 'merchant' as defined here roots in the 'law merchant' concept of a professional in business. . . ."

In construing a statute its words must be given their plain and ordinary meaning.

Questions

1. What is the written confirmation exception to the Statute of Frauds?
2. Why was the written confirmation exception not applied to Fallis?

Notes

1. Compare *Cook Grains* with this language in *Ohio Grain Co.* v. *Swisshelm* (40 Ohio App. 2d 203 [1973]).

   A buyer who agrees to purchase farm products at a stated price in cash may send to the seller a timely written confirmation specifying the terms, and the quality and standards required, and may hold a seller who has the knowledge or skill of merchants, to the terms and conditions specified, unless the seller gives timely notice of his objection.

   An experienced farmer, who previously sold soybeans, keeps abreast of the soybean market, and sells livestock and other farm products from time to time, is "chargeable with the knowledge or skill of merchants . . . in selling his current crop of soybeans."

2. The signature of each party to the agreement should be the one he or she ordinarily uses in business transactions, although the law does not make this requirement. It may be printed. It may be an initial, a mark, or any other symbol, as long as the party intends to authenticate the document. The signature need not appear at the end of the memorandum, but it must appear somewhere.

UNCONSCIONABLE

In addition to the traditional limitation on contractual freedom imposed by the concept of illegality, the law is evolving toward the requirement that contracts be fair and be formed in good faith. The law is becoming increasingly concerned with the use of superior bargaining power to obtain favorable terms from those who are unable to protect themselves.

In the case of sales under Article 2 of the UCC, the seller must act in good faith, which for a merchant-seller is defined as "honesty in fact and the observance of reasonable commercial standards of fair dealing in the trade" (UCC Section 2-103[1][b]). Other statutes, such as the Federal Automotive Dealer's Day in Court Act likewise are imposing duties of good faith bargaining. Such terms in the law empower the judges with greater latitude of interpretation to achieve "social justice." A more obvious example of expanding judicial power to modify contracts is the power afforded to the court to modify contractual terms if they are too harsh or oppressive to one of the two parties. Traditionally, the courts have refused to enforce a "too harsh" liquidated damage clause and in a more modern context, the UCC provides that

> If the court . . . finds the contract or any clause of the contract to have been unconscionable at the time it was made, the court may refuse to enforce the contract, or it may enforce the remainder of the contract without the unconscionable clause, or it may so limit the application of any unconscionable clause as to avoid any unconscionable result. UCC Section 2-302(1).

To exercise the unconscionability provision, the court need not receive proof of fraud. Whenever there is grossly disproportionate bargaining power between the parties, so that the weaker party "just signs on the dotted line," the court can modify the grossly unfair terms to avoid results which are contrary to public policy.

Campbell Soup Co. v. Wentz
172 F. 2d 80 (1948)
U.S. Court of Appeals (3d. Cir.)

On June 21, 1947, Campbell Soup Company (Campbell), a New Jersey corporation, entered into a written contract with George B. Wentz and Harry T. Wentz, who are Pennsylvania farmers, for delivery by the Wentzes to Campbell of all the Chantenay red cored carrots to be grown on fifteen acres of the Wentz farm during the 1947 season. The contract provides . . . for delivery of the carrots at the Campbell plant in Camden, New Jersey. The prices specified in the contract ranged from $23 to $30 a ton.

The Wentzes harvested approximately 100 tons of carrots from the fifteen acres covered by the contract. Early in January, 1948, they told a Campbell representative that they would not deliver their carrots at the contract price. The market price at the time was at least $90 per ton, and the Chantenay red cored carrots were virtually unobtainable. . . .

On January 9, 1948, Campbell [sued] . . . the Wentz brothers . . . to compel specific performance of the contract.

We think that on the question of adequacy of the legal remedy the case is one appropriate for specific performance. It was expressly found that at the time of the trial it was "virtually impossible to obtain Chantenay carrots in the open market."

. . . We see no reason why a court should be reluctant to grant specific relief when it can be given without supervision of the court or other time-consuming processes against one who has deliberately broken his agreement. Here the goods of the special type contracted for were unavailable on the open market, the plaintiff had contracted for them long ahead in anticipation of its needs, and had built up a general reputation for its products as part of which reputation uniform appearance was important. We think if this were all that was involved in the case specific performance should have been granted.

The reason that we shall affirm instead of reversing with an order for specific performance is found in the contract itself. We think it is too hard a bargain and too one-sided an agreement to entitle the plaintiff to relief in a court of conscience. For each individual grower the agreement is made by filling in names and quantity and price on a printed form furnished by the buyer. This form has quite obviously been drawn by skillful draftsmen with the buyer's interests in mind.

Paragraph 2 provides for the manner of delivery. Carrots are to have their stalks cut off and be in clean sanitary bags or other containers approved by Campbell. This paragraph concludes with a statement that Campbell's determination of conformance with specifications shall be conclusive.

The defendants attack this provision as unconscionable. We do not think that it is, standing by itself. We think that the provision is comparable to the promise to perform to the satisfaction of another and that Campbell would be held liable if it refused carrots which did conform to the specifications.

The next paragraph allows Campbell to refuse carrots in excess of twelve tons to the acre. The next contains a covenant by the grower that he will not sell carrots to anyone else except the carrots rejected by Campbell nor will he permit anyone else to grow carrots on his land. Paragraph 10 provides liquidation damages to the extent of $50 per acre for any breach by the grower. There is no provision for liquidated or any other damages for breach of contract by Campbell.

The provision of the contract which we think is the hardest is paragraph 9. . . . It will be noted that Campbell is excused from accepting carrots under certain circumstances. But even under such circumstances the grower, while he cannot say Campbell is liable to take the carrots, is not permitted to sell them elsewhere unless Campbell agrees. This is the kind of provision which the late Francis H. Bohlen would call "carrying a good joke too far." What the grower may do with his product under the circumstances set out is not clear. He has covenanted not to store it anywhere except on his own farm and also not to sell to anybody else.

We are not suggesting that the contract is illegal. Nor are we suggesting any excuse for the grower in this case who has deliberately broken an agreement entered into with Campbell. We do think, however, that a party who has offered and succeeded in getting an agreement as tough as this one is, should not come to a chancellor and ask court help in the enforcement of its terms. That equity does not enforce unconscionable bargains is too well established to require elaborate citation.

. . . As already said, we do not suggest that this contract is illegal. All we say is that the sum of its provisions drives too hard a bargain for a court of conscience to assist.

Questions

1. Why did the court think "damages" was an inadequate remedy and that specific performance was appropriate in this instance?
2. The court identified several provisions of the contract which it considered carefully drawn to protect the buyer's interest. Which of those provisions did the court find particularly "hardest" on the seller?
3. Did the court find the contract to be illegal? Did the court find any of the provisions in the contract unconscionable? Just what did the court rule?

PRODUCT LIABILITY

Product liability refers to those cases involving the liability of the seller, manufacturer, processor, or supplier for injuries caused to the person or property of the buyer or user because of a defect in the product sold. This area of the law has changed rapidly, producing pronounced effects on sellers of products. The result has been substantially to increase the liability of the seller, manufacturer, processor, and supplier of goods and the classes of injured parties who may seek recovery in such cases.

Initially, product liability was restricted in application to the sale of foodstuffs for human consumption. It has since been expanded to include almost any product that causes injuries to the person or property of the buyer. The seller can be held liable on the basis of negligence, breach of implied warranty, or strict liability.

NEGLIGENCE

Some jurisdictions adhere to the use of negligence as the theory of recovery in products liability cases. This theory requires that the plaintiff trace the defective condition of the product to a fault (negligence) in manufacturing. A manufacturer must exercise due care to make the product safe for the purpose for which it is intended. This requires the exercise of care in the design of the product, in the selection of materials and component parts, in inspection and testing, and in giving adequate warnings of any danger in the use of the product which an ordinary person might not be able to detect.

The development of manufacturer liability for negligent production of defective products was initially blocked by the doctrine of "privity." An English case in 1843 held that the breach of a contract to keep a passenger coach in good repair after sale provided no legal remedy to a passenger in the coach who was injured when it collapsed.[1] The court reasoned that the passenger, who was not a party to the contract involving the maintenance of the coach, was not in "privity of contract." To allow the passenger to recover, the judges argued, would lead to "the most absurd and outrageous consequences" with no limit to liability, unless the court confined liability to the contracting parties. This ruling later developed into a general rule that the original seller of goods was not liable for damages caused by defects in the goods to anyone except the immediate buyer; that is, the one in privity with the seller.

Later, both British and U.S. courts began to reject the strict privity requirement when dealing with goods that were considered inherently dangerous. In the case of *MacPherson* v. *Buick Motor Company*,[2] the manufacturer of an automobile with a defective wheel was held liable to the ultimate purchaser of the automobile who was injured when the defective wheel collapsed. The court held the manufacturer liable for its negligence—despite the absence of privity of contract between the manufacturer and MacPherson, the ultimate consumer who purchased through a retail distributor. Judge Cardozo wrote the following:

> If the nature of a thing is such that it is reasonably certain to place life and limb in peril when negligently made, it is then a thing of danger. Its nature gives warning of the consequences to be expected. If to the element of danger there is added knowledge that

the thing will be used by persons other than the purchaser and used wihout new tests, then irrespective of the contract, the manufacturer of this thing of danger is under a duty to make it carefully.

Cardozo's interpretation of "inherently dangerous" became the touchstone for the expansion of products liability cases. One writer has commented that

inherent danger was extended beyond Cardozo's interpretation to include physical harm to property, and even to negligence in the sale of goods, such as animal food, which involves no recognizable risk of personal injury, and are foreseeably dangerous only to property.[3]

Despite the breach in the wall of privity, it is still very difficult for an injured consumer to successfully pursue a products liability case on the basis of negligence. This is true because the plaintiff must prove a duty owed by the manufacturer or seller; the existence of a breach of that duty must be demonstrated; and a proximate causal connection between the plaintiff's injury and the defendant's breach of duty must be shown. Besides these difficult burdens of proof on the plaintiff-consumer, the defendant-manufacturer may also have a complete defense to negligence by proving the contributory negligence of the plaintiff or the assumption of risk of injury by the plaintiff.

The present state of the law of negligence by a manufacturer is best expressed in the *Restatement of the Law of Torts, Second,* Section 395, which provides the following:

A manufacturer who fails to exercise reasonable care in the manufacture of a chattel, which, unless carefully made, he should recognize as involving an unreasonable risk of causing substantial bodily harm to those who lawfully use it for a purpose for which it is manufactured and those whom the supplier should expect to be in the vicinity of its probable use, is subject to liability for bodily harm caused to them by its lawful use in a manner and for a purpose for which it is manufactured.

The liability for negligence of a seller other than the manufacturer (retailers and wholesalers) is set forth in Section 401. It provides the following:

A seller of a chattel manufactured by a third person who knows or has reason to know that the chattel is, or is likely to be, dangerous when used by a person to whom it is delivered or for whose use it is supplied, or to others whom the seller should expect to share in or be endangered by its use, is subject to liability for bodily harm caused thereby to them if he fails to exercise reasonable care to inform them of the danger or otherwise to protect them against it.

This liability is imposed on the seller (retailer or wholesaler) based on his or her "reason to know" the dangerous character of the product. The retailer's duty is to exercise reasonable care to inform the purchaser or user of this danger in order to protect the consumer from it. Section 402 excuses from liability the seller of goods manufactured by a third person if the seller does not know or have reason to know of the dangerous character of the goods. Moreover, Section

402 indicates that the retailer or wholesaler will not be liable for failure to inspect or test the goods before selling them. This Section, therefore, protects the retailer who sells goods that are prepackaged or placed in sealed containers by a manufacturer. The seller-retailer would not be liable for negligence based on the theory of failure to inspect. However, in those states utilizing an alternative theory of liability, the retailer may be liable even if not negligent.

LaRue v. National Union Electric Corp.
571 F. 2d 51 (1978)
U.S. Court of Appeals (5th Cir.)

Conrad LaRue brought this . . . action in January 1972, on behalf of his minor son Michael, for injuries suffered by Michael. The complaint charged National Union Electric Corp. with negligent design and manufacture of a vacuum cleaner. National Union denied all liability and alleged contributory negligence on the part of Michael. After a trial in March 1977 . . . the jury . . . [found] for Michael on the negligence count. The jury determined that $125,000 would fully compensate Michael but that his own comparative negligence required reduction of the award to $93,750. National Union and LaRue both appealed, the former . . . attacking the verdict as contrary to law . . . and the latter arguing the issue of comparative negligence should not have been submitted to the jury.

On January 25, 1971, Michael LaRue, then 11 years old, was playing with his parents' canister-type vacuum cleaner, a Eureka Model 842A. He and his sister were home because they had missed the bus for school; his father was at work and his mother in school. The previous evening his mother had taken out the two filters that rested above the fan housing and motor in order to clean them. The morning of the accident, the vacuum cleaner was left out in a hallway, plugged in, with the filters not yet replaced and the hood that covered its top half left open. . . .

According to Michael's testimony, he was sitting on the yellow plastic filter support, which in turn rested on the metal casing that covered the fan and engine, riding the vacuum cleaner as if it were a toy car. He was dressed in pajamas. His older sister was in another room watching television. At some point in his play the motor was turned on. Michael continued to ride the vacuum cleaner until his penis slipped through openings in the filter support and casing into the fan. He immediately suffered an amputation of the head of his penis and part of the shaft. He rushed outside to seek help, was taken to the hospital, and underwent the first of a number of complicated operations to repair the damage to his penis. . . .

The principal issue at trial was the adequacy of safety features in the Eureka vacuum cleaner in light of foreseeable risks of injury resulting from household use. The LaRues contended National Union had failed to take sufficient precautions both by not installing a shield over the opening in the engine and fan casing to prevent insertion of stray parts of the human body and by not using an "interlock" switch that would prevent the motor from turning on while the hood was up. The strongest evidence in support of these contentions was the testimony of plaintiff's expert, Dr. Paul, a design engineer on the MIT faculty. Dr. Paul . . . explained that the rotation of the fan at 15,000 rpm left it invisible. Someone fiddling around with the interior of the machine, and especially a child, would have no warning of the danger created by the sharp, quickly moving fan blades. Some amount of exposure to the risk was inherent in the design, as the filters that covered the fan casing periodically had to be removed. Dr. Paul testified that suction created by the fan was sufficient to pull in stray items through the overlarge openings. He asserted that the safety devices that could eliminate this risk—a shield or an interlock switch—were feasible and, at least with regard to the switch, inexpensive.

To demonstrate the reasonableness of installing a protective shield over the fan housing, plaintiff produced a Eureka 4001 vacuum cleaner, manufactured during the same period as the 842A model and marketed overseas. The 4001 was in all material respects identical to the 842A, except that it was wired to take the higher voltages used in Europe and contained a shield over the fan housing such as would have prevented Michael's accident. The shield was required by Swedish safety regulations. . . .

National Union . . . argues that regardless of the nature of the hazard presented by the vacuum cleaner, this accident resulted from unforeseeable misuse of the product for which the manufacturer cannot be charged with liability. That question was submitted to the jury as part of the issue of negligence. National Union . . . argues that as a matter of law this use and the ensuing accident were simply not foreseeable. . . .

In the analogous situation of a storeowner's duty of care to child invitees on the premises, the Supreme Judicial Court of Maine has ruled that the critical factor is

> the *reasonableness*, or the *unreasonableness*, of the risks of harm engendered by the premises, facilities, instrumentalities, or combinations thereof, in the light of the *totality of the circumstances*, as the ordinarily prudent storekeeper would apprehend the circumstances and foresee the dangers of harm generated by them—including the reasonably recognizable dangers resulting from the reasonably foreseeable *misuse* of the premises by children in the light of their known, or reasonably recognizable, propensities. *Orr v. First National Stores, Inc.*, 280 A.2d 785, 792 (Me. 1971) [Emphasis in original.]

In determining what kind of reasonable forseeable misuse might arise from the play of children, the court recognized

> that children as old as thirteen years of age are likely to act dangerously to themselves even though, upon reflection, they know better. *Id.* at 790.

It also observed:

> It should be emphasized that it is unessential that the *precise* manner in which injuries might have occurred, or were sustained, be foreseeable, or foreseen. It is sufficient that

there is a reasonable generalized gamut of greater than ordinary dangers of injury and that the sustaining of injury was within this range. . . .

It was undisputed that National Union realized that the Eureka 842A vacuum cleaner would be used in households where children would be present and appreciated the risks of children playing with the insides of the machine. Based on all the evidence presented at trial, there was a sufficient basis for holding that the vacuum cleaner presented an unreasonable risk of harm to children who might reasonably be foreseen to explore and fiddle with the device. The inadvertent intrusion of Michael's penis into the fan, perhaps the product of the machine's suction, fell within this class of dangers, even though the precise circumstances of the accident might have been improbable. Under the principles expressed in *Orr*, the district court had a sufficient basis for refusing to rule that as a matter of law the injury to Michael was so unforeseeable as to be outside the scope of National Union's duty to consumers of its product.

By the same token, we reject plaintiff's argument that the evidence concerning the hidden danger presented by the vacuum cleaner was so unequivocal as to bar the district court from letting the issue of Michael's own negligence go to the jury. Plaintiff exaggerates the strength of his own case. Evidence was presented suggesting that the vacuum cleaner motor was switched on as long as two minutes before the accident; during that time Michael continued to ride the machine. Perhaps, as plaintiff's expert contended, the fan blades rotated at too great a speed to be visible, but the jury well might have believed that the sound of the motor alone should have been enough to warn Michael that some danger existed. There was evidence that Michael was familiar with the operation of the machinery in general and engines in particular. The district court properly submitted the issue of comparative negligence to the jury.

Questions

1. Was the use of the machine as a toy car by a child "reasonably foreseeable" by the manufacturer?
2. What is "comparative negligence"? Was it properly applied in *LaRue*?

BREACH OF WARRANTY

A second type of theory of recovery against the seller of a defective product is called breach of warranty. A warranty under the law of sales (UCC Article 2) is an obligation imposed by law on the seller with respect to the goods. Such warranties can arise from (1) the mere fact of the transaction of sale (a warranty of title) or (2) by affirmations of fact or promise by the seller to the buyer (warranties of quality). The latter warranties are referred to as express warranties, which are explicit undertakings by the seller with respect to quality, description, or performability of the goods. For example, in *Baxter* v. *Ford Motor*

Company,[4] the court held that the manufacturer's advertisement of a "shatterproof" windshield made the defendant liable, when the windshield subsequently shattered and caused injuries to the plaintiff. These expressed warranties constitute a portion of the bargain between the parties. Accordingly, if the seller chooses not to give any expressed warranties, he or she is free to avoid this potential liability by refusing to affirm the quality or nature of the goods. Of course, the buyer is thereby put on notice and perhaps less likely to make the purchase.

In addition, the merchant-seller who deals in goods of a certain kind impliedly warrants the "merchantability" of those goods. This warranty is implied by law into the bargain without any express bargaining on the matter by the parties. To be merchantable, the goods must be of such quality as to pass in the market without objection and to be honestly resalable by the buyer in the normal course of business. The implied warranty of merchantability is an obligation on the merchant-seller that the goods are reasonably fit for the general purpose for which they are manufactured and sold and, also, that they are of fair, average, and merchantable quality. When goods are sold to a consumer, merchantability generally means reasonably fit for consumption.

The second implied warranty is the warranty of "fitness for *particular* purpose" which arises when a seller has reason to know the particular purpose of the buyer and the buyer is relying on the seller's skill and judgment in selecting goods to fit that particular purpose. Fitness for the buyer's particular purpose may be the same as merchantability. A restauranteur impliedly warrants that the meals are fit for the *particular* purpose and *ordinary* purpose for which goods are sold—human consumption.

The implied warranties are imposed on the seller by law, not by the bargaining of the parties. The UCC makes clear that the seller may modify or exclude these implied warranties with the buyer's consent; however, the disclaimers must be positive, explicit, unequivocal, and conspicuous, so that the buyer's acknowledgment of the change in implied warranties is clear. In addition, since the Code requires that notice of any breach of warranty be given to the seller in a reasonable time after the defect has occurred, the buyer's failure to notify the seller may result in being barred from any remedy.

Many states require that since the warranty extends with the contract of sale of the goods, the absence of a contractual relationship (privity) with the seller would preclude recovery by a victim that was not the buyer of the goods from the defendant-seller. However, many courts have abolished the requirement of privity. The Code itself has relaxed the requirement of privity of contract. It permits recovery for breach of warranty that causes injury to members of the family or the household of the buyer or guests to his or her home even though such persons are without privity of contract.

The contributory negligence of the buyer is no defense to an action for a breach of warranty. However, the buyer's discovery of a defect would preclude recovery against the seller for injuries caused by the known defect (voluntary assumption of risk).

Warranties are limited to sales of goods. No warranty attaches to the performance of a service. If the service is performed negligently, the cause of action accruing is for that negligence. In contrast, the case of a sale of goods gives rise to a breach of warranty action without proof of fault by the seller. Consequently, victims prefer a breach of warranty action over an action for negligence. Therefore, problems often arise over the determination of whether the transaction was a service or a sale. In one case, it was held that injuries to scalp and hair from the application of a product in a beauty treatment was not a sale and, consequently, no breach of warranty action could be maintained. The victim was left with only a negligence action in which she had to prove that the beauty operator failed to execise reasonable care. Contrast this result with the following case.

Newmark v. Gimbel's Inc.

246 A. 2d 11 (1968)
Supreme Court, Appellate Division of New Jersey

Mrs. Newmark sued for injury to her skin and loss of hair following a permanent wave treatment at defendant's beauty parlor. . . . She was waited on by one Valente, a beauty technician, who told her that her fine hair was not right for the special permanent and that she needed a "good" permanent wave. She agreed to this. . . .

Valente admitted that the permanent wave procedure followed was at his suggestion. It is conceded that the permanent wave solution he used was "Candle Glow," a product of Helene Curtis. Valente testified that the processing products he used were applied as they were taken from the original packages or containers, and that it was common for a customer to feel a burning or tingling sensation when the waving lotion was applied. He stated that persons were affected "in varying degrees" by the treatment. When he began the treatment there was "nothing wrong" with her hair or scalp. . . .

The core question here presented is whether warranty principles permit a recovery against a beauty parlor operator for injuries sustained by a customer as a result of use on the customer of a product which was selected and furnished by the beauty parlor operator. . . .

. . . In ruling that warranty did not apply here the trial judge reasoned that the transaction between the parties amounted to the rendition of services rather than the sale of a product, hence defendant could be held liable only for negligence in the performance of such services. Our consideration of the question convinces us that his ruling was a mistaken one.

It would appear clear that the instances in which implied warranties may be imposed are not limited to "sales" that come strictly within the meaning of Article 2 of the Uniform Commercial Code. . . .

In *Cintrone* v. *Hertz Truck Leasing*, 45 N.J. 434, 446 (1965), the court said:

There is no good reason for restricting such warranties to sales. Warranties of fitness are regarded by law as an incident of a transaction because one party to the relationship is in a better position than the other to know and control the condition of the chattel transferred and to distribute the losses which may occur because of a dangerous condition the chattel possesses. These factors make it likely that the party acquiring possession of the article will assume it is in a safe condition for use and therefore refrain from taking precautionary measures himself. . . .

The policy reasons applicable in the case of sales would likewise justify the extension of liability for breach of warranty to any commercial transaction where one person supplies a product to another, whether or not the transaction be technically considered as a sale. . . . The rationale underlying the liability of a retailer for defects in a product obtained from a reputable supplier and sold to a customer, has been explained as follows:

. . . If reliance upon the seller is needed, it may be found in the customer's reliance on the retailer's skill and judgment in selecting his sources of supply. Broader considerations are also urged. The retailer should bear this as one of the risks of his enterprise. He profits from the transaction and is in a fairly strategic position to promote safety through pressure on his supplier. Also, he is known to his customers and subject to their suits, while the maker is often unknown and may well be beyond the process of any court convenient to the customer. Moreover, the retailer is in a good position to pass the loss back to his supplier, either through negotiations or through legal proceedings. 2 Harper and James, *Torts*, §28.30, p. 1600 (1956).

Weighing the foregoing policy considerations, we are satisfied and hold that, stripped of its nonessentials the transaction here in question, consisting of the supplying of a product for use in the administration of a permanent wave to plaintiff, carried with it an implied warranty that the product used was reasonably fit for the purpose for which it was to be used.

Mrs. Newmark was a regular customer of defendant and had a weekly appointment to have her hair washed and set. On the day in question she received something in addition—a permanent wave. In essence, it involved application of a permanent wave lotion or solution and thereafter a neutralizer. The lotion was selected by one of defendant's operators who was familiar with her scalp and hair from current examination and prior visits. The product was secured from sources known to defendant and only defendant knew of any special instructions concerning its use. The risk from use of the lotion was incident to the operation of defendant's business, a business which yielded it a profit and placed it in a position to promote safety through pressure on suppliers. It was in a position to protect itself by making inquiry or tests to determine the susceptibility of customers to the use of the product, or by using another lotion which did not present the possibility of an adverse effect. It could secure indemnity from its suppliers through legal proceedings or otherwise. The fact that there was no separate charge for the product did not preclude its being considered as having been supplied to the customer in a sense justifying the imposition of an implied warranty against injurious defects therein. . . .

While the statement of facts presently before us leaves something to be desired, we are satisfied that the jury could have found from the evidence that the product was defective within the intent of the statute. In the first place the record does not show that plaintiff's dermatitis was the result of an allergic attack peculiar to her own sensitivities. Neither medical witness so testified. Second, the product was accompanied by an instruction in the form of a warning from which it could be inferred that its use, in the absence of certain precautions, could adversely affect an appreciable number of persons. Some support for such an inference is found in Valente's testimony that a burning or tingling sensation is fairly common (in such cases) and that each person was affected "in varying degrees." It is conceded that plaintiff testified that she had received permanent wave treatments prior to and for two years subsequent to the incident in question with no adverse effects to her hair or scalp.

It follows that the issue of defendant's liability for breach of implied warranties of fitness for purpose and merchantability should have been submitted to the jury.

Questions

1. Why did the trial judge decide there was no cause of action for breach of warranty?
2. What "policy reasons" justify the "extension of liability for breach of warranty to any commercial transaction where one person supplies a product to another, whether or not the transaction be technically considered as a sale"?
3. Forty-one states have enacted statutes which expressly provide that a blood transfusion is a service and not a sale, or alternatively state that the hospital is not liable in blood transfusions except for negligence or willful misconduct. Such statutes protect the hospital in the sale of blood which may contain a hepatitis virus because such viruses cannot be detected and excluded from blood components. Is this reason sufficient to override the policy reasons for imposing liability for defective goods in a "sale"?

Hunt v. Ferguson-Paulus Enterprises
415 P. 2d 13 (1966)
Supreme Court of Oregon

The plaintiff bought a cherry pie from the defendant through a vending machine owned and maintained by the defendant. On biting into the pie one of plaintiff's teeth was broken when it encountered a cherry pit. He brought this action to recover damages for the injury, alleging breach of warranty of fitness of the pie for human consumption. In a trial to the court without a jury the court found for the defendant and plaintiff has appealed.

Under . . . [the law] if the cherry pie purchased by the plaintiff from the defendant was not reasonably fit for human consumption because of the presence of the cherry pit there was a breach of warranty and plaintiff was entitled to recover his damages thereby caused.

In the consideration of similar cases some of the courts have drawn a distinction between injury caused by spoiled, impure, or contaminated food or food containing a foreign substance, and injury caused by a substance natural to the product sold. In the latter class of cases, these courts hold there is no liability on the part of the dispenser of the food. Thus in the leading case of *Mix* v. *Ingersoll Candy Co.*, 59 P. 2d 144, the court held that a patron of a restaurant who ordered and paid for chicken pie, which contained a sharp sliver or fragment of chicken bone, and was injured as a result of swallowing the bone, had no cause of action against the restauranteur either for breach of warranty or negligence. Referring to cases in which recovery had been allowed the court said:

All of the cases are instances in which the food was found not to be reasonably fit for human consumption, either by reason of the presence of a foreign substance, or an impure and noxious condition of the food itself, such as for example glass, stones, wires, or nails in the food served, or tainted, decayed, diseased, or infected meats or vegetables.

The court went on to say that:

. . . despite the fact that a chicken bone may occasionally be encountered in a chicken pie, such chicken pie, in the absence of some further defect, is reasonably fit for human consumption. Bones which are natural to the type of meat served cannot legitimately be called a foreign substance, and a consumer who eats meat dishes ought to anticipate and be on his guard against the presence of such bones.

Further the court said:

Certainly no liability would attach to a restaurant keeper for the serving of a T-bone steak, or a beef stew which contained a bone natural to the type of meat served, or if a fish dish should contain a fish bone, or if a cherry pie should contain a cherry stone—although it be admitted that an ideal cherry pie would be stoneless. 59 P.2d at 148.

The so-called "foreign-natural" test of the *Mix* case has been applied in the following cases: *Silva* v. *F. W. Woolworth Co.,* 83 P. 2d 76 (turkey bone in "special plate" of roast turkey); *Musso* v. *Picadilly Cafeterias,* 178 So. 2d 421 (cherry pit in a cherry pie); *Courter* v. *Dilbert Bros.,* 186 N.Y.S. 2d 334 (prune pit in prune butter); *Adams* v. *Great Atlantic & Pacific Tea Co.,* 112 S.E. 2d 92 (crystalized grain of corn in cornflakes); *Webster* v. *Blue Ship Tea Room Inc.,* 198 N.E. 2d 309 (fish bone in a fish chowder).

Other courts have rejected the so-called foreign-natural test in favor of what is known as the "reasonable expectation" test, among them the Supreme Court of Wisconsin, which, in *Betehia* v. *Cape Cod Corp.,* 103 N.W. 2d 64, held that a person who was injured by a chicken bone in a chicken sandwich served to him in a restaurant, could recover for his injury either for breach of an implied warranty or for negligence. "There is a distinction," the court said, "between what a consumer expects to find in a fish stick and in a baked or fried fish, or in a chicken sandwich made from sliced white meat and in roast chicken. The test should be what is reasonably expected by the consumer in the food as served, not what might be natural to the ingredients of that food prior to preparation. What is to be reasonably expected by the consumer is a jury question in most cases; at least, we cannot say as a matter of law that a patron of a restaurant must expect a bone in a chicken sandwich either because chicken bones are occasionally found there or are natural to chicken."

Among other decisions adopting the reasonable expectation test are: *Bonenberger* v. *Pittsburgh Mercantile Co.,* 28 A. 2d 913 (oyster shell in canned oysters used in making oyster stew); *Bryer* v. *Rath Packing Co.,* 156 A. 2d 442 (chicken bone in chow mein); *Varone* v. *Calaro,* 199 N.Y.S. 2d 755 (struvite in canned tuna).

In view of the judgment for the defendant, we are not required in this case to make a choice between the two rules. Under the foreign-natural test the plaintiff would be barred from recovery as a matter of law. The reasonable expectation test calls for determination of a question of fact. . . .

The court has found the fact in favor of the defendant and this court has no power to disturb the finding.

Questions

1. What is the foreign-natural test? How would it be applied in this instance to determine if a breach of the warranty of merchantability occurred?
2. What is the "reasonable expectation" test? According to this test, was there a breach of the warranty of merchantability?

STRICT LIABILITY

The most recent and far-reaching development in the field of products liability is that of strict liability in tort. The theory of strict liability, for those states which are adopting this approach, is best expressed in Section 402A of the *Restatement of Torts, Second,* which provides the following:

> (1) One who sells any product in a defective condition unreasonably dangerous to the user or consumer or to his property is subject to liability for physical harm thereby caused to the ultimate user or consumer, or to his property, if
>
> (a) the seller is engaged in the business of selling such a product (no distinction between a manufacturer or retailer), and
>
> (b) it is expected to and does reach the user or consumer without substantial change in the condition in which it is sold.
>
> (2) The rule stated in Subsection (1) applies although
>
> (a) the seller has exercised all possible care in the preparation and sale of his product, and
>
> (b) the user or consumer has not bought the product from or entered into any contractual relation with the seller.

It is to be emphasized that Subsection (2)(a) makes clear that negligence is not the basis of this liability. The seller may still be liable in spite of the fact that he or she "has exercised all possible care in the preparation and sale of his product."

In addition, (2)(b) indicates that a "contractual relation" or privity is not required in order to establish manufacturer liability. The elements of this action were summarized by the Supreme Court of Wisconsin in *Dippel* v. *Sciano*, 155 N.W. 2d 55 (1967), as follows:

From a reading of the plain language of the rule, the plaintiff must prove (1) that the product was in defective condition when it left the possession or control of the seller, (2) that it was unreasonably dangerous to the user or consumer, (3) that the defect was a cause (a substantial factor) of the plaintiff's injuries or damages, (4) that the seller engaged in the business of selling such product or, put negatively, that this is not an isolated or infrequent transaction not related to the principal business of the seller, and (5) that the product was one which the seller expected to and did reach the user or consumer without substantial change in the condition it was when he sold it.

This liability is imposed by law as a matter of public policy. It arises out of common law in tort and does not require any contract; therefore, it is not subject to any disclaimer or modification by contractual agreement. The expanding scope of this liability is being developed by the courts in various states.

At common law, contributory negligence of the plaintiff is a bar to his or her recovery on any action based on negligence of the defendant. However, under strict liability (or negligence) in a products liability case, the plaintiff's failure to discover the defect or to guard against the probability of its existence (contributory negligence) is no defense for the seller of a defective product. Nevertheless, the maker or seller of a product is entitled to assume that the product he or she sells will be put to its normal use. The plaintiff's use of the product in some unintended, unusual, or unforseeable manner will prevent recovery from the defendant on the ground of assumption of risk. Moreover, the plaintiff who used a product with a known defect would be precluded from recovery of injury resulting from the defect.

EMBS v. Pepsi-Cola Bottling Co. of Lexington, Kentucky, Inc.

528 S.W. 2d 703 (1975)
Court of Appeals of Kentucky

On the afternoon of July 25, 1970, plaintiff entered the self-service retail store operated by the defendant, Stamper's Cash Market, Inc., for the purpose of "buying soft drinks for the kids." She went to an upright soft drink cooler, removed five bottles and placed them in a carton. Unnoticed by her, a carton of Seven-Up was sitting on the floor at the edge of the produce counter about one foot from where she was standing. As she turned away from the cooler she heard an explosion that sounded "like a shotgun." When she looked down she saw a gash in her leg, pop on her leg, green pieces of bottle on the floor and the Seven-Up carton in the midst of the debris. She did not kick or otherwise come into contact with the carton of Seven-Up prior to the explosion. Her son, who was with her, recognized the green pieces of glass as part of a Seven-Up bottle.

She was immediately taken to the hospital by Mrs. Stamper, a managing agent of the store. Mrs. Stamper told her that a Seven-Up bottle had exploded and that several bottles had exploded that week. Apparently, all of the physical evidence went out with the trash. The location of the Seven-Up carton immediately before the explosion was not a place where such items were ordinarily kept.

The defendant, Arnold Lee Vice, was the distributor of Seven-Up in the Clark County area. . . .

The defendant, Pepsi-Cola Bottling Co. of Lexington, Kentucky, Inc., was the bottler who produced and supplied Vice with his entire stock of Seven-Up. . . .

In *Dealers Transport Co.* v. *Battery Distributing Co.,* 402 S.W. 2d 441 (1966), we adopted the view of strict liability in tort expressed in Section 402A of the American Law Institute's *Restatement, Second, Torts.* . . .

Our expressed public policy will be furthered if we minimize the risk of injury and property damage by charging the costs of injuries against the manufacturer who can procure liability insurance and distribute its expense among the public as a cost of doing business; and since the risk of harm from defective products exists for mere bystanders and passersby as well as for the purchaser or user, there is no substantial reason for protecting one class of persons and not the other. The same policy requires us to maximize protection for the injured third party and promote the public interest in discouraging the marketing of products having defects that are a menace to the public by imposing strict liability upon retailers and wholesalers in the distributive chain responsible for marketing the defective product which injures the bystander. The imposition of strict liability places no unreasonable burden upon sellers because they can adjust the cost of insurance protection among themselves in the course of their continuing business relationship.

We must not shirk from extending the rule to the manufacturer for fear that the retailer or middleman will be impaled on the sword of liability without regard to fault. Their liability was already established under Section 402A of the *Restatement of Torts 2d.* As a matter of public policy the retailer or middleman as well as the manufacturer should be liable since the loss for injuries resulting from defective products should be placed on those members of the marketing chain best able to pay the loss, who can then distribute such risk among themselves by means of insurance and indemnity agreements. . . .

The result which we reach does not give the bystanders a "free ride." When products and consumers are considered in the aggregate, bystanders, as a class, purchase most of the same products to which they are exposed as bystanders. Thus, as a class, they indirectly subsidize the liability of the manufacturer, middleman and retailer and in this sense do pay for the insurance policy tied to the product.

Public policy is adequately served if parameters are placed upon the extension of the rule so that it is limited to bystanders whose injury from the defect is reasonably foreseeable.

For the sake of clarity we restate the extension of the rule. The protections of Section 402A of the *Restatement, Second, Torts* extend to bystanders whose injury from the defective product is reasonably foreseeable. . . .

It matters not that the evidence be circumstantial for as Thoreau put it "Some circumstantial evidence is very strong, as when you find a trout in the milk." There are some accidents, as where a beverage bottle explodes in the course of normal handling, as to which there is common experience that they do not ordinarily occur without a defect; and this permits the inference of a defect. This is particularly true when there is evidence in the case of the antecedent explosion of other bottles of the same product.

In cases involving multiple defendants the better reasoned view places the onus of tracing the defect on the shoulders of the dealers and the manufacturer as a policy matter, seeking to compensate the plaintiff and to require the defendants to fight out the question of responsibility among themselves.

Questions

1. How is public policy best served by imposing strict liability on sellers, distributors, and manufacturers for defective products?
2. What is the limit of strict liability? Is the seller liable for all possible damages following from a defective product?

In many states, implied warranty of merchantability is more akin to the concept of strict liability in tort than it is to a warranty attached to a contract of sale. The court's desire to impose strict liability on the seller is merely camouflaged in contractual terms of warranty. Confusion in legal terminology results, but the result in increasing liability on sellers is the same. In those states adopting a strict liability theory in products liability, whether under Section 402A of the *Restatement of Torts* or under a strict liability theory of implied warranty, the courts are increasingly inclined to expand the concept of liability beyond the mere sale of goods.

INSURANCE CRISIS

The sharp increase in product liability awards for injured victims has escalated insurance premiums for product liability coverage. Often, smaller firms cannot afford to obtain liability coverage. However, the premiums are higher than required by the risk. One reason for this is the failure of insurance companies to segregate actuarial data for the proper assessment of a firm's liability loss experience. Another problem is the wide variation in state laws, which increases the range of probability of loss.

One suggestion to deal with the product liability insurance crisis is the Model Uniform Product Liability Act (UPLA). If the UPLA is voluntarily adopted by the states, more uniformity and predictability of product liability awards will likely stabilize insurance premiums. The UPLA adopts a strict liability standard for production defects and for disconformity with express warranties. In contrast, it utilizes a negligent standard for products with a defective design or inadequate warning labels. The contrasting legal theories of liability are based on the belief that the manufacturer should be better able to avoid production defects and unconforming warranties because these are violations of his or her own selected standards of performance. On the other hand, the failure to adequately design or label is a violation of outside standards based on the existing state-of-the-art knowledge. The UPLA grants the manufacturers the usual affirmative defenses, including contributory negligence, assumption of risk, and misuse or alteration of the product. However, it suggests a comparative responsibility approach in which the defenses do not fully bar recovery. Instead, the monetary award is reduced by an amount approximating the plaintiff's contribution to the injury. The UPLA also attempts to discourage frivolous consumer claims. Any consumer who sues without a legal or factual basis becomes liable for the defendant's reasonable attorney fees and the costs of the litigation. Because of the magnitude of the product liability awards and the corresponding insurance premiums, it seems likely that the UPLA or other acts incorporating its concepts will be enacted by the various states.

"UNFAIR" SELLING PRACTICES

It is clear that America has adopted the basic policy of competition as one of the means of social betterment. The competitive philosophy has even recognized and tolerated the more rigorous levels of competition that often cause harsh consequences to befall weaker or less efficient firms. These consequences are viewed as essential reallocations of the nation's scarce economic resources which in the long-run bestow more gains on society than the losses occasioned by the reallocative process.

Although the competitive process of trade warfare may be waged ruthlessly, there are certain rules of combat that must be observed. In the interest of the public and the competitors themselves, limits have been set by the law. Numerous practices have been designated as "unfair" competition, that is, beyond the traditional boundaries of reasonable business behavior. The courts have fashioned a body of laws which attempts to prohibit unfair competitive practices by either forcing violators to compensate competitors injured by the unfair competitive tactics or by issuing injunctions against the continuation of the unfair practice.

PALMING OFF

One large area of unfair competition is the fraudulent (false) marketing of one person's goods as those of another. This unlawful marketing tactic is often referred to as "palming off" or "passing off." It consists of false representations to the public which are likely to induce them to believe that the goods of the misrepresentor are those of another. This is often done by some sort of counterfeiting or imitating of the plaintiff's containers, trademark, trade names, the appearance of his or her place of business, or the physical appearance of the product sold. The test utilized in such cases is whether the resemblance is so great as to deceive the ordinary customer acting with the caution usually exercised in such transactions. If the customer could mistake one product for the other *because* of the false representation, this likelihood of confusion or deception is sufficient for the plaintiff to gain injunctive relief against the defendant's false representations. On the other hand, if the imitation does not involve a misrepresentation or a passing off, the result will be different, as illustrated in the following case.

Sears, Roebuck & Co. v. Stiffel Co.
376 U.S. 225 (1964)
Supreme Court of the United States

Justice Black

The question in this case is whether a State's unfair competition law can, consistently with the federal patent laws, impose liability for or prohibit the copying of an article which is protected by neither a federal patent nor a copyright. The respondent, Stiffel Company, secured design and mechanical patents on a "pole lamp"—a vertical tube having lamp fixtures along the outside, the tube being made so that it will stand upright between the floor and ceiling of a room. Pole lamps proved a decided commercial success, and soon after Stiffel brought them on the market, Sears, Roebuck & Company put on the market a substantially identical lamp, which it sold more cheaply, Sears' retail price being about the same as Stiffel's wholesale price. Stiffel then brought this action against Sears in the United States District Court . . . claiming in its first count that by copying its design Sears had infringed Stiffel's patents and in its second count that by selling copies of Stiffel's lamp Sears had caused confusion in the trade as to the source of the lamps and had thereby engaged in unfair competition under Illinois law. There was evidence that identifying tags were not attached to the Sears lamp although labels appeared on the cartons in which they were delivered to customers, that customers had asked Stiffel whether its lamps differed from Sears' and that in two cases customers who had bought Stiffel lamps had complained to Stiffel on learning that Sears was selling substantially identical lamps at a much lower price.

The District Court, after holding the patents invalid for want of invention, went on to find as a fact that Sears' lamp was "a substantially exact copy" of Stiffel's and that the two lamps were so much alike, both in appearance and in functional details, "that confusion between them is likely, and some confusion has already occurred." On these findings the court held Sears guilty of unfair competition, enjoined Sears "from unfairly competing with [Stiffel] by selling or attempting to sell pole lamps identical to or confusingly similar to" Stiffel's lamp, and ordered an accounting to fix profits and damages resulting from Sears' "unfair competition."

The Court of Appeals affirmed. That court held that, to make out a case of unfair competition under Illinois law, there was no need to show that Sears had been "palming off" its lamps as Stiffel lamps; Stiffel had only to prove that there was a "likelihood of confusion as to the source of the products"—that the two articles were sufficiently identical that customers could not tell who had made a particular one. Impressed by the "remarkable sameness of appearance" of the lamps, the Court of Appeals upheld the trial court's findings of likelihood of confusion and some actual confusion, findings which the appellate court construed to mean confusion "as to the source of the lamps." The Courts of Appeals thought this enough under Illinois law to sustain the trial court's holding of unfair competition, and thus held Sears liable under Illinois law for doing no more than copying and marketing an unpatented article. We granted *certiorari* to consider whether this use of a State's law of unfair competition is compatible with the federal patent law.

* * *

In the present case the "pole lamp" sold by Stiffel has been held not to be entitled to the protection of either a mechanical or a design patent. An unpatentable article, like an article on which the patent has expired, is in the public domain and may be made and sold by whoever chooses to do so. What Sears did was to copy Stiffel's design and to sell lamps almost identical to those sold by Stiffel. This it had every right to do under the federal patent laws. That Stiffel originated the pole lamp and made it popular is immaterial. "Sharing in the goodwill of an article unprotected by patent or trade-mark is the exercise of a right possessed by all—and in the free exercise of which the consuming public is deeply interested." To allow a State by use of its law of unfair competition to prevent the copying of an article which represents too slight an advance to be patented would be to permit the State to block off from the public something which federal law has said belongs to the public. The result would be that while federal law grants only 14 to 17 years' protection to genuine inventions, States could allow perpetual protection to articles too lacking in novelty to merit any patent at all under federal constitutional standards. This would be too great an encroachment on the federal patent system to be tolerated.

Sears has been held liable here for unfair competition because of a finding of likelihood of confusion based only on the fact that Sears' lamp was copied from Stiffel's unpatented lamp and that consequently the two looked exactly alike. Of course there could be "confusion" as to who had manufactured these nearly identical articles. But mere inability of the public to tell two identical articles apart is not enough to support an injunction against copying or an award of damages for copying that which the federal patent laws permit to be copied. . . . [B]ecause of the federal patent laws a State may not, when the article is unpatented and uncopyrighted, prohibit the copying of the article itself or award damages for such copying. The judgment below did both and in so doing gave Stiffel the equivalent of a patent monopoly on its unpatented lamp. That was error, and Sears is entitled to a judgment in its favor.

Questions

1. Why was Stiffel not able to succeed in his first count of patent infringement?
2. Was Sears palming off its lamps as Stiffel's?
3. Illinois law of unfair competition did not require a showing of palming off before the plaintiff was entitled to an injunction. Instead, an injunction was issued to prevent confusion. Did the Supreme Court feel Illinois' version of the law was compatible with the federal patent laws?
4. What two basic public policies are in conflict in this case—the fruits of competition versus the avoidance of consumer confusion? Which policy won? When would the other policy win?

Trademark Infringement

A trademark is a distinctive mark, word, letter, number, design, picture, or combination thereof which is affixed to goods and used by a business firm to identify the products it manufactures or sells. Trademarks may be registered with the U.S. Patent Office. The Lanham Act (Trademark Act of 1946) permits trademark registration and protection of a mark placed "on the goods or their containers or displays associated therewith or on the tags or labels affixed thereto."

Generally, generic or descriptive designations cannot be used as trademarks. This limitation protects against one firm monopolizing a word that generally describes a product of that industry. The following case further illustrates the issues involved in formulating a trademark and in protecting the mark from infringement. An infringement is a form of passing off, in that the infringer attempts to use the mark or some variation in order to cash in on the goodwill and reputation of the competitor's mark. As such, trademark infringement constitutes unfair competition.

Abercrombie & Fitch Co. v. Hunting World, Inc.
537 F. 2d 4 (1976)
U.S. Court of Appeals (2d Cir.)

This action by Abercrombie & Fitch Company (A&F), owner of well-known stores at Madison Avenue and 45th Street in New York City and seven places in other states, against Hunting World, Incorporated (HW), operator of a competing store on East 53rd Street, is for infringement of some of A&F's registered trademarks using the word "Safari." . . .

I.

The complaint, after describing the general nature of A&F's business, reflecting its motto "The Greatest Sporting Goods Store in the World," alleged as follows: For many years A&F has used the mark "Safari" on articles "exclusively offered and sold by it." Since 1936 it has used the mark on a variety of men's and women's outer garments. A&F has spent large sums of money in advertising and promoting products identified with its mark "Safari" and in policing its right in the mark, including the successful conduct of trademark infringement suits. HW, the complaint continued, has engaged in the retail marketing of sporting apparel including hats and shoes, some identified by use of "Safari" alone or by expressions such as "Minisafari" and "Safariland." Continuation of HW's acts would confuse and deceive the public and impair "the distinct and unique quality of the plaintiff's trademark." A&F sought an injunction against infringement and an accounting for damages and profits.

HW filed an answer . . . that "the word 'safari' is an ordinary, common, descriptive, geographic, and generic word" which "is commonly used and understood by the public to mean and refer to a journey or expedition, especially for hunting or exploring in East Africa, and to the hunters, guides, men, animals, and equipment forming such an expedition" and is not subject to exclusive appropriation as a trademark. . . .

II.

The cases, and in some instances the Lanham Act, identify four different categories of terms with respect to trademark protection. Arrayed in an ascending order which roughly reflects their eligibility to trademark status and the degree of protection accorded, these classes are (1) generic, (2) descriptive, (3) suggestive, and (4) arbitrary or fanciful. The lines of demarcation, however, are not always bright. Moreover, the difficulties are compounded because a term that is in one category for a particular product may be in quite a different one for another, because a term may shift from one category to another in light of differences in usage through time, because a term may have one meaning to one group of users and a different one to others, and because the same term may be put to different use with respect to a single product. In various ways, all of these complications are involved in the instant case.

A generic term is one that refers, or has come to be understood as referring, to the genus of which the particular product is species. At common law neither those terms which were generic nor those which were merely descriptive could become valid trademarks. While, as we shall see, the Lanham Act makes an important exception with respect to those merely descriptive terms which have acquired secondary meaning, it offers no such exception for generic marks. The Act provided for the cancellation of a registered mark if at any time it "becomes the common descriptive name of an article or substance." This means that even proof of secondary meaning, by virtue of which some "merely descriptive" marks may be registered, cannot transform a generic term into a subject for trademark. . . . [N]o matter how much money and effort the user of a generic term has poured into promoting the sale of its merchandise and what success it has achieved in securing public identification, it cannot deprive competing manufacturers of the product of the right to call an article by its name. . . . The pervasiveness of the principle is illustrated by a series of well-known cases holding that when a suggestive or fanciful term has become generic as a result of a manufacturer's own advertising efforts, trademark protection will be denied save for those markets where the term still has not become generic and a secondary meaning has been shown to continue. A term may thus be generic in one market and descriptive or suggestive or fanciful in another.

The term which is descriptive but not generic stands on a better basis. Although section 2(e) of the Lanham Act forbids the registrations of a mark which, when applied to the goods of the applicant, is "merely descriptive," Section 2(f) removes a considerable part of the sting by providing ". . . nothing in this chapter shall prevent the registration of a mark used by the applicant which has become distinctive of the applicant's goods in commerce" and that the Commissioner may accept, as *prima facie* evidence that the mark has become distinctive, proof of substantially exclusive and continuous use of the mark applied to the applicant's goods for five years preceding the application. . . . In the case [of generic terms] any claim to an exclusive right must be denied since this in effect would confer a monopoly not only of the mark but of the product by rendering a competitor unable effectively to name what it was endeavoring to sell. In the . . . case [of descriptive terms] the law strikes the balance, with respect to registration, between the hardships to a competitor in hampering the use of an appropriate word and those to the owner who, having invested money and energy to endow a word with the good will adhering to his enterprise, would be deprived of the fruits of his efforts.

The category of "suggestive" marks was spawned by the felt need to accord protection to marks that were neither exactly descriptive on the one hand nor truly fanciful on the other. . . . Having created the category the courts have had great difficulty in defining it. . . . [One] court has observed . . . that:

> A term is suggestive if it requires imagination, thought, and perception to reach a conclusion as to the nature of goods. A term is descriptive if it forthwith conveys an immediate idea of the ingredients, qualities, or characteristics of the goods.

Also useful is the approach taken by this court . . . that the reason for restricting the protection accorded descriptive terms, namely the undesirability of preventing an entrant from using a descriptive term for his product, is much less forceful when the trademark is a suggestive word since, as Judge Lumbard wrote,

> The English language has a wealth of synonyms and related words with which to describe the qualities which manufacturers may wish to claim for their products and the ingenuity of the public relations profession supplies new words and slogans as they are needed.

If a term is suggestive, it is entitled to registrations without proof of secondary meaning. Moreover, . . . the decision of the Patent Office to register a mark without requiring proof of secondary meaning affords a rebuttable presumption that the mark is suggestive or arbitrary or fanciful rather than merely descriptive.

It need hardly be added that fanciful or arbitrary terms enjoy all the rights accorded to suggestive terms as marks—without the need of debating whether the term is "merely descriptive" and with ease of establishing infringement. . . .

III.

We turn first to an analysis of A&F's trademarks to determine the scope of protection to which they are entitled. . . .

It is common ground that A&F could not apply "Safari" as a trademark for an expedition into the African wilderness. This would be a clear example of the use of "Safari" as a generic term. What is perhaps less obvious is that a word may have more than one generic use. The word "Safari" has become part of a family of generic terms which, although deriving no doubt from the original use of the word and reminiscent of its milieu, have come to be understood not as having to do with hunting in Africa, but as terms within the language referring to contemporary American fashion apparel. These terms name the components of the safari outfit well-known to the clothing industry and its customers: the "Safari hat," a broad flat-brimmed hat with a single, large band; the "Safari jacket," a belted bush jacket with patch pockets and a buttoned shoulder loop; when the jacket is accompanied by pants, the combination is called the "Safari suit." Typically these items are khaki-colored.

This outfit, and its components, were doubtless what Judge Ryan had in mind when he found that "the word 'safari' in connection with wearing apparel is widely used by the general public and people in the trade." The record abundantly supports the conclusion that many stores have advertised these items despite A&F's attempts to police its mark. In contrast, a search of the voluminous exhibits fails to disclose a single example of the use of "Safari," by anyone other than A&F and HW, on merchandise for which A&F has registered "Safari" except for the safari outfit and its components as described above.

What has been thus far established suffices to support the dismissal of the complaint with respect to many of the uses of "Safari" by HW. Describing a publication as a "Safariland Newsletter," containing bulletins as to safari activity in Africa, was clearly a generic use which is nonenjoinable. A&F also was not entitled to an injunction against HW's use of the word in advertising goods of the kind included in the safari outfit as described above. And if HW may advertise a hat of the kind worn on safaris as a safari hat, it may also advertise a similar brim as a minisafari. Although the issue may be somewhat closer, the principle against giving trademark protection to a generic term also sustains the denial of an injunction against HW's use of "Safariland" as a name of a portion of its store devoted at least in part to the sale of clothing as to which the term "Safari" has become generic.

A&F stands on stronger ground with respect to HW's use of "Camel Safari," "Hippo Safari," and Chukka "Safari" as names for boots imported from Africa. As already indicated, there is no evidence that "Safari" has become a generic term for boots. Since, as will appear, A&F's registration of "Safari" for use on its shoes has become incontestable, it is immaterial whether A&F's use of "Safari" for boots was suggestive or "merely descriptive."

HW contends, however, that even if "Safari" is a valid trademark for boots, it is entitled to the defense of "fair use" within Section 33(b)(4) of the Lanham Act. That section offers such a defense even as against marks that have become incontestable when the term charged to be an infringement is not used as a trademark "and is used fairly and in good faith only to describe to users the goods and services of such party, or their geographic origin."

Here, Lee Expeditions, Ltd., the parent company of HW, has been primarily engaged in arranging safaris to Africa since 1959; Robert Lee, the president of both companies, is the author of a book published in 1959 entitled "Safari Today—The Modern Safari Handbook" and has, since 1961, booked persons on safaris as well as purchased safari clothing in Africa for resale in America. These facts suffice to establish, absent a contrary showing, the defendant's use of "Safari" with respect to boots was made in the context of hunting and traveling expeditions and not as an attempt to garner A&F's good will. The district court here found the HW's use of "Camel Safari," "Hippo Safari," and "Safari Chukka" as names for various boots imported from Africa constituted "a purely descriptive use to apprise the public of the type of product by referring to its origin and use." The court properly followed the course sanctioned by this court in . . . [a previous case] by focusing on the "use of words, not on their nature or meaning in the abstract." When a plaintiff has chosen a mark with some descriptive qualities, he cannot altogether exclude some kinds of competing uses even when the mark is properly on the register. We do not have here a situation similar to those in . . . [previous cases] in . . . which we rejected "fair use" defenses, wherein an assertedly descriptive use was found to have been in a trademark sense. It is significant that HW did not use "Safari" alone on its shoes, as it would doubtless have done if confusion had been intended.

We thus hold that the district court was correct in dismissing the complaint.

Questions

1. Why cannot generic names be trademarked? Can a term that was registered as a fanciful trademark become generic over time and lose its trademark protection?
2. Can you supply examples of the use of the word *ivory* as a generic description of a product and as an arbitrary term applied to a product?
3. In the example of a "deep bowl spoon," which words are descriptive of the article and which are generic? On the other hand, when would "deep bowl" be a generic term?
4. Under what conditions will the Lanham Act allow the registration of a descriptive term as a trademark? What policy supports this rule?
5. If a person is able to register a mark without proof of secondary meaning, the Patent Office must have determined that the term was not merely descriptive. Does the conclusion of the Patent Office aid the registrant in an action against an alleged infringer?
6. A fanciful term usually means words invented solely for their use as trademarks. Can you supply an example?
7. An arbitrary term usually means a common term used in an unfamiliar way. Can you supply an example?
8. What advantages exist for the registrant when fanciful or arbitrary terms are used?
9. Why was the registrant's trademark, "Safari," not enforceable in the sale of safari outfits? Why was the Safari trademark generally enforceable in the sale of safari boots? Is use of the term Safari, in relation to the boots,

suggestive or merely descriptive? Is use of the term Safari, in relation to the boots, an "incontestable" (i.e., continuous five-year use) trademark? What is the effect of incontestability?

10. What is the defense of "fair use"? Why was the defendant entitled to assert this defense?

INTERNATIONAL TRADE CONTRACTS

International trade contracts often involve greater distances and longer periods of time before the goods are delivered and payment is required than contracts involving intranational trade. There are also a number of purely international risks, such as the involvement of the following:

1. More than one currency.
2. More than one government's regulation.
3. More than one legal system.
4. More than one language.
5. Import-export regulations.

However, despite the distance and time factors and the international risks, most of the obligations of the parties result from the placement of risks assigned by the contract itself.

Scherk v. Alberto-Culver Co.
417 U.S. 506 (1974)
Supreme Court of the United States

Justice Stewart

Alberto-Culver Co. is an American company incorporated in Delaware with its principal office in Illinois. It manufactures and distributes toiletries and hair products in this country and abroad. During the 1960's Alberto-Culver decided to expand its overseas operations, and as part of this program it approached Fritz Scherk, a German citizen residing at the time of trial in Switzerland. Scherk was the owner of three interrelated business entities, organized under the laws of Germany and Liechtenstein, that were engaged in the manufacture of toiletries and the licensing of trademarks for such toiletries. . . In February 1969 a contract was signed in Vienna, Austria, which provided for the transfer of the ownership of Scherk's enterprises to Alberto-Culver, along with all rights held by these enterprises to trademarks in cosmetic goods. The contract contained a number of express warranties whereby Scherk guaranteed the sole and unencumbered ownership of these trademarks. In addition, the contract contained an arbitration clause providing that "any controversy or claim [that] shall arise out of this agreement or the breach thereof" would be referred to arbitration before the International Chamber of Commerce in Paris, France, and that "[t]he laws of the State of Illinois, U.S.A. shall apply to and govern this agreement, its interpretation and performance."

The closing of the transaction took place in Geneva, Switzerland, in June 1969. Nearly one year later Alberto-Culver allegedly discovered that the trademark rights purchased under the contract were subject to substantial encumbrances that threatened to give others superior rights to the trademarks and to restrict or preclude Alberto-Culver's use of them. Alberto-Culver thereupon tendered back to Scherk the property that had been transferred to it and offered to rescind the contract. Upon Scherk's refusal, Alberto-Culver commenced this action . . . in a Federal District Court in Illinois, contending that Scherk's fraudulent representations concerning the status of the trademark rights constituted violations of § 10(b) of the Securities Exchange Act of 1934. . . .

In response, Scherk filed a motion to dismiss the action for want of personal and subject-matter jursdiction as well as on the basis of *forum non conveniens*, or, alternatively, to stay the action pending arbitration in Paris pursuant to the agreement of the parties. Alberto-Culver, in turn, opposed this motion and sought a preliminary injunction restraining the prosecution of arbitration proceedings. . . . The United States Arbitration Act, reversing centuries of judicial hostility to arbitration agreements, was designed to allow parties to avoid "the costliness and delays of litigation," and to place arbitration agreements "upon the same footing as other contracts. . . ." Accordingly the Act provides that an arbitration agreement such as is here involved "shall be valid, irrevocable, and enforceable, save upon such grounds as exist at law or in equity for the revocation of any contract." The Act also provides in § 3 for stay of proceedings in a case where a court is satisfied that the issue before it is arbitrable under the agreement, and § 4 of the Act directs a federal court to order parties to proceed to arbitration if there has been a "failure, neglect, or refusal" of any party to honor an agreement to arbitrate. . . . Alberto-Culver's contract to purchase the business entities belonging to Scherk was a truly international agreement. Alberto-Culver is an American corporation with its principal place of business and the vast bulk of its activity in this country, while Scherk is a citizen of Germany whose companies were organized under the laws of Germany and Liechtenstein. The negotiations leading to the signing of the contract in Austria and to the closing in Switzerland took place in the United States, England, and Germany, and involved consultations with legal and trademark experts from each of those countries and from Liechtenstein. Finally, and most significantly, the subject matter of the contract concerned the sale of business enterprises organized under the laws of and primarily situated in European countries, whose activities were largely, if not entirely, directed to European markets. . . . In this case, in the absence of the arbitration provision, considerable uncertainty . . . exists concerning the law applicable to the resolution of disputes arising out of the contract.

Such uncertainty will almost inevitably exist with respect to any contract touching two or more countries, each with its own substantive laws and conflict-of-law rules. A contractual provision specifying in advance the forum in which disputes shall be litigated and the law to be applied is, therefore, an almost indispensable precondition to achievement of the orderliness and predictability essential to any international business transaction. Furthermore, such a provision obviates the danger that a dispute under the agreement might be submitted to a forum hostile to the interests of one of the parties or unfamiliar with the problem area involved.

A parochial refusal by the courts of one country to enforce an international arbitration agreement would not only frustrate these purposes, but would invite unseemly and mutually destructive jockeying by the parties to secure tactical litigation advantages. In the present case, for example, it is not inconceivable that if Scherk had anticipated that Alberto-Culver would be able in this country to enjoin resort to arbitration he might have sought an order in France or some other country enjoining Alberto-Culver from proceeding with its litigation in the United States. Whatever recognition the courts of this country might ultimately have granted to the order of the foreign court, the dicey atmosphere of such a legal no-man's-land would surely damage the fabric of international commerce and trade, and imperil the willingness and ability of businessmen to enter into international commercial agreements.

An agreement to arbitrate before a specified tribunal is, in effect, a specialized kind of forum-selection clause that posits not only the situs of suit but also the procedure to be used in resolving the dispute. The invalidation of such an agreement in the case before us would not only allow the respondent to repudiate its solemn promise but would, as well, reflect a "parochial concept that all disputes must be resolved under our laws and in our courts. . . . We cannot have trade and commerce in world markets and international waters exclusively on our terms, governed by our laws, and resolved in our courts."

For all these reasons we hold that the agreement of the parties in this case to arbitrate any dispute arising out of their international commercial transaction is to be respected and enforced by the federal courts in accord with the explicit provisions of the Arbitration Act.

Questions

1. What are the purposes of the U.S. Arbitration Act?
2. Without the arbitration provision in the contract in *Scherk* v. *Alberto-Culver*, whose law and what court should decide contract disputes?
3. What facts in *Scherk* make this an international contract?

CONCLUSION

Of the marketing functions, perhaps none is more important than the function of selling the product. An important aspect of the selling function involves understanding and drafting advantageous sales contracts. The sales contract, whether domestic or international, is drafted to define the rights and duties of buyer and seller. Consequently, a broad understanding of the rules for formation of sales contracts is imperative in order for the merchant to understand the risk he or she assumes under the contract. An important risk that the merchant may want to avoid or reduce, to the extent permitted by law, is liability for product defects. Certainly, the merchant must learn to avoid overly generous expressions of warranty concerning product claims.

Although the marketing process involves the adoption of tactics that will obtain business contracts, some tactics have been ruled "out of the bounds" of reasonableness and lacking in social justification. The judicial process has developed a body of laws against "unfair competition." The rules of the judicial process have been reinforced by statutory measures, such as the Lanham Act which strengthens and enlarges the protections against unfair marketing tactics. Future business leaders must learn the proscribed practices and fashion appropriate policies to avoid their occurrence.

CASE PROBLEMS

1. A North Carolina consumer liberally applied deodorant from a can to his underarms and neck. He then put the can of deodorant down, walked across the room to where his shirt was, took up a cigarette and proceeded to light it with a match from a paper book of matches. When he struck the match, he heard a loud noise and he burst into blue flames. He sued the drugstore from which he had purchased the offending spray can. How will his chances for recovery vary according to the *theory* of product liability adopted in North Carolina?

2. Homeowner B stored a one-gallon container of gasoline near the base of his gas hot water heater. One day the can exploded with both B and B's house suffering burns. B is now suing the hot water heater manufacturer. Decide.

3. Evans gave the plaintiff an order for merchandise of the value of $686. The latter made a memorandum which he sent to Evans. The plaintiff shipped the goods. Defendant refused to accept them. Plaintiff sued for damages and the defendant pleaded the Statute of Frauds. Decide.

4. Miller Brewing Company argued it possessed a common law trademark for its "Lite" beer. Accordingly, Miller sued Heileman Brewing for its use of the word "Light" as a trademark for its beer. What was the result?

ENDNOTES

1. *Winterbottom* v. *Wright,* 10 M. & W. 109, 152 Eng. Rep. 402 (1842).
2. *MacPherson* v. *Buick Motor Co.,* 217 N.Y. 382, 111 N.E. 1050 (1916).
3. Prosser, *Law of Torts,* 4th ed. (Minneapolis, Minn.: West Pub. Co., 1971), p. 643.
4. *Haberman* v. *Sander,* 166 Wash. 453, 12 R. 2d 409, affirmed on rehearing (1932).

chapter 10

FINANCIAL TRANSACTIONS

Most societies that have developed a considerable amount of trade have found it expedient to use some form of commercial paper (negotiable instruments) to settle accounts between merchants. It is the use of these documents that facilitates the distribution of goods and services, since it is often impractical to transfer large sums of money with speed and safety.

Although there is evidence of usage earlier, it was during the late sixteenth and early seventeenth centuries that the use of commercial paper necessitated the creation of a special body of law. The commercial transactions of this period were primarily created at a local fair, which was authorized by the crown who conferred the privilege of the fair upon a nobleman or bishop. This privilege included the right to conduct court hearings in resolution of disputes between the merchants. The merchants, before moving on, wanted to settle their accounts at the fair. The decisions at these courts became known as the *law merchant,* with the custom and usage of the traders becoming an important aspect of this law. Later, whenever the courts of the crown were required to make decisions involving commercial transactions, they incorporated the *law merchant* in formulation of their common law decisions.

Commercial law in early America adopted the English common law and developed on a case-by-case basis. However, with each state having a separate legal system, unnecessary complexity evolved in multistate business transactions due to the diversity of rules in the various states. Merchants were faced with a variety of rules with regard to settling accounts with other merchants. Consequently, efforts were begun to provide more uniformity of law concerning business transactions.

In 1896 the National Conference of Commissioners on Uniform State Laws proposed the Negotiable Instruments Law (NIL) as part of their program to achieve uniformity. However, with differing judicial interpretations because of the ambiguities in the wording of the statute, the quest for uniformity was frustrated.

In 1952 the commissioners approved the Uniform Commercial Code (UCC) for submission to the states. Its purpose was to clarify and modernize business law, including the area of negotiable instruments. The Code has been adopted in its entirety in all states, except Louisiana which has adopted a portion of it. The Code was further clarified with a 1972 amendment. Presently, the UCC provides the basic legal framework for most business transactions.

The concept of "finance" has many different and broad connotations. Generally, however, it can be reduced to either (1) the lending of money or (2) the sale of goods with an extension of time for the payment of purchase price. In lending funds, business executives often employ the use of "negotiable instruments" whether the lending involves simple promissory notes or more complex corporate bonds.

The extension of time for payments in the sale of goods involves certain risks. One method often employed by merchants to reduce such risks is to ensure the right to repossess the goods if the debtor-buyer defaults in payment. To accomplish such results, the merchant must comply with the body of law known as "secured transactions."

The following materials explore the basic conceptual aspects of the law of "negotiable instruments" and "secured transactions."

COMMERCIAL PAPER

In the financial community, commercial paper is the term employed for short-term promissory notes issued by corporate borrowers for terms of 30 to 270 days. These are unsecured instruments, dependent on the financial strength of the issuing company, used to raise short-term financing. These notes are available in multiples of $100,000. Thus, when investors buy commercial paper, they are lending money to the issuing company.

In law, however, commercial paper (or negotiable instruments) are special types of contracts which are more extensively used than the definition of the financial community would suggest. Negotiable instruments are written in a special form requiring the future payment of money by one of the parties, either directly or through a third person. One of the parties has the contract right to receive payment of money and may transfer this right to other parties through what is called negotiations.

As commercial activity expanded in the sixteenth century, merchants found themselves short of cash. Buyers began to write short contracts that required their unconditional payment of money on the seller's demand (or at a stated time interval) as a substitute for an immediate cash payment. Since buyer-merchants appreciated this opportunity of delayed payment, they tended to pay the obligation on its due date. Later, as the practice expanded, the seller-merchants holding these contracts to receive future payment began to transfer them to their suppliers in payment for goods or debts. In effect, these payment-on-demand or future payment contracts began to pass as effective substitutes for money and serve as instruments for granting of credit.

It is important for the reader to remember that these contracts are to pass freely among merchants—as substitutes for money. Therefore, to facilitate this free transferability, the instrument must be readily identifiable. The following materials outline the essentials for formation of a negotiable instrument.

TYPES OF INSTRUMENTS

The UCC identifies four types of negotiable instruments that are employed as commercial paper: drafts, checks, certificates of deposit, and promissory notes.

A *draft* is a negotiable instrument by which one individual or firm orders another individual or firm to pay a sum of money to a third party. The person who draws up the instrument and orders payment is the drawer, the person to whom the instrument is addressed is the drawee, and the person to whom payment is made is the payee.

Sight and Time Drafts. A draft payable at sight is called a *sight draft.* A draft payable at a specific date or after a specific period of time is known as a *time draft.*

Trade Acceptance. The *trade acceptance* is used in commercial transactions by manufacturers and wholesalers in order to extend credit. The trade acceptance is drawn by the seller on the buyer, payable to the seller at a future time, for the sale price of goods. The seller sends the draft to the buyer, who *accepts* it. The buyer returns the accepted draft to the seller who may deposit it as collateral

$950.00 CLEVELAND, OHIO February 11, 19 ____

At sight -- PAY TO THE

ORDER OF Fredna Pearce

Nine hundred fifty and 50/100 - - - - - - - - - - - - - - - - - - DOLLARS

VALUE RECEIVED AND CHARGE TO ACCOUNT OF

TO Mary Lynn Britton SHARONANN APPLIANCES

No. 167 Gary, Indiana By Clara Bell

Figure 10-1. Sight draft.

for a loan or discount it with a financial institution. The buyer, by giving the trade acceptance, cannot later dispute the debt. As a result, the seller can more readily secure a loan on a negotiable trade acceptance than on an assignment of an open account. The trade acceptance is a convenient medium of trade which enables sellers to get cash and at the same time to extend credit to customers.

Banker's Acceptance. A *banker's acceptance* is a draft "accepted" by the buyer's bank, rather than by the buyer personally. However, before making a purchase, the buyer must make the necessary arrangements with the bank to accept the draft. For example, it might be necessary to deposit collateral or to keep a sufficient amount of money on deposit as a condition for the bank to accept the draft. In the latter situation, the bank is not making a loan, it is lending its creditworthiness to the buyer. The bank's payment on the draft makes it possible for the seller to obtain cash rather than extend credit to the buyer.

A *check* is a draft drawn on a bank and payable on demand. As with the draft, three original parties are involved: the drawer, the drawee bank, and the payee.

Cashier's Check. The *cashier's check* is a check drawn by a bank on itself. The bank is both the drawer and the drawee.

Bank Draft. A *bank draft* is a check drawn by a bank on another bank. It is necessary, therefore, that the drawer-bank have funds on deposit with the drawee-bank. Bank drafts are used because the bank usually has a more acceptable line of credit than an individual.

A *certificate of deposit* is an acknowledgment by a bank of its receipt of money with a duty to repay it. It is usually used to evidence a time deposit with a bank.

A *promissory note* is a written promise, other than a certificate of deposit, whereby one person or firm promises to pay a certain sum of money to another. The person who makes the promise is the maker; the person to whom the note is payable is the payee.

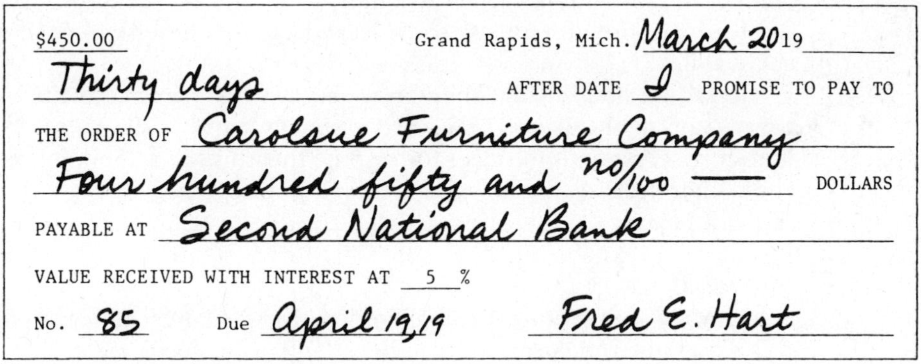

$450.00 Grand Rapids, Mich. March 20 19

Thirty days AFTER DATE I PROMISE TO PAY TO

THE ORDER OF Carolsue Furniture Company

Four hundred fifty and no/100 —— DOLLARS

PAYABLE AT Second National Bank

VALUE RECEIVED WITH INTEREST AT 5 %

No. 85 Due April 19, 19 Fred E. Hart

Figure 10-2. Promissory note.

REQUISITES FOR NEGOTIABILITY

To be negotiable (to qualify as negotiable paper), an instrument must meet certain requirements over and above those of a simple contract. It must

1. Be written.
2. Be signed by the maker or drawer.
3. Contain an unconditional promise or order to pay.
4. Be certain as to the sum of money.
5. Be payable on demand or at a definite time.
6. Be payable to "order" or to the "bearer."

MAGIC WORDS

Haggard v. Mutual Oil & Refining Co.
263 S.W. 745 (1924)
Court of Appeals of Kentucky

The single question presented by this appeal is whether or not the following check is a negotiable instrument:

$2,500.00 Winchester, Ky., July 10, 1920
The Winchester Bank, of Winchester, Ky.:
Pay to Arco Refinery Construction Company twenty-five hundred and no/100 dollars, for constructing refinery, switch, and loading racks, Win. Ky.

Mutual Oil & Refining Co.
By C. L. Bell, Pres.

"An instrument to be negotiable must conform to the following requirements: . . . (4) Must be payable to the order of a specified person or to bearer."

Since, as the check itself shows, and as is admittedly true, the [drawer], in issuing the check, drew a line through the printed words "or bearer," we need only to examine it to ascertain whether or not it was "payable to the order of a specified person," for unless so, it lacked one of the essentials prescribed for negotiability. . . .

It will be noticed that the above check is not payable to the order of the payee, nor to the payee or its order, but is payable simply to the payee. It therefore seems to us too clear for dispute that this check is not payable to order, and is therefore, as the lower court held, not negotiable.

Questions

1. Must an instrument contain either the word *order* or *bearer* on the face of the instrument in order to be a "negotiable instrument"?
2. Assuming the instrument is payable to bearer, does that mean the instru-

ment is the same as cash or currency as far as the risk of loss is concerned? Suppose you lose an instrument payable to bearer. If it is presented to the maker-payer, how would he or she know the instrument is being presented by a finder? (or thief?) If the maker paid the funds to the finder (or thief), should he or she be required to pay again to the true owner who lost the instrument? Does this suggest an obvious advantage of "order" instruments? Order instruments can be transferred only by the endorsement (or order) of the person whose name is designated as payee. Anyone taking or holding the order instrument without a valid endorsement does not have ownership over the instrument or a right to collect payment. The payer-maker could not pay the finder and discharge his or her duty to pay the person designated by the instrument or the endorsement.

3. Is a note made nonnegotiable because it contains a notation "as per contract"? Does this mean the note's promise to pay is "conditional"? In *D'Andrea* v. *Feinberg,* 256 N.Y.S. 2d 504 (1965) the Court made the following statement:

> The note meets all the requirements of section 3-104 of the U.C.C. with the possible exception that it does not contain an unconditional promise because of the legend "as per contract." Section 3-105(1)(c) expressly states that an unconditional promise "is not made conditional by the fact that the instrument . . . (c) refers to or states that it arises out of a separate agreement or refers to a separate agreement for rights as to prepayment or acceleration."
>
> The official comment on the above quoted provision . . . is that it was "intended to resolve a conflict, and to reject cases in which a reference to a separate agreement was held to mean that payment of the instrument must be limited in accordance with the terms of the agreement, and hence was conditioned by it." The court is satisfied that the legend "as per contract" does not affect the negotiability of an instrument as would a statement that the instrument "is subject to or governed by any other agreement."
>
> The court determines that the note being sued upon is a negotiable instrument.

4. Does a note payable "within 10 years after date" possess a definite maturity date? Is this language the same as "on or before"?

NEGOTIATION

The purpose of creating a negotiable instrument is to create an instrument that is readily transferable. Consequently, the law is designed to enhance that transferability. The method of transferring or negotiating an instrument depends on the terms of the instrument or the endorsements. If the instrument is order paper, it can be negotiated only by endorsement and delivery. If it is bearer paper, it may be negotiated by delivery alone.

An instrument payable to order must be negotiated by endorsement by the person to whom the instrument was made payable (payee). The endorsement must be placed on the instrument and is usually contained on the reverse side. When the endorser signs only his or her name, the endorsement is called a *blank endorsement* because it does not designate the person to whom the instrument is to be paid. Consequently, the effect of a blank endorsement is to make the instrument a "bearer" paper.

A *special endorsement* consists of the signature of the endorser and words designating the person to whom the endorser makes the instrument payable, that is, the endorsee. In effect, a special endorsement preserves the "order" status of the paper or transforms "bearer" paper into "order" paper.

A *restrictive endorsement* specifies a particular purpose of the endorsement and specifies the use that is to be made of the paper. The usual kind of restrictive endorsement is one "for deposit only." This endorsement indicates that the intent of the endorser is to have the instrument presented for payment and the proceeds deposited to his or her account.

Negotiations by blank, special, or restrictive endorsements (1) pass ownership of the instrument and (2) impose secondary liability on the endorser for the amount of the instrument. If the primary parties (maker or drawee-acceptor) fail to pay the holder of the instrument, the endorser may have to pay. In effect, the endorser's secondary liability is a conditional promise of payment if the primary party is unable or unwilling to pay. In order to obtain payment from the endorser, the holder must have (1) made a proper presentment for payment to the primary party and (2) given proper (timely) notice of dishonor (of the primary party's obligation to pay) to the endorser.

Should the endorser desire not to provide this conditional promise of payment to the endorsee, the endorser would utilize a *qualified endorsement,* which disclaims the secondary liability of the endorser. The qualified endorsement is created by including the words "without recourse" in the body of the endorsement. A qualified endorsement does not affect the passage of title to the negotiable instrument.

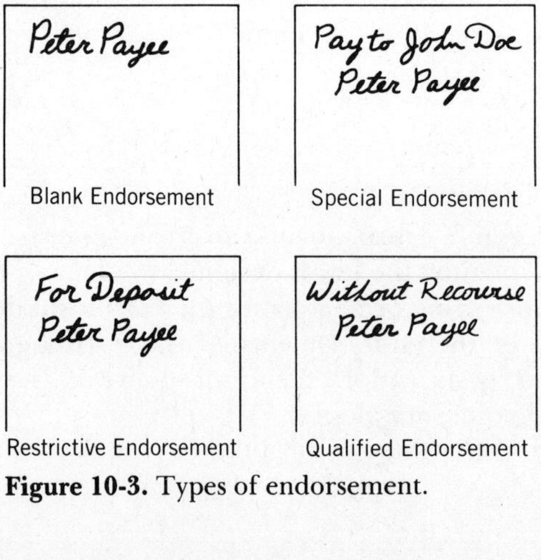

Figure 10-3. Types of endorsement.

A person who becomes a party to a negotiable instrument by adding his or her signature (credit), but who never obtains any ownership (benefits) of the paper, is called an *accommodation party.* For example, when a bank is unwilling to lend money to A on the strength of A's credit rating, B may sign the note as a comaker with A to bolster A's credit. In such instance, B is an accommodation maker. Moreover, if A was attempting to cash a check while in a strange city, B as a resident and depositor with a bank in that city could endorse A's check and thereby lend his or her credit to the check to induce the bank to cash the check. The accommodation party, whether a maker or endorser, receives no ownership interest in the instrument, but merely lends credit to support another party. If the accommodation party is required to pay the instrument, he or she may recover the amount of payment from the person accommodated.

ENDORSER'S SECONDARY LIABILITY

Hane v. Exten
259 A. 2d 290 (1969)
Court of Appeals, Maryland

John B. Hane is the indorsee of the note (made by) . . . Theta Electronic Laboratories, Inc. (Theta) in the stated amount of $15,377.07, with interest at six per cent per annum. The note was dated 10 August 1964; stipulated that the first monthly payment of $320.47 would be due five months from date, or on 10 January 1965; and that "in the event of the failure to pay the interest or principal, as the same becomes due on this Note the entire debt represented hereby shall at the end of thirty (30) days become due and demandable . . . ." The note was indorsed without recourse to Hane by George B. Thomson, the original payee, on 26 November 1965. A default having occurred in the making of the monthly payments, Hane . . . on 7 June 1967 sued Theta and Gerald M. Exten . . . who had [indorsed as an accommodation party on] . . . Theta's note. . . . From a judgment for the Extens, . . . Hane has appealed.

This case raises the familiar question: Must Hane show that the Extens were given notice of presentment and dishonor before he can hold them on their indorsement?

The court below, in finding for the Extens, relied on the provisions of Uniform Commercial Code. . . .

> Unless the indorsement otherwise specifies (as by such words as 'without recourse') every indorser engages that upon dishonor and any necessary notice of dishonor and protest he will pay the instrument according to its tenor at the time of his indorsement to the holder or to any subsequent indorser who takes it up.

§3-501(1)(b) provides that "Presentment for payment is necessary to charge any indorser" and §3-501(2)(a) that "Notice of any dishonor is necessary to charge any indorser," in each case subject, however, to the provisions of §3-511 which recite the circumstances under which notice of dishonor may be waived or excused, none of which is here present. §3-502(1)(a) makes it clear that unless presentment or notice of dishonor is waived or excused, unreasonable delay will discharge an indorser. . . .

There was testimony from which the trier of facts could find as he did that presentment and notice of dishonor were unduly delayed.

It is clear that Hane held the note from November, 1965, until some time in April 1967, before he made demand for payment. UCC §3-503(1)(d) provides that "Where an instrument is accelerated presentment for payment is due within a reasonable time after the acceleration." "Reasonable time" is not defined in §3-503, except that §3-503(2) provides, "A reasonable time for presentment is determined by the nature of the instrument, any usage of banking or trade and the facts of the particular case." But §1-204(2) characterizes it: "What is a reasonable time for taking any action depends on the nature, purpose and circumstances of such action."

Reasonableness is primarily a question for the fact finder. . . .

We see no reason to disturb the lower court's finding that Hane's delay of almost 18 months in presenting the note "was unreasonable from any viewpoint."

As regards notice of dishonor, §3-508(2) requires that notice be given by persons other than banks "before midnight of the third business day after dishonor or receipt of notice of dishonor." Exten, called as an adverse witness by Hane, testified that his first notice that the note had not been paid was . . . on 7 June 1967. Hane's brother testified that demand had been made about 15 April 1967. He was uncertain as to when he had given Exten notice of dishonor, but finally conceded that it was "within a week." The lower court found that the ambiguity of this testimony, coupled with Exten's denial that he had received *any* notice before 7 June fell short of meeting the three day notice requirement of the UCC. The date of giving notice of dishonor is a question of fact, solely for determination by the trier of facts.

In the absence of evidence that presentment and notice of dishonor were waived or excused, Hane's unreasonable delay discharged the Extens.

Questions

1. Did Hane unduly delay the presentment of the instrument for payment? When was the instrument to be presented for payment?
2. Did Hane give timely notice of the dishonor of the instrument? Within what time period was Hane required to give the notice of dishonor?
3. What is the legal result of Hane's failure to properly present the instrument for payment and failure to give notice of dishonor within the prescribed time period?
4. In *Hane* the time of presentment for payment was to be within a reasonable time after the instrument was accelerated (that is, all future payments are accelerated to a current date and presently due). Acceleration protects the creditor from having to sue for each monthly or yearly in-

stallment as it comes due. Rather, if a periodic payment is missed, the creditor can, if the note has an authorizing clause, accelerate and demand payment for all periodic payments (present and future) under the note. However, when a note is not accelerated, the holder of the note is to present it for payment, not within a reasonable time, but *on* the due date. Failure to make a timely presentment for payment will discharge the secondarily liable parties.

DRAWER'S SECONDARY LIABILITY

Gill v. Yoes
360 P. 2d 506 (1961)
Supreme Court of Oklahoma

The plaintiff in this case, Deane Gill, was the owner of an airplane which he had for sale. A man by the name of C. J. Hobson desired to buy this plane from Gill. The price of the plane was $8,000. Hobson agreed to buy the plane. He got the defendant Jackie Yoes to draw a draft on the Phoenix Savings and Loan Company of Muskogee, Oklahoma, in favor of Gill and gave the draft to Gill in payment for the plane. The defendant Jackie Yoes had no money in the Savings and Loan Company but had made application to it for a loan on property she owned but none was made to her. The draft was turned down by the Savings and Loan Company. Title to the plane was taken in the name of the defendant and application for registration in defendant's name was made. After the delivery of the plane Hobson took and flew it away and it was later destroyed in an accident. Soon after the draft was drawn it was presented for payment which was refused. Plaintiff immediately got in touch with the defendant and demanded that she make the draft good. This she refused to do, so the plaintiff brought suit on the draft.

The defendant claimed that she had nothing to do with the purchase of the plane except that she did sign the draft for $8,000 to pay for it; that she knew nothing about the dealings between Hobson and plaintiff; that she had no need for a plane and that she did not buy it. She did testify that she did try to borrow money from the Phoenix Savings and Loan Company on her property in Stigler, Oklahoma, but the loan was never completed. . . .

The case was tried by a jury and a verdict was rendered for the defendant. The plaintiff had moved for a directed verdict at the close of the defendant's case. . . .

By giving a negotiable instrument, . . . [the] drawer of the instrument . . . "engages that on due presentment the instrument will be . . . paid . . . according to its tenor. . . .

. . . There is no question in this case that the defendant executed the draft involved herein. It was on the strength of this draft that the airplane was turned over to Hobson. If this draft had not been delivered to plaintiff certainly he would not have executed the bill of sale and transferred the airplane. The defendant by her answer injected into this case the proposition that the draft given for the plane was for the benefit of a third party, one Hobson. It is really immaterial whether the draft was given for the purchase of the plane by either Hobson or the defendant just so long as it was given. . . .

The judgment is reversed with directions to the trial court to render judgment for the plaintiff.

Questions

1. What is the drawer's obligation under a negotiable draft or check? Are any conditions attached to the obligation?
2. Is the drawer's responsibility on a draft similar to the responsibility of an endorser?
3. Although secondary parties (endorsers and drawers) may be relieved from responsibility on a negotiable instrument because of improper presentment or improper notice of dishonor, primary parties (makers of notes and acceptors of drafts) are not thereby relieved for failure of proper presentment or notice of dishonor. The primarily obligated parties are forever bound to pay the instrument according to its terms. Why should a secondarily liable party (drawer or endorser) be relieved of liability on a delay of presentment or notice of dishonor? Consider the following situation:

   Joe Worker received his paycheck from his employer, Goodandrich, which was drawn on the First National Bank of Pleasantville. Joe Worker stopped by the saloon on his way home that evening and cashed the check by endorsement with Bart Barkeeper. Barkeeper held on to the check for a month before tendering it for payment to the First National Bank. During that month, the employer, Goodandrich, became insolvent and applied to the Bankruptcy Court for dissolution. Consequently, the bank, without any deposits by Goodandrich, refused to honor the check. Therefore, Barkeeper attempted to sue Joe Worker on his endorsement to make the check good. Would it be fair to Joe Worker to require that he pay the check when Barkeeper could have obtained full payment had he made a proper presentment of the check in the first part of the month? Barkeeper's delay forces someone to absorb the loss.

   Should Barkeeper or Joe Worker absorb the loss?

TRANSFEROR'S WARRANTIES

When one sells a negotiable instrument (by negotiating it for value), warranties are implied by law in this transfer. The transferor warrants the following:

1. He or she has good title to the instrument or is properly authorized to obtain payment.
2. All signatures are genuine or authorized.
3. The instrument has not been materially altered.

4. No defense of any party is good against him or her.
5. He or she has no knowledge of any insolvency proceedings against the maker or acceptor or the drawer of an unaccepted instrument.

Although the transferee of a negotiable instrument normally relies on the endorser's secondary liability as a protection against the insolvency of the primary party, the warranties may be important in certain instances: perhaps no endorsement was made, the endorsement was qualified (without recourse), or the transferee failed to make a proper presentment or to give proper notice of dishonor, all of which relieve the endorser of any secondary liability. In such cases, the transferee may sue the transferor if the transferor has breached any of the aforementioned warranties.

Suppose, for example, that Wayne obtained a negotiable instrument by fraudulent means and negotiated it to Percival with the endorsement "without recourse on me pay to the order of J. J. Percival, J. C. Wayne." When the instrument was dishonored by the maker, Percival sought to hold Wayne. Since Wayne signed "without recourse," Wayne could not be held on his endorsement. However, Wayne at the time of his transfer of the instrument to Percival knew of the maker's defense of fraud. Consequently, Wayne is liable for breach of the warranty that no defense of any party is good against him (Wayne). Percival could recover his loss from Wayne.

HOLDER IN DUE COURSE

An important concept of negotiable instruments is the "holder in due course" doctrine. This doctrine is designed to increase the effectiveness of instruments as substitutes for money by encouraging free transferability and by making them more desirable for investment purposes. To allow the instrument to circulate as freely as money itself, this rule of law gives a subsequent holder of the instrument (if qualified) greater rights to collect payment from the maker than the original payee had. For example, if a maker of a promissory note gives the note to a payee in payment for a refrigerator which was never delivered, the maker would not have to pay the party (payee) who sold the refrigerator. However, if the payee who sold the refrigerator had transferred the note to a "holder in due course," such holder could collect payment from the maker in spite of the nondelivery of the refrigerator. In effect, the rights of the holder (transferee) to collect are greater than the rights of the payee. This role of greater rights in the transferee is unique to commercial paper. Under contract law, any defense of the maker would be effective to stop payment to the payee or the transferee. Therefore, contrary to contract law, the holder in due course doctrine gives the holder a superior position (that is, the ability to collect payment regardless of the maker's defenses) and thereby encourages the potential purchaser of an instrument to take the paper. This doctrine allows negotiable instruments to circulate with greater freedom as substitutes for money (see Figure 10-4).

The normal path of a negotiable instrument is from the issuer to the payee

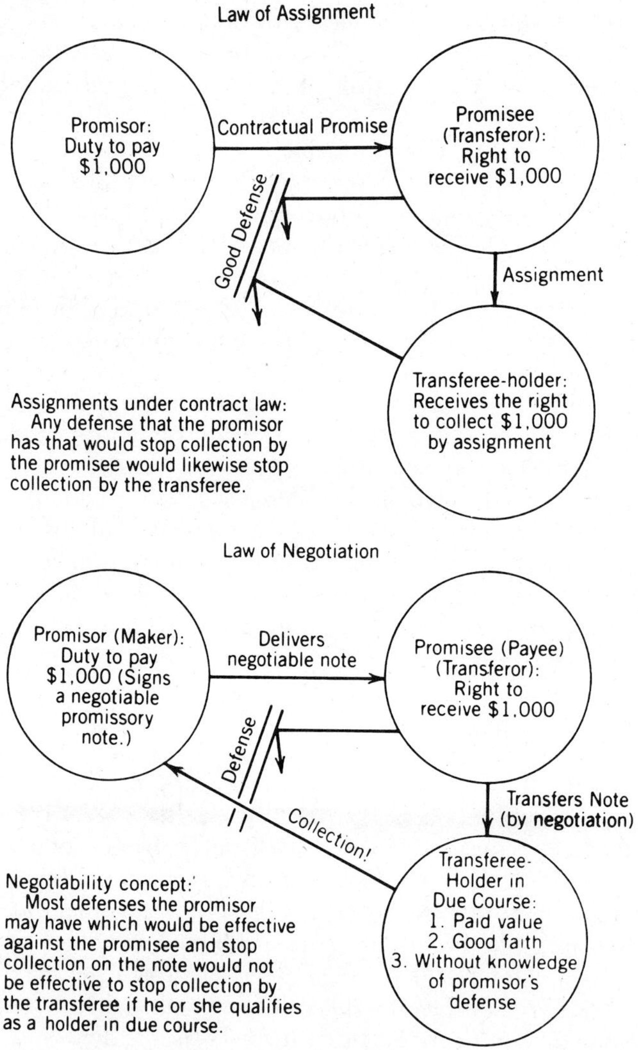

Figure 10-4. Figures contrasting law of assignment and law of negotiation.

and then through commercial channels, until it ultimately returns to the maker or drawee for payment.

Occasionally, when called on to pay on a negotiable instrument, the parties involved may raise defenses to avoid payment. Two classes of defenses are available to an individual from whom payment is requested: personal and real.

Personal Defenses

Personal defenses are based on circumstances collateral to the instrument itself. They may be raised to avoid payment to any holder except a holder in due course or a successor to a holder in due course. Personal defenses relate to the transaction for which the instrument was given and to losses resulting from negligence on the part of the primary party in creating and executing the instrument. They include fraud in the inducement; lack, failure, or illegality of consideration; set-offs, or counterclaims; nondelivery of a complete or an incomplete instrument; prior payment; and unauthorized completion of an incomplete but signed instrument.

Real Defenses

A real defense exists if it can be shown that no legal instrument was ever created or that liability on an instrument has been destroyed. Real defenses may be raised successfully against all holders. Real defenses arise in cases in which no instrument or liability was ever created or, if an instrument or liability was created, something has since destroyed its legal effect. Since no qualified instrument exists, no right or title passes to a holder in due course or, indeed, to any holder. Real defenses include forgery, fraud in the execution, lack of contractual capacity, illegality, duress, and material alteration.

Real and personal defenses are available to secondary as well as primary parties in suits brought by the holder. For example, an endorser may raise a real defense against any subsequent holder and may raise a personal defense against an immediate endorsee or against subsequent parties who are not holders in due course.

Illinois Valley Acceptance Corp. v. Woodard

304 N.E. 2d 859 (1975)
Court of Appeals of Indiana

Woodard was a part time salesman for Moody Manufacturing Company (Moody), a manufacturer of grain bins and grain handling equipment. In May of 1966, Moody, as "borrower," had entered into a Finance Agreement with Acceptance listed as "the lender." This agreement made provision, among other things, for Moody to sell acceptable accounts to Acceptance for face value with 15% being reserved for deductions, expenses, accumulated interest, etc. On the 24th of December, 1968, Woodard signed, as acceptor, the trade acceptance which is the subject of this litigation. Moody was the drawer and payee. At that time it was in blank with the face value subsequently being filled in for the face amount of $8,815.62. In the four or five years prior to 1968, Woodard had signed several trade acceptances in blank for Moody for the purposes of covering the purchase of materials which he sold. The face amount was ultimately to be filled in when it was determined how much he had ordered. The December, 1968, trade acceptance was endorsed by Moody's secretary and given to Acceptance several days after Woodard had signed it. Between February and April, 1970, and several months past the due date, Moody went bankrupt. When Acceptance presented the instrument for payment it was refused by Woodard. Additionally, Woodard never received the materials presented by the trade acceptance, nor was he aware it had been negotiated by Moody to Acceptance. . . .

This case is to be decided under the provisions of the Uniform Commercial Code. . . . It provides that only a holder can recover on the instrument. The applicable section reads:

(2) When signatures are admitted or established, production of the instrument entitles the holder to recover on it unless the defendant establishes a defense.

Acceptance's acknowledged status as a holder was not sufficient for it to recover because Woodard raised the defenses of fraud and failure of consideration, each a valid defense. These defenses, however, may have been cut off if Acceptance was a holder in due course. The holder in due course takes the instrument "free from all defenses of any party to the instrument with whom the holder has not dealt," subject to several exceptions. To avail itself of this "super-plaintiff" status, Acceptance had the burden of establishing by a preponderance of the evidence that it was "in all respects a holder in due course." "In all respects" means that Acceptance had to establish the existence of each of the elements set forth in 3-302. . . .

It provides:

(1) A holder in due course is a holder who takes the instrument

(a) for value; and

(b) in good faith; and

(c) without notice that it is overdue or has been dishonored or of any defense against or claim to it on the part of any person.

The evidence, when examined with the foregoing requisites in mind, establishes Acceptances as a holder in due course. Briefly summarized that evidence shows the trade acceptance being endorsed over to Acceptance by Moody. Moody in turn received a draft for 85% of the face value of the trade acceptance. There was nothing irregular with the acceptance and the transaction was similar to other prior transactions between the parties. At the time Acceptance had no knowledge that the trade acceptance had been signed in blank and that the goods had not been delivered.

A portion of Woodard's arguments appears to be directed to the questions of good faith and notice. . . .

The Finance Agreement, introduced into evidence by Woodard, may have been an attempt to establish something akin to the doctrine of close connectedness, characterized by Woodard as the lack of an arms-length transaction, for the purpose of showing that Acceptance was so closely related to Moody commercially that it knew, or should have known, either Moody was in poor financial shape or that it had not delivered the goods represented by the trade acceptance. Acceptance's summary judgment affidavit as well as the testimony given at the trial belies such a relationship.

Woodard further argues that there was no value given for the trade acceptance and that the Finance Agreement between Moody and Acceptance was merely a borrowing agreement. The evidence shows that Acceptance paid

Moody 85% of the face value of trade acceptance and held the remainder in reserve. There can be little question that the value concept was satisfied . . . .

Woodard's affirmative defense of want of consideration is not available against a holder in due course.

Turning next to the question of fraud, 3-305(2)(c) allows a defense against a holder in due course based upon "such misrepresentation as has induced the party to sign the instrument with neither knowledge nor reasonable opportunity to obtain knowledge of its character or its essential terms." The comments subsequent to this statute state that fraud in the essence or fraud in the factum is a valid defense against a holder in due course with the theory being that the "signature is ineffective because he did not intend to sign such an instrument at all." Woodard's past conduct in signing blank trade acceptances for Moody negates a defense based on the foregoing. Woodard testified he was familiar with the forms and knew they constituted a promise to pay. . . .

It is our conclusion that the evidence conclusively demonstrated Acceptance to be a holder in due course.

Questions

1. Was Acceptance a holder in due course? Did it give value? In good faith? Without notice of any defense?
2. What were Woodard's defenses? Why were these defenses not good against the holder in due course?

Burchett v. Allied Concord Financial Corp.

396 P. 2d 186 (1965)

Supreme Court of New Mexico

[Kelly was an agent selling aluminum siding for a firm named Consolidated Products. He talked with the Burchetts and their neighbors, the Beevers, at their homes offering to install aluminum siding on their houses for a stipulated price in exchange for their permission to use their houses as "show houses." Kelly told them they would receive a credit of $100 for each aluminum siding contract sold within a 25 mile radius and that such credit would be applied to their contractual indebtedness for installation of the siding on their homes. The couples believed that by this method they would receive the improvements for nothing. Kelly handed each couple a form of a printed contract to read. While they were reading the contracts, Kelly was filling out blanks on other forms. They signed, without reading, these forms filled out by Kelly, assuming them to be the same as those which they had read. The contracts clearly stated on the same pages on which the signatures of the purchasers appeared: "No one is authorized on behalf of this company to represent this job to be 'a sample home for a free job.' " What the couples had signed were notes and mortgages on their property to cover the cost of the aluminum siding and the contracts contained no mention of credits for "promoting" other sales. The aluminum siding was installed, although the jobs were not completely satisfactory. Shortly afterwards, the Burchetts and Beevers received letters from Allied Concord Financial Corp., informing them that it had purchased the notes and mortgages and that they were delinquent in their first payment. The Burchetts and the Beevers brought this action to have the notes and mortgages cancelled. The defendant, Consolidated Products, appeals from judgments avoiding the instruments.]

In both cases, the trial court found that the notes and mortgages, although signed by the plaintiffs, were fraudulently procured. The court also found that the defendant paid a valuable consideration for the notes and mortgages, although at a discount, and concluded as a matter of law that the defendant was a holder in due course. . . . The only real question in the case is whether, under these facts, plaintiffs, by substantial evidence, satisfied the provisions of the statute relating to their claimed defense as against a holder in due course.

In 1961, . . . our legislature adopted, with some variations, the Uniform Commercial Code. The provision of the code applicable to this case appears as . . . §3-305(2)(c) . . . which, so far as material, is as follows:

> To the extent that a holder is a holder in due course he takes the instrument free from
>
> (2) all defenses of any party to the instrument with whom the holder has not dealt except . . .
>
> (c) such misrepresentation as has induced the party to sign the instrument with neither knowledge nor reasonable opportunity to obtain knowledge of its character or its essential terms. . . .

* * *

We observe that the inclusion of subsection (2)(c) in §3-305 of the Uniform Commercial Code was an attempt to codify or make definite the rulings of many jurisdictions on the question as to the liability to a holder in due course of a party who either had knowledge, or a reasonable opportunity to obtain the knowledge, of the essential terms of the instrument, before signing. . . . Almost all of the courts that were called upon to rule on this question required a showing of freedom from negligence, in order to constitute a good defense against a bona fide holder of negotiable paper.

The reason for the rule . . . is that when one of two innocent persons must suffer by the act of a third, the loss must be borne by the one who enables the third person to occasion it.

. . . Thus the only question is whether, under the facts of this case, the misrepresentations were such as to be a defense as against a holder in due course.

Applying the elements of the test to the case before us, Mrs. Burchett was 47 years old and had a ninth grade education, and Mr. Burchett was approximately the same age, but his education does not appear. Mr. Burchett was a foreman of the sanitation department of the city of Clovis and testified that he was familiar with some legal documents. Both the Burchetts understood English and there was no showing that they lacked ability to read. Both were able to understand the original form of contract which was submitted to them. As to the Beevers, Mrs. Beevers was 38 years old and had been through the ninth grade. Mr. Beevers had approximately the same education, but his age does not appear. However, he had been working for the same firm for about nine years and knew a little something about mortgages, at least to the extent of having one upon his property. Mrs. Beevers was employed in a supermarket, and it does not appear that either of the Beevers had any difficulty with the English language and they made no claim that they were unable to understand it. Neither the Beevers nor the Burchetts had ever had any prior association with Kelly and the papers were signed upon the very day that they first met him. There was no showing of any reason why they should rely upon Kelly or have confidence in him. The occurrences took place in the homes of the defendants, but other than what appears to be Kelly's "chicanery," no reason was given which would warrant a reasonable person in acting as hurriedly as was done in this case. None of the defendants attempted to obtain any independent information either with respect to Kelly or Consolidated Products, nor did they seek out any other person to read or explain the instruments to them. As a matter of fact, they apparently didn't believe this was necessary because, like most people, they wanted to take advantage of "getting something for nothing." There is no dispute but that the plaintiff did not have actual knowledge of the nature of the instruments which they signed, at the time they signed them. Defendant urges that plaintiffs had a reasonable opportunity to obtain such knowledge but failed to do so, were therefore negligent, and that their defense was precluded.

We recognize that the reasonable opportunity to obtain knowledge may be excused if the maker places reasonable reliance on the representations. The difficulty in the instant case is that the reliance upon the representations of a complete stranger (Kelly) was not reasonable, and all of the parties were of sufficient age, intelligence, education, and business experience to know better .... See *First National Bank of Philadelphia* v. *Anderson,* which held that the mere failure to read a contract was not sufficient to allow the maker a defense under §3-305 of the Uniform Commercial Code. In our opinion, the plaintiffs here are barred for the reasons hereinabove stated.

Although we have sympathy with the plaintiffs, we cannot allow it to influence our decision. They were certainly victimized, but because of their failure to exercise ordinary care for their own protection, an innocent party cannot be made to suffer.

Questions

1. In *Burchett* the makers were asserting the defense of fraud. Since there are different kinds of fraud, the plaintiffs were attempting to assert the fraud that is a good defense against a holder in due course. This fraud is called fraud in the essence or fraud in the factum. How would you define this type of fraud?
2. Why were the plaintiffs not able to establish this fraud?

Notes

1. Allied Concord Financial Corp. was a holder in due course of the notes and mortgages. Suppose that subsequently, newspaper reports made known to the world the defenses of the makers. Thereafter, purchasers

of the notes, with notices of the defenses, could not become holders in due course. Purchasers would be most hesitant to buy the instrument. This inability of the present holder to further negotiate the instrument would frustrate the purpose of negotiable instrument law. Therefore, to avoid this result the Shelter Doctrine allows buyers of the instrument, in spite of their knowledge of the defenses of the maker at the time they purchased the instrument, to acquire the "rights" of the transferor-holder in due course. The doctrine "shelters" purchasers of an instrument from a holder in due course by giving the purchasers the rights of the seller (his or her holder in due course status). Since Allied Concord Financial Corp. could easily recover as a holder in due course, allowing its transferee to take Allied's "rights" as a holder in due course would not change the legal liabilities of the maker of the instrument. Consequently, the Shelter Doctrine enhances the marketability of the instrument by providing a "market" in which a holder in due course can more readily sell the instrument. Therefore, a purchaser from Allied Concord Financial Corp. could acquire the "rights" of a holder in due course even if they knew of the fraudulent transaction with the Burchetts and Beevers.

2. Because of cases like the Burchetts and the Beevers, numerous commentators have argued that the holder-in-due-course concept is an unfair law when applied in consumer sales. They maintain that financial institutions should not be allowed to collect payment from the consumer when the consumer has not received a fair value from the merchant-seller. State legislative and judicial attempts to modify the holder-in-due-course concept in consumer sales have been only modestly successful. Consequently, after several years of extensive hearings and investigations, the Federal Trade Commission in 1975 adopted a Trade Regulation Rule which provides that:

> In connection with any sale or lease of goods or services to consumers, in or affecting commerce as "commerce" is defined in the Federal Trade Commission Act, it is an unfair or deceptive act or practice within the meaning of Section 5 of that Act for a seller, directly or indirectly to:
>
> (a) Take or receive a consumer credit contract which fails to contain the following provision in at least ten point, bold face, type:
>
> **NOTICE**
>
> **ANY HOLDER OF THIS CONSUMER CREDIT CONTRACT IS SUBJECT TO ALL CLAIMS AND DEFENSES WHICH THE DEBTOR COULD ASSERT AGAINST THE SELLER OF GOODS OR SERVICES OBTAINED PURSUANT HERETO OR WITH THE PROCEEDS HEREOF, RECOVERY HEREUNDER BY THE DEBTOR SHALL NOT EXCEED AMOUNTS PAID BY THE DEBTOR HEREUNDER.**
>
> or, (b) Accept, as full or partial payment for such sale or lease, the *proceeds* of any purchase money loan (as purchase money loan is defined herein), unless any

consumer credit contract made in connection with such purchase money loan contains the following provision in at least ten point, bold face, type:

NOTICE
ANY HOLDER OF THIS CONSUMER CREDIT CONTRACT IS SUBJECT TO ALL CLAIMS AND DEFENSES WHICH THE DEBTOR COULD ASSERT AGAINST THE SELLER OF GOODS OR SERVICES OBTAINED PURSUANT HERETO OR WITH THE PROCEEDS HEREOF, RECOVERY HEREUNDER BY THE DEBTOR SHALL NOT EXCEED AMOUNTS PAID BY THE DEBTOR HEREUNDER

The FTC rule protects the rights of consumers who purchase on credit and incur obligations to financial institutions by preserving the consumers' claims and defenses. The consumers' claims and defenses could not be cut off by a purchaser of an instrument containing a "notice" like that above. Failure to include this notice provision subjects the merchant-seller to prosecution by the FTC for violating its rules. As a result, the holder in due course doctrine is no longer effective in retail installment sales to consumers. Results as occurred in *Burchett* will thereby be avoided.

UNAUTHORIZED ENDORSEMENTS

An unauthorized endorsement is wholly inoperative as the endorsement of the person whose name has been written. Accordingly, the possessor of "order" paper with such an endorsement is not the owner of the instrument. The following case deals with an unauthorized endorsement.

Salsman v. National Community Bank of Rutherford
246 A. 2d 162 (1968)
Supreme Court of New Jersey

Plaintiffs, payee and special indorsee of a check, sue defendant collecting bank for applying the proceeds of the check to the account of an attorney, Harold Breslow, who improperly indorsed the check. . . .

In May 1965 plaintiff Elizabeth A. Odgers (now Elizabeth A. Salsman) retained an attorney, Harold Breslow, to handle matters arising out of the death of her husband Arthur J. Odgers. . . .

Arthur J. Odgers had been an officer and stockholder in a company in which he had a one-third interest. He participated in the company's profit-sharing plan and had designated his wife as sole beneficiary. In payment of benefits under the plan, Mrs. Odgers received a cashier's check of the First National City Bank made out to her order in the amount of $159,770.02. The check is dated August 13, 1965. Breslow then informed Mrs. Odgers that the check was not hers but belonged to the estate, and that the proceeds must be held in a separate account for payment of taxes and other purposes. Mrs. Odgers was told by Breslow that the check "must be put in the estate account of Arthur Odgers." . . .

Breslow wrote on the back of the cashier's check, "Pay to the order of Estate of Arthur J. Odgers." He requested Mrs. Odgers to indorse the check in this fashion, and she did so. Under this special indorsement, when he was no longer in the presence of Mrs. Odgers, Breslow wrote, "Estate of Arthur J. Odgers—for deposit Harold Breslow, Trustee." Under this purported indorsement Breslow's secretary then wrote, "For deposit Harold Breslow Trustee." Mrs. Odgers had no knowledge of the subsequent indorsement. The check was then sent by mail to defendant National Community Bank of Rutherford for collection, and the proceeds were collected and deposited in Breslow's general trustee account. Defendant bank did not inquire into the authority of Breslow to indorse the checks for the estate. There was no estate account in defendant's bank, although Mrs. Odgers had qualified as administratrix of the estate on July 9, 1965.

From August 1965 until March 1966 Mrs. Odgers inquired of Breslow on many occasions as to the status of the profit-sharing funds. . . . As time passed Mrs. Odgers became more suspicious and began to investigate the disposition of the funds. . . .

Mrs. Odgers then contacted another attorney and he assisted her in further investigation. . . . An appointment was then made with Breslow for March 30. On that date, at his office, Breslow confessed to Mrs. Odgers and her present husband, Salsman, that he had appropriated the funds to his own use. . . . Breslow has since pleaded guilty to the charge of embezzlement and misappropriation of funds and is presently serving a prison sentence. He also resigned from the New Jersey Bar. In April 1966 Mrs. Odgers started an action against Breslow and on June 3, 1966, obtained judgment in her favor. Some monies were recovered by execution on that judgment. The balance not yet recovered is $117,437.43. . . .

In the absence of defenses such as negligence, estoppel or ratification, the payee is entitled to recover against a bank making collection from the drawee based upon a forged or unauthorized indorsement of a check. . . . This has been the established law throughout the country. . . .

The check in question was indorsed by the payee, Mrs. Odgers, to the order of the Estate of Arthur J. Odgers. There was no valid indorsement thereafter by the estate of Arthur J. Odgers. [The UCC] provides that an instrument may be payable to the order of "an estate, trust or fund, in which case it is payable to the order to the representative of such estate, trust or fund . . . ." The check was not indorsed by the administratrix of the estate, the only person who had authority in law to indorse the check. Breslow was not a trustee of the estate, and the purported indorsement for the estate by "Harold Breslow, Trustee" was unauthorized and ineffective. Breslow testified that he never told plaintiff that he would act as her agent. His purported indorsement was not authorized as the agent for the administratrix nor as a representative of the estate. . . .

The check in question could not be negotiated without an authorized indorsement of the special indorsee, the estate of Arthur J. Odgers. [The UCC] provides that "Any unauthorized signature is wholly inoperative as that of the person whose name is signed unless he ratifies it or is precluded from denying it . . . ." There is no evidence in this case which shows a ratification by Mrs. Odgers of the conduct of Breslow; there has been nothing shown to preclude her from denying the indorsements in question, and there is no evidence of any negligence on her part which contributed to the misapplication of the funds.

Mrs. Odgers had relied upon an attorney who was then reputable. She followed his instructions and was not negligent in assuming that the check would be deposited into the estate account after she indorsed it to the order of the estate. . . . Although she had not signed signature cards as administratrix in order to open such an account, Mrs. Odgers cannot be held negligent on the theory that she should have suspected that the check might not have been deposited in an estate account. Mrs. Odgers made repeated inquiries concerning the funds and was given various explanations by Breslow as to their disposition and as to her inability to deal with them at the stage in the administration of the estate. Her conduct was not unreasonable or imprudent.

Receiving the funds without a proper indorsement and crediting the funds to one not entitled thereto constitutes a conversion of the funds. A holder is one who receives an instrument which is indorsed to his order or in blank. . . .

The bank cannot be a holder, or a holder in due course . . . without a valid indorsement of this check by the estate of Arthur J. Odgers. 3-419(1)(c) provides that an instrument is converted when it is paid on a forged indorsement. 1-201(43) provides that an unauthorized signature or indorsement is one made without authority (actual, implied or apparent) and includes a forgery. . . .

3-419(3) clearly implies the liability of a depositary or collecting bank in conversion when it deals with an instrument or its proceeds on behalf of one who is not the true owner, where the bank does not act in accordance with "reasonable commercial standards." Defendant did not act in accordance with reasonable commercial standards. . . . In *Teas* v. *Third National Bank and Trust Co.*, the Court . . . held . . . that a depository bank was derelict in its duty to the check's payee in failing to inquire as to an attorney's right to indorse the check and place the proceeds in his own account to his own credit. The court held that the form of the checks, payable to an executor and to an estate, put the bank on notice that the attorney had no power to do what he did, and that the bank's breach of its duty to make appropriate inquiry rendered it liable to the payee . . . .

In the present case there are sufficient facts to justify the conclusion that defendant bank is liable regardless of how we view the conduct of Mrs. Odgers in giving the check to Breslow. . . . [T]he indorsement purportedly made on behalf of the estate was a "for deposit" indorsement, a restrictive indorsement. This is another fact which should have alerted the bank to a misapplication of the funds. . . .

Thus, even if the indorsement for the estate had been authorized, defendant bank would be liable for failing to deposit the proceeds to the credit of the estate as required by that indorsement.

Questions

1. What kind of endorsement did Mrs. Odgers make on the back of the cashier's check from the insurance company? Did Breslow have the authority to endorse for the estate of Arthur J. Odgers?
2. Did the National Community Bank of Rutherford have a valid endorsement (ownership) for collection of the proceeds of the check? What should the bank have done to protect itself from this type of error?
3. Was the National Community Bank of Rutherford negligent in another regard? What did the "for deposit only" endorsement indicate? What was the bank's duty in relation to this restrictive endorsement?

IMPOSTER RULE

The UCC contains a body of rules involving situations in which the payee's name on a negotiable instrument is forged but the endorsement is ruled effective. The law makes the forgery effective only for the purpose of transferring the loss away from the bank, which normally would absorb the loss because it dealt with an instrument with a forged endorsement. The loss is transferred to the drawer of the instrument because his or her behavior has been less than acceptable to society's standards in relation to negotiable instruments. The following case illustrates one of those instances. The reader should consider the question of who, between the drawer of the check and the bank who paid over a forged endorsement, should bear the loss?

Philadelphia Title Insurance Co. v. Fidelity-Philadelphia Trust Co.

212 A. 2d 222 (1965)
Supreme Court of Pennsylvania

Edmund Jezemski and Paula Jezemski were husband and wife, estranged and living apart. Edmund Jezemski was administrator and sole heir of his deceased mother's estate, one of the assets of which was premises 1130 North Fortieth Street, Philadelphia. Mrs. Jezemski, without her husband's knowledge, arranged for a mortgage to be placed on this real estate. This mortgage was obtained for Mrs. Jezemski though John M. McAllister, a member of the Philadelphia Bar, and Anthony DiBenedetto, a real estate dealer, and was to be insured by Philadelphia Title Insurance Company, the plaintiff. Shortly before the date set for settlement at the office of the title company, Mrs. Jezemski represented to McAllister and DiBenedetto that her husband would be unable to attend the settlement. She came to McAllister's office in advance of the settlement date, accompanied by a man whom she introduced to McAllister and DiBenedetto as her husband. She and this man, in the presence of McAllister and DiBenedetto, executed a deed conveying the real estate from the estate to Edmund Jezemski and Paula Jezemski . . . and also executed the mortgage . . . which had been prepared. McAllister and DiBenedetto, accompanied by Mrs. Jezemski, met at the office of the title company on the date appointed for settlement, the signed deed and mortgage were produced, the mortgagee handed over the amount of the mortgage, and the title company delivered its check to Mrs. Jezemski for the net proceeds of $15,640.82, made payable . . . to Mr. and Mrs. Jezemski individually and Mr. Jezemski as administrator of his mother's estate. . . .

Paula Jezemski, one of the payees . . . presented [the check], with purported endorsements of all the payees, at the Penns Grove National Bank and Trust Company in Penns Grove, New Jersey, for cash. Edmund Jezemski received none of the proceeds, either individually or as administrator of the estate of Sofia Jezemski; and it is conceded that the endorsements purporting to be his were forged. The Penns Grove bank negotiated the check through the Philadelphia National Bank, and it was eventually paid by Fidelity-Philadelphia Trust Company, which charged the amount of the check against the deposit account of plaintiff. . . .

There is no question that the man whom Mrs. Jezemski introduced to McAllister and DiBenedetto was not Edmund Jezemski, her husband. It was sometime later that Edmund Jezemski, when he tried to convey the real estate, discovered the existence of the mortgage. When he did so he instituted an action in equity which resulted in the setting aside of the deed and mortgage and the repayment of the fund advanced by the mortgagee.

The parties do not dispute the proposition that as between the payor bank (Fidelity-Philadelphia) and its customer (Title Company), the former must bear the loss occasioned by the forgery of a payee's endorsement (Edmund Jezemski) upon a check drawn by its customer and payed by it. . . .

However, the bank argues that this case falls within an exception to the above rule, making the forged indorsement of Edmund Jezemski's name effective so that Fidelity-Philadelphia was entitled to charge the account of its customer, the Title Company, who was the drawer of the check. The exception asserted by the bank is found in §3-405(1)(a) of the Uniform Commercial Code-Commercial Paper which provides:

> An indorsement by any person in the name of a named payee is effective if (a) an imposter by use of the mails or otherwise has induced the maker or drawer to issue the instrument to him or his confederate in the name of the payee . . . .

The lower court found and the Title Company does not dispute that an imposter appeared before McAllister and DiBenedetto, impersonated Mr. Jezemski, and, in their presence, signed Mr. Jezemski's name to the deed, bond and mortgage; that Mrs. Jezemski was a confederate of the imposter; that the drawer, Title Company, issued the check to Mrs. Jezemski naming her and Mr. Jezemski as payees; and that some person other than Mrs. Jezemski indorsed his name on the check. In effect, the only argument made by the Title Company to prevent the applicability of Section 3-405(1)(a) is that the imposter, who admittedly played a part in the swindle, *did not "by the mails or otherwise" induce the Title Company* to issue the check within the meaning of Section 3-405(1)(a). The argument must fail.

Both the words of Section 3-405(1)(a) and the official Comment thereto leave no doubt that the imposter can induce the drawer to issue him or his confederate a check within the meaning of the section even though he does not carry out his impersonation before the very eyes of the drawer. Section 3-405(1)(a) says the inducement might be by "the mails or otherwise." . . .

Moreover, the Legislature's use of the word "otherwise" and the Comment, which suggests that results should not turn upon "the type of fraud which the particular imposter committed," indicates that the Legislature did not intend to limit the applicability of the section to cases where the imposter deals directly with the drawer (face-to-face, mails, telephone, etc.). Naturally, the Legislature could not have predicted and expressly included all the ingenious schemes designed and carried out by imposters for the purpose of defrauding the makers or drawers of negotiable instruments. Something had to be left for the courts by way of statutory construction. For purposes of imposing the loss on one of two "innocent" parties, either the drawer who was defrauded or the drawee bank which payed out on a forged endorsement, we see no reason for distinguishing between the drawer who is duped by an impersonator communicating directly with him through the mails and a drawer who is duped by an impersonator communicating indirectly with him through third persons. Thus, both the language of the Code and common sense dictate that the drawer must suffer the loss in both instances. . . .

Questions

1. How could the bank protect itself from this type of loss? Who is in a better position to stop this type of injury—the bank or the drawer?
2. Suppose Widget Co. employs a bookkeeper, Smart, who prepares company paychecks. Smart prepares a paycheck for eight hours of overtime work to Joe Worker. However, Joe never worked the overtime and doesn't expect or receive the check. Smart endorses "Joe Worker" and then deposits the check to his own account. When the check clears, it is returned to Widget Co. who allows Smart to reconcile the bank statement. After several years of this practice, the Widget Co. sues the bank for paying on checks with forged endorsements. Should Widget Co. recover against the bank?

NEGLIGENT PREPARATION OF CHECKS

Park State Bank v. Arena Auto Auction, Inc.
207 N.E. 2d 158 (1965)
Appellate Court of Illinois

This case comes into Court by reason of certain mistakes made by employees of the involved parties following the normal routine of customary business details so characteristic of the rapidly changing society and world in which we live.

Defendant, Arena Auto Auction, Inc., created the problem brought to court by the issuance of its check dated December 17, 1963, and by the mailing of it to Plunkett Auto Sales, Rockford, Illinois. For clarity's sake, we will refer to the Rockford Plunkett and the Alabama Plunkett by the geographical designations rather than by their corporate names. . . . Rockford Tom Plunkett might well have felt, upon receiving said check, that he was the recipient of some give-away or promotional scheme, for it later appears that he had sold no merchandise, a fact of which he was well aware, to the Defendant. We might visualize Rockford Tom Plunkett as a fast-thinking, old-time horse trader, now engaged in the business of buying and selling used automobiles. He, being well known to the Plaintiff Bank by reason of his borrowing and having cashed one previous check of the Defendant, after holding this check from December 17th or 18th until January 3rd, 1964, and after due reflection on his part, signed his name to the check and presented it for payment to Charlotte Parish, head teller, who, promptly and without question, turned over to him the check-designated sum of $1,435.00.

On January 9, 1964, the said check was returned to the Plaintiff Bank by reason of a stop-payment order by the maker, and came into the hands of the Assistant Vice-President, Mr. Marconi, whose duties are to assist in the operation of the financial institution, to know its customers, and, equally, to earn a profit for the Plaintiff. Vice-President Marconi promptly called his personal friend, Jack Clark of the Arena Auto Auction, Inc., who, to cover the shortcomings of his secretary, called at the Plaintiff Bank on January 10, 1964, to make the explanation. Now, Jack Clark, being in the business of operating an automobile auction and using the speed of their operation to explain the error, commented thus: "This guy here (meaning Rockford Tom Plunkett) wasn't supposed to get the check. It was another Plunkett in Alabama. But Alabama Plunkett wasn't in our books, so that's why our gals sent the check to Rockford Plunkett, and that's why we stopped payment on our check."

But, to put the frosting on the cake, or as Counsel put it, to add insult to injury, Defendant, Arena Auto Auction, Inc., issued their second check in the same amount to the same payee, and again sent the check to Rockford Tom Plunkett. Again we can visualize quick-thinking Rockford Tom Plunkett's surprise, for this truly must come from the money tree. He loses no time in going to the same financial institution as before. Not so fortunate on this second occasion, poor Rockford Tom Plunkett, as he tendered the second check, is questioned as to why payment was stopped on the first one. In his effort to secure quick payment he stated, "This check is to replace the first. Cash this check, give me back the first one, and I will return it to the Arena Auto Auction."

Mindful of the first experience, the Vice-President was reluctant to follow this advice and informed poor Tom that he was in difficulty. Rockford Tom Plunkett, seeing that the Vice-President could be right, promptly left the State of Illinois and established his abode in a more sunny climate. . . .

So now we find the Plaintiff Bank in the embarrassing position of having cashed a check and having had payment of that check stopped. Desirous of not losing money, they start suit to recover from the Arena Auto Auction. . . . [The trial judge] . . . decided in favor of the Plaintiff and against the Arena Auto Auction, Inc., who appeals to this Court.

From a purely legal point of view, there are two questions raised. First, did Rockford Tom Plunkett commit a forgery by signing his own name to a check ostensibly issued to him? Without passing on the very technical question of whether or not these facts constitute a forgery, this is apparently admitted by all parties concerned, for they cite cases in the Trial Court and in this Court, holding that a forgery passes no title by which one can recover as a bar to the Plaintiff recovering. The Plaintiff Bank relies upon Chapter 26, Illinois Revised Statutes, 1963, Section 3-406; which, being a new section of our Commercial Code, is as follows:

> Any person who by his negligence substantially contributes to a material alteration of the instrument or to the making of an unauthorized signature is precluded from asserting the alteration or lack of authority against a holder in due course or against a drawee or other payor who pays the instrument in good faith in accordance with the reasonable commercial standards of the drawee's or payor's business.

Without repeating the various errors previously recited, it appears to this Court presumptuous on the part of Arena Auto Auction, Inc., Defendant, to insist that they did nothing for which they should be held accountable. We point out the interval of lapsed time before they, in their fast-thinking, fast-operating business, decide first to stop payment.

Second, bearing in mind the erroneous sending of a second check to the same payee, and considering the custom of the trade as set forth by the testimony of the several gentlemen of the financial world as to the routine handling of checks in banking institutions, it is our considered conclusion that to require the recipient Bank to stop and question persons known to that Bank and presenting checks in routine business and issued by makers likewise known to the Bank, would be placing cogs in the wheels of business, which, in turn, would bring those wheels of the banking business to an astounding and abrupt halt. This, as we see it, was neither the intent nor the purpose of our legislators in passing the section in our Commercial Code to which reference was made.

We, therefore and accordingly, do conclude that the Trial Court was correct in holding that the Defendant, by their own negligence, substantially assisted in making it possible that an unauthorized person's signature passed title to the funds represented by said check.

Questions

1. Did Rockford Tom Plunkett commit forgery by signing his own name to a check which was meant to be issued to another?
2. The court determined that the Arena Auto Auction, Inc., was precluded from recovery because of its negligence. What did the court identify as negligent behavior?

SECURED TRANSACTIONS

A secured credit sale is a sale in which possession of certain property passes to the buyer but the seller retains a "security interest" in the goods until the buyer has paid in full. The seller's security interest entitles him or her to repossess the goods when the buyer fails to make a required payment or in some other way commits a breach of the purchase contract.

A security interest for the protection of the creditor arises when the debtor grants such security interest to the creditor by a written security agreement signed by the debtor and describes the property involved, called collateral. The description of the collateral need only reasonably identify such property and is sufficient when it would enable a third person aided by additional information to determine which goods were involved. The security interest of the creditor and the right of repossession can be effective not only against the debtor, but also against the creditors of the debtor and purchasers of the collateral from the debtor (if the creditor takes the appropriate legal steps).

When the creditor's security interest becomes effective against third persons (in addition to the debtor), it is said to be "perfected." The usual way of perfecting a security interest is to file a "financing statement" in the public recorder's office. The filing of this document gives "notice" to other parties of the existence of the secured transaction between the debtor and creditor. As such, other parties may modify their transactions and dealings with the debtor in light of this knowledge concerning the secured creditor's priority over the collateral in the hands of the debtor.

The law covering "secured transactions" is embodied in Article 9 of the UCC. Article 9 defines different categories of goods which may be used as collateral. A consumer good is a good that is used or bought primarily for personal, family, or household purposes. It is the intended use, rather than the nature of the article, which determines its definition. For example, any goods purchased for resale to consumers would not be a consumer good in the hands of such resaler. Instead, goods purchased by a merchant for resale are categorized as inventory. Equipment used in the business, on the other hand, is neither a consumer good nor inventory. The filing requirements and other rules of law vary depending on the category of goods involved.

CREATION OF THE SECURITY INTEREST

Mosley v. Dallas Entertainment Company, Inc.
496 S.W. 2d 237 (1973)
Court of Civil Appeals of Texas

Dallas Entertainment Company, Inc. sued Bill Mosley for conversion of a cash register alleging that plaintiff was a secured party under a security agreement covering the cash register and that defendant, Mosley, had purchased the cash register from the plaintiff's debtor without its consent and had sold same to a third party. The trial court sitting without a jury, granted judgment against defendant, Bill Mosley, in the amount of $950.00, from which judgment defendant . . . appeals. . . .

The evidence shows that in June, 1970, plaintiff, Dallas Entertainment Company, Inc., was the holding company for a private club located in Dallas and known as the Music Box. Plaintiff sold the entire club to Follies Buffet of Dallas, Inc. Among the various items of personal property allegedly sold with the club was a certain cash register. In connection with the sale of the club, a financing statement was prepared showing Dallas Entertainment Company as the secured party and Follies Buffet of Dallas, Inc., as debtor. The financing statement was filed in the office of the Texas Secretary of State on July 2, 1970. . . .

Defendant, Bill Mosley, was in the business of buying and selling used cash registers and does not dispute the fact that he purchased the cash register from Follies Buffet in December, 1970, and that he subsequently sold the cash register to a customer in the course of his business. It is not contended that defendant had actual knowledge of plaintiff's alleged security interests in the cash register. . . .

. . . Defendant attacks the judgment on the ground that there is no evidence or alternatively that the evidence is insufficient to show plaintiff was a secured party under a Security Agreement executed by the debtor because plaintiff failed to produce a written security agreement. . . .

In reply plaintiff contends first that there is competent oral testimony to prove the existence of a security agreement and second that the financing statement itself amounts to a security agreement. . . .

In paragraph 5 of the Uniform Commercial Code Comment following Section 9.203, we find this statement:

> The formal requisites stated in this Section are not only conditions to the enforceability of a security interest against third parties. They are in the nature of a Statute of Frauds. Unless the secured party is in possession of the collateral, his security interest, absent a writing which satisfies subsection (1)(b), is not enforceable even against the debtor, and cannot be made so on any theory. . . .

In *American Card Company, Inc. v. H. M. H. Co.,* 196 A. 2d 150 (1966), the court specifically rejected the argument that the security agreement could be established by parol, stating that oral assertions were without probative force to supply the absence of a required security agreement in writing. . . .

Since the foregoing statute requires the secured party to show that the debtor has signed a security agreement containing a description of the collateral, we hold that the oral testimony of the secured party is without probative force to establish a security interest for the simple reason that it fails to satisfy the statutory requirement that the security agreement be in writing and signed by the debtor.

This brings us to the question of whether the judgment may be sustained on the theory that the financing statement amounts to a security agreement. The financing statement in this case appears to have been written on the Secretary of State's standard form. As noted above, it recites a general description of the collateral in which a security interest is claimed. It is signed by the creditor, plaintiff, and by a party alleged to be the agent of Follies. . . . Nowhere in the instrument does it grant the creditor a security interest in the collateral nor does it identify the obligation owed to the creditor.

The code makes no provisions for a naked financing statement to be enforced as a security agreement. It merely gives notice of the existence of a security interest but in itself does not create a security interest. A financing statement cannot serve as a security agreement where it does not grant the creditor an interest in the collateral and does not identify the obligation owed to the creditor. Since the financing statement offered by plaintiff fails to contain any language showing the alleged debtor granted the creditor (plaintiff) an interest in the collateral and since plaintiff was unable to produce a written security agreement signed by defendant, plaintiff failed to establish a cause of action. It therefore follows that the judgment must be reversed and rendered in favor of defendant.

Questions

1. Why did the court rule the proffered evidence could not be used to establish the existence of a security agreement?
2. Why was the financing statement not sufficient as a security agreement? Did the financing statement omit some "magic word"?
3. What are the basic elements of a security agreement? What are the basic elements of the financing statement?

PURCHASE MONEY SECURITY INTERESTS

Often a person desires to purchase goods but lacks the cash or the necessary credit rating to get the goods on open credit, so the seller retains a security interest in the goods sold. Or the potential buyer secures financing from a third party who takes a security interest in the goods purchased to secure the repayment of the loan. Either type of arrangement is called a "purchase money security interest" because the security interest is taken or retained to secure the payment of the *purchase* price. Consequently, a purchase money security interest arises whenever the lender supplies the funds that purchase the collateral. Since the lender is supplying funds to purchase goods on credit and thereby aiding the selling of goods which help promote the health of the nation's economy, the purchase money security interest holder is often given a preferred status under the law.

"FLOATING LIEN"

The "floating lien" concept was created with the enactment of Article 9 of the UCC. To create the security interest in goods called a floating lien, the Code requires a written security agreement with certain provisions. The security agreement must include a provision that the collateral, *whenever acquired,* secures the indebtedness under the agreement. This provision permits the goods, which may be broadly defined as all inventory or equipment, to vary. The items of inventory or equipment may be sold and replaced with subsequent purchases which immediately become subject to the secured party's interests. It is not necessary to create a new security agreement each time items are sold and replaced. The new items automatically become covered by the previous security agreement. It is as though there is "a floating lien," hovering above the collateral (inventory or equipment) at all times, despite sales or replacements in the broadly described collateral. The concept of a floating lien eliminates the burden of repetitious filing that was required under prior law. Once the floating lien holder has filed the financing statement in the recorder's office, no additional filing is needed as the inventory is sold or replaced. The financing statement is considered "notice" to all other would-be creditors of the debtor that the secured party has an interest in the goods in the hands of the debtor. Other creditors informed by the financing statement of the debtor-creditor relationship may modify their credit extension policies accordingly.

Often the floating lien language (whenever acquired) is followed by a provision covering *future advances* of funds. This provision means that new advances of funds can be made by the lender to the debtor and these funds are secured by the prior security interest which was created in the security agreement of the original loan. Therefore, the amount of the indebtedness may vary under this provision as payments of the debt are made and as the lender may choose to extend more loans to the debtor for additional inventory. A future advances provision makes unnecessary the execution of a new security agreement each time new funds are lent. When both the future advances provision and the after-acquired property clause are combined, the items of the collateral may change without defeating the secured party's interest in the collateral and new funds may be advanced to the debtor to secure new inventory on a continuous basis. The once executed security agreement and the once filed financing statement are sufficient for this continuing relationship between the debtor and creditor for an extended period of time (usually five years). The floating lien concept and the future advances concept eliminated the repetitious creation of security agreements and financing statements required under the old law. As such, Article 9 greatly improves the processes of financing inventory and equipment.

The security interest holder of a floating lien is capable of being made secondary in priority to the collateral by two parties. First, a purchaser from the merchant-debtor in an ordinary business transaction takes title to the goods free of the lender's security interest. This, of course, is what the lender expects, in that he or she anticipates repayment of the loan from the proceeds of such sale.

The holder of the floating lien may not recover the good sold to the purchaser if the lien holder is unable to secure repayment of the debt from the debtor-merchant.

Second, the holder of a floating lien may become secondary in priority to a subsequent creditor who lends funds to the debtor on a purchase money basis. The sale of goods to the debtor-merchant on a purchase-money-security-interest basis creates a security interest in such seller that takes priority over the floating lien if the purchase money seller files a financing statement within 10 days of giving possession of the sold item to the debtor-merchant and, in addition, notifies the floating lien holder of this sale on a purchase money basis. In this way, the debtor-merchant may expand his or her inventory lines or equipment needs and thereby secure new lines of credit from different sources in spite of the floating lien which hovers over all the inventory or equipment. The new items are exempt from the floating lien and, instead, are pledged to the purchase-money-security-interest holder. However, should the seller on a purchase money basis not comply with necessary steps to gain priority over the floating lien, the goods would come under the floating lien of the original lender, who would gain priority to those goods on the debtor's default.

AFTER-ACQUIRED PROPERTY

National Cash Register Company v. Firestone & Co.

191 N.E. 2d 471 (1963)
Supreme Court of Massachusetts

The underlying question is the relative standing of two security interests. On June 15, 1960, the plaintiff, a manufacturer of cash registers, and one Edmond Carroll, doing business in Canton as Kozy Kitchen, entered into a conditional sale contract for a cash register. On November 18, 1960, the defendant, which was in the financing business, made a loan to Carroll, who conveyed certain personal property to the defendant as collateral under a security agreement. The defendant filed a financing statement with the Town Clerk of Canton on November 22, 1960. Between November 19 and November 25 the plaintiff delivered a cash register to Carroll in Canton. On November 25, the contract of June 15 was canceled and superseded by a new contract for the same cash register but provided for different terms of payment. The plaintiff filed a financing statement with respect to this contract with the Town Clerk of Canton on December 20 and with the Secretary of State on December 21. Carroll subsequently became in default both on the contract with the plaintiff and on the security agreement with the defendant. In December the defendant took possession of the cash register, and although notified on January 17, 1961, of the plaintiff's asserted right sold it at auction on the following day.

The defendant's security agreement recites that Carroll in consideration of $1,911 paid by it does "hereby grant, sell, assign, transfer and deliver to Grantee the following goods, chattels, and automobiles, namely: The business located at and numbered 574 Washington Street, Canton, Mass. together with all its good-will, fixtures, equipment and merchandise. The fixtures specifically consist of the following: *All contents of luncheonette including equipment such as: booths and tables; stand and counter; tables; chairs; booths; steam tables; salad unit; potato peeler; U.S. Slicer; range; case; fryer; compressor; bobtail; milk dispenser; silex; 100 Class air conditioner; signs; pastry case; mixer; dishes; silverware; tables; hot fudge; Haven Ex.; 2 door stationwagon 1957 Ford A57R107215* together with all property and articles now, and which may hereafter be, used or mixed with, added or attached to, and/or substituted for, any of the foregoing described property."

In the defendant's financing statement the detailed description of the "types (or items) of property" is the same as the words in supplied italics in the security agreement. There is no specific reference to a cash register in either document, and no mention in the defendant's financing statement of property to be acquired thereafter.

Under the Uniform Commercial Code after-acquired property, such as this cash register, might become subject to the defendant's security agreement when delivered and likewise its delivery under a conditional sale agreement with retention of title in the plaintiff would not, in and of itself, affect the rights of the defendant. Although the plaintiff could have completely protected itself by perfecting its interest before or within ten days of the delivery of the cash register to Carroll, it did not try to do so until more than ten days after delivery. Thus the principal issue is whether the defendant's earlier security interest effectively covers the cash register. . . .

Contrary to the plaintiff's contention, we are of opinion that the security agreement is broad enough to include the cash register, which concededly did not have to be specifically described. The agreement covers "All contents of luncheonette including equipment such as," which we think covers all those contents and does not mean "equipment, to wit." There is a reference to "all property and articles now, and which may hereafter be, used . . . with, [or] added . . . to . . . any of the foregoing described property." We infer that the cash register was used with some of the other equipment even though the case stated does not expressly state that the luncheonette was operated.

We now come to the question whether the defendant's financing statement should have mentioned property to be acquired thereafter before a security interest in the cash register could attach. The code . . . reads in part: "A financing statement is sufficient if it is signed by the debtor and the secured party, gives an address of the secured party from which information concerning the security interest may be obtained, gives a mailing address of the debtor and contains a statement indicating the types, or describing the items, or collateral."

In this official comment to this section appears the following: "2. This Section adopts the system of 'notice filing' which has proved successful under the Uniform Trust Receipts Act. What is required to be filed is not, as under chattel mortgage and conditional sales acts, the security agreement itself, but only a simple notice which may be filed before the security interest attaches or thereafter. The notice itself indicates merely that the secured party who has filed may have a security interest in the collateral described. Further inquiry from the parties concerned will be necessary to disclose the complete state of affairs. Section 9-208 provides a statutory procedure under which the secured party, at the debtor's request, may be required to make disclosure. Notice filing has proved to be of great use in financing transactions involving inventory, accounts and chattel paper, since it obviates the necessity of refiling on each of a series of transactions in a continuing arrangement where the collateral changes from day to day. Where other types of collateral are involved, the alternative procedure of filing a signed copy of the security agreement may prove to be the simplest solution."

The framers of the Uniform Commercial Code, by adopting the "notice filing" system, had the purpose to recommend a method of protecting security interest which at the same time would give subsequent potential creditors and other interested persons information and procedures adequate to enable the ascertainment of the facts they needed to know. In this respect the completed Code reflects a decision of policy reached after several years' study and discussion by experts. We conceive our duty to be the making of an interpretation which will carry out the intention of the framers of uniform legislation. . . .

In view of the broad purposes of the act we do not give a restrictive construction to the provision which sets forth what constitutes a "sufficient" financing statement. The defendant's financing statement is signed by the debtor and the secured party and gives both the address of the latter from which information is to be obtained and the mailing address of the debtor. It is argued, however, that the "statement indicating the types, or describing the items, of collateral" is inadequate because it fails to include a reference to the after-acquired clause of its security agreement, and so is not a reasonable identification of the cash register. . . .

The words, "All contents of luncheonette," including, as we have held, all equipment, were enough to put the plaintiff on notice to ascertain what those contents were. This is not a harsh result as to the plaintiff, to which, as we have indicated, [the UCC] made available a simple and sure procedure for completely protecting its purchase money security interest.

Questions

1. In the *NCR* case, did the financing statement of Firestone contain an "after-acquired property" clause? Was its inclusion necessary to make the "after-acquired property" language of the security agreement effective?
2. Did Firestone's financing statement contain "notice" of the after-acquired property clause in the security agreement?
3. The court said that NCR could have protected itself from defendant's floating lien. How?

PROTECTION FROM A BONA FIDE PURCHASER OF COLLATERAL

Sterling Acceptance Co. v. Grimes
168 A. 2d 600 (1961)
Supreme Court of Pennsylvania

Sterling Acceptance Company brought action . . . against Patrick Grimes, Jr. and George Homish to obtain possession of a 1958 Dodge automobile which Grimes had purchased new from Homish, a dealer. . . .

Homish, who traded as Homish Sales & Service, was an automobile dealer in Aliquippa, Beaver County, for approximately 40 years. On May 29, 1958, he sold Grimes a new 1958 Dodge automobile for which Grimes paid him the sale price in full, including the sales tax and the fee for registration of the title. Grimes paid Homish $2,060 in cash and transferred to Homish title to a 1955 Dodge automobile for which he was given an allowance of $1,636.14. Possession of the new Dodge was given to Grimes. An application for title to the new car was signed by Grimes and given to Homish for mailing to the Bureau of Motor Vehicles in Harrisburg. The purchase of the automobile by Grimes was made from Homish's inventory in the ordinary course of Homish's business at his place of business in Aliquippa. When the certificate of title did not arrive, Grimes contacted Homish several times, and was told that the delay was caused by the authorities in Harrisburg. Finally, after frequent evasions, Homish told Grimes that he was in financial difficulties and that he had not mailed the application for the certificate of title.

Over two years prior to the sale of the Dodge to Grimes, a Blanket Security Agreement was filed by the acceptance company in the office of the Prothonotary of Beaver County. The agreement covered a security interest of the plaintiff in the sale of all new and used vehicles by Homish. This agreement was filed in compliance with §9-302 of the Uniform Commercial Code. . . .

Article 9 of the Uniform Commercial Code deals with secured transactions, including liens on personal property intended to be sold in the ordinary course of business. Section 9-307 provides: "(1) In the case of inventory . . . a buyer in ordinary course of business takes free of a security interest even though perfected and even though the buyer knows of the terms of the security agreement." . . .

According to the comment on §9-307 of the Uniform Commercial Code, "The theory is that when goods are inventory or when proceeds are claimed the secured party contemplates that his debtor will make sales, and so the debtor has effective power to do so, even though his buyers know the goods they buy were subject to the security interest."

Under the provision of the Uniform Commercial Code, the plaintiff must look to Homish for repayment of the loan it made to him, and not to the automobile in the possession of Grimes, who paid the full purchase price to Homish.

Questions

1. UCC Section 2-403 provides that"(2) any entrusting of possession of goods to a merchant who deals in goods of that kind gives him power to transfer all rights of the entruster to a buyer in ordinary course of business. (3) 'Entrusting' includes any delivery and any acquiescence in retention of possession regardless of any condition expressed between the parties to the delivery or acquiescence and regardless of whether the procurement of the entrusting or the possessor's disposition of the goods have been such as to be larcenous under the criminal law."

   Can you think of specific situations of "entrusting"? What do you suspect is the policy reason for such a law?
2. UCC Section 9-302(2) provides that "the filing provisions of this Article do not apply . . . to a security interest . . . (b) in property subject to a statute of this state which provides for central filing of, or which requires indication on a certificate of title of, such security interests in such property. Compliance with any such statute is equivalent to filing under this article."

   Can you think of any such property in your state subject to central filing or a certificate of title on which security interests are noted?

CONSUMER SALE OF COLLATERAL

In *Sterling Acceptance* v. *Grimes,* Section 9-307(1) says the buyer takes free of a security interest in goods classified as "inventory." Does this cover goods pledged to a merchant-creditor in the hands of a consumer-debtor who chooses to sell the goods? The next case deals with this problem.

U.G.I. v. McFalls
18 D&C 2d 713 (1959)
United States Bankruptcy Court

The complaint avers as follows: "On September 13, 1957, the plaintiff and Robert Henry, of 23 Parkside Avenue, Lancaster, Pennsylvania, entered into a written security agreement lease by which plaintiff sold to the said Robert Henry one household laundry dryer described in the security agreement lease as CD-85 Whirlpool Dryer. The dryer was delivered by the plaintiff to Robert Henry on September 18, 1957. By the terms of said security agreement lease, title to the dryer did not pass to Robert Henry until payments totaling $204.97 had been made to the plaintiff and a bill of sale for the dryer given by the plaintiff to Robert Henry. . . .

In the month of January, 1958, Robert Henry failed to pay an installment of $8.54 due at that time under the said security agreement lease and has not paid any amount whatsoever since that time. By the terms of said security agreement lease, upon default in the payment of any installment for a period of ten days, the plaintiff is entitled to possession of the dryer. On or about the early part of March, 1958, Robert Henry sold and delivered the dryer to the defendant. The defendant is a dealer in used household appliances and purchased the dryer for purposes of resale. On July 8, 1958, the plaintiff demanded of the defendant the return of the dryer to it but the defendant refused to return the dryer, and refuses to return the dryer at the present time. The value of the dryer at the time of its conversion by the defendant was $180.00."

Defendant, William H. McFalls, . . . raises but one question, namely: Does plaintiff have a cause of action against defendant because of plaintiff's failure to file a financing statement in accordance with the Uniform Commercial Code?

The Uniform Commercial Code defines "consumer goods" as goods "used or bought for use primarily for personal, family or household purposes." There can be no question, therefore, that the description in the complaint of the article sold to Robert Henry as "one household laundry dryer" is within the above definition of "consumer goods." The question then is, does plaintiff bring itself within the exception of the Uniform Commercial Code which provides as follows: "A financing statement must be filed to perfect all security interests except . . . a purchase money security interest in consumer goods; but filing is required if the goods are part of the realty or a motor vehicle required to be licensed."

. . . Under [the] Code ". . . these transactions might qualify as purchase money security interests that would be effective without filing." This court is in accord with this statement and finds that plaintiff has brought itself within [the] exception of the Uniform Commercial Code.

This then leaves one remaining question, was defendant a buyer of goods, such as is contemplated in the code, which provides as follows: "In the case of consumer goods . . . a buyer takes free of a security interest even though perfected if he buys without knowledge of the security interest for value and for his own personal, family or household purposes or his own farming operations unless prior to the purchase the secured party has filed a financing statement covering such goods."

We have previously stated that the goods purchased by defendant were clearly "consumer goods" and were not purchased for defendant's own personal family or household purposes. Since . . . it is averred that defendant is a dealer in used household appliances and purchased the dryer for purposes of resale, plaintiff therefore did not have to file a financial statement covering such goods as provided by the Uniform Commercial Code . . . and defendant did not purchase the same from Robert Henry free of the security interest of plaintiff.

Questions

1. A purchase money security interest in consumer goods can be "perfected" without filing. What does this mean?
2. Without filing, does the purchase money security interest holder in consumer goods have protection against other creditors of the debtor? Against *all* buyers from the debtor? Or only against *some* buyers from the debtor?

REPOSSESSION PROCESS

Benschoter v. First National Bank of Lawrence

542 P. 2d 1042 (1975)
Supreme Court of Kansas

This is an appeal from an order of the trial court granting a creditor judgment thereby affirming the creditor's "self-help" repossession of the plaintiff's property (pledged as security for a loan) pursuant to [UCC] 9-503. The provision . . . reads:

> Unless otherwise agreed a secured party has on default the right to take possession of the collateral. In taking possession a secured party may proceed without judicial process if this can be done without breach of the peace or may proceed by action. . . .

The plaintiff first argues the due process requirements of the Fourteenth Amendment of the United States Constitution requires that he should have been given notice and a prior hearing. . . . Under this clause, state action is necessary to invoke the Fourteenth Amendment. Acts of private individuals, however discriminatory or wrongful, are outside the scope of the Fourteenth Amendment.

The state action test is generally met when conduct formerly private becomes so entwined with governmental policies and so impregnated with governmental character as to become subject to the constitutional limitations placed upon state action. The courts have never attempted the impossible task of formulating an infallible test for determining whether the state in any of its manifestations has become significantly involved in private conduct. Only by sifting facts and weighing circumstances on a case-by-case basis can a non-obvious involvement of the state in private conduct be attributed its true significance.

The plaintiff's primary argument is that the state has passed a law which authorizes or encourages "self-help repossession" so state action must be present. But the Federal Circuit Courts have unanimously rejected this argument. The state courts have also unanimously rejected this contention. . . .

One reason for the almost unanimous acceptance of self-help repossession is that 9-503 did not change the common law or the previously codified statutory law. The right to peaceful self-help repossession of property under circumstances such as are here involved, far from being a right created by 9-503, has roots deep in the common law. . . . Therefore, 9-503 injects no new element upon which a finding of state action may be based.

Had 9-503 changed our law, a finding of state action would still not be required.

Statutes regulate many forms of private activities in some manner or another. Subjecting all behavior that conforms to some statute to complete due process guarantees would emasculate the state action concept and create chaos in our society.

Recent United States Supreme Court cases have held that conforming to some state regulation is not sufficient state action to trigger application of the

Fourteenth Amendment. (*Moose Lodge No. 107* v. *Irvis*, 407 U.S. 163, [conforming to liquor regulations]; and *Jackson* v. *Metropolitan Edison Co.*, 419 U.S. 345, [conforming to utility tariffs].) The same is true when a creditor conforms to 9-503, no state action is present. . . .

Plaintiff further relies on several of the more modern creditors' rights cases. *Sniadach* v. *Family Finance Corp.*, 395 U.S. 337, (prejudgment garnishment of wages); and *Fuentes* v. *Shevin*, 407 U.S. 67, (prejudgment replevin statute). These decisions of the United States Supreme Court reversed state laws which allowed state agents, the state court in *Sniadach* and the sheriff in *Fuentes*, to seize property without prior notice and prior hearings.

Here no state official, be he judge, clerk of the court or police officer, is involved in the prejudgment self-help repossession of the collateral. As such no state action is present. . . .

The plaintiff suggests that the better course of action would be for the bank and other secured parties to institute legal proceedings pursuant to 9-503, under which "the secured party" may "proceed by action." However, that is not necessary. The secured party may choose the remedy it wishes: either self-help repossession or judicial action in accordance with the due process guarantees of the Fourteenth Amendment.

Commentaries on the practical and economic aspects of self-help repossession make a strong argument that absent self-help repossession credit would be more restricted or would cost more or both. . . .

Debtors are not without remedy. If the bank or secured party repossesses before default, or breaches the peace during repossession after default, it may be liable for damages.

A default having been established, the next question is whether the defendant took repossession of the secured property by "stealth" and thereby committed a "breach of the peace" under the facts in this case. The plaintiff asserts that the defendant used "stealth" to effect the repossession because the repossession occurred without the plaintiff's knowledge and arguably, at a time when the defendant knew the plaintiff would not be at his place of residence. The deposition testimony of the parties submitted to the court for consideration upon the motion for summary judgment fails to bear out the plaintiff's contention that defendant knew the plaintiff would not be home. In fact, the plaintiff's deposition testimony tends to establish the contrary. To support the plaintiff's assertion that "stealth" is part of a breach of the peace the plaintiff argues it should be defined to cover, without more, a repossession that is effected without the debtor's knowledge. . . .

Here plaintiff had knowledge that the property might be taken. He had received repeated warnings from the defendant and he *agreed to the taking of repossession upon his continued default*. . . . Thus the defendant had permission to be on the property, both from the plaintiff and his seventeen-year-old son at the time of their entry. Had the seventeen-year-old son refused to let the defendant repossess (*Morris* v. *Bk. & TR Co.*, 21 Ohio St. 2d 25, 254 N.E. 2d 683 [1970]), or had he requested the defendant to wait until his father returned, a different case might be presented (*Luthy* v. *Philip Werlein Co.*, 163 La. 752, 112 So. 709 [1927].) . . . .

As a matter of law this court cannot say "stealth," as the term is used in the context of this case by the plaintiff, constitutes a "breach of the peace."

. . . [S]tealth, in the sense of the debtor's lack of knowledge of the creditor's repossession, does not make an otherwise lawful repossession an unlawful repossession.

White and Summers in their Handbook of the Law under the Uniform Commercial Code, discuss the essential requirement that repossession be peaceful and what constitutes a breach of the peace, as follows:

> . . . To determine if a breach of the peace has occurred, courts inquire mainly into: (1) whether there was entry by the creditor upon the debtor's premises; and (2) whether the debtor or one acting on his behalf consented to the entry and repossession.

Using this basis for any analysis the trial court correctly found there was no breach of the peace in this case.

Questions

1. In *Benschoter* why did the court reject the plaintiff's argument that "self-help repossession" authorized by statute amounts to "state action"?
2. Are there any good reasons for private repossessions? Why not force all creditors to proceed by judicial action?
3. Private repossession is permissible only if obtained without breach of the peace. Is it a "breach of the peace" for a creditor to repossess the property without giving the debtor any notice of the repossession? May the creditor repossess over the protests of the debtor? Or the debtor's family? Or may the creditor break and enter?

CONCLUSION

Commercial paper is a contract that calls for the future payment of money by one of the parties, either directly or through another party designated to make payment. It may also be described as a contract that evidences a right to receive money; this right may be transferred by a process called negotiation, which serves as a substitute for money. Commercial paper furnishes the means by which the greater part of commerce and business in the United States is conducted.

In order to enable commercial paper to efficiently perform these functions, certain rules were devised to identify the negotiable contract and distinguish it from other contracts. Other rules, such as the holder in due course doctrine and the shelter doctrine, are designed to enhance the transferability of the paper.

Whereas commercial paper is a money substitute, a secured transaction involves the lending of money and the establishment of legal priority in the lender to some property owned by the debtor to ensure that a debt is repaid on the due date. The security interest is created by the execution by the parties of a document called a security agreement. The secured party normally obtains priority to the collateral pledged by the debtor by filing a financing statement which gives notice to other potential creditors of the debtor. The collateral provides a fund of monies from which the creditor may collect his or her debt in the event of nonpayment by the debtor.

The laws of negotiable instruments and secured transactions are reasonably efficient in fashioning short-term financial obligations that facilitate the exchange of economic values. Besides recent reform efforts to protect consumers from the holder in due course doctrine and to protect debtors from creditor repossession without due process notice and hearing, the rules of negotiable instruments and secured transactions are stable and enduring.

CASE PROBLEMS

1. Three individuals held equal interests in an option for the purchase of certain land which they planned to acquire and either erect thereon a shopping plaza or sell for profit. Payments were made periodically to maintain the option, and at one point the need arose for $20,340. One member of the group, Glenna, paid $6,780 on her own behalf and advanced $6,780 on behalf of each of the other two members, receiving in return a promissory note from each which read as follows:

   > $6,780.00 May 15, 1967
   >
   > As below after date for value received I promise to pay to the order of Glenna E. Mosley six thousand seven hundred eighty and no/100 dollars with interest at the rate of six (6) per centum per annum at simple interest.
   >
   > Due when land in Kent, Ohio, is sold or when shopping center is finished.
   >
   > (signature)

   Are the notes negotiable?

2. Plaintiff, the holder, sued the maker on a note due January 1, 1977. Plaintiff bought the note from a bank in February 1977, the bank having previously acquired it from a holder in due course. Defendant contends that plaintiff is not a holder in due course since he bought the instrument after its maturity. Decide.

3. Defendant sold furniture to a customer who gave his name as Norton, receiving in payment a note, secured by a mortgage on the furniture, that he endorsed "without recourse" and sold to plaintiff. When the maker of the note later defaulted, it was discovered that his name was actually Morton, and that he had a very bad credit rating and a prison record. Plaintiff brought an action to recover the money paid to defendant for the note. Decide.

4. A financing statement described the collateral as 800 head of cattle, plus "any increase thereof by birth or purchase." The security agreement mentioned only 800 head of cattle. A dispute later arose regarding cattle purchased by the debtor after the closing of the deal. Are the subsequently purchased cattle included in the security interest?

part three
PRESERVING COMPETITIVE MARKETS

From earliest history of the United States, American society has had a firm faith in the workings of a free-market economy. Protection against those who might exploit or abuse society in the production and distribution of the nation's goods and services was to be effectuated through the forces of competition. Although this belief in the virtue of competition in society continues even today, the government has found it necessary to change its role from that of a passive observer of economic activity to one of modern-day protector of "competition," the theory being that by protecting and preserving competition, America will continue to reap the benefits of a free economy except for the historical role of a limited government.

In the last part of the nineteenth century, a device known as a trust became a popular tool for gaining monopolistic control of industries. The majority of the stock of competing companies would be transferred to a board of trustees and the previous stockholders would receive trust certificates naming them as beneficiaries entitled to dividends from the companies through the trust. The trustee board would be composed of various directors from the companies in the industry. The board would then make policy decisions for the supposedly competing companies and, in effect, run the legally separate companies in a monopolistic manner. It was this use of the trust device that brought on the "trust busting" era (which tried to eliminate this type of trust purpose not the trust device itself). The laws enacted to eliminate monopolistic practices in industry became known as antitrust laws. These laws do not outlaw legitimate uses of trusts; rather they are designed to promote competition.

Of course, the decisions concerning a change in the role of government and the variety of methods to be employed in regulating competition have not been accomplished without opposition. Certainly, the policy choices selected to preserve competition have not received universal acceptance.

Part Three scans the historical development of antitrust laws and presents the various viewpoints concerning appropriate antitrust policy. The basic substantive rules relating to the structure of industries and the conduct of the firms are discussed.

chapter 11

REGULATION OF MONOPOLIES

Monopoly, or *monopoly power,* has been defined by the Supreme Court as the power or ability to fix or control prices in, or exclude competitors from, a relevant market. Not all monopolies, however, have been declared illegal. In certain situations a monopoly or exclusive privileges may be granted by federal, state, or local government. In other cases, monopoly may occur when only one firm survives because of its efficiency in organization, production, or the quality and utility of its products. What is legally proscribed, therefore, is the act of or attempt at "monopolization," which involves an analysis of the intent of the firm whose large market control and practices are questioned.

In the United States, the trust device was employed to acquire monopoly power. The trust device is a judicial creation of the Chancery Court of England. American courts adopted it as a unique and flexible method for dispositions of property. It is a fiduciary relationship with respect to property, whereby the person who holds title to the property is subjected to equitable duties to deal with the property for the benefit of another person. A fiduciary relationship involves a duty on the part of the fiduciary (trustee) to act for the benefit of the second party, called the beneficiary. In a trust, the trustee holds title to property and controls or manages the property for the beneficiary. The trustee has received the property from the party (settlor) setting up the trust, who commands the trustee as to his or her duties in regard to the property and to whom the property benefits are to be distributed. The trustee is legally bound to follow the instructions as set forth in the instrument that created the trust. The trust device has many very legitimate and socially desirable purposes. The will of parents who die at an early age can bequeath title to their property to a trustee for the benefit of the orphaned children. An individual could grant funds to a trustee to be invested for income which is to be used for charitable or scientific purposes. The variety of trust purposes is almost as wide as one's imagination.

In the latter half of the nineteenth century, however, the trust device was also used for the purpose of gaining monopolistic control of industries. The majority of the stock of competing companies was transferred to a board of trustees, and the previous stockholders received trust certificates naming them as beneficiaries entitled to dividends coming from the companies through the trust. The trustee board would be composed of various directors from the companies in the industry. This board made policy decisions for the supposedly competing companies and, in effect, ran the legally separate companies in a monopolistic manner. This use of the trust device produced the era of "trust busting" (that is, eliminating this type of trust purpose, not the trust device itself). "Antitrust" laws were enacted to eliminate monopolistic practices in industry. These laws do not outlaw legitimate uses of trusts but promote competition. In interpreting the first antitrust law, the Sherman Act, Justice Black made the following statement:

> The Sherman Act was designed to be a comprehensive charter of economic liberty aimed at preserving free and unfettered competition as a rule of trade. It rests on the premise that the unrestrained interaction of competitive forces will yield the best allocation of our economic resources, the lowest prices, the highest quality and the greatest material progress while at the same time providing an environment conducive to the preservation of our democratic political and social institutions. But even were that premise open to question, the policy unequivocally laid down by the Act is competition. *Northern Pac. R. Co.* v. *U.S.*, 356, U.S. 1, 4 (1958).

THE GOALS OF ANTITRUST

Justice Black predicated his understanding of the antitrust laws on the notion that competitive markets provide (1) "the best allocation of our economic resources [and] the lowest prices" (economic efficiency), (2) "the highest quality and the greatest material progress" (technological innovation and invention), and (3) "an environment conducive to the preservation of our democratic political and social institutions" (maintenance of political freedoms). Others have argued that competitive markets provide an equitable dispersion of income among society's participants (market valuation of worth and, hence, income levels) and that competitive markets, with flexible pricing and wage rates, make governmental policies of economic stabilization work better.

An ideological commitment to competition permeates society and is often supported by an almost religious fervor. It is not surprising, therefore, that statutory and common law reflect this ideological commitment to the competitive market system. However, although nearly everyone is in favor of competition, there is a great deal of debate concerning the degree or type of competition sufficient to bring about its benefits—in other words, what type of competition is to be accepted as a public policy *norm* against which to judge whether an industry is sufficiently competitive. The determination of this policy norm is subject to considerable debate. There are basically three schools of thought (approaches) concerning the appropriate norm of "workable competition."

CONDUCT APPROACH

Advocates of the conduct approach argue that certain business practices which interfere with the efficient operation of the competitive marketplace should be reasonably identified and outlawed. They argue that standards of illegal "conduct" must be identified so that business managers will have "fairly definite standards" to guide their behavior. They conclude that the criterion of *intent* to commit these illegal acts establishes a sensible test for determining antitrust enforcement. In effect, prohibition of illegal overt actions and behaviors should be the only basis for judicial action in the field of antitrust. Since attorneys, who enforce antitrust law, are trained and conditioned to prosecution against behavior or conduct rather than mere status, the conduct approach has had a definite impact on the evolving antitrust laws.

STRUCTURALIST APPROACH

Structuralists believe that a norm of workable competition can be formulated from classical economic theory, which can be modified for a realistic economic setting. They maintain that certain structural characteristics of an industry can be identified and that these characteristics can be applied to any specific industry on a case-by-case basis to determine whether antitrust enforcement is needed. Industries lacking these characteristics should be restructured through dismemberment orders. Such structural characteristics of a workably competitive market would include the following:

1. An appreciable number of traders (absence of concentration).
2. No firm powerful enough to be able to coerce its rivals.
3. Responsiveness of the market participants to economic incentives (rather than political purposes).
4. Minimization of product differentiation.
5. Reasonable opportunity for entry by new rivals.

These market structure tests place primary emphasis on limiting the economic power in the hands of private parties. Structuralists seek to employ antitrust laws to ensure the continued existence of the competitive system, with checks and balances against any private attempts to control the market. Structuralists also favor alternative governmental policies that encourage small businesses, the use of government procurement and surplus property programs to establish competing firms, and the imposition of taxes on increased advertising expenditures which can destroy the independence of consumers. However, remedies, such as divestiture of existing large firms, would be the more desired remedy of the structuralists.

PERFORMANCE APPROACH

The pure economic performance test to determine appropriate antitrust policy includes criteria such as the following:

1. Is the industry economically efficient?
2. Is it technologically progressive?
3. Does it show a reasonable and socially useful profit pattern?
4. Does it have as much freedom of entry as the nature of the industry will permit?
5. Is it well suited to serve national defense needs?

Negative answers to these questions suggest the need for antitrust action. Positive answers to these questions suggest immunity from antitrust attack. However, it is extremely difficult to devise tests of performance that can be applied by the courts. The literature of performance economists summarize some of the tests as follows:

1. Whether the firm is progressive in product and process innovation.
2. Whether cost reductions are passed on to consumers promptly.
3. Whether investment is excessive in relation to output.
4. Whether the profits are continually and substantially higher than in industries exhibiting similar trends in sales and costs and innovations.
5. Whether competitive effort concentrates mainly on selling activities rather than improvements in services and products and price reductions.

To the extent that performance of the firm or industry, as measured by these criteria, is determined to be acceptable, antitrust attack on the industry is deemed inappropriate. Obviously, the pronouncements of large firms adopt the performance criteria and argue that their particular firm should not be subjected to antitrust action because their performance is acceptable.

Other viewpoints concerning the level of competition could be presented, but these will suffice to indicate that the phrase *workable competition* means different things to different people. Most economists recognize that the classical economic model of "pure competition" does not provide a *norm* for enforcement of the antitrust laws. Instead, a pragmatic approach to determining appropriate "competitive markets" is utilized by each of the three schools of thought discussed here. However, the debate to determine an acceptable pragmatic norm of workable competition among these approaches is continuous. For example, the structuralists of today argue for a policy that would prohibit the oil companies from also having interests in coal or atomic energy firms. Performance advocates maintain that such a structural limitation on oil companies would be inappropriate if adequate performance (that is, technological advancement and cross-utilization of technology by oil and coal companies) could be obtained by the combination of alternative energy source firms. More often than not, performance economists do not find a need for antitrust enforcement. Other aspects of the debate between these schools of thought will be discussed throughout the remainder of this chapter and the next.

MONOPOLIZATION

Economists have prepared descriptions of competition, whether pure or imperfect, and its opposite extreme of monopoly. Based on certain assumptions, the competitive models suggest that competition will achieve higher levels of production with lower prices than a monopoly, which seeks to restrain output to capture higher prices. As a result, few people advocate the creation of monopoly if a competitive market structure is a viable alternative. It was the belief that monopolies are undesirable which led to the enactment of Section 2 of the Sherman Act. Section 2 outlaws monopolizations, attempts to monopolize, and conspiracies to monopolize. Congress outlawed monopolization and then, in effect, passed the buck to the courts to further articulate this law in specific situations. The courts have had a difficult time in applying this law. One reason for this is that economic theory, as illustrated by the differing views of the conduct, structuralist, or performance schools of thought, has been little help. In addition, public consensus concerning specific cases has been lacking. As a result, the courts' decisions have been subjected to criticism and ridicule by those holding to one or more of the opposing economic viewpoints.

Section 2 of the Sherman Act uses the word *monopolize*. The statutory language does not say that monopoly is prohibited but rather that "to monopolize" is to transgress the law. Monopolize was not defined by the statute, so such definition had to be determined by the courts. The Supreme Court has indicated that monopolization exists when two elements are present. First, the possession of monopoly power in the relevant market must be established, and second, the willful (intentional) acquisition or maintenance of that power must be shown. In *Standard Oil* v. *U.S.*, 221 U.S. 1 (1911) the Supreme Court determined that Standard Oil's unification of power and control over petroleum and its products was the result of combinations, not of normal methods of industrial development. These large combinations afforded Standard Oil better than 90 percent control of the oil market, which equalled monopoly power. Coupled with these combinations were certain patterns of conduct that were essentially predatory. These predatory actions were sufficient evidence to establish Standard Oil's intent to monopolize. The use of predatory behavior as evidence of "intent" established a behavioral or conduct approach to the determination of illegality under Section 2.

In *U.S.* v. *U.S. Steel Corp.*, 251 U.S. 417 (1920), the Supreme Court found no violation of Section 2 and asserted the following:

> The corporation is undoubtedly of impressive size and it takes an effort of resolution not to be affected by it or to exaggerate its influence. But we must adhere to the law and the law does not make mere size an offense or the existence of unexerted power an offense. It, we repeat, requires overt acts.

This statement, when coupled with the previous case against Standard Oil, has been characterized as the "abuse theory" of monopoly. Under this theory the government must establish the monopolistic intent of the defendant with proof of overt acts and conduct which abuse the competitors. Without actions by the defendant indicating a wrongful intent, the government would be unable to prove the abuse of monopoly power.

The abuse theory of monopoly is consistent with the conduct approach for antitrust laws. Only the abusive practices and conduct of the defendant are outlawed. To the structuralist economists, a monopoly which restricts production and raises its price is contrary to the public interest, whether overt predatory conduct can be shown or not. It matters not how the monopolist obtained power or maintains its position. Consequently, the criticisms of some economists and growing public concern over the inadequacy of the abuse theory (the conduct approach) caused the government to consider a different approach in the Alcoa case.

THE ALCOA CASE

In 1937 the Justice Department charged the Aluminum Company of America, Alcoa, with illegal monopolization. Alcoa was formed in 1888 to exploit patents it held on the basic process for producing aluminum. After the basic patents expired in 1909, there were several attempts to enter the industry, but none were successful. During these early years, Alcoa had been involved in various litigations involving patents, merger disputes, international cartelization, and price discrimination.

The District Court absolved Alcoa on the charge of monopolization on the basis of the *U.S. Steel* decision. The Justice Department appealed, but a quorum of six justices could not be obtained in the Supreme Court. Four Supreme Court justices disqualified themselves because they had been associated with the prior litigation against Alcoa. A congressional amendment of the Judicial Code established a court of appeals to serve, in such circumstances, as the court of last resort. The case was then sent to the Court of Appeals in the second circuit. A three-member panel of judges, with Judge Learned Hand presiding, heard the appeal. As in all monopolization cases, the court had to determine if Alcoa possessed monopoly power in the relevant market and if that power was intentionally obtained and maintained.

Determination of whether Alcoa possessed monopoly power turned on how the market in which Alcoa operated was defined. This is so because monopoly power cannot be measured in the abstract. It has significance only in relation to a defined market within meaningful boundaries. Consequently, the issues of monopoly and market are intertwined. Proper delimitation of the market involves a consideration of what set of near substitutes should be considered as the "product" market. The market definition also requires an inquiry into substitution, both in production and in use of the items traded in the market.

In the Alcoa case the court dismissed the possibility of substitution on the production side. The court felt the highly specialized aluminum refining facilities precluded the possibility of other companies converting their plants to produce aluminum. Moreover, on the demand side, aluminum's unique properties led the court to summarily exclude other metals such as steel, copper, and magnesium. Although such exclusion was perhaps unjustified by the facts (some users viewed other metals as substitutes for aluminum in many applications), the court nevertheless limited its analysis to alternative definitions of Alcoa's aluminum ingot market share (none of which need be discussed). Suffice it to say that Judge Hand concluded that Alcoa's 90 percent control of the virgin aluminum market "is enough to constitute a monopoly." Having found that Alcoa possessed a monopoly of the aluminum market, the court had to determine whether Alcoa's intent to achieve that position was sufficiently proven to establish a monopolization violation under Section 2.

United States v. Aluminum Co. of America

148 F. 2d 416 (1945)
U.S. Court of Appeals, 2d Cir.

Circuit Judge Hand

It is undisputed that throughout [a 28-year] period "Alcoa" continued to be the single producer of "virgin" ingot in the United States; and the plaintiff argues that this without more was enough to make it an unlawful monopoly. . . . "Alcoa's" position is that its monopoly was not retained by unlawful means, but was the result of a growth which the Act does not forbid, even when it results in a monopoly. . . .

"Alcoa" was free to raise its prices as it chose, since it was free from domestic competition, save as it drew other metals into the market as substitutes. Was this a monopoly within the meaning of §2? The judge found that, over the whole half century of its existence, "Alcoa's" profits upon capital invested, after payment of income taxes, had been only about ten percent, and, although the plaintiff puts this figure a little higher, the difference is negligible.

This assumed, it would be hard to say that "Alcoa" had made exorbitant profits on ingot. . . . But the whole issue is irrelevant anyway, for it is no excuse for "monopolizing" a market that the monopoly has not been used to extract from the consumer more than a "fair" profit. The Act has wider purposes. Indeed even though we disregarded all but economic considerations, it would by no means follow that such concentration of producing power is to be desired, when it has not been used extortionately. . . . In any event the mere fact that a producer, having command of the domestic market, has not been able to make more than a "fair" profit, is no evidence that a "fair" profit could not have been made at lower prices. . . . True, it might have been thought adequte to condemn only those monopolies which could not show that they had exercised the highest possible ingenuity, had adopted every possible economy, had anticipated every conceivable improvement, stimulated every possible demand. No doubt, that would be one way of dealing with the matter. . . . Be that as it may, that was not the way that Congress chose; it did not condone "good trusts" and condemn "bad" ones; it forbad all. Moreover, in so doing it was not necessarily actuated by economic motives alone. It is possible, because of its indirect social or moral effect, to prefer a system of small producers, each dependent for his success upon his own skill and character, to one in which the great mass of those engaged must accept the direction of a few. These considerations, which we have suggested only as possible purposes of the Act, we think the decisions prove to have been in fact its purposes. . . .

It does not follow because "Alcoa" had such a monopoly, that it "monopolized" the ingot market: it may not have achieved monopoly; monopoly may have been thrust upon it. If it had been a combination of existing smelters which united the whole industry and controlled the production of all aluminum ingot, it would certainly have "monopolized" the market. In several decisions the Supreme Court has decreed the dissolution of such combinations, although they had engaged in no unlawful trade practices. . . . We may start therefore with the premise that to have combined ninety percent of the producers of ingot would have been to "monopolize" the ingot market; and, so far as concerns the public interest, it can make no difference whether an existing competition is put an end to, or whether prospective competition is prevented. . . . Nevertheless, it is unquestionably true that from the very outset the courts have at least kept in reserve the possibility that the origin of a monopoly may be critical in determining its legality. . . . This notion has usually been expressed by saying that size does not determine guilt; that there must be some "exclusion" of competitors; that the growth must be something else than "natural" or "normal"; that there must be a "wrongful intent," or some other specific intent; or that some "unduly" coercive means must be used. . . .

What engendered these compunctions is reasonably plain; persons may unwittingly find themselves in possession of a monopoly, automatically so to say: that is, without having intended either to put an end to existing competition, or to prevent competition from arising when none had existed; they may become monopolists by force of accident. . . . A market may, for example, be so limited that it is impossible to produce at all and meet the cost of production except by a plant large enough to supply the whole demand. Or there may be changes in taste or in cost which drive out all but one purveyor. A single producer may be the survivor out of a group of active competitors, merely by virtue of his superior skill, foresight, and industry. In such cases, a strong argument can be made that, although the result may expose the public to the evils of monopoly, the Act does not mean to condemn the resultant of those very forces which it is its prime object to foster. The successful competitor, having been urged to compete, must not be turned upon when he wins. . . .

It would completely misconstrue "Alcoa's" position in 1940 to hold that it was the passive beneficiary of a monopoly, following upon an involuntary elimination of competitors by automatically operative economic forces.

There were at least one or two abortive attempts to enter the industry, but "Alcoa" effectively anticipated and forestalled all competition, and succeeded in holding the field alone. True, it stimulated demand and opened new uses for the metal, but not without making sure that it could supply what it had evoked. There is no dispute as to this; "Alcoa" avows it as evidence of the skill, energy and initiative with which it has always conducted its business; as a reason why, having won its way by fair means, it should be commended, and not dismembered. . . .

The only question is whether it falls within the exception established in favor of those who do not seek, but cannot avoid, the control of a market. It seems to us that that question scarcely survives its statement. It was not inevitable that it should always anticipate increases in the demand for ingot and be prepared to supply them. Nothing compelled it to keep doubling and redoubling its capacity before others entered the field. It insists that it never excluded competitors; but we can think of no more effective exclusion than progressively to embrace each new opportunity as it opened, and to face every newcomer with new capacity already geared into a great organization, having the advantage of experience, trade connections and the elite of personnel. Only in case we interpret "exclusion" as limited to manoeuvers not honestly industrial, but actuated solely by a desire to prevent competition, can such a course, indefatigably pursued, be deemed not "exclusionary." So to limit it would in our judgment emasculate the Act; would permit just such consolidations as it was designed to prevent. . . .

We disregard any question of "intent." The plaintiff was seeking to show that many transactions, neutral on their face, were not in fact necessary to the development of "Alcoa's" business, and had no motive except to exclude others and perpetuate its hold upon the ingot market. . . . The plaintiff has so satisfied us, and the issue of intent ceases to have any importance; no intent is relevant except . . . an intent to bring about the forbidden act.

In order to fall within Section 2, the monopolist must have both the power to monopolize, and the intent to monopolize. To read the passage as demanding any "specific" intent, makes nonsense of it, for no monopolist monopolizes unconscious of what he is doing. So here, "Alcoa" meant to keep, and did keep, that complete and exclusive hold upon the ingot market with which it started. That was to "monopolize" that market, however innocently it otherwise proceeded.

Questions

1. Is the approach in the Alcoa case a conduct approach (abuse theory)?
2. How did the court define the market in the Alcoa case?
3. What was the court's response to Alcoa's assertion that it was a "good"

monopoly and charged only "fair" prices? Is this assertion relevant to a structuralist? To a performance economist?

4. Did Alcoa "intend" to monopolize? What proof of intent did the court require? Is the court's approach that of a structuralist or of a performance economist?
5. What is a "thrust upon" defense? Can you give examples? Was the monopoly of Alcoa "thrust upon" it? Is a newspaper firm in a town with only one newspaper an illegal monopoly?

Remedial action in the Alcoa case was deferred until after World War II. During the war, the government built aluminum producing plants which were operated by Alcoa. After the war, the government's plants were sold to the newly formed Reynolds Metals and Kaiser Aluminum. Thereafter, the district court concluded that with the two new competitors, Alcoa did not need to be fragmented.

The Alcoa decision was broadly endorsed by the Supreme Court in subsequent decisions. The approach in *Alcoa* overturned the *Standard Oil* and *U.S. Steel* precedents. It became possible to infer illegal monopolization from the mere possession and continuation over time of monopoly power without evidence of unreasonable practices driving competitors from the market. In 1948 Justice Douglas, in speaking for a 6–1 majority upholding a monopolization charge, stated that "monopoly power, whether lawfully or unlawfully acquired, may itself constitute an evil and stand condemned under Section 2 even though it remains unexercised."[1]

THE dUPONT CASE

The decision in *United States* v. *duPont* in 1956 shattered the hardline structuralist approach against dominant firms of the Alcoa decision. In *duPont*, the Justice Department argued for a narrow definition of the market embracing only cellophane sales. The government emphasized cellophane's unique properties, substantial price differences between cellophane and other packaging materials, and the unusually high profits realized by cellophane sales. However, duPont argued that the relevant market included all "flexible wrapping materials" because there was a high cross-elasticity of demand between cellophane and other flexible wrapping materials. Within this broadly defined market, cellophane embraced only an 18 percent share.

DuPont dominated the cellophane market by virtue of patents acquired from abroad and from its own improvement inventions. duPont also settled with an American company that had challenged duPont's patent claims by working out a licensing arrangement. The government argued that these patent arrangements justified an inference of illegal intent to monopolize. The district court disagreed with both the government's definition of the market and its proof of intent to monopolize.

United States v. duPont & Co.

351 U.S. 377 (1956)

Supreme Court of the United States

Justice Reed

. . . Market delimitation is necessary . . . to determine whether an alleged monopolist violates § 2. The ultimate consideration in such a determination is whether the defendants control the price and competition in the market for such part of trade or commerce as they are charged with monopolizing. Every manufacturer is the sole producer of the particular commodity it makes but its control in the above sense of the relevant market depends upon the availability of alternative commodities for buyers: i.e., whether there is a cross-elasticity of demand between cellophane and the other wrappings. This interchangeability is largely gauged by the purchase of competing products for similar uses considering the price, characteristics and adaptability of the competing commodities. . . .

If a large number of buyers and sellers deal freely in a standardized product, such as salt or wheat, we have complete or pure competition. Patents, on the other hand, furnish the most familiar type of classic monopoly. As the producers of a standardized product bring about significant differentiations of quality, design, or packaging in the product that permit differences of use, competition becomes to a greater degree incomplete and the producer's power over price and competition greater over his article and its use, according to the differentiation he is able to create and maintain. A retail seller may have in one sense a monopoly on certain trade because of location, as an isolated country store or filling station, or because no one else makes a product of just the quality or attractiveness of his product, as for example in cigarettes. Thus one can theorize that we have monopolistic competition in every nonstandardized commodity with each manufacturer having power over the price and production of his own product. However, this power that, let us say, automobile or soft-drink manufacturers have over their trademarked products is not the power that makes an illegal monopoly. Illegal power must be appraised in terms of the competitive market for the product.

Determination of the competitive market for commodities depends on how different from one another are the offered commodities in character or use, how far buyers will go to substitute one commodity for another. For example, one can think of building materials as in commodity competition but one could hardly say that brick competed with steel or wood or cement or stone in the meaning of Sherman Act litigation; the products are too different. This is the interindustry competition emphasized by some economists.

On the other hand, there are certain differences in the formulae for soft drinks but one can hardly say that each one is an illegal monopoly. Whatever the market may be, we hold that control of price or competition establishes the existence of monopoly power under § 2. Section 2 requires the application of a reasonable approach in determining the existence of monopoly power. . . . This of course does not mean that there can be a reasonable monopoly.

* * *

The Relevant Market . . . [W]here there are market alternatives that buyers may readily use for their purposes, illegal monopoly does not exist merely because the product said to be monopolized differs from others. If it were not so, only physically identical products would be a part of the market. To accept the Government's argument, we would have to conclude that the manufacturers of plain as well as moistureproof cellophane were monopolists, and so with films such as Pliofilm, foil, glassine, polyethylene, and Saran, for each of these wrappings materials is distinguishable. These were all exhibits in the case. New wrappings appear, generally similar to cellophane: is each a monopoly? What is called for is an appraisal of the "cross-elasticity" of demand in the trade. . . . The varying circumstances of each case determine the result. In considering what is the relevant market for determining the control of price and competition, no more definite rule can be declared than that commodities reasonably interchangeable by consumers for the same purposes make up that "part of the trade or commerce," monopolization of which may be illegal. . . .

. . . In determining the market under the Sherman Act, it is the use or uses to which the commodity is put that control. The selling price between commodities with similar uses and different characteristics may vary, so that the cheaper product can drive out the more expensive. Or, the superior quality of higher priced articles may make dominant the more desirable. Cellophane costs more than many competing products and less than a few. But whatever the price, there are various flexible wrapping materials that are bought by manufacturers for packaging their goods in their own plant or sold to converters who shape and print them for use in the packaging of the commodities to be wrapped. . . .

It may be admitted that cellophane combines the desirable elements of transparency, strength and cheapness more definitely than any of the others. . . .

But, despite cellophane's advantages, it has to meet competition from other materials in every one of its uses. . . . Thus, cellophane shares the packaging market with others. The overall result is that cellophane accounts for 17.9% of flexible wrapping materials, measured by the wrapping surface. . . .

An element for consideration as to cross-elasticity of demand between products is the responsiveness of the sales of one product to price changes of the other. If a slight decrease in the price of cellophane causes a considerable number of customers of other flexible wrappings to switch to cellophane, it would be an indication that a high cross-elasticity of demand exists between them; that the products compete in the same market. The court below held that the "[g]reat sensitivity of customers in the flexible packaging markets to price or quality changes" prevented duPont from possessing monopoly control over price. The record sustains these findings.

We conclude that cellophane's interchangeability with the other materials mentioned suffices to make it a part of this flexible packaging material market.

The Government stresses the fact that the variation in price between cellophane and other materials demonstrates they are noncompetitive. As these products are all flexible wrapping materials, it seems reasonable to consider, as was done at the trial, their comparative cost to the consumer in terms of square area. Cellophane costs two or three times as much, surface measure, as its chief competitors for the flexible wrapping market, glassine and greaseproof papers. Other forms of cellulose wrappings and those from other chemical or mineral substances, with the exception of aluminum foil, are more expensive. The uses of these materials, . . . are largely to wrap small packages for retail distribution. The wrapping is a relatively small proportion of the entire cost of the article. Different producers need different qualities in wrappings and their need may vary from time to time as their products undergo change. But the necessity for flexible wrappings is the central and unchanging demand. We cannot say that these differences in cost gave duPont monopoly over prices in view of the findings of fact on that subject. . . .

The facts above considered dispose also of any contention that competitors have been excluded by duPont from the packaging material market. That market has many producers and there is no proof duPont ever has possessed power to exclude any of them from the rapidly expanding flexible packaging market. . . . The record shows the multiplicity of competitors and the financial strength of some with individual assets running to the hundreds of millions.

The "market" which one must study to determine when a producer has monopoly power will vary with the part of commerce under consideration. The tests are constant. That market is composed of products that have reasonable interchangeability for the purposes for which they are produced—price, use and qualities considered. While the application of the tests remains uncertain, it seems to us that duPont should not be found to monopolize cellophane when that product has the competition and interchangeability with other wrappings that this record shows.

Questions

1. By a narrow definition of the market, the courts may find a monopoly (as in the Alcoa case) or they may determine that no monopoly exists (as in *duPont*) when a broad definition of the market is accepted. What is the test to define the "product market"? Does the application of this test in any factual situation afford considerable leeway to the court?
2. The Alcoa decision emphasized the lack of interchangeability of production facilities which provided Alcoa with the illegal monopolization power to exclude competitors or to control price. In contrast, the *duPont* decision emphasized the interchangeability of the produced goods despite the inability of others to produce cellophane. Which of these two cases creates a better approach for Section 2?
3. Does the company that produces Dr. Pepper soft drink possess an illegal monopoly?
4. Is interindustry competition to be included in the definition of the product market?
5. Why did the Supreme Court not consider the issue of whether duPont's patent practices justified an inference of intent to monopolize?

WILLFUL AND EXCLUSIONARY PRACTICES

The principal litigated victory of the government in the late 1960s was the *Grinnell* case.[2] This case restated the elements that constitute monopolization under Section 2, that is, "the possession of monopoly power in the relevant market and . . . the willful acquisition or maintenance of that power as distinguished from growth or development as a consequence of a superior product, business acumen, or historic accident." This statement seems to revive some elements of the abuse theory of older decisions by placing increased emphasis on the willfulness of the monopolist. *Grinnell*'s requirement to separate "willful acquisition or maintenance" of monopoly power from "growth or development" through superior products, business acumen, or historic accident has become a difficult task in subsequent cases.

The Grinnell test makes it clear that mere possession of monopoly power to control market prices is not sufficient to establish a violation of Section 2. It must also be shown that the power was *willfully* acquired or maintained. The cases have established that a firm which has monopoly control of a market may not engage in practices that are designed to continue such control. The principal conduct attributed to Alcoa in support of the assertion that it had monopolized the market for aluminum ingots was its practice of expanding existing plants and constructing new facilities in anticipation of increased demand for the product. This expansion of capacity had the effect of discouraging and frustrating entry into the field by other firms. Judge Learned Hand delineated the proper means of analyzing the conduct of a firm with monopoly power by writing, "The only question is whether it falls within the exception established in favor of those who do not seek, but cannot avoid, the control of the market."[3] Reviewing Alcoa's expansion policy, the court stated that it could "think of no more effective exclusion than to embrace every new opportunity as it opened."[4]

One point made clear by the Alcoa decision is that the conduct of firms with monopoly power is viewed differently from that of firms without such power. It leads to the conclusion that firms with monopoly power may not maintain that power through means that are not economically inevitable. This conclusion follows naturally from the strong policy of the antitrust laws to which monopoly is repugnant. Some monopolies must be tolerated because they are inevitable, natural, or "thrust upon" their owners. But where a firm with monopoly power interferes with natural economic forces which would otherwise dissipate its monopoly, the law rightfully condemns it.

The question of defining appropriate limits on permissible business behavior by a monopoly is perplexing. On one hand, monopoly power and the market dislocations it generates are abhorrent to an effective competitive system. On the other hand, it is fundamental to Section 2 enforcement that a monopolist will not be penalized if its success derives solely from its superior skill, foresight, and industry. However, these eloquent statements are difficult to apply sensibly and consistently in specific situations. For example, the word *willful* suggests that intent is the critical element in determining whether conduct by a monopolist is legal or not. Although many have argued that intent is an ambiguous indicator, the courts nevertheless accept testimony and corporate documents of plans and correspondence which may reveal corporate intent to monopolize.

Also, the language in the Alcoa case suggests that *any* exclusionary business behavior, at least where not economically inevitable, would violate Section 2. Some have pointed out that there are many forms of conduct not economically inevitable which can have an exclusionary effect and which it would clearly be unwise policy to deter. For example, a monopolist may improve its product and succeed thereby in obtaining additional business. Or the monopolist may improve its production facilities so as to become more efficient and then pass that efficiency along to consumers in the form of lower prices. Such conduct, it is argued, may actually exclude existing or potential rivals but surely should not be considered illegal under Section 2.[5]

Perhaps a fairer and more effective description of permissible behavior by a monopolist must proceed beyond loose language dealing with intent or exclusion and come to grips with the specific conduct engaged in by the monopolist. A description of permissible behavior by a monopolist must inquire whether the conduct at issue was *unreasonably* exclusionary or anticompetitive, that is, whether the anticompetitive effects of a practice outweigh its procompetitive consequences, taking into account whether the same procompetitive consequences could have been achieved through a less restrictive alternative action. The search for clear guidelines to identify only *unreasonable* exclusionary behavior, however, is continuous but rarely satisfying to all. For example, consider the following discussion concerning the appropriate pricing policies of a monopolist.

PRICING POLICIES OF A MONOPOLIST

It frequently occurs that a business rival (sometimes a new entrant) cuts price significantly below the price of a monopolist in order to take away part of its market. Assuming the monopolist responds with a price cut of its own, in what circumstances would such behavior violate Section 2 of the Sherman Act?

No Price Response

It is possible to argue that a monopolist should not be permitted to engage in responsive price cuts at all when a new, smaller challenger appears on a scene. If a legally mandated supracompetitive price were imposed, smaller rivals would eventually cut into the market share of the monopolist until its market position fell below the monopoly level. At that point the monopolist would be free to respond with any price strategy it felt would be effective.

New entrants protected by a legally mandated umbrella price of the monopolist may themselves charge higher prices than would otherwise be the case. The whole industry could become economically inefficient for the period of time the administered price umbrella was in effect. Also, the legally mandated umbrella price creates extremely burdensome administrative problems in supporting the monopolist's pricing policy. For example, suppose the monopolist improves the quality of its products. The court would have to judge what constitutes a fair increase in price to take into account the more attractive features introduced. No increase in price for a better quality item would have the same effect on the new entrant as a price cut. These and other objections to the no response rule has led to its rejection by the courts.

Discriminatory Pricing

One rule could require that a monopolist not respond to a new challenge by lowering prices strategically in competitive markets. This rule requires that the monopolist not discriminate in price between geographic markets or between product categories. Consequently, if there is to be a price reduction, it must be across the board.

The district court in *Grinnell* discussed the issue of discriminatory pricing, and the Supreme Court affirmed the district court's decision with little more than a passing reference to this issue. The court acknowledged that Grinnell had reduced its prices in competitive markets and raised prices in markets in which it faced no competition. Accordingly, the court approved of the govenment's proposal to require Grinnell to sell on nondiscriminatory terms. In the *United Shoe Machinery* case, the court acknowledged that a discriminatory pricing policy may not be "predatory, abusive, or coercive," but nevertheless could be "in economic effect, exclusionary" and hence a violation of Section 2.[6] Although the authority of precedents is not overwhelming, it could be a dangerous practice for a monopolist to engage in discriminatory pricing which may have the "exclusionary effect" of eliminating the new competition.

Predatory Pricing

Professors Areeda and Turner have argued that predatory or exclusionary pricing by a monopolist should be assessed by a series of cost-based rules.[7] Their rule states that a monopolist should be held to be violating Section 2 only when it sells "below cost," defining cost as average *variable* cost. They assert that a firm that is selling at a short-term profit-maximizing price is clearly not a predator even though it may be selling below its full cost. On the other hand, when a firm sells at less than average variable cost, it is taking an out-of-pocket loss on every unit sold. Such conduct can only be explained as part of a strategy to drive rivals out of business and then recoup the earlier losses with larger than competitive prices. Also, sales at such low prices raise the specter that success in the market will depend not on the relative efficiency of rivals, but on which seller has a sufficiently long purse to subsidize these unit-by-unit competitive losses. Thus, Areeda and Turner argue that a price at or above average variable cost is presumed nonpredatory; a price below is conclusively presumed unlawful. This rule provides sufficient guidance as to permissible pricing behavior for a monopolist and the courts alike. Several courts of appeal and district courts have recently adopted the below average variable cost rule to test for predatory pricing, but in limited circumstances.[8]

A different cost-based rule is suggested by Professor Posner, who defines predatory pricing as (1) selling below average variable cost (Areeda–Turner rule) or (2) "pricing at a level calculated to exclude from the market an equally or more efficient competitor" (Posner's rule).[9] Posner adopts a rebuttable presumption that predation is selling below average *total* cost with intent to exclude a competitor. A defendant could rebut the *prima facie* case of predation by showing, because of change in supply and demand, that its average total costs were not the correct guide to efficient pricing. This formulation apparently is predicated on the belief that an average variable cost rule (Areeda–Turner rule) would be too permissive and would allow a monopolist to eliminate a competitor whose long-run cost may be equal to or lower than the monopolist's. Short-term costs are invariably lower than long-run costs because the former may not include a variety of past expenses which have become a fixed cost for existing competitors but are yet to be incurred by the new entrant. Allowing existing firms to ignore previous fixed costs by pricing according to their present variable costs will force a new entrant to absorb losses on its initial fixed costs.

Several courts have recognized the problem identified by Posner and attempted to deal with it by adopting a two-step test for predatory pricing.[10] The first standard to determine predation is whether the price is below the average variable cost (Areeda–Turner rule). Even if it is not, a violation can still occur if it is below the average total cost and barriers to entry are high. The theory appears to be that if entry barriers are high, a monopolist can drive equally efficient or nearly as efficient rivals out of business (or discipline them into a compliant posture through price wars), and then raise its price to above competitive levels to reap monopoly profits before new entrants can create a competitive market.

Professor Scherer has concluded that it may be socially undesirable to allow price cutting to eliminate competitors when the monopolist's position is attained by an "image advantage." When image superiority is created in the consumers' minds by advertising and trademarking an item, the firm is able to maintain a price premium. Professor Scherer has written as follows:

> An image advantage . . . enhances the dominant firm's incentive to cut prices temporarily to exclude less favored rivals. What society obtains following successful image-induced exclusionary pricing is not the freeing of resources that can be employed more effectively elsewhere, but rather, higher prices and profits accompanied by increased consumption of the "premium" product. . . . I find it hard to avoid a value judgment that temporary price cutting to eliminate producers handicapped only by an inferior brand image is socially undesirable.[11]

Scherer's conclusion and Posner's rule were applied in the Federal Trade Commission (FTC) case against Borden and its monopolization of the processed lemon juice market.[12] The FTC concluded that the 30 percent price advantage achieved through successful differentiation of the ReaLemon brand, served as an instrument by which Borden could control prices and entry into the processed lemon juice market. The FTC found that although Borden did not sell below average variable cost, it did price below average total cost with the intent to exclude competitors (in violation of Posner's rule). The FTC concluded that, "the effect of Borden's spurious product differentiation, making it necessary for competitors to sell considerably below ReaLemon, created a circumstance where [Borden's reduced prices which were still above average variable] . . . cost could, as the record indicates, be predatory in the sense that even equally efficient competitors could be driven from the market." The ReaLemon case and others utilizing Posner's rule for predatory pricing are presently on appeal. Whether Posner's rule will be uniformly adopted and applied in future cases depends on its acceptance in the appellate courts.

FTC ENFORCEMENT

The basic authority of the FTC is enforcement of all antitrust laws and of Section 5 of the FTC Act which outlaws "unlawful methods of competition" among competitors. This latter provision was conceived as protection for honest businesses from competitors utilizing unfair competitive practices. The FTC is empowered by the statute to conduct investigations to determine if any business firm is in violation of Section 5. Whenever the commission has "reason to believe" that any party is violating Section 5, it is authorized to issue a complaint against the party. The courts have upheld the authority of the FTC to outlaw a practice as an "unfair method of competition" though the practice is not yet a full-blown antitrust violation under the Sherman Act.[13]

The FTC instigated some actions beginning in the late 1960s to reorganize monopolistic industries. For example, one FTC action involved a complaint against the Xerox Corporation for its monopolization of the plain paper copier business. Xerox settled through a consent order and agreed to make its extensive portfolio of copying machine patents available for licensing at a royalty rate not exceeding 1.5 percent (to all except IBM).[14]

In an effort to extend its authority under Section 5 even further, the FTC issued a complaint against a "shared monopoly" situation which would not normally be a provable violation under Section 2 of the Sherman Act.[15] None of the firms alone could be charged with monopolization under Section 2 of the Sherman Act because no firm by itself controlled a dominant share of the market. The case involved the three leading ready-to-eat (i.e., cold) breakfast cereal manufacturers. During the late 1960s, 81 percent of the total sales of cereal were made by the three leading sellers. As usual, the cereal makers urged a much broader market definition which would encompass such other breakfast foods as hot cereals, toast, waffles, and bacon and eggs.

The behavior of the three leading cereal makers embodied a high degree of parallelism and respect for mutual interdependence. Kellogg exercised price leadership and the other firms followed. List price reductions were rare and secret price cutting was unknown. As a result, the cereal makers maintained prices at twice the level of their manufacturing costs. Prices were high enough for them to spend 16 cents per sales dollar on advertising and still realize an after-tax return on assets between 1958 and 1970 of roughly twice the average for all manufacturing corporations.

Kellogg and General Mills had always refused to engage in private label cereal production. Post quit the private brand distribution in the 1960s even though internal analyses showed sizable private label accounts to be quite profitable.

With the leading cereal producers charging high prices and realizing supranormal profits, one may well wonder why new firms did not enter to erode these high profits. Economies of scale do not appear to be the answer, because minimum optimum scale appears to involve no more than 4 to 6 percent of the market.[16] Consequently, the FTC concluded and argued that opportunities for profitable new entry had been preempted largely by the existing sellers' proliferation of product brands. A firm attempting to gain a product differentiation advantage to facilitate its entry found that the established sellers had created such a diversity of product variants that a new brand entrant would hardly be noticed without enormous promotional expenditures. There may be little evidence of explicit intent by the cereal makers to preclude entry by the proliferation of products, but the entry-deterring *effects* of brand proliferation have been widely known to marketing managers since the 1960s, if not earlier.

The evidence of parallel noncompetitive behavior in private brands, overall monopolistic profits, persistently high concentration levels, and a plausible mechanism (brand proliferation) of collective market share maintenance was deemed insufficient to conclude the practice of illegal monopolization under Section 5 of the FTC Act. The administrative law judge dismissed the FTC complaint in September 1981, saying FTC counsel had not proved the charge that the companies' conduct illegally interferred with the ability of new firms to enter the market. The judge said that brand proliferation is "nothing more than the introduction of new brands, which is a legitimate means of competition. [The companies] engaged in intense, unrestrained and uncoordinated competition in the introduction of new products."[17] The judge's decision was not reversed by the full commission.

If monopolization had been found, the FTC indicated that a structural reorganization would be required. The FTC wanted three new competitors spun off from Kellogg, one from General Mills, and one from General Foods. Beyond this, the FTC asked that many of the cereal formulas and trademarks be made available for licensing to rivals. Licensees would thereby be able to use, for example, the name Cheerios and indicate that they had followed the original formula under strict quality-control standards. Companies would distinguish their Cheerios with a prominent company name identification. Consequently, it would be possible to have Jones' Cheerios and Smith's Cheerios as well as General Mills' Cheerios. The FTC felt that this would encourage new price-oriented competition.

It is clear that the cereal case was uncommonly innovative. For one, it alleged monopolization by oligopolists rather than by a dominant firm. Second, the theory of entry preclusion argued (brand proliferation) was novel. And, third, the request for a trademark licensing remedy to enhance price competition was unusual.

PROPOSALS OF REFORM

It is difficult to determine the impact of the existing monopolization doctrines on American industries. Many suppose that they have at least discouraged the more blatant predatory behavior. Also, many have argued that the fear of Section 2 may have induced some leading sellers to restrain their competitive efforts so as not to exceed the range of a 60 to 64 percent market share that Judge Learned Hand had identified as the threshold of monopoly.

Apart from these behavioral modifications, the direct impact of Sherman Act, Section 2, in lessening market concentration has been more modest. Scherer has indicated that between 1890 and 1970 "the courts have ordered structural reorganization in only 32 Section 2 cases—all but 7 of them before 1950."[18] One reason for this relatively small reorganization effort is judicial reluctance to impose structural remedies. The courts often perceive the monopolists as "efficient and progressive." The courts often seem unconvinced that restructuring will bring about the theoretical benefits of workable competition.

Another factor that has hindered the enforcement of Section 2 is the complexity and cost of major monopolization suits. The Justice Department is believed to have expended at least $10 million in the IBM suit alone. IBM was believed to have spent $100 million in legal fees and related expenses in defending itself against charges of Section 2 violations.[19] Presentation of the government's case against IBM took nearly three years, and that does not include the time IBM took to present its defense. Widespread dissatisfaction with the protracted litigation has resulted in a series of proposals to streamline the procedures. The National Commission for the Review of Antitrust Laws and Procedures issued its first report in January 1979.[20] Some of the views expressed therein were enacted in the antitrust procedural improvements legislation of 1980. As one improvement, the statute broadened the range of practices which a delaying attorney could be personally liable for if the practices in question are engaged in "unreasonably and vexatiously." Although these procedures may be helpful in moving the case along, it may well be nearly impossible to vastly speed up the handling of large antitrust cases if the estimates are correct that IBM gained at least $2 million a day for each day of delay.[21]

Proposals have also been made suggesting changes in the substantive law itself. A task force established by President Johnson recommended in 1968 a new concentrated industries act. This proposal would have set up structural criteria to judge whether oligopolistic industries needed to be reorganized and established a specially constituted court of economic, legal, and organizational specialists. In 1972 and in 1973, the late Senator Phillip Hart introduced an industrial reorganization bill. In his proposal the existence of a monopoly power would be presumed if a company's after-tax return on stockholders' equity exceeded 15 percent for five consecutive years. Other precise tests were included to identify monopoly power. The proposal required divestiture of firms possessing monopoly power and would be enforced by a specially constituted industrial reorganization commission. Neither the concentrated industries bill nor the industrial reorganization bill were able to attract sufficient votes for congressional passage.

In 1976 Senator Hart proposed a "no-fault" monopolization bill which would amend the Sherman Act, Section 2, by eliminating the government's burden to prove intent to monopolize. His proposal allowed two defenses for the companies found to possess monopoly power. They could escape fragmentation only by demonstrating that their power came solely from legally acquired and used patents or that divestiture would cause a loss of substantial scale economies. Senator Hart's proposal did not gain sufficient congressional support to be voted out of committee. However, the first report of the National Commission for the Review of Antitrust Laws and Procedures indicated that the no-conduct (or no-fault) monopolization concept needed further study.

CONCLUSION

Governmental regulation of industrial structure seems to favor the maintenance of the existing industry structure. Such conservatism is based on the recognition that the U.S. economic system performs relatively well in comparison with other systems throughout the world. Instead of utilizing the antitrust law for structural reform, alternative governmental policies (as explored in subsequent chapters) have been utilized to modify business behavior. Nevertheless, structuralists maintain that the rising tide of economic concentration threatens economic and political liberties as much as it erodes economic efficiencies. The continuing debate between structuralists and performance economists has been manifested in the bills placed before Congress.

Besides the bills already mentioned, structurally oriented senators have proposed alternative methods for dealing with concentrated industry structure. They have proposed legislation to deal specifically with a single industry or firm. One bill proposed breaking up AT&T, prior to AT&T's settlement of divestiture with the Justice Department. The petroleum industry competition bill called for the oil industry to eliminate its vertically integrated status among the 18 largest oil firms in the United States. Another bill proposed that the oil industry be prohibited from acquiring firms in other basic energy areas, such as coal or atomic energy. These proposals and others that are sure to be presented in the future deserve attention by business people. Increased research and more information are surely needed to formulate future public policies on the critical issues of appropriate industry structure.

CASE PROBLEMS

1. IBM marketed electronic data processing equipment which consisted of central processing units plus various peripheral devices such as magnetic tapes, disk and drum information storage components, memory units, and terminal devices such as printers. The peripheral devices are connected by plugs to the central processing units, and several other companies market peripheral components which are plug compatible with IBM central processing units (CPUs). Peripheral devices are not interchangeable on CPUs of various manufacturers, but at a modest cost, manufacturers can alter the plug interfaces so as to make their devices plug compatible with the products of other CPU manufacturers such as Univac, Burroughs, and Honeywell.

   IBM launched a marketing strategy to meet the competitive threat of plug compatible suppliers of peripheral devices. One such supplier, which specialized in producing devices plug compatible with IBM CPUs, brought a Section 2 action to prevent IBM from implementing its marketing strategy.

   Apply the *DuPont* decision to determine the relevant market. What would be the effect of the existence of relatively high cross-elasticity of demand between IBM CPU plug compatible and nonplug compatible devices?

2. IBM has obtained a position of monopoly power in the peripheral equipment market by research and technical innovations. In response to the challenge of Telex and other producers of peripheral equipment, IBM lowered its prices on peripheral equipment. What facts and tests would be relevant in deciding if IBM's actions were lawful?

3. For 15 years, the *Lorain Journal* was the only daily newspaper in a town of 52,000 and served 99 percent of Lorain families. When a local radio station was established, the *Journal* refused to publish advertisements for businesses that advertised over the radio station as well. Does the *Journal,* as a monopolist, have the right to refuse to deal with whatever advertisers it chooses? Does the Sherman Act apply to competition between industries? Would the *Journal's* actions constitute a violation of Section 2 of the Sherman Act?

4. Kodak, a film and camera monopolist, was in a position to set industry standards. Competitors argued that because of Kodak's dominant position, it must make sufficient advance information of its product innovations available to its competitors so that they can also introduce copies of the new product at the same time as Kodak introduces its new product. In support of a Section 2, Sherman Act, charge, the competitors argued that Kodak's failure to "predisclose" its new products to competitors is anticompetitive conduct.

END NOTES

1. *U.S.* v. *Griffith Amusement Company,* 334 U.S. 100, 105 (1948).
2. *U.S.* v. *Grinnell Corp.,* 384 U.S. 563 (1966).
3. *U.S.* v. *Alcoa,* 148 F. 2d at 431.

4. Ibid.
5. Ibid., p. 21, 518.
6. *U.S.* v. *United Show Machinery Corp.,* 110 F. Supp. 295, 340–41.
7. P. Areeda and D. Turner, "Predatory Pricing and Related Practices Under Section 2 of the Sherman Act," 88 *Harv. L. Rev.* 697 (1975).
8. See, *Janich Bros., Inc.* v. *American Distilling Co.,* 570 F. 2d 848 (9th Cir., 1977), cert. denied, 47 U.S.L.W. 3195 (Oct. 2, 1978); *Pacific Engr. & Prod. Co.* v. *Kerr-McGee Corp.,* 551 F. 2d 790 (10th Cir.), cert. denied, 98 S. Ct. 234 (1977).
9. R. Posner, *Antitrust Law: An Economic Perspective,* 188 (1976).
10. See, *International Air Industries, Inc.* v. *American Excelsior Co.,* 517 F. 2d 714, 734 (5th Cir., 1975), cert. denied, 424 U.S. 940 (1976). *I.L.C. Peripherals Leasing Corp.* v. *IBM* (1978–2), Trade Cases, Para. 62,177 (N.D. Cal., 1975) at 75,256–57.
11. Scherer, "Predatory Pricing and the Sherman Act: A Comment," 89 *Harv. L. Rev.* 869, 889 (1976).
12. *FTC* v. *Borden,* 92 F.T.C. 669 (1978).
13. *FTC* v. *Brown Shoe Co.,* 384 U.S. 316 (1965).
14. *In re Xerox Corp.,* 86 F.T.C. 364 (1975).
15. *In re Kellogg et al.,* filed January 25, 1972.
16. F. M. Scherer, *Industrial Market Structure and Economic Performance,* 2d ed. (Chicago, Ill.: Rand McNally, 1980), p. 539.
17. *FTC News Summary,* Vols. 50–81, September 18, 1981.
18. Ibid., p. 540.
19. Ibid., p. 541.
20. L. Lempert, "Antitrust Reform Faces Long, Winding Road," *Legal Times,* September 15, 1980.
21. W. Shepherd and C. Wilcox, *Public Policy Toward Business* (Homewood, Ill.: Richard D. Irwin, Inc., 1979), pp. 148–49.

chapter 12

REGULATION OF MERGERS

A *merger* is the uniting of formerly independent enterprises under a single ownership. It involves the complete acquisition of the stock of another corporation and then the termination of the acquired corporation as a corporate entity. A merger may also be effected through the outright purchase of the assets of another enterprise. If the acquiring and acquired firms continue their existence, the union of the firms is technically referred to as an acquisition, not a merger.

Absent any attempt to monopolize, internal growth of assets is generally recognized as a legitimate method of corporate expansion. However, external growth through mergers and acquisitions of separate firms which were formerly independent enterprises often has the effect of reducing competition and tending toward a monopoly.

HISTORICAL PERSPECTIVES

MOTIVES FOR MERGERS

A *horizontal* merger unites the ownership of side-by-side competitors. It combines like plants (such as steel mills) which produce the same product and sell in the same geographic market. A *vertical* merger unites suppliers and users in the chain of production and distribution. It brings under one ownership the control of unlike plants producing different products but related in the successive stages of production or marketing. Vertical mergers are usually referred to as "integration." A *conglomerate* merger may be classified as one of three main forms: (1) product extension, (2) market extension, or (3) pure diversification. When the acquired and acquiring firm are in allied or closely related fields, so that the acquisition extends the acquired company's product line (for example, a soap company acquiring a liquid bleach firm), the combination is referred to as a product extension merger. A market extension merger involves the acquisition of a like firm which operates in a different geographic market (for example, a beer firm in the Midwest acquiring a beer firm in California). A pure conglomerate merger is one in which the acquiring firm and the acquired firm are in totally unrelated fields (for example, an oil firm and a fire insurance company).

Merger actions are taken for different reasons of business advantage. The main categories of gains to the firm include the following:

1. Market power. The merger may increase the combined firm's market power by increasing its market share or by erecting higher entry barriers. Market power, in turn, provides opportunities for higher prices and profits for the firm.
2. Technical economies. A merger may help firms achieve economies of scale and lower average unit costs. There may be economies of scale in conducting research and development as a firm expands. The combined firm may be able to economize on management services by having a common central pool of financial planners, accountants, market researchers, labor relations specialists, lawyers, and the like. Vertical economies achieved through vertical integration may avoid the cost of extra material handling, uncertainty, or reprocessing. It may also be possible to obtain some economies by pooling diverse enterprises to reduce risks.
3. Pecuniary economies. Mergers may create pecuniary gains by the firm's larger purchases of raw materials, advertising space, managerial talent, capital, or other inputs. Tax benefits of the merger may enhance pecuniary gain also.
4. New market entry. Entry into new markets is usually easier through mergers than by "starting from scratch." Such mergers may not confer market power or achieve technical or pecuniary economies but merely provide the nucleus for the acquiring firm to venture into new areas.
5. Salvage of failing companies. Many mergers involve the absorption of a failing company. Failure, of course, means imminent bankruptcy, which often involves a financial insolvency of a short-term nature. The infusion of new capital by the acquiring firm revives the failing company.
6. Takeovers. A takeover involves an action by one firm to seize, or take over, another firm whose management appears inefficient. The firm attempting the takeover typically makes a tender offer for a controlling block of the stock of the acquired company at a price above the current market price. The acquiring company believes it can manage the company so much better that profits in the acquired firm will rise sufficiently to offset the premium paid for the stock.

In many instances, mergers have increased industrial efficiency and improved a firm's position as a competitor. On the other hand, mergers often result in larger firms which gain discretionary control over prices through the elimination of smaller competitors. The separation of economically efficient mergers from mergers that enhance market power to the detriment of society is not always easy. Moreover, differing economic perspectives (structuralists or performance economists) have made consensus on a merger policy even more difficult to obtain.

MERGER ACTIVITY

There have been three major periods of merger activity in the United States.[1] The first great boom was from 1897 to 1904. The mergers of this period were primarily horizontal and resulted in the formation of firms with 60 to 90 percent control of the market in many industries. It was the era of financial capitalism and of the creation of dominant firms in major industries. This merger wave stopped primarily because of changing stock market and economic conditions but also because of Theodore Roosevelt's antitrust enforcement in 1902.

The second active merger period occurred in the 1920s. It mainly resulted in the formation of oligopolies which replaced the industry structure of one large dominant firm. The mergers of this period tended to create second and third-ranking firms to compete with the existing dominant firms. This merger activity, like the first, came to an end with the change in economic conditions that occurred in the 1930s.

The third merger period, in the 1960s, mainly involved conglomerate mergers. Although horizontal and vertical mergers continued, conglomerate mergers became very popular. This merger activity took a pronounced dip in the late 1960s as the stock market dropped over 40 percent. In addition, antitrust enforcement against mergers, particularly conglomerate mergers, during the period 1969–1971 helped reverse the continuing growth in conglomerate mergers.

THE EVOLUTION OF STATUTORY LAW

Mergers were initially challenged under the Sherman Act. Early government successes in prohibiting mergers were largely limited to railroad consolidations.[2] Subsequent efforts to use the Sherman Act against mergers were unsuccessful. The most famous defeat for the Justice Department occurred in 1948 when it lost its suit against the U.S. Steel Corporation's acquisition of the Consolidated Steel Corporation. The merger was allowed by the Supreme Court even though Consolidated accounted for 11 percent of the structural steel and plate fabrication activity in the Pacific and Mountain states and U.S. Steel controlled 39 percent of all raw steel ingot capacity.[3]

In contrast to the Supreme Court's unwillingness to interpret the Sherman Act as an effective weapon against industrial consolidation by mergers, Congress expressed consternation about mergers and acquisitions and their effect in reducing competition or tending toward a monopoly. Congress first attempted to formulate a merger policy in the Clayton Act of 1914. Section 7 of the Clayton Act established guidelines as to when mergers were to be held illegal. It differed from the Sherman Act in that "actual" restraints or monopolization did not have to be proven. The Clayton Act was designed to stop anticompetitive mergers before they resulted in the creation of a monopoly. This purpose was to be accomplished by the method of making illegal those mergers that "may" lessen competition. By lowering the government's burden of proof from an *actual* anticompetitive effect to a *probable* anticompetitive effect, Congress anticipated that anticompetitive activities, such as mergers, would be arrested in their early stages. This concept of attacking evil practices in their incipiency is carried throughout the major sections of the Clayton Act.

Despite the intentions of Congress, the original language of Section 7 of the Clayton Act possessed several loopholes which vastly reduced its effectiveness in preventing mergers. The original text included language that made it necessary for the merger to eliminate competition between the "acquiring" and the "acquired" firms in order to be illegal. If competition *between* these two firms is eliminated, they must first be in competition with one another. Consequently, the acquiring-acquired language indicated that Section 7 applied only to horizontal mergers (that is, those companies which compete with one another). Therefore, vertical or conglomerate mergers were felt to be free of Section 7 attack until the Justice Department decided to test this language in the late 1940s. In addition, the original language prohibited only the acquisition of *stock* in another company if the probable effect would be to substantially lessen competition. Therefore, any combination of companies, including horizontal, that wanted to avoid Section 7 would not acquire the *stock* of the acquired firm. Instead, acquisition of *assets* was used to avoid Section 7's prohibition of *stock* acquisitions. As a consequence, Section 7 of the Clayton Act had only a minimal effect in prohibiting mergers. Indeed, so ineffective was Section 7 that antitrust enforcement officials reverted to the use of the Sherman Act in an effort to prohibit mergers. For example, the government's attempt to prohibit the previously discussed merger of U.S. Steel with Consolidated Steel in the 1940s was prosecuted under the Sherman Act rather than Section 7 of the Clayton Act. However, in that case and in others the Sherman Act was also found inadequate for preventing mergers.

In 1950, the Celler–Kefauver Amendment modified Section 7 of the Clayton Act. This amendment omitted the acquiring-acquired language to indicate that horizontal, vertical, or conglomerate mergers were illegal if they had the probable effect of substantially lessening competition. In addition, the acquisition of stock or *assets* was made illegal if it had the prohibited anticompetitive effect. The two major loopholes of the original Section 7 language consequently were closed by the Celler–Kefauver Amendment. The amended Section 7 now reads, in part, as follows:

> That no person engaged in commerce, or in any activity affecting commerce shall acquire, directly or indirectly, the whole or any part of the stock or other share capital and no person subject to the jurisdiction of the Federal Trade Commission shall acquire the

whole or any part of the assets of another person engaged also in commerce or in any activity affecting commerce, where in any line of commerce or in any activity affecting commerce in any section of the country, the effect of such acquisition may be substantially to lessen competition, or to tend to create a monopoly.

From the legislative history and from the omission of the acquiring-acquired language, it was clear that the amended Section 7 was intended to apply to mergers of every type. Any type of merger that has the probability of lessening competition "in any line of commerce" (product market) or "in any section of the country" (geographic market) was declared illegal. Accordingly, any use of Section 7 to challenge a merger begins with the definition of the relevant product and geographic markets, followed by the determination of the probable effect of the merger in the relevant markets.

In spite of Congress's recognition that some mergers might bring about economic efficiencies, it outlawed mergers which had the probable effect of substantially reducing competition in the relevant product or geographic markets. Congress made no provision for an "economic efficiencies" defense to a Section 7 charge. Consequently, the courts have not generally made substantial inquiry into the economic efficiencies alleged to have been accrued by virtue of any proposed merger. Instead, the court's analysis has concentrated on the probable anticompetitive impact of the merger.

HORIZONTAL MERGERS

To observe the principles applied by the courts in interpreting the new Section 7 of the Clayton Act, it is necessary to examine the leading decisions. Often the decisions of the courts involve mergers that contain a mixture of horizontal, vertical, and conglomerate characteristics. Nevertheless, the basic policies and principles enunciated by the court for the various types of mergers can be discussed separately, beginning with the basically horizontal-type merger.

BETHLEHEM-YOUNGSTOWN

The first major government victory under the new Section 7 involved Bethlehem Steel Corporation's proposed merger with Youngstown Sheet and Tube.[4] Bethlehem Steel Corporation, the nation's second largest producer of steel, handled 16.3 percent of total U.S. ingot capacity. Youngstown Sheet and Tube Company was the sixth largest producer, with 4.6 percent of national ingot capacity. Bethlehem argued that the merger did not have the probability of substantially lessening competition because the two companies essentially sold in two different geographical submarkets. Bethlehem argued that this was essentially a market extension merger because Bethlehem, which sold most of its output in the East, did not directly compete with Youngstown, which primarily sold in the Midwest.

Only about 10 percent of the combined output of Bethlehem and Youngstown was shipped to customers in overlapping geographic territories. The trial court rejected this characterization of the proposed merger and held that the freight cost barriers to interpenetration of regional markets were overcome sufficiently to view the market as nationwide in scope. Accordingly, the court felt a merger combining 16.3 and 4.6 percent of national capacity had the probability of substantially lessening competition in the national market.

Bethlehem attempted to justify the merger by arguing that it would enable Bethlehem to compete more effectively with the largest steel producer, U.S. Steel. In particular, Bethlehem argued that it had no plant in the Chicago area and shipped into Chicago less than 1 percent of its output. Bethlehem argued that the acquisition of the Chicago facilities of Youngstown would create more vigorous competition with U.S. Steel in this area. Furthermore, Bethlehem declared that it would not otherwise enter this geographical market.

The trial judge rejected Bethlehem's pro-competitive argument by asserting that Congress "made no distinction between good mergers and bad mergers. It condemned all which came in reach of the prohibition of Section 7." Furthermore, the court was not convinced that the merger was the only means to increase the supply of steel in the Chicago area. Accordingly, the trial court enjoined the merger. Bethlehem did not appeal. A few years later, Bethlehem developed a modern steel-making facility in the Chicago area and Youngstown invested $450 million to modernize its Chicago works.

BROWN-KINNEY

The first Supreme Court case interpreting the new Section 7 of the Clayton Act was decided in 1962. It involved the effort of Brown Shoe Company to merge with G. R. Kinney Company. Brown was the fourth largest shoe manufacturer in the United States in 1955, with approximately 4 percent of the national output. Kinney was the 12th largest manufacturer, with 0.5 percent of output. There was no contention in the suit that the merger posed a threat to horizontal competition in shoe manufacturing. Instead, debate centered on competition in shoe retailing. Brown owned and operated approximately 470 of the nation's 22,000 retail shoe outlets, and franchised 760 other independent retail outlets. Kinney owned and operated more than 350 retail stores. The Supreme Court's analysis of the boundaries of the product and geographic markets has provided the basic criteria for determination of relevant markets.

Brown Shoe Co. v. United States
370 U.S. 296 (1962)
Supreme Court of the United States

Chief Justice Warren

This suit . . . [alleges] that a contemplated merger between the G. R. Kinney Company, Inc. (Kinney), and the Brown Shoe Company, Inc. (Brown) . . . would violate §7 of the Clayton Act. . . . The complainant sought injunctive relief . . . to restrain consummation of the merger.

* * *

The Product Market

The outer boundaries of a product market are determined by the reasonable interchangeability of use or the cross-elasticity of demand between the product itself and substitutes for it. However, within this broad market, well-defined submarkets may exist which, in themselves, constitute product markets for antitrust purposes.

. . . The boundaries of such a submarket may be determined by examining such practical indicia as industry or public recognition of the submarket as a separate economic entity, the product's peculiar characteristics and uses, unique production facilities, distinct customers, distinct prices, sensitivity to price changes, and specialized vendors. Because §7 of the Clayton Act prohibits any merger which may substantially lessen competition "in *any* line of commerce," it is necessary to examine the effects of a merger in each such economically significant submarket to determine if there is a reasonable probability that the merger will substantially lessen competition. If such a probability is found to exist, the merger is proscribed.

Applying these considerations to the present case, we conclude that the record supports the District Court's finding that the relevant lines of commerce are men's, women's, and children's shoes. These product lines are recognized by the public; each line is manufactured in separate plants; each has characteristics peculiar to itself rendering it generally noncompetitive with the other; and each is, of course, directed toward a distinct class of customers.

* * *

The Geographic Market

The criteria to be used in determining the appropriate geographic market are essentially similar to those used to determine the relevant product market. . . . Moreover, just as a product submarket may have §7 significance as the proper "line of commerce," so may a geographic submarket be considered the appropriate "section of the country." The geographic market selected must, therefore, both "correspond to the commercial realities" of the industry and be economically significant. Thus, although the geographic market in some instances may encompass the entire Nation, under other circumstances it may be as small as a single metropolitan area. . . .

The District Court found that the effects of [the retail] . . . aspect of the merger must be analyzed in every city with a population exceeding 10,000 and its immediate contiguous surrounding territory in which Brown and Kinney sold shoes at retail through stores they either owned or controlled. . . .

We therefore agree that the District Court properly defined the relevant geographic markets in which to analyze this merger as those cities with a population exceeding 10,000 and their environs in which both Brown and Kinney retailed shoes through their own outlets. Such markets are large enough to include the downtown shops and suburban shopping centers in areas contiguous to the city, which are the important competitive factors, and yet are small enough to exclude stores beyond the immediate environs of the city, which are of little competitive significance.

The Probable Effect of the Merger

The market share which companies may control by merging is one of the most important factors to be considered when determining the probable effects of the combination on effective competition in the relevant market. In an industry as fragmented as shoe retailing, the control of substantial shares of the trade in a city may have important effects on competition. If a merger achieving 5 percent control were now approved, we might be required to approve future merger efforts by Brown's competitors seeking similar market shares. The oligopoly Congress sought to avoid would then be furthered and it would be difficult to dissolve the combinations previously approved. Furthermore, in this fragmented industry, even if the combination controls but a small share of a particular market, the fact that this share is held by a large national chain can adversely affect competition. Testimony in the record from numerous independent retailers, based on their actual experience in the market, demonstrates that a strong, national chain of stores can insulate selected outlets from the vagaries of competition in particular locations and that the large chains can set and alter styles in footwear to an extent that renders the independents unable to maintain competitive inventories. . . .

Other factors to be considered in evaluating the probable effects of a merger in the relevant market lend additional support to the District Court's conclusion that this merger may substantially lessen competition. One such factor is the history of tendency toward concentration in the industry. As we have previously pointed out, the shoe industry has, in recent years, been a prime example of such a trend. . . .

. . . By the merger in this case, the largest single group of retail stores still independent of one of the large manufacturers was absorbed into an already substantial aggregation of more or less controlled retail outlets. As a result of this merger, Brown moved into second place nationally in terms of retail stores directly owned. Including the stores on its franchise plan, the merger placed under Brown's control almost 1,600 shoe outlets, or about 7.2 percent of the Nation's retail "shoe stores" as defined by the Census Bureau, and 2.3 percent of the Nation's total retail shoe outlets. We cannot avoid the mandate of Congress that tendencies toward concentration in industry are to be curbed in their incipiency, particularly when those tendencies are being accelerated through giant steps striding across a hundred cities at a time. In the light of the trends in this industry we agree with the Government and the court below that this is an appropriate place at which to call a halt.

. . . We hold that the District Court was correct in concluding that this merger may tend to lessen competition substantially in the retail sale of the men's, women's and children's shoes in the overwhelming majority of those cities and their environs in which both Brown and Kinney sell through owned or controlled outlets.

Questions

1. What criteria did the Court identify for determination of a relevant product submarket?
2. What geographic submarket did the Court adopt?
3. What "probable anticompetitive effects" of this proposed merger did the Court identify?

DEFINING THE MARKET

In *Brown Shoe* the Supreme Court established criteria for defining markets. These criteria provide considerable latitude for the courts in determining the relevant market. Review of two decisions applying the *Brown Shoe* criteria can illustrate the eclectic approach of the Court.

The first case involves the acquisition of the Rome Cable Corporation by the Aluminum Company of America.[5] Alcoa produced various types of aluminum electrical conductor cable, and Rome specialized in copper conductor cable but used aluminum in about 10 percent of its cables. The district court found Rome's share (0.3 percent) of the *bare aluminum* cable market to be too small to threaten any substantial lessening of competition when added to Alcoa's 32.5 percent share. When the *insulated and bare aluminum* was combined with the *insulated and bare copper,* again the market shares were too small for illegality. Nevertheless, the Supreme Court reversed the district court decision and held that the *combined insulated and bare aluminum* wire and cable market, with all copper products excluded, could be utilized to test the legality of the merger. The Court argued that the price of aluminum conductors was generally less than the price of comparable copper conductors and a price change for copper conductors did not cause a responsive change in the aluminum conductor prices or vice versa. The Court concluded that the addition of Rome's 1.3 percent share of this market to Alcoa's 27.8 percent share constituted a substantial lessening of competition.

The second case involves a proposed merger between the Continental Can Company, second largest maker of tin cans in the United States, and the Hazel-Atlas Glass Company, the third largest bottle manufacturer.[6] Continental held 33 percent of the market for tin cans and Hazel-Atlas held 10 percent of the market for glass bottles. The trial court found cans and bottles to be separate product markets and, hence, concluded that competition was not substantially reduced by the merger. On appeal, the Supreme Court pointed out that tin cans and glass bottles were closely competitive in many applications with buyers switching from one type of container to another. The Court wrote that

> In defining the product market . . . we must recognize meaningful competition where it is found to exist. . . . [T]hough the interchangeability of use may not be so complete and the cross-elasticity of demand not so immediate as in the case of most intraindustry mergers,

> there is over the long run the kind of customer response to innovation and other competitive stimuli that brings the competition between these two industries within §7's competition-preserving proscriptions. . . . That there are price differentials between the two products or that the demand for one is not particularly or immediately responsive to changes in the price of the other are relevant matters but not determinative of the product market issues. . . . Where the area of effective competition cuts across industry lines, so must the relevant line of commerce.[7]

In the relevant market of metal cans and glass bottles combined, Continental held second place, with a 22 percent share, and Hazel-Atlas held sixth place with a 3 percent share. According to the Court, these percentages were too high for the merger to be legal.

These two decisions of the Supreme Court illustrate the wide extremes (some say inconsistency) that the courts are willing to accept in defining "sensitive competitive relations" that courts feel are worthy of preservation. It appears that "markets" can be easily gerrymandered to accomplish the overall philosophical desires of the Court either to stem the concentration of economic power through mergers or to permit mergers perceived to enhance economic efficiencies.

DETERMINING "PROBABLE EFFECT"

The *Brown Shoe* decision indicated that several basic elements should be reviewed in determining the "probable effect" of a proposed merger. The Court felt the combination of the percentages of the defined market held by the two merging parties was one of the most important factors to be considered. Second, the combined market share must be functionally viewed in terms of the industry. In a fragmented industry, even small market shares by the merging parties can adversely affect competition, particularly if the relatively small combination involves one of the largest firms in that industry. Third, the Court pointed out that "the history of tendency toward concentration in the industry" is an important factor to be considered.

These factors, first articulated in *Brown Shoe*, became determinative standards in subsequent cases. The court was willing to use the statistical market data and industry trends toward concentration for a determination of "probable effect." The dissenting justices criticized the Court's approach as amounting to an almost *per se* rule. Structuralists, of course, have favored this approach to halt the continuing trend toward concentration. Performance economists, on the other hand, argue that several pro-competitive mergers or mergers advancing the levels of economic efficiency have also been prohibited and, consequently, society's interests are not being advanced by an almost *per se* illegality based on percentages alone. Nevertheless, the success of the Justice Department in gaining verdicts that outlawed mergers during the 1960s led to the establishment of the Department of Justice Merger Guidelines.

MERGER GUIDELINES

The 1968 Merger Guidelines emphasized market structure as the basic determinant of whether mergers would be challenged by the Department of Justice. The guidelines distinguished between concentrated industries. In less concentrated industries, mergers may be allowed that would not be tolerated in oligopolistic industries. The guidelines were not law but were criteria for use by the Department of Justice in its determination of which mergers to challenge in the courts. However, because the Justice Department had been so successful in gaining favorable verdicts during the sixties, many merger proposals were forestalled when the parties determined that they would be challenged under the guidelines. The guidelines were revised by the Department of Justice in 1982. A summary explanation of the new guidelines is presented at the end of this chapter. But before a discussion of these new guidelines is proper, other types of mergers should be examined.

VERTICAL MERGERS

When a firm has successive stages in the production or distribution of finished goods or services, it is said to be *vertically integrated.* On the positive side, vertical integration may generate economies of scale. However, competition must remain effective after the merger if society is to share such cost savings through lower prices for consumers. Unfortunately, vertically integrated firms may also follow business practices which weaken or destroy their nonintegrated or less-integrated rivals. For example, the vertically integrated firm may be in a position to exclude non- or less-integrated firms from the best sources of supply or from retail outlets. This is referred to as a supply squeeze and involves either a refusal to sell to non- or less-integrated firms or a preferential allocation of raw materials to the subsidiaries of the integrated firms. Second, the vertically integrated firm may be in a position to control the prices and profits of its non- or less-integrated rivals by employing a price squeeze. The vertically integrated firm either (1) sells to its distributor at a lower price than to independent rivals, while maintaining the price at the retail level, or (2) reduces its price (and profit) at the retail level when consumer demand declines, but maintains the prices for the primary materials sold to non- or less-integrated rivals.

To provide equal access to suppliers and outlets, public policy could prohibit vertical integration altogether. Already the federal government and many states have laws that prohibit distillers from engaging in the retailing of liquors. It is possible that Congress could decide that divestiture is appropriate policy in many highly integrated industries, such as aluminum, copper, oil, or steel. Without outright prohibition, Congress has found it necessary in certain instances to require integrated firms to give fair allocation of supplies to non- or less-integrated rivals.[8] Absent specific legislation of prohibition or allocation, Congress has permitted vertical integration, particularly if achieved without mergers. However, vertical mergers may have an exclusionary *effect*, which has led

Congress to include such vertical mergers in the amended Section 7 of the Clayton Act.

The firm seeking a vertical merger argues its purpose is to assure itself of a source of supply or of an outlet. However, the courts must be careful to weigh this "legitimate business purpose" for an ensured supply for the merged firm against the *effect* of the merger on the ability of the non- or less-integrated firms to obtain supplies or outlets.

BROWN-KINNEY

The first decision applying the new language of Section 7 of the Clayton Act to a vertical acquisition involved the merger of the Brown Shoe Company with G. R. Kinney Company. The horizontal aspects (in retailing) of this merger were discussed previously. However, because Brown was primarily engaged in manufacturing and Kinney in retailing, the vertical aspects of this merger were even more important to the companies involved and to the Court.

Brown Shoe Co. v. United States
370 U.S. 296 (1962)
Supreme Court of the United States

Chief Justice Warren

The District Court found a "definite trend" among shoe manufacturers to acquire retail outlets. . . .

And once the manufacturers acquired retail outlets, the District Court found there was a "definite trend" for the parent-manufacturers to supply an ever increasing percentage of the retail outlets' needs, thereby foreclosing other manufacturers from effectively competing for the retail accounts. Manufacturer-dominated stores were found to be "drying up" the available outlets for independent producers.

* * *

Brown Shoe

Brown Shoe was found not only to have been a participant, but also a moving factor, in these industry trends. . . . [I]n 1951, Brown . . . began to seek retail outlets by acquisitions. . . .

The acquisition of these corporations was found to lead to increased sales by Brown to the acquired companies. . . .

During the same period of time, Brown also acquired the stock or assets of seven companies engaged solely in shoe manufacturing. As a result, in 1955, Brown was the fourth largest shoe manufacturer in the country, producing about 4% of the Nation's total footwear production.

Kinney

Kinney is principally engaged in operating the largest family-style shoe store chain in the United States. At the time of trial, Kinney was found to be operating over 400 such stores in more than 270 cities. These stores were found to make about 1.2% of all national retail shoe sales by dollar volume. . . .

The Vertical Aspects of the Merger

Economic arrangements between companies standing in a supplier-customer relationship are characterized as "vertical." The primary vice of a vertical merger or other arrangement tying a customer to a supplier is that, by foreclosing the competitors of either party from a segment of the market otherwise open to them, the arrangement may act as a "clog on competition," . . . which "deprive[s] . . . rivals of a fair opportunity to compete." Every extended vertical arrangement by its very nature, for at least a time, denies to competitors of the supplier the opportunity to compete for part of or all of the trade of the customer-party to the vertical arrangement. However, the Clayton Act does not render unlawful all such vertical arrangements, but forbids only those whose effect "may be substantially to lessen competition, or to tend to create a monopoly" "in any line of commerce in any section of the country.". . .

* * *

. . . [W]e conclude that the record supports the District Court's finding that the relevant lines of commerce are men's, women's, and children's shoes. These product lines are recognized by the public; each line is manufactured in separate plants; each has characteristics peculiar to itself rendering it generally noncompetitive with the other; and each is, of course, directed toward a distinct class of customers.

The Geographic Market

. . . [T]he relevant geographic market is the entire Nation. The relationships of product value, bulk, weight and consumer demand enable manufacturers to distribute their shoes on a nationwide basis, as Brown and Kinney, in fact, do. . . .

The Probable Effect of the Merger

* * *

Since the diminution of the vigor of competition which may stem from a vertical arrangement results primarily from a foreclosure of a share of the market otherwise open to competitors, an important consideration in determining whether the effect of a vertical arrangement "may be substantially to lessen competition, or to tend to create a monopoly" is the size of the share of the market foreclosed. . . .

[Another] . . . important such factor to examine is the very nature and purpose of the arrangement. . . .

* * *

. . . In 1955, the date of this merger, Brown was the fourth largest manufacturer in the shoe industry while Kinney . . . owned and operated the largest independent chain of family shoe stores in the Nation. Thus, in this industry, no merger between a manufacturer and an independent retailer could involve a larger potential market foreclosure. Moreover, it is apparent both from past behavior of Brown and from the testimony of Brown's President, that Brown would use its ownership of Kinney to force Brown shoes into Kinney stores. . . .

Another important factor to consider is the trend toward concentration in the industry. . . .

The existence of a trend toward vertical integration, which the District Court found, is well substantiated by the record. Moreover, the court found a tendency of the acquiring manufacturers to become increasingly important sources of supply for their acquired outlets. The necessary corollary of these trends is the foreclosure of independent manufacturers from markets otherwise open to them. . . .

* * *

The District Court's findings, and the record facts . . . convince us that the shoe industry is being subjected to just such a cumulative series of vertical mergers which, if left unchecked, will be likely "substantially to lessen competition."

Questions

1. Kinney held 1 percent of the national sales of men's shoes, 1.5 percent of the national sales of women's shoes, and 2 percent of the national sales of children's shoes. Since Brown supplied 7.9 percent of Kinney's requirements following the merger, the share of the market foreclosed ranged from 0.08 percent for men's shoes (1 times 7.9 percent) to 0.16 percent for children's shoes (2 times 7.9 percent). Are these shares substantial? Is there any indication that Brown would continue to limit its supply to Kinney to the 7.9 percent?
2. Why is the existence of a trend toward vertical integration an important criterion in determining the probable effect of the merger?

CONGLOMERATE MERGERS

Economic analysis reveals that conglomerate mergers may adversely affect competition.

First, conglomerate mergers may *entrench* oligopoly in various industries by weakening the competitive ability of the independent firms. The large acquiring firm uses nonprice forms of competition (brand differentiation) to enhance the market power of the acquired company. Independents, without sufficient financial resources to compete on nonprice terms, lose their competitiveness, for, if the smaller firms attempt to compete too vigorously on price, the larger merged firm can utilize discriminatory and exclusionary practices to discipline its smaller rival. Large multiproduct firms can utilize (a) product discrimination, in the form of either saturation advertising or one-product price cutting, (b) geographic price discrimination, (c) business reciprocity, or (d) tie-in sales as retaliation against any smaller rivals showing some price independence. Thereafter, fear of these retaliatory practices can force smaller firms into compliant postures and discourage potential entrants. In either case, oligopoly is solidified and oligopolistic nonprice competition replaces price competition.

Second, a conglomerate merger may lessen competition by eliminating the potential entrance of the merging party into the industry on an independent basis. This is usually referred to as the elimination of a "potential competitor." In addition, present members of the industry may perceive the potential entrant as on the edge of the industry and about to enter. Such perception can exert a competitive effect on the performance of the present members of the industry. This "edge effect" is eliminated when the firm enters the industry by merger.

Third, the Supreme Court held that the "reciprocity" made possible by some acquisitions introduces "an irrelevant and alien factor" into the choice among competing products. Reciprocity, at the least, creates "a priority on the business at equal prices." Reciprocal trading may not involve bludgeoning or coercion but may flow from more subtle arrangements. Threatening withdrawal of orders if products of an affiliate cease to be bought or basing future purchases on the condition of receipt of orders for products of that affiliate are examples of subtle, but nonetheless, anticompetitive reciprocal practices. Reciprocity in trading as a result of an acquisition violates Section 7 if the probability of a lessening of competition is shown.

Congress, in passing the Celler-Kefauver Act of 1950, recognized the potential anticompetitive effects that may follow from a conglomerate merger. However, since 1950 the antitrust enforcement agencies have challenged comparatively few conglomerate mergers. The two major victories of the government enunciated the three basic doctrines outlawing conglomerate mergers.[9] When conglomerate mergers create probabilities of (1) reciprocity, (2) oligopolistic entrenchment, or (3) elimination of *potential* competitors, they may be illegal.

FTC v. Procter & Gamble Co.

386 U.S. 568 (1966)

Supreme Court of the United States

Justice Douglas

This is a proceeding by the Federal Trade Commission charging . . . that Procter's acquisition of Clorox might substantially lessen competition or tend to create a monopoly in the production and sale of household liquid bleaches.

At the time of the merger, in 1957, Clorox was the leading manufacturer in the heavily concentrated household liquid bleach industry. It is agreed that household liquid bleach is the relevant line of commerce. The product is used in the home as a germicide and disinfectant, and, more importantly, as a whitening agent in washing clothes and fabrics. It is a distinctive product with no close substitutes. Liquid bleach is a low-price, high-turnover consumer product sold mainly through grocery stores and supermarkets. The relevant geographical market is the Nation and a series of regional markets. Because of high shipping costs and low sales price, it is not feasible to ship the product more than 300 miles from its point of manufacture. Most manufacturers are limited to competition within a single region since they have but one plant. Clorox is the only firm selling nationally; it has 13 plants distributed throughout the Nation. Purex,

Clorox's closest competitor in size, does not distribute its bleach in the northeast or mid-Atlantic States; in 1957, Purex's bleach was available in less than 50% of the national market.

At the time of the acquisition, Clorox was the leading manufacturer of household liquid bleach, with 48.8% of the national sales—annual sales of slightly less than $40,000,000. Its market share had been steadily increasing for the five years prior to the merger. Its nearest rival was Purex, which . . . accounted for 15.7% of the household liquid bleach market. The industry is highly concentrated; in 1957, Clorox and Purex accounted for almost 65% of the Nation's household liquid bleach sales, and, together with four other firms, for almost 80%. The remaining 20% was divided among over 200 small producers. . . .

Since all liquid bleach is chemically identical, advertising and sales promotion are vital. In 1957 Clorox spent almost $3,700,000 on advertising, imprinting the value of its bleach in the mind of the consumer. In addition, it spent $1,700,000 for other promotional activities. The Commission found that these heavy expenditures went far to explain why Clorox maintained so high a market share despite the fact that its brand, though chemically indistinguishable from rival brands, retailed for a price equal to or, in many instances, higher than its competitors.

Procter is a large, diversified manufacturer of low-price, high-turnover household products sold through grocery, drug, and department stores. Prior to its acquisition of Clorox, it did not produce household liquid bleach. . . . Procter has been marked by rapid growth and diversification. It has successfully developed and introduced a number of new products. Its primary activity is in the general area of soaps, detergents, and cleansers. . . . Procter was the dominant factor in this area. It accounted for 54.4% of all packaged detergent sales. The industry is heavily concentrated—Procter and its nearest competitors, Colgate-Palmolive and Lever Brothers, account for 80% of the market.

In the marketing of soaps, detergents, and cleansers, as in the marketing of household liquid bleach, advertising and sales promotion are vital. In 1957, Procter was the Nation's largest advertiser, spending more than $80,000,000 on advertising and an additional $47,000,000 on sales promotion. Due to its tremendous volume, Procter receives substantial discounts from the media. As a multi-product producer Procter enjoys substantial advantages in advertising and sales promotion. Thus, it can and does feature several products in its promotions, reducing the printing, mailing, and other costs for each product. It also purchases network programs on behalf of several products, enabling it to give each product network exposure at a fraction of the cost per product that a firm with only one product to advertise would incur. . . .

The decision to acquire Clorox was the result of a study conducted by Procter's promotion department designed to determine the advisability of entering the liquid bleach industry. The initial report noted the ascendancy of liquid bleach in the large and expanding household bleach market, and recommended that Procter purchase Clorox rather than enter independently. Since a large investment would be needed to obtain a satisfactory market share, acquisition of the industry's leading firm was attractive. . . .

All mergers are within the reach of Section 7, and all must be tested by the same standard, whether they are classified as horizontal, vertical, conglomerate or other. As noted by the Commission, this merger is neither horizontal, vertical, nor conglomerate. Since the products of the acquired company are complementary to those of the acquiring company and may be produced with similar facilities, marketed through the same channels and in the same manner, and advertised by the same media, the Commission aptly called this acquisition a "product-extension merger":

> By this acquisition . . . Procter has not diversified its interests in the sense of expanding into a substantially different, unfamiliar market or industry. Rather, it has entered a market which adjoins, as it were, those markets in which it is already established, and which is virtually indistinguishable from them insofar as the problems and techniques of marketing the product to the ultimate consumer are concerned. As a high official of Procter put it, commenting on the acquisition of Clorox, "While this is a completely new business for us, taking us for the first time into the marketing of a household bleach and disinfectant, we are thoroughly at home in the field of manufacturing and marketing low priced, rapid turn-over consumer products.". . .

The anticompetitive effects with which this product-extension merger is fraught can easily be seen: (1) the substitution of the powerful acquiring firm for the smaller, but already dominant, firm may substantially reduce the competitive structure of the industry by raising entry barriers and by dissuading the smaller firms from aggressively competing; (2) the acquisition eliminates the potential competition of the acquiring firm.

The liquid bleach industry was already oligopolistic before the acquisition, and price competition was certainly not as vigorous as it would have been if the industry were competitive. Clorox enjoyed a dominant position nationally, and its position approached monopoly proportions in certain areas. The existence of some 200 fringe firms certainly does not belie that fact. Nor does the fact, relied upon by the court below, that, after the merger, producers other than Clorox "were selling more bleach for more money than ever before." In the same period, Clorox increased its share from 48.8% to 52%. The interjection of Procter into the market considerably changed the situation. There is every reason to assume that the smaller firms would become more cautious in competing due to their fear of retaliation by Procter. It is probable that Procter would become the price leader and that oligopoly would become more rigid.

The acquisition may also have the tendency of raising the barriers to new entry. The major competitive weapon in the successful marketing of bleach is advertising. Clorox was limited in this area by its relatively small budget and its inability to obtain substantial discounts. By contrast, Procter's budget was much larger; and, although it would not devote its entire budget to advertising Clorox, it could divert a large portion to meet the short-term threat of a new entrant. Procter would be able to use its volume discounts to advantage in advertising Clorox. Thus, a new entrant would be much more reluctant to face the giant Procter than it would have been to face the smaller Clorox.

Possible economies cannot be used as a defense to illegality. Congress was aware that some mergers which lessen competition may also result in economies but it struck the balance in favor of protecting competition.

The Commission also found that the acquisition of Clorox by Procter eliminated Procter as a potential competitor. The Court of Appeals declared that this finding was not supported by evidence because there was no evidence that Procter's management had ever intended to enter the industry independently and that Procter had never attempted to enter. The evidence, however, clearly shows that Procter was the most likely entrant. Procter has recently launched a new abrasive cleaner in an industry similar to the liquid bleach industry, and had wrested leadership from a brand that had enjoyed even a larger market share than had Clorox. Procter was engaged in a vigorous program of diversifying into product lines closely related to its basic products. Liquid bleach was a natural avenue of diversification since it is complementary to Procter's products, is sold to the same customers through the same channels, and is advertised and merchandised in the same manner. Procter had substantial advantages in advertising and sales promotion, which, as we have seen, are vital to the success of liquid bleach. No manufacturer had a patent on the product or its manufacture, necessary information relating to manufacturing methods and processes was readily available, there was no shortage of raw material, and the machinery and equipment required for a plant of efficient capacity were available at reasonable cost. Procter's management was experienced in producing and marketing goods similar to liquid bleach. Procter had considered the possibility of independently entering but decided against it because the acquisition of Clorox would enable Procter to capture a more commanding share of the market.

It is clear that the existence of Procter at the edge of the industry exerted considerable influence on the market. First, the market behavior of the liquid bleach industry was influenced by each firm's predictions of the market behavior of its competitors, actual and potential. Second, the barriers to entry by a firm of Procter's size and with its advantages were not significant. There is no indication that the barriers were so high that the price Procter would have to charge would be above the price that would maximize the profits of the existing firms. Third, the number of potential entrants was not so large that the elimination of one would be insignificant. Few firms would have the temerity to challenge a firm as solidly entrenched as Clorox. Fourth, Procter was found by the Commission to be the most likely entrant.

Questions

1. What is a product-extension merger?
2. What were the anticompetitive effects of the "deep pockets" of Procter and Gamble? In other words, what would be the competitive effect if Procter and Gamble's financial resources were made available to Clorox to market a product that involves extensive promotional expenditures to differentiate its otherwise competitively identical product?

3. What is a potential competitor? What is the competitive *effect* of a potential entrant?
4. What is the competitive *effect* of Procter and Gamble at the edge of the liquid bleach industry?

THE "EDGE EFFECT"

One of the earliest cases concerning "potential competition" involved a firm that had repeatedly considered entering the market into which it merged.[10] The fact that this firm had tried to enter the new market independently made its status as a source of competition clear. However, most potential entry cases are not so simple. In Procter and Gamble (P&G), the appellate court had found that there was no evidence P&G intended to enter the liquid household bleach market on its own. The Supreme Court disagreed, as previously mentioned, concluding that P&G had all the resources needed to enter on its own, had entered similar markets without mergers, and was the most likely entrant into the liquid bleach market.

In 1971, the Supreme Court further defined the potential competition doctrine. Falstaff Brewing Co., the fourth largest producer of beer in the United States, acquired the Narragansett Brewing Co., the leading seller in New England.[11] Since Falstaff executives testified they would not have built a brewery on their own in New England, the district court ruled that Falstaff had no intent to enter the New England market and, therefore, could not be eliminated as a potential competitor by merging. On appeal, the Supreme Court said the following:

> The specific question . . . is not what Falstaff's internal company decisions were but whether, given its financial capabilities and conditions in the New England market, it would be reasonable to consider it a potential entrant into that market. . . . [I]f it would appear to rational beer merchants in New England that Falstaff might well build a new brewery . . . then its entry by merger becomes suspect. . . . The district court should therefore have appraised the economic facts about Falstaff in the New England market in order to determine whether in any realistic sense Falstaff could be said to be a potential competitor . . . so positioned on the edge of the market that it exerted beneficial influence on competitive conditions in that market.[12]

On remand, the trial court reconsidered the evidence and concluded that Falstaff was not a *perceived* potential entrant and, therefore, the merger was allowed to stand. The lower court felt that brewers in New England were too involved in an intense rivalry among themselves to be influenced by Falstaff's remote threat.

A year later, the Supreme Court restated its view of the edge effect of the potential competition doctrine:

> Unequivocable proof that an acquiring firm actually would have entered *de novo* but for a merger is rarely available. . . . Thus, . . . the principal focus of the doctrine is on the likely

effects of the premerger position of the acquiring firm on the fringe of the target market. . . . [A] market extension merger may be unlawful if the target market is substantially concentrated, if the acquiring firm has the characteristics, capabilities, and the economic incentive to render it a perceived potential *de novo* entrant, and if the acquiring firm's premerger presence on the fringe of the target market in fact tempered oligopolistic behavior on the part of the existing participants in the market.[13]

This instruction from the Supreme Court requires lower courts to determine whether the acquiring firm's premerger posture as a possible entrant constrained the pricing policies of the firms already in the industry. This is a difficult burden of proof imposed on the antitrust enforcers, who attempt to utilize the potential competition doctrine to stop market extension and product extension mergers. It is likely to reduce the effectiveness of the potential competition doctrine to forestall conglomerate mergers.

The Supreme Court has not yet been subjected to one version of the potential competition doctrine referred to as the "toehold" acquisition. Under this doctrine, a large conglomerate acquisition of a leading seller in a concentrated industry would be challenged because a less anticompetitive entry is available. The large conglomerate could have acquired a smaller industry participant (a toehold) and built its acquisition into a competitive challenger. Although without Supreme Court endorsement, the toehold theory has been widely discussed in the lower courts and among antitrust authorities. Its purpose, like the potential competition doctrine itself, is to preserve the opportunity for deconcentration of oligopolistic markets by requiring likely entrants to enter *de novo* or by toehold acquisition rather than by acquisition of competitive significant firms in those markets. The lower courts, in applying this doctrine, have looked to a variety of factors, including concentration level entry barriers, the capacity of the outside firm to enter *de novo* or by toehold acquisition, the deconcentration effect of such entry, and the number of other potential entrants.

NEW MERGER GUIDELINES

U.S. Department of Justice Explanation and Summary of the Merger Guidelines

(June 14, 1982)

Attorney General William French Smith today announced guidelines which outline the standards now in use by the Department of Justice in determining what mergers it will challenge.

The new guidelines replace those issued by the Department in 1968. In 44 pages they outline the general principles and specific standards the Department's Antitrust Division uses in screening the hundreds of mergers it examines every year.

The Attorney General emphasized that the guidelines are not a comprehensive statement of the circumstances considered by the Department in determining whether to challenge a merger. Their purpose is to provide guidance to the business community, private lawyers and others in anticipating what standards will be used and how they will be applied. For that reason, he noted, they give as much attention to situations in which a challenge is unlikely as to those in which a challenge is likely.

Usually a challenge comes in the form of a civil suit by the Antitrust Division charging a violation of Section 7 of the Clayton Act or Section 1 of the Sherman Act—both of which prohibit anticompetitive mergers. Such a suit often seeks divestiture of the acquired firm or one or more units of either firm in order to remove the anticompetitive problem. Such suits are frequently settled by consent decree. The Department generally requires prior elimination of the competitive problem before entering into such court-enforced settlements. Sometimes proposed mergers are abandoned after the Department threatens suit.

The 1968 Guidelines

Though it was made clear when the 1968 guidelines were issued that they would be revised as time went by, no formal changes were ever published. The standards employed in analyzing mergers have changed substantially since that time, however. For that reason, the new guidelines differ considerably from the old ones, although the new guidelines simply reflect the standards and policy now in use.

The 1968 guidelines dealt with three kinds of mergers—horizontal, vertical and conglomerate. Horizontal mergers are those between competitors, such as two auto makers. Vertical mergers are those involving firms in the same supply chain, such as a manufacturer of a product and the distributor of the same product. Conglomerate mergers are those between firms in different lines of business or between firms in the same line of business in economically separate geographic regions.

The 1968 guidelines set forth standards for each of the three kinds of mergers. The new guidelines have only two categories—horizontal and non-horizontal mergers.

The New Guidelines

The main purpose of the Department's merger enforcement is the prevention of mergers that make easier the exercise of market power—the ability of one or more firms to raise prices above a competitive level. All the standards mentioned in the guidelines involve factors bearing on that ability. The purpose of the guidelines is to prevent the monopolization or cartelization—control by one or by several firms—of any significant economic markets.

In general the new guidelines may allow some horizontal mergers that the old guidelines would have challenged, and generally provide for the challenge of other mergers only where there are indications that there would be some horizontal effect, real or potential. In other words, they usually require an indication of harm to competition by affecting firms in competition with one another. Those changes reflect the gradual trends in judicial merger decisions and Department of Justice enforcement practices between 1968 and the beginning of the 1980s. In addition, the new guidelines reflect some changes in emphasis which began with this Administration in early 1981.

The purpose of the new guidelines is to reflect the current emphasis—both in the Antitrust Division and in the courts—on the need for economic evidence of harm or potential harm to competition before a merger will be challenged. The new guidelines were designed to quantify the standards applied to the extent that is practicable. Where numbers are not applicable, efforts were made to state in detail the kinds of factors that would be weighed.

In analyzing any merger, it is first necessary to determine the relevant market or markets in which competitive harm may occur as a result of the merger. For instance, two merging grocery chains may be operating nationally with direct competition in dozens of major cities. To remove the competitive problems of a merger it could be necessary for them to spin off to third parties one of the stores in each of those cities, so that the merger would no longer reduce competition. If, on the other hand, they were only in competition in two cities in the Midwest, the sale of one outlet in each of those two cities might solve the problem.

In determining whether or not the risk of harm to competition is enough to warrant a challenge by the Antitrust Division, one of the most important factors is the level of concentration in that particular market, whether it be a national market for a particular drug or a local market for freshly baked doughnuts.

The Herfindahl Index

One significant change from the 1968 guidelines is the use of a different index to measure market concentration.

The 1968 guidelines used the four-firm concentration ratio to measure market shares. The four-firm concentration ratio is the sum of the percentage market shares of the top four firms in the market.

The new guidelines use the Herfindahl index instead. That index is calculated by squaring the percentage market share of each firm in the market and then adding those squares.

The Herfindahl index was chosen because it gives a more accurate measure of market structure than the four-firm concentration ratio. For instance, if there were a market in which four firms each had a 15 percent share and 40 firms each had a one percent share, and a second market where one firm had 57 percent of the market and the remaining 43 firms one percent each, the four-firm concentration ratios would be identical—60 percent each.

The Herfindahls for those two markets would be far from the same, however. The first market would have an index of 940 and the second an index of 3,292—more than three times as great. In the first market, the Department's concern about mergers would be relatively low, and in the second, quite high. In actually applying the Herfindahl index to a merger situation two figures are important—the index of concentration after the merger, and how much that differs from the index before the merger.

Market Definition

A second significant change from the 1968 guidelines is the fact that the new guidelines discuss the process of market definition in considerable detail. Defining the relevant market is one of the most important steps in merger analysis, because what market is selected and how that market is defined can be vital in determining whether or not the merger is deemed anticompetitive enough to warrant challenge by the Antitrust Division.

Since the relevant market chosen for analysis is the foundation on which all later analysis depends, the principles applied in market definition should be consistent. Although market definition will always depend on the specific facts in each case, the guidelines describe general principles that will be applied consistently in this process, which will still involve a fair amount of judgment and discretion on the part of those making the analysis.

Throughout the section of the guidelines dealing with market definition is an emphasis on defining a market in terms of the underlying concern about market power that is the basis for the guidelines themselves. The goal of market definition is to identify and consider all the firms that would have to cooperate in order to raise prices above the competitive level and keep them there.

For instance, the guidelines suggest that in considering whether to include a particular product or firm in the market it may be useful to hypothesize a small price increase, and then consider whether such an action would be likely to cause customers to shift to a different supplier or a different product. If a sufficient number of customers would shift to a substitute product or another supplier to make a price increase unprofitable, the market probably needs to be expanded to include that product or that supplier.

Once the market is defined, the guidelines provide standards for analyzing the merger. The standards applied depend on whether the merger is horizontal—in which the merging firms are in the same market—or non-horizontal—which includes all other mergers.

Since the bulk of mergers that pose competitive problems are horizontal ones, the guidelines focus primarily on them.

Horizontal Mergers

The standards applied to horizontal mergers fall into three general areas. They are the level of concentration in the market after the merger, the ease of entry by other firms into the market, and a series of factors bearing on the ease or profitability of collusion.

Market concentration is important because it is much easier to raise prices above a competitive level and keep them there in a highly concentrated market.

Ease of entry is important because if enough firms can enter by constructing new facilities or converting existing ones, an effort to increase price would not be profitable because other firms could be drawn in and drive prices down.

Ease and profitability of collusion are important because there is less likelihood that firms will try to get together to raise prices above a competitive level when it is difficult or unprofitable.

What Mergers Will Be Challenged

In analyzing market concentration in a horizontal merger the guidelines use the post-merger Herfindahl index to set forth three levels of concentration:

—where the post-merger market is "unconcentrated," that is, where even after the merger the Herfindahl is below 1,000. In such an "unconcentrated" market the Department would be unlikely to challenge any merger. An index of 1,000 indicates the level of concentration that exists, for instance, in a market shared equally by 10 firms.

—where the post-merger market is "moderately concentrated," with an index between 1,000 and 1,800, a challenge would still be unlikely, provided the merger increases the index by less than 100 points. If the merger increases the index by more than 100 points, a challenge by the Antitrust Division would be more likely than not, with the decision being based on the extent of the increase, the ease of entry, and the presence or absence of other relevant factors specified in the guidelines.

—where the post-merger market is "highly concentrated," resulting in an index above 1,800, challenge is unlikely where the merger produces an increase of less than 50 points. If the merger produces an increase in the index between 50 and 100 points, challenge is more likely than not, again depending on the size of the increase, ease of entry and other factors as specified. If the merger produces an increase in the index of more than 100 points, challenge is likely. An index of 1800 indicates the level of concentration that exists, for instance, in a market shared equally by approximately six firms (5.56 equally-sized firms, to be precise).

In addition, if the leading firm in the market has a market share of 35 percent or more and is about twice as large as the second largest firm or larger, the Department is likely to challenge a merger by the largest firm with any firm having at least one percent of the market. In such a case, the only possible mitigating factor to be considered by the Department would be ease of entry.

A shorthand way to calculate the increase in the Herfindahl index that would be created by any merger is to multiply the percentage shares of the two merging firms and then double the product. For instance, the merger of a 25 percent firm with a two percent firm would give an increase of 100 points ($25 \times 2 \times 2$), and the merger of two firms with seven percent each would yield an increase of 98 points ($7 \times 7 \times 2$).

Converted into the Herfindahl measurement, the 1968 guidelines stated that a challenge was likely for mergers that increased concentration by 30–40 points in highly concentrated markets (four-firm concentration of 75% or more) and by 50–90 points in less highly concentrated markets (four-firm concentration of less than 75%).

Unlike the new guidelines, however, the old guidelines did not state that mergers producing smaller increases in concentration would not be challenged.

Similarly, the old guidelines did not recognize an unconcentrated region where challenges were generally unlikely.

New Entry

The inferences drawn from the concentration numbers above may be adjusted to take account of very easy entry to the market. The reason that ease of entry is so important is that where firms not already in the market can enter it very easily, inferences drawn from the post-merger concentration index can be misleading. Because ease of entry cannot be expressed in market statistics, it has to be looked at as an independent consideration but one which the guidelines make clear is very significant.

Other Factors

Compared to the old guidelines, the new guidelines identify a much larger number of additional factors that the Department will consider in deciding whether to challenge a merger.

The other factors to be considered are ones which might justify some adjustment in the inferences to be drawn from the post-merger concentration. The guidelines state that, where relevant, these factors will be used to resolve close cases.

These factors generally deal with the ease and profitability of collusion among sellers to raise prices above competitive levels. They fall into four rough categories, dealing with:

- the nature of the product and the terms of sale;
- availability to firms in the market of information about specific transactions and buyer market characteristics;
- conduct of firms in the market;
- market performance.

Within each category, the relevance of the factors to the likelihood of collusion is explained. For instance, with homogeneous products, the number of issues on which competitors must agree in order to raise prices is smaller, thus making effective collusion more likely.

Factors that may make a challenge more likely include:

- extreme homogeneity of product;
- substantial gaps between the products in the market and the next best substitute;
- particularly strong similarities in the products of the merging firms compared to the products of other firms in the market;
- readily accessible information about specific transactions in the market;
- a market for the product in which buyers' orders are frequent, regular and small compared to the total output of the typical firm in the market;
- evidence of prior horizontal collusion among firms in the market;
- use by substantially all the firms in the market of mandatory delivered pricing, or exchange of sensitive price or output information, or collective standardization of characteristics of the product which were at one time the basis

for competition, or price protection clauses, or the fact that the acquired firm has been an unusually competitive force in the market, or the fact that before the merger the market appears to be operating in a non-competitive way.

The only factor discussed in the horizontal section that would make a challenge less likely is extreme heterogeneity of the relevant product. A footnote, however, points out that a similar situation may exist where there is rapid technological change or where supply arrangements consist of many complicated terms in addition to price. Those three factors make successful collusion more difficult.

Non-horizontal Mergers

The guidelines make clear that although non-horizontal mergers are less likely to harm competition, they are not always innocuous. They make plain that much of what is said about horizontal mergers could also be applied to non-horizontal mergers—such as the discussion of market concentration, ease of entry and other factors—and they discuss five non-horizontal theories of liability.

The five non-horizontal theories of liability under which such mergers might be challenged are:

- the elimination of specific potential entrants into the market;
- the creation of barriers to entry to the market through vertical mergers;
- the facilitation of collusion through vertical mergers which integrate the firms to include the retail level;
- the elimination through vertical merger of a disruptive buyer;
- the evasion of rate regulation.

For each of the five theories the guidelines describe the possible harm and the conditions necessary for that harm to occur.

Defenses

In a concluding section dealing with defenses to an antitrust challenge to a merger, the guidelines indicate that only in extraordinary cases will the Department consider a claim of efficiencies as a mitigating factor to a merger that would otherwise be challenged. They also indicate that a stringent analysis will be applied to the so-called "failing firm" defense, a doctrine which may immunize otherwise anticompetitive mergers. Before recognizing the defense, the Department will require that the failure of the firm is very likely and that no less anticompetitive acquisition be available.

Conclusions

The guidelines do not oblige the Department or the Antitrust Division to consider or ignore any factors in analyzing mergers. That consideration will still, as in the past, require the exercise of judgment and discretion. The purpose of the guidelines is to reduce uncertainty to the reasonable minimum consistent with an uncertain and evolving area. For those seeking more certainty as to the

Department's enforcement intent, specific proposed conduct may be described to the Department as part of the Business Review Letter procedure, and a letter dealing with the enforcement intent of the Department, where appropriate, will be sent in return.

The guidelines represent more than a year of work by the economists and lawyers of the Antitrust Division, and were prepared at the direction of, and with the active involvement of, William F. Baxter, Assistant Attorney General in charge of the Antitrust Division.

Questions

1. How do the guidelines define market power?
2. What does the Herfindahl Index measure?
3. What is the "goal of market definition"? How does it suggest a means for defining the relevant market?
4. In a horizontal merger situation, what three standards are applied to determine if the merger should be challenged?
5. When is a market considered unconcentrated, moderately concentrated, or highly concentrated?
6. Why is ease of entry significant in determining whether to challenge a merger?
7. What other factors should be reviewed to determine whether to challenge a merger?
8. What are the five theories of liability under which non-horizontal mergers may be challenged?
9. What defenses are available for merging firms?

CONCLUSION

Since the early 1960s, merger policy in the United States has become more strict and consistent. The lines defining illegal mergers have become reasonably clear. Horizontal mergers that appreciably increase market shares, especially if in concentrated industries, are likely to be held illegal. Vertical mergers that substantially foreclose competitors from suppliers or outlets or raise entry barriers are normally decreed illegal. Conglomerate mergers involving reciprocity or the elimination of potential entrants will likewise be challenged.

U.S. merger policy attempts to retain industries with firms possessing small market shares and to promote entry. However, industry structure predating this new merger policy has not been affected. Merger policy has not sought to restructure existing firms. Instead, it seeks to avoid increasing levels of industry concentration. Consequently, one major criticism of U.S. merger policy is its *status quo* hardening of industrial structure. Large firms are privileged to retain their size while gaining an unintended immunity from the takeover process.

Critics further argue that the strict rules of U.S. merger policy have prevented smaller firms from merging to gain the size that firms predating this policy have obtained.

On the other hand, structuralists have argued that the looseness of the conglomerate merger guidelines allows more conglomerate mergers than it prohibits. They point out that the failure to retard conglomerate mergers has led to an increase in the overall aggregate economic concentration. This increased concentration is achieved with little evidence that conglomerate mergers enhance industrial efficiency.[14] Consequently, these critics call for congressional intervention to stop conglomerate mergers that confer little social benefit but conflict with the societal goal of decentralizing economic power.

Merger policy is not wanting for critics who suggest reform, but no group of critics has been successful in convincing Congress of the need to modify its legislative policy on mergers. This congressional inactivity suggests general approval by Congress of the merger policy that has been fashioned through legislative, judicial and enforcement processes.

CASE PROBLEMS

1. Brunswick Corporation is one of the two largest manufacturers, distributors, and financiers of bowling alley equipment. Until the early 1960s it did not operate recreational bowling centers itself.

   In the early 1960s the bowling recreation industry began a decline and an alarming number of Brunswick's customers defaulted on payments. Rather than repossess the equipment for resale, Brunswick began to take over the failing bowling centers by purchase of stock or assets, and keep them operating when they otherwise would have failed. Brunswick carried out such takeovers if its new Bowling Centers Operations Division determined that a center could produce a positive cash flow.

   A competing operator of bowling centers in several cities over the country sued Brunswick, alleging a Section 7 violation by a "deep pocket" manufacturer integrating vertically forward into local markets, causing a potential lessening of horizontal competition on the local level. Because of Brunswick's acquisitions, the local competitors did not realize the increase in their market shares they had anticipated, and, it was contended, reduced the income they would have made as a result of failures of bowling houses within local markets.

   Was an injury sustained by the plaintiff which Section 7 was intended to prevent? Why?

2. Arrow Brands, Inc., was in the business of purchasing aluminum foil in large quantities from manufacturers and converting it into "florist foil" by coloring and embossing it. The converted foil was then sold to wholesale florist supply houses. Although 200 companies in the United States were engaged in the business of converting foil into decorative foil, only eight served the florist

industry, with the remainder converting foil for innumerable other decorative wrapping purposes. Arrow accounted for 33 percent of annual florist foil wholesale sales in the United States market.

Theoretically, any of the 200 foil converters could supply florist foil, used for covering clay and plastic pots and as decoration in arrangements, because decorative foil used in the florist trade is physically not distinguishable from foil decorated by coloring, laminating, or embossing but used for potato wrap, cheese wrap, medicine containers, and so on. However, of the 192 million pounds of converted aluminum foil shipped annually in the United States, 9.7 million pounds consisted of decorative foil, and of that decorative foil, less than 1.5 million pounds went to the florist trade, virtually all of which was shipped by the eight firms, including Arrow, catering to that trade. Also, users of decorative foil, other than florists and florist supply houses, do not purchase from the florist foil converters.

A lower price prevails in the market for florist foil than for colored or embossed aluminum foil sold in the same weight units and gauged at the same thickness. Florist foil brings $.75 to $.85 per unit, whereas other decorative foils are priced at approximately $1.15 to $1.22 per unit.

Arrow and other florist foil converters purchased their plain foil from Reynolds Metals Company among other producers. Plain or raw foil costs contribute 70 percent of the total cost of production.

Following the acquisition, Arrow lowered its prices, and by 1957 it had increased sales 18.9 percent over its 1955 sales volume. Five of Arrow's seven competitors' sales in 1957 were 14 to 47 percent below 1955 sales.

The FTC found a violation of Section 7 of the Clayton Act and ordered divestiture. Reynolds appealed, arguing that the converting and supplying of florist foil is not a "line of commerce" distinct from the converting and supplying of other decorative foils. It was not contended that Reynolds' acquisition of Arrow was likely to have an anticompetitive effect on the market for *all* decorative foils.

What is the relevant "line of commerce"?

3. In the mid-1970s, Atlantic Richfield Company (Arco) was the 13th largest publicly held corporation in terms of assets and ranked 15th in terms of sales and revenues. It produced petroleum products and natural gas, and had never engaged in the copper business. Since the late 1960s, high-level Arco management recognized a need for diversification and favored diversification into the copper industry only if it could be accomplished by large acquisition rather than by original entry or toehold acquisition.

   The Anaconda Company was a fully integrated copper and aluminum company, ranking third in the industry for the mining of copper ore, and fourth in the refined copper market. Anaconda's market shares were 8.27 percent for copper ore and 9.78 for refined copper. The three leaders in the refined copper market control 60 percent of the market.

   Original entry into the copper industry entails outlays from $200 million to $450 million for discovery and development of an exploitable ore deposit, which could take 10 years or more, development of technical expertise, and construction of smelting facilities. Total entry time could range up to 20 years.

In 1967, Arco and Anaconda agreed to merge, with Anaconda to become a wholly owned subsidiary of Arco. The Federal Trade Commission sought to enjoin the merger on the basis that a violation of Section 7 of the Clayton Act would result, on the theory of actual potential entry.

What are the results?

4. Cargill Inc., a huge, privately owned corporation, had been involved for over 100 years in grain trading in the midwest and had acquired river barges and towboats which were used to carry not only grain but also other bulk commodities. By 1973 Cargill was involved in vegetable oil processing, sugar trading, ore and metal mining, ocean shipping, flour milling, corn wet milling, manufacture of industrial chemicals, production of animal feeds, fertilizers, and poultry products, and salt mining. After forming a planning committee and receiving its recommendations for company expansion, Cargill made a tender offer for all outstanding shares of stock in Missouri Portland Cement Co. (MP), a manufacturer of cement operating three plants on the Missouri and Ohio Rivers.

   Missouri Portland Cement sold its cement in an 11-state area, along with several dozen competitors including 8 of the 10 largest cement producers in the country. MP was the 20th-largest national producer, possessing 2 percent of national cement production capacity and 8 percent of capacity in its 11-state area. The cement industry could be characterized as oligopolistic.

   MP sued Cargill to enjoin the acquisition, on the basis that such an acquisition or merger would result in a violation of Section 7 of the Clayton Act. MP argued that Cargill was attempting a "product-extension merger" as was attempted by Proctor and Gamble with Clorox. MP further analogized that Cargill's "deep pocket" would enable it to raise entry barriers or discourage competition in the cement industry.

   How would you characterize the acquisition of Missouri Portland Cement by Cargill? What economic effect would you expect it to have on the cement market? Would a Section 7 violation result? Is *Proctor and Gamble* applicable to this situation?

END NOTES

1. See Ralph L. Nelson, *Merger Movements in American Industry—1890–1956* (Princeton: Princeton University Press, 1962).
2. *U.S.* v. *Northern Securities Co.*, 193 U.S. 197 (1904).
3. *U.S.* v. *Columbia Steel Co.*, 334 U.S. 495 (1948).
4. *U.S.* v. *Bethlehem Steel Co.*, 168 F. Supp. 576 (1958).
5. *U.S.* v. *Aluminum Company of America*, 377 U.S. 271.
6. *U.S.* v. *Continental Can Co.*, 217 F. Supp. 761 (1963); 378 U.S. 441 (1964).
7. 378 U.S. 441, 449, 455, 457 (1964).
8. During the oil shortage of the 1970s, Congress mandated that large vertically inte-

grated oil companies share their scarce supplies of crude oil with refineries that had little or no crude oil production (Energy Petroleum Act of 1973).

9. The two cases are *FTC* v. *Consolidated Foods*, 380 U.S. 592 (1965), which outlawed probable reciprocity, and *FTC* v. *Procter and Gamble*, 386 U.S. 568 (1966), which utilized "entrenchment" and "potential competition" doctrines.
10. *U.S.* v. *El Paso Natural Gas Co.*, 376 U.S. 651 (1964).
11. *U.S.* v. *Falstaff Brewing Corp.*, 332 F. Supp. 970 (1971), 410 U.S. 526 (1973).
12. 410 U.S. 526, 533–534, 532 (1973).
13. *U.S.* v. *Marine Bancorporation*, 418 U.S. 602, 624–625 (1974).
14. F. M. Scherer, *Industrial Market Structure and Market Performance*, 2d ed. (Chicago: Ill.: Rand McNally, 1980), p. 563.

chapter 13

HORIZONTAL COMBINATIONS

One of the premises of an effective competitive system is that rivals act independently in determining price, quality, and other terms of trade. Such competitive action among sellers affords the buyers an opportunity to find the lowest price offered by the suppliers.

On the other hand, profit-oriented competitors are tempted to unite on price or other terms of trade. By avoiding price or other types of competition, it is possible for the firms to raise prices above the level that would result from independent competitive action. Even Adam Smith, the often-quoted author of the *Wealth of Nations* which proclaimed the virtues of freely competitive enterprise, warned, "people of the same trade seldom meet together, even for merriment and diversion, but the conversation ends in a conspiracy against the public, or in some contrivance to raise prices."[1]

Only if rivals act independently in regard to competitive matters, can society be assured that the efficiency, equity, and progress associated with a competitive system will be achieved. Accordingly, public policy has long recognized that joint action which restrains competition should normally be prohibited. However, society has not always been successful in identifying and suppressing joint actions in the form of contracts, trusts, conspiracies, or other collusions.

RULE OF REASON

The rules of law on collusion of competitors followed by the courts prior to the adoption of the federal and state antitrust statutes were based on English common law. The common law permitted restraints on competition that were merely ancillary to some legitimate business purpose, but voided those contracts whose main object was to restrict competition. For example, a contract of employment restraining an employee, should he or she quit or be terminated, from subsequently competing with the employer was held lawful if the restraint imposed was reasonable in time (limited to a number of years) and in area (limited to a geographical area). This restraint was considered ancillary to the basic employment contract, that is, it allowed the employer to train the employee without fear of the employee's immediate exit as a competitor. Likewise, a restraint on one's freedom to exercise one's trade, if accepted in selling the business, was held valid if it was reasonable in time and area because it was ancillary to the sale of the business. Because social purposes, such as employment training or the sale of businesses, were being furthered by these contracts and because they did not involve substantial restraints on competition, the common law allowed enforcement. In contrast, the common law courts would not enforce contracts among competitors to fix prices on their goods. These types of contracts were considered contrary to the public interest. Therefore, the basic rule of reasonableness (rule of reason) governed the enforcement of the common law restraint of trade. However, as agreements among competitors found alternative means of private enforcement through pools or the trust arrangement, it became apparent that the passive approach of nonenforceability of the contract followed by the common law was an inadequate protection for the public. A positive approach was needed to combat the problem of the trusts and collusion in American industries. Consequently, Congress enacted the Sherman Act.

Section 1 of the Sherman Act provides that "every contract, combination, . . . or conspiracy, in restraint of trade or commerce . . . is . . . illegal." This section imposes the positive duty on the federal government to enforce the policy of maintaining the principles of market price (competitively determined) in the conduct of business. Since expressed standards for identifying a "restraint of trade" were not specified in the law, the federal courts have had to develop and apply such standards as were found necessary to preserve competition.

Section 1 of the Sherman Act declares "every" contract, combination, or conspiracy in restraint of trade to be illegal. In interpreting this provision, the obvious question arises: Are *reasonable* restraints of trade that were lawful under the common law made unlawful by Section 1? In other words, does the word *every* in Section 1 mean "every"—including those reasonable common law restraints—and thereby outlaw *all* restraints on trade? Initially, the Supreme Court answered this question affirmatively in writing,

> . . . [T]he plain and ordinary meaning of such language is not limited to that kind of contract alone which is in unreasonable restraint of trade, but all contracts are included in

such language, and no exception or limitation can be added without placing in the Act that which has been omitted by Congress. *U.S.* v. *Trans-Missouri Freight Association,* 166 U.S. 290 (1896).

This language by the Supreme Court indicates that the justices were following a "plain meaning" rule of statutory interpretation. They believed the plain meaning of the words as employed in the statute were the best evidence of the intention of Congress. They argued that if the legislators had meant something else, different words would have been used to indicate the alternative meaning. The dissenting justices favored a "purpose construction." They felt the statute should be interpreted in light of its purpose rather than the strictly literal meaning of the language employed in the statute.

In 1911, the Court decided to adopt the purpose approach. The Court determined that the elimination of reasonable restraints of trade that were lawful under the common law was not within the purpose of the Sherman Act. Consequently, a "rule of reason" approach was accepted as the proper method of interpreting the Sherman Act. So, though the act itself may say "every" restraint of trade, the judicial interpretations of the act have added the requirement of "unreasonableness" before the restraint of trade is to be ruled illegal. This rule of reason was first enunciated in the monopolization case against the Standard Oil trust in 1911. However, one of the most frequently cited statements of the rule of reason is that of Justice Brandeis in *Chicago Board of Trade* v. *U.S.*, 246 U.S. 231, 238 (1918):

The true test of legality is whether the restraint imposed is such as merely regulates and perhaps thereby promotes competition or whether it is such as may suppress or even destroy competition. To determine that question the court must ordinarily consider the facts peculiar to the business to which the restraint is applied; its condition before and after the restraint was imposed; the nature of the restraint and its effect, actual or probable. The history of the restraint, the evil believed to exist, the reason for adopting the particular remedy, the purpose or end sought to be attained, are all relevant facts. This is not because a good intention will save an otherwise objectionable regulation or the reverse; but because knowledge of the intent may help the court to interpret facts and to predict consequences.

PRICE-FIXING

Businesspeople freely accept and publicly proclaim the advantages of competition and the free market. They maintain that the self-regulating aspects of competition promote the public welfare by ensuring lower prices and greater productivity. However, businesspeople also recognize that in planning for productive operations and in the development of marketing strategy, cooperation among competitors may reduce the hazards associated with the competitive process. When such agreements are made between competitors at the same level of the distribution process, the agreements are considered horizontal combinations. Obvious examples include the agreements of manufacturers to fix prices they charge to the public, or wholesalers agreeing not to sell competing goods in each other's assigned territory. Such horizontal combinations eliminate competition between competing rivals. Society is then faced with higher prices and no alternative source of supplies. Because most of these practices present obvious harm to the competitive process, the courts have treated them as containing no redeeming social or economic value and, hence, unreasonable *per se*. However, in many instances the conspiring merchants have attempted to convince the court that they set or fix only "reasonable" prices and achieve only "reasonable" profits as a result of the price-fixing agreement. In the following case, the conspirators also argued that their buying program to support prices merely eliminated "ruinous competition."

U.S. v. Socony-Vacuum Oil Co.
310 U.S. 150 (1939)
Supreme Court of the United States

Justice Douglas

The court charged the jury that it was a violation of the Sherman Act for a group of individuals or corporations to act together to raise the prices to be charged for the commodity which they manufactured where they controlled a substantial part of the interstate trade and commerce in that commodity. The court stated that where the members of a combination had the power to raise prices and acted together for that purpose, the combination was illegal and that it was immaterial how reasonable or unreasonable those prices were or to what extent they had been affected by the combination. . . .

In *United States* v. *Trenton Potteries Co.,* 273 U.S. 392, this Court sustained a conviction under the Sherman Act where the jury was charged that an agreement on the part of the members of a combination, controlling a substantial party of an industry, upon the prices which the members are to charge for their commodity is in itself an unreasonable restraint of trade without regard to the reasonableness of the prices or the good intentions of the combining units. . . . This court reviewed the various price-fixing cases under the Sherman Act . . . and said ". . . it has since often been decided and always assumed that uniform price-fixing by those controlling in any substantial manner a trade or business in interstate commerce is prohibited by the Sherman Law, despite the reasonableness of the particular prices agreed upon." This Court pointed out that the so-called "rule of reason" had not affected this view of the illegality of price-fixing agreements. And in holding that agreements "to fix or maintain prices" are not reasonable restraints of trade under the statute merely because the prices themselves are reasonable, it said . . .

> The aim and result of every price-fixing agreement, if effective, is the elimination of one form of competition. The power to fix prices, whether reasonably exercised, or not, involves power to control the market and to fix arbitrary and unreasonable prices. The

reasonable price fixed today may through economic and business changes become the unreasonable price of tomorrow. Once established, it may be maintained unchanged because of the absence of competition secured by the agreement for a price reasonable when fixed. Agreements which create such potential power may be held to be in themselves unreasonable or unlawful restraints, without the necessity of minute inquiry whether a particular price is reasonable or unreasonable as fixed and without placing on the government in enforcing the Sherman Law the burden of ascertaining from day to day whether it has become unreasonable through the mere variation of economic conditions. . . .

Thus, for over forty years this Court has consistently and without deviation adhered to the principle that price-fixing agreements are unlawful *per se* under the Sherman Act and that no showing of so-called competitive abuses or evils which those agreements were designed to eliminate or alleviate may be interposed as a defense.

Questions

1. Did the Court accept the notion that reasonable prices and reasonable profits are justifications for price-fixing?
2. Is the elimination of "ruinous competition" a justification for establishing a price-fixing scheme?
3. If the Supreme Court accepted reasonable prices and profits as justification for price-fixing and ruled that such pricing and profits were reasonable, what would have to be done if the parties later changed their price structure? Would the Supreme Court become like a price control board? Do you think the Court wanted to get into such an activity?
4. When is an activity considered "unreasonable *per se*"? What reasons can be given for having such a rule? The Supreme Court said the following:

   . . . [T]here are certain agreements or practices which because of their pernicious effect on competition and lack of any redeeming virtue are conclusively presumed to be unreasonable and therefore illegal without elaborate inquiry as to the precise harm they have caused or the business excuse for their use. This principle of *per se* unreasonableness not only makes the type of restraints which are proscribed by the Sherman Act more certain to benefit everyone concerned, but it also avoids the necessity for an incredibly complicated and prolonged economic investigation into the entire history of the industry involved, as well as related industries, in an effort to determine at large whether a particular restraint has been unreasonable—an inquiry so often wholly fruitless when undertaken. *Northern Pac. R. Co.* v. *United States,* 356 U.S. 1 (1957).

PROOF OF CONSPIRACY

Price-fixing has been ruled unreasonable *per se* since *U.S.* v. *Trenton Potteries* (1927). Enforcement officials have consistently taken legal action against schemes to rig, control, or stabilize prices. No anticompetitive scheme is frowned on more than a price-fixing combination. Consequently, the Department of Justice believes that everyone should understand the illegality of price-fixing. Therefore, the Department of Justice often brings *criminal* charges against participants of a price-fixing conspiracy. A criminal violation of the Sherman Act can be a felony and result in imprisonment for up to three years. The act authorizes the imposition of fines of $100,000 per count for an individual and a $1,000,000 fine per count for a corporation. These criminal penalties were upgraded in 1976 from more lenient provisions in the original Sherman Act. The increase in the level of penalties and the increased willingness of enforcement officials to proceed with criminal suits suggests that more prosecution and stiff sentencing of antitrust violators may well occur in the future. Business executives have been imprisoned for participation in price-rigging schemes.

Some businesspeople attempt to circumvent the price-fixing prohibitions by concealing their conspiracy from the public. Historically, such conspiracies have been proven by presenting in evidence the actual documents or contracts of the price-fixing scheme. When such documents are not prepared or not discovered, circumstantial evidence is presented to establish the conspiracy. Meetings of competitors are often used as evidence of a conspiracy. In addition, business firms that sell their products at the same price are behaving "parallel," and such behavior may imply a conspiracy. "Conscious parallelism" of the competitors in following the same practices is often asserted as evidence of conspiracy. The following case deals with the question of evidence of conspiracy and whether the "parallel behavior" of several competitors was the result of the independent business judgment by each competitor or the result of a conspiracy.

Esco Corporation v. United States
340 F. 2d 1000 (1965)
U.S. Court of Appeals (9th Cir.)

This is an appeal from a jury verdict convicting appellant corporation of violating Section 1 of the Sherman Act by means of its participation in an alleged price-fixing conspiracy, admittedly a *per se* violation of the Act. . . .

The "central criminal design" charged herein was the restraint of trade by fixing prices on stainless steel pipe and tubing within the described market area. But, it is contended, Esco's "relationship" to the two . . . [Los Angeles] meetings and the Salt Lake City meeting of the competitors was "perfectly legal. . . ." [Defendant's] counsel [argues] "there is a compelled inference" that Tubesales, the biggest competitor, called the meeting "not to ask for agreement, but simply to announce" its own pricing plans. Were we triers of fact, we might well ask if this were so, what purpose was to be served by a meeting of competitors?

Nor are we so naive as to believe that a formal signed-and-sealed contract or written resolution would conceivably be adopted at a meeting of price-fixing conspirators in this day and age. In fact, the typical price-fixing agreement is usually accomplished in a contrary manner.

While particularly true of price-fixing conspiracies, it is a well recognized law that any conspiracy can ordinarily only be proved by inferences drawn from relevant and competent circumstantial evidence, including the conduct of the defendants charged. . . . A knowing wink can mean more than words. Let us suppose five competitors meet on several occasions, discuss their problems, and one finally states—"I won't fix prices with any of you, but here is what I am going to do—put the price of my gidget at X dollars, now you all do what you want." He then leaves the meeting. Competitor number two says—"I don't care whether number one does what he says he's going to do or not; nor do I care what the rest of you do, but I am going to price my gidget at X dollars." Number three makes a similar statement—"My price is X dollars." Number four says not a word. All leave and fix "their" prices at "X" dollars.

We do not say the foregoing illustration compels an inference in this case that the competitors' conduct constituted a price-fixing conspiracy, including an agreement to so conspire, but neither can we say, as a matter of law, that an inference of no agreement is compelled. As in so many other instances, it remains a question for the trier of fact to consider and determine what inference appeals to it (the jury) as most logical and persuasive after it has heard all the evidence as to what these competitors had done before such meetings, and what actions they took thereafter, or what actions they did not take.

An accidental or incidental price uniformity, or even "pure" conscious parallelism of prices is, standing alone, not unlawful. Nor is an individual competitor's sole decision to follow a price leadership standing alone, a violation of law. But we do not find that factual situation here.

It is not necessary to find an express agreement, either oral or written, in order to find a conspiracy, but it is sufficient that a concert of action be contemplated and that defendants conform to the arrangement. . . . Mutual consent need not be bottomed on express agreement, for any conformance to an agreed or contemplated pattern of conduct will warrant an inference of conspiracy. . . . An exchange of words is not required. . . . Thus not only action, but even a lack of action, may be enough from which to infer a combination or conspiracy. . . .

Applying these rules to the facts at hand, the jury came to an opposite conclusion from that which [Esco] urges, and the fact that Esco's involvement was in but two of ten allegedly conspiratorial situations does not absolve Esco from participation in the entire conspiracy if its involvement in the two was unlawful and knowingly and purposely performed. We hold that sufficient evidence existed for the jury to find participation in a price-fixing conspiracy.

Questions

1. How many different types of evidence of a conspiracy or agreement are discussed in *Esco*?
2. Is pure "conscious parallelism" illegal? Is it evidence? Is it enough evidence to have a jury decide? What can the defendants do to rebut the evidence of their "parallel" behavior to avoid an adverse jury verdict?
3. Is price leadership illegal?
4. Do you think it is wise to attend your competitor's announcement of new pricing plans? Is it ever wise to consult with your competitors concerning prices?

MODERN PRICE-FIXING

The prices for many public purchases and construction projects are set by competitive bidding. Specifications for the project are published and bids are invited. Later, the sealed bids are opened, with the lowest bid winning. Sometimes bidding rings are formed whereby the bids are rigged so that the ring's chosen winner submits the lowest bid (but a bid higher than under a truly competitive bidding process). These rings are clearly illegal under Section 1 of the Sherman Act.

The most famous bidding ring involved the makers of heavy, electrical equipment, prosecuted and convicted in 1960.[2] The conspirators, including General Electric and Westinghouse, had met under assumed names in various meeting places, ranging from luxury hotels to backwoods cabins in Canada. They had utilized codes in written correspondence, which was sent to their home addresses rather than to their offices. Verbal communications were limited to public telephones. Despite their efforts to maintain secrecy, 29 companies and 45 of their officers pleaded guilty or offered no defense in criminal suits when faced with the evidence the government had acquired. Seven officers served brief jail sentences and the companies were fined $1.9 million. Thereafter, over 1,900 private treble-damage suits were filed by victims of the illegal price rigging, and over $405 million was paid out by the conspirators to settle the suits.

Thereafter, to avoid the strong price competition in the turbine-generator market following the breakup of the conspiracy, General Electric (GE) announced in 1963 a new pricing system. The price system involved the publication of a price formula, publication of all orders and prices offered, and a "price protection" clause in all sales contracts which guaranteed customers that discounts from the formula system would be retroactively applied to all sales during the preceding six months. This self-penalty provision and publication of pricing data assured GE's competitors that it would not give selective price discounts. Westinghouse immediately copied GE's plan, and identical price levels followed. The Justice Department did not challenge this arrangement until the 1970s. Finally, a consent decree was negotiated in December 1976, in which the pricing scheme was withdrawn, but no penalties or damages were assessed against General Electric or Westinghouse.[3]

Questions

1. The private utilities that purchased the electrical generators from the price-fixers did not complain of the high prices. In addition, the damage claims of the utilities were regarded by many as meek. Can you offer an explanation of why these regulated utilities were not more aggressive?
2. Which method of "price fixing" is safer for the company—GE's secret rendezvous with competitors or announced pricing systems? Is either method acceptable to the public?

Beyond the big case against GE and Westinghouse, other price-fixng agreements were prosecuted in the 1960s on a wide range of national markets, such as eye glasses, soap, cheese, watches, electrical lamps, explosives, typewriters, ball bearings, newspaper print, stainless steel, fertilizer, and chemicals. Even small-scale price-fixing arrangements were attacked in such markets as auto body repairs, fire extinguishers, ready mix cement, Hawaiian package tours, paper labels, Korean wigs, timber, Utah egg dealers, construction firms, gypsum, industrial laundries, school dairy products, travel agents, and bakeries.

One of the larger cases in the 1970s involved 23 major producers of paper board boxes used for food, drugs, household supplies, and textiles.[4] The criminal suits against 48 corporate officials resulted in *nolo contendere* pleas or convictions. In prosecuting these cases, the Department of Justice announced new and tougher guidelines for price-fixing penalties. The guidelines call for an average 18-month jail term, an average $50,000 fine, and fines on the company equaling 10 percent of sales in the product. Nevertheless, the judge refused the Department of Justice's recommendation and set jail sentences which averaged 10 days for 15 of the 49 managers found guilty. Fines assessed by the judge averaged $5,000.

Questions

1. Is the variety of products involved in price-fixing schemes surprising? Is this "record" embarrassing to the business community?
2. Are the Department of Justice's guidelines for price-fixing penalties too tough? Were the sentences imposed by the trial judge too lenient?

UNRECOVERABLE DAMAGES

In the *Illinois Brick*[5] case, consumers of concrete block sued to recover damages caused by price-fixing by producers. The consumers were represented by the attorney general of Illinois. The Supreme Court held that these consumers could not recover because they were only "indirect" purchasers who had bought from wholesalers. The Court held that the wholesalers, the direct purchasers, could sue because they were in privity with the price fixers. The Court was fearful of "multiple liability" if it permitted the consumer, the remote purchaser, to recover damages also. The Court avoided this possibility by ruling that the remote purchaser could not recover any damages passed on by the wholesalers.

The *Illinois Brick* decision could restrict the deterrent force of private treble-damage claims against price fixers. It is conceivable that wholesalers could pass on the price rigging charges and suffer no harm. Such wholesalers would lack incentive to file antitrust claims against their suppliers. And if the wholesalers chose not to sue to recoup their "higher costs," the final consumer would have no recourse.

Questions

1. Should the difficulty of assigning damages between the wholesalers and consumers preclude the consumers' right to sue?
2. Should Congress, by amending the antitrust laws, overturn the *Illinois Brick* decision?

EXCHANGE OF PRICE INFORMATION

U.S. v. Container Corp.
393 U.S. 333 (1968)
Supreme Court of the United States

Justice Douglas

This is a civil antitrust action charging a price-fixing agreement in violation of Section 1 of the Sherman Act.

The case as proved is unlike any other price decisions we have rendered. There was here an exchange of price information but no agreement to adhere to a price schedule as in . . . *United States* v. *Socony-Vacuum Oil Co.* . . . There was here an exchange of information concerning specific sales to identified customers, not a statistical report on the average cost to all members, without identifying the parties to specific transactions. Here all that was present was a request by each defendant of its competitor for information as to the most recent price charged or quoted, whenever it needed such information and whenever it was not available from another source. Each defendant on receiving that request usually furnished the data with the expectation that it would be furnished reciprocal information when it wanted it. That concerted action is of course sufficient to establish the combination or conspiracy, the initial ingredient of a violation of Section 1 of the Sherman Act.

There was of course freedom to withdraw from the agreement. But the fact remains that when a defendant requested and received price information, it was affirming its willingness to furnish such information in return.

* * *

The defendants account for about 90% of the shipment of corrugated containers from plants in the Southeastern United States. While containers vary as to dimensions, weight, color, and so on, they are substantially identical, no matter who produces them, when made to particular specifications. The prices paid depend on price alternatives. Suppliers when seeking new or additional business or keeping old customers, do not exceed a competitor's price. It is common for purchasers to buy from two or more suppliers concurrently. A defendant supplying a customer with containers would usually quote the same price on additional orders, unless costs had changed. Yet where a competitor was charging a particular price, a defendant would normally quote the same price or even a lower price.

The exchange of price information seemed to have the effect of keeping prices within a fairly narrow ambit. Capacity has exceeded the demand from 1955 to 1963, the period covered by the complaint, and the trend of corrugated container prices has been downward. Yet, despite this excess capacity and the downward trend of prices, the industry has expanded in the Southeast from 30 manufacturers with 49 plants to 51 manufacturers with 98 plants. An abundance of raw materials and machinery makes entry into the industry easy with an investment of $50,000 to $75,000.

The result of this reciprocal exchange of prices was to stabilize prices though at a downward level. Knowledge of a competitor's price usually meant matching that price. The continuation of some price competition is not fatal to the Government's case. The limitation or reduction of price competition brings the case within the ban, for as we held in *United States* v. *Socony-Vacuum Oil Co.*, interference with the setting of price by free market forces is unlawful *per se.* Price information exchanged in some markets may have no effect on a truly competitive price. But the corrugated container industry is dominated by relatively few sellers. The product is fungible, and the competition for sales is price. The demand is inelastic, as buyers place orders only for immediate, short-run needs. The exchange of price data tends toward price uniformity. For a lower price does not mean a larger share of the available business but a sharing of the existing business at a lower return. Stabilizing prices as well as raising them is within the ban of Section 1 of the Sherman Act. As we said in *United States* v. *Socony-Vacuum Oil Co.,* "in terms of market operations stabilization is but one form of manipulation." The inferences are irresistible that the exchange of price information has had an anticompetitive effect in the industry, chilling the vigor of price competition.

Price is too critical, too sensitive a control to allow it to be used even in an informal manner to restrain competition.

Questions

1. Is the exchange of price information by competitors illegal *per se*? Is the purpose of the exchange to fix prices? Is the effect of the exchange to fix prices?
2. The first element of a Section 1 violation, the joint action, is clearly established by the agreement to exchange price information. However, the government has to establish that the effect of the exchange of price information is to stabilize or fix prices. What proofs were offered in *Container Corporation* of price stabilization?

A trade association is a voluntary association of business competitors existing for the purpose of promoting their businesses through cooperative activity. Most trade associations engage in collecting and disseminating price information. A trade association of hardwood manufacturers operated an interchange of reports on inventory, production, prices, and sales, with a commentary added by the compiler of statistics. In reporting their information to the association, the members disclosed prices on closed transactions, current prices being offered, and future price intentions. The association reports identified sellers and their price quotations and the names of buyers associated with particular purchases. Moreover, the reports of the association were not available to buyers. When the Department of Justice charged the plan constituted a combination to restrain pricing in hardwood lumber, the association members argued that "perfect competition," as economic theory explains, requires those participating in the market to have complete knowledge of market conditions. This information exchange, they argued, was simply the means of providing market information to industry sellers.

The Supreme Court rejected the defendants' arguments and held the association's activities in violation of Section 1. The Court remarked that the published reports were not available to both sellers and buyers as is theorized in "perfect competition." Moreover, the Court pointed out that the competitive market process and its market information flow do not include a "skilled interpretor . . . to insistently recommend harmony of action likely to prove profitable in proportion as it is unitedly pursued."[6]

Questions

1. If a trade association is to have a price reporting service, what ingredients should it avoid in order to be lawful?
2. Many have argued that nonmembers of a trade association cannot be certain that the data furnished by a group of sellers is correct. Accordingly, they have urged that price reporting in industries become a public function to be handled by the government or a regulated enterprise. Do you agree?

ALLOCATING MARKETS

Agreements between competitors to divide markets on a customer or geographic basis are often referred to as horizontal customer or territorial allocations. These agreements can have a greater anticompetitive effect than price fixing among competitors because price fixers may still compete on product quality or additional services rendered. In contrast, competitors who agree not to compete in geographic markets or for different customers completely eliminate competition.

Almost from the beginning, the court has declared that allocation of markets among competitors is illegal *per se*. Two modern cases have reaffirmed that position.

In 1967 the Supreme Court held the division of markets accomplished by a trademark licensing system was illegal.[7] There were 30 licensees who owned substantially all the stock of the licenser, Sealy. Sealy's board of directors was composed of five members from the licensee-stockholder group. The Court characterized the licenser as a joint venture of the stockholder-licensees and, therefore, a horizontal combination. Since the licenser, dominated by the licensees, allocated exclusive territories to the licensees, the Court found this territorial arrangement to be a horizontal market allocation by the licensees and illegal *per se*.

In the *Topco* case, regional supermarket chains joined together to form Topco Associates, Inc., as a group-buying operation.[8] Topco thereafter obtained private label brands for its members. Members of the Topco combination limited the location of their stores to designated territories which eliminated intrabrand competition between them. They argued there were still plenty of other grocery stores within the territories in which they had eliminated competition among themselves. Topco members argued that their arrangement enabled them to compete more vigorously with the private labels of the national chains (interbrand competition). The lower court agreed with Topco and dismissed the case. The Supreme Court reversed in 1972 and found the allocation of territories to be a horizontal restraint and, therefore, a *per se* violation of Section 1. The Supreme Court noted that Topco had no authority under the Sherman Act to determine the respective values of intrabrand and interbrand competition. The Court, in both *Sealy* and *Topco,* was not willing to balance the pro-competitive effects in the interbrand market against the elimination of intrabrand competition among private brand sellers.

GROUP BOYCOTTS

Klor's v. Broadway-Hale Stores
359 U.S. 207 (1959)
Supreme Court of the United States

Justice Black

Klor's, Inc., operates a retail store on Mission Street, San Francisco, California; Broadway-Hale Stores, Inc., a chain of department stores, operates one of its stores next door. The two stores compete in the sale of radios, television sets, refrigerators and other household appliances. . . .

Klor's brought this action for treble damages and injunction in the United States District Court.

In support of its claim Klor's . . . [alleged]: [M]anufacturers and distributors of such well-known brands as General Electric, RCA, Admiral, Zenith, Emerson and others have conspired among themselves and with Broadway-Hale either not to sell to Klor's or to sell to it only at discriminatory prices and highly unfavorable terms. Broadway-Hale had used its "monopolistic" buying power to bring about this situation. . . . The concerted refusal to deal with Klor's has seriously handicapped its ability to compete and has already caused it a great loss of profits, goodwill, reputation and prestige.

The defendants did not dispute these allegations, but sought summary judgment and dismissal of the complaint for failure to state a cause of action. They submitted unchallenged affidavits which showed that there were hundreds of other household appliance retailers, some within a few blocks of Klor's who sold many competing brands of appliances, including those the defendants refused to sell to Klor's. From the allegations of the complaints, and from the affidavits supporting the motion for summary judgment, the District Court concluded that the controversy was a "purely private quarrel" between Klor's and Broadway-Hale, which did not amount to a "public wrong proscribed by the [Sherman]

Act." On this ground the complaint was dismissed and summary judgment was entered for the defendants. . . . [I]t held that here the required public injury was missing since "there was no charge or proof that by any act of defendants the price, quantity, or quality offered the public was affected, nor that there was any intent or purpose to effect a change in, or an influence on, prices, quantity, or quality. . . ." The holding, if correct, means that unless the opportunities for customers to buy in a competitive market are reduced, a group of powerful businessmen may act in concert to deprive a single merchant, like Klor, of the goods he needs to compete effectively. . . .

We think Klor's allegations clearly show one type of trade restraint and public harm the Sherman Act forbids, and that defendants' affidavits provide no defense to the charges. Section 1 of the Sherman Act makes illegal any contract, combination, or conspiracy in restraint of trade. . . . In the landmark case of *Standard Oil Co.* v. *United States,* 221 U.S. 1, this court read Section 1 to prohibit those classes of contracts or acts which the common law deemed to be undue restraints of trade and those which new times and economic conditions would make unreasonable. . . . The Court recognized that there were some agreements whose validity depended on the surrounding circumstances. It emphasized, however, that there were classes of restraints which from their "nature or character" were unduly restrictive, and hence forbidden by both the common law and the statute. . . . Group boycotts, or concerted refusals by traders to deal with other traders, have long been held to be in the forbidden category. They have not been saved by allegations that they were reasonable in the specific circumstances, nor by a failure to show that they "fixed or regulated prices, parcelled out or limited production, or brought about a deterioration in quality."

* * *

Plainly the allegations of this complaint disclose such a boycott. This is not a case of a single trader refusing to deal with another, nor even of a manufacturer and a dealer agreeing to an exclusive distributorship. Alleged in this complaint is a wide combination consisting of manufacturers, distributors and a retailer. This combination takes from Klor's its freedom to buy appliances in an open competitive market and drives it out of business as a dealer in the defendants' products. It deprives the manufacturers and distributors of their freedom to sell to Klor's at the same prices and conditions made available to Broadway-Hale, and in some instances forbids them from selling to it on any terms whatsoever. It interferes with the natural flow of interstate commerce. It clearly has, by its "nature" and "character" a monopolistic tendency. As such it is not to be tolerated merely because the victim is just one merchant whose business is so small that his destruction makes little difference to the economy. Monopoly can as surely thrive by the elimination of such small businessmen, one at a time, as it can by driving them out in large groups. In recognition of this fact the Sherman Act has consistently been read to forbid all contracts and combinations "which 'tend to create a monopoly,'" whether "the tendency is a creeping one" or "one that proceeds at full gallop."

Questions

1. The district court ruled that these facts merely demonstrated the existence of a "private dispute" without any "public wrong." What did the court mean by no "public wrong proscribed by the Act"?
2. Why did the Supreme Court feel these facts reveal a "public wrong"?
3. Would there be illegal behavior if each distributor independently refused to deal with Klor?

RELATIONS WITH COMPETITORS

Cases have revealed that Section 1 of the Sherman Act prohibits conspiracies that unreasonably restrain trade. Some kind of *joint or concerted* action between two or more persons or companies must exist for Section 1 of the Sherman Act to apply. But there need not be anything so formal as a written contract; "understandings" are enough, and these can be inferred by the court or jury from the way the parties have conducted themselves. Any kind of a mutual understanding which gives the parties a basis for expecting that a business practice or decision will be adopted by one and all, or at least not opposed by the others, is sufficient to establish joint action.

For Section 1 to be violated, the joint action must have as its *purpose or effect* an unreasonable restraint of trade. If the *purpose* is unreasonable, it does not matter whether the action taken by the parties is successful or fails. Such restraints of trade that are in their purpose considered unreasonable are identified as *per se* violations. Federal enforcement policy allows criminal prosecution for these *per se* offenses, which include the following.

Price-Fixing. This agreement need not be on a specific price. The law is violated by agreements on maximums or minimums, on a common sales agent, on terms or conditions of sale such as credit terms or discounts, or even on the mere exchange or price information if this has a stabilizing effect on prices. The agreement of price-fixing schemes can be inferred from a course of conduct or from a history of telephone calls, meetings, and the like between competitors followed by uniform price action. Price-fixing, in whatever form, is the antitrust violation most frequently prosecuted criminally.

Dividing Territory. Competitors may not agree as to geographical areas in which each will or will not sell. Any course of action whereby competitors avoid each other's territory may be a basis for a court finding of such an illegal agreement.

Dividing Customers. Competitors may not agree that each will sell to a particular customer or class of customers and not to another. Neither may competitors agree on which of them will make any specific sales.

Dividing Products. Basically, competitors may not agree that one will not make or sell products made or sold by another.

Limiting Production. Competitors may not agree to restrict or limit production or production capacity. Violations of this form often involve a quota system.

Boycotting. Competing sellers must not agree among themselves not to sell to a particular customer or reseller, whatever the reason.

Suppression of Quality Competition. Competitors may not agree to restrict the development of improvements in the quality of their products. Nor may competitors agree to limit research for quality improvements. Most agreements of this type are, in effect, agreements not to compete and are contrary to the basic purpose of antitrust laws.

To avoid suspicion of a *per se* violation, there should be no conversations or communications of any kind with competitors concerning these kinds of agreements. If any communications are made, a document should be prepared indicating the extent of the conversation and how the conversation was limited to avoid any violation of antitrust law. If one of these subjects comes up in conversation at a trade meeting attended by company employees, employees should terminate the conversation immediately or leave the gathering. Again, documentation of the incident should be recorded indicating the facts and the employee's noninvolvement. In all *per se* situations it makes no difference that an apparently sound business consideration may be involved also. There are no acceptable excuses or such a thing as being just a "little bit" guilty.

Besides the *per se* offenses under the Sherman Act, the legality of other joint action by competitors turns on the reasonableness, under the circumstances, of any restraint on competition. Reasonableness of such restraints is measured in terms of both the purpose of the restraint and its effect on competition. All these potential restraints must be tested on an individual basis. However, one should remember that a reasonable business purpose will not excuse joint action which has an unreasonable effect on competition.

Joint activities of competitors to present views or make recommendations to governmental bodies are exempt from antitrust laws if they are limited to good faith efforts to influence governmental policy. However, the courts have ruled that such action must not be a mere sham to accomplish an otherwise illegal purpose.[9] Therefore, before engaging with other companies in joint presentations to governmental bodies, each proposal should be reviewed to make certain that the project cannot be asserted to be a sham and thus lose its antitrust exemption status.

CONCLUSION

The long trend of cases against anticompetitive horizontal combinations has created rather clear lines against price-fixing and related collusive activities. However, the continuing successful prosecutions against these practices reveal that outright collusion still exists. The remedies imposed by the courts include fines and injunctive orders to stop conspiring. Many criticize these remedies as too weak and call for higher fines against conspirators to eliminate the profits obtained by conspiracy.

Beyond these underground conspiracies, implicit or tacit collusion is widespread. The horizontal merger movements of past eras have made a significant portion of American industry oligopolistic. When a small group of firms make up an industry, coordinated selling and pricing become not only possible but probable in light of the sellers' recognition of their interdependence. Price cuts are not made because competitors can easily retaliate, and all sellers would gain less revenue if the demand for the product was not sufficiently elastic. Likewise, price increases are followed, and identical prices result from these supposedly independent but concurrent actions of the major sellers. Smaller sellers are not likely to be aggressive price competitors because of their fear of retaliation by the giants. The result of this interdependence is often characterized as noncompetitive price-fixing. And as the cases reveal, present antitrust laws do not afford much opportunity of relief for the public.

Structural economists have criticized the failure to dissolve dominant firms in oligopolistic situations. However, the Department of Justice has been rebuffed by the courts in its effort to secure divestiture of oligopolistic firms. Moreover Congress has not seen fit to modify the Sherman Act to apply to price leadership or oligopolistic industry structure. Consequently, antitrust efforts against horizontal combinations forming joint price and marketing policies have been mixed—lenient penalties have been given in cases of strict illegality for conspiracies and no success has resulted against the problem of oligopoly.

CASE PROBLEMS

1. A shipyard on Staten Island was sold by Bethlehem Steel to a trading company. The deed included a covenant, binding on all subsequent purchasers, that the property would not be used for the construction or repair of ships or harbor craft (except pleasure craft) for 20 years. Sound Ship Company, a corporation in the business of building and repairing barges, wanted to purchase the shipyard from the trading company and sought a waiver of the deed restriction by Bethlehem, which was refused unless Sound Ship paid an additional $250,000. Sound Ship leased property elsewhere and eventually went out of business.

   Bethlehem had remained in the ship construction and repair business in New York harbor at another site but sold the Staten Island yard because of a decline in the shipbuilding industry.

   Sound Ship claims that the deed covenant violates Section 1 of the Sherman Act, entitling Sound Ship to treble damages. What is the result?
2. In order to "protect the manufacturer, laborer, retailer and consumer" from the marketing of copies of original clothing and textile designs, textile and garment manufacturers formed the Fashion Originators' Guild of America. To prevent the practice they characterized as "style piracy," guild members obtained agreements from retailers across the nation under which the retail-

ers were to cooperate with the guild by refusing to stock "copies" of guild members' original designs. In addition, member textile manufacturers agreed to sell fabric only to garment manufacturers dealing with cooperating retailers. Members' prices and production were not regulated or affected, nor did the quality of their products deteriorate. "Copies" consistently sold at lower prices than originals. Garment and textile designs are not protected under copyright or patent law.

Are the guild's practices lawful?

3. The American Medical Association (AMA) restricts a doctor's solicitation of patients by advertising. It also restricts competition among doctors for a job in a hospital or business. Further, the AMA labels unethical the participation of a doctor with nonphysicians such as dentists or psychologists in the ownership or management of a health care organization. Are these restraints on physicians by the AMA in violation of antitrust?

4. Beer wholesalers generally extended credit to their retailers in the Fresno area for periods between 30 and 42 days at no interest, and precise credit terms for various individual retailers varied considerably. The wholesalers then began to restrict the credit they offered, and eventually stopped extending credit at all.

   A group of beer retailers contends that these actions constitute an illegal *per se* horizontal agreement to fix prices. The wholesalers believe that the elimination of credit terms is not price-fixing.

   What is your analysis?

END NOTES

1. Adam Smith, *Wealth of Nations* (London: J. M. Dent and Sons, Ltd., 1970), Vol. 1, Book 1, Chapter 10, Part II, p. 117.
2. See John G. Fuller, *The Gentlemen Conspirators* (New York: Grove Press, 1962).
3. *U.S.* v. *General Electric Co.,* "plaintiff's memorandum in support of a proposed modification to the final judgment entered on October 1, 1962, against each defendant," December 1976.
4. *U.S.* v. *Alton Box Board Co.,* 76 CR 199, N.D. Ill. (1977).
5. *Illinois Brick Co.* v. *Illinois,* 431 U.S. 720 (1977).
6. *American Column and Lumber Co.* v. *U.S.,* 257 U.S. 377, 394–412 (1912).
7. *U.S.* v. *Sealy, Inc.,* 388 U.S. 350 (1976).
8. *U.S.* v. *Topco Associates, Inc.,* 405 U.S. 596 (1972).
9. *California Motor Transport Co.* v. *Trucking Unlimited,* 404 U.S. 508 (1972).

chapter 14

VERTICAL COMBINATIONS

Since the manufacturer, wholesaler, and retailer are not operating at the same level of distribution, they are often not in direct competition with each other. However, the manufacturer and distributor may desire to enter into contractual relations that restrict competition. For example, a manufacturer may desire to impose resale restrictions on the distributors, thereby controlling the distributors' resale price, the territorial area of resale, or the customers to whom the distributor may resell. Beyond these efforts to impose resale policies, the manufacturer may also desire to restrict the distributors' freedom to sell competing brands, known as an exclusive dealing arrangement. These vertical resale restrictions and exclusive dealing arrangements are vertical agreements between manufacturers and distributors and, as such, are different from the horizontal agreements studied in Chapter 13.

As noted in Chapter 13, joint action by sellers or by buyers to eliminate competition among themselves is illegal. However, joint action by a seller and a buyer, a vertical arrangement, may also result in lessening of competition, as was suggested in the analysis of vertical mergers in Chapter 12. Consequently, vertical contractual arrangements often have been challenged as contrary to antitrust goals. Vertical arrangements usually involve vertically imposed price control, consumer or territorial divisions, or exclusive dealings.

REASONS FOR VERTICAL COMBINATIONS

It should first be made clear that no manufacturer desires to allow its retailers to make above-normal profits. Such a position would imply that the manufacturer is willing to pay more than necessary for retailing services. Above-normal profits can be achieved by retailers only if they restrict sales to gain higher prices. Such sales restrictions could reduce the manufacturer's sales and, in effect, take money out of the manufacturer's own pocket. Consequently, when manufacturers attempt to impose vertical restraints on resale, it is because they believe such policies will induce dealer behavior that will make the distribution process more efficient. Additional profits for the retailer resulting from the manufacturer-imposed restrictions are gained at the retail level in exchange for distribution efficiencies or expanded sales efforts which also accrue to the advantage of the manufacturer. The expanded sales through retail promotion may reduce unit costs for the manufacturer. The consumer may share these lower costs through long-term price reductions and obtain more services from the retail outlets.

The most common justification raised for vertical restraints is the optimization of sales effort by dealers through the elimination of "free riding." Selling involves the provision of information and persuasion. It is in the nature of some products that dealers may need to invest money and time in carrying a full line of models for display, instructing sales personnel in the product's features and comparative advantages, and explaining the product and its uses to potential consumers. The dealer, of course, will do these things only if the cost can be recaptured in the price at which the product is sold. Nevertheless, some dealers will perceive the opportunity to avoid these costs and capture the consumer by offering a lower price. Such dealers take a "free ride" on the other dealers' sales efforts. If free riding becomes common, no dealer will find it worthwhile to provide the sales effort that the manufacturer believes is optimal in the distribution of the products.

For the manufacturer to ensure optimal dealer sales effort and avoid free riding, the manufacturer may divide dealer territories or fix minimum resale prices. When the product is of such a nature that it can be sold effectively through one or a few outlets in a given area, the manufacturer may employ the use of a few outlets with restricted market areas. However, where using many outlets in an area is a preferable marketing strategy, the manufacturer may choose to maintain the resale price charged by dealers. Such resale restrictions eliminate competition between the dealers who sell the manufacturer's brand. Alternative brands of other manufacturers continue to compete in the marketplace for the consumers' dollars. Consequently, vertical restraints eliminate *intrabrand* competition, but may enhance *interbrand* competition.

Many economists suggest that the degree to which vertical restraints are exercised should be left to the free determination of the marketplace. However, other economists have asserted that the elimination of intrabrand competition by the use of vertical restraints may be part of a method or means to achieve conspiratorial horizontal restraints by the manufacturer. If manufacturers agree to fix prices, they would have the ability, if vertical restraints were lawful, to impose their price-fixing scheme not only at the manufacturing level but also at the retail level. Consequently, they argue that it is preferable to disallow intrabrand restrictions at the retail level to frustrate manufacturer efforts to extend their conspiratorial price-fixing scheme all the way through the distribution channels. This is especially true, they argue, because the courts have been unwilling to eliminate monopolistic and oligopolistic industry structure at the manufacturing level. Consequently, tacit collusion and follow-the-leader pricing of competitors in oligopolistic industries make it easy for the manufacturer-competitors to achieve parallel behavior without being condemned by antitrust laws. With lawful vertical price-fixing, they can extend their power to the retail level. On the other hand, those in favor of vertical arrangements argue that the conspiracies by manufacturers should be detected at their source. Efficient distribution operations created by vertical restraints should not be outlawed as a technique to frustrate alleged conspiratorial conduct on a horizontal level.

Many opponents of vertical arrangements have argued that in some industries the intrabrand competition eliminated by vertical restraints is significant competition that should not be lost. The elimination of any intrabrand competition in industries where only a few brands exist would have adverse effects on consumer welfare. Even where brands proliferate, it is often asserted that intrabrand competition, for example in the auto industry, is significant. A vertical arrangement for an auto brand (Chevrolet, for instance) would eliminate significant price competition between dealerships selling the same brand. It is argued that such competition is too significant to be eliminated.

It is also argued that the higher profits achieved for retailers under a resale price maintenance program make possible larger expenditures for nonprice forms of competition only in the short run. In the long run, the higher prices and profits may simply invite proliferation of outlets or the entry of minor brands. Excess capacity thus develops at the distributor's level, with rising average costs and falling profits. Thereafter, distributors press the manufacturer to provide wider margins by raising the resale price or by reducing the factory price. Usually, opponents to vertical price-fixing argue, higher prices for consumers would result. They point to the studies that have found certain branded items could be purchased at prices averaging 19 percent lower in those areas where *intrabrand* price competition was possible than in those areas where the manufacturer eliminated such competition.

Finally, opponents argue that the independent judgment of small retailers is destroyed by vertical restraints and America's "free" economy is thereby eroded. Also, resale price maintenance is argued to contain an inflationary bias. All the arguments, both for and against vertical arrangements, have gained some constituency and force in the fashioning of antitrust rules. Since economists have differed in their prescriptions regarding vertical arrangements, lawmakers have also vacillated and developed inconsistent rules.

VERTICAL PRICE RESTRAINTS

Vertical price control involves a manufacturer imposing a fixed price on the wholesaler or retailer as the product travels through the distribution channel to its final consumers. Such vertical control of prices after the manufacturer has passed title to others is often called *resale* price maintenance. This practice is usually limited to a manufacturer that is able to identify its product in the resale market in order to enforce compliance with its resale pricing policy. Therefore, resale price maintenance is usually applied in the sale of brand name products.

Usually, vertical price control is effected by means of a contract between a manufacturer and its distributors. The manufacturer inserts its desired resale price in the sales-purchase agreement, and the buyer promises to abide by the seller's desires. If the buyer fails to adhere to the fixed price, the seller can sue for damages if this type of provision is upheld as lawful.

FAIR TRADE LAWS

The antitrust authorities have historically argued that vertical contracts to fix resale prices are illegal restraints of trade in violation of Section 1 of the Sherman Act. As early as 1911, in *Dr. Miles Medical Co.* v. *John D. Park & Sons,* the Supreme Court held that contractual agreements designed to maintain retail prices after the manufacturer had parted with title to the goods were injurious to the public interest and illegal.[1] However, proponents of the practice of resale price maintenance have made various attempts to persuade Congress to legalize the practice. The impact of the Great Depression and the growth of chain and cut-rate stores solidified the efforts of various groups of small retailers and wholesalers (particularly druggists) for legalization of resale price maintenance, which they designated as "fair trade." The first "fair trade" act was passed by the California Legislature in 1931. In 1933 the California statute was amended so that a single agreement between a manufacturer and a distributor to fix the resale price of a trademarked product was to be applicable to all other distributors in the state even though the other distributors did not sign the price-maintenance contract. This *nonsigners* provision made the resale price control law a potent method for enforcing resale price maintenance on distributors. Any distributor having notice of the contractual arrangement with other dealers and not conforming to the resale prices so fixed was subject to legal suit for violating the price-fixing provision.

Since the initial resale price control laws applied only to intrastate transactions, the trade groups sought legalization of resale price maintenance contracts in the course of interstate commerce. Congress reacted with the passage of the Miller-Tydings Act in 1937 and added a nonsigner provision in the McGuire Act in 1952. These acts legalized resale price agreements in interstate commerce and removed these contracts from the prohibitions of the Sherman Act.

The fair trade movement was successful in obtaining laws in all states except

Missouri, Texas, and Vermont, and the District of Columbia. The movement peaked in the early 1950s with 1,600 manufacturers enforcing fair trade agreements.[2] However, legal setbacks at the state level and the growing pressures of competition slowly eroded the successes of the fair trade movement.

Besides the states that never passed the fair trade laws, several additional states, through their courts, ruled the fair trade statute legally unenforceable. Over a dozen other states refused to enforce the nonsignor provisions which were declared to be an unconstitutional deprivation of due process of law for the nonsignors. Consequently, retailers in more than 20 states were able to ignore the manufacturers' prescribed minimum prices. Moreover, enterprising businesspeople opened mail order houses in nonfair trade areas and shipped branded merchandise at reduced prices to customers in the fair trade states. Federal courts had ruled that the states could not enjoin the shipment of interstate merchandise into their area.[3] Moreover, in the fair trade states, the more aggressive retailers chose to ignore fair trade laws and forced the manufacturers to decide whether to initiate legal proceedings to enforce compliance and alienate an important, high-volume retailer or to ignore the retailers' actions. With some large retailers ignoring the price minimum and with the out-of-state mail order houses undercutting the price minimum, many manufacturers abandoned the retail price maintenance program completely. Others introduced new product lines to be sold at uncontrolled retail prices in competition with their fair traded items. By 1974, the value of fair traded items fell from the estimated 10 percent of retail sales in 1959 to 4 percent.[4] In 1975, so few supported the fair trade laws that 15 states repealed their statutes and Congress repealed the Miller-Tydings and McGuire Acts.[5] The abolition of the fair trade laws did not seem to have a perceptible effect because the forces of competition had already eroded the effects of the fair trade laws.

REFUSALS TO DEAL

As previously mentioned, the Supreme Court held in the 1911 *Dr. Miles* case that contracts designed to maintain resale prices after the manufacturer had parted with title to the goods were illegal. However, in 1919 the Supreme Court allowed resale price maintenance in *U.S.* v. *Colgate & Co.*, 250 U.S. 300 (1919). Colgate did not have contractual agreements with its dealers to maintain the resale price. Instead, it announced that it would refuse to deal with those distributors that did not cooperate with the announced resale price expected by Colgate. The Supreme Court held that Colgate could not be charged with an *agreement* to vertically fix prices. The Colgate decision was distinguished from previous cases which were based on contracts between the manufacturer and the dealer. Thus, although the results (resale price maintenance) were the same in *Dr. Miles* and *Colgate,* the techniques used to achieve those results were different. Consequently, vertical price-fixing was both legal and illegal, depending on the technique employed.

The following case represents an effort by the Supreme Court to cut back the utilization of the Colgate doctrine to achieve resale price maintenance.

United States v. Parke, Davis & Co.
363 U.S. 29 (1960)
Supreme Court of the United States

Justice Brennan, Jr.

The Government . . . [alleged] that Parke Davis conspired and combined, in violation of Section 1 of the [Sherman] Act, with retail and wholesale druggists . . . to maintain the wholesale and retail prices of Parke Davis pharmaceutical products. . . .

Parke Davis makes some 600 pharmaceutical products which it markets nationally through drug wholesalers and drug retailers. The retailers buy these products from the drug wholesalers or make large quantity purchases directly from Parke Davis. Sometime before 1956 Parke Davis announced a resale price maintenance policy in its wholesalers' and retailers' catalogues. . . .

There are some 260 drugstores in Washington D.C., and some 100 in Richmond, Virginia. . . . There are five drug wholesalers handling Parke Davis products in the locality who do business with the drug retailers. The wholesalers observed the resale prices suggested by Parke Davis. However, during the spring and early summer of 1956, drug retailers in the two cities advertised and sold several Parke Davis vitamin products at prices substantially below the suggested minimum retail prices. . . . The Baltimore office manager of Parke Davis in charge of the sales district which included the two cities sought advice from his head office on how to handle this situation. The Parke Davis attorney advised that the company could legally "enforce an adopted policy arrived at unilaterally" to sell only to customers who observed the suggested minimum resale prices. He further advised that this meant that "we can lawfully say, 'we will sell you only so long as you observe such minimum retail prices' but cannot say 'we will sell you only if you agree to observe such minimum retail prices,' since . . . agreements as to resale price maintenance are invalid." Thereafter in July the branch manager put into effect a program for promoting observance of the suggested minimum retail prices by the retailers involved. The program contemplated the participation of the five drug wholesalers. In order to insure that retailers who did not comply would be cut off from sources of supply, representatives of Parke Davis visited the wholesalers and told them, in effect, that not only would Parke Davis refuse to sell to wholesalers who did not adhere to the policy announced in its catalogue, but also that it would refuse to sell to wholesalers who sold Parke Davis products who did not observe the suggested minimum retail prices. Each wholesaler was interviewed individually but each was informed that his competitors were also being apprised of this. The wholesalers without exception indicated a willingness to go along.

Representatives called contemporaneously upon the retailers involved, individually, and told each that if he did not observe the suggested minimum retail prices, Parke Davis would refuse to deal with him, and that furthermore he would be unable to purchase any Parke Davis products from the wholesalers. Each of the retailers was also told that his competitors were being similarly informed.

Several retailers refused to give any assurances of compliance and continued after the July interviews to advertise and sell Parke Davis products at prices below the suggested minimum retail prices. Their names were furnished by Parke Davis to the wholesalers. Thereafter, Parke Davis refused to fill direct orders from such retailers and the wholesalers likewise refused to fill their orders. This ban was not limited to the Parke Davis products being sold below the suggested minimum prices but included all the company's products, even those necessary to fill prescriptions. . . .

* * *

The program upon which Parke Davis embarked to promote general compliance with its suggested resale prices plainly exceeded the limitations of the *Colgate* doctrine and . . . effected arrangements which violated the Sherman Act. Parke Davis did not content itself with announcing its policy regarding retail prices and following this with a simple refusal to have business relations with any retailers who disregarded that policy. Instead, Parke Davis used the refusal to deal with the wholesalers in order to elicit their willingness to deny Parke Davis products to retailers and thereby help gain the retailers' adherence to its suggeted minimum retail prices. The retailers who disregarded the price policy were promptly cut off when Parke Davis supplied the wholesalers with their names. . . . In thus involving the wholesalers to stop the flow of Parke Davis products to the retailers, thereby inducing retailers' adherence to its suggested retail prices, Parke Davis created a combination with the retailers and the wholesalers to maintain retail prices and violated the Sherman Act. Although Parke Davis' orginally announced wholesalers' policy would not under *Colgate* have violated the Sherman Act if its action thereunder was the simple refusal without more to deal with wholesalers who did not observe the wholesalers' Net Price Selling Schedule, that entire policy was tainted with the "vice of . . . illegality," when Parke Davis used it as the vehicle to gain the wholesalers' participation in the program to effectuate the retailers' adherence to the suggested retail prices. . . .

Questions

1. What was the advice of the Parke Davis attorney? Was it correct in light of the Colgate doctrine?
2. What did Parke Davis do that "went beyond" a mere refusal to deal and transformed their unilateral behavior into bilateral or group practice?
3. Considering the *Parke Davis* decision, is it possible to utilize the Colgate doctrine to achieve resale price maintenance when the manufacturer sells through wholesalers?

CONSIGNMENTS

A manufacturer may send goods to a dealer for sale to the public with the understanding that the manufacturer is to remain the owner of the goods and the dealer is to act as the manufacturer's agent in making the sale. The device of entrusting another person with the possession of property for the purpose of sale is commonly referred to as *selling on consignment.* Since the goods are still the property of the manufacturer, may the manufacturer set the dealer's resale price of the items? In other words, may selling on consignment provide an alternative means of achieving resale price maintenance? The Supreme Court has said that the use of a consignment device in connection with a short-term lease to coerce administered resale prices in a vast distribution system is illegal under the antitrust laws.[6] Hence, the manufacturer's use of the consignment device to maintain resale prices will not necessarily protect the consignor from a charge of violation of Section 1.

CRIMINAL CHARGES AND COSTS

It should be noted that the Justice Department has obtained criminal indictments against business firms that conspire to maintain resale prices. Historically, utilization of criminal proceedings for price-fixing has been restricted generally to horizontal price-fixing. But a recent grand jury indictment against a manufacturer for arranging price-fixing among the parties of a vertical supply chain serves as a stark reminder that vertical price-fixing is perceived by some (the Carter Administration) to be just as obnoxious to society as horizontal price-fixing.[7] However, the Reagan Administration officials have announced that they do not regard vertical price-fixing as obnoxious. Consequently, antitrust enforcement by the Justice Department against vertical price maintenance during Reagan's term of office has been relaxed.

The cost of vertical price-fixing can be substantial. The aforementioned distributor who was indicted for vertical price-fixing also has been sued for violation of the Sherman Act by the attorney general in Massachusetts.[8] Bringing the action on behalf of the state as *parens patriae* for all natural persons residing in Massachusetts, the attorney general charged that the price fixing conspiracy resulted in higher prices in Massachusetts, which entitled the attorney general to seek treble damages on behalf of all natural persons residing within Massachusetts. In addition, the attorney general is seeking an injunction to stop the vertical price-fixing practices as well as the cost of the suit, which includes a reasonable attorney's fee. This state action, and others of the same kind, illustrate the critical dangers associated with agreements to vertically fix prices. For example, it is reported that attorney generals in six states have won more than $12 million in settlements from Levi Strauss & Co. since its settlement with the Federal Trade Commission on charges that it fixed the resale price of its jeans.[9]

VERTICAL NONPRICE RESTRAINTS

Vertical arrangements between a seller and a customer can give rise to the imposition of *customer limitations* on resale. This restraint involves a manufacturer granting a distributor the right to sell its product and binding the retailer not to resell to particular customers, such as discount houses, public agencies, or industrial users. The manufacturer may want to reserve these accounts for itself without competition from its distributors.

Vertical arrangements also can be used by the seller to impose *territorial limitations* on sales made by its customers. This restraint involves a manufacturer giving a distributor exclusive sales rights in a particular area on the distributor's promise not to sell in another dealer's territory. This arrangement restricts the final purchaser to buying the brand from the distributor that serves its particular territory. This arrangement has various names, such as exclusive agency, exclusive selling, closed territory, or territorial safety.

The courts have permitted manufacturers to contractually make a buyer primarily responsible for adequately serving a given territorial area, even though the buyer thereby may not have the time and resources to trade elsewhere outside the assigned area. The manufacturer thereby achieves some informal but practical territorial division. The courts also allow the seller to insist on delivery to a designated location only and to prohibit "branching" by the dealer. This "location" clause also provides a form of territorial division of the market at the retail level. Either a "primary responsibility" clause or a "location" clause in sales contracts can provide sellers with a semblance of territorial division which is normally lawful because neither clause involves a complete restriction on the buyer from making sales elsewhere. Only practical constraints, brought about by the primary responsibility or location clauses, restrict the buyer to the assigned area or to the store location.

Some manufacturers, however, attempt to impose more complete territorial and customer resale restraints on their buyers. In *U.S.* v. *Schwinn,* 388 U.S. 365 (1967), the Supreme Court ruled that customer and territorial restrictions on buyers' resale policies were *per se* unreasonable. Strangely, the Court ruled that Schwinn's consignment sales, which imposed the same customer and territorial restraints, were to be tested by the rule of reason. On application of the reasonableness test in the bicycle market, the Court determined that Schwinn's use of customer and territorial restrictions in consignment sales were lawful because interbrand competition was sufficiently strong and the intrabrand restriction imposed by Schwinn was insignificant in the bicycle market. Though the customer and territorial restrictions imposed on the outright sales were the same as those imposed in the consignment sales in terms of market effect, the Court ruled the restraints in the outright sales to be unreasonable *per se* without any analysis of the market effect. This dichotomy in approach which determines legality by the contractual method of sale was highly criticized in the legal and economic literature. Lower courts increasingly displayed ingenuity in finding interpretive ways around the *Schwinn* rule for *per se* illegality of vertical restraints in *sale* situations. Finally, the Supreme Court decided to reconsider Schwinn's strict rule of sale illegality which ignored market realities.

Continental T.V., Inc. v. GTE Sylvania, Inc.
433 U.S. 36 (1977)
Supreme Court of the United States

[In an attempt to improve its market position by attracting more aggressive and competent retailers, Sylvania limited the number of retail franchises granted for any given area and required each franchisee to sell its products only from the location at which it was franchised. Petitioner, one of Sylvania's franchised retailers, claimed that Sylvania had violated Section 1 of the Sherman Act by entering into and enforcing franchise agreements that prohibited the sale of Sylvania's products other than from specified locations.]

Justice Powell

Both Schwinn and Sylvania sought to reduce but not to eliminate competition among their respective retailers through the adoption of a franchise system. . . . [T]he Schwinn franchise plan included a location restriction similar to the one challenged here. These restrictions allowed Schwinn and Sylvania to regulate the amount of competition among their retailers by preventing a franchise from selling franchised products from outlets other than the one covered by the franchise agreement. To exactly the same end, the Schwinn franchise plan included a companion restriction, apparently not found in the Sylvania plan, that prohibited franchised retailers from selling Schwinn products to nonfranchised retailers. In *Schwinn* the Court expressly held that this restriction was impermissible under the broad principle stated there. In intent and competitive impact, the retail customer restriction in *Schwinn* is indistinguishable from the location restriction in the present case. In both cases the restrictions limited the freedom of the retailer to dispose of the franchised products as he desired. The fact that one restriction was addressed to territory and the other to customers is irrelevant to functional antitrust analysis, and indeed, to the language and broad thrust of the opinion in *Schwinn*.

* * *

In essence, the issue before us is whether *Schwinn's per se* rule can be justified. . . .

The market impact of vertical restrictions is complex because of their potential for a simultaneous reduction of intrabrand competition and stimulation of interbrand competition. . . .

Vertical restrictions reduce intrabrand competition by limiting the number of sellers of a particular product competing for the business of a given group of buyers. Location restrictions have this effect because of practical constraints on the effective marketing area of retail outlets. Although intrabrand competition may be reduced, the ability of retailers to exploit the resulting market may be limited both by the ability of consumers to travel to other franchised locations and, perhaps more importantly, to purchase the competing products of other manufacturers. . . .

Vertical restrictions promote interbrand competition by allowing the manufacturer to achieve certain efficiencies in the distribution of his products. These "redeeming virtues" are implicit in every decision sustaining vertical restrictions under the rule of reason. Economists have identified a number of ways in which manufacturers can use such restrictions to compete more effectively against other manufacturers. For example, new manufacturers and manufacturers entering new markets can use the restrictions in order to induce competent and aggressive retailers to make the kind of investment of capital and labor that is often required in the distribution of products unknown to the consumer. Established manufacturers can use them to induce retailers to engage in promotional activities or to provide service and repair facilities necessary to the efficient marketing of their products. Service and repair are vital for many products, such as automobiles and major household appliances. The availability and quality of such services affect a manufacturer's good will and the competitiveness of his product. Because of market imperfections such as the so-called "free rider" effect, these services might not be provided by retailers in a purely competitive situation, despite the fact that each retailer's benefit would be greater if all provided the services than if none did. . . .

The question remains whether the *per se* rule stated in *Schwinn* should be . . . abandoned in favor of a return to the rule of reason. . . .

. . . Such restrictions, in varying forms, are widely used in our free market economy. As indicated above, there is substantial scholarly and judicial authority supporting their economic utility. There is relatively little authority to the contrary. Certainly, there has been no showing in this case, either generally or with respect to Sylvania's agreements, that vertical restrictions have a "pernicious effect on competition" or that they "lack . . . any redeeming virtue." Accordingly, we conclude that the *per se* rule stated in *Schwinn* must be overruled. . . .

In sum, we conclude that the appropriate decision is to return to the rule of reason that governed vertical restrictions prior to *Schwinn*.

Questions

1. When is a *per se* unreasonable rule appropriate?
2. Why was Schwinn's *per se* rule against resale restraints considered inappropriate?
3. What business reasons or pro-competitive effects did the court identify that may result from vertical resale restrictions?
4. The Court in a footnote in *Continental T.V.* provided this analysis in upholding Sylvania's vertical restriction under the rule of reason:

   Interbrand competition is the competition among the manufacturers of the same generic product—television sets in this case—and is the primary concern of antitrust law. The extreme example of a deficiency of interbrand competition is monopoly, where there is only one manufacturer. In contrast, intrabrand competiton is the competition between the distributors—wholesale or retail—of the product of a particular manufacturer.

The degree of intrabrand competition is wholly independent of the level of interbrand competition confronting the manufacturer. Thus, there may be fierce intrabrand competition among the distributors of a product produced by a firm in a highly competitive industry. But when interbrand competition exists, as it does among television manufacturers, it provides a significant check on the exploitation of intrabrand market power because of the ability of consumers to substitute a different brand of the same product.

Does this suggest the circumstances under which the courts would prohibit an intrabrand restraint?

EXCLUSIVE SUPPLY ARRANGEMENT

Supply contracts often contain a clause requiring the buyer not to handle the products of a competitive supplier. The buyer is required by the exclusive supply contract to buy all of its supplies of the product from the contractually designated supplier. This vertical arrangement is termed an exclusive supply or an exclusive dealing contract. Another form of exclusive supply contract is a requirements contract which commits a buyer to purchase from the seller all (or substantially all) of its requirements of a product and, thus, by *implication* to promise not to buy elsewhere. Consequently, the buyer's commitment not to buy elsewhere may be embodied in a clause of the exclusive supply contract itself or it may be implied, as in a requirements contract. Nevertheless, the effect of the various types of contracts is the same.

The commercial purpose of exclusive dealing contracts is to secure the undivided attention of the distributor in promoting the product of the manufacturer to the consumer. Distributors enter into exclusive dealing contracts to secure a dependable source of supply or to obtain assistance from the manufacturer in sales promotion.

Exclusive supply contracts can also operate to lessen competition through the *exclusion* of rival suppliers. If the exclusive supply contract is for a long duration, competing suppliers are denied access to the buyer for a long period of time. The rival suppliers lose the buyer as an outlet for their products. Exclusive dealing can be especially detrimental to small suppliers who lack the large volume of sales required for a dealer to maintain its business on an exclusive basis without selling competitive brands. Also, if all or most of an industry is utilizing exclusive dealing arrangements, entry of new firms at the manufacturing level is impossible without the new entrant's creation of its own distribution outlets. This fact, of course, raises the cost of entry and reduces the potential of new competitors.

CLAYTON ACT, SECTION 3

Congressional concern with the potential anticompetitive effects of exclusive dealing arrangements led to the enactment of a provision in the Clayton Act which limits its practice. Section 3 of the Clayton Act makes it illegal for any person "to lease or make a sale . . . of . . . commodities, whether patented or unpatented, . . . on the condition, agreement or understanding that the lessee or purchaser thereof shall not use or deal in the . . . commodities of a competitor . . . of the lessor or seller, where the effect of such . . . [arrangement] may be to substantially lessen competition or tend to create monopoly in any line of commerce." Consequently, whether any particular exclusive dealing agreement is prohibited by Section 3 depends in each case on the determination of the *probable effect* of the agreement in substantially lessening competition in the relevant product market. Early Supreme Court cases determining the *substantiality* of the "probable effect" have been characterized as follows:

> Where the alleged violator dominated or was a leader in the industry, proof of such fact was . . . determined to be a sufficient predicate from which to conclude that the use of exclusive-dealing contracts was violative of Section 3 and other factors appeared to have been largely ignored. [Later] . . . the Supreme Court extended the rule to business organizations enjoying a powerful, though clearly not dominant, position in the trade and doing a substantial share of the industry's business by means of these contractual provisions and [the Court] tacitly approved the trial court's refusal to consider other economic effects or merits of the system employed. *Dictograph Products* v. *FTC,* 217 F. 2d 812 (1954).

The Supreme Court's utilization of such tests as "dominance of the seller" or a "powerful position" which included a "substantial share of the industry's business" without inquiry into the economic effects or merits of the exclusive dealing system amounts to an almost *per se* test of illegality by a firm that has a substantial share of the market. This test of substantiality was so strict that almost all exclusive dealings were illegal. This test became known as the "quantitative substantiality" test because the Court emphasized the dollar volume of commerce tied-up in the exclusive-dealing contracts. The court said that if a "not insubstantial amount of commerce was affected," then the exclusive-dealing contracts were illegal. The Court made no further inquiry concerning economic effects and made no market analysis of the impact of the exclusive-dealing arrangements. This quantitative substantiality test and its almost *per se* determination of illegality received mixed reviews in the legal and economic literature. The Supreme Court retreated from this strict test in the following case and approved a more lenient test, which is generally referred to as "qualitative substantiality."

Tampa Electric Co. v. Nashville Co.
365 U.S. 320 (1960)
Supreme Court of the United States

[Tampa Electric Co., a public utility in Florida, contracted with Nashville Coal Company for its expected coal requirements for two new electrical generating units to be constructed. The agreement required Tampa Electric to purchase all its requirements of coal for a period of twenty years. Before the first shipment of coal was to be delivered, Nashville Coal Company advised Tampa Electric that the contract was illegal under the anti-trust laws and that no coal would be delivered. Tampa Electric purchased its coal requirements elsewhere and sued Nashville Coal for breach of contract.]

Justice Clark

. . . [The District Court and the Court of Appeals] . . . admitted that the contract "does not expressly contain the 'condition' " that Tampa Electric would not use or deal in the coal of [defendant's] competitors. Nonetheless, they reasoned, the "total requirements" provision had the same practical effect, for it prevented Tampa Electric for a period of 20 years from buying coal from any other source. . . . [B]oth courts found that the "line of commerce" on which the restraint was to be tested was coal. . . . Both courts compared the estimated coal tonnage as to which the contract pre-empted competition for 20 years, namely, 1,000,000 tons a year by 1961, with the previous annual consumption of peninsular Florida, 700,000 tons. Emphasizing that fact as well as the contract value of the coal covered by the 20-year term, i.e., $128,000,000, they held that such volume was not "insignificant or insubstantial" and that the effect of the contract would "be to substantially lessen competition," in violation of the [Clayton] Act. Both courts were of the opinion that in view of the executory nature of the contract, judicial enforcement of any portion of it could not be granted without directing a violation of the Act itself, and enforcement was, therefore, denied.

Application of Section 3 of the Clayton Act

* * *

In practical application, even though a contract is found to be an exclusive-dealing arrangement, it does not violate the section unless the court believes it probable that performance of the contract will foreclose competition in a substantial share of the line of commerce affected. Following the guidelines of earlier decisions, certain considerations must be taken. *First,* the line of commerce, i.e., the type of goods, wares, or merchandise, etc., involved must be determined, where it is in controversy on the basis of the facts peculiar to the case. *Second,* the area of effective competition in the known line of commerce must be chartered by careful selection of the market area in which the seller operates, and to which the purchaser can practicably turn for supplies. In short, the threatened foreclosure of competition must be in relation to the market affected. . . .

Third, and last, the competition foreclosed by the contract must be found to constitute a substantial share of the relevant market. That is to say, the opportunities for other traders to enter into or remain in that market must be significantly limited. . . .

To determine substantiality in a given case, it is necessary to weigh the probable effect of the contract on the relevant area of effective competition, taking into account the relevant strength of the parties, the proportionate volume of commerce involved in relation to the total volume of commerce in the relevant market area, and the probable immediate and future effects which pre-emption of that share of the market might have on effective competition therein. It follows that a mere showing that the contract itself involves a substantial number of dollars is ordinarily of little consequence.

The Application of Section 3 Here

In applying these considerations to the facts of the case before us, it appears that both the Court of Appeals and the District Court have not given the required effect to a controlling factor in the case—the relevant competitive market area. This omission, by itself, requires reversal, for, as we have pointed out, the relevant market is the prime factor in relation to which the ultimate question, whether the contract forecloses competition in a substantial share of the line of commerce involved, must be declared. . . .

Relevant Market of Effective Competition

* * *

We are persuaded that on the record in this case, neither peninsular Florida, nor the entire State of Florida, nor Florida and Georgia combined constituted the relevant market of effective competition. . . . By far the bulk of the overwhelming tonnage marketed from the same producing area as serves Tampa is sold outside of Georgia and Florida, and the producers were "eager" to sell more coal in those States. While the relevant competitive market is not ordinarily susceptible to a "metes and bounds" definition, . . . it is of course the area in which [defendant] and the other 700 producers effectively compete.

The record shows that, like the [defendant], they sold bituminous coal "suitable for [Tampa's] requirements," mined in parts of Pennsylvania, Virginia, West Virginia, Kentucky, Tennessee, Alabama, Ohio and Illinois. We take notice of the fact that the approximate total bituminous coal product in the year 1954 from the districts in which these 700 producers are located was 359,289,000 tons, of which some 290,567,000 tons were sold on the open market. Of the latter amount, some 78,716,000 tons were sold to electric utilities. . . . From these statistics it clearly appears that the proportionate volume of the total relevant coal product as to which the challenged contract pre-empted competition, less than 1%, is, conservatively speaking, quite insubstantial. A more accurate figure, even assuming pre-emption to the extent of the maximum anticipated total requirements, 2,250,000 tons a year, would be .77%.

Effect on Competition in the Relevant Market

It may well be that in the context of antitrust legislation protracted requirements contracts are suspect, but they have not been declared illegal *per se*. . . . It is urged that the present contract pre-empts competition to the extent of purchases worth perhaps $128,000,000, and that this "is, of course, not insignificant or insubstantial." While $128,000,000 is a considerable sum of money, even in these days, the dollar volume, by itself, is not the test, as we have already pointed out.

The remaining determination, therefore, is whether the pre-emption of competition to the extent of the tonnage involved tends to substantially foreclose competition in the relevant coal market. We think not. That market sees an annual trade in excess of 250,000,000 tons of coal and over a billion dollars—multiplied by 20 years it runs into astronomical figures. There is here neither a seller with a dominant position in the market as in *Standard Fashions;* nor myriad outlets with substantial sales volume, coupled with an industrywide practice of relying upon exclusive contracts, as in *Standard Oil.* . . .

On the contrary, we seem to have only that type of contract which "may well be of economic advantage to buyers as well as to sellers." *Standard Oil Co.* v. *United States.* In the case of the buyer it "may assure supply," while on the part of the seller it "may make possible the substantial reduction of selling expenses, give protection against price fluctuations, and . . . offer the possibility of a predictable market." The 20-year period of the contract is singled out as the principal vice, but at least in the case of public utilities the assurance of a steady and ample supply of fuel is necessary in the public interest. In weighing the various factors, we have decided that in the competitive bituminous coal marketing area involved here, the contract sued upon does not tend to foreclose a substantial volume of competition.

Questions

1. How did the lower courts define the competitive geographical market? Did the Supreme Court agree?
2. How did the lower courts determine the "substantiality" of the probable anticompetitive effect? What is the proper test to determine "substantiality" of the probable anticompetitive effect?

REFUSAL TO SELL TO NONEXCLUSIVE DEALERS

Many large suppliers achieve exclusive dealing arrangements without contractual provisions prohibiting the dealer from buying elsewhere. Instead, the manufacturers, relying on the Colgate doctrine, refuse to sell to dealers that will not handle only their products. Any dealers that stock competing lines of merchandise would have their supplies cut off by these manufacturers.

Most firms, in dropping the contractual provisions for exclusive dealing to avoid Section 3 of the Clayton Act, have inserted an "adequate representation" clause that requires the dealer to adequately represent the manufacturer's interest in an assigned area. Any number of reasons, such as failure to promote sales or to secure a certain volume of sales, may provide grounds for the manufacturer to assert that the dealer is not adequately representing the manufacturer, and therefore cancel their trading relationship. Often, manufacturers argue that the handling of products provided by rival suppliers precludes the dealer from adequately representing the manufacturer's interest. Consequently, the "adequate representation" clause in combination with the *Colgate* right of refusing to deal provides an alternative method of securing an effective exclusive dealing arrangement.

FRANCHISES

The typical franchise contract involves a franchisor who grants the franchisee the right to operate a busines in a certain manner in a designated area and to use the franchisor's trademark or trade name in the operation. Because the franchisor normally has substantially more bargaining power than the franchisee, the franchise agreements contain provisions that restrict the franchisee's freedoms. Franchisees often agree not to compete with other franchised dealers in another territory. Franchisees also often agree not to sell competitors' brands from the franchised outlet. Franchise agreements sometimes require the franchisee to purchase supplies and services from the franchisor. Often the restrictions imposed in franchise contracts violate the antitrust laws. However, Congress has also enacted the federal trademark statute, the Lanham Act. This act requires franchisors to exercise control over the use of their trademark so as not to misrepresent the source of trademarked goods. Consequently, franchisors must exercise stringent quality control to maintain consistency in all franchised outlets to protect the product represented by the trademark. Quality variance would negatively affect the public's attitude toward the mark in an economic sense and conflict with the policies of the Lanham Act. Consequently, some of the restrictions placed on franchisees may be motivated by the franchisor's desire to maintain quality control as required by the Lanham Act.

TIE-IN ARRANGEMENTS

A tie-in agreement is a refusal by a seller to sell or lease one product or service unless another product or service is also bought or leased. In effect, the distributor forces its buyers to take a less-desirable product or service (the tied product) in order to obtain a more wanted item (the tying product). The courts have said that ordinarily there can be hardly any reason for tying two goods together except to use one's power over the tying product or service to gain a market for the tied product. Tie-in agreements limit competition in the market for the tied product in that rival sellers in the tied product must overcome their competitor's economic power over the tying product to gain access to the available buyers of tied products. Because of this anticompetitive effect, tie-in arrangements receive close scrutiny by the courts, which find the tie-in illegal if the firm (1) has sufficient economic power in the tying product (2) to restrict competition in the tied product market. For example, it is normally unreasonable to require that a buyer finance his or her purchase through the seller or to require that lessees of equipment use the lessor's supplies in the equipment. The courts generally give tie-ins an almost *per se* status of illegality unless the seller can produce an exceptional justification.

The tie-in may be justified if the seller can prove that the new technology involved in a sensitive piece of equipment functions properly only if the seller's repair parts and service are used. If this is true, and only as long as this is true, the tie-in for repair parts and service would not be unreasonable. Besides this new technology justification, which was first expressed in *Jerrold Electronics,*[10] and the quality control justification made by the Lanham Act, other tie-ins have received a rather inhospitable reception by the courts.

Principe v. McDonald's Corp.

631 F. 2d 303 (1980)
U.S. Court of Appeals (4th Cir.)

This appeal presents the question of whether a fast food franchise that requires its licensees to operate their franchises in premises leased from the franchisor is guilty of an illegal tying arrangement in violation of Section 1 of the Sherman Act. . . .

I

The . . . Principes . . . are franchisees of McDonald's hamburger restaurant[s] in Hopewell, Virginia . . . [and] in Colonial Heights. . . .

They filed this action . . . alleging . . . McDonald's violated federal antitrust laws by tying store leases and $15,000 security deposit notes to the franchise rights at the Hopewell and Colonial Heights stores. . . .

II

At the time this suit was filed, McDonald's consisted of at least four separate corporate entities. McDonald's Systems, Inc. controlled franchise rights and licensed franchisees to sell hamburgers under the McDonald's name. Franchise Realty Interstate Corporation (Franchise Realty) acquires real estate, either by purchasing or long term lease, builds McDonald's hamburger restaurants, and leases them either to franchisees or to a third corporation, McOpCo. McOpCo, which is not a party to this suit, operates about one-fourth of the McDonald's restaurants in the United States as company stores. Straddling this triad is McDonald's Corporation, the parent, who owns all the stock of the other defendants.

McDonald's is not primarily a fast food retailer. While it does operate over a thousand stores itself, the vast majority of the stores in its system are operated by franchisees. Nor does McDonald's sell equipment or supplies to its licensees. Instead its primary business is developing and collecting royalties from limited menu fast food restaurants operated by independent business people.

McDonald's develops new restaurants according to master plans . . . and . . . uses demographic data generated by the most recent census and its own research in evaluating potential sites. . . .

* * *

After the specifics of each proposed new restaurant are approved, McDonald's decides whether the store will be company operated or franchised.

If the decision is to franchise the store, McDonald's begins the process of locating a franchisee. . . .

Meanwhile, Franchise Realty acquires the land, either by purchase or long term lease and constructs the store. Acquisition and development costs averaged over $450,000 per store in 1978. All McDonald restaurants bear the same distinctive features with a few exceptions due to architectural restrictions: the golden arches motif, the brick and glass contruction and the distinctive roofline. According to the defendants, these features identify the stores as a McDonald's even where zoning restrictions preclude other advertising or signs.

As constructed, McDonald's restaurants are finished shells; they contain no kitchen or dining room equipment. Furnishing store equipment is the responsibility of the operator, whether a franchisee or McOpCo. McDonald's does provide specifications such equipment must meet, but does not sell the equipment itself.

Having acquired the land, begun construction of the store, and selected an operator, McDonald's enters into two contracts with the franchisee. Under the first, the franchise agreement, McDonald's grants the franchisee the rights to use McDonald's food preparation system and to sell food products under the McDonald's name. The franchisee pays a $12,500 franchise fee and agrees to remit three percent of his gross sales as a royalty in return. Under the second contract, the lease, McDonald's grants the franchisee the right to use the particular store premises to which his franchise pertains. In return, the franchisee pays a $15,000 refundable security deposit (as evidence of which he receives a twenty year non-negotiable non-interest bearing note) and agrees to pay eight and one half percent of his gross sales as rent. These payments under the franchise and lease agreements are McDonald's only sources of income from its franchised restaurants. The franchisee also assumes responsibility under the lease for building maintenance, improvements, property taxes and other costs associated with the premises. Both the franchise agreement and the lease generally have twenty year durations, both provide that termination of one terminates the other, and neither is available separately.

III

The Principes argue McDonald's is selling not one but three distinct products, the franchise, the lease, and the security deposit note. The alleged antitrust violation stems from the fact that a prospective franchisee must buy all three in order to obtain the franchise.

As evidence that this is an illegal tying arrangement, the Principes point to the unfavorable terms on which the franchisees are required to lease their stores. Not only are franchisees denied the opportunity to build equity and depreciate their property, but they must maintain the building, pay for improvements and taxes, and remit 8.5 percent of their gross sales as rents. In 1978 the gross sales of the Hopewell store generated about $52,000 in rent. That figure nearly equalled Franchise Realty's original cost for the site and corresponds to more than a fourth of the original cost of the entire Hopewell restaurant complex. At that rate of return, the Principes argue, Franchise Realty will have recouped its entire investment in four years and the remainder of the lease payments will be pure profit. The Principes contend that the fact the store rents are so high proves that McDonald's cannot sell the leaseholds on their own merits.

Nor has McDonald's shown any need to forbid its licensees to own their own stores, the Principes say. Appellants contend that McDonald's is the only fast food franchisor that requires its licensees not only to pay royalties but to lease their own stores. McDonald's could maintain its desired level of uniformity by requiring franchisees to locate and construct stores according to company specifications. The company could even provide planning and design assistance as it apparently does in connection with food purchasing and restaurant management. The Principes argue McDonald's has not shown that the success of its business or the integrity of its trademarks depends on company ownership of all store premises.

A separate tied product is the note that evidences the lessee's $15,000 security deposit, according to the appellants. The Principes argue the security deposit really is a mandatory contribution to McDonald's working capital, not security against damage to the store or breach of the lease contract. By tying the purchase of these $15,000 twenty year non-negotiable non-interest bearing notes to that of the franchise, McDonald's allegedly has generated a capital fund that totalled over $45 million in 1978. It is argued that no one would purchase such notes on their own merits. The Principes assert that only by requiring franchisees to purchase the notes as a condition of obtaining a franchise has McDonald's been able to sell them at all.

McDonald's responds that it is not in the business of licensing use of its name, improving real estate for lease, or selling long term notes. Its only business is developing a system of hamburger restaurants and collecting royalties from their sales. The allegedly tied products are but parts of the overall bundle of franchise benefits and obligations. According to McDonald's, the appellants are asking the court to invalidate the way McDonald's does business and to require it to adopt the licensing procedures of its less successful competitors. Federal antitrust laws do not compel such a result, McDonald's contends.

* * *

IV

As support for their position, the Principes rely primarily on the decision of the Ninth Circuit in *Siegel* v. *Chicken Delight, Inc.*, one of the first cases to address the problem of franchise tie-ins. Chicken Delight was what McDonald's characterizes as a "rent a name" franchisor: it licensed franchisees to sell chicken under the Chicken Delight name but did not own store premises or fixtures. The company did not even charge franchise fees or royalties. Instead, it required its franchisees to purchase a specified number of cookers and fryers and to purchase certain packaging supplies and mixes exclusively from Chicken Delight. These supplies were priced higher than comparable goods of competing sellers. A class composed of franchisees challenged the tying arrangements as a violation of the Sherman Act. The district court held for the franchisees and Chicken Delight appealed.

In addressing Chicken Delight's argument that the allegedly tied products all were essential components of the franchise system, the Ninth Circuit looked to the "function of the aggregation." Viewing the essence of a Chicken Delight franchise as the franchisor's trademark, the court sought to determine whether requiring franchisees to purchase common supplies from Chicken Delight was necessary to ensure that their operations lived up to the quality standards the trademark represented. Judged by this standard, the aggregation was found to consist of separate products:

> This being so, it is apparent that the goodwill of the Chicken Delight trademark does not attach to the multitude of separate articles used in the operation of the licensed system or in the production of its end product. It is not what is used, but how it is used and what results that have given the system and its end product their entitlement to trademark protection. It is to the system and the end product that the public looks with the confidence that established goodwill has created.

In the court's view, Chicken Delight had attempted to "extend trademark protection to common articles (which the public does not and has no reason to connect with the trade-mark)," a classic kind of illegal tying arrangement.

The Principes urge this court to apply the *Chicken Delight* reasoning to invalidate the McDonald's franchise lease note aggregation. They urge that McDonald's can protect the integrity of its trademarks by specifying how its franchisees shall operate, where they may locate their restaurants and what types of buildings they may erect. Customers do not and have no reason to connect the building's owner with the McDonald's operation conducted therein. Since company ownership of store premises is not an essential element of the trademark's goodwill, the Principes argue, the franchise, lease and note are separable products tied together in violation of the antitrust laws. In *Philips* v. *Crown Central Petroleum Corporation,* this court . . . noted that "the very essence of a franchise is the purchase of several related products in a single competitively attractive package." Franchising has come a long way since the decision in *Chicken Delight.*

Without disagreeing with the result in *Chicken Delight,* we conclude that the Court's emphasis in that case upon the trademark as the essence of a franchise is too restrictive. Far from merely licensing franchisees to sell products under its trade name, a modern franchisor such as McDonald's offers its franchisees a complete method of doing business. It takes people from all walks of life, sends them to its management school, and teaches them a variety of skills ranging from hamburger grilling to financial planning. It installs them in stores whose market has been researched and whose location has been selected by experts to maximize sales potential. It inspects every facet of every store several times a year and consults with each franchisee about his operation's strengths and weaknesses. Its regime pervades all facets of the business, from the design of the menu board to the amount of catsup on the hamburgers, nothing is left to chance. This pervasive franchisor supervision and control benefits the franchisee in turn. His business is identified with a network of stores whose very uniformity and predictability attracts customers. In short, the modern franchisee pays not only for the right to use a trademark but for the right to become a part of a system whose business methods virtually guarantee his success. It is often unrealistic to view a franchise agreement as little more than a trademark license.

Given the realities of modern franchising, we think the proper inquiry is not whether the allegedly tied products are associated in the public mind with the franchisor's trademark, but whether they are integral components of the business method being franchised. Where the challenged aggregation is an essential ingredient of the franchised system's formula for success, there is but a single product and no tie in exists as a matter of law.

Applying this standard to the present case, we hold the lease is not separable from the McDonald's franchise to which it pertains. McDonald's practice of developing a system of company owned restaurants operated by franchisees has substantial advantages, both for the company and for franchisees. It is part of what makes a McDonald's franchise uniquely attractive to franchisees.

First, because it approaches the problem of restaurant site selection systematically, McDonald's is able to obtain better sites than franchisees could select. Armed with its demographic information, guided by its staff of experts and unencumbered by preferences of individual franchisees, McDonald's can wield its economic might to acquire sites where new restaurants will prosper without undercutting existing franchisees' business or limiting future expansion. Individual franchisees are unlikely to possess analytical expertise, undertake elaborate market research or approach the problem of site selection from an area wide point of view. Individual franchisees benefit from the McDonald's approach because their stores are located in areas McDonald's has determined will produce substantial fast food business and on sites where that business is most likely to be diverted to their stores. Because McDonald's purposefully locates new stores where they will not undercut existing franchisees' business, McDonald's franchisees do not have to compete with each other, a substantial advantage in the highly competitive fast food industry.

Second, McDonald's policy of owning all of its own restaurants assures that the stores remain part of the McDonald's system. McDonald's franchise arrangements are not static: franchisees retire or die; occasionally they do not live up to their franchise obligations and must be replaced; even if no such contingency intervenes, the agreements normally expire by their own terms after twenty years. If franchisees owned their own stores, any of these events could disrupt McDonald's business and have a negative effect on the system's goodwill. Buildings whose architecture identified them as former McDonald's stores would sit idle or be used for other purposes. Replacement franchisees would have to acquire new and perhaps less desirable sites, a much more difficult and expensive process after the surrounding business area has matured. By owning its own stores, McDonald's assures its continued presence on the site, maintains the store's patronage even during management changes and avoids the negative publicity of having former McDonald's stores used for other purposes. By preserving the goodwill of the system in established markets, company store ownership produces attendant benefits for franchisees.

Third, because McDonald's acquires the sites and builds the store itself, it can select franchisees based on their management potential rather than their real estate expertise or wealth. Ability to emphasize management skills is important to McDonald's because it has built its reputation largely on the consistent quality of its operations rather than on the merits of its hamburgers. A store's quality is largely a function of its management. McDonald's policy of owning its own stores reduces a franchisee's initial investment, thereby broadening the applicant base and opening the door to persons who otherwise could not afford a McDonald's franchise. Accordingly, McDonald's is able to select franchisees primarily on the basis of their willingness to work for the success of their operations. Their ability to begin operating a McDonald's restaurant without having to search for a site, negotiate for the land, borrow hundreds of thousands of dollars and construct a store building is of substantial value to franchisees.

Finally, because both McDonald's and the franchisee have a substantial financial stake in the success of the restaurant, their relationship becomes a sort of partnership that might be impossible under other circumstances. McDonald's spends close to half a million dollars on each new store it establishes. Each franchisee invests over $100,000 to make the store operational. Neither can afford to ignore the other's problems, complaints or ideas. Because its investment is on the line, the Company cannot allow its franchisees to lose money. This being so, McDonald's works with its franchisees to build their business, occasionally financing improvements at favorable rates or even accepting reduced royalty payments in order to provide franchisees more working capital.

All of these factors contribute significantly to the overall success of the McDonald's system. The formula that produced systemwide success, the formula that promises to make each new McDonald's store successful, that formula is what McDonald's sells its franchisees. To characterize the franchise as an unnecessary aggregation of separate products tied to the McDonald's name is to miss the point entirely. Among would be franchisees, the McDonald's name has come to stand for the formula, including all that it entails. We decline to find that it is an illegal tie in.

Questions

1. What is the main argument of the plaintiff that the lease is an illegal tie-in with the franchise? What is the argument that the security deposit is an illegal tie-in with the franchise?
2. Does the court disagree with the result obtained in the *Chicken Delight* decision? How did the court justify its treatment of the franchise-lease-deposit aggregation as a single product?
3. Would this court approve of a situation where McDonald's required all franchisees to purchase their meat supplies from McDonald's?

CONCLUSION

In light of the differing economic arguments both supporting and condemning vertical arrangements, it is not surprising that lawmakers have vacillated in the formulation of public policy positions concerning vertical arrangements.

For one, the law has condemned vertical price-fixing through contracts, but permitted such control if accomplished by the right to refuse to deal. At the same time, Congress allowed vertical price-fixing for a period of time in the "fair trade" laws. Presently, the fair trade laws have been repealed and the Colgate doctrine is so restricted that few firms would rely on it as authority for vertical price-fixing. Consequently, historical vacillation has been replaced in the post-war years with a clear public policy denunciation of vertical price controls. However, this certainty has again been shaken by the doubts expressed by the Reagan Administration concerning the appropriateness of outlawing vertical price restraints.

Second, the courts have ruled that vertical nonprice restraints are to be judged by the rule of reason, which generally permits intrabrand restraints as long as sufficient interbrand competition exists. This permissiveness allows some customer territorial division which protects distributors' margins as much as a resale price maintenance program would. This *per se* condemnation of high retail margins through vertical price-fixing but rule-of-reason permissiveness for such margins accomplished through customer or territorial divisions is inconsistent, though apparently explained by the less-restrictive nature of the latter technique.

Exclusive supply contracts were interpreted to be almost *per se* illegal in the 1950s. Subsequent litigation relaxed this strict illegality. In addition, the "adequate representation" clause and the right to refuse to deal have provided an alternative method of securing exclusive dealing.

The modern relaxation of the rules against nonprice resale restraints and exclusive dealing is perhaps partially explained by the fact that contractual vertical arrangements are less obtrusive than vertical mergers. Vertical mergers are even more restrictive than simple contractual restriction. It eliminates the independent status of the distributor altogether and enhances the overall level of economic concentration. Yet historically, vertical mergers were not outlawed as rigidly as contractual vertical arrangements. Inadvertently, the strict posture of the law against contractual vertical arrangements fostered the vertical merger movement as an alternative to contractual vertical control. Recognition of this unintended consequence may partially explain the relaxation of the rules against contractual restraints.[11] Now, the more generally lawful and less restrictive contractual combinations may replace the feeling by manufacturers that only through vertical mergers were they able to achieve retailer control.

Finally, the courts seem to be developing a more lenient attitude toward tie-ins in franchise situations. The court's adoption of an "essential ingredient" test to avoid the existence of a tied product provides wide latitude for franchisors in developing franchise packages.

CASE PROBLEMS

1. The B&R Ice Cream franchise requires the franchisee not to carry any other brands of ice cream for sale from the B&R franchise outlet. What questions would you ask to determine if this practice is lawful?

2. A licensor of patents, trademarks, and trade names on bedding products sells advertising and promotional goods and products to its licensees, as well as mattress ticking, inner spring assemblies, labels, and so on. Each licensee is required to execute a franchise agreement which prescribes a territory in which the licensee will operate, called its "area of primary reponsibility."

   Each licensee is required by the franchise to participate in a "pass-over" plan. Under this plan a licensee is not prohibited from selling outside its area of primary responsibility, but if it should do so, the licensee making the sale must pay 7 percent of its gross receipts from the sale to the licensee in whose area the sale was made.

   An independent accounting firm had examined the expenses of the licensees at the request of the licensor, and found that the licensees' fixed selling expenses were 2 percent and its fixed advertising expenses were 5 percent. The licensor believes that a licensee should be compensated for these expenses if a competitor sells in its area.

   Is this plan lawful? What effect would it have on your evaluation if the profit margin on each sale was 4 percent or if the fixed selling expenses totaled only 5 percent?

3. Clairol markets Miss Clairol hair coloring products through two distinct channels of trade. Miss Clairol "salon" product is sold through distributors only to beauty salons and beauty schools. Miss Clairol "retail" product is sold by the company either directly to large retail chains or to wholesalers who in turn sell to retail stores for ultimate resale to the general public for home use. This dual distribution system has existed since Clairol entered the retail market in the 1950s.

   Clairol charges a substantially lower price for its salon product ($6.12 per dozen) than it charges for the products it sells to the retail trade ($11.67 per dozen) for resale to the general public.

   Each bottle of the retail Miss Clairol is enclosed in an individual yellow carton, bearing the conspicuous cautionary statement of possible skin irritation and the necessity of a preliminary test. It also indicates the product must not be used for dyeing the eyelashes or eyebrows; to do so may cause blindness. Each retail carton also contains a carefully prepared and copyrighted booklet providing detailed information and instructions to enable the untrained consumer to obtain safe and satisfactory results.

   Clairol packages its Miss Clairol salon product in a six-pack carton with only one sheet of instructions describing the antiallergy test. The salon instructional sheet does not contain the warning that preliminary patch and strand tests should be given before each application of the product.

   Clairol wrote letters to each salon distributor threatening termination if they sell the salon product to retailers. Are Clairol's policies lawful?

4. U.S. Steel Home Credit Corp., a wholly owned subsidiary of U.S. Steel Corp., was offering 100 percent financing to home developers in the Louisville, Kentucky, area during a period of years when no other lending institution in that area could match U.S. Steel Home Credit Corp. credit terms and interest rates. Once such developer alleged, in a suit against U.S. Steel and the U.S.

Home Credit Corp., that in order to obtain loans from the credit corporation, it had to use the funds to purchase prefabricated homes from U.S. Steel Corp. at "unreasonably high prices" and erect the homes on lots also purchased with borrowed funds.

The plaintiff-developer alleged the credit corporation's lending arrangements were considered "uniquely advantageous" to developers and were used to tie-in U.S. Steel's prefab homes.

What arguments might U.S. Steel and its subsidiary raise in defense?

END NOTES

1. *Dr. Miles Medical Co.* v. *John D. Park & Sons Co.,* 220 U.S. 373 (1911).
2. James C. Johnson and Louis E. Boone, "Farewell to Fair Trade," *MSU Business Topics,* Spring 1976, p. 25.
3. *Bissell Carpet Sweeper Co.* v. *Masters Mail Order Co. of Washington,* 240 F. 2d 684 (1957); and *General Electric Co.* v. *Masters Mail Order Co. of Washington,* 244 F. 2d 681 (1957), cert. denied.
4. See "Fair-Trade Laws May Be Retired by Congress," *Chicago Tribune,* February 10, 1975, citing a Consumer Union's estimate.
5. Public Law 94-145.
6. *Simpson* v. *Union Oil Co.,* 377 U.S. 13 (1964).
7. *U.S.* v. *Cuisinarts, Inc.,* Crim No. H-80-49; Civ. No. H-80-559, D. Conn., Sept. 17, 1980.
8. *Massachusetts* v. *Cuisinarts, Inc.,* Dkt. No. 80-2430-K, D. Mass., Oct. 10, 1980.
9. Robert E. Taylor, "Litvack Gets Attention of Business with Novel Antitrust Prosecution," *Wall Street Journal,* Oct. 31, 1980.
10. *U.S.* v. *Jerrold Electronics Corp.,* 365 U.S. 567 (1961).
11. Justice Douglas (dissenting) felt the requirements contracts employed by Standard Stations, Inc., were relatively less innocuous than the alternatives (agency devices or acquisition) available to the large oil companies. *Standard Oil Co. of Calif.* v. *United States,* 337 U.S. 293, 320 (1949).

chapter 15

PRICE DISCRIMINATION

Price discrimination is usually associated with some degree of market power and the absence of market forces. In markets with *open* price publicity, a seller would not normally be able to make some buyers pay a higher price while giving others a lower price for the same commodity. Instead, buyers asked to pay the higher price would turn to another seller. However, when *covert* price concessions are granted, buyers are unaware of the discrimination and do not pressure the seller to set uniform prices for all customers. Moreover, if price discrimination is openly practiced, unfavored buyers who continue to patronize the seller must have no alternative source of supply, that is, the seller possesses some monopoly power. Consequently, price discrimination is either an indicator of some degree of monopoly power or of incomplete (covert) competition.

There are three basic methods by which price discrimination may be exercised. First, the seller may discriminate between *customers* by charging a higher price to those who can afford to pay or who lack the power to buy from a substitute seller. Second, a seller may discriminate between purchasers in *different localities*. This geographic price discrimination may involve the practice of charging higher prices on a national basis while the seller receives a reduced price on shipments into a particular local market, or higher prices on domestic sales than on international sales (dumping). Third, price discrimination may be practiced by selling substantially identical products under *different labels or brands* at substantial differences in price. For example, petroleum refineries sell gasoline under different brand names, one at a higher price than the other.

EFFECTS ON COMPETITION

Price discrimination can affect market structure and the vigor of competition. It may strengthen or weaken competition, depending on the type of price discrimination utilized.

Some economists have argued that price discrimination can enhance competition by facilitating experimentation in pricing. Sellers will be willing to experiment with prices if such changes can be restricted to test markets. In this way, the seller can reduce the consequences of an adverse reaction by consumers or a business rival.

Another pro-competitive effect is often called the "erosion theory." It maintains that unsystematic price discrimination has a tendency to undermine oligopolistic discipline. Sellers who are eager to utilize excess capacity may grant secret, discriminatory price concesssions. But as word leaks out, other sellers match or undercut the secret discounts. As the price concessions spread, list prices become increasingly unrealistic and sellers may lose confidence in their rivals' willingness to cooperate to achieve a common price policy. In effect, the discriminatory lower price made available to one or a few buyers, it is said, may thereupon erode the published or uniform oligopolistic price and eventually become a price reduction available to all.

Those who do not accept the erosion theory argue that if the seller made the discriminatory lower price to retain or obtain a buyer's patronage, the buyer must presently have an alternative source of supply at a lower price. Either the buyer could obtain the product from another firm in the industry, probably one of the smaller independents, or the buyer could vertically integrate to produce the good for itself. If the buyer has these options, opponents of the erosion theory argue, then price discrimination is unnecessary as a competitive process because the real competition is the alternative available to the buyer. Therefore, instead of eroding the oligopolistic price structure, the price discrimination will more likely erode the enlargement of the alternative options available to the buyer; that is, it will eliminate the small independent seller or discourage the buyer from vertical integration. Consequently, opponents of the erosion theory view price discrimination as a technique utilized by oligopolistic firms to lower prices in certain product or geographic areas as a competitive response to the smaller firms. They lower prices in a discriminatory fashion rather than uniformly to all buyers. This price discrimination becomes a disciplinary action against a smaller firm. Therefore, price discrimination enables the large firm to "erode" small, independent competing sellers rather than the oligopolistic price structure.

Moreover, the erosion theory does not consider that the secret price concessions may be obtained only by large buyers who thereby obtain substantial cost advantages over smaller competing buyers. Consequently, the smaller competitors faced with higher purchasing costs and lower profits may be forced out of business without regard to their efficiency.

Even the proponents of the erosion theory recognize that discriminatory price concessions must be granted on an unsystematic basis. This is conceded because systematic price discrimination is likely to weaken competition by entrenching firms in their position of power. For example, a firm's dominant position in an industry could be entrenched if it received discriminatory price concessions from suppliers and granted discriminatory price reductions to large buyers. Competitors of the dominant firm which do not receive the price concessions from the suppliers would be at an obvious cost disadvantage. Moreover, the dominant firm's price concessions to large purchasers make it difficult for competing sellers to secure orders. In this manner, American Can Company was able to maintain its dominant position in the tin can industry by both receiving from suppliers and granting to large customers *systematic* discriminatory price concessions.[1]

Another sort of systematic discriminatory pricing involves the acceptance of lower rates of return on product lines that face competition and maintaining high margins on product lines that do not face stiff competitors.

In summation, various types of systematic price discrimination can strengthen monopoly positions by permitting large firms (1) to enjoy input costs lower than their smaller rivals (2) by foreclosing other sellers from buyers who receive special discounts for concentrated purchases from the monopolist and (3) by making entry into narrow segments of the market difficult or impossible because of narrow profit margins. On the other hand, economists differ as to whether *unsystematic* price discrimination can have a pro-competitive effect by undermining oligopolistic discipline. Instead, some economists insist *unsystematic* price discrimination is a "disciplinary" technique used by large firms to force smaller firms into compliance policies.

PUBLIC POLICY ON PRICE DISCRIMINATION

With so many types and effects of price discrimination, it is difficult to form a consensus on appropriate public policy and to draft a discerning statute which would discourage undesirable price discrimination while permitting desirable ones.

Besides congressional efforts to eliminate price discrimination by railroads in the Interstate Commerce Act, the first statutory prohibition of price discrimination was embodied in Section 2 of the 1914 Clayton Act. It outlawed price discrimination where the effect "may be to substantially lessen competition or tend to create a monopoly." Price discrimination, based on differences in the grade, quality, or quantity of the commodity sold was exempted. The quantity exemption proved to be a giant loophole, so that enforcement of the law was not spectacular. Of the 43 complaints by the FTC charging illegal price discrimination between 1914 and 1936, in only eight of these was the government able to claim success.[2]

The growth of chain stores in the 1920s and 1930s led to a Federal Trade

Commission (FTC) investigation of chain store practices. The FTC report concluded that one reason for the decline of independent retailers was the ability of giant chains to obtain discriminatory price concessions from their suppliers. The chains passed the savings from these lower costs on to the consumer in lower prices, which drew away customers from smaller retailers. The report concluded that 15 percent of the chain's selling price advantage over independents was accountable to the induced price discrimination.[3] To eliminate this advantage derived from exerting purchasing leverage, the commission recommended strengthening of the law.

Congressional reaction to the FTC report was the amendment of Section 2 of the Clayton Act through the enactment of the Robinson–Patman Act of 1936. Congress sought to protect small independent enterprises from the price discrimination practices of large firms in both their sales and purchasing functions. Consequently, many assert that the purpose of the act is to reduce price discrimination as a competitive weapon and preserve small businesses. The preservation of small businesses, however, may be inconsistent with economic efficiency and consumer welfare. Although the appropriateness of the goals of the Robinson–Patman Act are still debated, the greater prosecutorial success of the FTC under the amended Section 2 cannot be disputed. Since its enactment, the FTC has issued over a thousand cease and desist orders against price discrimination practices.[4]

ROBINSON–PATMAN ACT

The Robinson–Patman Act has two main purposes, which are as follows:

1. The prevention of a seller from using its profits on higher priced interstate sales to unfairly subsidize its lower price in a regional market in competition with a regional seller.
2. The prevention of buyers from using their large purchasing power to exact discriminatory prices from suppliers to the unfair disadvantage of smaller buyers.

To protect these small sellers and buyers, the Robinson–Patman Act makes it illegal to charge different prices for different buyers for goods of like grade and quality when the effect of the differences in prices may substantially lessen competition. To determine whether a Robinson–Patman violation is present under Section 2(a) of the act, one should ask the following questions:

1. Has the company made sales at different prices within a reasonably contemporaneous time period (this time period may vary depending on the competitive market, but six months is a good rule of thumb)?
2. Has one of the two sales involving different prices occurred in interstate commerce (price discrimination occurring totally intrastate is not covered by the act)?

3. Are the products sold of like grade and quality (that is, of substantial physical and chemical identity without any significant difference from the commercial standpoint and regardless of different "branding")?
4. Have the sales resulted in probable injury to competition at the seller, buyer, or subbuyer level?

If any of these elements is absent, no Robinson–Patman violation has occurred. Even if the four criteria of a Section 2(a) violation are present, the defendant may still avoid conviction of violation of the law if he or she is able to prove a "justification" for the price discrimination. The act authorizes three justifications.

One justification for price discrimination under the law is "difference in cost of manufacturer, sale, or delivery resulting from the differing methods or quantities in which such commodities are . . . sold or delivered." However, this defense is largely an illusion.

In determining costs, the FTC considers only "full cost," that is, variable costs plus an appropriate share of total overhead. Full costing does not permit a seller to demonstrate that the lower price is justified because it completely covers variable cost and makes some partial contribution to overhead costs. The FTC feels variable cost pricing would defeat the purpose of the Robinson–Patman Act. Consequently, the FTC argues that the Robinson–Patman Act requires each customer to bear its proportionate share of the total cost. The imposition of the full-cost rule leads to inherently arbitrary judgments, since accounting theory provides no uniquely correct way of prorating fixed or joint costs.

Because of the difficulty in proving that the accounting standards utilized in the cost defense are the only or most appropriate standards, the defendant normally cannot establish the defense with acceptable evidence. Because of the debates concerning techniques of overhead cost allocation, the seller often fails to carry the burden of proof that the lower price was cost justified. Between 1936 and 1954 only 11 attempts were made to utilize the cost defense in cases brought before the FTC. Of these, only two were fully successful.[5] Apart from the difficult task of proving the defense in litigation, the defendant may find more success in convincing the FTC at the informal investigatory stage that its cost data justify its price differential.

A second justification provided under the law is the privilege of charging different prices because of "changing conditions affecting the market for or the marketability of the goods concerned." This defense can be easily demonstrated by actual or eminent deterioration of perishable goods or obsolescence of seasonal goods. It also covers price changes resulting from inflation or other changing market conditions. Distress sales under court order or discontinuance of business would likewise be protected.

The last justification under the act is embodied in Section 2(b). This section grants the seller the privilege of lowering a price in good faith to meet a price offered by a competitor. This defense has received considerable use in litigated cases and will be more fully discussed in the cases to follow.

Section 2(c) of the Robinson–Patman Act outlaws "phoney brokerage." Brokerage payments may not be paid by a seller to a buyer or an agent of the buyer except for services rendered to the seller. Often buyers attempt to bypass brokers of the seller and then seek the commission the broker normally earns from the seller. However, the buyer has not rendered services to the seller and is not entitled to such brokerage commission. The buyer has rendered service to himself or herself in bypassing the broker. These "phoney brokerage" allowances are illegal *per se*.

As the interpretations to Section 2(c) have evolved, mediaries are likely to be classified as wholesalers entitled to a wholesalers' functional discount if they customarily take title to goods being distributed, assume the risk of price fluctuations, and maintain warehouses and inventories. Any firm performing less than these functions is apt to be called a broker. Such brokers can earn a fee only for services rendered to the seller. Drawing a line between services rendered to the seller or buyer is obviously difficult and tends to eliminate any payments except to clearly recognized wholesalers or to bona fide brokers. Phoney brokers owned and set up by large buyers in order to obtain a brokerage commission (discount) from the seller are illegal.

Many large companies, nevertheless, are able to escape Section 2(c) violation by purchasing the entire output of their suppliers or by purchasing only from suppliers who employ no brokers. As a consequence, Section 2(c) may operate to the disadvantage of medium-sized buyers who have less flexibility in choosing sources of supply. Moreover, Section 2(c) may cause the unnecessary preservation of possibly uneconomic brokerage functions. Because of these and other shortcomings, there is rather widespread sentiment for the repeal of Section 2(c).

COMPETITIVE INJURY

Price discrimination of goods of like grade and quality is illegal only if the (1) effect of such discrimination in any line of commerce may substantially lessen competition or (2) injure or prevent competition with any person who either (a) grants or (b) knowingly receives the benefit of such discrimination or (c) customers of either of them. This language appears to indicate and the effect of court decisions seem to support, that the first part of this law protects against injury to competition whereas the second part covers injury to a competitor. However, the courts have never officially recognized the concept of injury to a competitor unless such injury is a substantial injury to competition also. Rather than to merely protect a competitor, the FTC has chosen to use the test of injury to competition. Of course, private litigants favor the use of the more easily proven injury to a competitor (namely, themselves) test. Some courts tend to find competitive injury whenever an injury to a competitor occurs, which causes some confusion as to which legal standard is to be applied.

From the language of the act, it is possible to have competitive injury on various levels of business operations. For example, if interstate seller A's price discrimination causes his or her (probably smaller, regional) competitive seller B

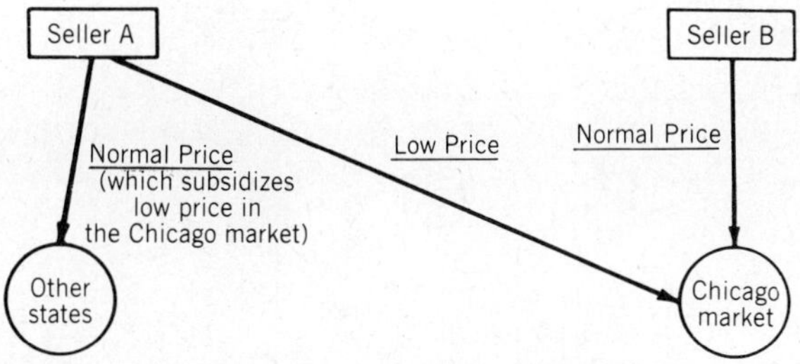

Figure 15-1. Seller-level (primary-line) injury.

to suffer injury, this would be primary-line or seller-level injury. Seller A could sell in most markets at a high price to subsidize the lower price in the market competing with Seller B. This seller-level injury is illustrated in Figure 15-1.

If the manufacturer sells his or her products at different prices to buyers who compete with each other, the price discrimination will cause competitive injury at the buyers' level. This is called secondary line injury and is diagrammed in Figure 15-2.

A third-line injury occurs when the customers of the supplier's buyer are discriminated against in prices. This level is a more controversial means of showing competitive injury, and lawsuits alleging third-line injuries rarely occur. Theoretically, it is possible for price discrimination to exist where no primary-line injury is present and the secondary-level buyers do not compete with each other, so that secondary-level injury is absent also. Nevertheless, if a lower price to a secondary-level buyer allows that buyer to pass on a lower price to customers who compete with customers of another secondary-level supplier, competitive injury occurs on the third level, as diagrammed in Figure 15-3.

Injury to the vigor of competition from the practice of price discrimination is clear when individual competitors are so lethally injured that they withdraw from the market, leaving fewer rivals competing more cautiously thereafter. However, courts have been willing to infer competitive injury even though rivals have not been literally driven from the market. The evidence needed to deter-

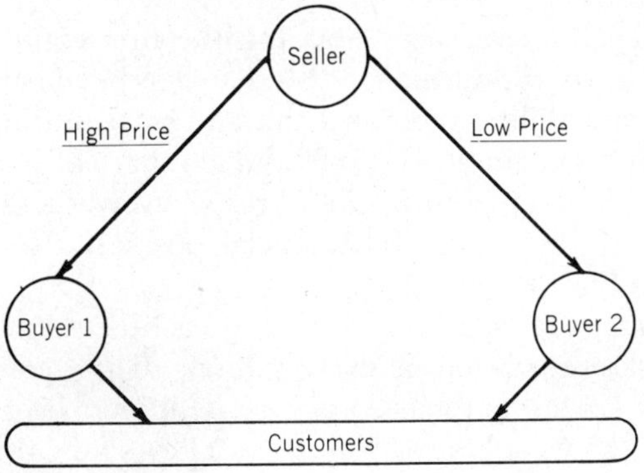

Figure 15-2. Buyer-level (secondary-line) injury.

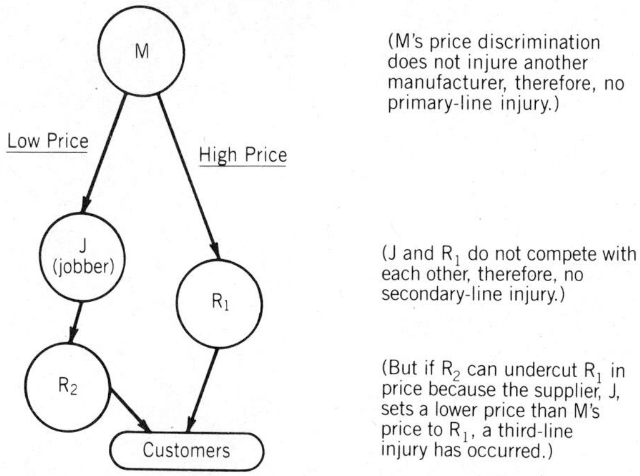

Figure 15-3. Sub-buyer-level (third-line) injury.

mine the requisite competitive injury has varied in court decisions, and its adequacy is continually debated.

PROOF OF COMPETITIVE INJURY

Utah Pie Co. v. Continental Baking Co.
386 U.S. 685 (1967)
Supreme Court of the United States

Justice White

This suit for treble damages . . . was brought by petitioner, Utah Pie Company, against [defendants], Continental Baking Company, Carnation Company and Pet Milk Company. The complaint charged . . . violations by each [defendent] of Section 2(a) of the Clayton Act as amended by the Robinson–Patman Act. . . . The jury found for petitioner on the price discrimination charge. . . .

The product involved is frozen dessert pies. . . . The period covered by the suit comprised the years 1958, 1959, and 1960 and the first eight months of 1961. Petitioner is a Utah corporation which for 30 years has been baking pies in its plant in Salt Lake City and selling them in Utah and surrounding States. It entered the frozen pie business in late 1957. . . . Utah Pie's share of this market in those years was 66.5%, 34.3%, 45.5%, and 45.3%, respectively, its sales volume steadily increasing over the four years. Its financial position also improved. Petitioner is not, however, a large company. . . .

Each of the [defendants] is a large company and each of them is a major factor in the frozen pie market in one or more regions of the country. Each entered the Salt Lake City frozen pie market before petitioner began freezing dessert pies. None of them had a plant in Utah. . . . They sold primarily on a delivered price basis.

The major competitive weapon in the Utah market was price. The location of petitioner's plant gave it natural advantages in the Salt Lake City marketing area and it entered the market at a price below the then going prices for [defendant's] comparable pies. For most of the period involved here its prices were the lowest in the Salt Lake City market. It was, however, challenged by each of the [defendants] at one time or another and for varying periods. There was ample evidence to show that each of the [defendants] contributed to what proved to be a deteriorating price structure over the period covered by this suit, and each of the [defendants] in the course of the ongoing price competition sold frozen pies in the Salt Lake market at prices lower than it sold pies of like grade and quality in other markets considerably closer to its plants. . . .

Petitioner's case against Continental is not complicated. . . . Effective for the last two weeks of June it offered its 22-ounce frozen apple pies in the Utah area at $2.85 per dozen. It was then selling the same pies at substantially higher prices in other markets. The Salt Lake City price was less than its direct cost plus an allocation for overhead. . . .

The Court of Appeals concluded that Continental's conduct had had only minimal effect, that it had not injured or weakened Utah Pie as a competitor, that it had not substantially lessened competition and that there was no reasonable possibility that it would do so in the future.

We differ with the Court of Appeals. Its opinion that Utah was not damaged as a competitive force apparently rested on the fact that Utah's sales volume continued to climb in 1961. . . . But this retrospective assessment fails to note that Continental's discriminatory below-cost price caused Utah Pie to reduce its price to $2.75. The jury was entitled to consider the potential impact of Continental's price reduction absent any responsive price cut by Utah Pie. . . . The jury could rationally have concluded that had Utah not lowered its price, Continental, which repeated its offer once, would have continued it. . . . It could also have reasonably concluded that a competitor who is forced to reduce his price to a new all-time low in a market of declining prices will in time feel the financial pinch and will be a less effective competitive force. . . .

Section 2(a) does not forbid [all] price competition. . . . But Congress has established some ground rules for the game. Sellers may not sell like goods to different purchasers at different prices if the result may to be injure competition in either the sellers' or the buyers' market unless such discriminations are justified as permitted by the Act. This case concerns the sellers' market. In the context, the Court of Appeals placed heavy emphasis on the fact that Utah Pie constantly increased its sales volume and continued to make a profit. But we disagree with its apparent view that there is no reasonably possible injury to competition as long as the volume of sales in a particular market is expanding and at least some of the competitors in the market continue to operate at a profit. Nor do we think that the Act only comes into play to regulate the conduct of price discriminators when their discriminatory prices consistently undercut other competitors. It is true that many of the primary line cases that have reached the courts have involved blatant predatory price discriminations employed with the hope of immediate destruction of a particular competitor. On the question of injury to competition such cases present courts with no difficulty, for such pricing is clearly within the heart of the proscription of the Act. Courts and commentators alike have noted that the existence of predatory intent might bear on the likelihood of injury to competition. In this case there was some evidence of predatory intent with respect to each of these [defendants]. There was also other evidence upon which the jury could rationally find the requisite injury to competition. . . . We believe that the Act reaches price discrimination that erodes competition as much as it does price discrimination that is intended to have immediate destructive impact. In this case, the evidence shows a drastically declining price structure which the jury could rationally attribute to continued or sporadic price discrimination. The jury was entitled to conclude that "the effect of such discrimination," by each of these [defendants], "may be substantially to lessen competition . . . or to injure, destroy, or prevent competition with any person who either grants or knowingly receives the benefit of such discrimination. . . ." The statutory test is one that necessarily looks forward on the basis of proved conduct in the past.

Questions

1. What evidence did the Court of Appeals rely on to determine that there was no "probable injury to competition"?
2. Must a predatory price discrimination be employed with the hope of immediate destruction of a particular competitor?
3. What evidence existed as to Continental's predatory intent? What motive could Continental have in selling its pies below cost?
4. Would Pet Milk's insertion of an "industrial spy" into Utah Pie's plant be evidence of predatory intent?

The *Utah Pie* decision has been criticized for protecting a seller whose cost advantage (lower transportation cost) made it quite able to protect itself. The controversy in this case also includes the argument over what constitutes predatory pricing. Below total cost pricing was accepted as evidence of predatory intent. However, recent cases reveal some appellate courts have rejected primary-line injury claims because prices had not been cut below average *variable* costs (see Areeda–Turner test in Chapter 11).[6] The Areeda–Turner test has been criticized by Posner and others when the pricing decision of the seller is supported by substantial monopoly power (entry barriers), as in the Borden *ReaLemon* case. Consequently, the controversy over predatory pricing formulas continues unabated, and Supreme Court clarification is sorely needed.

SECONDARY-LINE INJURIES

In secondary-line cases a clearer standard of competitive injury has been adopted. Beginning with the *Morton Salt* case in 1948, the Supreme Court observed that Morton established a quantity discount schedule which lowered the price for carload lots and lowered the price even further on the basis of total annual purchases. The discount schedule permitted the largest buyers to gain prices below those of smaller rivals. The Court found the price scheme to be an illegal injury to competition and wrote the following:

> The legislative history of the Robinson–Patman Act makes it abundantly clear that Congress considered it to be an evil that a large buyer could secure a competitive advantage over a smaller buyer solely because of the large buyer's quantity purchasing ability. . . . [I]n enacting the Robinson–Patman Act Congress was especially concerned with protecting small businesses which were unable to buy in quantities, such as the merchants here who purchased in less-than-carload lots. . . . That respondents quantity discounts did result in price differentials between competing purchasers sufficient in amount to influence their resale price of salt was shown by evidence. This showing in itself was adequate to support the Commission's appropriate finding that the effect of such discriminations "may be substantially to lessen competition . . . and to prevent competition."[7]

Subsequent secondary-line cases have indicated that the price differentials must be large enough and given over a sufficient period of time to have a significant effect on sales and market shares before an inference of a competitive injury can be made. A 1965 appellate court has written as follows:

> [I]t seems well established that where the record indicates a price differential subtantial enough to cut into the purchaser's profit margin and discloses a reduction which would afford the favored buyer a significant aggregate saving that, if reflected in a resale price cut, would have a noticeable effect on the decisions of customers in the retail market, an inference of injury may properly be indulged.[8]

THE 2(b) DEFENSE

When a *prima facie* Section 2(a) price discrimination violation has been found, Section 2(b) of the Robinson–Patman Act permits a seller to rebut the *prima facie* presumption of illegality by showing that its lower price was "made in good faith to meet an equally low price of competitor."

The *Standard Oil of Indiana* case[9] established the meeting competition defense as a complete defense to a charge of injurious price discrimination. The FTC had charged Standard Oil with illegal discrimination in selling its Red Crown gasoline in the Detroit area to four independent gasoline dealers who received a price lower than that charged to other Red Crown dealers competing with the favored four dealers. Standard insisted it was simply meeting the lower price quoted by competitors, namely, a small independent refinery named Red Indian. Red Indian sold on a uniform price basis and normally had lower prices than the giant oil firms in order to secure retail outlets. The FTC refused to accept Standard's defense as an absolute defense where the discriminatory pricing caused competitive injury at the retail level.

The court of appeals upheld the commission's decision that the probable injury to competition was to be weighed against the claimed advantage of the business practice of price discrimination. If the government could show that substantial injury to competition was reasonably probable, this would outweigh the need for Standard Oil of Indiana to retain customers by price discrimination. Standard Oil appealed this decision to the Supreme Court.

Prior to the Supreme Court's decision, the commission changed its attitude and in substance adopted the erosion theory. It felt price discrimination should be permitted in industries in which economic power had become concentrated in the hands of a few sellers. In such oligopolistic industries, the FTC recognized that price competition is almost nonexistent. Usually the only form of price competition is secret price concessions, such as Standard Oil made to the four independent retailers. The commissioners reasoned that if the Robinson–Patman Act was applied so as to require equal treatment of all customers, it might stifle this limited price competition in oligopolistic industries. By permitting some price discrimination, the commissioners accepted the erosion theory and its notion that some price competition would develop by allowing secret price discriminations. Consequently, in June 1949, the commission publicly announced its preference that the good faith meeting of competition defense be made absolute.[10] The commission's new policy reduced the likelihood of success by the government's attorneys in defending the court of appeals' decision.

In 1951, the Supreme Court reversed the court of appeals in the *Standard Oil of Indiana* decision.[11] The Court ruled that even though competition among customers is injured, a seller may justify a lower discriminatory price to some customers if it showed that the lower price was made in good faith to meet the equally low price of a competitor.

Those who reject the erosion theory believe the *Stndard Oil of Indiana* decision was a mistake. They contend that price discrimination by a large seller discourages price competition by small competitors, such as Red Indian. Their argument is as follows:

> Red Indian is faced with the consequence of continuing to lower its price in a financial war with Standard Oil of Indiana which is supporting its selective price reductions with higher prices charged elsewhere. In time, Red Indian will learn not to wage financial warfare with giant firms and will adopt a compliant price policy consistent wih the pricing policies dictated by the larger firms. The real competitive factor, Red Indian, will be eroded by allowing the large firms the privilege of price discrimination. There will not be, as the erosion theory predicts, an erosion of the price level adopted by oligopolistic firms. Instead, the price discrimination becomes a tool for large firms to discipline smaller rivals who "dare" to lower their price below that level considered tolerable by the giants. Real price competition from smaller firms will "erode" away.

Despite the continuing debate, the good faith meeting of competition defense is an absolute defense, regardless of the existence of any competitive injury. The following case, *Cadigan* v. *Texaco*, is illustrative of the present policy.

Cadigan v. Texaco, Inc.

492 F. 2d 383 (1974)
U.S. Court of Appeals (9th Cir.)

[A former operator and lessee of Texaco service station brought suit against Texaco alleging that Texaco's sale of gasoline to Wickland Oil, a station across the street, at prices lower than the prices paid to Texaco by the plaintiff was a violation of the Robinson–Patman Act.]

* * *

Section 2(b) provides a complete defense to a *prima facie* case of price discrimination, despite any adverse effect on competition created by the price differential. The sole permissible inference which may be drawn from the uncontroverted facts is that Texaco offered the discriminatory discounts in a good faith effort to secure Wickland's business by matching prices offered by Texaco's competitors, Humble and American. . . . Plaintiff . . . contends that . . . defendants, not having shown that the prices of Texaco's competitors were lawful, failed to bring themselves within the Section 2(b) proviso. We reject this contention. A defendant need not prove the actual lawfulness of his competitor's price in order to secure the protection of the proviso. The well established rule is that Section 2(b) is satisfied unless it appears that the defendant either knows the price being met is unlawful or that it is inherently unlawful.

Plaintiff has offered no proof to suggest that the competitor's prices were unlawful, much less that Texaco knew them to be such.

Finally, [plaintiff] argues that the Section 2(b) defense can be asserted only when the price discrimination is made to retain old customers, and not, as in this case, when a seller meets competitive prices in order to obtain a new customer. The distinction is unsound and has been rejected by the courts, *Sunshine Biscuits, Inc.* v. *FTC,* 306 F. 2d 48 (7th Cir., 1962); and is not applied by the Federal Trade Commission, *see* Beatrice Foods Co., Trade Reg. Rep. 19,045 (FTC 1970).

We agree with the Seventh Circuit that:

> If, in situations where the Section 2(b) proviso is applicable, sellers could grant good faith competitive price reductions only to old customers in order to retain them, competition for new customers would be stifled and monopoly be fostered. In such situations an established seller would have a monopoly of his customers and a seller entering the market would not be permitted to reduce his price to compete with his established rivals unless he could do so on a basis such as cost justification. Moreover, the distinction would create a forced price discrimination between a seller's existing customers to whom he had lawfully lowered his price under Section 2(b) and a prospective new customer. These results, we believe, are incompatible with the purpose for which the Robinson–Patman Act was enacted.

Questions

1. Is the "good faith meeting of competition" defense a complete defense to a *prima facie* case of price discrimination?
2. To take advantage of the 2(b) defense, must the seller prove the lawfulness of the competitor's price which it is meeting?
3. May the 2(b) defense be utilized "aggressively" to obtain new customers? Or is the 2(b) defense limited to the retention of old customers (defensive use)?

BUYER LIABILITY

Section 2(f) of the Robinson–Patman Act reveals that "it shall be unlawful for any person engaged in commerce, in the course of such commerce, knowingly to induce or receive a discrimination in price which is prohibited by this section."

From this language, it is easy to determine that the *buyer* may be in violation of this act also. The buyer has committed a violation if he or she (1) receives an unlawful price discrimination and (2) has knowledge of its illegality. From the landmark *Automatic Canteen* case, the Court ruled that the FTC has the burden of "coming forward with evidence" on the buyer's knowledge of illegality and that this burden extends to establishing that the buyer lacked knowledge of cost justification of the price discrimination.[12] However, the FTC may establish its burden by "trade experience" evidence. In an FTC decision, it was established that the FTC need only show that the buyer "should have known" that the price discrimination received was not justified by costs or by meeting competition and, therefore, the buyer had a "duty to inquire."[13]

Great A&P Tea Co. v. FTC

440 U.S. 69 (1979)
Supreme Court of the United States

Justice Stewart

The question presented in this case is whether the petitioner, the Great Atlantic and Pacific Tea Company (A&P), violated Section 2(f) of the Robinson–Patman Act, by knowingly inducing or receiving illegal price discriminations from the Borden Company (Borden).

The alleged violation was reflected in a 1965 agreement between A&P and Borden under which Borden undertook to supply "private label" milk to more than 200 A&P stores in a Chicago area that included portions of Illinois and Indiana. This agreement resulted from an effort by A&P to achieve cost savings by switching from the sale of "brand label" milk (milk sold under the brand name of the supplying dairy) to the sale of "private label" milk (milk sold under the A&P label).

To implement this plan, A&P asked Borden, its longtime supplier, to submit an offer to supply under private label certain of A&P's milk and other dairy product requirements. After prolonged negotiations, Borden offered to grant A&P a discount for switching to private label milk provided A&P would accept limited delivery service. Borden claimed that this offer would save A&P $410,000 a year compared to what it had been paying for its dairy products. A&P, however, was not satisfied with this offer and solicited offers from other dairies. A competitor of Borden, Bowman Dairy, then submitted an offer which was lower than Borden's. [Court footnote reads: "The Bowman bid would have produced estimated annual savings of approximately $737,000 for A&P as compared with the first Borden bid, which would have produced estimated annual savings of $410,000."]

At this point, A&P's Chicago buyer contacted Borden's chain store sales manager and stated, "I have a bid in my pocket. You [Borden] people are so far out of line it is not even funny. You are not even in the ball park." When the Borden representative asked for more details, he was told nothing except that a $50,000 improvement in Borden's bid "would not be a drop in the bucket."

Borden was thus faced with the problem of deciding whether to rebid. A&P at the time was one of Borden's largest customers in the Chicago area. Moreover, Borden had just invested more than five million dollars in a new dairy facility in Illinois. The loss of the A&P account would result in underutilization of this new plant. Under these circumstances, Borden decided to submit a new bid which doubled the estimated annual savings to A&P, from $410,000 to $820,000. In presenting its offer, Borden emphasized to A&P that it needed to keep A&P's business and was making the new offer in order to meet Bowman's bid. A&P then accepted Borden's bid after concluding that it was substantially better than Bowman's.

* * *

Section 2(f) provides:

> That it shall be unlawful for any person engaged in commerce, in the course of such commerce, knowingly to induce or receive a discrimination in price *which is prohibited by this section.* (Emphasis added.)

Liability under Section 2(f) thus is limited to situations where the price discrimination is one "which is prohibited by this section." While the phrase "this section" refers to the entire Section 2 of the Act, only subsections (a) and (b) dealing with seller liability involve discriminations in price. Under the plain meaning of Section 2(f), therefore, a buyer cannot be liable if a *prima facie* case could not be established against a seller or if the seller has an affirmative defense. In either situation, there is no price discrimination "prohibited by this section."

The derivative nature of liability under Section 2(f) is dependent on seller liability under Section 2(a).

The derivative nature of liability under Section 2(f) was recognized by this Court in *Automatic Canteen Co. of America* v. *FTC,* 346 U.S. 61. In that case, the Court stated that even if the Commission has established a *prima facie* case of price discrimination, a buyer does not violate Section 2(f) if the lower prices received are either within one of the seller's defenses or not known by him not to be within one of those defenses. . . . The Court thus explicitly recognized that a buyer cannot be held liable under Section 2(f) if the lower prices received are justified by reason of one of the seller's affirmative defenses.

The petitioner, relying on this plain meaning of Section 2(f) and the teaching of the *Automatic Canteen* case, argues that it cannot be liable under Section 2(f) if Borden had a valid meeting competition defense. The respondent, on the other hand, argues that the petitioner may be liable even assuming that Borden had such a defense. The meeting competition defense, the respondent contends, must in these circumstances be judged from the point of view of the buyer. Since A&P knew for a fact that the final Borden bid beat the Bowman bid, it was not entitled to assert the meeting competition defense even though Borden may have honestly believed that it was simply meeting competition. Recognition of a meeting competition defense for the buyer in this situation, the respondent argues, would be contrary to the basic purpose of the Robinson–Patman Act to curtail abuses by large buyers.

The short answer to these contentions of the respondent is that Congress did not provide in Section 2(f) that a buyer can be liable if the seller has a valid defense. The clear language of Section 2(f) states that a buyer can be liable only if he receives a price discrimination "prohibited by this section." If a seller has a valid meeting competition defense, there is simply no prohibited price discrimination.

* * *

In the *Automatic Canteen* case, the Court warned against interpretations of the Robinson–Patman Act which "extend beyond the prohibitions of the Act and, in so doing, help give rise to a price uniformity and rigidity in open conflict with the purposes of other antitrust legislation." Imposition of Section 2(f) liability on the petitioner in this case would lead to just such price uniformity and rigidity.

In a competitive market, uncertainty among sellers will cause them to compete for business by offering buyers lower prices. Because of the evils of collusive action, the Court has held that the exchange of price information by competitors violates the Sherman Act. *United States* v. *Container Corp.*, 393 U.S. 333. Under the view advanced by the respondent, however, a buyer, to avoid liability, must either refuse a seller's bid or at least inform him that his bid has beaten competition. Such a duty of affirmative disclosure would almost inevitably frustrate competitive bidding and, by reducing uncertainty, lead to price matching and anticompetitive cooperation among sellers.

* * *

As in the *Automatic Canteen* case, we decline to adopt a construction of Section 2(f) that is contrary to its plain meaning and would lead to anticompetitive results. Accordingly, we hold that a buyer who has done no more than accept the lower of two prices competitively offered does not violate Section 2(f) provided the seller has a meeting competition defense.

* * *

Under the circumstances of this case, Borden did act reasonably and in good faith when it made its second bid. The petitioner, despite its longstanding relationship with Borden, was dissatisfied with Borden's first bid and solicited offers from other dairies.

* * *

Thus Borden was informed by the petitioner that it was in danger of losing its A&P business in the Chicago area unless it came up with a better offer. It was told that its first offer was "not even in the ball park" and that a $50,000 improvement "would not be a drop in the [bucket]." In light of Borden's established business relationship with the petitioner, Borden could justifiably conclude that A&P's statements were reliable and that it was necessary to make another bid offering substantial concessions to avoid losing its account with the petitioner.

Borden was unable to ascertain the details of the Bowman bid. It requested more information about the bid from the petitioner, but this request was refused. It could not then attempt to verify the existence and terms of the competing offer from Bowman without risking Sherman Act liability. Faced with a substantial loss of business and unable to find out the precise details of the competing bid, Borden made another offer stating that it was doing so in order to meet competition. Under these circumstances, the conclusion is virtually inescapable that in making that offer Borden acted in a reasonable and good-faith effort to meet its competition, and therefore was entitled to a meeting competition defense.

Since Borden had a meeting competition defense and thus could not be liable under Section 2(b) the petitioner who did no more than accept that offer cannot be liable under Section 2(f).

Questions

1. The FTC argued that the purpose of the Robinson–Patman Act is to curtail abuses by large buyers. Does the result of the *A&P* decision curtail the opportunities for abuses by large buyers? Does it offer the seller an easily proven affirmative defense which may be utilized also by the big buyer to the potential harm of other competing buyers? Will large buyers be able to receive substantial price concessions as a result of the *A&P* decision without incurring Robinson–Patman Act liability?
2. The Supreme Court warned that the FTC's interpretation of the act would extend beyond the prohibitions of the Robinson–Patman Act and lead to price uniformity and rigidity. How does the Court reach this conclusion?
3. The Supreme Court in a footnote indicated that A&P was not a "lying buyer" and the Court, therefore, did not need to decide whether such a buyer could be liable under Section 2(f) even if the seller had a meeting competition defense. In addition, a dissenting justice argued that a buyer who induces the lower bid by *misrepresentation* should not escape Robinson–Patman Act liability. Do these statements imply a warning to buyers as to the negotiation ploys that they might utilize?

EQUALITY IN PROMOTION

Sections 2(d) and 2(e) of the Robinson–Patman Act seek to afford equitable treatment to competing customers of the seller. These sections require that promotional payments, services, or facilities (such as advertising allowances or display materials) must be extended by the seller on proportionately equal terms to all the seller's customers who compete with each other. The law does not require that probable adverse competitive effect be shown for violation of these sections to occur. Rather, damages from the loss of the promotional service or allowance or to the buyer's "business stature" will suffice for the award of a pecuniary recovery to the buyer. Equitable promotional services to all customers should be the general rule of the seller, unless the seller can justify failure to provide equitable treatment of promotional services on the ground that it was meeting in good faith a competing offer of assistance by a competitor.

CONCLUSION

Price discrimination is a widespread business practice that has both favorable and unfavorable effects on competition. Consequently, the purpose of the law prohibiting price discrimination was to be specifically aimed only at the anticompetitive evils created by the buying power and selling practices of big business which injure smaller competitors. By overprotecting these competitors, the Robinson–Patman Act has become controversial because it is in conflict with the accepted antitrust purpose of protecting competition, not competitors.

In addition, many argue that the act is conceptually complex, resulting in myriad interpretations, some of which have expanded the law beyond its narrowly conceived purpose and caused a chilling effect on the vigor of price flexibility and competition.

Efforts to repeal or reform the Robinson–Patman Act have consistently met with stern opposition from the lobbies of small business. In its present form, the act is difficult to comply with; particularly in industries with sensitive price competition. To avoid violating the act, a fundamental understanding of the provisions of the law by all levels of management is imperative.

CASE PROBLEMS

1. Hanson, a glass retailer, sued Pittsburgh Plate Glass Industries, Inc. (PPG), under the Robinson–Patman Act, claiming that PPG sold to Hanson's competitors at prices lower than those offered to Hanson. Hanson purchased glass at 62 cents per foot, which was cut to his size specifications. A competitor purchased standard stock sizes of identical glass at 35 cents per foot. Does PPG have a defense to this price discrimination charge?

2. Borden produced evaporated milk, canned the product, and marketed it bearing several labels, including Borden's own brand label and those for several customers' private brands. Evaporated milk bearing the Borden brand was sold at prices above that bearing private brand labels, both at wholesale and retail levels. At the retail level, a definite brand preference for Borden milk was found to exist, a certain segment of the market being willing to pay a higher price for the Borden label. The FTC charged Borden Co. with price discrimination, and Borden argued that the consumer brand preference rendered the products commercially different and, therefore, of differ-

ent "grades" even though the canned milk was physically identical and of equal quality. Are Borden's products of "like grade and quality"?

3. Central Ice Cream Co. sued Golden Road Ice Cream Co. under the Robinson–Patman Act. Central claims Golden Road offered special price concessions to Central's customers in order to secure their patronage. Both companies manufacture ice cream in Illinois, and they compete in selling to retailers in the Chicago area. Does the Robinson–Patman Act apply?

4. Forelco sold its pocket calculator throughout the United States for around $100 a unit. The retailers then would mark up from that price and sell to the consuming public. In an effort to improve its market penetration in the South, Forelco implemented the policy of a reduced price in the southern states. What questions would you ask to determine if Forelco's pricing policies violated the Robinson–Patman Act?

END NOTES

1. *U.S.* v. *American Can Co.,* 230 F. 859, 256 U.S. 706 (1921); and see James W. McKie, *Tin Cans and Tin Plate* (Cambridge, Mass.: Harvard University Press, 1959), pp. 58–64, 160–82.
2. See Corwin D. Edwards, *The Price Discrimination Law* (Washington, D.C.: Brookings Institution, 1959), p. 6.
3. U.S. Federal Trade Commission, *Final Report on the Chain Store Investigation* (Washington, D.C.: U.S. Government Printing Office, 1934), p. 55.
4. U.S., Congress, House, Committee on Small Businesses, Ad Hoc Subcommittee on Antitrust, Robinson–Patman Act, and Related Matters Hearings, *Recent Effort to Amend or Repeal the Robinson–Patman Act,* Pt. 2, 94th Cong., 1st. sess., 1976, pp. 186–91.
5. See the *Report of the Attorney General National Committee to Study Antitrust Laws* (1955), p. 171.
6. See, *Pacific Eng. & Prod. Co. of Nev.* v. *Kerr-McGee Corp.,* 551 F. 2d 790 (10th Cir., 1977), and *International Air Inds.* v. *American Excelsior Co.,* 517 F. 2d 714 (5th Cir., 1975), cert. denied in both cases.
7. *FTC* v. *Morton Salt Co.,* 334 U.S. 37, 43, 47 (1948).
8. *Foremost Dairies, Inc.* v. *FTC,* 348 F. 2d 674, 680 (1965).
9. *Standard Ohio Co.* v. *FTC,* 340 U.S. 231 (1951).
10. Hearings before Subcommittee, No. 1 of the House Committee of the Judiciary on S. 1008, 81st Cong. 1st. sess., June 8 and 14, 1949, p. 61.
11. *Standard Oil Co.* v. *FTC,* 340 U.S. 231 (1951).
12. *Automatic Canteen Co. of Am.* v. *FTC,* 346 U.S. 61 (1953).
13. *Fred Meyer, Inc.* v. *FTC,* 359 F. 2d 351 (9th Cir. 1966).

part four
GOVERNMENT REGULATIONS

The birth of the United States and *laissez-faire* economics occurred in the same era, both in reaction to British mercantilism and its government-dictated economic policies. Because of this heritage of a limited role of government, Americans have tended to overlook the fact that governmental domination over economic affairs has been the norm in history and a relatively free market economy the exception. Instead, Americans have viewed their short history, with its reliance on the market mechanism and on relative freedom from governmental restraint, as the natural state of a national economy. Consequently, the subsequent development of government regulations of business has resulted only when the populace perceived failures of the market system.

Adam Smith popularized the "invisible hand" concept—the idea that an individual who "intends only his own gain" is, nevertheless, "led by an invisible hand to promote . . . the public interest." The dominant tendency of thought ever since seems to have been that decisions reached individually will, in fact, be the best decisions for an entire society. But consider Garrett Hardin's "Tragedy of the Commons."

> The tragedy of the commons develops in this way. Picture a pasture open to all. It is to be expected that each herdsman will try to keep as many cattle as possible on the commons. Such an arrangement may work reasonably satisfactorily for centuries because tribal wars, poaching, and disease keep the numbers of both man and beast well below the carrying capacity of the land. Finally, however, . . . the inherent logic of the commons remorselessly generates tragedy.

> As a rational being, each herdsman seeks to maximize his gain. Explicitly or implicitly, more or less consciously, he asks, "What is the utility to me of adding one more animal to my herd?". . . Since the herdsman receives all the proceeds from the sale of the additional animal, the positive utility is nearly +1. . . . Since, however, the effects of overgrazing are shared by all the herdsmen, the negative utility for any particular decision-making herdsman is only a fraction of −1.
>
> Adding together the component partial utilities, the rational herdsman concludes that the only sensible course for him to pursue is to add another animal to his herd. And another; and another. . . . But this is the conclusion reached by each and every rational herdsman sharing a commons. Therein is the tragedy. Each man is locked into a system that compels him to increase his herd without limit—in a world that is limited. Ruin is the destination toward which all men rush, each pursuing his own best interest in a society that believes in the freedom of the commons. Freedom in a commons brings ruin to all.

What kind of market failure has Hardin identified? How does the market system deal with externalities or public goods? How is the political authority to deal with socially erroneous private decisions? One instance in American history is particularly illustrative of the two main political reactions to the "tragedy of the commons."

Under oil and gas law, the "rule of capture" allows the owner of a track of land to produce oil and gas from beneath his or her land even if some oil and gas which has migrated from beneath the neighbors' land is included. Moreover, the owner will not be liable to neighbors even if his or her production has caused the migration. The neighbors' only defense to the rule of capture is to capture the oil or gas first. The result of this rule was a rush to drill by all property owners. However, when a field is developed too rapidly, the natural energy of a reservoir is dissipated in a manner that reduces the total recovery from a reservoir. Is this a tragedy of the commons? Is this waste a failure of the market system that can only be prevented by regulation?

Also, the rule of capture has the effect of bringing large amounts of oil to the surface for storage and sale in excess of a market demand that will support a price to cover the cost recovery. Is the resulting "destructive competition" in need of regulation for the social good? Are the costs of storing large amounts of oil on the surface, which could have been left in the reservoir, a waste of economic resources?

The problems of ecological waste and excessive competition resulting from the failure of the "invisible hand" to promote the public interest have been the major economic and political problems of the 20th century. Excessive competition has spawned private cartels which were either outlawed by antitrust or socially approved as long as public participation (regulation) was included. The prodigy of ecological waste, whether human or natural resources, has been labor laws and environmental protection laws adopting a variety of regulatory techniques. All these have resulted from society's perception of market failure which needed governmental solution. Even the strongest advocates of reliance on the market system have admitted that certain circumstances require governmental intervention.

Indeed, for much of the past century, the central issue of government economic policy has been whether to accept big business with direct governmental control of business policies or to reject such control and rely on antitrust enforcement and positive support of competition through encouragement of new entrants and subsidization of marginal producers. America's ambivalence toward big business has been reflected in cycles of expanded antitrust enforcement and relaxation or, alternatively, more regulation and deregulation. The elements of these competing approaches to the problem of market failure can be found in government policy of almost any time period. For example, in the presidential campaign of 1912 Theodore Roosevelt, who had gained a reputation as a "trust buster" in the decade before, accepted the trend toward consolidation of large enterprises and the existence of monopoly power and, instead, argued for regulation, which he felt would achieve the approximate results of competition, rather than the promotion of competition itself. And today, the debate between political parties concerning the appropriate role of government in dealing with market failures is no less intense, particularly when one notes that *regulatory* failure often seems as prevalent as market failure.

The chapters in Part Four contain materials that reveal the separate methods of government regulation dealing with various aspects of market failure. Each chapter will expose the historical movements that led to the societal decision to adopt government regulation over the respective subject areas and will discuss the substantive provisions of the regulatory techniques employed.

chapter 16

CONSUMER PROTECTION LAWS

Classical economists have advanced the theory of consumer sovereignty as an essential ingredient of free competitive markets. Informed consumers with equal bargaining power were to interact with sellers in the marketplace to establish mutually satisfactory bargains. Government protection of either consumers or producers was considered unnecessary. *Caveat emptor*—let the buyer beware—was accepted public policy because the seller and the buyer generally had equal knowledge of the simple goods that revealed their quality through inspection. In effect, consumers could protect themselves. The consumer could avoid unsafe products because most goods did not contain hidden defects or dangerous tendencies. Consumers could protect themselves against fraud or deceit with nontechnical wares because they could, by inspection, inform themselves concerning the attributes of the product. In addition, the large number of sellers in the competitive market provided the consumer with the right to choose among producers and, thereby, forced producers to supply satisfactory quality and service at a fair price. And because the buyer and seller often dealt face to face, the consumers' complaints fell on the sympathetic ears of producers who, in their desire to make sales, responded to the consumers' voice.

During the final years of the nineteenth century, however, the marketplace began to change. New technology developed more sophisticated products, and producers began to organize into larger and fewer economic units. Initial outcries for consumer or public protection brought about congressional regulation of monopolistic practices of railroads and the passage of the antitrust laws. Subsequent legislation included the Federal Trade Commission (FTC) Act in 1914 to prevent "unfair methods of competition" and to abort the trends toward monopoly. In 1938, the Wheeler–Lea Amendment broadened the FTC's authority to prevent "unfair and deceptive practices" by business which are deemed unfair or deceptive to consumers.

Other laws of consumer protection have been created in more recent times. Although the development of these laws continues to be sporadic, President Kennedy's address concerning consumer protection in 1962 brought clarity and definition to the problems of consumers. The president asserted four basic rights of the consumer:

1. The right to choose (variety in product sources).
2. The right to be informed (avoid deceptions).
3. The right to safety (avoid hazardous goods).
4. The right to be heard (to assert consumer interest in the formulation of governmental policy).

These rights as enunciated by the President gave direction to the "consumer movement" throughout the 1960s and 1970s. They also provide some insights into probable future trends and legislation. For example, recent consumer advocates have advanced the notion that consumers should also have the *right to recover*. The right of recovery is considered an essential consumer right, necessary to protect the other four fundamental consumer rights. However, consumer rights, as advocated, have not been completely fulfilled in law. Consequently, the debate over the content and passage of consumer protection laws is continuous. This chapter attempts to provide a basic understanding of the principles of law that have been fashioned to protect the consumer.

CONSUMER'S RIGHT TO CHOOSE

The consumer's right to choose involves the assurance, whenever possible, of access to a variety of products and services at competitive prices. In effect, the consumer's right to choose is primarily protected by the market system itself. Competitive vendors provide a variety of goods from which the consumer may exercise independent choice for products and prices that suit the consumer's taste. However, when vendors cooperate with one another in contravention of the competitive process, the consumer's choice for products or competitive prices is likely to be reduced. The response of the political process to such industry cooperation has been the enactment of antitrust laws to protect the competitive process. The theory, substance, and process of the antitrust laws has been fully explained in previous chapters. Suffice it to say at this point that both private and public remedies are provided by the antitrust statutes in an effort to protect the consumer's right to choice. To the extent that antitrust laws are ineffective in eliminating industry collusion or concentration which reduce the competitive process, the consumer's right to choice will likely be impaired. Consequently, consumer groups continue to support efforts to improve antitrust laws and resist efforts of other groups that seek relaxation of antitrust rules.

CONSUMER'S RIGHT TO BE INFORMED

COMMERCIAL ADVERTISING

In 1942, the Supreme Court in *Valentine* v. *Chrestensen,* 316 U.S. 52, held that commercial advertising was not protected by the First Amendment right of free speech. In effect, the First Amendment imposed no restraints on governmental regulation of commercial advertising. The fact that advertising was a form of speech, a means of communicating ideas or information, and literally within the First Amendment's language was ignored by the Court. Consequently, the government and, in particular, the FTC had authority to regulate advertising without such government action being construed an infringement on the advertiser's right to free speech. In so doing, the FTC had almost total authority to determine the meaning of the advertisement and to issue broad "fencing in" orders to avoid recurrence of the "illegal" ad.

However, in 1975 the Court began to critically examine its position concerning commercial speech. Then, in *Virginia State Board* v. *Virginia Citizens Consumer Council,* 425 U.S. 748 (1976), the Court held that even if the advertiser's interest is "a purely economic one," it "hardly disqualifies him from protection under the First Amendment." The Court added the following:

> It is a matter of public interest that [private economic] decisions in the aggregate, be intelligent and well-informed. To this end, the free flow of commercial information is indispensable. . . . [E]ven if the First Amendment were thought to be primarily an instrument to enlighten public decision making in a democracy, we could not say that free flow of [commercial] information does not serve that goal.

However, the Court emphasized that its decision that "commercial speech, like other varieties, is protected" does not mean "it can never be regulated in any way." The Court acknowledged that reasonable "time, place, and manner" restrictions on speech are valid. The Court added that

> untruthful speech, commercial or otherwise, has never been protected for its own sake. . . . Obviously, much commercial speech is not provably false, or even wholly false, but only deceptive or misleading. We foresee no obstacle to a state's dealing effectively with this problem.

This language quickly dispells any foolish notion that the Court was attempting to repeal the Federal Trade Commission Act or any other laws prohibiting false and deceptive advertising. The Court wanted to make sure that its decision was not misconstrued as giving commercial speech the same degree of constitutional protection as political and literary speech. Advertising is to become constitutionally protected speech, but advertisers do not need or deserve as much protection as politicians and editorial writers.

Deceptive Advertising

FTC v. Colgate-Palmolive Co.

380 U.S. 374 (1964)
Supreme Court of the United States

Chief Justice Warren

The basic question before us is whether it is a deceptive trade practice to represent falsely that a televised test, experiment, or demonstration provides a viewer with visual proof of a product claim, regardless of whether the product claim is itself true.

The case arises out of an attempt by defendant Colgate-Palmolive Company to prove to the television public that its shaving cream, "Rapid Shave," . . . could soften even the toughness of sandpaper. Each of the commercials contained the same "sandpaper test." The announcer informed the audience that, "To prove RAPID SHAVE'S super-moisturizing power, we put it right from the can onto this tough, dry sandpaper. It was apply . . . soak . . . and off in a stroke." While the announcer was speaking, Rapid Shave was applied to a substance that appeared to be sandpaper, and immediately thereafter a razor was shown shaving the substance clean. The Federal Trade Commission issued a complaint against respondent Colgate . . . charging that the commercials were false and deceptive. The evidence before the . . . Administrative Law Judge (ALJ) disclosed that . . . the substance resembling sandpaper was in fact a simulated prop, or "mock-up," made of plexiglass to which sand had been applied. . . .

The Commission . . . found that the undisclosed use of a plexiglass substitute for sandpaper was . . . a material misrepresentation that was a deceptive act. . . . [T]he Commission found that viewers had been misled into believing they had seen it done with their own eyes. As a result of these findings the Commission entered a cease-and-desist order against the [defendant]. . . .

We accept the Commission's determination that the commercials involved in this case contained [the] representation . . . that the viewer was seeing this experiment for himself . . . which was clearly false. The parties agree that Section 5 prohibits the intentional misrepresentation of any fact which would constitute a material factor in a purchaser's decision whether to buy. They differ, however, in their conception of what "facts" constitute a "material factor" in a purchaser's decision to buy. [Defendant] submits, in effect, that the only material facts are those which deal with the substantive qualities of a product. The Commission, on the other hand, submits that the misrepresentation of *any* fact so long as it materially induces a purchaser's decision to buy is a deception prohibited by §5.

* * *

. . . We find an especially strong similarity between the present case and those cases in which a seller induces the public to purchase an arguably good product by misrepresenting his line of business, by concealing the fact that the product is reprocessed, or by misappropriating another's trademark. In each the seller had used a misrepresentation to break down what he regards to be an annoying or irrational habit of the buying public—the preference for particular manufacturers or known brands regardless of a product's actual qualities, the prejudice against reprocessed goods, and the desire for verification of a product claim. In each case the seller reasons that when the habit is broken the buyer will be satisfied with the performance of the product he receives. . . . It is generally accepted that it is a deceptive practice to state falsely that a product has received a testimonial from a respected source. In addition, the Commission has consistently acted to prevent sellers from falsely stating that their product claims have been "certified." We find these situations to be indistinguishable from the present case. We can assume that in each the underlying product claim is true and in each the seller actually conducted an experiment sufficient to prove to himself the truth of the claim. But in each the seller has told the public that it could rely on something other than his word concerning both the truth of the claim and the validity of his experiment. We find it an immaterial difference that in one case the viewer is told to rely on the word of a celebrity or authority he respects, in another on the word of a testing agency, and in the present case on his own perception of an undisclosed simulation. . . .

We agree with the Commission, therefore, that the undisclosed use of plexiglass in the present commercials was a material deceptive practice. . . . Nor was it necessary for the Commission to conduct a survey of the viewing public before it could determine that the commercials had a tendency to mislead, for when the Commission finds deception it is also authorized, within the bounds of reason, to infer that the deception will constitute a material factor in a purchaser's decision to buy. . . .

We turn our attention now to the order issued by the Commission. . . .

The Court of Appeals has criticized the reference in the Commission's order to "test, experiment or demonstrate" as not capable of practical interpretation. It could find no difference between the Rapid Shave commercial and a commercial which extolled the goodness of ice cream while giving viewers a picture of a scoop of mashed potatoes appearing to be ice cream. We do not understand this difficulty. In the ice cream case the mashed potato prop is not being used for additional proof of the product claim, while the purpose of the Rapid Shave commercial is to give the viewer objective proof of the claims made. If in the ice cream hypothetical the focus of the commercial becomes the undisclosed potato prop and the viewer is invited, explicitly or by implication, to see for himself the truth of the claims about the ice cream's rich texture and full color, and perhaps compare it to a "rival product," then the commercial has become similar to the one now before us. Clearly, however, a commercial which depicts happy actors delightedly eating ice cream that is in fact mashed potatoes or drinking a product appearing to be coffee but which is in fact some other substance is not covered by the present order.

* * *

In commercials where the emphasis is on the seller's word, and not on the viewer's own perception, the defendants need not fear that an undisclosed use of props is prohibited by the present order. On the other hand, when the commercial not only makes a claim, but also invites the viewer to rely on his own perception for demonstrative proof of the claim, the defendants will be aware that the use of undisclosed props in strategic places might be a material deception. We believe that defendants will have no difficulty applying the Commission's order to the vast majority of their contemplated future commercials.

Questions

1. For an advertising misrepresentation to be illegal, must it relate false information about the substantive qualities of the product or misrepresent any fact that may induce a purchaser to buy the product?
2. Should misrepresenting mock-ups be allowed on television if the substantive facts behind the mock-up are true?
3. An advertisement showing a family enjoying ice cream uses mashed potatoes for ice cream because of the hot lights in filming. Is this an illegal mock-up?
4. Must the Commission conduct a survey of the viewing public to determine if a commercial has a tendency to mislead? Must the Commission put some individual on the stand who will admit to being deceived?

Other FTC enforcement actions have further defined "deceptive trade practices" in relation to product claims. For example, misrepresenting a business or trade as a mill, manufacturer, or wholesaler when the seller merely performs a retailing function has been held deceptive. The deceptive use of trademarks or trade names is also outlawed. For example, Carter Products, Inc., was forced to excise the word *liver* from its trademark when it was demonstrated that the drug had no effect on the liver.

False product claims of composition, quality, quantity, characteristics, or effectiveness of the product are illegal. For example, Algoma Lumber Co. was prevented from the selling of yellow pine as "California white pine." Also, Winsted Hosiery Co. was prohibited from labeling as "wool" some underwear manufactured from partly wool ingredients.

Corrective Advertising

The remedy of "corrective advertising" requires the advertiser to run advertising disclosures of wrongdoing or of false impressions previously created by the advertiser. There have been consent orders in which companies have agreed to 12 months of advertising disclosures that correct previous false impressions created by their advertising. However, the companies have not admitted to any wrongdoing or to the FTC's authority to order such corrective advertising. For example, ITT Continental Baking Corp. agreed to a 12-month advertising disclosure that Profile Bread was not a dietary product. Ocean Spray Cranberries, Inc., likewise, admitted in corrective ads that cranberry juice had more "energy" only because it contained more calories. However, in the following case the FTC "ordered" the corrective advertising and the defendant, Warner-Lambert, challenged the authority of the commission to issue such an order.

Warner-Lambert Co. v. FTC
562 F. 2d 749 (1977)
U.S. Court of Appeals (D.C. Cir.)

The Warner-Lambert Company petitions for review of an order of the Federal Trade Commission requiring it to cease and desist from advertising that its product, Listerine antiseptic mouthwash, prevents, cures, or alleviates the common cold. The FTC order further requires Warner-Lambert to disclose in future Listerine advertisements that: ". . . Listerine will not help prevent colds or sore throats or lessen their severity." . . .

Listerine has been on the market since 1879. Its formula has never changed. Ever since its introduction it has been represented as being beneficial in certain respects for colds, cold symptoms, and sore throats. Direct advertising to the consumer, including the cold claims as well as others, began in 1921. . . .

Petitioner contends that even if its advertising claims in the past were false, the portion of the Commission's order requiring "corrective advertising" exceeds the Commission's statutory power. The argument is based upon a literal reading of Section 5 of the Federal Trade Commission Act, which authorizes the Commission to issue "cease and desist" orders against violators and does not expressly mention any other remedies. The Commission's position, on the other hand, is that the affirmative disclosure that Listerine will not prevent colds or lessen their severity is absolutely necessary to give effect to the prospective cease and desist order; a hundred years of false cold claims have built up a large reservoir of erroneous consumer belief which would persist unless corrected, long after petitioner ceased making the claims.

Petitioner's narrow reading of Section 5 was at one time shared by the Supreme Court. . . .

But the modern view is very different. In 1963 the Court ruled that the Civil Aeronautics Board has authority to order divestiture in addition to ordering cessation of unfair methods of competition by air carriers. *Pan American World Airways, Inc.* v. *United States,* 371 U.S. 296 (1963). The CAB statute, like Section 5, spoke only of the authority to issue cease and desist orders, but the Court said, "[W]here the problem lies within the purview of the Board, . . . Congress must have intended to give it authority that was ample to deal with the evil at hand. . . . [The] power to order divestiture need not be explicitly included in the powers of an administrative agency to be part of its arsenal of authority. . . ."

Later, in *FTC* v. *Dean Foods Co.,* the Court applied *Pan American* to the Federal Trade Commission. In upholding the Commission's power to seek a preliminary injunction against a proposed merger, the Court held that it was not necessary to find express statutory authority for the power. "Such ancillary powers have always been treated as essential to the effective discharge of the Commission's responsibilities."

Thus it is clear that the Commission has the power to shape remedies which go beyond the simple cease and desist order. Our next inquiry must be whether a corrective advertising order is for any reason outside the range of permissible remedies. . . .

According to petitioner, "The first reference to corrective advertising in Commission decisions occurred in 1970, nearly fifty years and untold numbers of false advertising cases after passage of the Act." In petitioner's view, the late emergence of this "newly discovered" remedy is itself evidence that it is beyond the Commission's authority. This argument fails on two counts. First the fact that an agency has not asserted a power over a period of years is not proof that the agency lacks such power. Second, and more importantly, we are not convinced that the corrective advertising remedy is really such an innovation. The label may be newly coined, but the concept is well established. It is simply that under certain circumstances an advertiser may be required to make affirmative disclosure of unfavorable facts.

One such circumstance is when an advertisement that did not contain the disclosure would be misleading. For example, the Commission has ordered the sellers of treatments for baldness to disclose that the vast majority of cases of thinning hair and baldness are attributable to heredity, age, and endocrine balance (so-called "male pattern baldness") and that their treatment would have no effect whatever on this type of baldness. It has ordered the promoters of a device for stopping bedwetting to disclose that the device would not be of value in cases caused by organic defects or diseases. And it has ordered the makers of Geritol, an iron supplement, to disclose that Geritol will relieve symptoms of tiredness only in persons who suffer from iron deficiency anemia, and that the vast majority of people who experience such symptoms do not have such a deficiency.

Each of these orders was approved on appeal over objections that it exceeded the Commission's statutory authority. . . .

Affirmative disclosure has also been required when an advertisement, although not misleading if taken alone, becomes misleading considered in light of past advertisements. For example, for 60 years Royal Baking Powder Company has stressed in its advertising that its product was superior because it was made with cream of tartar, not phosphate. But, faced with rising costs of cream of tartar, the time came when it changed its ingredients and became a phosphate baking powder. It carefully removed from all labels and advertisements any reference to cream of tartar and corrected the list of ingredients. But the new labels used the familiar arrangement of lettering, coloration, and design, so that they looked exactly like the old ones. A new advertising campaign stressed the new low cost of the product and dropped all reference to cream of tartar. But the advertisements were also silent on the subject of phosphate and did not disclose the change in the product.

The Commission held, and the Second Circuit agreed, that the new advertisements were deceptive, since they did not advise consumers that their reasons for buying the powder in the past no longer applied. The court held that it was proper to require the company to take affirmative steps to advise the public. To continue to sell the new product on the strength of the reputation attained through 60 years of its manufacture and sale and wide advertising of its superior powder, under an impression induced by its advertisements that the product purchased was the same in kind and as superior as that which had been so long manufactured by it, was unfair alike to the public and to the competitors in the baking powder business.

It appears to us that the order in *Royal* . . . [was] the same kind of remedy the Commission has ordered here. Like Royal . . . , Listerine has built up over a period of many years a widespread reputation. When it was ascertained that that reputation no longer applied to the product, it was necessary to take action to correct it. Here, as in *Royal,* it is the accumulated impact of *past* advertising that necessitates disclosure in *future* advertising. To allow consumers to continue to buy the product on the strength of the impression built up by prior advertising—an impression which is now known to be false—would be unfair and deceptive.

Having established that the Commission does have the power to order corrective advertising in appropriate cases, it remains to consider whether use of the remedy against Listerine is warranted and equitable. . . .

The Commission has adopted . . . [a] standard for the imposition of corrective advertising . . . [which] dictates two factual inquiries: (1) did Listerine's advertisements play a substantial role in creating or reinforcing in the public's mind a false belief about the product? and (2) would this belief linger on after the false advertising ceases? It strikes us that if the answer to both questions is not yes, companies everywhere may be wasting their massive advertising budgets. Indeed, it is more than a little peculiar to hear petitioner assert that its commercials really have no effect on consumer belief.

. . . [In any case] the Commission adduced survey evidence to support both propositions. We find that . . . survey data and the expert testimony interpreting them constitute substantial evidence in support of the need for corrective advertising in this case.

Finally, petitioner challenges the duration of the disclosure requirement. By its terms it continues until respondent has expended on Listerine advertising a sum equal to the average annual Listerine advertising budget for the period April 1962 to March 1972. That is approximately ten million dollars. Thus if petitioner continues to advertise normally the corrective advertising will be required for about one year. We cannot say that is an unreasonably long time in which to correct a hundred years of cold claims. But, to petitioner's distress, the requirement will not expire by mere passage of time. If petitioner cuts back its Listerine advertising, or ceases it altogether, it can only postpone the duty to disclose. The Commission concluded that correction was required and that a duration of a fixed period of time might not accomplish that task, since petitioner could evade the order by choosing not to advertise at all. The formula settled upon by the Commission is reasonably related to the violation it found.

Questions

1. The FTC Act authorizes the commission to issue cease and desist orders. It does not expressly mention other remedies, such as corrective advertis-

ing. Does this mean that the FTC does not possess the authority to order corrective advertising?

2. What particular precedents did the court of appeals cite as containing essentially the same kind of remedy that the commission ordered against Warner-Lambert?
3. When does the commission feel corrective advertising is an appropriate remedy? What factual inquiries are necessary to impose corective advertising?
4. A mail survey study was conducted before and during the corrective ad campaign.[1] The results showed the number of people who considered a mouthwash's ability to prevent colds or sore throats dropped from 31 percent before the corrective campaign to 25 percent when it was over. The study found that although the usage of Listerine for clean breath remained the same, there was about a 40 percent drop in the amount of the mouthwash used for colds and sore throats. In contrast, 42 percent of the respondents still believe colds and sore throat effectiveness was the principal Listerine advertising theme and 39 percent of Listerine users reported they still use mouthwash to relieve or prevent a cold or sore throat. A second study concluded that viewers apparently understood the commercial's primary purpose as not to communicate the correction but to promote the product. What is your opinion of the effectiveness of the corrective advertising remedy?

Proposed "Deceptive" Standard

The new FTC officials under the Reagan Administration have urged Congress to adopt a standard that uses the "reasonable consumer" as the key in determining whether an act or advertising is deceptive.[2] According to the new officials, an act or practice should be considered deceptive only if it is likely to mislead individuals to their detriment, while they act reasonably under the circumstances. Three examples of the types of claims the commission should not pursue were detailed: the claims about taste or scent; obviously exaggerated claims, such as "put a tiger in your tank"; and correctly stated expert opinions unless all reasonable experts disagree. These officials argue that all of these claims are useful to consumers and seldom, if ever, lead to consumer injury. Such claims, they explain, may inform consumers about subjective product characteristics, help them remember the advertising, and provide easy access to expert opinion.

Under this revised standard of deception, cases such as *Listerine* would continue to be challenged because Listerine's ad would likely lead reasonable consumers to believe that Listerine prevents and cures cold, when, in fact, it does not. On the other hand, another recent case, *Kroger,* would not hold up under the proposed standard. The commission challenged Kroger's comparative-price ads on the grounds that they implicitly represented the price surveys as methodologically sound. However, new FTC officials point out that Kroger's ads frequently emphasized the informality of the surveys and, therefore, would not mislead a "reasonable" consumer. They argue that this sort of ad would not be challenged under the newly proposed deceptive standard.

The FTC officials admit that some groups, such as children, need more protection than reasonable adults. They argue that camera angles and photographic techniques that may exaggerate the speed or size of a toy, for example, may mislead a reasonable child but not a reasonable adult.

Whether Congress adopts this new standard for deception or not, the new leadership at the FTC is likely to follow some variety of this reasoning in its enforcement activities.

"Unfairness" Doctrine

Besides FTC enforcement actions against deceptive practices in relation to product claims, various "unfair" product claims may be held to be illegal. The FTC has argued that advertising product claims for which the advertiser possesses no substantiation is deceptive. The substantiation requirement developed from the FTC's conclusion that the proliferation of highly technical products places the consumer at a distinct disadvantage in knowledge and ability to evaluate product claims. Consequently, the FTC feels that if it can prove the advertiser lacked a "reasonable basis" for its claim, the advertiser's claim is deceptive because the advertiser has impliedly claimed to have such "reasonable basis." Alternatively, the commission argues that unsubstantiated claims are unfair to consumers even if the claim, in fact, is true. One type of unfair claim is an improper uniqueness claim. For example, ITT Continental Baking Company was not allowed to claim that its enriched bread possessed a unique feature (nutritional) when it merely contained ingredients that are in all manufacturers' bread. Likewise, Firestone's "safe" tire was held to be an unfair uniqueness claim. Its tire, like Continental Baking's bread, possessed no uniqueness in comparison with competing brands and the assertion in the ads was unfair to consumers.

However, perhaps no case has done more to delineate the parameters of the commission's powers to regulate unfair practices than the 1972 case of *FTC* v. *Sperry & Hutchinson Co.*, 405 U.S. 233. In that case the court of appeals stated that for the alleged act complained of to be a violation of Section 5 it must be (1) a *per se* violation of antitrust policy, (2) a violation of the letter of the Sherman, Clayton, or Robinson–Patman Acts, or (3) a violation of the spirit of these acts as recognized by the Supreme Court. The Supreme Court disagreed with the views of the court of appeals and concluded the following:

> . . . [L]egislative and judicial authorities alike convince us that the Federal Trade Commission does not arrogate excessive power to itself if, in measuring a practice against the elusive, but congressionally mandated standard of fairness, it . . . considers public values beyond simply those enshrined in the letter of the law or encompassed in the spirit of the antitrust laws.

The Court even offered some guidelines in a footnote for determining the existence of "unfairness." The Court cited a previous FTC suggestion that a three-factor test could be employed. The factors include (1) whether the practice offends public policy as it has been established by statutes, the common law, or otherwise; (2) whether it is immoral, unethical, oppressive, or unscrupulous; and (3) whether it causes substantial injury to consumers or competitors.

Thereafter, the commission promulgated standards for determining unfairness which balanced consumer injury against commercial necessity. The difficulty with the initial standards announced by the commission is that consumer injury is not always quantifiable (for example, damage from emotional distress or effect on future employment). Therefore, the balancing process is not predictable if the weights of the various factors involved are not precise. Consequently, it is clear to many that the balancing test needs considerable clarification before it can become an effective tool in regulation of unfair practices.[3]

When Congress renewed the FTC's rule-making powers in 1975, the FTC announced its intention to promulgate rules under the unfairness doctrine. The FTC proposed rules that probably would have banned all children's advertising, under the unfairness notion that even if such ads were truthful, they were unfair when aimed at a particularly vulnerable audience. The FTC also initiated proceedings for possible "unfair" regulations in the funeral industry. However, in 1980 Congress expressed its objections to the FTC's rule-making efforts utilizing the unfairness doctrine. The FTC Improvements Act of 1980 terminated the rule-making proceedings on children's advertising. Moreover, the act stated that unfairness cannot be used as a basis for a trade regulation *rule* concerning advertisements aimed at children. Finally, the 1980 act forbad the FTC to use any funds for the years 1980 to 1982 to initiate rule-making proceedings involving *unfair* acts or practices. After 1982 the FTC is again empowered to issue industry-wide rules that are based on unfairness. Meanwhile, the commission remains free to challenge in an adjudicatory context any commercial advertising that the commission determines to be unfair.

Future Advertising Regulations

Under the Reagan Administration, the FTC will likely restrict its prosecution efforts to outright fraud and deception. However, some writers have suggested that marketing and psychological research is likely to influence advertising regulation in the future.[4]

Prosecution of "deception" may well expand to include "tricks of phrasing" that deliberately mislead consumers. Marketing research already discusses the effects of incomplete comparisons, hedge words, and puffery on the consumers' cognitive processing of information. Such research may well influence future FTC prosecutorial decision making concerning deception.

Psychological research also reveals that "emotional" advertising which associates the product with the "good life" influences consumer behavior. Although consumers deny they believe such associations implied by the ads, research suggests that the subconscious which is conditioned by the ad often directs irrational behavior in consumers. Since proof of deception requires evidence that the ad has the capacity to create misleading *beliefs,* the deception doctrine provides little protection for consumers from emotional claims consumers stress they do not believe. Consequently, if such emotional commercials are to be regulated, the unfairness doctrine will need to be expanded.

Conservative economists contend that consumers are rational decision makers when they choose to purchase heavily advertised products because such advertisers with large advertising outlays possess great incentives to ensure the quality of their brands. However, this theoretical assertion is not convincingly supported by empirical research and ignores the ethical question of whether the consumers will even buy such items in the absence of emotional advertisements. Consequently, the results of such cognitive and emotional research will likely challenge the FTC's future fashioning of policy positions concerning deceptive and unfair advertising.

Little–FTC Acts

In an effort to gain state aid to combat unfair trade practices, the Federal Trade Commission proposed a draft of an *Unfair Trade Practices and Consumer Protection Law* for states to enact. Forty-three states have enacted some version of this proposal, and six other states and the District of Columbia have adopted a variation of the *Uniform Consumer Sales Practice Act,* which was developed by the National Conference of Commissioners of Uniform State Laws. Consequently, 50 jurisdictions have enacted laws more or less like the Federal Trade Commission Act to prevent deceptive and unfair trade practices within their respective jurisdictions. In Alabama, which does not have such a law, a Consumer Protection Council is charged with the responsibility of creating fair consumer finance transactions. Alabama's Commissioner of Agriculture and Industries is empowered to seek proper "marking and labeling" of products and remove "misbranded" articles from commerce.

These "Little-FTC" acts typically contain authorization for the administrating authority to conduct investigations through the use of subpoenas, to issue cease and desist orders, or to obtain court injunctions to halt the use of anticompetitive, deceptive, or unfair trade practices. Rules and regulations may be issued under the statutes in 31 states. The following case illustrates the utilization of these state laws in the protection of the consumer's right to be correctly informed.

People Ex Rel. Dunbar v. Gym of America, Inc.

493 P. 2d 660 (1972)
Supreme Court of Colorado

The trial court held that the Colorado Consumer Protection Act is so vague and uncertain that it does not furnish a standard sufficiently definite to give notice of meaning to persons affected thereby and is thus in contravention of state and federal due process. In support of this conclusion, [defendant] claims that certain key words . . . in the statute are either not defined at all or are so inadequately defined that one cannot determine which trade practices are allowed and which are prohibited. . . .

We note that this statute is concerned with proscribing certain kinds of specific *future* conduct. As such, the statute provides sanctions of purely prospective effect, such as the restraining orders, injunctions, and assurances of discontinuance found in Section 7. This, of course, means that when the attorney general seeks an injunction he is not demanding that the defendant be punished with a penal sanction, but rather that the defendant be restrained from acting unlawfully in the future. It is unnecessary that such a statute provide absolutely precise warning before its equitable sanctions are applied. The adjudication itself provides notice to the defendant, and is prospective in its application. The result is that the defendant is provided with the explicit terms of the decree or order to tell him what practices are allowed without incurring penalties. Therefore, as will be seen below, a statute such as this whose sanctions are injunctions or assurances of discontinuance need not be as precise as a statute where the sanction is penal or criminal.

One should also take note . . . that the statute's subject matter . . . is the Colorado version of the Uniform Deceptive Trade Practices Act. It is clearly enacted to control various deceptive trade practices in dealing with the public and as such is obviously designed to both declare and enforce an important public policy. More significantly, the utility of general standards of actionability with respect to deceptive trade practices has been repeatedly recognized. . . .

The question before the Court now is whether the . . . challenged phrases—"bait and switch," "disparagement," and "tie-in sales," as used in the Consumer Protection Act are so vague as to render their meaning unintelligible to people affected by them. We believe that all . . . terms are not unconstitutionally vague. . . .

The statute's "bait and switch" terminology is attacked on the ground that it has no commonly understood meaning and is therefore unconstitutionally vague. This argument must fall for several reasons. First, Section 2(1) (a) (o) (i) *specifically defines* "bait and switch" advertising which "consists of an attractive but insincere offer to sell a product or service which the seller in truth does not intend or desire to sell." Second, "bait and switch" advertising and selling techniques have long been recognized in the legal literature and have long been subject to equitable sanctions.

The use of the term "disparagement" in the statute is attacked on the basis that it has no widely understood meaning. It may be true that the Colorado Consumer Protection Act does not specifically define "disparagement" anywhere, but, in our view, the word "disparagement" has such a common meaning that to define it would be an exercise in redundancy. The legal literature contains many instances of the use of the word "disparagement" when dealing with forbidden trade practices.

In *Electrolux,* the New York Court of Appeals enjoined a sales promotion scheme whereby a business firm first advertised a product at a very attractive price in order to invite inquiry, then disparaged or "knocked" the product when members of the public made inquiry, and finally offered another item for sale which was more expensive than the first but which seemed like a "bargain" in comparison to the disparaged product that was originally advertised. This deceptive use of advertising as a lure to sell other nonadvertised products or services is exactly the kind of trade practice which the Colorado Consumer Protection Act and the Uniform Deceptive Trade Practices Act . . . prohibit. This is also the "disparagement" that Gym of America is accused of engaging in when it allegedly told members of the public that club privileges on terms as advertised would not be valuable because the advertised terms were too short in duration to be of any benefit to their health, while an expensive membership of a longer period of time would be quite helpful.

[Defendant's] last contention concerning the statute's purported vagueness is that the Act's "tie-in-sales" language is too ambiguous and uncertain to meet due process requirements. This argument must also fall for several reasons. The Colorado Consumer Protection Act specifically defines "tie-in-sales" to mean an "undisclosed condition to be met prior to selling the advertised product or service." Furthermore, the concept of a "tie-in-sale" is not new to the law as its practice has long been prohibited by the anti-trust laws. These guideposts, added to the fact that a "tie-in-sale," like "disparagement," and "bait and switch" tactics, is not a new or unfamiliar term to most business enterprises, leads us to conclude that its use in the Colorado Consumer Protection Act does establish a standard against which one's business and trade activities can be tested. There is a definite background of experience and precedent to illuminate the meaning of the words employed in the statute. No one would reasonably be misled thereby.

Questions

1. Why is it not necessary that a statute, such as the Colorado Consumer Protection Act, provide absolutely precise language in outlawing certain activity?
2. What is a "bait and switch" sales tactic?
3. What is the "disparagement" sales tactic?
4. What is a "tie-in-sales" tactic?
5. How do these rules protect the consumer's right to be correctly informed?

FAIR LABELING

Closely related to the regulation of advertising and deceptive sales practices is the regulation of labeling and marking of products. Numerous federal statutes have been designed to give the consumer more accurate information about the product or precise warnings as to the dangers in the use of the product. Particular federal labeling statutes include the Fair Packaging and Labeling Act, the Fair Products Labeling Act, the Wool Products Labeling Act, the Cigarette Labeling and Advertising Act, and the Federal Hazardous Substances Labeling Act. Other statutes designed to protect the consumer from personal harm or economic loss also regulate labeling and disclosure of information.

The Fair Packaging and Labeling Act of 1966 directs the Federal Trade Commission (in the case of most commodities) to promulgate labeling requirements (1) pertaining to the identification of the commodity's manufacturer, packer, or distributor; (2) pertaining to the location and legibility of a statement of net quantity of the contents; and (3) pertaining to any description in terms of weight, volume, or size. The act authorizes the issuance of labeling regulations to prevent consumer deception and to determine what size packages may be represented by words such as *small, medium,* and *large.* The act grants additional authority to regulate the use of "cents-off" or "economy" sizes for packaging. It also requires a listing of the ingredients of commodities and authorizes regulations to prohibit "nonfunctional slack fill" or "packaged air."

Labeling Standards

The implementation of labeling laws is seldom easy. For example, in 1966 Congress recognized that there was great consumer confusion as to the quality of tires offered for sale to the public and the meaning of the variety of trade terminology used in marketing new passenger car tires. This conclusion led to a provision in the National Traffic and Motor Vehicle Safety Act of 1966 that a system be established to assist the consumer in making an informed choice in purchasing new tires. The Department of Transportation (DOT) Act required the secretary of transportation to develop a "uniform quality grading system for motor vehicle tires." However, because of the failure of the tire industry to initially provide test and cost information requested by DOT and because of the technical difficulties in developing acceptable tire testing procedures, the tire-grading system was not implemented until 1979. Besides the long delays in establishing product labeling standards, there is the inherent problem of creating standards themselves. Either the producers or consumers or both may be disappointed with the established standards. Consider the dispute in the following case.

Federation of Homemakers v. Hardin

328 F. Supp. 181 (1971)
U.S. District Court (D.C.)

[T]he Federation of Homemakers, a consumer organization dedicated to protecting the integrity of food products, challenges the use of "All Meat" labels on frankfurters when such products actually contain up to 15 percent of non-meat ingredients. . . .

The underlying statute in this case is the Wholesome Meat Act, enacted to protect the health and welfare of consumers by ensuring that they have access to wholesome and properly marked meats. . . .

The sections of the Wholesome Meat Act relating to misleading labeling, prohibit any meat product from being sold under a label which is misleading and provides a procedure whereby the Secretary [of Agriculture] may enforce the prohibition. . . .

In reviewing the adoption of a regulation by an agency under its rule-making procedures, the Court is limited to considering whether the administrative action was "arbitrary, capricious, an abuse of discretion, or otherwise not in accordance with law." In this matter, the Secretary's determination that "All

Meat" labels were authorized for frankfurters which contained up to 15 percent of non-meat ingredients represented a codification of a term in common use in the meat industry. However, there is nothing in the record to suggest that this "term of art" is understood by the general public.

The primary purpose of the Wholesome Meat Act is to benefit the consumer and to enable him to have a correct understanding of and confidence in meat products purchased. Prohibitions against mislabeling are an integral part of this purpose. Clearly, any rule-making procedure conducted under this Act which fails to primarily emphasize the understanding of the consumer is a procedure not conducted "in accordance with [the applicable] law" (the Act).

The leading case in this jurisdiction on the problem of mislabeling is *Armour and Company* v. *Freeman*. . . . The Court stated:

> To measure whether a label employing ordinary words of common usage is false or not, the words must be taken in their ordinary meaning. . . .

This Court finds the *Armour* case controlling. In applying the "ordinary meaning" test to the word "all," it is clear when that adjective is used on a label with the word "meat," the common understanding is that it describes a substance that is *totally and entirely* meat. The application of the "All Meat" label to frankfurters that are 15 percent nonmeat is a contradiction in terms and is misleading within the meaning of . . . [the Act]. The use of the term "All Meat" or "All (*species*)" as applied to frankfurters is invalid, and the defendants should be enjoined from permitting any frankfurter product to be so labeled.

Questions

1. Why did the Secretary of Agriculture adopt a rule for labeling frankfurters "all meat" when they may contain up to 15 percent nonmeat ingredients?
2. What was the reasoning of the Court in rejecting the secretary's rule?

FEDERAL WARRANTY LEGISLATION

Consumers perceive warranties as added assurance of quantity and value. They assume that product performance is guaranteed if a written warranty accompanies its purchase. They view warranty provisions as a means of consumer redress for defective products. On the other hand, marketers often regard warranties as promotional devices rather than additional benefits for the consumer. They also view warranties as legal instruments which limit their obligations to consumers. The result of these opposing viewpoints has been consumer confusion in comprehending warranty messages. The "legalese" language employed in warranties impedes the message to the consumers that the seller intends to limit his or her responsibilities in relation to the product sold. The resulting consumer dissatisfaction with warranties as an assurance of quality and consumer frustration with attempts to gain "satisfaction" through complex warranty provisions caused Congress to respond with the Magnuson–Moss Warranty Act, which became law in 1975. Even though the Warranty Act went into effect in 1975, its full impact was not immediately felt, because it provides only an outline of principles which must be further defined and implemented through rules promulgated by the Federal Trade Commission.

The Warranty Act has five primary purposes:

1. To improve the adequacy of warranty information available to consumers.
2. To prevent deception with respect to warranties.
3. To improve competition in warranties in the marketing of consumer products.
4. To improve incentives for product reliability.
5. To encourage warrantors to establish informal dispute settlement mechanisms.

Although the act imposes no requirement that a consumer product be expressly warranted or any requirement regarding the duration of expressed warranties, it does impose certain disclosure requirements and standards on warrantors who choose to give written warranties. Failure to comply with the act's standards for warranties will subject the warrantor to action by the FTC or to action by a consumer class-action suit, if consumers have been damaged by the warrantor's failure to comply. The act authorizes the Court to award the consumer his or her legal expenses, incuding attorney's fees, as part of a judgment in favor of the consumer.

The act applies when a written warranty is given in connection with the sale of consumer products— "any tangible personal property which is distributed in commerce and which is normally used for personal, family or household purposes." A warranty which is unambiguous and applies solely to services or workmanship is not covered by the act. However, should the written warranty affirm both product performance and workmanship, such as basement waterproofing, it will be interpreted as a warranty subject to the terms of the act. A service contract may not be a warranty, but the act nevertheless stipulates that the terms of the service contract must be fully, clearly, and conspicuously disclosed in simple and readily understood language.

Since products are capable of both personal and commercial uses, the "normal use" of the product is determinative in defining the scope of the act. For example, the "normal use" of passenger autos is for personal or household purposes and, consequently, the auto warranty must comply with the act as a consumer product. Finally, it should be noted that the act does not apply to any warranty given in connection with the sale of real estate.

When a written warranty is given on a consumer product which costs the consumer more than $10, the warranty must be clearly and conspicuously designated a "full warranty" or a "limited warranty." If a warranty is designated a full warranty, it must meet the act's minimum standards for warranty:

1. There must be no charge for repairing the product if there is a defect within the warranty period.
2. There must be no limitation on the duration of implied warranties.
3. Any exclusion or limitation of consequential damages for breach of express or implied warranty must appear clearly and conspicuously on the face of the warranty.
4. If the product cannot be repaired after a reasonable number of attempts, the consumer is permitted to elect either a replacement without charge or a refund.

The consumer's choice of refund or replacement is often referred to as a "lemon-aid" provision because it aids a consumer who purchased a "lemon." Unfortunately, most consumers are not aware that "lemon-aid" is served only to those who purchase products under a "full warranty."

Two additional requirements for full warranties under the act are as follows:

1. Warranty terms cannot be limited to the original purchaser only, but must extend to each purchaser who is a consumer of the product within the warranty period.
2. The warrantor may not impose any unreasonable duties on consumers as a condition of securing performance under the warranty.

Although the act did not establish any criteria for determining what is a "reasonable" duty to impose on a consumer, the FTC is authorized to develop rules to define such duties in detail. Any warranty that does not meet the minimum standards for a full warranty must be designated as a "limited warranty."

Under the FTC Warranty Rule 702, sellers have the affirmative duty to make the text of the witten warranties available for the buyer's review prior to sale. A variety of techniques are allowed by the FTC to accomplish this purpose. Rule 701 establishes the requirements for disclosures of warranty terms. It requires that the terms of the warranty clearly and conspicuously disclose the following:

1. The identity of the party to whom the warranty is extended.
2. A clear identification of products, parts, or characteristics covered and excluded by the warranty.
3. A statement of what the warrantor will do in the event of a defect or failure of the product to perform.
4. The point in time in which the warranty becomes effective if different from the purchase date.
5. A step-by-step explanation of the procedure which the consumer should follow to obtain performance under the warranty.
6. Information respecting any informal dispute settlement mechanism adopted by the warrantor.

7. Certain mandatory statements if limitations are imposed on duration of implied warranties or consequential damages.
8. A statement that the warranty confers specific legal rights.

The act allows warrantors an option to establish an informal dispute settlement procedure for resolving consumer complaints arising out of warranty obligations. Rule 703 defines the duties of the warrantor and the minimum requirements that must be met if the warrantor elects to implement such an informal procedure. The informal procedure must be disclosed in the written warranty and the warrantor must fund and operate the mechanism so that it is provided free of charge to consumers. If the warrantor provides such a mechanism, consumers may not bring civil suits under the act until the dispute has been submitted to the informal proceedings. Although the decision of the informal proceedings is not binding on the parties, it is admissible in evidence in subsequent civil suits relating to the matter decided.

Questions

1. How has the Warranty Act expanded the consumer's right to be informed?
2. What are the rights of the consumer under a "full warranty"?

CONSUMER'S RIGHT TO SAFETY

The consumer's right to safety involves protection against the marketing of goods that are hazardous to health, life, or economic well-being. The consumer's right to safety found initial expression in the judicial doctrines that began the erosion of the concept of *caveat emptor*. Judges developed rules which express the notion that consumers are entitled to some reasonable quality in goods to avoid personal harm. The result has been a substantial increase in the liability of the seller of a defective good and an increase in the classes of injured parties who may seek recovery in such cases (see Chapter 8).

The judicial approach to dealing with sellers of defective goods is one of compensating the consumer for injuries sustained from the defective product. The tort system is founded on the belief that the cost of the award to the injured consumer will motivate the manufacturer to improve production processes to avoid such costs arising from defective goods. However, society felt other *preventive* measures were necessary; consequently, legislation attempting to prevent the marketing of unsafe products was created.

National product safety legislation consisted of a series of isolated statutes designed to remedy specific hazards existing in a narrow range of product categories. For example, the Federal Food and Drug Administration (FDA) was founded in 1931 to be responsible for the safety of drugs and medical devices and the purity of foods. In addition, food additives, color additives, antibiotic drugs, insulin, and most prescription drugs have been made subject to premarketing approval by the FDA. Veterinary drugs are regulated to ensure that they are safe, effective, and properly labeled. The FDA licenses the production of vaccine, serums, and other biological drugs and regulates bloodbanks. The FDA also enforces radiation safety standards for products such as X-ray equipment, colored television, lasers, sun lamps, and microwave ovens.

The Flamable Fabrics Act of 1953 was passed after serious injuries and deaths had resulted from the ignition of clothes made from synthetic fibers. This act empowers the Federal Trade Commission to enforce its provisions.

The National Hazardous Substances Labeling Act of 1960 mandates warnings on labels of potentially hazardous substances such as cleaning agents and paint removers. The Child Protection Act of 1966 outlaws the marketing of potentially harmful toys and other articles intended for children.

The National Traffic and Motor Vehicle Safety Act of 1966 is related specifically to automobiles and assigned to the National Highway Traffic Safety Administration (NHTSA) in the Department of Transportation. The NHTSA writes and enforces safety standards which set minimum performance levels for certain parts in motor vehicles and for the vehicle as a unit. Its jurisdiction includes automobiles, trucks, buses, recreational vehicles, motorcycles, bicycles, mopeds, and all related accessory equipment. The NHTSA also publishes information on car carriers and baby seats used in cars. The agency pursues allegations of vehicle defects both to ensure manufacturer compliance with federal standards and to identify all vehicle defects that may lie outside the applicability of the standards. The agency possesses strong powers to enforce its safety standards.

The congressional legislation designed to protect consumers includes the Public Health Smoking Act and the Poison Prevention Packaging Act in 1970 and the Lead-Based Paint Elimination Act in the following year. However, Congress finally determined that the continued passage of legislation fragmented over various consumer items was an insufficient process that left other products involving hazards to the consumer without any controls. Consequently, in 1972 Congress passed the Consumer Product Safety Act, which had broad powers to cover a host of consumer products.

CONSUMER PRODUCT SAFETY COMMISSION

The Consumer Product Safety Act created a five-member Consumer Products Safety Commission (CPSC) whose major goal is to substantially reduce injuries associated with consumer products in or around the home, schools, and recreational areas. Congress directed the commission to protect the public against unreasonable risk of injury associated with consumer products, to develop uniform safety standards for consumer products and minimize conflicting state and local regulations, and to promote research and investigation into the causes and prevention of product-related deaths, illnesses, and injuries. The commission sets and enforces mandatory safety standards for consumer products and, in certain instances, bans hazardous products. The commission deals with over

10,000 consumer products—from architectural glass, stairs, and power tools to stoves, ladders, and lawnmowers.

A major function of the commission is to gather and disseminate information related to product injuries. The commission can require manufacturers and distributors to establish and maintain books and records and make available such information as the commission deems necessary. The law requires manufacturers to conduct testing programs to ensure that their products conform to established safety standards. The law holds manufacturers accountable for knowing all safety criteria applicable to their products, for testing the products, and for maintaining technical data relating to the performance and safety of the products. This information may have to be given to the consumer when purchasing the product. The commission can require the use of specific labels that set forth the results of product testing. It also operates the National Electronic Injury Surveillance System, which monitors over 100 hospital emergency rooms nationwide for injuries associated with consumer products.

The manufacturer can be required to take corrective steps if it becomes aware of a product defect that could create a substantial product hazard. The manufacturer may be required to publicize this information to consumers. The commission can compel a manufacturer to refund the purchase price of the product, less a reasonable allowance for use, or to replace the product with a like or equivalent product that complies with the consumer product safety rules. The commission also seeks to reduce product-related injury to consumers by mandating better designs in product instruction sheets. It is empowered to set product-safety standards and to ban those products which present "real" hazards to consumers.

The Consumer Product Safety Act also transferred the authority for enforcing the Federal Hazardous Substances Act, Flamable Fabric Act, Poison Prevention Packaging Act, and Refrigerator Safety Act to the Consumer Product Safety Commission.

Knowing violation of consumer product safety rules will subject the violator to a civil penalty of $2,000 for each offense or the maximum penalty of $500,000 for any related series of violations. Criminal penalties of $50,000, a year in jail, or both, can result when the act is knowingly and willfully violated after having received notice of noncompliance. In addition, the commission can bring action to restrain the distribution of any consumer products that do not comply with its safety rules.

D. D. Bean & Sons v. Consumer Products Safety Commission

574 F. 2d 643 (1978)
U.S. Court of Appeals (1st Cir.)

Petitioner D. D. Bean & Sons Co. (Bean), a manufacturer of paper bookmatches . . . , seeks review of the Consumer Product Safety Commission's matchbook safety regulations. . . . The Commission stated that the proposed regulation was "designed to reduce or eliminate . . . [e]ye injuries sustained by persons who use bookmatches that fragment and cause particles from such matches to lodge in a person's eye. . . ."

The Commission's final rule contained the following design or "general" requirements. . . .

No matchhead in the matchbook shall be split, chipped, cracked, or crumbled.

The rule also listed the following "performance requirement" with which matchbooks must comply:

A matchbook is defective . . . if it has, when tested. . . .
(b) A splint that separates into two or more pieces.
(c) A matchhead that produces fragments. . . .

The Commission will test for violations in accordance with detailed testing procedures that are set out at length in the Rule. The testing procedures call for a visual, post-manufacture inspection of matchbooks to insure compliance with the "general" requirements governing such matters as . . . splitting . . . of matchheads, etc. "Performance" defects are to be minimized by more elaborate testing. Samples from a lot are to be . . . tested under laboratory conditions for the incidence of fragmentation. . . .

In ascertaining the sufficiency of the basis for the Commission's Rule we shall first inquire whether there is substantial evidence for its findings that . . . the listed hazard is in fact such. If it is, we shall next inquire whether the requirements addressed to . . . [the] hazard have been shown to be likely to reduce or eliminate it at a reasonable cost. Only after the existence of [the] hazard and the likelihood of its reduction at a reasonable cost have been established by the Commission may it be said that the requirements are "reasonably necessary."

The Commission's performance standards are fashioned to reduce the occurrence of matchhead fragmentation, and heads breaking off matches. . . . The date from the Commission's survey of hospital emergency rooms and other studies indicate that roughly one-third of reported match-related injuries consist of fragments lodging in the eye. There are also some reported cases where a flaming fragment ignited a victim's clothing. One study indicated that entire matchheads occasionally fly off upon ignition, lodging in the eye or on clothing. We think therefore that there is sufficient evidence in the record to support the Commission's finding that a substantial hazard exists from matchhead fragmentation. We also think that the Commission was entitled to adopt the "general" requirements addressed to the fragmentation hazard. These call essentially for assurance that the matchbooks and matches do not contain obvious defects such as broken splints and matchheads and projecting staples which could lead to particles flying off when a match is struck. Compliance with these requirements may be insured by visual testing, a procedure which is presently the industry norm. . . . And the design requirements themselves merely amount to insisting that the manufacturer produce matchbooks and matches that, on their face, do not contain obvious defects that seem logically to relate to a fragmentation risk. Since the cost of testing to ensure compliance with the general requirements geared to meeting the fragmentation hazard will therefore be slight, and the object of the requirement—ensuring a properly functioning product—seems only reasonable, we think that these requirements can be said to be "reasonably necessary" to reduce the risk from fragmentation.

However, we are not satisfied that the Commission has carried its burden of showing that the "performance" requirements geared to fragmentation are "reasonably necessary to eliminate or reduce" the risk to any significant degree. Performance requirements, unlike design requirements, cannot be tested for visually. The Commission itself concedes "that the principal cost effects on producers will arise from implementation of testing programs." Hence the effectiveness of these performance requirements in reducing risk is a matter of considerable importance.

There is a complete absence from the record of evidence tending to show the causes of fragmentation. The Commission has evidently proceeded on the assumption that the fragmentation results from defective manufacturing procedures and will show up upon testing at the plant. However, manufacturers, in submissions to the Commission, asserted that experience showed that post-manufacturer factors such as high humidity, perspiration, or misuse by consumers were principally responsible for fragmentation.

In view of the lack of evidence establishing the causes of fragmentation, and of the manufacturers' submissions claiming that post-manufacture handling causes most fragmentation, it is a large assumption that fragmentation is almost wholly attributable to the manufacturing process. Even then, the Commission's position on fragmentation establishes only that, at most "gross manufacturing errors" will be detected. But there is no evidence in the record from which the Commission could have determined that "gross errors," much less occasional defects occur with any frequency. It is just as possible to hypothesize that post-manufacture handling is the principal cause of fragmentation. We therefore think it speculative for the Commission to find, on the present record, that the proposed fragmentation performance requirements will result in a significant decrease on the fragmentation risk. In view of this, the substantial, added cost of testing to insure compliance with the performance requirements cannot be justified. . . .

Questions

1. What is the difference between a "design" or "general" requirement and a "performance" requirement? How was the manufacturer to ensure compliance with the design requirements? With the performance requirements?
2. What was the consumer hazard in *Bean*? Were the requirements to reduce the hazard obtainable "at reasonable cost" to the manufacturer in relation to the likely benefits of reducing the consumer hazard?

In late 1978, the CPSC released its interpretative statement of the reporting requirements under the Consumer Product Safety Act. The CPSC allows five days for "reportable knowledge" to travel from "an official or employee who may reasonably be expected to be capable of appreciating the significance of the information" to the Chief Executive Office (CEO). Unless a written delegation of authority has been filed with CPSC, the CEO must notify the commission within 24 hours of receiving reportable information. Reporting may be delayed an additional 10 days if the firm feels an investigation is needed to determine reportability. The commission will usually require a much more detailed "full report" at a later date. A knowing failure to report can result in a civil penalty (fine); and a knowing and willful failure can result in a criminal penalty. It should be noted that the original equipment manufacturer and the component manufacturer are equally liable under the reporting requirements.

Under the new CPSC reporting policy, efficient internal procedures will be essential to ensure that product safety information reaches the reporting officer. Internal controls will also be important to monitor the system to be sure that all the information is being transmitted quickly and accurately. People should be designated within the company (more than one if possible, to ensure cross checking) to bear responsibility for reporting to top officials even the slightest chance that a defect may be occurring. Employees should be notified in writing that they are expected to report possible product defects and all part suppliers should likewise be notified that the company expects immediate reporting of any possible defects that may cause a safety hazard. Once the reporting system is set up and a specific routine becomes mandatory, it should be regularly reviewed for effectiveness.

As a result of the Supreme Court decision, denying OSHA the right to inspect without a warrant, the CPSC has reevaluated its own inspection procedures and determined that, henceforward, manufacturers would be given advance notice of CPSC inspections. The notice would include a statement describing the purpose of the inspection and the nature of the information sought. Besides inspecting the premises, the CPSC inspector can obtain information from employees, examine all records, books, and documents, and obtain samples of any items and materials or substances necessary to an effective inspection. Should the employer refuse admittance to the CPSC official, the commission may seek compulsory process by a search warrant, subpoena, or witnesses or order an investigational hearing.

MANAGER'S ACCOUNTABILITY

Governmental inspection of the production, processing, and storage facilities of an industry is an important means of preventing dangerous goods from reaching the consumer. However, for the government's inspection and warning system to work effectively, managers of business firms must instigate appropriate action to eliminate the discovered violations. The following case illustrates the increasingly strict standards that the law has developed to help ensure appropriate managerial action after governmental warnings.

U.S. v. Park

721 U.S. 658 (1975)
Supreme Court of the United States

[Acme Markets, Inc. is a national retail food chain with over 800 retail outlets and 12 warehouses. Acme Markets, Inc. and its chief Executive Officer, Park, were charged with criminal violations of the Federal Food, Drug, and Cosmetic Act. It was alleged that Acme Markets, Inc. held food in a building accessible and exposed to contamination by rodents. In April, 1970 the FDA advised Park by letter of the unsanitary conditions in Acme's warehouse. A second inspection by the FDA in March, 1972 revealed continued evidence of rodent activity in the building. While Acme pleaded guilty, Park pleaded not guilty. Park moved for a judgment of acquittal on the grounds that the evidence did not show that he was personally concerned in this violation. He maintains that he directed a divisional vice president to investigate the situation and take corrective action. Park stated that he did not believe there was anything else he could have done more constructively than what he had done. Park was found guilty by a jury and sentenced to pay a fine of $50 on each of five counts. The Court of Appeals reversed.]

Chief Justice Burger

The rule that corporate employees who have "a responsible share in the furtherance of the transaction which the statute outlaws" are subject to the criminal provision of the Act was not formulated in a vacuum. Cases under the Federal Food and Drugs Act of 1906 reflected the view both that knowledge or intent were not required to be proved in prosecutions under its criminal provision, and that responsible corporate agents could be subjected to the liability thereby imposed. Moreover, the principle had been recognized that a corporate agent, through whose act, default, or omission the corporation committed a crime, was himself guilty individually of that crime. The principle had been applied whether or not the crime required "consciousness of wrongdoing," and it has been applied not only to those corporate agents who themselves committed the criminal act, but also to those who by virtue of their managerial positions or other similar relations to the act could be deemed responsible for its commission.

In the latter class of cases, the liability of managerial officers did not depend on their knowledge of, or personal participation in, the act made criminal by the statute. Rather, where the statute under which they were prosecuted dispensed with "consciousness of wrongdoing," an omission or failure to act was deemed a sufficient basis for a responsible corporate agent's liability. It was enough in such cases that, by virtue of the relationship he bore to the corporation, the agent had the power to have prevented the act complained of. . . .

. . . [T]he Court has reaffirmed the proposition that "the public interest in the purity of its food is so great as to warrant the imposition of the highest standard of care on distributors." In order to make "distributors of food the strictest censors of their merchandise," the Act punishes "neglect where the law requires care, or inaction where it imposes a duty." "The accused, if he does not will the violation, usually is in a position to prevent it with no more care than society might reasonably expect and no more exertion than it might reasonably exact from one who assumed his responsibilities." Similarly, . . . the court of appeals have recognized that those corporate agents vested with the responsibility, and power commensurate with that responsibility, to devise whatever measures are necessary to ensure compliance with the Act bear a "responsible relationship" to, or have a "responsible share" in, violations.

Thus . . . the cases . . . reveal that in providing sanctions which reach and touch the individuals who execute the corporate mission—and this is by no means necessarily confined to a single corporate agent or employee—the Act imposes not only a positive duty to seek out and remedy violations when they occur but also and primarily a duty to implement measures that will insure that violations will not occur. The requirements of foresight and vigilance imposed on responsible corporate agents are beyond question demanding, and perhaps onerous, but they are no more stringent than the public has a right to expect of those who voluntarily assume positions of authority in business enterprises whose services and products affect the health and well-being of the public that supports them. . . .

The Act does not . . . make criminal liability turn on "awareness of some wrongdoing" or "conscious fraud." The duty imposed by Congress on responsible corporate agents is, we emphasize, one that requires the highest standard of foresight and vigilance, but the Act, in its criminal aspect, does not require that which is objectively impossible. The theory upon which responsible corporate agents are held criminally accountable for "causing" violations of the Act permits a claim that a defendant was "powerless" to prevent or correct the violation to "be raised defensively at a trial on the merits." If such a claim is made, the defendant has the burden of coming forward with evidence, but this does not alter the Government's ultimate burden of proving beyond a reasonable doubt the defendant's guilt, including his power, in light of the duty imposed by the Act, to prevent or correct the prohibited condition. Congress has seen fit to enforce the accountability of responsible corporate agents dealing with products which may affect the health of consumers by penal sanctions cast in rigorous terms, and the obligation of the courts is to give them effect so long as they do not violate the Constitution.

Questions

1. Do managerial officers have to know of, or personally participate in the activity before they can be convicted of a crime?
2. Just what was the criminal behavior of Parks? Was he "powerless" to prevent the violation?
3. A previous court decision dealing with the same problem recognized that the act dispenses with the need to prove "consciousness of wrongdoing." As such, it may result in a hardship as applied to those who share "responsibility in the business process." But, the Court added, "In such matters the good sense of prosecutors, the wise guidance of trial judges, and

the ultimate judgment of juries must be trusted." Are these sufficient protections against a "hardship" prosecution?

FINANCIAL SAFETY

Recent legislation and FTC rule-making authority have been directed toward the protection of the consumer's "financial safety." Financial safety of the consumer involves protection from economic loss occurring by some method other than personal physical harm. For example, the Fair Credit Reporting Act of 1970 was passed by Congress to protect consumers from the circulation of inaccurate or obsolete information, and ensure that consumer reporting agencies exercise their responsibilities in a manner that is fair and equitable to consumers. Under the law the consumer has the right to be told the name of the consumer reporting agency that prepared the consumer report used to deny the consumer either credit, insurance, or employment. Although the consumer does not have the right to request a copy or physically examine the file of the credit bureau, the consumer must be told the nature, substance, and sources of the information (except medical) collected. The consumer also has the right to have incomplete or incorrect information reinvestigated and inaccurate or unverifiable information removed from his or her files. Those individuals who previously received the incomplete information must be notified by the agency that such information has been deleted from the consumer's file. When a dispute between the consumer and the reporting agency exists over information in the consumer's file, the consumer has the right to have his or her version of the dispute placed in the file and included in future consumer reports.

To protect the privacy of the consumer, he or she must be notified by any business that is seeking information about him or her, which would constitute an "investigative consumer report." After notification, the consumer may request from that business more information about the nature and scope of the investigation and have the resulting report withheld from anyone who under the law does not have a legitimate business need for the information. The consumer, of course, can discover the nature and substance (but not the sources) of the information that was collected for the report. Adverse information of the consumer which is over seven years old may be removed from the files, except for bankruptcy, which must remain in the file for 14 years. The consumer is empowered to sue the reporting agency for damages if it negligently violates the law. The consumer can collect attorney fees and court costs if successful.

The Fair Credit Reporting Act also deals with credit cards, as is revealed in the following case.

National Commercial Bank & Trust Co. v. Malik

339 N.Y.S. 2d 605 (1972)

Supreme Court, Albany County, N.Y.

. . . [T]he plaintiff seeks to recover the sum of $3,304.01 for unauthorized purchases made through the use of a Master Charge credit card which was issued by the plaintiff to Thomas S. Eldridge and his wife Ann R. Eldridge. While shopping at the defendant's gift store on April 13, 1971, Mrs. Eldridge used the credit card to make a purchase and inadvertently left the card at the defendant's store, and it was found by one of the defendant's employees. Mrs. Eldridge was notified by a telephone call from the defendant's employee that the credit card was there and she then requested that the credit card be held for her until she could pick it up on April 19, 1971. The defendant's employee agreed to hold it for her. Thereafter, the credit card disappeared from defendant's possession and was used to make unauthorized purchases of $3,304.01. The credit card was subsequently recovered by the authorities on April 23, 1971 at a store in Albany. On June 30, 1971, Thomas S. Eldridge and his wife Ann R. Eldridge assigned to the plaintiff all claims which they then had against the defendant resulting from the above-described events.

The complaint of the plaintiff assignee contains . . . [two] causes of action. The first cause of action is predicated upon the fact that defendant wrongfully allowed the credit card to fall into the possession of unauthorized persons who used it to make unauthorized purchases. . . . The second cause of action states that the loss of the credit card and the consequent damages were caused by the negligence of the defendant. . . .

. . . The Federal Truth in Lending Act, 15 U.S.C., Section 1643(a) states, in part, as follows:

> A cardholder shall be liable for the unauthorized use of a credit card only if the card is an accepted credit card, the liability is not in excess of $50, the card issuer gives adequate notice to the cardholder of the potential liability, the card issuer has provided the cardholder with a self-addressed, prestamped notification to be mailed by the cardholder in the event of the loss or theft of the credit card, and the unauthorized use occurs before the cardholder has notified the card issuer that an unauthorized use of the credit card has occurred or may occur as the result of loss, theft, or otherwise. . . .

Section 1643(c) makes this the greatest liability that can be imposed on a card holder regardless of all other applicable laws or agreements. Section 1643(d) states that the liability imposed by this section is the only liability to which a card holder can be subject for the unauthorized use of his credit card. Section 1643(b) places the burden of proof on the card issuer to show that the conditions of liability for the unauthorized use of a credit card as set forth in subsection (a) have been met.

The plaintiff does not contend that it complied with the Truth in Lending Act.

The assignors, the Eldridges, under the existing circumstances of this case and under the applicable statutes, cannot be and were not subject to any liability for the misuse of their credit card and therefore suffer no damages through the loss of the card. The claims of the plaintiff assignee, herein, are therefore claims without damages.

The other . . . cause of action based on negligence . . . must also fail. . . . Liability for negligence depends on the existence of a duty or obligation recognized by law by one party to another; the breach of that duty; and a finding that the proximate cause of that breach resulted in damages, and actual loss or damage, and that the plaintiff be free of contributory negligence. The plaintiff herein fails to establish any of these elements.

Questions

1. There are a series of conditions that must exist before a card holder can be liable for unauthorized use of a credit card. What are those conditions?
2. If the Eldridges were not liable, why couldn't the defendant store be liable? Was the store liable for negligence?

Fair Debt Collection Practices

The Fair Debt Collection Practices Act, which became effective in 1978, prohibits abusive, deceptive, and unfair debt collection practices by debt collectors. The law will not permit collectors to use unjust means when attempting to collect a debt. Obviously, the law does not cancel genuine debts owed by the consumer. The law indicates that a debt collector may not contact the consumer in person at inconvenient or unusual times and places. The consumer can even stop a debt collector from contacting him or her by requesting this in writing. The debt collector must not tell anyone else that the consumer owes money or utilize postcards or envelopes which identify the debt collector. The debt collector may not use threats or violence, repetitious phone calls, or advertise the consumer's debt. The debt collector may not use any false statements—such as implying that the collector represents the government, is an attorney, or that the consumer has committed a crime. Moreover, the debt collector may not say that any action will be taken against the consumer which cannot legally be taken.

The consumer has the right to sue the debt collector within one year from the date the law was violated for any damages suffered. The consumer is entitled to court costs and attorney fees if the violation is proven. Class action by consumers is authorized up to $500,000.

Home Solicitation Sales

A number of statutes or administrative rules are aimed at the evils involved in home solicitation sales. To avoid the "slick-talking" sales representatives or high-pressure sales tactics sometimes employed, the statute provides the consumer with a chance to think things over during a "cooling-off period." If the consumer decides against the purchase, the law usually affords a right of cancellation. The following case involves the consumer's effort to utilize state law, federal law, and finally an administrative rule to avoid a home solicitation sale.

Donnelly v. Mustang Pools, Inc.
374 N.Y.S. 2d 967 (1975)
Supreme Court of New York

On September 5, 1974, the plaintiffs and the defendant entered into an agreement for the construction of a 17 × 35 in-ground pool at the residence of plaintiffs. The contract provided for a cash price of $5,500.00. By the terms of the contract, the plaintiffs were credited with a $50.00 down payment, leaving a balance of $5,450.00. The contract also provided that a payment was due November 1st in the amount of $1,800.00, leaving a balance of $3,650.00. The contract further provided that the sum of $3,000.00 would be paid upon delivery of the pool equipment; another $350.00 would be paid when the construction was half-completed and, finally, the balance of $300.00 was due on completion. The installment was to begin, as near as the Court is able to determine, in the Spring of 1975.

After the execution of the contract, the plaintiffs had second thoughts about the construction of this pool and sought to be relieved of whatever liability they might have under the contract. Sometime after the 23rd of April, 1975, the plaintiffs commenced this action against the defendant alleging in substance that the defendant failed and neglected to furnish plaintiffs with a statement of their right to cancel the contract within three days, allegedly as required by Article 10-A of the Personal Property Law and Regulation Z of the Federal Consumer Credit Code. Plaintiffs claim that because of the failure of the contract to provide for the right of cancellation, they have the right to rescind the contract absolutely. . . .

Article 10-A of the Personal Property Law of the State of New York attempts to deal with the problems created by the so-called "door-to-door" sales. This Article of the Personal Property Law states as its purpose: ". . . to afford consumers, subjected to high pressure door-to-door sales tactics, a 'cooling-off' period." That Article defines a consumer transaction wherein the money, property, or service which is the subject of the transaction is primarily for personal, family or household purposes.

There is no question that this agreement entered into between the parties for the construction of a pool at the residence of plaintiffs falls within the meaning of the definition as set forth in Section 426.

Article 10-A, §426.2 of the Personal Property Law defines a home solicitation sale as a consumer transaction in which payment of the purchase price *is deferred over time,* and the Seller or a person acting for him, is a person doing business who engages in a personal solicitation of the sale. The Buyer's agreement or purchase offer is made at a place other than the place of business of the Seller or a person acting for him.

The contract was executed at the residence of the plaintiffs and it meets one part of the definition of a home solicitation sale. However, the fact that the payments were not required to be made over a period of time, notwithstanding that payments were to be made at certain scheduled times prior to completion of the installation of the pool, does not bring the transaction within Article 10-A of the Personal Property Law. The contract, under a fair interpretation of all its terms, was a cash transaction upon completion and was not a "time payment plan" embracing the payment for the construction of the pool after its completion. Thus, the transaction, viewed as a whole, is a cash transaction, payable on completion and does not come within the definition of a home solicitation sale as set forth in Article 10-A of the Personal Property Law.

Plaintiffs contend, in the alternative, that the transaction is governed by Regulation Z pursuant to the Federal Truth-in-Lending Act. The plaintiffs, relying on Regulation Z, claim that the fact that payments were required in more than four installments brings the transaction within the purview of Regulation Z, requiring a three day cooling off period which was, concededly, not contained in the contract in dispute. Subdivision (a) of §1635 of Title 15 of U.S. Code provides, as it applies to this dispute:

In the case of any consumer credit transaction in which a security interest is retained or acquired in any real property which is used or is expected to be used as the residence of the person to whom credit is extended, the obligor shall have the right to rescind the transaction until midnight the third business day following the consummation of the transaction or the delivery of the disclosures required under this part, whichever is later. . . .

Subdivision (k) of §226.2 of Regulation Z provides:

"Consumer credit" means credit offered or extended to a natural person . . . for which either a finance charge is or may be imposed or which pursuant to an agreement, is or may be payable in more than four installments.

It appears therefore that the key to bringing this transaction within the purview of Regulation Z is the offering or extending of credit for which either a finance charge *is or may be imposed* or which pursuant to an agreement *is or may be payable in more than four installments*. . . .

If you included the down payment, the contract in question would be clearly within the ambit of §226.2(k) of Regulation Z, thus requiring the three day notice of cancellation in the contract in question.

The Court has examined the Truth-in-Lending Manual Supplement, Appendix E. submitted by the attorneys for the defendant. Advisory Letter No. 695, dated July 6, 1973, states that the staff's view is that in computing the number of installments, any down payment is not considered to be an installment for purposes of §226.2(k) of Regulation Z.

In view of this, and since the contract calls for only four installment payments, exclusive of the down payment, the contract does not come within the notice of cancellation requirements of Regulation Z.

However, the plaintiffs are not without hope to extricate themselves from what they feel to be a difficult situation.

On October 18, 1972, the Federal Trade Commission promulgated a Trade Regulation Rule concerning a cooling-off period for door-to-door sales. . . . The Rule provides that . . . it constitutes an unfair and deceptive act or practice for any seller to fail to furnish the buyer with a fully completed copy of the contract, and which contains a statement in substantially the following form:

> You, the buyer, may cancel this transaction at any time prior to midnight of the third business day after the date of this transaction. See the attached notice of cancellation form for an explanation of this right.

The Rule also defines a door-to-door sale as a sale, lease, or rental of consumer goods or services with a purchase price of $25.00 or more, whether under a single or multiple contracts, in which the Seller or his representative personally solicits the sale, including those in response to or following an invitation by the Buyer, and the Buyer's agreement or offer to purchase is made at a place other than the place of business of the Seller.

Clearly, the transaction with which we are concerned falls within the definition of the door-to-door sale as set forth in the Federal Trade Commission Regulation Rule effective June 7, 1974.

As pointed out earlier in this decision, the contract contained no notice of cancellation provision. The contract, although it did not fall within the purview of Article 10-A of the Personal Property Law of New York or Regulation Z, does fall within the purview of the Federal Trade Commission rule.

Accordingly, since the contract failed to contain the required notice concerning the right to cancel the transaction, and in view of the fact that it did not contain the necessary notice of cancellation as required by the above referred to Trade Regulation Rule, the Court hereby declares that the contract entered into between the plaintiffs and the defendant is in violation of that Regulation and is therefore subject to cancellation by plaintiffs.

Questions

1. Why was the Personal Property Law in the State of New York ineffective as a means of cancellation for the consumer?
2. Why was the Truth-in-Lending Act's cancellation provision not available to the consumer?
3. What scheme of regulation is utilized by the Federal Trade Commission to provide cooling-off periods in door-to-door sales?
4. How do these laws protect the consumer's financial safety?

CONSUMER'S RIGHT TO BE HEARD

The consumer's right to be heard includes the right to receive full consideration of the consumer's interests in the formulation of governmental policy. Increasingly, this right includes the right to fair and active participation by consumer advocates in hearings that formulate governmental policy.

As mentioned in Chapter 3, the imbalance of consumer advocacy in administrative hearings has been increasingly recognized in judicial decisions. In *United Church of Christ* v. *FCC,* 359 F. 2d 994 (D.C. Cir. 1966), the court of appeals ordered some "audience participation" in proceedings before the FCC. The court determined that unless consumers could be heard, there might be no one bringing the consumers' views to the attention of the administrative body in an effective manner. As this case indicates, there is a growing body of case law in which the courts are requiring federal agencies to take into account the consumer groups that are being affected by the agency's decisions.

Consumers have also sought legislation which improves the consumers' voice. For example, many states have enacted an "office of consumers' council" to represent utility customers in utility regulation hearings. Also, the Federal Public Utility Regulatory Policies Act (PURPA) of 1978 grants the consumer the right to intervene in state public utility regulation hearings.

There has also been a consumer movement to establish a federal consumer protection agency to represent the consumer interest in other federal agencies. In 1971, the House of Representatives passed a consumer protection agency bill by a vote of 344 to 44. However, the Senate did not pass a similar version, and by 1975, the vote in the House on the proposed agency was only 208 to 199. In February of 1978 the House scuttled the consumer protection agency bill by a 227 to 198 vote. The proponents of consumer advocacy have since proposed acts that would authorize federal agencies to pay the fees of lawyers and expert witnesses who participate in agency proceedings. When individuals and organizations that represent a consumer or public interest viewpoint would be foreclosed from participation because the cost of representation would be prohibitive or the financial interest of the consumer groups would be too small in relation to the cost of representation, such participants would be eligible for payment from the agency. The consumer proponents feel that such "participation acts" do not have the same effect as the creation of an office of consumer representation. They feel the participation approach carries less of a "big government" connotation which was utilized to defeat the consumer protection agency bill. Those consumer groups "representing" the consumers are likely to continue to pursue efforts to improve their voice before governmental bodies.

CONSUMER'S RIGHT TO RECOVER

Recent consumer advocates have advanced the notion that "wronged" consumers should have the right to recover monies. The right of recovery is considered an essential remedy, necessary to protect the other fundamental consumer rights. However, this advocated consumer right has not been completely fulfilled in law.

At common law the consumer's remedy for deception and misrepresentation by the seller was an action for the tort of fraud. However, the elements to establish fraud are difficult barriers for the consumer to surmount. As a consequence, the consumer's right to recover was and continues to be frustrated often. Therefore, alternative means of establishing the consumer's right to recover are slowly evolving.

The FTC Improvement Act of 1975 provides that the FTC may seek "rescision or reformation of contracts, the refund of money or return of property, (or) the payment of damages" on behalf of consumers. This provision empowers the FTC to bring an action on behalf of consumers and seek recovery of monies for the consumers. However, private actions by consumers under the FTC Act are still forbidden.

The Consumer Product Safety Commission has been empowered to compel a manufacturer to refund the purchase price of the product, less a reasonable allowance for use, or to replace the product with a like or equivalent product that complies with the consumer product safety rules. In like manner, the Department of Transportation's enforcement of the National Traffic and Motor Vehicle Safety Act against Firestone Tire and Rubber Company resulted in an agreement by Firestone to refund or replace a tire it sold which was alleged to be unsafe for consumers.

On the state level, "Little-FTC" acts authorize state officials to seek restitution for aggrieved consumers in 47 jurisdictions. Moreover, 16 states allow for consumer class actions. Individual private actions by a consumer are authorized in 42 states.

Although the consumer's right to recover is being increasingly recognized in legislation, the right of recovery has not become as fully established as most consumer groups have requested. However, the following materials on the Truth-in-Lending Act illustrate how the "right of recovery" can be built into the statute as an inducement for the seller to comply with the law.

TRUTH IN LENDING

Title 1 of the Consumer Credit Protection Act is more often referred to as the Truth-in-Lending Act. Section 102(a) reveals the purposes of Congress:

> The Congress finds that economic stabilization would be enhanced and the competition among various financial institutions . . . would be strengthened by the informed use of credit. The informed use of credit results from an awareness of the cost thereof by consumers. It is the purpose of this title to assure a meaningful disclosure of credit terms so that the consumer will be able to compare more readily the various credit terms available to him and avoid the uninformed use of credit. . . .

The act authorizes the Federal Reserve Board to prescribe regulation Z to effectuate the purposes of the act and prevent circumvention or evasion thereof. Regulation Z attempts to let consumers (borrowers) know the cost of credit so they can compare costs between various credit sources. Regulation Z applies to credit card issuers and any individual or organization that extends or arranges consumer credit for which a finance charge is or may be payable or which is repayable by agreement in more than four installments. The law obviously applies to all financial institutions and may also apply to department stores, automotive, furniture, and appliance dealers, artisans such as plumbers and electricians, and professional people.

Failure to make disclosures as required under the Truth-in-Lending Act subjects the violator to suit for actual damages by consumers plus twice the amount of the finance charge in the case of a credit transaction, as well as court costs and attorneys fees. Willfully or knowingly violating the act or Regulation Z can result in criminal action and fines up to $5,000 or imprisonment for up to one year, or both. In addition, failure to comply with the fair credit billing provisions can result in a forfeiture penalty of up to $50.

General Finance Corp. v. Garner
556 F. 2d 772 (1977)
U.S. Court of Appeals (5th Cir.)

In 1974, Ernest Garner purchased a car from Cantrell's Auto Sales in Columbus, Georgia. Garner signed a conditional sales contract granting the seller a security interest in the car. The contract required Garner to make 30 monthly payments of $86.19 each for a total of $2,585.70. In the same document, Cantrell's Auto Sales assigned the contract to General Finance Corp.

The record indicates that Garner made 11 monthly payments on the car. On February 11, 1975, after Garner made the payment that was due for that month, he filed . . . a petition for relief under Chapter XIII of the Bankruptcy Act. Garner proposed to pay his creditors all that he owed them through the extension mechanism provided by Chapter XIII. Garner's plan called for a monthly payment to General Finance in the amount of $47.88.

General Finance rejected the plan. It filed a reclamation petition seeking possession of the car. Garner answered the petition alleging that the conditional sales contract violated the federal Truth-in-Lending Act. The bankruptcy judge agreed with Garner that the contract violated the Truth-in-Lending Act. The Court concluded that Garner was entitled to a statutory penalty of $1,000.00 and to an attorney's fee of $150.00. The Court, however, did not order General Finance to pay the penalty directly:

> The proof of claim filed by General Finance Corporation is in the amount of $1,637.61. We shall apply the $1,000.00 to this claim and allow the claim in the amount of $637.61. This would appear preferable to requiring General Finance Corporation to pay the sum of $1,000.00 to the debtor and increasing the payments under the plan to General Finance Corp. to $86.19 per month. The Chapter XIII Trustee should be instructed to pay to General Finance Corp. the sum of $47.88 per month as proposed in the original plan until General Finance Corporation has received the total of $637.61. . . .

The district court approved the bankruptcy judge's conclusion that the conditional sales contract violated the disclosure provisions of the Truth-in-Lending Act and the Federal Reserve Board's regulations thereunder (Regulation Z), because the disclosure statement on the contract did not call attention to a provision in small type on the reverse side of the document dealing with a security interest in future indebtedness. . . .

The Truth-In-Lending Act requires the creditor in the kind of transaction involved here to disclose

> [a] description of any security interest held or to be retained or acquired by the creditor in connection with the extension of credit, and a clear identification of the property to which the security interest relates.

The Federal Reserve Board's regulations require

> If after-acquired property will be subject to the security interest, or if other or future indebtedness is or may be secured by any such property, this fact shall be clearly set forth in conjunction with the description or identification of the type of security interest held, retained or acquired.

The future indebtedness term on the reverse side of the conditional sales contract here seems clearly to fall within the language both of the Act and of Regulation Z. . . .

. . . General Finance contends that the spirit of the Truth-in-Lending Act will be served if disclosure is made at the time of any future advances, the theory being that Garner could then choose to go elsewhere for credit. This notion has been rejected by the Federal Reserve Board. Section 226.8(b)(5) . . . provides in part that

> [i]f after-acquired property will be subject to the security interest, or *if other or future indebtedness* is or may be secured by any such property, *this fact shall be clearly set forth* in conjunction with the description or identification of the type of security interest held, retained or acquired.

While this language is not without ambiguity . . . it is at least clear that the creditor may not wait until the future transaction to tell the debtor about the future indebtedness provision. . . .

The implication of General Finance's argument is that it should be of no moment to the potential borrower that he is binding the collateral to cover any future debts owed to the creditor. We think, on the contrary, that Congress meant for the potential debtor to have such information when deciding whether he ought to deal with a particular lender. . . .

Questions

1. What did General Finance Company fail to disclose in its credit terms with Garner which violated the Truth-in-Lending Act? What did this failure cost General Finance?
2. Do you agree that the consumer has the right to be informed of "credit terms" and of the various "security interests" retained by the creditor?

CONCLUSION

The changing conditions of the marketplace (long distribution channels) and the changing characteristics of the distributed products (more technologically complex) have brought about societal reaction to counterbalance the manufacturer's distance from the consumer and the manufacturer's higher level of product knowledge. Because consumers became increasingly unable to judge or discover dangerous tendencies in products, new legal theories have evolved to aid the consumers. Judicial pronouncements abolished the legal doctrine of privity and adopted new legal theories of strict liability of manufacturers of defective products which cause consumer injury. Legislative bodies created administrative agencies which are charged with the task of improving consumer knowledge of products and of preventing distribution of dangerous products. In effect, the legal process has been utilized to modify perceived defects in the effective operation of the market system. The legal process, even with its limitations, will undoubtedly continue to be utilized to improve the operation of the private economic system.

CASE PROBLEMS

1. A floor wax manufacturer markets a product under the name "Continental Six Month Floor Wax" for general home use. Some of the manufacturer's tests showed that following wear simulating six months of home traffic, some of the wax "would be left sticking to a floor." The FTC contends that this name constitutes deceptive advertising and has ordered that the words *Six Month* be deleted from the name. Would you consider the name to be deceptive?

2. Litton Industries, Inc. has advertised its microwave ovens are superior to others and that independent technicians prefer Litton ovens over competing products. The survey to substantiate the ad only surveyed Litton service agencies. The technicians interviewed, who "chose" Litton ovens over other products, were not always experienced in servicing all brands they compared. Is this "substantiation" sufficient to support the ads against an FTC charge of deceptive advertising?

3. Charles of the Ritz Rejuvenescence Cream was advertised as containing a "vital organic ingredient" and "essences and compounds" which bring to one's skin quickly "the clear radiance . . . the petal-like quality and texture of youth" and it "restores natural moisture necessary for a live, healthy skin" so that one's "face need know no drought years," but have "a bloom that is wonderfully rejuvenating" and is "constantly active in keeping your skin clear, radiant and young looking." The FTC sought to prohibit the advertisement as deceptive. Charles of the Ritz contended that a consumer would not be deceived by such an ad, in that "no straight-thinking person could believe that its cream would actually rejuvenate." Must the FTC produce a person who will admit to being "deceived" by these ads?

4. The Pratts purchased a motor home from the Norris Agency, a Winnebago dealership outside of Cleveland, Ohio, after test driving it. A Norris employee delivered the vehicle to the Pratts's home in Erie, Pennsylvania. Four days after delivery, the Pratts tried to use the motor home two or three times and compiled a list of complaints ranging from a transmission that would only allow operation in reverse to a clipped signal light. GM, which manufactured the chassis, arranged for replacement of the transmission at a GM agency in Erie as well as for adjustments to the brakes which Mr. Pratts claimed were "spongy" with excessive pedal travel. During the four weeks it took to make these repairs, the Pratts were provided with another vehicle by Winnebago. Also during this time, the Pratts decided that they no longer wanted the vehicle and asked Norris to replace the vehicle or return their money.

   The Pratts' complaints included a leaking roof in the kitchen area, oil leaks from the lighting system support generator, faulty generator operation, failure of the driver's seat to lock into driving position, a faulty cab air conditioner, fluid leaks from power steering hoses, loose wiring on furnace gas valve controls, a damaged trim panel on the dashboard, windshield wipers making an incomplete stroke, a loosely fastened clearance light by the radio antenna, plus various others. The GM and Winnebago warranties require the Pratts to return the motor home to the Norris Agency or some other authorized dealer for repairs. The distance involved was over 100 miles, and the Pratts refused to transport the vehicle to Ohio because they claimed the brakes were unsafe, it would cost $300 for a tow to Norris Agency, the 30-day temporary license supplied by the dealer had expired, and they would have to pay $1,200 tax to register the vehicle in Pennsylvania when they no longer wished to keep the motor home.

   The Pratts sued for a refund under the Magnuson Moss Act which provides that a warrantor of a consumer product must permit a refund or replacement without charge if the product contains defects after a reasonable number of attempts by the warrantor to remedy the defects. The Pratts feel that they need only notify Norris of the defects and cannot be required to return the home from a distance of over 100 miles for repairs. If the vehicle were returned, GM and Winnebago could remedy the defects within two or three days at a cost to them of about $500.

   What are Winnebago and GM's responsibilities under the Magnuson Moss Act?

END NOTES

1. As reported in *FTC News Summary*, Vol. 5–82 (October 30, 1981): 1–2.
2. *FTC News Summary*, Vol. 25–82 (April 9, 1982): 1–2.
3. Robert W. Schupp, "Unfairness Doctrine—The Death of an Administrative Standard?" *Business Law Review*, Vol. 15, No. 2 (Winter 1980–81): 12–18.
4. O. Lee Reed, "The Next 25 Years of Advertising Regulation," *The Collegiate Forum* (Princeton, N.J.: Dow Jones & Co., Inc., Fall 1981), p. 7.

chapter 17

SECURITIES REGULATION: THE ISSUING OF SECURITIES

Although securities and the trading of securities have deep historical roots, laws regulating the securities trading process are of more recent origin. The speculative pricing of securities in uncharted stock companies of England caused Parliament to pass the South Sea Bubble Act of 1720, which substantially prohibited the formation of unchartered corporations and outlawed the dishonest issuance of securities of unchartered companies. In the United States, however, the laws dealing with transactions in securities were not passed until states authorized general incorporation statutes during the industrialization process following the Civil War.

HISTORICAL BACKGROUND

BLUE-SKY LAWS

Nearly every state in the country has laws regulating the issuance of securities to its residents. The purpose of such laws is to prevent abuses by promoters of speculative ventures. To avoid fraudulent sales of securities, states passed "blue-sky" laws, so named because a judge once referred to a fraudulent security as having no more value "than so many feet of blue sky."

The blue-sky laws differ from state to state. Most states have a *fraud-type* law which imposes penalties if evidence indicates fraudulent sale of securities. A securities violation can result in criminal prosecution and injunctions barring future utilization of such practices. Other states require *registration of brokers and dealers* who sell securities. Such laws were enacted in an effort to regulate the person who sells securities in those states. Still other states utilize *registration of information* about the issuer with some state official. The laws of these states empower state officials to determine whether the securities themselves are "fair" deals for the buying public. For example, in California, a security offering must meet a "fair, just, and equitable" standard before the security can be registered for distribution.

NEED FOR FEDERAL LEGISLATION

The absence of blue-sky laws in some states and the inadequacy of such laws in other states allowed fraudulent and deceptive sales of securities to continue in spite of the laws of some states. The most widely used method of evading state blue-sky laws was to operate across state lines.

The speculative securities market of the 1920s afforded numerous opportunities for abuses in the trading of securities. One practice involved price manipulation through "wash sales" or "matched orders." Through successive buy and sell orders brokers created a false impression of market activity and of higher prices. Brokers using these devices reaped profits before the price collapsed to true market levels. Another practice involved issuing false and misleading statements in order to profit at the expense of unwary investors. Finally, the misuse of corporate information by "inside" corporate officials allowed them to trade with misinformed stockholders and investors before important inside information became public.

Before the "market crash" in the fall of 1929, the New York Stock Exchange (NYSE) had an aggregate value of about $89 billion. However, in 1932 the aggregate value of NYSE stocks was only about $15 billion. This traumatic drop in stock value, which probably could not have been prevented by legislation, nevertheless caused a social awakening to the need for federal legislation to deal with abusive practices in securities transactions.

FEDERAL SCHEME OF REGULATION

When Congress determined to regulate securities, it had the advantage of surveying the various state efforts at security regulation before determining the federal approach to this problem. Congress rejected the notion that a federal bureaucracy should make a judgment concerning the worth or fairness of securities offered to the public. Instead, Congress utilized concepts embodied in blue-sky laws which include the designation of fraudulent activities, the registration of dealers in securities, and the registration of information about the issuers of securities to be offered to the public. The essence of the federal approach is disclosure. The drafters of the federal laws viewed the responsibility of the federal government as being one primarily to assure investors of access to enough information to enable them to arrive at rational decisions. The fundamental purpose of securities law is to substitute the philosophy of full disclosure for the philosophy of *caveat emptor* and thus achieve a higher standard of business ethics in the securities industry.

SECURITIES AND EXCHANGE COMMISSION

The Securities and Exchange Commission (SEC) was created by the Securities Exchange Act of 1934. As an independent, bipartisan agency, it administers laws that seek to protect investors and the general public in securities transactions. Laws administered by the SEC are briefly explained in Table 17-1. The commission also advises federal courts in corporate reorganization proceedings under Chapter 11 of the National Bankruptcy Act. It studies any proposed reorganization plan and issues a report on whether the proposal is fair, feasible, and equitable.

The commission is composed of five members who are appointed by the president, with the advice and consent of the Senate. The commissioners hold five-year terms which are staggered so that one expires on June 5 of each year. The chairman of the commission is designated by the president, and no more than three members of the commission may be from the same political party.

Table 17-1
LAWS ADMINISTERED BY THE SEC

Securities Act of 1933	Previously administered by the Federal Trade Commission, this law is now under the jurisdiction of the SEC. It provides that securities which are offered to the public must be registered with the SEC unless there is a specific exemption for the transaction. Assuming no exemption, the registration statement containing a prospectus must be filed giving specified information and the SEC will judge the completeness and accuracy of the filing. The prospectus then must be delivered to potential buyers as a means of disclosing critical information about the company. There are specific penalties for material misstatement in registration.
Securities Exchange Act of 1934	This act created the SEC and is concerned with the trading of securities. The companies listed on stock exchanges or having more than 500 shareholders must file certain regular reports with the SEC, including a Form 10-K annually, and Form 10-Q quarterly, annual proxy statements, and a

Table 17-1 (*Continued*)
LAWS ADMINISTERED BY THE SEC

	Form 8-K for special events. The 1934 act also contains a general fraud provision applicable to all securities sold in interstate commerce, even though they are exempt from registration.
Public Utility Holding Company Act of 1935	This act was enacted to correct abuses in the financing and operation of electric and gas public-utilities holding-company systems. Such systems had been complicated by the formation of large holding companies on top of the operating companies and a substantial amount of pyramiding.
Trust Indenture Act of 1939	This act requires that publicly held debt be issued pursuant to contract, an indenture, which must contain specific provisions to protect the public. For each debt issued, there must be a trustee who is obligated in the event of default to protect the public debt holder as if the trustee were acting prudently on his own behalf.
Investment Company Act of 1940	This act subjects investment holding companies (mutual funds) to certain statutory prohibitions and to commission regulation deemed necessary to protect the interest of investors and the public. The commission does not supervise the investment activities of these companies, but the law requires disclosure of their financial condition and investment policies to afford investors full and complete information about their activities.
Investment Advisers Act of 1940	This act establishes a pattern of regulation of investment advisers. It requires that persons or firms who engage for compensation in the business of advising others about their securities transactions must register with the commission and conform their activities to statutory standards designed to protect the interests of investors.
Securities Investor Protection Act of 1970	This act created the Securities Investor Protector Corporation (SIPC), a nonprofit organization whose membership comprises the brokers and dealers registered under the 1934 act and members of the national securities exchanges. The SIPC creates a fund by collecting fees from the membership which is used for the protection of investors to a limit of $500,000 for each customer and a maximum of $100,000 for cash claims from each customer. The SEC has regulatory authority over the SIPC.
Foreign Corrupt Practices Act of 1977	This act makes it a criminal offense for any United States business enterprise to offer a bribe to a foreign official for the purpose of obtaining or directing business to any person. It also amends the 1934 act to require registrants to maintain reasonably complete and accurate records and to devise sufficient systems of internal accounting controls.

ISSUANCE OF SECURITIES

The financial community that deals in securities may be divided into two activities: the *distribution* (issuance) of securities and the *trading* of securities (Chapter 18). The *distribution* involves the raising of capital for corporations and government entities through the new issuance of securities. The distribution function is often called underwriting, and this activity is principally regulated by the Securities Act of 1933. On the other hand, trading of securities involves transactions whereby outstanding securities are traded or bought and sold among members of the public. Transactions are often executed through professional financial houses, through the exchanges, or through the over-the-counter market. These secondary transactions are regulated primarily by the Securities Exchange Act of 1934.

SECURITIES ACT OF 1933

The Work of the SEC

(Published by the SEC, October 1980)
SECURITIES ACT OF 1933

This "truth in securities" law has two basic objectives: (a) to provide investors with material financial and other information concerning securities offered for public sale; and (b) to prohibit misrepresentation, deceit and other fraudulent acts and practices in the sale of securities generally (whether or not required to be registered).

Registration of Securities

The first objective applies to securities offered for public sale by an issuing company or any person in a control relationship to such company. Before the public offering of such securities, a registration statement must be filed with the commission by the issuer, setting forth the required information. When the statement has become effective, the securities may be sold. The purpose of registration is to provide disclosure of financial and other information on the basis of which investors may appraise the merits of the securities. To that end, investors must be furnished with a prospectus (selling circular) containing the salient data set forth in the registration statement to enable them to evaluate the securities and make informed and discriminating investment decisions.

The Registration Process

To facilitate the registration of securities by different types of issuing companies, the Commission has prepared special registration forms which vary in their disclosure requirements to provide disclosure of the essential facts pertinent in a given type of offering while at the same time minimizing the burden and expense of compliance with the law. In general, the registration forms call for disclosure of information such as (1) a description of the registrant's properties and business, (2) a description of the significant provisions of the security to be offered for sale and its relationship to the registrant's other capital securities, (3) information about the management of the registrant, and (4) financial statements certified by independent public accountants.

The registration statement and prospectus become public immediately on filing with the Commission; but it is unlawful to sell the securities until the effective date. After the filing of the registration statement, the securities may be offered orally or by certain summaries of the information in the registration statement as permitted by rules of the Commission. The Act provides that registration statements shall become effective on the 20th day after filing (or on the 20th day after the filing of the last amendment thereto); but the Commission, in its discretion, may advance the effective date if . . . such action is deemed appropriate.

Registration statements are examined by the Division of Corporation Finance for compliance with the disclosure requirements. If a statement appears to be materially incomplete or inaccurate, the registrant usually is informed by letter and given an opportunity to file correcting or clarifying amendments. The Commission, however, has authority to refuse or suspend the effectiveness of any registration statement if it finds, after hearing, that material representations are misleading, inaccurate, or incomplete. Accordingly, if material deficiencies in a registration statement appear to stem from a deliberate attempt to conceal and mislead, or if the deficiencies otherwise are of such nature as not to lend themselves readily to correction through the informal letter process, the Commission may conclude that it is in the public interest to resort to a hearing to develop the facts by evidence and to determine on the evidence whether a stop order should issue refusing or suspending effectiveness of the statement.

A stop order is not a permanent bar to the effectiveness of the registration statement or sale of the securities, for the order must be lifted and the statement declared effective if amendments are filed correcting the statement in accordance with the stop order decision. The Commission may issue stop orders after the sale of securities has been commenced or completed. Although losses which may have been suffered in the purchase of securities are not restored to investors by the stop order, the Commission's decision and the evidence on which it is based may serve to put investors on notice of their rights and aid in their own recovery suits.

This examination process naturally contributes to the general reliability of the registration disclosures—but it does not give positive assurance of the accuracy of the facts reported. Even if such a verification of the facts were possible, the task, if not actually prohibitive, would involve such a tremendous undertaking (both in time and money) as to seriously impede the financing of business ventures through the public sale of securities.

PENDING REGISTRATION

Section 5 of the 1933 act contains a double prohibition. First, it is unlawful for any person to *offer to sell* a security unless a registration statement has been *filed* with the SEC. Second, it is unlawful to *sell* a security unless a registration statement is *effective.* These prohibitions, in effect, mean that only when a preliminary prospectus has been filed is it permissible for the securities to be offered to the public, but no sales can take place until the prospectus has become effective. The preliminary prospectus contains wording in red ink which declares that the instrument is subject to amendment and that the securities described in the prospectus may not be sold prior to the time the registration statement becomes effective. Because of the red ink utilized in the preliminary prospectus, it is often referred to as a "red herring."

The period of time between the preliminary filing and the effective date is known as the waiting period, during which the public may become familiar with the new proposed offering. The management of the offering company must be careful during this period to avoid publicity which "puffs" the value of the company securities. The SEC's Release 5180 urges companies to respond factually to unsolicited inquiries from securities analysts during this period, but companies often limit communication while "in registration." Companies desire to avoid inadvertently violating the 1933 Act by releasing a statement that could be perceived by the SEC as initiating the type of publicity that would subject the company's new offer to a SEC stop order. A stop order can have disastrous consequences because the timing of the offering of securities is critical in ever-changing financial markets.

SECTION 2: A "SECURITY"

Section 2 of the 1933 act defines a "security." The section includes any note, stock, treasury stock, investment contract, guarantee, warrant, and any interest or instrument commonly known as a security. However, there are many cases in which various obscure financial instruments are determined to be securities, as the following case illustrates.

SEC v. Glenn W. Turner Enterprises, Inc.
474 F. 2d 476 (1973)
U.S. Court of Appeals (9th Cir.)

This is an appeal from an order granting the SEC a preliminary injunction. The injunction prohibits offering and selling by defendants of certain of their "Adventures" and "Plans." . . . Dare To Be Great, Inc. (Dare), a Florida corporation is a wholly owned subsidiary of Glenn W. Turner Enterprises, Inc. The individual defendants are, or were, officers, directors, or employees of the defendant corporations.

The trial court's findings, which are fully supported by the record, demonstrate that defendant's scheme is a gigantic successful fraud. The question presented is whether the "Adventure" or "Plan" enjoined are "securities" within the meaning of the federal securities laws. . . .

The five courses offered by Dare ostensibly involve two elements. In return for his money, the purchaser is privileged to attend seminar sessions and receives tapes, records, and other material, all aimed at improving self-motivation and sales ability. He also receives, if he purchases either Adventure III or IV or the $1,000 Plan, the opportunity to help to sell the courses to others; if successful he receives part of the purchase price as his commission. There is no doubt that this latter aspect of the purchase is in all respects the significant one. . . .

It is apparent from the record that what is sold is not of the usual "business motivation" type of courses. Rather, the purchaser is really buying the possibility of deriving money from the sale of the plans by Dare to individuals whom the purchaser has brought to Dare. The promotional aspects of the plan, such as seminars, films, and records, are aimed at interesting others in the Plans. Their value for any other purpose, is, to put it mildly, minimal.

Once an individual has purchased a Plan, he turns his efforts toward bringing others into the organization, for which he will receive a part of what they pay. His task is to bring prospective purchasers to "Adventure Meetings."

These meetings are like an old time revival meeting, but directed toward the joys of making easy money rather than salvation. Their purpose is to convince prospective purchasers, or "prospects," that Dare is a sure route to great riches. . . .

Once he has bought a plan that empowers him to help sell the plans to others, the task of the purchaser is to find prospects and induce them to attend Adventure Meetings. He is not to tell them that Dare To Be Great, Inc. is involved. Rather, he catches their interest by intimating that the result of attendance will be significant wealth for the prospect. It is at the meetings that the sales effort takes place. The "salesman" is told that to maximize his chances of success he should impart an aura of affluence, whether spurious or not—to pretend that through his association with Dare he has obtained wealth of no small proportions. The training that he has received at Dare is educating him on this point. He is told to "fake it 'til you make it," or to give the impression of wealth even if it has not been attained. He is urged to go into debt if necessary to purchase a new and expensive automobile and flashy clothes, and to carry with him large sums of money, borrowing if necessary, so that it can be ostentatiously displayed. The purpose of all this is to put the prospect in a more receptive state of mind with respect to the inducements that he will be subject to at the meetings. . . .

The 1933 and 1934 Acts are remedial legislation, among the central purposes of which is full and fair disclosure relative to the issuance of securities. It is a familiar canon of legislative construction that remedial legislation should be construed broadly. The Acts were designed to protect the American public from speculative or fraudulent schemes of promoters. For that reason Congress defined the term "security" broadly, and the Supreme Court in turn has construed the definition liberally. . . . In *SEC* v. *W. J. Howey Co.* the Court stated that the definition of a security "embodies a flexible rather than a static principle, one that is capable of adaptation to meet the countless and variable schemes devised by those who seek the use of the money of others on the promise of profits." . . .

In *SEC* v. *W. J. Howey Co.* the Supreme Court set out its by now familiar definition of an investment contract:

> The test is whether the scheme involves an investment of money in a common enterprise with profits to come solely from the efforts of others.

In *Howey* the Court held that a land sales contract for units of a citrus grove, together with a service contract for cultivating and marketing the crops, was an investment contract and hence a security. The Court held that what was in essence being offered was "an opportunity to contribute money and to share in the profits of a large citrus fruit enterprise managed and partly owned by respondents." The purchasers had no intention themselves of either occupying the land or developing it; they were attracted only "by the prospects of a return on their investment." It was clear that the profits were to come "solely" from the efforts of others.

For purposes of the present case, the sticking point in the *Howey* definition is the word "solely," a qualification which of course exactly fitted the circumstances in *Howey*. All the other elements of the *Howey* test have been met here. There is an investment of money, a common enterprise, and the expectation of profits to come from the efforts of others. Here, however, the investor, or purchaser, must himself exert some efforts if he is to realize a return on his initial cash outlay. He must find prospects and persuade them to attend Dare Adventure Meetings, and at least some of them must then purchase a plan if he is to realize that return. Thus it can be said that the returns or profits are not coming "solely" from the efforts of others.

We hold, however, that in light of the remedial nature of the legislation, the statutory policy of affording broad protection to the public and the Supreme Court's admonitions that the definition of securities should be a flexible one, the word "solely" should not be read as a strict or literal limitation on the definition of an investment contract, but rather must be construed realistically, so as to include within the definition those schemes which involve in substance, if not form, securities. . . .

Strict interpretation of the requirement that profits to be earned must come "solely" from the efforts of others has been subject to criticism. Adherence to such an interpretation could result in a mechanical, unduly restrictive view of what is and what is not an investment contract. It would be easy to evade by adding a requirement that the buyer contribute a modicum of effort. Thus the fact that the investors here were required to exert some efforts if a return were to be achieved should not automatically preclude a finding that the Plan or Adventure is an investment contract. To do so would not serve the purpose of the legislation. Rather we adopt a more realistic test, whether the efforts made by those other than the investor are the undeniably significant ones, those essential managerial efforts which affect the failure or success of the enterprise.

In this case, Dare's source of income is from selling the Adventures and the Plan. The purchaser is sold the idea that he will get a fixed part of the proceeds of the sales. In essence, to get that share, he invests three things: his money, his efforts to find prospects and bring them to the meetings and whatever it costs him to create an illusion of his own affluence. He invests them in Dare's get-rich-scheme. What he buys is a share of the proceeds of the selling efforts of Dare. Those efforts are the . . . [basis] of the scheme; those efforts are what keeps it going; those efforts are what produces the money which is to make him rich. In essence, it is the right that he buys. In our view, the scheme is no less an investment contract merely because he contributes some effort as well as money to get into it.

Let us assume that in *Howey* the sales and service agreements had provided that the buyer was to buy and plant the citrus trees. Unless he did so, there would be no crop to cultivate, harvest and sell, no moneys in which he could share. The essential nature of the scheme, however, would be the same. He would still be buying, in exchange for money, trees and planting, a share in what he hoped would be the company's success in cultivating the trees and harvesting and marketing the crop. We cannot believe that the Court would not have held such a scheme to be an investment contract. So here. Regardless of the fact that the purchaser here must contribute something besides his money, the essential managerial efforts which affect the failure or success of the enterprise are those of Dare, not his own. . . .

Questions

1. What is the definition of a security? What are the elements of the *Howey* test?
2. To create a security, must the profit to be realized from the investment of money be gained "solely" from the efforts and management of others?

EXEMPTIONS

Because the definition of security under Section 2 is so broad and all-encompassing, Section 5 appears to prohibit the sale of any security without an effective registration statement. However, Section 3 of the 1933 act exempts certain securities and Section 4 exempts certain transactions from the registration requirements. Section 3 exempts commercial paper, securities of government, banks, charitable organizations, savings and loan associations, common carriers, insurance policies, annuity contracts, and securities issued in bankruptcy reorganizations. In addition, "intrastate offerings" are exempt. However, to qualify as an "intrastate offering" certain elements must be established. The following case illustrated the difficulties of complying with the "intrastate offering" exemption.

Intrastate Offering

SEC v. McDonald Investment Co.

343 F. Supp. 343 (1972)
U.S. District Court, Minnesota

The question presented to the court is whether the sale exclusively to Minnesota residents of securities, consisting of unsecured installment promissory notes of the defendants, a Minnesota corporation, whose only business office is situate(d) in Minnesota, is exempt from the filing of a registration statement under § 3(a)(11) of the 1933 Securities Act, when the proceeds from the sale of such notes are to be used principally, if not entirely, to make loans to land developers outside of Minnesota. . . .

Plaintiff, the Securities and Exchange Commission, instituted this lawsuit. . . . The defendants are McDonald Investment Company, a Minnesota corporation, and H. J. McDonald, the company's president, treasurer, and owner of all the company's outstanding common stock. Plaintiff requests that the defendants be permanently enjoined from offering for sale and selling securities without having complied with the registration requirements of Section 5 of the Act. . . .

Section 3(a)(11) of the Act, however, sometimes called the intrastate exemption, exempts from registration:

> (11) Any security which is a part of an issue offered and sold only to persons resident within a single State or Territory, where the issuer of such security is a person resident and doing business within or, if a corporation, incorporated by and doing business within, such State or Territory. . . .

The plaintiff predicates its claim for a permanent injunction on the ground that the defendants will be engaged in a business where the income producing operations are located outside the state in which the securities are to be offered and sold and therefore not available for the 3(a)(11) exemption. . . .

In *Truckee* v. *Showboat* the exemption was not allowed because the proceeds of the offering were to be used primarily for the purpose of a new unrelated business in another state, i.e., a California corporation acquiring and refurbishing a hotel in Las Vegas, Nevada. Likewise, in *Chapman* v. *Dunn* the 3(a)(11) exemption was unavailable to an offering by a company in one state, Michigan, of undivided fractional oil and gas interests located in another state, Ohio. The *Dunn* court specifically stated at page 159:

> . . . in order to qualify for the exemption of § 3(a)(11), the issuer must offer and sell his securities only to persons resident within a single State and the issuer must be a resident of that same State. *In addition to this, the issuer must conduct a predominant amount of his business within his same State.* This business which the issuer must conduct within the same State refers to the income producing operations of the business in which the issuer is selling the securities. . . . [Emphasis added]

This language would seem to fit the instant case where the income producing operations of the defendant, after completion of the offering, are to consist entirely of earning interest on its loans and receivables invested outside the state of Minnesota. While the defendant will not participate in any of the land developer's operations, nor will it own or control any of the operations, the fact is that the strength of the installment notes depends perhaps not legally, but practically, to a large degree on the success or failure of land developments located outside Minnesota, such land not being subject to the jurisdiction of the Minnesota court. The investor obtains no direct interest in any business activity outside of Minnesota, but legally holds only an interest as a creditor of a Minnesota corporation, which of course would be a prior claim on the defendant's assets over the shareholder's equity. . . .

This case does not evidence the deliberate attempt to evade the Act as in the example posed by plaintiff of a national organization or syndicate which incorporates in several or many states, opens an office in each and sells securities only to residents of the particular state, intending nevertheless to use all the proceeds whenever realized in a venture beyond the boundaries of all, or at best all but one of the states. Defendant corporation on the contrary has been in business in

Minnesota for some period of time, is not a "Johnny come lately" and is not part of any syndicate or similar enterprise; yet to relieve it of the federal registration requirements where none or very little of the money realized is to be invested in Minnesota, would seem to violate the spirit if not the letter of the Act. . . .

Exemptions under the Act are strictly construed, with the burden of proof on the one seeking to establish the same.

Defendant notes that agreements with land developers will by their terms be construed under Minnesota law; that the income producing activities will be the earnings of interest which occurs in Minnesota; that the Minnesota registration provides at close proximity all the information and protection that any investor might desire; that whether or not registered with the Securities and Exchange Commission, a securities purchaser has the protection of 15 U.S.C. § 77e which attaches liability to the issuer whether or not registration of the securities are exempted for fraudulent or untrue statements in a prospectus or made by oral communications; that plaintiff blurs the distinction between sale of securities across state lines and the operation of an intrastate business; and that if injunction issues in this case it could issue in any case where a local corporation owns an investment out of the particular state in which it has its principal offices and does business such as accounts receivable from its customers out of state. While these arguments are worthy . . . on balance and in carrying out the spirit and intent of the Securities Act of 1933, plaintiff's request for a permanent injunction should be granted.

Questions

1. Must the revenue from the security sales be applied or invested in the state itself to come within the "intrastate offering" exemption?
2. Should the intrastate offering exemption be narrowly or broadly interpreted?
3. Does the reasoning in the *McDonald Investment Co.* decision make it difficult to comply with the intrastate offering exemption?

To avoid confusion concerning the scope of the intrastate offering exemption, the SEC has adopted Rule 147 which outlines a series of guidelines to determine the applicability of a Section 3 exemption. Under Rule 147, a firm incorporated and doing 80 percent of its business within a state may sell its securities without registering them if at least 80 percent of the proceeds of the offering are used within the state and all offerees are residents of that state. In addition, resales of the stock for nine months must be limited to state residents and the stock certificates must bear a legend indicating these restrictions. As one can imagine, the limitations of Rule 147 are too severe for it to be widely utilized. Therefore, businesses with a substantial volume of interstate sales or interstate purchases of the stock would be denied an intrastate offering exemption.

Private Placements

Section 4 provides that the registration requirements shall be inapplicable to "transactions by an issuer not involving any public offering." The courts have struggled to come up with a useful definition of a "nonpublic offer," which is often referred to as a private placement. The following case illustrates some of the appropriate criteria used by the courts to determine whether or not the offering is nonpublic.

Hill York Corp. v. American International Franchises, Inc.
488 F. 2d 680 (1971)
U.S. Court of Appeals (5th Cir.)

It is conceded that no registration statement had been filed with the SEC in connection with this offering of securities. The defendants contend, however, that the transactions come within the exemptions to registration found in . . . Section 4(2). Specifically, they contend that the offering of securities was not a public offering. . . .

The SEC has stated that the question of public offering is one of fact and must depend upon the circumstances of each case. We agree with this approach. . . .

The following specific factors are relevant:

1. *The number of offerees and their relationship to each other and to the issuer.*
In the past the SEC has utilized the arbitrary figure of twenty-five offerees as a litmus test of whether an offering was public. A leading commentator in the field has noted, however, that in recent years the SEC has increasingly disavowed any safe numerical test. . . . Obviously, however, the more offerees, the more likelihood that the offering is public. The relationship between the offerees and the issuer is most significant. If the offerees know the issuer and have special knowledge as to its business affairs, such as high executive officers of the issuer would possess, then the offering is apt to be private. The Supreme Court laid special stress on this consideration in *Ralston Purina* by stating that "[t]he focus of the inquiry should be on the need of the offerees for the protections afforded by registration. The employees here were not shown to have access to the kind of information which registration would disclose." Also to be considered is the relationship between the offerees and their knowledge of each other. For example, if the offering is being made to a diverse and unrelated group, i.e. lawyers, grocers, plumbers, etc., then the offering would have the appearance of being public; but an offering to a select group of high executive officers of the issuer who know each other and of course have similar interests and knowledge of the offering would more likely be characterized as a private offering.
2. *The number of units offered.*
Here again there is no fixed magic number. Of course, the smaller the number of units offered, the greater the likelihood the offering will be considered private.
3. *The size of the offering.*
The smaller the size of the offering, the more probability it is private.

4. *The manner of offering.*
   A private offering is more likely to arise when the offer is made directly to the offerees rather that through the facilities of public distribution such as investment bankers or the securities exchanges. In addition, public advertising is incompatible with the claim of private offering.

Even an objective testing of these factors without determining whether a more comprehensive and generalized prerequisite has been met, is insufficient. . . . "The design of the statute is to protect investors by promoting full disclosure of information thought necessary to informed investment decisions." Thus the ultimate test is whether " 'the particular class of persons affected need the protection of the Act.' " . . . The evidence indicates that this offering was limited to sophisticated businessmen and attorneys who planned to do business with the new firm. . . .

The defendants rely most strongly on the fact that the offering was made only to sophisticated businessmen and lawyers and not the average man in the street. Although this evidence is certainly favorable to the defendants, the level of sophistication will not carry the point. In this context, the relationship between the promoters and the purchasers and the "access to the kind of information which registration would disclose" become highly relevant factors. . . . Obviously if the plaintiffs did not possess the information requisite for a registration statement, they could not bring their sophisticated knowledge of business affairs to bear in deciding whether or not to invest in this franchise sales center. There is abundant evidence to support the conclusion that the plaintiffs did not in fact possess the requisite information. The plaintiffs were given: 1. a brochure representing that the defendants had just left the very successful firm of Nationwide, but without disclosing the fact that Nationwide was then under investigation by the SEC; 2. a brochure representing Browne as an expert in capitalization consulting, when in fact he had no expertise in such consulting; 3. a brochure stating that the franchise fee would be 25,000 dollars, when in fact the franchise fee turned out to be 25,000 dollars plus a 1,000 dollar per month royalty; 4. a brochure representing that the existing sales centers were successfully operating, without disclosure of the fact that most of them were under investigation by various state securities commissions. No reasonable mind could conclude that the plaintiffs had access to accurate information on the foregoing points since the only persons who reasonably could have relieved their ignorance were the ones that told them the untruths in the first instance. This proof . . . inexorably leads to the conclusion that even the most sanguine of the purchasers would have entertained serious, if not fatal, doubts about investing in this scheme if completely accurate information had been furnished.

While defendants allude to other evidence in this case, the paucity of evidence pertaining to the relative considerations remains stark. The record contains no evidence as to the number of offerees. The fact that there were only thirteen actual purchasers is of course irrelevant. We do know that the purchasers were a diverse and unrelated group, or at least this was so at the time the offering occurred. Furthermore, the defendants admit that the plantiffs had never met or in any way communicated with them prior to purchasing their stock. . . .

This Court reviews cases, it neither tries nor retries fact issues. . . . Faced with the state of evidentiary development when the parties rested, the court below could properly reach the same conclusion as the court in *Repass* v. *Rees,* 174 F. Supp. 898, 904 (D. Colo. 1959):

> . . . there is no evidence as to the experience of the buyers other than the plaintiffs. And there is no evidence as to how many offers were made to other persons, or the experience of those persons. The defendants did not testify that they had made no other offers. Without such evidence in the record the Court cannot determine whether the class needed protection. It was incumbent on the defendants to submit this evidence. Since they did not, they must suffer the consequences.

Questions

1. What are the relevant factors identified by the court to be considered in determining whether the offer is "public"? What is the "ultimate test"?
2. If the securities are offered to "sophisticated businessmen and lawyers," will this entitle the offering to be designated as private?
3. On what other issues did the court say that evidence was lacking which would be necessary to establish the nature of a private offering?

In 1974 the SEC adopted Rule 146, which defines criteria to establish the clearly legal "private placement." However, if one is not able to fully comply with all the criteria of Rule 146, the offering may be held nevertheless to be a private offering under case law. Consequently, lawyers in the securities field try to comply with Rule 146 as much as possible in an effort to satisfy the court of the private nature of the offering. The provisions of Rule 146 require that there be a limitation of offerees to around 35 persons, that no solicitation or general advertising be undertaken, that the offerees or their representative be sophisticated investors with access to or disclosure of company information (by employment or economic bargaining power), and that the purchasers buy the securities for their own account without intent to resell.

Resale of Privately Placed Securities

After having acquired securities in a private placement, the investor is prohibited from reselling the securities unless he or she complies with the provisions of Rule 144. Following Rule 144 is the only way for persons who have purchased securities under a private placement to resell their securities without being designated "underwriters" who are selling securities without registration. Rule 144 requires that the securities be held for two years from the date of the purchase and that the amount of distribution must be limited to less than 1 percent of the average market trading volume within a four-week period. In addition, information must be delivered to the public prior to such distributions. This requirement means the company must have "gone public" (through registration) so that the general public will have information with which to evaluate whether to purchase stock. If the company has not gone public, the seller should follow Rule 237, which requires a holding period of five years and a sale within a one-year period of no more than $50,000 worth of securities or 1 percent of the securities outstanding in a particular class, whichever is the lesser.

Small Issue Exemptions

In an effort to aid small businesses in their attempts to raise risk capital, the SEC has an exemption from the registration requirements for issues smaller than $1,500,000. The commission's promulgated Regulation A covers these situations. Under a "Reg. A" procedure, the offeror prepares a short form of registration to be filed with the nearest SEC regional office.

A second exemption for small offerings is provided by SEC Rule 240. To qualify, the issuer cannot sell more than $100,000 of securities within any 12-month period. Sales to full-time employees of the issuer are excluded from the $100,000 figure, regardless of their degree of sophistication. However, there can be no more than 100 holders of the securities issued by the corporation, and no general solicitation of the public is permitted. A simplified report of the security sales is filed with the SEC regional office.

Finally, Rule 242 enlarges the small offering exemption to $2 million in securities within any six-month period if sales are made to an unlimited number of "accredited persons." Accredited persons include institutional investors, purchasers of at least $100,000 in securities, and the issuer's executive officers and directors. A corporation may also sell to as many as 35 nonaccredited investors. However, if nonaccredited persons are avoided, the corporation need not furnish the accredited persons with any prospectus-type information. The inclusion of nonaccredited persons in the sale requires the company to furnish a simplified prospectus to all purchasers.

Compliance with any of the regulations authorizing small offerings that are exempt from registration does not also exempt the issuer or others from the antifraud provisions of the securities laws.

ANTIFRAUD PROVISION

The 1933 act contains a general antifraud provision in Section 17(a). This provision outlaws fraudulent transactions in securities whether or not the security is entitled to an exemption from registration. The following case illustrates the utilization of this antifraud provision.

SEC v. Manor Nursing Centers, Inc.
458 F. 2d 1082 (1972)
U.S. Court of Appeals (2d Cir.)

The conduct of appellants in connection with the public offering of Manor shares, upon analysis, demonstrates beyond a peradventure of a doubt that they violated the antifraud provisions of the federal securities laws—§ 17(a) of the 1933 Act and § 10(b) of the 1934 Act.

The gravamen of this case is that each of the appellants participated in a continuing course of conduct whereby public investors were fraudulently induced to part with their money in the expectation that Manor and the selling stockholders would return the money if all Manor shares were not sold and all the proceeds from the sale were not received by March 8, 1970. It is undisputed that, as of March 8, Manor and the selling stockholders had not sold all the 450,000 shares and that all the proceeds expected from the sale had not been received. Moreover, it is clear that all appellants knew, or should have known, that the preconditions for their retaining the proceeds of the offering had not been satisfied. Nevertheless, rather than complying with the terms of the offering by returning the funds of public investors, appellants retained these funds for their own financial benefit. This misappropriation of the proceeds of the Manor offering constituted a fraud on public investors and violated the antifraud provisions of the federal securities laws. . . .

It also is clear that appellants violated the antifraud provisions of the federal securities laws by offering Manor shares when they knew, or should have known, that the Manor prospectus was misleading in several material respects. After the registration statement became effective on December 8, 1969, at least four developments occurred which made the prospectus misleading: the public's funds were not returned even though the issue was not fully subscribed; an escrow account for the proceeds of the offering was not established; shares were issued for consideration other than cash; and certain individuals received extra compensation for agreeing to participate in the offering. These developments were not disclosed to the public investors. That these developments occurred after the effective date of the registration statement did not provide a license to appellants to ignore them. Post-effective developments which materially alter the picture presented in the registration statement must be brought to the attention of public investors. "The effect of the antifraud provisions of the Securities Act (§ 17(a)) and of the Exchange Act (§ 10(b) and Rule 10b-5) is to require the prospectus to reflect any post-effective changes necessary to keep the prospectus from being misleading in any material respect."

While appellants admit that public investors were defrauded, they seek to exculpate themselves from liability for their acts by arguing that they acted in good faith.

We hold, however, that the evidence established that appellants . . . did not act in good faith. Feinberg, as the district court properly found, has had considerable experience in complex financing arrangements. Thus, it would strain credulity to suggest that Feinberg did not know that the closing . . . was invalid. . . .

Ezrine's claim that he acted in good faith likewise is belied by the evidence adduced at trial. As an experienced securities lawyer, he was well aware that failure to correct a misleading prospectus and retention of the proceeds even through the issue had not been fully subscribed constituted violations of the antifraud provisions of the securities laws. Indeed, Ezrine's knowledge that the federal securities laws required public disclosure of developments which occurred subsequent to the effective date of the registration statement is indicated by his supplementing the Manor prospectus on February 24 to reflect [a new participant] in the offering as an underwriter. . . .

Having concluded that appellants had violated the federal securities laws, the district court permanently enjoined all appellants . . . from further violations of the antifraud provisions of the 1933 and 1934 Acts. . . .

In addition to granting the SEC's request for injunctive relief, the district court ordered appellants to disgorge all the proceeds . . . received in connection with the public offering of Manor stock; appointed a trustee to receive such funds, to distribute them to defrauded public investors and to report to the court on the true state of affairs; and, to prevent a wasting of assets, ordered a temporary freeze on appellants' assets pending transfer of the funds to the trustee.

Questions

1. Identify the fraudulent activities of the defendants in *Manor Nursing Center.*
2. Must a prospectus be "up-dated" by subsequent developments which would be materially important to public investors?
3. Why were the defendants unable to convince the court that they had acted in good faith?
4. What actions did the court take to protect public investors?

LIABILITIES FOR ILLEGAL SALES AND REGISTRATION

The SEC can enjoin the illegal distribution of securities without a registration statement and obtain a $5,000 fine or up to five years imprisonment for violation of the 1933 act. Private parties also have the right to litigate securities violations under the 1933 act.

Under Section 12(1) purchasers of securities may directly sue for rescission or damages any person who violated Section 5 by selling the securities to them without the required registration. Section 12(2) imposes liability for material misstatements or omissions in the distribution of securities. Since Section 12 contains a requirement of "privity," purchasers may sue only their immediate sellers and not the issuer. Consequently, Section 12 is drafted to impose potential liability on *broker-dealers* who violate the act in merchandising of securities.

Section 11 of the 1933 act contains potential liability for the *issuer* of a security should a registration statement be filed which contains material misstatements or omissions. Section 11 entitles any person acquiring a security not knowing of the misstatement or omission to sue every person who has signed the registration statement, including the issuer. All directors who have signed the registration statement and the underwriters who have also signed are subject to suit. Even a director who has not signed the registration statement may not be relieved of potential liability. However, Section 11 also provides that no person, other than the issuer, shall be liable if the person can establish his or her "due diligence" defense. The following case illustrates the efforts of the defendants to establish their due diligence defense.

Escott v. BarChris Construction Corp.
283 F. Supp. 643 (1968)
U.S. District Court (S.D.N.Y.)

The action is brought under Section 11 of the Securities Act of 1933. Plaintiffs allege that the registration statement with respect to these debentures filed with the Securities and Exchange Commission, which became effective on May 16, 1961, contained false statements and material omissions.

Defendants fall into three categories: (1) the persons who signed the registration statement; (2) the underwriters, consisting of eight investment banking firms, led by Drexel & Co. (Drexel); and (3) BarChris's auditors, Peat, Marwick, Mitchell & Co. (Peat, Marwick). . . .

It is a prerequisite to liability under Section 11 of the Act that the fact which is falsely stated in a registration statement, or the fact that is omitted when it should have been stated to avoid misleading, be "material." . . .

Early in the history of the Act, a definition of materiality was given in *Matter of Charles A. Howard,* 1 S.E.C. 6.8 (1934), which is still valid today. A material fact was there defined as:

". . . a fact which if it had been correctly stated or disclosed would have deterred or tended to deter the average prudent investor from purchasing the securities in question." . . .

Judged by this test, there is no doubt that many of the misstatements and omissions in this prospectus were material. This is true of all of them which relate to the state of affairs in 1961, i.e., the overstatement of sales and gross profit for the first quarter, the understatement of contingent liabilities as of April 30, the overstatement of orders on hand and the failure to disclose the true facts with respect to officers' loans, customers' delinquencies, application of proceeds and the prospective operation of several alleys. . . .

The "Due Diligence" Defenses

Every defendant . . . has pleaded these affirmative defenses. Each claims that (1) as to the part of the registration statement purporting to be made on the authority of an expert (which for convenience, I shall refer to as the "expertised portion"), he had no reasonable ground to believe and did not believe that there were any untrue statements or material omissions, and (2) as to the other parts of the registration statement, he made a reasonable investigation, as a result of which he had reasonable ground to believe and did believe that the registration statement was true and that no material fact was omitted. . . .

The only expert, in the statutory sense, was Peat, Marwick, and the only parts of the registration statement which purported to be made on the authority of an expert were the portions which purported to be made on Peat, Marwick's authority. . . .

I turn now to the question of whether defendants have proved their due diligence defenses.

Russo

Russo was, to all intents and purposes, the chief executive officer of BarChris. He was a member of the executive committee. He was familiar with all aspects of the business. He was personally in charge of dealings with the factors. He talked with customers about their delinquencies. . . .

In short, Russo knew all the relevant facts. He could not have believed that there were no untrue statements or material omissions in the prospectus. Russo has no due diligence defenses.

Vitolo and Pugliese

They were the founders of the business. . . . Vitolo was president and Pugliese was vice president. . . .

Vitolo and Pugliese are each men of limited education. It is not hard to believe that for them the prospectus was difficult reading, if indeed they read it at all. . . .

The liability of a director who signs a registration statement does not depend upon whether or not he read it or, if he did, whether or not he understood what he was reading.

And in any case, Vitolo and Pugliese were not as naive as they claim to be. They were members of BarChris's executive committee. At meetings of that committee BarChris's affairs were discussed at length. They must have known what was going on. Certainly they knew of the inadequacy of cash in 1961. They knew of their own large advances to the company which remained unpaid. . . .

All in all, the position of Vitolo and Pugliese is not significantly different, for present purposes, from Russo's. They could not have believed that the registration statement was wholly true and that no material facts had been omitted. And in any case, there is nothing to show that they made any investigation of anything which they may not have known about or understood. They have not proved their due diligence defenses.

Kircher

Kircher was treasurer of BarChris and its chief financial officer. He is a certified public accountant and an intelligent man. He was thoroughly familiar with BarChris's financial affairs. . . . He knew of the customers' delinquency problem. . . .

Moreover, as a member of the executive committee, Kircher was kept informed as to those branches of the business of which he did not have direct charge. . . .

Kircher worked on the preparation of the registration statement. . . . He supplied information . . . about the company's business. He read the prospectus and understood it. He knew what it said and what it did not say.

Kircher's contention is that he had never before dealt with a registration statement, that he did not know what it should contain, and that he relied wholly on [the attorneys] and Peat, Marwick to guide him. . . .

There is an issue of credibility here. In fact, Kircher was not frank in dealing with [the attorneys]. He withheld information from them. But even if he had told them all the facts, this would not have constituted the due diligence contemplated by the statute. Knowing the facts, Kircher had reason to believe that the expertised portion of the prospectus, i.e., the 1960 figures, was in part incorrect. He could not shut his eyes to the facts and rely on Peat, Marwick for that portion.

As to the rest of the prospectus, knowing the facts, he did not have a reasonable ground to believe it to be true. On the contrary, he must have known that in part it was untrue. Under these circumstances, he was not entitled to sit back and place the blame on the lawyers for not advising him about it.

Kircher has not proved his due diligence defenses. . . .

Birnbaum

Birnbaum was a young lawyer, admitted to the bar in 1957, who, after brief periods of employment by two different law firms and an equally brief period of practicing in his own firm, was employed by BarChris as house counsel and assistant secretary in October 1960. Unfortunately for him, he became secretary and a director of BarChris on April 17, 1961, after the first version of the registration statement had been filed with the Securities and Exchange Commission. He signed the later amendments, thereby becoming responsible for the accuracy of the prospectus in its final form. . . .

One of Birnbaum's more important duties, first as assistant secretary and later as full-fledged secretary, was to keep the corporate minutes of BarChris and its subsidiaries. This necessarily informed him to a considerable extent about the company's affairs. Birnbaum was not initially a member of the executive committee, however, and did not keep its minutes at the outset. . . .

It seems probable that Birnbaum did not know of many of the inaccuracies in the prospectus. He must, however, have appreciated some of them. In any case, he made no investigation and relied on the others to get it right. . . . [H]e was entitled to rely upon Peat, Marwick for the 1960 figures, for as far as appears, he had no personal knowledge of the company's books of account or financial transactions. But he was not entitled to rely upon Kircher and [attorneys] for the other portions of the prospectus. As a lawyer, he should have known his obligations under the statute. He should have known that he was required to make a reasonable investigation of the truth of all the statements in the unexpertised portion of the document which he signed. Having failed to make such an investigation, he did not have reasonable ground to believe that all these statements were true. Birnbaum has not established his due diligence defenses except as to the audited 1960 figures.

Auslander

Auslander was an "outside" director, i.e., one who was not an officer of BarChris. He was chairman of the board of Valley Stream National Bank in Valley Stream, Long Island. In February 1961 Vitolo asked him to become a director of BarChris. Vitolo gave him an enthusiastic account of BarChris's progress and prospects. As an inducement, Vitolo said that when BarChris received the proceeds of a forthcoming issue of securities, it would deposit $1,000,000 in Auslander's bank. . . .

Auslander was elected a director on April 17, 1961. The registration statement in its original form had already been filed, of course without his signature. On May 10, 1961, he signed a signature page for the first amendment to the registration statement which was filed on May 11, 1961. This was a separate sheet without any document attached. Auslander did not know that it was a signature page for a registration statement. He vaguely understood that it was something "for the SEC."

Auslander attended a meeting of BarChris's directors on May 15, 1961. At that meeting he, along with the other directors, signed the signature sheet for the second amendment which constituted the registration statement in its final form. Again, this was only a separate sheet without any document attached. Auslander never saw a copy of the registration statement in its final form.

At the May 15 directors' meeting, however, Auslander did realize that what he was signing was a signature sheet to a registration statement. This was the first time that he had appreciated that fact. A copy of the registration statement in its earlier form as amended on May 11, 1961, was passed around at the meeting. Auslander glanced at it briefly. He did not read it thoroughly.

At the May 15 meeting, Russo and Vitolo stated that everything was in order and that the prospectus was correct. Auslander believed this statement.

In considering Auslander's due diligence defenses, a distinction is to be drawn between the expertised and nonexpertised portions of the prospectus. As to the former, Auslander knew that Peat, Marwick had audited the 1960 figures. He believed them to be correct because he had confidence in Peat, Marwick. He had no reasonable ground to believe otherwise.

As to the non-expertised portions, however, Auslander is in a different position. . . .

It is true that Auslander became a director on the eve of the financing. He had little opportunity to familiarize himself with the company's affairs. The question is whether, under such circumstances, Auslander did enough to establish his due diligence defense with respect to the non-expertised portions of the prospectus. . . .

Section 11 imposes liability in the first instance upon a director, no matter how new he is. He is presumed to know his responsibility when he becomes a director. He can escape liability only by using that reasonable care to investigate the facts which a prudent man would employ in the management of his own property. In my opinion, a prudent man would not act in an important matter without any knowledge of the relevant facts, in sole reliance upon representations of persons who are comparative strangers and upon general information which does not purport to cover the particular case.

To say that such minimal conduct measures up to the statutory standard would, to all intents and purposes absolve new directors from responsibility merely because they are new. This is not a sensible construction of Section 11, when one bears in mind its fundamental purpose of requiring full and truthful disclosure for the protection of investors.

I find and conclude that Auslander has not established his due diligence defense. . . .

Grant

Grant became a director of BarChris in October 1960. His law firm was counsel to BarChris in matters pertaining to the registration of securities. . . .

Grant is sued as a director and as a signer of the registration statement. This is not an action against him for malpractice in his capacity as a lawyer. Nevertheless, in considering Grant's due diligence defenses, the unique position which he occupied cannot be disregarded. As the director most directly concerned with writing the registration statement and assuring its accuracy, more was required of him in the way of reasonable investigation than could fairly be expected of a director who had no connection with this work. . . .

I find that Grant honestly believed that the registration statement was true and that no material facts had been omitted from it.

In this belief he was mistaken, and the fact is that for all his work, he never discovered any of the errors or omissions. . . .

Grant contends that a finding that he did not make a reasonable investigation would be equivalent to a holding that a lawyer for an issuing company, in order to show due diligence, must make an independent audit of the figures supplied to him by his client. I do not consider this to be a realistic statement of the issue. There were errors and omissions here which could have been detected without an audit. The question is whether, despite his failure to detect them, Grant made a reasonable effort to that end. . . .

It is claimed that a lawyer is entitled to rely on the statements of his client and that to require him to verify their accuracy would set an unreasonably high standard. This is too broad a generalization. It is all a matter of degree. To require an audit would obviously be unreasonable. On the other hand, to require a check of matters easily verifiable is not unreasonable. Even honest clients can make mistakes. The statute imposes liability for untrue statements regardless of whether they are intentionally untrue. The way to prevent mistakes is to test oral information by examining the original written record. . . .

Grant was entitled to rely on Peat, Marwick for the 1960 figures. He had no reasonable ground to believe them to be inaccurate. But of the matters which were not within the expertised portion of the prospectus . . . Grant was obliged to make a reasonable investigation. I am forced to find that he did not make one. . . . In my opinion, this finding on the evidence in this case does not establish an unreasonably high standard in other cases for company counsel who are also directors. Each case must rest on its own facts. I conclude that Grant has not established his due diligence defenses except as to the audited 1960 figures.

The Underwriters and Coleman

The underwriters other than Drexel made no investigation of the accuracy of the prospectus. They all relied upon Drexel as the "lead" underwriter.

Drexel did make an investigation. The work was in charge of Coleman, a partner of the firm. . . . Drexel's attorneys acted as attorneys for the entire group of underwriters. . . .

* * *

It is impossible to lay down a rigid rule suitable for every case defining the extent to which such verification must go. It is a question of degree, a matter of judgment in each case. In the present case, the underwriters' counsel made almost no attempt to verify management's representations. I hold that that was insufficient.

On the evidence in this case, I find that the underwriters' counsel did not make a reasonable investigation of the truth of those portions of the prospectus which were not made on the authority of Peat, Marwick as an expert. Drexel is bound by their failure. It is not a matter of relying upon counsel for legal advice. Here the attorneys were dealing with matters of fact. Drexel delegated to them, as its agent, the business of examining the corporate minutes and contracts. It must bear the consequences of their failure to make an adequate examination.

The other underwriters, who did nothing and relied solely on Drexel and the lawyers, are also bound by it. It follows that although Drexel and the other underwriters believed that those portions of the prospectus were true, they had no reasonable ground for that belief, within the meaning of the statute. Hence, they have not established their due diligence defenses, except as to the 1960 audited figures.

The same conclusions must apply to Coleman. He made no investigation after he became a director. When it came to verification, he relied upon his counsel to do it for him. Since counsel failed to do it, Coleman is bound by that failure. Consequently, in his case also, he has not established his due diligence defense as to the audited 1960 figures.

Peat, Marwick

Section 11(b) . . . defines the due diligence defense for an expert. Peat, Marwick has pleaded it.

The part of the registration statement purporting to be made upon the authority of Peat, Marwick as an expert was the 1960 figures. . . . [The] question is whether at that time Peat, Marwick, after reasonable investigation, had reasonable ground to believe and did believe that the 1960 figures were true and that no material fact had been omitted from the registration statement which should have been included in order to make the 1960 figures not misleading. In deciding this issue, the court must consider not only what Peat, Marwick did in its 1960 audit, but also what it did in its subsequent "S-1 review." The proper scope of that review must also be determined. . . .

Most of the actual work was performed by a senior accountant, Berardi. . . .

It is unnecessary to recount everything that Berardi did in the course of the audit. We are concerned only with the evidence relating to what Berardi did or did not do with respect to those items which I have found to have been incorrectly reported in the 1960 figures in the prospectus. . . .

First and foremost is Berardi's failure to discover that [a subsidiary] . . . had not been sold. This error affected both the sales figure and the liability side of the balance sheet.

As to factors' reserves, it is hard to understand how Berardi could have treated this item as entirely a current asset when it was obvious that most of the reserves would not be released within one year. If Berardi was unaware of that fact, he should have been aware of it.

Berardi erred in computing the contingent liability on Type B leaseback transactions at 25 percent. Berardi did not examine the documents which are in evidence which established that BarChris's contingent liability on this type of transaction was in fact 100 percent. Berardi did not make a reasonable investigation in this instance.

The S-1 Review

The purpose of reviewing events subsequent to the date of a certified balance sheet (referred to as an S-1 review when made with reference to a registration statement) is to ascertain whether any material change has occurred in the company's financial position which should be disclosed in order to prevent the balance sheet figures from being misleading. The scope of such a review, under generally accepted auditing standards, is limited. It does not amount to a complete audit.

Peat, Marwick prepared a written program for such a review. I find that this program conformed to generally accepted auditing standards. . . .

Berardi made the S-1 review in May 1961. He devoted a little over two days to it, a total of 20½ hours. He did not discover any of the errors or omissions pertaining to the state of affairs in 1961 which I have previously discussed at length, all of which were material. The question is whether, despite his failure to find out anything, his investigation was reasonable within the meaning of the statute.

What Berardi did was to look at a consolidating trial balance as of March 31, 1961, which had been prepared by BarChris, compare it with the audited December 31, 1960, figures, discuss . . . certain unfavorable developments which the comparison disclosed, and read certain minutes. He did not examine any "important financial records" other than the trial balance. . . .

In substance, what Berardi did is similar to what Grant . . . did. He asked questions, he got answers which he considered satisfactory, and he did nothing to verify them. . . .

Since he never read the prospectus, he was not even aware that there had ever been any problem about loans from officers.

There had been a material change for the worse in BarChris's financial position. That change was sufficiently serious so that the failure to disclose it made the 1960 figures misleading. Berardi did not discover it. As far as results were concerned, his S-1 review was useless.

Accountants should not be held to a standard higher than that recognized in their profession. I do not do so here. Berardi's review did not come up to that standard. He did not take some of the steps which Peat, Marwick's written program prescribed. He did not spend an adequate amount of time on a task of this magnitude. Most important of all, he was too easily satisfied with glib answers to his inquiries.

This is not to say that he should have made a complete audit. But there were enough danger signals in the materials which he did examine to require some further investigation on his part. Generally accepted accounting standards required such further investigation under these circumstances. It is not always sufficient merely to ask questions.

Here again, the burden of proof is on Peat, Marwick. I find that the burden has not been satisfied. I conclude that Peat, Marwick has not established its due diligence defense.

Questions

1. As to the nonexpert portion of the registration statement, what must a director do to establish a "due diligence" defense?
2. Identify some of the things that the "insiders" failed to do to establish their reasonable investigations and reasonable belief in the accuracy of the registration statement?
3. What did the underwriters fail to do to establish their due diligence defense?
4. What did the expert accountants have to do to establish their due diligence defense? What did they fail to do to establish the defense?

CONCLUSION

The Securities Act of 1933 is basically a registration of information law which is designed to give the prospective investor more information about the management and finances of the corporation when the firm seeks to sell its securities to the public. Some opponents of the disclosure doctrine argue that its costly operation imposes artificial barriers of entry which inefficiently allocate capital. On the other hand, supporters of the disclosure system maintain that it is necessary to protect the "purity" of the securities distribution system and the confidence of the investors which is essential to the process of raising capital investments.

CASE PROBLEMS

1. A pension plan entered into under a collective-bargaining agreement between a local labor union and employer trucking firms required all employees to participate in a pension plan but not to pay anything into it. All contributions to the plan were to be made by employers at a specified amount per week for each worker-week covered employment. To be eligible for a pension, an employee was required to have 20 years of continued service. Peti-

tioner employee, who had over 20 years' service, was denied a pension on retirement because of a break in service. He then brought suit in Federal District Court, alleging that the union and the trustee of the pension funds had misrepresented and omitted a statement of material facts with respect to the value of a covered employee's interest in the pension plan, and that such misstatements and omissions constituted a fraud in connection with the sale of a security in violation of Section 10(b) of the Securities Exchange Act of 1934 and Rule 10b-5. As a prerequisite matter, the district court held that petitioner's interest in the pension fund constituted a "security" within the meaning of the Securities Act because the plan created an "investment contract." Do you agree?

2. Defendant engaged in a fraudulent "short selling" scheme by placing orders with brokers to sell certain shares of stock which he believed had peaked in price and which he falsely represented that he owned. Gambling that the price would decline substantially before he was required to deliver the securities, he planned to take offsetting purchases through other brokers at lower prices. But the market price rose sharply before the delivery date so that defendant was unable to make covering purchases and never delivered the securities. Consequently, the brokers were unable to deliver the securities to the investor-purchasers and were forced to borrow stock to make the delivery. In order to return the borrowed stock the brokers had to purchase replacement shares on the open market at the now higher prices, a process known as "buying in." The investors were thereby shielded from direct injury, but the brokers suffered substantial financial losses. The district court found defendant guilty of employing "a scheme and artifice to defraud" in the sale of securities in violation of Section 17(a)(1) of the Securities Act of 1933, which makes it unlawful "for any person in the offer or sale of any securities . . . directly or indirectly . . . to employ any device, scheme, or artifice to defraud." The court of appeals, though finding the evidence sufficient to establish that defendant had committed fraud, vacated the conviction on the ground that the purpose of the Securities Act was to protect investors from fraudulent practices in the sale of securities and that since defendant's fraud injured only brokers and not investors, defendant did not violate Section 17(a)(1). Is the court of appeals correct?

3. A limited partnership agreement divided partners into "participants" whose capital contributions were to be applied first to defray intangible expenses incurred in the partnership's oil drilling venture, and "special participants" whose capital was to be used for tangible drilling expenses. One of the two original special participants, PMC and ITR Corp., located four participants to join the partnership. PMC attracted only Doran, who became a special participant. Doran was the fourth person contacted by PMC in regard to joining in the venture.

   A broker had linked PMC and Doran. PMC sent Doran some drilling logs and technical maps and informed him that two of the four wells planned had been completed. Doran contributed $25,000 down and assumed liability on a $113,643 note owed by PMC to an outsider. Doran's share of production payments was to be used to make payments on the note, and Doran's name was added to the note as obligor directly to the outsider. He contracted to hold PMC harmless on the liability.

Because of a state law violation in the operation of the wells, the wells were sealed by a state authority for 388 days. The note went into default; the outsider took judgment against Doran and PMC. Doran seeks federal court relief voiding his agreements with PMC and the limited partnership because he was sold a security that was not registered.

What defense might PMC offer for not registering?

4. Bangor Corporation in its registration statement listed its 98.7 percent holding in Bangor and Aroostook Railroad (BAR) at $18.4 million. The Bangor Corporation failed to disclose that it had negotiated for a sale of the BAR at a price substantially below $18.4 million. The board had authorized Hutchins to enter into a deal to sell BAR to Amos on whatever terms he decided were best. The agreement that was entered into resulted in Bangor sustaining a $13.8 million book loss and a reduction in retained earnings from $37.9 million to $20.5 million.

   First Boston was the underwriter reviewing the registration statement and had ready access to the books and records of Bangor. It examined the minutes of the Bangor board meeting and questioned Bangor's management regarding the BAR. It was informed that there were no plans at that time to dispose of the railroad. First Boston did not seek verification of the official answer that a sale was not anticipated at that time, nor did it talk to officials at Amos after it discovered from the minutes that Amos was the likely buyer.

   Is First Boston's action sufficient to support a due diligence defense when charged as a participant in the registration of a misleading registration statement?

chapter 18

SECURITIES REGULATION: THE TRADING OF SECURITIES

After the original issuance of securities from the corporation to the public, such securities are traded among members of the public. To improve the fairness of the trading process, Congress passed the Securities Exchange Act of 1934, which extended the "disclosure" doctrine of investor protection to the securities listed and registered for public trading on national securities exchanges. And in 1964 the Securities Acts Amendment applied the disclosure and reporting provisions to equity securities of hundreds of companies traded over-the-counter (if their assets exceed $1 million and their shareholders number 500 or more). The requirements of the 1934 Act as amended impose new responsibilities on corporations and individuals, as explained in the following excerpt from a SEC publication.

SECURITIES AND EXCHANGE ACT OF 1934

The Work of the SEC

(SEC, 1980)

Corporate Reporting

Companies which seek to have their securities listed and registered for public trading on . . . an exchange must file a registration application with the exchange and the

Commission. A similar registration form must be filed by companies whose equity securities are traded over-the-counter if they meet the size test. . . . The Commission's rules prescribed the nature and content of these registration statements, including certified financial statements. Their data are generally comparable to, but less extensive than, the disclosures required in Securities Act registration statements. Following the registration of their securities, such companies must file annual and other periodic reports to keep current the information contained in the original filing. Copies of any of the reported data may be obtained from the Commission at nominal cost. . . .

The law prescribes penalties for filing false statements and reports with the Commission, as well as provision for recovery by investors who suffer losses in the purchase or sale of registered securities in reliance thereon.

Proxy Solicitations

Another provision of this law governs the solicitation of proxies (votes) from holders of registered securities (both listed and over-the-counter), whether for the election of directors or for approval of other corporate action. In any such solicitation, whether by the management or minority groups, disclosure must be made of all material facts concerning the matters on which such holders are asked to vote; and they must be afforded an opportunity to vote "Yes" or "No" on each matter. Where a contest for control of the management of a corporation is involved, the rules require disclosure of the names and interests of all "participants" in the proxy contest. Holders of such securities thus are enabled to vote intelligently on corporate actions requiring their approval. The Commission's rules require that proposed proxy material be filed in advance for examination by the Commission for compliance with the disclosure requirements.

Tender Offer Solicitations

In 1968, Congress amended the Exchange Act to extend its reporting and disclosure provisions to situations where control of a company is sought through a tender offer or other planned stock acquisition of over 10 percent of a company's equity securities. The amount was reduced to 5 percent by an amendment in 1970. These amendments and Commission rules thereunder require disclosure of pertinent information by the person seeking to acquire over 5 percent of the company's securities by direct purchase or by tender offer, as well as by any persons soliciting shareholders to accept or reject a tender offer. Thus, as with the proxy rules, public investors who hold stock in the subject corporation may now make informed decisions on take-over bids.

* * *

Margin Trading

The statute also contains provisions governing margin trading in securities. It authorizes the Board of Governors of the Federal Reserve System to set limitations on the amount of credit which may be extended for the purpose of purchasing or carrying securities. The objective is to restrict the excessive use of the nation's credit in the securities markets. While the credit restrictions are set by the Board, investigation and enforcement is the responsibility of the Commission.

Market Surveillance

The Securities Exchange Act also provides a system for regulating securities trading practices in both the exchange and the over-the-counter markets. In general, transactions in securities which are effected otherwise than on national securities exchanges are said to take place "over the counter." Designed to protect the interests of investors and the public, these provisions seek to curb misrepresentations and deceit, market manipulation and other fraudulent acts and practices and to establish and maintain just and equitable principles of trade conducive to the maintenance of open, fair and orderly markets.

While these provisions of the law establish the general regulatory pattern, the Commission is responsible for promulgating rules and regulations for their implementation. Thus, the Commission has adopted regulations which, among other things, (1) define acts or practices which constitute a "manipulative or deceptive device or contrivance" prohibited by the statute, (2) regulate short selling, stabilizing transactions and similar matters, (3) regulate the hypothecation of customers' securities and (4) provide safeguards with respect to the financial responsibility of brokers and dealers.

Registration of Exchanges and Others

In addition, the law as amended requires registration with the Commission of (1) "national securities exchanges" (those having a substantial securities trading volume); (2) brokers and dealers who conduct securities business in interstate commerce; (3) transfer agents; (4) clearing agencies; (5) municipal brokers and dealers; and (6) securities information processors.

To obtain registration, exchanges must show that they are so organized as to be able to comply with the provisions of the statute and the rules and regulations of the Commission and that their rules contain provisions which are just and adequate to insure fair dealing and to protect investors.

Each exchange is a self-regulatory organization, and its rules, among other things, must provide for the expulsion, suspension or other disciplining of member broker-dealers for conduct inconsistent with just and equitable principles of trade. While the law contemplates that exchanges shall have full opportunity to establish self-regulatory measures insuring fair dealing and the protection of investors, it empowers the Commission by order, rule or regulation to amend the rules of exchanges with respect to various phases of their activities and trading practices if necessary to effectuate the statutory objective. For the most part, exchange rules and revisions thereof suggested by exchanges or by the Commission reach their final form after discussion between representatives of the exchange and the Commission without resort to formal proceedings.

By an amendment to the law enacted in 1938, Congress also provided for creation of a self-regulatory organization to prevent fraudulent and manipulative acts and practices, to promote just and equitable principles of trade among over-the-counter brokers and dealers. One such association, the National Association of Securities Dealers, Inc., is registered with the Commission under this provision of the law. The establishment, maintenance and enforcement of a voluntary code of business ethics is one of the principal features of this provision of the law.

Not all broker-dealer firms are members of the NASD; thus, some are not subject to supervision and control by the agency. To equalize the regulatory pattern, Congress provided in the 1964 Amendments that the Commission should untertake to establish investor safeguards applicable to non-NASD firms comparable to those applicable to NASD members. Among the controls adopted by the Commission is a requirement that persons associated with non-NASD firms meet certain qualification standards similar to those applied by the NASD to its members.

Broker-Dealer Registration

Applications for registration as broker-dealers and amendments thereto are examined by the Office of Reports and Information Services with the assistance of the Division of Market Regulation. The registration of brokers and dealers engaged in an interstate over-the-counter securities business also is an important phase of the regulatory plan of the Act. They must conform their business practices to the standards prescribed in the law and the Commission's regulations for the protection of investors (as well as to the fair trade practice rules of their association); in addition, . . . they may violate these regulations only at the risk of possible loss of registration with the Commission and the right to continue to conduct an interstate securities business, or of suspension or expulsion from the association and loss of the benefits of such membership.

Investigation and Enforcement

It is the duty of the Commission under the laws it administers to investigate complaints or other indications of possible law violations in securities transactions, most of which arise under the Securities Act of 1933 and the Securities Exchange Act of 1934. Investigation and enforcement work is conducted both by the Commission's Regional Offices and the Division of Enforcement.

Most of the Commission's investigations are conducted privately, the facts being developed to the fullest extent possible through informal inquiry, interviewing of witnesses, examination of brokerage records and other documents, reviewing and trading data and similar means. The Commission, however, is empowered to issue subpoenas requiring sworn testimony and the production of books, records and other documents pertinent to the subject matter under investigation; in the event of refusal to respond to a subpoena, the Commission may apply to a Federal court for an order compelling obedience thereto.

Inquiries and complaints of investors and the general public provide one of the primary sources of leads for detection of law violations in securities transactions. Another is the surprise inspections by Regional Offices of the books and records of brokers and dealers to determine whether their business practices conform to the prescribed rules. Still another is the conduct of inquiries into market fluctuations in particular stocks which appear not to be the result of known developments affecting the issuing company or of general market trends.

The more general types of investigations concern the sale without registration of securities subject to the registration requirement of the Securities Act, and misrepresentation or omission of material facts concerning securities offered for sale (whether or not registration is required). The anti-fraud provisions of the law also apply equally to the *purchase* of securities, whether involving outright misrepresentations or the withholding or omission of pertinent facts to which the seller was entitled. For example, it is unlawful in certain situations to purchase securities from another person while withholding materal information which would indicate that the securities have a value substantially greater than that at which they are being acquired. Such provisions of the law apply not only to transactions between brokers and dealers and their customers but also to the reacquisition of securities by an issuing company or its "insiders."

Other types of inquiries relate to the manipulation of the market prices of securities; the misappropriation or unlawful hypothecation of customers' funds or securities; the conduct of a securities business while insolvent; the purchase or sale of securities by a broker-dealer, from or to his customers, at prices not reasonably related to the current market prices therefore; and violation by the broker-dealer of his responsibility to treat his customers fairly.

The most common of the latter type of violation involves the broker-dealer who, on gaining the trust and confidence of a customer and thereby establishing an agency relationship demanding the highest degree of fiduciary duty and care, takes secret profits in his securities transactions with or for the customer over and above the agreed brokerage (agency) commission. For example, the broker-dealer may have purchased securities from customers at prices far below, or sold securities to customers at prices far above, their current market prices. In most such cases, the broker-dealer subjects himself to no risk of loss, since his purchases from customers are made only if he can make simultaneous sales of the securities at prices substantially in excess of those paid to the customer, and his sales to customers are made only if he can make simultaneous purchases of the securities at prices substantially lower than those charged the customer. Or the firm may engage in large-scale in-and-out transactions for the customer's account ("churning") to generate increased commissions, usually without regard to any resulting benefit to the customer.

There is a fundamental distinction between a broker and a dealer; and it is important that investors should understand the difference. The *broker* serves as the customer's *agent* in buying or selling securities *for* his customer. As such, he owes the customer the highest fiduciary responsibility and care and may charge only such agency commission as has been agreed to by the customer. On the other hand, a *dealer* acts as a principal and buys securities *from* or sells securities *to* his customers. In such transactions, the dealer's profit is measured by the difference between the prices at which he buys and sells securities. Since the dealer is operating for his own account, he normally may not charge the customer a fee or commission for services rendered. Even in the case of such dealer transactions, however, the Commission and the courts have held that the conduct of a securities business carries with it the implied representation that customers will be dealt with fairly and that dealers may not enter into transactions with customers at prices not reasonably related to the prevailing market. The law requires that there be delivered to the customer a written "confirmation" of each transaction disclosing whether the securities firm is acting as a principal for its own account or as an agent for the customer (and, if the latter, the broker's compensation from all sources.)

Statutory Sanctions

It should be understood that Commission investigations (which for the most part are conducted in private) are essentially fact-finding inquiries. The facts so developed by the staff are considered by the Commission only in determining whether there is *prima facie* evidence of a law violation and whether an action should be commenced to determine whether, in fact, a violation actually occurred and, if so, whether some sanction should be imposed.

Assuming that the facts show possible fraud or other law violation, the laws provide several courses of action or remedies which the Commission may pursue:

a. *Civil injunction.* The Commission may apply to an appropriate United States District Court for an order enjoining those acts or practices alleged to violate the law or Commission rules.
b. *Criminal prosecution.* If fraud or other willful law violation is indicated, the Commission may refer the facts to the Department of Justice with a recommendation for criminal prosecution of the offending persons. The Department, through its local United States Attorneys (who frequently are assisted by Commission attorneys), may present the evidence to a Federal grand jury and seek an indictment.
c. *Administrative remedy.* The Commission may, after hearing, issue orders suspending or expelling members from exchanges or the over-the-counter dealers association; denying, suspending or revoking the registrations of broker-dealers; or censuring individuals for misconduct or barring them (temporarily or permanently) from employment with a registered firm.

Broker-Dealer Revocations

All of these sanctions may be applied to any person who engages in securities transactions violative of the law, whether or not he is engaged in the securities business. However, the administrative remedy is generally only invoked in the case of exchange or association members, registered brokers or dealers, or individuals who may associate with any such firm. In any such administrative proceeding, the Commission issues an order specifying the acts or practices alleged to have been committed in violation of law and directing that a hearing be held for the purpose of taking evidence thereon. At the hearing, counsel for the Division of Enforcement (often a Regional Office attorney) undertakes to establish for the record those facts which support the charge of law violation, and the respondents have full opportunity to cross-examine witnesses and to present evidence in defense. The procedure followed in the conduct of such proceedings . . . [conform to the Administrative Procedure Act]. If the Commission in its ultimate decision of the case finds that the respondents violated the law, it may take remedial action as indicated above. Such action may effectively bar a firm from the conduct of a securities business in interstate commerce or on exchanges or an individual from association with a registered firm—subject to the respondent's right to seek judicial review of the decision by the appropriate United States Court of Appeals.

* * *

SHORT-SWING PROFITS

Section 16 of the 1934 Act attempts to prohibit the use of inside information by insiders to reap profits on short-swing transactions in securities markets. Section 16(a) requires that all directors, officers, and beneficial owners of at least 10 percent of the stock file a form with the SEC disclosing the amount of securities of the issuer they hold. Subsequently, a report must be filed whenever a change in beneficial ownership occurs during any calendar month. These reports are public information and are scrutinized by individuals who may be interested in instituting lawsuits against the insiders. Section 16(b) allows recovery of short-swing profits realized by a director, officer, or 10 percent beneficial stockowner resulting from any sale or purchase, or purchase and sale, of any equity security of the company within a period of less than six months. The suit may be instituted by the company or by any owner of stock of the company, if the company refuses to bring suit within 60 days after request by the complaining stockholder. It is possible for an individual to purchase one share of the company stock and bring suit in the name of the company to recover short-swing profits. The person's motivation for bringing the suit is often explained by the right of the person's attorney to claim an attorney's fee out of the short-swing profits recovered by the suit. In this manner, private litigants serve as "enforcers" of Section 16.

A person may be held to be a "beneficial" owner of securities which are legally owned by a spouse, minor children, or any relative who resides in his or her home. Moreover, securities owned by a trustee who is under the direction of an insider also are considered to be beneficially owned by the insider.

In determining whether a short-swing profit has been secured, the courts arbitrarily match purchases and sales during any six-month period. For example, consider the following transactions:

Day 1—a purchase of 100 shares @ $10 per share.
Day 2—a sale of 100 shares @ $8 per share.
Day 3—a purchase of 100 shares @ $5 per share.
Day 4—a sale of 100 shares @ $3 per share.

It would appear that in this declining price market the insider has suffered losses. However, the court would compare the purchase at $5 per share with the sale at $8 per share and determine a short-swing profit has been obtained. In addition, the courts have held that any losses incurred during the six-month period (the purchase at $10 per share and the sale at $3 per share) could not be used as a set-off against the profits obtained during the same period. Consequently, the insider would be obligated to pay the short-swing profit to the corporation.

INSIDER TRADING

SEC v. Texas Gulf Sulphur Company
401 F. 2d 833 (1968)
U.S. Court of Appeals (2d Cir.)

This action was commenced by the Securities and Exchange Commission (the SEC) against Texas Gulf Sulphur Company (TGS) and several of its officers, directors and employees, to enjoin certain conduct by TGS and the individual defendants said to violate Section 10(b) of the Act, and Rule 10 b-5 (the Rule), promulgated thereunder, and to compel the rescission by the individual defendants of securities transactions assertedly conducted contrary to law. . . .

This action derives from the exploratory activities of TGS begun in 1957 on the Canadian Shield in eastern Canada. . . . These operations resulted in the detection of numerous anomalies, i.e., extraordinary variations in the conductivity of rocks, one of which was on the Kidd 55 segment of land located near Timmins, Ontario.

. . . Drilling of the initial hole, K-55-1, at the strongest part of the anomaly was commenced on November 8 and terminated on November 12 at a depth of 655 feet. Visual estimates . . . of the core of K-55-1 indicated an average copper content of 1.15% and an average zinc content of 8.64% over a length of 599 feet. This visual estimate convinced TGS that it was desirable to acquire the remainder of the Kidd 55 segment, and in order to facilitate this acquisition TGS President Stephens instructed the exploration group to keep the results of K-55-1 confidential and undisclosed even as to other officers, directors, and employees of TGS. The hole was concealed and a barren core was intentionally drilled off the anomaly. Meanwhile, the core of K-55-1 had been shipped to Utah for chemical assay which, when received in early December, revealed an average mineral content of 1.18% copper, 8.26% zinc, and 3.94% . . . of silver per ton over a length of 602 feet. These results were so remarkable that neither Clayton, an experienced geophysicist, nor four other TGS expert witnesses, had ever seen or heard of a comparable initial exploratory drill hole in a base metal deposit. So, the trial court concluded, "There is no doubt that the drill core of K-55-1 was unusually good and that it excited the interest and speculation of those who knew about it." By March 27, 1964, TGS decided that the land acquisition program had advanced to such a point that the company might well resume drilling, and drilling was resumed on March 31.

During this period, from November 12, 1963 when K-55-1 was completed, to March 31, 1964 when drilling was resumed, certain of the individual defendants . . . purchased TGS stock or calls thereon. Prior to these transactions these persons had owned 1135 shares of TGS stock and possessed no calls; thereafter they owned a total of 8235 shares and possessed 12,300 calls. . . .

When drilling was resumed on March 31, hole K-55-3 was commenced 510 feet west of K-55-1 and was drilled easterly at a 45° angle so as to cross K-55-1 in a vertical plane. Daily progress reports of the drilling of this hole K-55-3 and of all subsequently drilled holes were sent to defendants. . . . On the basis of these findings relative to the foregoing drilling results, the trial court concluded . . . that "There was real evidence that a body of commercially mineable ore might exist." . . .

Rule 10b-5, on which this action is predicated, provides:

> It shall be unlawful for any person, directly or indirectly, by the use of any means or instrumentality of interstate commerce, or of the mails, or of any facility of any national securities exchange.
>
> (1) to employ any device, scheme, or artifice to defraud,
> (2) to make any untrue statement of a material fact or to omit to state a material fact necessary in order to make the statements made, in the light of the circumstances under which they were made, not misleading, or
> (3) to engage in any act, practice, or course of business which operates or would operate as a fraud or deceit upon any person,
> in connection with the purchase or sale of any security.

Rule 10b-5 was promulgated pursuant to the grant of authority given the SEC by Congress in Section 10(b) of the Securities Exchange Act of 1934. By that Act Congress purposed to prevent inequitable and unfair practices and to insure fairness in securities transactions generally, whether conducted face-to-face, over the counter or on exchanges. The Act and the Rule apply to the transactions here, all of which were consummated on exchanges. . . . [T]he rule is based in policy on the justifiable expectation of the securities marketplace that all investors trading on impersonal exchanges have relatively equal access to material information. The essence of the Rule is that anyone who, trading for his own account in the securities of a corporation has "access, directly or indirectly, to information intended to be available only for corporate purpose and not for the personal benefit of anyone" may not take "advantage of such information knowing it is unavailable to those with whom he is dealing," i.e., the investing public. Insiders, as directors or management officers are, of course, by this Rule, precluded from so unfairly dealing, but the Rule is also applicable to one possessing the information who may not be strictly termed an "insider" within the meaning of Sec. 16(b) of the Act. Thus, anyone in possession of material inside information must either disclose it to the investing public, or, if he is disabled from disclosing it in order to protect a corporate confidence, or he chooses not to do so, must abstain from trading in or recommending the securities concerned while such inside information remains undisclosed. So, it is here no justification for insider activity that disclosure was forbidden by the legitimate corporate objective of acquiring options to purchase the land surrounding the exploration site; if the information was, as the SEC contends, material, its possessors should have kept out of the market until disclosure was accomplished.

Material Inside Information

An insider is not, of course, always foreclosed from investing in his own company merely because he may be more familiar with company operations than are outside investors. An insider's duty to disclose information or his duty to abstain from dealing in his company's securities arises only in "those situations which are essentially extraordinary in nature and which are reasonably certain to have a substantial effect on the market price of the security if [the extraordinary situation is] disclosed."

Nor is an insider obligated to confer upon outside investors the benefit of his superior financial or other expert analysis by disclosing his educated guesses or predictions. The only regulatory objective is that access to material information be enjoyed equally, but this objective requires nothing more than the disclosure of basic facts so that outsiders may draw upon their own evaluative expertise in reaching their own investment decisions with knowledge equal to that of the insiders. . . .

. . . [M]aterial facts include not only information disclosing the earnings and distributions of a company but also those facts which affect the probable future of the company and those which may affect the desire of investors to buy, sell, or hold the company's securities. . . .

The core of Rule 10b-5 is the implementation of the congressional purpose that all investors should have equal access to the rewards of participation in securities transactions. It was the intent of Congress that all members of the investing public should be subject to identical market risks—which market risks include, of course, the risk that one's evaluative capacity or one's capital available to put at risk may exceed another's capacity or capital. The insiders here were not trading on an equal footing with the outside investors. They alone were in a position to evaluate the probability and magnitude of what seemed from the outset to be a major ore strike; they alone could invest safely, secure in the expectation that the price of TGS stock would rise substantially in the event such a major strike should materialize, but would decline little, if at all, in the event of failure, for the public, ignorant at the outset of the favorable probabilities would likewise be unaware of the productive exploration, and the additional exploration costs would not significantly affect TGS market prices. Such inequities based upon unequal access to knowledge should not be shrugged off as inevitable in our way of life, or in view of the congressional concern in the area, remain uncorrected.

We hold, therefore, that all transactions in TGS stock or calls by individuals apprised of the drilling results of K-55-1 were made in violation of Rule 10b-5. Inasmuch as the visual evaluation of that drill core (a generally reliable estimate though less accurate than a chemical assay) constituted material information, those advised of the results of the visual evaluation as well as those informed of the chemical assay traded in violation of law.

Questions

1. What is the purpose of Rule 10b-5? How did the defendants violate this rule?
2. When are "insiders" precluded from trading in securities of the company they represent?
3. Must a corporation immediately disclose all material information?
4. Is the definition of an "insider" under Rule 10b-5 more extensive than that under 16(b)?

The insiders of Texaco Gulf Sulphur who were found to be in violation of Rule 10b-5 were ordered to pay money into an escrow account with the company which was to be used to pay parties injured by their illegal trading on inside information. The amount each had to pay into the fund was determined by comparing the price of Texas Gulf Sulphur stock after the disclosure of the extraordinary information with the purchase price paid by the insider prior to disclosure. The difference plus interest was to be disgorged from the insiders.

In addition, some of the individual defendants were enjoined from violating this aspect of the securities law again. Any future violation by these defendants would subject them to a contempt of court charge and the possibility of a prison sentence.

However, trying to stop insiders from using "inside information" illegally to make money in the stock market is difficult. A study by an investment banking concern shows a clear pattern of preannounced buying in stocks of companies that have become targets of tender offers or involved in merger negotiations. The study examined the premiums above market prices offered for target companies' shares. The study calculated the premium's percentage above market values one month before the initial takeover announcement and one day before the announcement. In a sample of 24 unopposed cash offers in the first three quarters of 1980, it was revealed that the average premium shrank to 60 percent the day before the announcement from 82 percent the month before. Although some of the premium shrinkage can be attributed to the acquiring companies' acquisition of shares in the open market to gain a "toehold," a large portion of the premium shrinkage results from leaks, rumors, and more buying prior to the announcement.

SEC officials investigate suspicious stock-price movements. They often have to sift through mounds of data to connect buyers with the sellers and piece together a relationship between the trader and those who have inside information. Despite the difficulty, in the late 1970s the commission increased its efforts to obtain prosecution against violators of the insider trading rules.

In November 1980, the government obtained a guilty plea from a prominent takeover attorney who had been retained as legal counsel by a corporation that proposed to repurchase a large number of its shares at a premium above the market price. The attorney promptly purchased over 3,000 shares of the stock prior to the announced repurchase program.

In the last few years the SEC has brought about 25 civil suits charging investors with trading on the basis of nonpublic information. For example, the SEC obtained a consent order against a stockbroker and his father for trading on confidential takeover information leaked by a paralegal employee of a law firm. The stockbroker was fired by his employer and his personal transactions based on insider information were canceled. In addition, the New York Stock Exchange barred the stockbroker from employment in any capacity with any member firm for four years. The stockbroker's father, who obtained the inside information from his son, agreed to give up the almost $100,000 in profit he netted while trading on the confidential tip. In most civil suits of this type the violators settled the charges of the SEC by negotiating a consent order in which they neither admit nor deny guilt but agree to relinquish their alleged insider trading profits.

Although the SEC has been successful in many civil cases, the Supreme Court overturned the insider-trading criminal conviction of an employee of a financial printing company. The employee had deduced the identities of takeover targets from legal documents he had helped print. His transactions based on this information resulted in handsome profits which, in settlement of the civil charges with the SEC, he agreed to return to the sellers of the shares. His criminal conviction was appealed to the Supreme Court which issued the following decision.

Chiarella v. U.S.

445 U.S. 222 (1980)
Supreme Court of United States

Justice Powell

* * *

In January 1978, petitioner was indicted on 17 counts of violating Sec. 10(b) of the Securities Exchange Act of 1934 and SEC Rule 10b-5. After petitioner unsuccessfully moved to dismiss the indictment, he was brought to trial and convicted on all counts.

The Court of Appeals for the Second Circuit affirmed petitioner's conviction. . . .

* * *

This case concerns the legal effect of the petitioner's silence. The District Court's charge permitted the jury to convict the petitioner if it found that he willfully failed to inform sellers of target company securities that he knew of a forthcoming takeover bid that would make their shares more valuable.

Although the starting point of our inquiry is the language of the statute, Sec. 10(b) does not state whether silence may constitute a manipulative or deceptive device. Section 10(b) was designed as a catch-all clause to prevent fraudulent practices. But neither the legislative history nor the statute itself affords specific guidance for the resolution of this case. When Rule 10b-5 was promulgated in 1942, the SEC did not discuss the possibility that failure to provide information might run afoul of Sec. 10(b).

The SEC took an important step in the development of Sec. 10(b) when it held that a broker-dealer and his firm violated that section by selling securities on the basis of undisclosed information obtained from a director of the issuer corporation who was also a registered representative of the brokerage firm. In *Cady, Roberts & Co. (1961),* the Commision decided that a corporate insider must abstain from trading in the shares of his corporation unless he has first disclosed all material inside information known to him.

* * *

The Commission emphasized that the duty arose from (i) the existence of a relationship affording access to inside information intended to be available only for a corporate purpose, and (ii) the unfairness of allowing a corporate insider to take advantage of that information by trading without disclosure.

That the relationship between a corporate insider and the stockholders of his corporation gives rise to a disclosure obligation is not a novel twist of the law. At common law, misrepresentation made for the purpose of inducing reliance upon the false statement is fraudulent. But one who fails to disclose material information prior to the consummation of a transaction commits fraud only when he is under a duty to do so. And the duty to disclose arises when one party has information "that the other (party) is entitled to know because of a fiduciary or similar relation of trust and confidence between them." In its *Cady, Roberts* decision, the Commission recognized a relationship of trust and confidence between the shareholders of a corporation and those insiders who have obtained confidential information by reason of their position with that corporation. This relationship gives rise to a duty to disclose because of the "necessity of preventing a corporate insider from taking advantage of the uninformed minority stockholders."

The Federal courts have found violations of Sec. 10(b) where corporate insiders used undisclosed information for their own benefit. The cases also have emphasized, in accordance with the common-law rule, that "the party charged with failing to disclose market information must be under a duty to disclose it." Accordingly, a purchaser of stock who has no duty to a prospective seller because he is neither an insider nor a fiduciary has been held to have no obligation to reveal material facts.

* * *

Thus, administrative and judicial interpretations have established that silence in connection with the purchase or sale of securities may operate as a fraud actionable under Sec. 10(b) despite the absence of statutory language or legislative history specifically addressing the legality of nondisclosure. But such liability is premised upon a duty to disclose arising from a relationship of trust and confidence between parties to a transaction. Application of a duty to disclose prior to trading guarantees that corporate insiders, who have an obligation to place the shareholder's welfare before their own, will not benefit personally through fraudulent use of material nonpublic information.

In this case, the petitioner was convicted of violating Sec. 10(b) although he was not a corporate insider and he received no confidential information from the target company. . . . Petitioner's use of that information was not a fraud under Sec. 10(b) unless he was subject to an affirmative duty to disclose it before trading. In this case, the jury instructions failed to specify any such duty. In effect, the trial court instructed the jury that petitioner owed a duty to everyone; to all sellers, indeed, to the market as a whole. The jury simply was told to decide whether petitioner used material, nonpublic information at a time when "he knew other people trading in the securities market did not have access to the same information."

. . . The Court of Appeals, like the trial court, failed to identify a relationship between petitioner and the sellers that could give rise to a duty. Its decision thus rested solely upon its belief that the federal securities laws have "created a system providing equal access to information necessary for reasoned and intelligent investment decisions." The use by anyone of material information not generally available is fraudulent, this theory suggests, because such information gives certain buyers or sellers an unfair advantage over less informed buyers and sellers.

This reasoning suffers from two defects. First, not every instance of financial unfairness constitutes fraudulent activity under Sec. 10(b). Second, the element required to make silence fraudulent—a duty to disclose—is absent in this case. No duty could arise from petitioner's relationship with the sellers of the target company's securities, for petitioner had no prior dealings with them. He was not their agent, he was not a fiduciary, he was not a person in whom the sellers had placed their trust and confidence. He was, in fact, a complete stranger who dealt with the sellers only through impersonal market transactions.

We cannot affirm petitioner's conviction without recognizing a general duty between all participants in market transactions to forgo actions based on material, nonpublic information. Formulation of such a broad duty, which departs radically from the established doctrine that duty arises from a specific relationship between two parties, should not be undertaken absent some explicit evidence of congressional intent.

* * *

We see no basis for applying such a new and different theory of liability in this case. As we have emphasized before, the 1934 Act cannot be read " 'more broadly than its language and the statutory scheme reasonably permit.' " Section 10(b) is aptly described as a catch-all provision, but what it catches must be fraud. When an allegation of fraud is based upon nondisclosure, there can be no fraud absent a duty to speak. We hold that a duty to disclose under Sec. 10(b) does not arise from the mere possession of nonpublic market information. The contrary result is without support in the legislative history of Sec. 10(b) and would be inconsistent with the careful plan that Congress has enacted for regulation of the securities markets.

Questions

1. The Supreme Court indicated that liability permised on a duty to disclose arises from a relationship of trust and confidence between parties to the transaction. What confidential relationship is usually involved in an insider trading situation which creates a duty to disclose?
2. Did the defendant-buyer owe a duty to the sellers of securities from whom he purchased?

Later in 1980, the Security and Exchange Commission reinforced its longstanding ban against trading in securities on the basis of "inside" information. Because the Supreme Court appeared to create an exception to this prohibition in *Chiarella*, the agency adopted changes in its rules intended to cover investors who buy stock on the basis of solid information that the issuing company is about to become the target of a tender offer. In general, the new rule bars anyone from trading on a tip about a pending tender offer unless the information is disclosed to the person on the other side of the transaction. Both givers and receivers of the tips are covered by the prohibition. The SEC attorneys acknowledge that defining a tip may be somewhat troublesome in practice. They indicated that the rule is not intended to cover "rumors heard on the street" or "casual and innocently motivated social discourse." In contrast, if the investor knows or has reason to know that the information comes from the target company, the acquiring company or the companies' respective agents, such as lawyers and investment bankers, he or she is precluded from trading on the basis of such inside information. In effect, the new rule is limited to people who are involved in the tender-offer process and to those who get information from them. Whether this new rule will be upheld by the Supreme Court remains in doubt.

ACCOUNTANTS AND RULE 10b-5

If accountants (or attorneys and underwriters) were to participate intentionally in a fraudulent or misleading scheme, they would clearly be violating Rule 10b-5.

However, it is a more difficult question to determine if the accountant should be liable to third parties for negligent failure to expose a client corporation's fraud. The following case examines this specific question.

Ernst & Ernst v. Hochfelder

425 U.S. 185 (1976)
Supreme Court of the United States

Justice Powell

Petitioner, Ernst & Ernst, is an accounting firm. From 1946 through 1967 it was retained by First Securities Company of Chicago (First Securities), a small brokerage firm and member of the Midwest Stock Exchange and of the National Association of Securities Dealers, to perform periodic audits of the firm's books and records. In connection with these audits Ernst & Ernst prepared for filing with the Securities and Exchange Commission (the Commission) the annual reports required of First Securities under § 17(a) of the 1934 Act. . . .

Respondents were customers of First Securities who invested in a fraudulent securities scheme perpetrated by Leston B. Nay, president of the firm and owner of 92 percent of its stock. Nay induced the respondents to invest funds in "escrow" accounts that he represented would yield a high rate of return. Respondents did so from 1942 through 1966, with the majority of the transactions occurring in the 1950's. In fact, there were no escrow accounts as Nay converted respondents' funds to his own use immediately upon receipt. These transactions were not in the customary form of dealings between First Securities and its customers. The respondents drew their personal checks payable to Nay or a designated bank for his account. No such escrow accounts were reflected on the books and records of First Securities, and none was shown on its periodic accounting to respondents in connection with their own investments. Nor were they included in First Securities' filings with the Commission. . . .

This fraud came to light in 1968 when Nay committed suicide, leaving a note that described First Securities as bankrupt and the escrow accounts as "spurious." Respondents subsequently filed this action for damages against Ernst & Ernst. . . . The complaint charged that Nay's escrow scheme violated § 10(b) and Commission Rule 10b-5, and that Ernst & Ernst had "aided and abetted" Nay's violations by its "failure" to conduct proper audits of First Securities. As revealed through discovery, respondents' cause of action rested on a theory of negligent nonfeasance. The premise was that Ernst & Ernst had failed to utilize "appropriate auditing procedures" in its audits of First Securities, thereby failing to discover internal practices of the firm said to prevent an effective audit. The practice principally relied on was Nay's rule that only he could open mail addressed to him at First Securities or addressed to First Securities to his attention, even it it arrived in his absence. Respondents contended that if Ernst & Ernst had conducted a proper audit, it would have discovered this "mail rule." The existence of the rule then would have been disclosed in reports to the Exchange and to the Commission by Ernst & Ernst as an irregular procedure that prevented an effective audit. This would have revealed the fraudulent scheme. Respondents specifically disclaimed the existence of fraud or intentional misconduct on the part of Ernst & Ernst. . . .

We granted *certiorari* to resolve the question whether a private cause of action for damages will lie under § 10(b) and Rule 10b-5 in the absence of any allegation of "scienter"—intent to deceive, manipulate, or defraud. . . .

Section 10(b) makes unlawful the use or employment of "any manipulative or deceptive device or contrivance" in contravention of Commission rules. The words "manipulative or deceptive" used in conjunction with "device or contrivance" strongly suggests that § 10(b) was intended to proscribe knowing or intentional misconduct. . . .

In its *amicus curiae* brief, however, the Commission contends that nothing in the language "manipulative or deceptive device or contrivance" limits its operation to knowing or intentional practices. In support of its view, the Commission cites the overall congressional purpose in the 1933 and 1934 Acts to protect investors against false and deceptive practices that might injure them. . . . The Commission then reasons that since the "effect" upon investors of given conduct is the same regardless of whether the conduct is negligent or intentional, Congress must have intended to bar all such practices and not just those done knowingly or intentionally. The logic of this effect-oriented approach would impose liability for wholly faultless conduct where such conduct results in harm to investors, a result the Commission would be unlikely to support. . . . The argument simply ignores the use of the words "manipulative," "device," and "contrivance," terms that make unmistakable a congressional intent to proscribe a type of conduct quite different from negligence. Use of the word "manipulative" is especially significant. It is and was virtually a term of art when used in connection with securities markets. It connotes intentional, or wilful conduct designed to deceive or defraud investors by controlling or artificially affecting the price of securities. . . .

. . . The Commission contends, however, that subsections (2) and (3) of Rule 10b-5 are cast in language which—if standing alone—could encompass both intentional and negligent behavior. These subsections respectively provide that it is unlawful "[t]o make any untrue statement of a material fact or to omit to state a material fact necessary in order to make the statements made, in light of the circumstances under which they were made, not misleading . . ." and "to engage in any act, practice, or course of business which operates or would operate as a fraud or deceit upon any person. . . ." Viewed in isolation the language of subsection (2), and arguably that of subsection (3), could be read as proscribing, respectively, any type of material misstatement or omission, and any course of conduct, that has the effect of defrauding investors, whether the wrongdoing was intentional or not.

We note first that such a reading cannot be harmonized with the administrative history of the rule, a history making clear that when the Commission adopted the rule it was intended to apply only to activities that involved scienter. More importantly, Rule 10b-5 was adopted pursuant to authority granted the Commission under § 10(b). The rulemaking power granted to an administrative agency charged with the administration of a federal statute is not the power to make law. Rather, it is " 'the power to adopt regulations to carry into effect the will of Congress as expressed by the statute.' " . . . Thus, despite the broad view of the Rule advanced by the Commission in this case, its scope cannot exceed the power granted the Commission by Congress under § 10(b). For the reasons stated above, we think the Commission's original interpretation of Rule 10b-5 was compelled by the language and history of § 10(b) and related section of the Acts. . . . When a statute speaks so specifically in terms of manipulation and deception, and of implementing devices and contrivances—the commonly understood terminology of international wrongdoing—and when its history reflects no more expansive intent, we are quite unwilling to extend the scope of the statute to negligent conduct. . . .

Questions

1. What do the respondents contend was the "error" of Ernst & Ernst in auditing First Securities? Was the error intentional or fraudulent? Was the error negligent misrepresentation? Did the Court decide whether Ernst & Ernst was negligent?
2. Should the language "manipulative or deceptive device or contrivance" limit the use of Rule 10b-5 to "intentional" practices?
3. What impact did the administrative history of the rule have on the Court's interpretation?

FRAUD BY INVESTMENT ADVISERS

The Investment Advisers Act of 1940 requires that persons who advise others on a compensatory basis about their transactions in securities must register with the commission and conform their activities to statutory standards which protect investors. The act contains provisions governing investment advisers much like the Securities Exchange Act provisions that govern the activities of brokers and dealers who merchandise securities. The registration of investment advisers can be denied, suspended, or revoked if the commission determines such action is in the public interest. The act also contains antifraud provisions which empower the commission to adopt rules that define fraudulent and manipulative acts and practices. The following case is illustrative of the SEC's determination of fraudulent activities by investment advisers.

SEC v. Capital Gains Research Bureau

375 U.S. 180 (1963)
Supreme Court of the United States

Justice Goldberg

We are called upon in this case to decide whether under the Investment Advisers Act of 1940 the Securities and Exchange Commission may obtain an injunction compelling a registered investment adviser to disclose to his clients a practice of purchasing shares of a security for his own account shortly before recommending that security for long-term investment and then immediately selling the shares at a profit upon the rise in the market price following the recommendation. The answer to this question turns on whether the practice—known in the trade as "scalping"—"operates as a fraud or deceit upon any client or prospective client" within the meaning of the Act. We hold that it does and that the Commission may "enforce compliance" with the Act by obtaining an injunction requiring the adviser to make full disclosure of the practice to his clients. . . .

An adviser who, like respondents, secretly trades on the market effect of his own recommendation may be motivated—consciously or unconsciously—to recommend a given security not because of its potential for long-run price increase (which would profit the client), but because of its potential for short-run price increase in response to anticipated activity from the recommendation (which would profit the adviser). An investor seeking the advice of a registered investment adviser must, if the legislative purpose is to be served, be permitted to evaluate such overlapping motivations, through appropriate disclosure, in deciding whether an adviser is serving "two masters" or only one, "especially . . . if one of the masters happens to be economic self-interest." Accordingly, we hold that the Investment Advisers Act of 1940 empowers the courts, upon a showing such as that made here, to require an adviser to make full and frank disclosure of his practice of trading on the effect of his recommendations.

In *Capital Gains,* the Supreme Court held that a showing of intent to defraud (scienter) by the investment adviser was not required. This conclusion rested on the revelation by the legislative history that the "Investment Advisers Act of 1940 . . . reflects a congressional recognition 'of the delicate fiduciary nature of an investment advisory relationship,' as well as a congressional intent to eliminate, or at least to expose, all conflicts of interest which might incline an investment adviser—consciously or unconsciously—to render advice which was not disinterested." To require proof of intent, the Court reasoned, would run counter to the expressed intent of Congress. This rationale was again approved by the Supreme Court in *Aaron* v. *SEC,* 100 S.Ct. 1945 (1980).

FOREIGN CORRUPT PRACTICES ACT

The scandal of illegal corporate payments in the 1970s was largely uncovered by the SEC. The staff of the SEC heard testimony in the Senate Watergate Hearings that the Republican Party regularly received secret donations from corporations in violation of the maximum amount that corporations are legally permitted to contribute to political parties. Thereafter, the SEC brought suits against a few corporations, alleging such secret payments were improperly withheld from the disclosure documents that the corporations were required to file with the commission. However, since corporate disclosure regulation pursuant to the Securities Acts is limited to *material* information, corporate officials often asserted that the SEC cannot require the disclosure of most secret corporate payments for political or foreign bribes, because the amounts were usually small compared to sales or earnings of the company. The SEC argued, nevertheless, that information that reflects the integrity of management, or the integrity of the company's books and records, is material even if the dollar amount is very small. Since secret corporate payments often involve mislabeling of accounts in the books and records, the SEC contended that the transactions are generally material and required disclosure.

The SEC argued further that books and records must be accurately maintained for the company's financial statements to be relied on by stockholders. Congressional agreement with the SEC's position was subsequently evidenced in the Foreign Corrupt Practices Act (FCPA) of 1977, which amended the 1934 Securities Act in prohibiting the making of false entries in books and records of publicly traded companies. The act requires that the company's books, records, and accounts accurately and fairly reflect, in reasonable detail, the transactions and dispositions of the company's assets. Since the reliability of the company's books and records depends on the effectiveness of the company's system of internal accounting controls, the act also requires that each company devise and maintain a system of internal accounting controls sufficient to provide reasonable assurances that accurate records are being kept. Companies found to have willfully violated the accounting standards provisions of the FCPA are subject to fines of not more than $10,000 or imprisonment of not more than five years or both. The possibility also exists that a violating company may be subject to civil litigation brought by third parties.

The sections of the act that deal with "foreign corrupt practices" are quite limited in scope, but can involve a fine of up to $1 million for a violation. There are five separate parts that make up a violation: (1) the use of an instrumentality of interstate commerce (such as the telephone or mails) in furtherance of (2) a payment, or even an offer to pay, "anything of value," directly or indirectly, (3) to any foreign official with discretionary authority or to any foreign political party or foreign political candidate, (4) if the purpose of the payment is the "corrupt" one of getting the recipient to act (or refrain from acting) (5) in such a way as to assist the company in obtaining or retaining business for or with or directing business to any person.

The act provides that a foreign official does not include any government employee whose duties are "essentially ministerial or clerical." Consequently, there is no prohibition against paying substantial sums to minor officials, so long as their duties are ministerial or clerical. Such payments are frequently called "grease" or "facilitating" payments to minor foreign officials to get them to perform customary services that they might refuse to perform, or perform only slowly, in the absence of such payments.

For the payments to be illegal under the act, the word "corruptly" is used to make clear that the offer, payment, promise, or gift must be intended to induce the recipient to misuse his or her official position to wrongfully direct business to the payor or the client, or to obtain preferential legislation or regulation. The word "corruptly" connotes an evil motive or purpose, but there is no requirement that the payment violate the law of the host country for it to be labeled "corrupt."

Though not in the act itself, Congress made clear in its hearings that it did not attempt to outlaw an extortion payment. However, no precise guidance is provided in this area except that Congress expects the U.S. diplomatic service to render aid to American businesses abroad who are threatened by extortion.

CORPORATE GOVERNANCE

The SEC has often settled suits of alleged wrongdoing by corporate officials by requiring the defending companies to appoint "independent" persons to investigate the full extent of wrongdoing. In-house investigators were either outside directors of the company or specially hired lawyers and accountants who were to report to a committee of the board of directors, such as an audit committee. This technique became the basis of the SEC's handling of the "Corporate Payment Scandal." The SEC requested companies to participate in a "voluntary disclosure program." Almost 400 companies agreed to conduct independent internal investigations and make the findings available to the SEC. A summary of the internal investigation was reported to investors. The SEC also required the participating companies to develop corporate codes of conduct which prohibit illegal payments, require proper record keeping, and prohibit other types of unethical conduct. The codes also established compliance and monitoring procedures so that, in effect, the codes became in-house extensions of the securities laws.

As a "voluntary disclosure program" indicates, corporate disclosure regulation appears to be expanding from merely providing information to investors. Instead, disclosure rules are becoming instruments for social regulation. Critics of the "corporate system" have asserted that companies are "undemocratic" because management controls the nomination procedures for the board of directors. Opposing shareholders must bear an expensive proxy fight to nominate any other person for a directorship. As a response to these criticisms, Congress and the SEC held public hearings on corporate governance in 1977. Most reform proposals have involved the corporate disclosure machinery as a means for shareholders to gain greater control over boards of directors. Such reforms attempt to make companies more responsible, accountable, and democratic.

Athough it already requires many shareholder social accountability proposals to be included in management's proxy materials, the SEC appears to believe that an increase in federal intervention into corporate control is unjustified by past corporate transgressions. The SEC is satisfied with the disclosure program and hopes to convince Congress not to set precedence in government regulation of corporate decision making.

In an attempt to stave off tougher congressional legislation (federal chartering, public directors, or business-in-the-sunshine board meetings), the SEC considered developing new disclosure rules for directors. Future proxy statements may include materials concerning the composition and responsibilities of the board's audit, nominating, conflicts of interest, and compensation committees. Increased disclosure concerning the business and personal relationship between directors and management may be required in proxy materials. Information concerning the directors' attendance at meetings, other directorships held, reasons for director resignations, and director compensation may become required disclosure items, also. Finally, rules relating to increased shareholder participation in director elections may follow.

CRITICISMS AND REFORMS

New academic theories and congressional criticism have raised fundamental questions about the federal disclosure system of security regulation. These questions will undoubtedly affect the future course of innovation in this field. One fundamental issue is whether disclosure is an effective remedy to deal with the ills that affect the securities markets. For example, the federal securities laws were passed in part as a reaction to the 1929 stockmarket crash. However, the federal securitics laws have not prevented continuing gyration in securities markets. The goal of stability in the financial markets has not been achieved. Yet, in theory, full information revealed by the disclosure system should result in more stable prices. However, conclusions on this matter are difficult to determine since the instability of markets may result more from uncertainty and imperfection of financial and economic predictions and forecasts, rather than from the failure of securities laws to make adequate disclosures of historical facts.

Connected with this criticism is the debate about historical cost financial statements. Such statements do not reflect current market values or provide information of future projection, which are more valuable to the professional or average investor. In addition, the overly permissible treatment of accounting standards tends to destroy the comparability of financial information published through the registration process. Historically, the SEC has essentially delegated the regulation of accounting principles to the accounting profession. In January of 1977, however, a Senate subcommittee led by Senator Lee Metcalf lambasted the SEC and the accounting profession. Senator Metcalf reported:

> Corporations presently have substantial discretion in choosing among alternative accounting standards to report similar business transactions. As a result, the amounts of earnings or losses reported to the public can vary drastically depending on which accounting alternatives are chosen. . . . In particular, I am disturbed by two . . . findings. The first is the extraordinary manner in which the SEC has insisted upon delegating its public authority and responsibilities on accounting matters to private groups with obvious self-interests in the resolution of such matters. The second is the alarming lack of independence and the lack of dedication to public protection shown by the large accounting firms.

As a consequence of the Metcalf report, the SEC is likely to place increasing pressure on the accountants' Financial Accounting Standards Board to set more specific accounting standards to allow for comparability of financial statements. The flexibility of accounting standards will probably be reduced and the relationship of the SEC to the accounting profession will continue to be a source of controversy for years to come.

One example of the continuing efforts of the SEC in prodding the accounting profession to make the financial statements more accurately reflect reality is the SEC accounting release which requires the disclosure of replacement costs in addition to historical costs. This involves the SEC's efforts to make financial statements reflect current value.

Another example of SEC reform is its new rule which allows companies to make projections (forecasts) in financial information. Because of the value of such data to security analysts, the SEC is likely to continue these efforts. The SEC was previously concerned that companies would use overly optimistic forecasts. The SEC has now adopted guides which encourage projections by absolving a company of liability if its forecast is competently prepared but is later shown to have been inaccurate. The SEC's voluntary program of guidelines encourages the publishing of financial projections in reports, proxy, and registration statements. Nearly all the details of the forecast, including the items to be projected, assumptions underlying the projections, projection periods and frequency, and third-party review are left to the discretion of management. As a further inducement to disclose, the SEC has adopted a so-called safe-harbor rule, which would shelter the company and its management from liability for projections that fail the test of time. The forecasts made must be (1) "reasonably prepared" and (2) "disclosed in good faith." The safe-harbor rule covers stockholder reports and commission filings. Many observers believe that after some years of voluntary forecasting, the program may be made mandatory.

Another criticism of the present disclosure system is that the disclosed data are beyond the skills and background of the average investor to understand. The system attempts to protect relatively unsophisticated individuals who are presently inundated with overly complex material. It will be a continuing problem of the SEC to develop simpler documents and otherwise provide a more meaningful disclosure to the average investor.

Companies and critics have complained also of the extensive paperwork that must be filed with the commission. The Advisory Committee on Corporate Disclosure has recommended that the SEC create one "continuous disclosure report" which could be used for all 1933 and 1934 Act filings. Furthermore, the American Law Institute has proposed a bill to Congress which combines the 1933 and 1934 Acts. The new act would deemphasize the company's public offerings of securities and make the company's annual report the "key-disclosure document."

Finally, some have argued that the disclosures mandated by the securities laws have not been effective in preventing fraud. They maintain that scandals such as BarChris, Manor Nursing Centers and Equity Funding were not prevented by the securities law. However, it is impossible to know what frauds would have been perpetrated had the securities laws not been enacted. The incidence of fraud and manipulation may well have been reduced by virtue of disclosure requirements. The fact that some frauds are perpetrated does not preclude the possible conclusion that other frauds have been prevented by the securities laws. Moreover, many have argued that the requirement of full disclosure not only results in the prevention of fraud but also reduces shareholder-management conflicts of interest and deters other questionable practices.

CONCLUSION

The efforts of the SEC are designed to promote investor confidence in American capital markets by the extension of the "disclosure" doctrine to securities listed on the national exchanges. No one doubts that these disclosure practices involve a great deal of cost. However, the confidence of investors is essential to the preservation of the vigor of the capital-raising system of the United States. Only a few would contend that the economic and social benefits accruing from the laws enhancing the capital-raising system are less than the costs associated with securities regulations.

CASE PROBLEMS

1. The petitioner was a managerial employee at E. L. Aaron & Co. (the firm), a registered broker-dealer with its principal office in New York City. Among other responsibilities at the firm, the petitioner was charged with supervising the sales made by its registered representatives and maintaining the so-called due diligence files for these securities in which the firm served as a market maker. One such security was the common stock of Lawn-A-Mat Chemical & Equipment Corp. (Lawn-A-Mat), a company engaged in the business of selling lawn care franchises and supplying its franchisees with products and equipment.

   Between November 1974 and September 1975, two registered representatives of the firm conducted a sales campaign in which they repeatedly made false and misleading statements in an effort to solicit orders for the purchase of Lawn-A-Mat common stock. During the course of this promotion, they informed prospective investors that Lawn-A-Mat was planning or in the process of manufacturing a new type of small car, and that the car would be marketed within six weeks; Lawn-A-Mat, however, had no such plans. The two registered representatives also made projections of substantial increases in the price of Lawn-A-Mat common stock and optimistic statements concerning the company's financial condition. These projections and statements were without basis in fact, since Lawn-A-Mat was losing money during the relevant period.

Upon receiving several complaints from prospective investors, an officer of Lawn-A-Mat informed the representatives that their statements were false and misleading and requested them to cease making such statements. This request went unheeded.

Thereafter, an attorney representing Lawn-A-Mat communicated with the petitioner twice by telephone. In these conversations, he informed the petitioner that the representatives were making false and misleading statements and described the substance of what they were saying. The petitioner, in addition to being so informed, had reason to know that the statements were false, since he knew that the reports in Lawn-A-Mat's due diligence file indicated a deteriorating financial condition and revealed no plans for manufacturing a new car. The petitioner took no affirmative steps to prevent the recurrence of the misrepresentations. The petitioner's only response to the telephone calls was to inform the representatives of the complaints. Otherwise, the petitioner did nothing to prevent the two registered representatives under his direct supervision from continuing to make false and misleading statements in promoting Lawn-A-Mat common stock.

In February 1976, the commission filed a complaint in the district court against the petitioner in connection with the offer and sale of Lawn-A-Mat common stock. In seeking preliminary and final injunctive relief, the commission alleged that the petitioner had violated and aided and abetted violations of Section 10(b) of the 1934 Act and Rule 10b-5. The gravamen of the charges against the petitioner was that he knew or had reason to know that the employees under his supervision were engaged in fraudulent practices but failed to take adequate steps to prevent those practices from continuing.

Following a trial, the district court found that the petitioner had violated and aided and abetted violation of Section 10(b) and Rule 10b-5 during the Lawn-A-Mat sales campaign and enjoined him from future violations of these provisions. The district court's finding of violations was based on its factual finding that the petitioner had intentionally failed to discharge his supervisory responsibility to stop his employees from making statements to prospective investors that the petitioner knew to be false and misleading. The district court concluded that the fact that the petitioner "intentionally failed to terminate the false and misleading statements made by his employees, knowing them to be fraudulent, is sufficient to establish his scienter under the securities laws."

The Court of Appeals for the Second Circuit declined to decide the question whether the petitioner's conduct would support a finding of scienter. It held, instead, that when the commission is seeking injunctive relief, "proof of negligence alone will suffice" to establish a violation of Section 10(b) and Rule 10b-5. Will the court of appeal's conclusion be upheld on appeal?

2. An independent public accountant, M., audited Yale Company's financial statements for inclusion in its 19XX annual report to stockholders and certified the figures contained in the statements. This annual report was prepared in April of the following year, 19YY. The accountant was then

engaged by Yale to conduct some special studies relating to its internal functioning. In the process, M. discovered that the figures in the annual report for 19XX were substantially false and misleading. In June 19YY, Yale filed its form 10-K Report with the SEC, containing the same financial statement as the annual report.

M. is sued by members of the trading public who relied on the published financial statements. Do they have a cause of action against M.?

3. A customer of a brokerage firm charged the firm with churning his account, a deceptive device under Section 10(b), Securities Exchange Act. The investor, Buckley, was interested in speculation and was "intensely interested" in his account. At the end of a four-year period with the firm, the account had a deficit of $332,000, and Buckley owed the firm $75,000 in commissions. The account had been very active, and even though 80 or 90 percent of the transactions resulted from the firm's suggestions, Buckley did often reject the firm's recommendations and sometimes initiated transactions himself. Buckley was a Cornell University graduate in economics and international marketing and subscribed to various financial journals.

   Each year, total purchases on the account averaged approximately seven times the sum invested by Buckley.

   Evaluate Buckley's claim.

4. In a meeting between a financial analyst and the chief financial adviser for Liggett and Myers, Inc., the analyst asked whether earnings for the second quarter would be down and received an affirmative answer. He inquired whether this was a "good possibility," and the answer again was yes, but the financial adviser then asked the analyst to keep this information confidential. The analyst relayed this information to a stockbroker friend who, that same day, sold 1,800 shares of Liggett and Myers stock for his customers. The following day Liggett and Myers released a preliminary earning report showing the decline in second-quarter earnings. The report was published in the *Wall Street Journal* the day after it was released.

   Has Liggett and Myers, Inc., violated Rule 10b-5?

chapter 19

LABOR-MANAGEMENT RELATIONS LAWS

The years after the Civil War were a time of building industrial empires. The technological developments of the Industrial Revolution created a need for large-scale industrial establishments. The increasing concentration of economic power was not greatly reduced by the passage of the Sherman Act. However, the growth of the large corporations had significant consequences for workers. It ended the personal relationship that had existed between the employer and employee and put the employee at a considerable bargaining disadvantage. Unionism appeared to be essential to give laborers an opportunity to deal with their employers on an equal basis.

As a consequence of the changing economic conditions, modern labor laws regulate nearly all aspects of the relationship between employer and employee. Employers must concern themselves not only with the National Labor Relations Act but also with fair employment practices, fair labor standards, minimum wage, workers' compensation, unemployment compensation, safety rules, and numerous other legislative prohibitions and regulations. Nevertheless, collective bargaining is the heart of labor law. Despite the detailed regulations provided by law, it is the negotiation and administration of the collectively bargained labor contracts that primarily guarantee the social and economic security that American workers enjoy. As a result, modern unions and collective bargaining have emerged as significant institutions. Moreover, the evolving legal doctrines concerning labor disputes focus attention on the limitations of law. It is largely through the private arena, grievance, and arbitration procedures, that detailed regulations most vitally affecting workers in their daily lives are made.

Within the context of this understanding the question arises, "What role should the court play?" The following cases elaborate some of the history involved in the legislation of labor laws, some of the basic legislative pronouncements themselves, and the appropriate role for the courts. Within the context of particular labor disputes, the reader may gain a more significant understanding of the tremendous social issues involved.

ANTITRUST AND ANTI-INJUNCTION

NORRIS–LAGUARDIA ACT

In 1932 Congress passed the Federal Anti-injunction Act (Norris–LaGuardia Act). The act protects legitimate union activity from federal court injunctions attempting to prohibit such activity. The act was passed as a congressional disapproval of the courts' utilization of injunctions in spite of the Clayton Act which had, without clarity, exempted labor activities from the antitrust laws. As a consequence, the provisions of the Norris–LaGuardia Act divest federal courts of injunctive power in cases growing out of a "labor dispute," unless the private complainant can prove in court, under cross-examination, the following elements:

1. Unlawful acts have been threatened or committed.
2. Injury to property will result.
3. Injury to complainant will be greater than injury to defendant unless the unlawful acts are enjoined.
4. Complainant has no adequate "damages" remedy.
5. Public officials (police) are unable or unwilling to provide protection to the complainant's property.
6. Complainant must petition the court with "clean hands" by having made reasonable efforts to negotiate a settlement.

Since all these elements will be difficult to establish, private parties (employers) will most likely be unable to obtain a federal court injunction against labor activities. Even if an injunction is issued, it can enjoin only the specific acts complained of in the petition.

A "labor dispute" is broadly defined in the act to include a list of events in which the federal courts are restricted in the issuance of injunctions against labor activities. Consequently, federal courts are denied the power to issue an injunction to prohibit such "labor disputes" as ceasing or refusing to perform work, joining a labor organization, assembling peacefully, advising others, or giving publicity to any labor dispute. Nor can the federal courts issue injunctions to prohibit the paying of strike or unemployment benefits that may be available to participants in a labor dispute.

The anti-injunction provisions of the Norris–LaGuardia Act establish a policy which is in opposition to the policy of the antitrust laws. Yet, the anti-injunction law does not repeal antitrust laws. Therefore, the courts must "accommodate" or reconcile the two acts, just as the Court attempted in *Allen Bradley*.

Allen Bradley Co. v. Local Union No. 3
325 U.S. 797 (1945)
Supreme Court of the United States

Justice Black

Our problem in this case is a very narrow one—do labor unions violate the Sherman Act when, in order to further their own interests as wage earners, they aid and abet businessmen to do the precise things which that Act prohibits?

The Sherman Act as originally passed contained no language expressly exempting any labor union activities. Sharp controversy soon arose as to whether the Act applied to unions. . . .

Federal Courts . . . applied the law to unions in a number of cases. Injunctions were used to enforce the Act against unions. At the same time, employers invoke injunctions to restrain labor union activities even where no violation of the Sherman Act was charged.

Vigorous protest arose from employee groups. The unions urged congressional relief from what they considered to be two separate, but partially overlapping evils—application of the Sherman Act to unions, and issuance of injunctions against strikes, boycotts and other labor union weapons. . . . All of this is a part of the well-known history of the era between 1890 and 1914.

To amend, supplement, and strengthen the Sherman Act against monopolistic business practices, and in response to the complaints of the unions against injunctions and application of the Act to them, Congress in 1914 passed the Clayton Act. . . .

. . . Section 6 declared that labor was neither a commodity nor an article of commerce, and that the Sherman Act should not be "construed to forbid the existence and operation of labor, agricultural, or horticultural organizations, instituted for the purposes of mutual help. . . ." Section 20 limited the power of the courts to issue injunctions in a case "involving or growing out of a labor dispute over terms or conditions of employment. . . ." It declared that no restraining order or injunction should prohibit certain specified acts, and further declared that no one of these specified acts should be "held to be violations of any law of the United States." This Act was broadly proclaimed by many as labor's "Magna Carta," wholly exempting labor from any possible inclusion in the antitrust legislation; others, however, strongly denied this.

This Court later declined to interpret the Clayton Act as manifesting a congressional purpose wholly to exempt labor unions from the Sherman Act. . . .

Again the unions went to Congress. They protested against this Court's interpretation, repeating the arguments they had made against application of the Sherman Act to them. Congress adopted their viewpoint, at least in large part, and . . . passed the Norris–LaGuardia Act. That Act greatly broadened the meaning this court had attributed to the words, "labor dispute," further restricted the use of injunctions in such a dispute, and emphasized the public importance under modern economic conditions of protecting the rights of concerted activities for the purpose of collective bargaining or other mutual aid and protection." . . .

The result of all this is that we have two declared congressional policies which it is our responsibility to try to reconcile. The one seeks to preserve a competitive business economy; the other to preserve the rights of labor to organize to better its conditions through the agency of collective bargaining. We must determine here how far Congress intended activities under one of these policies to neutralize the results envisioned by the other.

Aside from the fact that the labor union here acted in combination with the contractors and manufacturers, the means it adopted to contribute to the combination's purpose fall squarely within the "specified acts" declared by Sec. 20 not to be violations of federal law. . . . Consequently, had there been no union-contractor-manufacturer combination, the union's actions here, coming as they did within the exemptions of the Clayton and Norris–LaGuardia Acts, would not have been violations of the Sherman Act. We pass to the question of whether unions can with impunity aid and abet business men who are violating the Act. . . .

It must be remembered that the exemptions granted the unions were special exceptions to a general legislative plan. The primary objective of all the antitrust legislation has been to preserve business competition and to proscribe business monopoly. It would be a surprising thing if Congress, in order to prevent a misapplication of that legislation to labor unions, had bestowed upon such unions complete and unreviewable authority to aid business groups to frustrate its primary objective. For if business groups, by combining with labor unions, can fix prices and divide up markets, it was little more than a futile gesture for Congress to prohibit price fixing by business groups themselves. Seldom, if ever, has it been claimed before, that by permitting labor unions to carry on their own activities, Congress intended completely to abdicate its constitutional power to regulate interstate commerce and to empower interested business groups to shift our society from a competitive to a monopolistic economy. Finding no purpose of Congress to immunize labor unions who aid and abet manufacturers and traders in violating the Sherman Act, we hold that the district court correctly concluded that the respondents had violated the Act.

Our holding means that the same labor union activities may or may not be in violation of the Sherman Act, dependent upon whether the union acts alone or in combination with business groups. This, it is argued, brings about a wholly undesirable result—one which leaves labor unions free to engage in conduct which restrains trade. But the desirability of such an exemption of labor unions is a question for the determination of Congress. It is true that many labor union activities do substantially interrupt the course of trade and that these activities, lifted out of the prohibitions of the Sherman Act, include substantially all, if not all, of the normal peaceful activities of labor unions. . . .

Thus, these congressionally permitted union activities may restrain trade in and of themselves. There is no denying the fact that many of them do so, both directly and indirectly. Congress evidently concluded, however, that the chief objective of antitrust legislation, preservation of business competition, could be accomplished by applying the legislation primarily only to those business groups which are directly interested in destroying competition.

Questions

1. In its early history, was the Sherman Act applied to union activities?
2. Does the Clayton Act "wholly exempt" labor unions from the Sherman Act? When might a labor union violate the Sherman Act?
3. Are agricultural associations exempt from antitrust laws?
4. What is the purpose of the Norris–LaGuardia Act? Does it prohibit a federal court injunction against unilateral labor activities that restrain trade?
5. Is it the intention of Congress that the Sherman Act apply only against employer combinations and not labor combinations?

The Court in *Allen Bradley* stated that the union could have achieved its purpose by acting alone. Such results would be "the natural consequence of labor union activities exempted by the Clayton Act from the coverage of the Sherman Act." However, any *agreement* between the union and the employer whereby the union imposes certain restrictions on other employers would not be exempt from an antitrust charge. For example, in the *United Mine Workers* v. *Pennington,* 381 U.S. 657 (1965), the Court ruled that

> a union forfeits its exemption from the antitrust laws when it is clearly shown it has agreed with one set of employers to impose a certain wage scale on other bargaining units. One group of employers may not conspire to eliminate competitors from the industry and the union is liable with the employers if it becomes a party to the conspiracy. This is true even though the union's part in the scheme is an undertaking to secure the same wages, hours, or other conditions of employment from the remaining employers in the industry.

Although the union may not agree with the employer to impose a certain wage scale on another employer, the Court said that

> the union may make wage agreements with the multi-employer bargaining unit and may in pursuance of its own union interests seek to obtain the same terms from other employers. No case under the antitrust laws could be made out on evidence limited to such union behavior.

The Court has subsequently made the following statement:

> Union success in standardizing wages ultimately will affect price competition among the employers, but the goals of federal labor law never could be achieved if this effect on business competition were held a violation of the antitrust laws. The Court therefore has

acknowledged that labor policy requires tolerance for the lessening of business competition. *Connell Co.* v. *Plumbers and Steamfitters,* 421 U.S. 616 (1975).

NATIONAL LABOR RELATIONS ACT

Congress determined that the denial by some employers of the right of employees to organize and collectively bargain led to strikes and other forms of industrial strife which had the effect of obstructing commerce. They felt the inequality of bargaining power between employees who did not possess full freedom of association and employers who were organized in the corporate form substantially burdened the free flow of commerce. Consequently, Congress declared that the policy of the United States, through the National Labor Relations Act of 1932, was to eliminate these obstructions by encouraging the practice and procedure of collective bargaining. This involved the protection of the exercise by workers of the full freedom to self-organize and designate representatives of their own choosing to negotiate terms and conditions of their employment with their employers.

The National Labor Relations Board was created by Section 3 of the act and consists of five members, appointed by the president with the advice and consent of the Senate. The board shall have the authority to make, amend, and rescind such rules and regulations as may be necessary to carry out the provisions of the act.

The two most important portions of the National Labor Relations Act are Sections 7 and 8. Section 7 as originally enacted reads as follows:

> Employees shall have the right to self-organization, to form, join or assist labor organizations, to bargain collectively through representatives of their own choosing, and to engage in other concerted activities for the purpose of collective bargaining or other mutual aid or protection.

There are three parts to the right guaranteed by Section 7. First, employees are secured the freedom to form, join, or assist labor organizations. Second, they are guaranteed the right to engage in concerted activities, such as strikes and picketing. Without the right to engage in strikes and picketing, the other rights may have been nothing more than empty slogans. Third, employees are guaranteed the right "to bargain collectively through representatives of their own choosing."

The rights granted to employees in Section 7 are protected against employer interference by Section 8, which details five prohibited practices by employers deemed unfair to labor.

Section 8(a)(1) declares it to be an unfair labor practice for an employer to "interfere with, restrain, or coerce employees in the exercise of rights guaranteed in Section 7." This provision outlaws such antiunion tactics as beating of labor organizers, company lock-outs of employees to destroy efforts to organize a union, and other use of the employer's economic power to prevent unionization. This section also prohibits some subtle antiunion tactics, such as carefully timing wage increases to demonstate to employees that nothing would be gained by joining a union.

Section 8(a)(2) outlaws "company unions" which are dominated and controlled by the company. Such "company unions" granted the employees the *form* of an organization, but denied them any substantive rights in control. Section 8(a)(3) prohibits discrimination in the hiring or firing of employees to influence union affiliation. Subsection (4) provides protection for employees against reprisals from the company because of the employee's filing of charges with or giving testimony to the National Labor Relations Board. Section 8(a)(5) declares that it is an unfair labor practice for the company to refuse to bargain collectively with the duly designated representative of the employees.

The National Labor Relations Board has exclusive jurisdiction over both unfair labor practices and questions of which union organization is to represent the employees. The board has the authority to designate or separate the employees into appropriate "bargaining units." The employees of each bargaining unit by majority vote determine if they desire a union and which union will represent the unit. Such elections are controlled by the labor laws. The following cases illustrate situations in which alleged Section 8 violations occurred.

INTERFERENCE WITH UNIONIZING

NLRB v. Gissel Packing Co., Inc.
395 U.S. 575 (1969)
Supreme Court of the United States

Chief Justice Warren

When petitioner's president first learned of the Union's drive in July, he talked with all of his employees in an effort to dissuade them from joining a union. He particularly emphasized the results of the long 1952 strike, which he claimed "almost put our company out of business," and expressed worry that the employees were forgetting the "lessons of the past." He emphasized, secondly, that the Company was still on "thin ice" financially, that the Union's "only weapon is to strike," and that a strike "could lead to the closing of the plant," since the parent company had ample manufacturing facilities elsewhere. He noted, thirdly, that because of their age and the limited usefulness of their skills outside their craft, the employees might not be able to find re-employment if they lost their jobs as a result of a strike. Finally, he warned those who did not believe that the plant could go out of business to "look around Holyoke and see a lot of them out of business." The president sent letters to the same effect to the employees in early November, emphasizing that the parent company had no reason to stay in Massachusetts if profits went down.

During the two or three weeks immediately prior to the election . . . the president sent the employees a pamphlet captioned "Do you want another 13-

week strike?" stating that "We have no doubt that the Teamsters Union can again close the Wire Weaving Department and the entire plant by a strike. We have no hopes that the Teamsters Union Bosses will not call a strike. . . . The Teamsters Union is a strike-happy outfit." Similar communications followed . . . including one stressing the Teamsters' "hoodlum control." . . . He repeated that the Company's financial condition was precarious; that a possible strike would jeopardize the continued operation of the plant; and that age and lack of education would make re-employment difficult. The Union lost the election 7-6, and then filed both objections to the election and unfair labor practice charges which were consolidated for hearing before the [administrative law judge].

The Board agreed with the trial [judge] that the president's communications with his employees, when considered as a whole, "reasonably tended to convey to the employees the belief or impression that selection of the Union in the forthcoming election could lead [the Company] to close its plant, or to the transfer of the weaving production with the resultant loss of jobs to the wire weavers." Thus, the Board found that under the "totality of the circumstances," petitioner's activities constituted a violation of Section 8(a)(1) of the Act. The Board further agreed with the trial [judge] that petitioner's activities, because they "also interfered with the exercise of a free and untrammeled choice in the election," and "tended to foreclose the possibility" of holding a fair election required that the election be set aside. . . . Consequently, the Board set the election aside, entered a cease-and-desist order, and ordered the Company to bargain on request. . . .

We [next] consider petitioner['s] . . . First Amendment challenge to the holding of the Board. . . .

Any assessment of the precise scope of employer expression, of course, must be made in the context of its labor relations setting. Thus, an employer's rights cannot outweigh the equal rights of the employees to associate freely, as those rights are embodied in §7 and protected by §8(a)(1) and the proviso to §8(c). And any balancing of those rights must take into account the economic dependence of the employees on their employers, and the necessary tendency of the former, because of that relationship, to pick up intended implications of the latter that might be more readily dismissed by a more disinterested ear. Stating these obvious principles is but another way of recognizing that what is basically at stake is the establishment of a nonpermanent, limited relationship between the employer, his economically dependent employee and his union agent, not the election of legislators or the enactment of legislation whereby that relationship is ultimately defined and where the independent voter may be freer to listen more objectively and employers as a class freer to talk.

Within this framework, we must reject the Company's challenge to the decision below and the findings of the Board on which it was based. The standards used below for evaluating the impact of an employer's statements are not seriously questioned by petitioner and we see no need to tamper with them here. Thus, an employer is free to communicate to his employees any of his general views about unionism or any of his specific views about a particular union, so long as the communications do not contain a "threat of reprisal or force or promise of benefit." He may even make a prediction as to the precise effects he believes unionization will have on his company. In such a case, however, the prediction must be carefully phrased on the basis of objective fact to convey an employer's belief as to demonstrably probable consequences beyond his control or to convey a management decision already arrived at to close the plant in case of unionization. If there is any implication that an employer may or may not take action solely on his own initiative for reasons unrelated to economic necessities and known only to him, the statement is no longer a reasonable prediction based on available facts but a threat of retaliation based on misrepresentation and coercion, and as such without the protection of the First Amendment. We therefore agree with the court below that "conveyance of the employer's belief, even though sincere, that unionization will or may result in the closing of the plant is not a statement of fact unless, which is most improbable, the eventuality of closing is capable of proof." As stated elsewhere, any employer is free only to tell "what he reasonably believes will be the likely economic consequences of unionization that are outside his control," and not "threats of economic reprisal to be taken solely on his own volition."

Equally valid was the finding by the court and the Board that petitioner's statements and communications were not cast as a prediction of "demonstrable economic consequences," but rather as a threat of retaliatory action. The Board found that petitioner's speeches, pamphlets, leaflets, and letters conveyed the following message: that the company was in precarious financial condition: that the "strike-happy" union would in all likelihood have to obtain its potentially unreasonable demands by striking, the probable result of which would be a plant shutdown, as the past history of labor relations in the area indicated; and that the employees in such a case would have great difficulty finding employment elsewhere. In carrying out its duty to focus on the question, "What did the speaker intend and the listener understand," the Board could reasonably conclude that the intended and understood import of that message was not to predict that unionization would inevitably cause the plant to close but to threaten to throw employees out of work regardless of the economic realities. In this connection, we need go no further than to point out (1) that petitioner had no support for its basic assumption that the union, which had not yet even presented any demands, would have to strike to be heard, and that it admitted at the hearing that it had no basis for attributing other plant closings in the area to unionism; and (2) that the Board has often found that employees, who are particularly sensitive to rumors of plant closings, take such hints as coercive threats rather than honest forecasts.

Questions

1. Labor laws limit the employer's free speech. What are the limitations on the employer's speech?
2. How did the Court justify this limitation on the free speech of the employer?

COMPANY UNION

NLRB v. Post Publishing Company

311 F. 2d 565 (1962)
U.S. Court of Appeals (7th Cir.)

This case is before us on the petition of the National Labor Relations Board for enforcement of its order issued against respondent . . . , The Post Publishing Company, on March 15, 1962. . . .

The Board found, in agreement with the trial [judge], that respondent violated §8(a)(2) of the Act by offering contributing financial and other assistance and support of the Appleton Post-Crescent Craftsmen's Union, herein called PCCU.

At the time of the dispute in question, PCCU was an independent union and since 1921 had been the lawfully recognized bargaining agent and representative of respondent's mechanical employees.

The charging party in this case is Appleton, International Typographical Union, AFL-CIO, herein called ITU. It was seeking to replace PCCU as the bargaining representative of respondent's mechanical employees. Thus, it appears at the outset that respondent found itself in the middle of a representation dispute between the two unions. . . .

On April 4, 1961, ITU held an organizational meeting for employees in Appleton which was attended by some mechanical employees of respondent.

Subsequently, following an exchange of correspondence between respondent and ITU, the latter demanded recognition as the representative of a majority of the mechanical employees. Respondent refused such recognition because of its current contract with PCCU.

Subsequently, ITU . . . charged respondent with . . . giving PCCU illegal support by allowing it to use respondent's cafeteria for union meetings, giving PCCU illegal support by permitting it to print its union notices on respondent's machines, and furnishing PCCU illegal support by permitting it to retain the profits from the operation of the cafeteria and coffee vending machine.

The trial [judge] found that the conduct complained of in the [first] and [second] charges, standing alone, would not constitute a type of "support" that amounted to a violation of the Act.

However, on the [third] charge, he ruled that the receipt of profits from the operation of the cafeteria and coffee vending machine was violative of the Act. He then considered the conduct alleged in charges 1 and 2 as contributing to such violation as a part of an overall pattern of continued and substantial support of PCCU "which was well calculated to coerce and restrain employees in the exercise of their right freely to choose or change their bargaining representative."

The Board approved and adopted the trial [judge's] report without change and entered an appropriate order thereon.

The trial [judge] agreed there was no evidence showing that respondent had made use of this "support" to gain concessions from PCCU in bargaining and that respondent had not threatened to discontinue such "support" if the employees left PCCU and joined ITU.

The narrow issue before us is whether the granting of annual financial benefits of its 38-year history of amicable relationship with this independent union, constituted illegal financial support by respondent in violation of the Act.

At the outset the resolution of this issue must be made in the light of the Board's concession that *there is no claim that respondent was the motivating factor in the organization of PCCU* and that *no claim is made that respondent dominated this independent union.*

We conclude that the Board erred in failing to properly distinguish between "support" and "cooperation." The findings of proscribed support under the Act are unsupported by substantial evidence in the record considered as a whole and are contrary to law.

The course of conduct engaged in by respondent in its relationship with PCCU follows that pattern of friendly and courteous cooperation, or even generous action, of the sort we feel brings about the end result in labor-management relations sought by the underlying philosophy motivating the National Labor Relations Act.

This course of conduct flows directly from union request. Absent any showing of employer domination, we fail to find in the record that showing of proscribed motivation warranting an inference drawn by the Board that it was calculated to unlawfully coerce or restrain the employees in their right to freely choose or change their bargaining representative.

The fact that the union members chose to eliminate dues and forego the provision for many fringe benefits to its members was a decision it made. Respondent did not participate in any way in the decision of the union as to how it would derive its income, or in what manner it would incur expenses in the conduct of its business. All that respondent did was to assist the employees in carrying out their independent activities. No one ever complained until a representation dispute was precipitated. That complaint was made by the dominant international organization in its effort to oust the small independent group. . . .

We have carefully reviewed the many cases cited by the Board. In practically all of them, the facts clearly demonstrate antiunion bias by the employer, financial support combined with union domination by the employer, discriminatory discharges, threats or other unfair labor practices interwoven with acts of alleged illegal financial support. Such is not the case here.

We hold, absent any showing of employer motivation in the original organization of the independent union or any showing of subsequent employer domination thereof, that a course of conduct over a period of years by an employer in its amicable relationship for 38 years with an independent union acting as a bargaining agent for employees . . . under the circumstances as herein earlier set forth is a permissible form of friendly cooperation designed to foster and resulting in uninterrupted harmonious labor-management relations, and is not the form of "support" designed to interfere with, restrain or coerce employees in the free exercise of their right to choose or change their bargaining representative.

For the foregoing reasons, we deny the Board's petition for enforcement of its order against respondent.

SECTION 8(a)3

This section prevents an employer from discharging or refusing to hire an employee as a technique to encourage or discourage membership in a labor organization. However, it does not restrict the employer in a normal exercise of its judgment in selecting or discharging employees for proper cause. Nevertheless, the question arises as to whether the employer may close its shop and open another business elsewhere to avoid unionization of the plant, or whether the employer can choose to go out of business altogether in order to avoid unionization. The following excerpt provides some answers.

Textile Workers Union v. Darlington Manufacturing Co.
380 U.S. 263 (1965)
Supreme Court of the United States

Justice Harlan

We are not presented here with the case of a "runaway shop," whereby Darlington would transfer its work to another plant or open a new plant in another locality to replace its closed plant. Nor are we concerned with a shutdown where the employees, by renouncing the union, could cause the plant to reopen. Such cases would involve discriminatory employer action for the purpose of obtaining some benefit in the future from the new employees. We hold here only that when an employer closes his entire business, even if the liquidation is motivated by vindictiveness towards the union, such action is not an unfair labor practice. . . .

The closing of an entire business, even though discriminatory, ends the employer-employee relationship; the force of such a closing is entirely spent as to that business when termination of the enterprise takes place. On the other hand, a discriminatory partial closing may have repercussions on what remains of the business, affording employer leverage for discouraging the free exercise of §7 rights among remaining employees of much the same kind as that found to exist in the "runaway shop" and "temporary closing" cases. Moreover, a possible remedy open to the Board in such a case, like the remedies available in the "runaway shop" and "temporary closing" cases, is to order reinstatement of the discharged employees in the other parts of the business. No such remedy is available when an entire business has been terminated. By analogy to those cases involving a continuing enterprise we are constrained to hold, in disagreement with the Court of Appeals, that a partial closing is an unfair labor practice under §8(a)(3) if motivated by a purpose to chill unionism in any of the remaining plants of the single employer and if the employer may reasonably have foreseen that such closing will likely have that effect.

Questions

1. What is a "runaway shop"? Is it illegal?
2. Is termination of a business in violation of Section 8(a)3?

BARGAIN IN GOOD FAITH

NLRB v. Katz
369 U.S. 736 (1961)
Supreme Court of the United States

Justice Brennan

Is it a violation of the duty "to bargain collectively" imposed by §8(a)(5) of the National Labor Relations Act for an employer, without first consulting a union with which it is carrying on bona fide contract negotiations, to institute changes regarding matters which are subjects of mandatory bargaining under §8(d) and which are in fact under discussion? The National Labor Relations Board answered the question affirmatively in this case, in a decision which expressly disclaimed any finding that the totality of the respondents' conduct manifested bad faith in the pending negotiations. . . .

. . . [T]he union['s] charge of unfair labor practices particularly referred to three acts by the company: unilaterally granting numerous merit increases on October 1956 and January 1957; unilaterally announcing a change in sick-leave policy in March 1957; and unilaterally instituting a new system of automatic wage increases during April 1957. As the ensuing litigation has developed, the company has defended against the charges along two fronts: First, it asserts that the unilateral changes occurred after a bargaining impasse had developed through the union's fault in adopting obstructive tactics. According to the Board, however, "the evidence is clear that the [company] undertook its unilateral actions before negotiations were discontinued, or before, as we find on the record, the existence of any possible impasse." There is ample support in the record considered as a whole for this finding of fact. . . .

The second line of defense was that the Board could not hinge a conclusion that Section 8(a)(5) had been violated on unilateral actions alone, without making a finding of the employer's subjective bad faith at the bargaining table . . . .

The duty "to bargain collectively" enjoined by §8(a)(5) is defined by §8(d) as the duty to "meet . . . and confer in good faith with respect to wages, hours, and other terms and conditions of employment." Clearly, the duty thus defined may be violated without a general failure of subjective good faith: for there is no occasion to consider the issue of good faith if a party has refused even to negotiate *in fact*—"to meet . . . and confer"—about any of the mandatory subjects. A refusal to negotiate *in fact* as to any subject which is within §8(d), and about which the union seeks to negotiate, violates §8(a)(5) though the employer has every desire to reach agreement with the union upon an over-all collective agreement and earnestly and in all good faith bargains to that end. We hold that an employer's unilateral change in conditions of employment under negotiation is similarly a violation of §8(a)(5), for it is a circumvention of the duty to negotiate which frustrates the objectives of §8(a)(5) as much as does a flat refusal.

The unilateral actions of the respondent illustrate the policy and practical considerations which support our conclusion. . . . It is clear at a glance that the automatic wage increase system which was instituted unilaterally was considerably more generous than that which had shortly theretofore been offered to and rejected by the union. Such action conclusively manifests bad faith in the negotiations, and so would have violated Section 8(a)(5) even . . . though no additional evidence of bad faith appeared. An employer is not required to lead with his best offer; he is free to bargain. But even after an impasse is reached he has no license to grant wage increases greater than any he has ever offered the union at the bargaining table, for such action is necessarily inconsistent with a sincere desire to conclude an agreement with the union. . . .

. . . Unilateral action by an employer without prior discussion with the union does amount to a refusal to negotiate about the affected conditions of employment under negotiation, and must of necessity obstruct bargaining, contrary to the congressional policy. . . . It will rarely be justified by any reason of substance. It follows that the Board may hold such unilateral action to be an unfair labor practice in violation of Section 8(a)(5), without also finding the employer guilty of over-all subjective bad faith.

Questions

1. What was the 8(a)(5) violation in *NLRB* v. *Katz*?
2. The duty to bargain collectively is defined in Section 8(d). This duty relates only to certain mandatory subjects. What are they?
3. Is the refusal to "meet . . . and confer" about a mandatory subject a violation of 8(a)5?

LABOR-MANAGEMENT RELATIONS ACT

The Labor-Management Relations Act of 1947 (Taft–Hartley Act) was the product of diverse forces. Many business firms continued to attack "unionism" and gladly joined in the effort to develop an antiunion law. Others criticized the unions for abuse of power. John L. Lewis and the United Mine Workers had carried on two long strikes during World War II in defiance of the government. There were news reports that many so-called labor unions were really rackets and controlled by unsavory individuals. Often violence was promoted by union leaders when peaceful measures failed to achieve union objectives. In a few unions the membership rolls were closed to outsiders and jobs passed from father to son. Others criticized the use of secondary boycotts by unions to achieve their purposes. The Taft–Hartley Act attempted to deal with these perceived problems by amending the National Labor Relations Act and in formulating other policies for labor law.

Several changes in labor law were created by the Taft–Hartley Act. First, the labor injunction was revived in a modified and restrictive form. As one example, an injunction could be secured by the National Labor Relations Board to eliminate statutorily defined unfair union practices. Second, Section 7 of the National Labor Relations Act was amended to allow individuals the freedom to refrain from union activities as a right equal to Section 7's previously announced right to join a union. Moreover, Section 8 of the National Labor Relations Act was amended [8(b)(1)] to prohibit union restraint or coercion of workers who attempted to exercise the right not to join the union.

Prior to 1947 the union could secure a "union security" provision in the contract negotiated with the employer whereby the employer would refuse to hire those who were not members of the union. In effect, the union determined who would be hired. This system was called a closed shop and was outlawed by the Taft–Hartley Act. Instead, the Taft–Hartley amendments to the NLRA established that the employer could legally agree to a union membership provision only if it allowed the employer to select employees without regard to prehired union membership. Membership in the union could only be required after 30 days of employment. If the employee thereafter refused to pay union initiation fees and dues, the membership provision of the collectively bargained contract would require the employer to discharge the employee. This type of union security agreement is referred to as a union shop.

Although the rules of federal law apply to all employers whose operations affect interstate commerce, Congress has chosen to explicitly exclude employers from the permissible union shop provisions of federal law in those states that have enacted the so-called right-to-work laws. Section 14(b) of the NLRA excludes state employers when state law refuses to enforce any contractual commitments of employers and unions which attempt to mandate membership in labor organizations. Twenty states have enacted such laws which, in effect, outlaw union shops in their jurisdictions.

Besides the amendment of Section 8 to protect the right of the individual worker to refrain from union membership, subsections (2) through (6) of Section 8(b) also outlawed the following concerted union activities:

(2) attempt to cause an employer to discriminate against an employee, except where the employee fails to pay dues,
(3) refusal to bargain in good faith with the employer,
(4) strikes to compel an employer to commit some unfair labor practice or secondary boycotts: i.e. the refusal to work for employer A, unless he ceases to do business with employer B, with whom the union has its real dispute,
(5) requirements of excessive or discriminatory initiation fees,
(6) "feather-bedding" practices of pay without work performed.

The following cases discuss portions of Section 8(b) and relate in more detail some of the particular union practices held to be illegal.

FAIR REPRESENTATION

Local Union, No. 12, United Rubber Workers v. NLRB
368 F. 2d 12 (1966)
U.S. Court of Appeals (5th Cir.)

At the outset it must be reiterated that every union decision which may in some way result in overriding the wishes . . . of . . . even an appreciable number of employees, does not in and of itself constitute a breach of the fiduciary duty of fair representation. Even in the administration stage of the bargaining contract . . . , the union must necessarily retain a broad degree of discretion in processing individual grievances. Thus, where the union after a good faith investigation of the merits of a grievance, concludes that the claim is insubstantial and refuses to encumber further its grievance channels by continuing to process the unmeritorious claim, its duty of fair representation may well be satisfied. Such good-faith effort to represent fairly the interests of individual employees, however, is not evidenced in this controversy. To the contrary, Local 12 in open disregard of the recommendations of its International has continued to refuse to represent the vital interests of a segment of its membership. . . . Undoubtedly, the duty of fair representation can be breached by discriminatory inaction in refusing to process a grievance as well as by active conduct on the part of the union. . . .

We thus conclude that where the record demonstrates that a grievance would have been processed to arbitration but for arbitrary and discriminatory reasons, the refusal to so process it constitutes a violation of the union's duty to represent its members "without hostile discrimination, fairly, impartially, and in good faith."

Similarly, with respect to the grievances concerning the segregated nature of plant facilities, the union not only refused to process such claims but actively opposed desegregation of shower and toilet facilities. It is impossible for us to look upon such conduct as anything other than an effort to discriminate against Negro employees with respect to conditions of employment. . . . As the Board properly concluded, "whatever may be the bases on which a statutory representative may properly decline to process grievances, the bases must bear a reasonable relation to the Union's role as bargaining representative or its functioning as a labor organization; manifestly racial discrimination bears no such relationship."

. . . Local 12, in refusing to represent the complainants in a fair and impartial manner, thereby violated section 8(b)(1)(A) by restraining them in the exercise of their Section 7 right to bargain collectively through their chosen representatives.

Questions

1. May the union refuse to further prosecute a grievance of an individual union member? What valid justification might be advanced by the union for refusing to prosecute a union member's claim?
2. Why was the refusal to prosecute grievances of union members by Local Union No. 12 in violation of federal law?

SECONDARY BOYCOTTS

NLRB v. Local 825, International Union of Operating Engineers
400 U.S. 297 (1971)
Supreme Court of the United States

Justice Marshall

In this case we are asked to determine whether strikes by Operating Engineers at the site of the construction of a nuclear power generator plant at Oyster Creek, New Jersey, violated §8(b)(4)(B) of the National Labor Relations Act. Although the National Labor Relations Board found the strikes to be in violation of this section, the Court of Appeals refused to enforce the Board's order. . . .

The general contractor for the project, Burns & Roe, Inc., subcontracted all of the construction work to three companies—White Construction Co., Chicago Bridge & Iron Co., and Poirier and McLane Corp. All three employed operating engineers who were members of Local 825, International Union of Operating Engineers. But White, unlike Chicago Bridge and Poirier, did not have a collective-bargaining agreement with Local 825.

In the latter part of September 1965, White installed an electric welding machine and assigned the job of pushing the buttons that operated the machine to members of the Ironworkers Union, who were to perform the actual welding. Upon learning of this work assignment, Local 825's job steward and its lead engineer threatened White with a strike if operating engineers were not given the work. White, however, refused to meet the demand. On September 29, 1965, the job steward and lead engineer met with the construction manager for Burns, the general contractor. They informed him that the members of Local 825 working at the jobsite had voted to strike unless Burns signed a contract, which would be binding on all three subcontractors as well as Burns, giving Local 825 jurisdiction over all power equipment, including electric welding machines, operated on the jobsite. On October 1, after White and Burns refused to accede to the demands, the operating engineers employed by Chicago Bridge and Poirer as well as those employed by White walked off the job. . . .

Congressional concern over the involvement of third parties in labor disputes not their own prompted §8(b)(4)(B). This concern was focused on the "secondary boycott," which was conceived of as pressure brought to bear, not "upon the employer who alone is a party [to a dispute], but upon some third party who has no concern in it" with the objective of forcing the third party to bring pressure on the employer to agree to the union's demands.

Section 8(b)(4)(B) is, however, the product of legislative compromise and also reflects a concern with protecting labor organizations' right to exert legitimate pressure aimed at the employer with whom there is a primary dispute. This primary activity is protected even though it may seriously affect neutral third parties.

Thus there are two threads to §8(b)(4)(B) that require disputed conduct to be classified as either "primary" or "secondary." And the tapestry that has been woven in classifying such conduct is among the labor law's most intricate. But here the normally difficult task of classifying union conduct is easy. As the Court of Appeals said, the "record amply justifies the conclusion that [Burns and the neutral subcontractors] were subjected to coercion in the form of threats or walkouts, or both." And, as the Board said, it is clear that this coercion was designed "to achieve the assignment of [the] disputed work" to operating engineers.

Local 825's coercive activity was aimed directly at Burns and the subcontractors that were not involved in the dispute. The union engaged in a strike against these neutral employers for the specific, overt purpose of forcing them to put pressure on White to assign the job of operating the welding machine to operating engineers. . . . It was . . . using a sort of pressure that was unmistakably and flagrantly secondary.

Local 825's . . . operating engineers sought to force Burns to bind all the subcontractors on the project to a particular form of job assignments. The clear implication of the demands was that Burns would be required either to force a change in White's policy or to terminate White's contract. The strikes shut down the whole project. If Burns was unable to obtain White's consent, Local 825 was apparently willing to continue disruptive conduct that would bring all the employers to their knees.

Certainly, the union would have preferred to have the employers capitulate to its demands; it wanted to take the job of operating the welding machines away from the ironworkers. It was willing, however, to try to obtain this capitulation by forcing neutrals to compel White to meet union demands. To hold that this flagrant secondary conduct with these most serious disruptive effects was not prohibited by §8(b)(4)(B) would be largely to ignore the original congressional concern. . . .

Since the Court of Appeals did not believe that §8(b)(4)(B) was applicable, it did not consider the propriety of the portion of the Board's order relating to that section. . . . [S]o we must remand these cases for the Court of Appeals to consider whether the order is necessary to further the goals of the Act.

Questions

1. What is a primary boycott by a union? What is a secondary boycott?
2. Why should secondary boycotts be illegal?

INFORMATIONAL PICKETING

NLRB v. Fruit Packers
377 U.S. 58 (1963)
Supreme Court of the United States

Justice Brennan

Under . . . the National Labor Relations Act, as amended, it is an unfair labor practice for a union . . . [to use secondary picketing] with the object of "forcing . . . any person to cease using, selling, handling, transporting, or otherwise dealing in products of any other producer. . . ." A proviso excepts, however, "publicity, *other than picketing,* for the purpose of truthfully advising the public . . . that a product or products are produced by an employer with whom the labor organization has a primary dispute and are distributed by another employer, as long as such publicity does not have an effect of inducing any individual employed by any person other than the primary employer in the course of his employment to refuse to pick up, deliver, or transport any goods, or not to perform any services, at the establishment of the employer engaged in such distribution." The question in this case is whether the respondent unions violated this section when they limited their secondary picketing of retail stores to an appeal to the customers of the stores not to buy the products of certain firms against which one of the respondents was on strike.

Respondent Local 760 called a strike against fruit packers and warehousemen doing business in Yakima, Washington. The struck firms sold Washington State apples to the Safeway chain of retail stores in and about Seattle, Washington. Local 760 . . . instituted a consumer boycott against the apples in support of the strike. They placed pickets who walked back and forth before the customers' entrances of 46 Safeway stores in Seattle. The pickets—two at each of 45 stores and three at the 46th store—wore placards and distributed handbills which appealed to Safeway customers, and to the public generally, to refrain from buying Washington State apples, which were only one of numerous food products sold in the stores. Before the pickets appeared at any store, a letter was delivered to the store manager informing him that the picketing was only an appeal to his customers not to buy Washington State apples, and that pickets were being expressly instructed "to patrol peacefully in front of the consumer entrances of the store, to stay away from the delivery entrances and not to interfere with the work of your employees, or with deliveries to or pickups from your store." A copy of written instructions to the pickets—which included the explicit statement that "you are also forbidden to request that the customers not patronize the store"—was enclosed with the letter. Since it was desired to assure Safeway employees that they were not to cease work, and to avoid any interference with pickups or deliveries, the pickets appeared after the stores opened for business and departed before the stores closed. At all times during the picketing, the store employees continued to work, and no deliveries of pickups were obstructed. Washington State apples were handled in normal course by both Safeway employees and the employees of the other employers involved. Ingress and egress by customers and others was not interfered with in any manner.

A complaint issued on charges that this conduct violated §8(b)(4) as amended . . . that "by literal wording of the proviso (to Section 8(b)(4)) as well as through the interpretive gloss placed thereon by its drafters, consumer picketing in front of a secondary establishment is prohibited."

The Board's reading of the statute—that the legislative history and the phrase "other than picketing" in the proviso reveal a congressional purpose to outlaw all picketing directed at customers at a secondary site—necessarily rested on the finding that Congress determined that such picketing always threatens, coerces or restrains the secondary employer. . . [However], throughout the history of federal regulation of labor relations, Congress has consistently refused to prohibit peaceful picketing except where it is used as a means to achieve specific ends which experience has shown are undesirable. We have recognized this congressional practice . . . reflect[s] concern that a broad ban against peaceful picketing might collide with the guarantees of the First Amendment.

We have examined the legislative history of the amendments to §8(b)(4), and conclude that it does not reflect with the requisite clarity a congressional plan to proscribe all peaceful consumer picketing at secondary sites, and, particularly, any concern with peaceful picketing when it is limited, as here, to persuading Safeway customers not to buy Washington State apples when they traded in the Safeway stores. All that the legislative history shows in the way of an "isolated evil" believed to require proscription of peaceful consumer picketing at secondary sites, was its use to persuade the customers of the secondary employer to cease trading with him in order to force him to cease dealing with, or to put pressure upon, the primary employer. This narrow focus reflects the difference between such conduct and peaceful picketing at the secondary site directed only at the struck product. In the latter case, the union's appeal to the public is confined to its dispute with the primary employer, since the public is not asked to withhold its patronage from the secondary employer, but only to boycott the primary employer's goods. On the other hand, a union appeal to the public at the secondary site not to trade at all with the secondary employer goes beyond the goods of the primary employer, and seeks the public's assistance in forcing the secondary employer to cooperate with the union in its primary dispute. This is not to say that this distinction was expressly alluded to in the debates. It is to say, however, that the consumer picketing carried on in this case is not attended by the abuses at which the statute was directed. . . .

Peaceful consumer picketing to shut off all trade with the secondary employer unless he aids the union in its dispute with the primary employer, is poles apart from such picketing which only persuades his customers not to buy the struck product. The proviso indicates no more than that the Senate conferees' constitutional doubts led Congress to authorize publicity other than picketing which persuades the customers of a secondary employer to stop all trading with him, but not such publicity which has the effect of cutting off his deliveries or inducing his employees to cease work. On the other hand, picketing which persuades the customers of a secondary employer to stop all trading with him was also to be barred.

In sum, the legislative history does not support the Board's finding that

Congress meant to prohibit all consumer picketing at a secondary site, having determined that such picketing necessarily threatened, coerced, or restrained the secondary employer. Rather, the history shows that Congress was following its usual practice of legislating against peaceful picketing only to curb "isolated evils."

This distinction is opposed as "unrealistic" because, it is urged, all picketing automatically provokes the public to stay away from the picketed establishment. The public will, it is said, neither read the signs and handbills, nor note the explicit injunction that "This is not a strike against the store or market." Be that as it may, our holding today simply takes note of the fact that Congress has never adopted a broad condemnation of peaceful picketing, such as that urged upon us by petitioners and an intention to do so is not revealed with the "clearest indication in the legislative history," which we require.

Questions

1. What "evil" was Congress legislating against in Section 8(b)4?
2. Why did Congress feel the "proviso" was necessary in this legislation?
3. As a result of the decision in *Fruit Packers,* under what conditions is "secondary picketing" permitted?
4. Could a radio publicity compaign *without secondary picketing* be directed to consumers requesting their *total* boycott of retailers selling goods of the primary employer?
5. Could publicity be directed to employees or deliverypersons of a secondary employer?

FEATHERBEDDING OR MAKE-WORK

NLRB v. Gamble Enterprises
345 U.S. 117 (1952)
Supreme Court of the United States

Justice Burton

The question here is whether a labor organization engages in an unfair labor practice, within the meaning of §8(b)(6) of the National Labor Relations Act, as amended by the Labor Management Relations Act, 1947, when it insists that the management of one of an interstate chain of theaters shall employ a local orchestra to play in connection with certain programs, although that management does not need or want to employ that orchestra. . . .

For generations professional musicians have faced a shortage in the local employment needed to yield them a livelihood. They have been confronted with the competition of military bands, traveling bands, foreign musicians on tour, local amateur organizations and, more recently, technological developments in reproduction and broadcasting. To help them conserve local sources of employment, they developed local protective societies. Since 1896, they also have organized and maintained on a national scale the American Federation of Musicians, affiliated with the American Federation of Labor. By 1943, practically all professional instrumental performers and conductors in the United States had joined the Federation. . . .

The Federation uses its nationwide control of professional talent to help individual members and local unions. It insists that traveling band contracts be subject to its rules, laws and regulations. Article 18, §4, of its By-Laws provides: "Traveling members cannot, without the consent of a Local, play any presentation performances in its jurisdiction unless a local house orchestra is also employed."

From this background we turn to the instant case. For more than 12 years the Palace Theater in Akron, Ohio, has been one of an interstate chain of theaters managed by respondent, Gamble Enterprises, Inc., which is a Washington corporation with its principal office in New York. Before the decline of vaudeville and until about 1940, respondent employed a local orchestra of nine union musicians to play for stage acts at that Theater. When a traveling band occupied the stage, the local orchestra played from the pit for the vaudeville acts and, at times, augmented the performance of the traveling band.

Since 1940, respondent has used the Palace for showing motion pictures with occasional appearance of traveling bands. Between 1940 and 1947, the local musicians, no longer employed on a regular basis, held periodic rehearsals at the theater and were available when required. When a traveling band appeared there, respondent paid the members of the local orchestra a sum equal to the minimum union wages for a similar engagement but they played no music.

The Taft–Hartley Act, containing §8(b)(6), was passed, over the President's veto, June 23, 1947, and took effect August 22. Between July 2 and November 12, seven performances of traveling bands were presented on the Palace stage. Local musicians were neither used nor paid on those occasions. They raised no objections and made no demands for "stand-by" payments. However, in October, 1947, the American Federation of Musicians, Local No. 24 of Akron, Ohio, here called the union, opened negotiations with respondent . . . for the latter's employment of a pit orchestra of local musicians whenever a traveling band performed on the stage. The pit orchestra was to play overtures, "intermissions" and "chasers" (the latter while patrons were leaving the theater). The union required acceptance of this proposal as a condition of its consent to local appearances of traveling bands. Respondent declined the offer and a traveling band scheduled to appear November 20 canceled its engagement on learning that the union had withheld its consent.

* * *

In 1949, respondent filed charges with the National Labor Relations Board asserting that the union was engaging in the unfair labor practice defined in §8(b)(6). . . .

We accept the finding of the Board, made upon the entire record, that the union was seeking actual employment for its members and not mere "stand-by" pay. The Board recognized that, formerly, before §8(b)(6) had taken effect, the union had received "stand-by" payments in connection with traveling band appearances. Since then, the union has requested no such payments and has received none. It has, however, requested and consistently negotiated for actual employment in connection with traveling band and vaudeville appearances. It has suggested various ways in which a local orchestra could earn pay for performing competent work and, upon those terms, it has offered to consent to the appearance of traveling bands which are Federation-controlled. Respondent, with equal consistency, has declined these offers as it had a right to do.

Since we and the Board treat the union's proposals as in good faith contemplating the performance of actual services, we agree that the union has not, on this record, engaged in a practice proscribed by §8(b)(6). It has remained for respondent to accept or reject the union's offers on their merits in the light of all material circumstances. We do not find it necessary to determine also whether such offers were "in the nature of an exaction." We are not dealing here with offers of mere "token" or nominal services. The proposals before us were appropriately treated by the Board as offers in good faith of substantial performances by competent musicians. There is no reason to think that sham can be substituted for substance under §8(b)(6) any more than under any other statute. Payments for "standing-by," or for the substantial equivalent of "standing-by," are not payments for services performed, but when an employer receives a bona fide offer of competent performance of relevant services, it remains for the employer, through free and fair negotiation, to determine whether such offer shall be accepted and what compensation shall be paid for the work done.

Questions

1. What is featherbedding? Had the local musicians in *Gamble Enterprises* ever engaged in featherbedding?
2. What is make-work? Is it illegal?

FEDERAL PREEMPTION

Through constitutional decisions the Supreme Court has allocated to Congress the power (1) to enact national labor legislation and (2) to forbid the application of State laws in labor relations. The Congress may choose not to exercise this power or to use only part. However, the actual enactment of federal legislation does not necessarily exclude the jurisdiction of state tribunals nor the application of state law. But the expansion of national power over industrial relations raised significant questions concerning the portion of government power shared between the states and the nation.

First, how far does actual federal regulation of labor relations extend? The National Labor Relations Act is the most significant labor legislation in the United States. In upholding the constitutionality of the NLRA, the Supreme Court assumed without so holding that the act asserted federal power to the outermost limits of the commerce power. But in fact, the National Labor Relations Board exercises more narrow jurisdiction. Congress has never appropriated sufficient funds to the board to fully cover the scope of the act. Therefore, through self-restraint imposed by limited funds and administrative discretion, several million employees and employers are left outside the board's jurisdiction. In the 1957 decision of *Guss* v. *Utah Labor Relations Board,* 353 U.S. 1, the Supreme Court held that state agencies could not take jurisdiction in areas over which the NLRB declined to exercise its statutory jurisdiction. The result was a "no man's land" in which the federal agency declined to act and the states were excluded by federal legislation. Finally in 1959, the Congress allowed the state law to operate in the area over which the NLRB had declined to exercise jurisdiction. The same legislation prohibits the NLRB from any further contractions of its jurisdiction.

Second, how far does federal regulation of labor relations exclude the application of supplementary state law? The Court has determined that, with limited exceptions, the states have no authority over the aspects of labor relations under NLRB jurisdiction. A state may not decide questions of union representation, remedy employer unfair labor practices, or regulate the concerted activities (picketing and strikes) of employees when such activities are arguably within the jurisdiction of the NLRB. These activities lie within the protection of Section 7 or the prohibition of Section 8 of the NLRA. As such, they are areas that are exclusive to the NLRB and excluded from state courts. The principal judge-made exception is the power of state courts to enjoin or award damages resulting from conduct marked by violence or imminent threats to public order. Previously in *San Diego Building Trades Council* v. *Garman*, 359 U.S. 236 (1959), the court had concluded that the states need not yield jurisdiction "where the activity regulated was a merely peripheral concern of the Labor Management Relations Act. . . . Or where the regulated conduct touched interests so deeply rooted in local feeling and responsibility that, in the absence of compelling congressional direction, we could not infer that Congress had deprived the States of the power to act." Consequently, states may legislate to supplement the federal law if such legislation does not concern an area of labor relations arguably within the area covered by federal legislation. The "peripheral" aspects of labor relations are within the reach of state legislation.

COURT ENFORCEMENT OF LABOR CONTRACTS

As previously indicated, the Norris–LaGuardia Act generally prohibits federal court injunctions in labor disputes. However, Section 301 of the Taft–Hartley Act provides that unions may sue and be sued as an entity. Suits for violation of labor contracts may be brought in any district court and money judgments against labor unions or the employer may be obtained. However, the language of the Taft–Hartley Act did not expressly overrule the Norris–LaGuardia anti-injunction provisions. Thereafter, the question naturally arose as to whether the courts could use an injunction against either party to a labor contract who refused to abide by the collective bargaining agreement.

In *Textile Workers Union* v. *Lincoln Mills*, 353 U.S. 448 (1957), the Supreme Court held that Section 301 of the Labor-Management Act authorizes federal courts to fashion a body of federal law for the enforcement of collective bargaining agreements and includes within that federal law specific performance of promises to arbitrate grievances under collective bargaining agreements. This construction of Section 301 means that the agreement to arbitrate grievance disputes, contained in a collective bargaining agreement, can be specifically enforced by court injunctions.

However, in 1962 the Supreme Court held in *Sinclair Refining Co.* v. *Atkinson*, 370 U.S. 195, that the anti-injunction provisions of the Norris–LaGuardia Act precluded a federal district court from enjoining a strike in breach of a no-strike obligation under a collective bargaining agreement, even though that agreement contained provisions, enforceable under Section 301(a) of the Labor-Management Relations Act for binding arbitration of the grievance dispute concerning which the strike was called. The Court reexamined its holding in *Sinclair* in the following case.

Boys Markets, Inc. v. Retail Clerks Local 770

398 U.S. 235 (1970)

Supreme Court of the United States

Justice Brennan

In February 1969, at the time of the incidents that produced this litigation, petitioner and respondent were parties to a collective bargaining agreement which provided that all controversies concerning its interpretation or application should be resolved by adjustment and arbitration procedures set forth therein and that during the life of the contract, there should be "no cessation or stoppage of work, lock-out, picketing or boycotts. . . ." The dispute arose when petitioner's frozen foods supervisor and certain members of his crew who were not members of the bargaining unit began to rearrange merchandise in the frozen food cases of one of petitioner's supermarkets. A union representative insisted that the food cases be stripped of all merchandise and be restocked by union personnel. When petitioner did not accede to the union's demand, a strike was called and the union began to picket petitioner's establishment. Thereupon petitioner demanded that the union cease work stoppage and picketing and sought to invoke the grievance and arbitration procedures specified in the contract. . . .

The Norris–LaGuardia Act was responsive to a situation totally different from that which exists today. In the early part of this century, the federal courts generally were regarded as allies of management in its attempt to prevent the organization and strengthening of labor unions; and in this industrial struggle the injunction became a potent weapon which was wielded against the activities of labor groups. . . .

In 1932 Congress attempted to bring some order out of the industrial chaos that had developed and to correct the abuses which had resulted from the interjection of the federal judiciary into union-management disputes on the behalf of management. Congress, therefore, determined initially to limit severely the power of the federal courts to issue injunctions "in any case involving or growing out of any labor dispute. . . ." Even as initially enacted, however, the prohibition against federal injunctions was by no means absolute. Shortly thereafter Congress passed the Wagner Act, designed to curb various management activities which tended to discourage employee participation in collection action.

As labor organizations grew in strength and developed toward maturity, congressional emphasis shifted from protection of the nascent labor movement to the encouragement of collective bargaining and to administrative techniques for the peaceful resolution of industrial disputes. This shift in emphasis was accomplished, however, without extensive revision of many of the older enactments, including the anti-injunction section of the Norris–LaGuardia Act. Thus it became the task of the courts to accommodate, to reconcile the older statutes with the more recent ones.

* * *

The *Sinclair* decision, however, seriously undermined the effectiveness of the arbitration technique as a method peacefully to resolve industrial disputes without resort to strikes, lockouts, and similar devices. Clearly employers will be wary of assuming obligations to arbitrate specifically enforceable against them when no similar efficacious remedy is available to enforce the concomitant undertaking of the union to refrain from striking. On the other hand, the central purpose of the Norris–LaGuardia Act to foster the growth and viability of labor organizations is hardly retarded—if anything, this goal is advanced—by a remedial device which merely enforces the obligation that the union freely undertook under a specifically enforceable agreement to submit disputes to arbitration. We conclude, therefore, that the unavailability of equitable relief in the arbitration context presents a serious impediment to the congressional policy favoring the voluntary establishment of a mechanism for the peaceful resolution of labor disputes, that the core purpose of the Norris–LaGuardia Act is not sacrificed by the limited use of equitable remedies to further this important policy, and consequently that the Norris–LaGuardia Act does not bar the granting of injunctive relief in the circumstances of the instant case.

Questions

1. Why was the *Sinclair* decision considered wrongfully decided?
2. What reasons were cited by the Court for allowing court enforcement (injunctions) of "no strike" provisions in collectively bargained contracts?

SUITS FOR DAMAGES

In a long line of decisions defining the conditions for federal court suits over violations of collective-bargaining agreements, the Supreme Court began with the decision in the early 1960s that individual union officials could not be held liable for damages caused by a strike in violation of a contract. Later in 1979, the

Court ruled that the union, itself, could not be sued for damages for a wildcat strike not sanctioned by the union. Finally, in 1981 the Court ruled that employers cannot sue their workers for damages caused by wildcat strikes. Instead, the Court said employers have alternative steps to handle wildcat strikes. Wildcat strikers can be fired or disciplined. Moreover, the employer can obtain an injunction to halt a wildcat walkout that could have been arbitrated as provided by the contract. Thus, Section 301 of the Taft–Hartley Act allows a damages remedy for breach of the no-strike provision of a collective-bargaining agreement only against *unions*, not *individuals*, and only when the unions participated in or authorized the strike.

ARBITRATION

Labor arbitration is the process in which a neutral third party, selected jointly by labor and management, decides a dispute which the parties have been unable to resolve. The arbitrator's decision is final and binding and enforceable through the courts. The Supreme Court has approved of labor arbitration in a series of cases in 1960. These cases establish arbitration as the preeminent process in deciding contract disputes. In one case, the company refused to arbitrate what the lower court called a frivolous and patently baseless claim by the union. Consequently, the lower court held the employer was not subject to arbitration under the labor contract. The Supreme Court reversed the lower court's determination and ordered arbitration. The Court identified the proper role of the lower courts in the following language:

> The collective agreement calls for the submission of grievances in the categories which it describes, irrespective of whether a court may deem them to be meritorious. In our role of developing a meaningful body of law to govern the interpretation and enforcement of collective bargaining agreements, we think special heed should be given to the context in which collective bargaining agreements are negotiated and the purpose which they are intended to serve. . . . The function of the court is very limited when the parties have agreed to submit all questions of contract interpretation to the arbitrator. It is confined to ascertaining whether the party seeking arbitration is making a claim which on its face is governed by the contract. Whether the moving party is right or wrong is a question of contract interpretation for the arbitrator. In these circumstances the moving party should not be deprived of the arbitrator's judgment, when it was his judgment and all that it connotes that was bargained for.
>
> The courts, therefore, have no business weighing the merits of the grievance, considering whether there is equity in a particular claim, or determining whether there is a particular language in the written instrument which will support the claim. The agreement is to submit all grievances to arbitration, not merely those which the court will deem meritorious. The processing of even frivolous claims may have therapeutic values of which those who are not a part of the plant environment may be quite unaware.
>
> The union claimed in this case that the company had violated a specific provision of the contract. The company took the position that it had not violated that clause. There was, therefore, a dispute between the parties as to "the meaning, interpretation and

application" of the collective bargaining agreement. Arbitration should have been ordered. When the judiciary undertakes to determine the merits of a grievance under the guise of interpreting the grievance procedure of collective bargaining agreements, it usurps a function which under that regime is entrusted to the arbitration tribunal. *United Steelworkers of Am.* v. *American Mfg. Co.,* 363 U.S. 564 (1960).

Questions

1. Is the Court to separate frivolous and meritorious claims before ordering arbitration?
2. What therapeutic value could result from processing even frivolous claims?

NATIONAL EMERGENCIES

The Taft–Hartley Act sets forth detailed procedures to govern strikes which are deemed to create a national emergency. The act provides that if the President believes a strike will imperil the national health or safety, he may impanel a board of inquiry. This board is directed to investigate the causes and circumstances of the labor controversy and report to the President. After reviewing the report, the President may direct the attorney general to petition a federal district court for an injunction. If the district court finds the continuation of the strike will imperil the national health and safety, the court has jurisdiction to enjoin the strike. Thereafter, bargaining between the parties is to continue under the aid of the Federal Mediation and Conciliation Service. After 60 days, the board of inquiry must submit another report detailing the current status of the dispute and the employer's last offer of settlement. Within the next 15 days, a vote is to be taken among the employees to determine whether they will agree to accept the last offer of the employer. If no settlement is reached, the injunction is dissolved at the end of 80 days.

The hope of the "80-days cooling-off period" is that the parties will be able to reach an agreement. If no agreement is reached, the employees may strike again and no further injunctions are provided by law. Accordingly, Congress must deal with the "national emergency" in some fashion. In 1963, the railroad unions threatened a strike because the railroad companies had proposed modifications of certain work rules. In an effort to avoid the strike, Congress enacted a law requiring compulsory arbitration over the two most controversial work rule changes (the retention of stokers on diesels and the size and complement of train crews). The arbitration panel satisfactorily settled the controversy and avoided the strike. Most elements in American industry and labor would reject the compulsory arbitration alternative as a solution to major labor disputes; nevertheless compulsory arbitration has been utilized on one occasion and thus the possibility of its subsequent employment cannot be ruled out. The fear by both labor and management of congressional action often helps formulate an agreement.

LABOR-MANAGEMENT REPORTING AND DISCLOSURE ACT

The Labor-Management Reporting and Disclosure Act of 1959 (Landrum–Griffin Act) regulates the internal affairs of unions. During the 1950s, congressional hearings produced evidence of misconduct by the officials of some unions. To cope with the abuses, such as embezzlement and "sweetheart" contracts with employers, Congress enacted a wide variety of provisions. Certain provisions, often referred to as a union member's "bill of rights," require elections to be held periodically for union officers and that union members be assured the right to vote, nominate candidates, run for office, or comment on qualifications of candidates for office. Moreover, union members were given the right to attend membership meetings and participate in the voting and deliberations of such meetings. Other provisions of the act require filing of extensive information concerning the financial affairs of the union and its officials. The act outlaws embezzlement of union funds and restricts the making of loans by the union to its officials in excess of a stipulated amount.

In *Hall* v. *Cole*, 83 LRRN 1390 (1973), a union member introduced a set of resolutions alleging undemocratic actions and misguided policies on the part of union officers in the Seafarers Union. When the resolutions were defeated by the union membership, the member was expelled from the union on the grounds that the resolutions violated a union rule prohibiting "deliberate and malicious vilification with regard to execution of the duties of any office." Finding no success with efforts to secure an intraunion remedy, the expelled member filed suit under the Labor-Management Reporting and Disclosure Act, claiming that his expulsion violated the union member's right of free speech. The courts regained union membership for the petitioner and awarded $5,500 in legal fees. The petitioner's vindication of free speech rights was conceived by the courts to have worked to the benefit of all members of the union and, hence, justified the union's bearing the expense of the petitioner's litigation.

When members of the unions feel their rights under the Labor-Management Reporting and Disclosure Act have been violated and internal union procedures are exhausted, the union member may complain to the secretary of labor who, after investigation, may bring an action in court for the vindication of the union member's rights.

Trbovich v. United Mine Workers of America

404 U.S. 528 (1972)
Supreme Court of the United States

Justice Marshall

The Secretary of Labor instituted this action under §402(b) of the Labor-Management Reporting and Disclosure Act of 1959 (LMRDA), to set aside an election of officers of the United Mine Workers of America (UMWA), held on

December 9, 1969. He alleged that the election was held in a manner that violated the LMRDA in numerous respects, and he sought an order requiring a new election to be held under his supervision.

Petitioner, a member of the UMWA, filed the initial complaint with the Secretary that eventually led him to file this suit. Petitioner now seeks to intervene in the litigation pursuant to Fed. Rule Civ. Proc. 24(a), in order (1) to urge two additional grounds for setting aside the election, (2) to seek certain specific safeguards with respect to any new election that may be ordered, and (3) to present evidence and argument in support of the Secretary's challenge to the election. The District Court denied his motion for leave to intervene, on the ground that the LMRDA expressly stripped union members of any right to challenge a union election in the courts, and gave that right exclusively to the Secretary.

The LMRDA was the first major attempt of Congress to regulate the internal affairs of labor unions. Having conferred substantial power on labor organizations, Congress began to be concerned about the danger that union leaders abuse that power, to the detriment of the rank-and-file members. Congress saw the principle of union democracy as one of the most important safeguards against such abuse, and accordingly included in the LMRDA a comprehensive scheme for the regulation of union elections.

Title IV of the statute establishes a set of substantive rules governing union elections, and it provides a comprehensive procedure for enforcing those rules. Any union member who alleges a violation may initiate the enforcement procedure. He must first exhaust any internal remedies available under the constitution and bylaws of his union. Then he may file a complaint with the Secretary of Labor, who "shall investigate" the complaint. Finally, if the Secretary finds probable cause to believe a violation has occurred, he "shall . . . bring a civil action against the labor organization" in federal district court to set aside the election if it has already been held, and to direct and supervise a new election. With respect to elections not yet conducted, the statute provides that existing rights and remedies apart from the statute are not affected. But with respect to an election already conducted, "[T]he remedy provided by this subchapter . . . shall be exclusive."

The critical statutory provision for present purposes is § 403, making suit by the Secretary the "exclusive" post-election remedy for a violation of Title IV. This Court has held that § 403 prohibits union members from initiating a private suit to set aside an election. But in this case, petitioner seeks only to participate in a pending suit that is plainly authorized by the statute; it cannot be said that his claim is defeated by the bare language of the Act. The Secretary, relying on legislative history, argues that § 403 should be construed to bar intervention as well as initiation of a suit by the members. In his view the legislative history shows that Congress deliberately chose to exclude union members entirely from any direct participation in judicial enforcement proceedings under Title IV. The Secretary's argument rests largely on the fact that two alternative proposals figured significantly in the legislative history of Title IV, and each of these rejected bills would have authorized individual union members to bring suit. In the words of the District Court:

> We think that Congress considered two alternatives—suit by union members and suit by the Secretary—and then chose the latter alternative and labelled it 'exclusive' deprives this Court of jurisidiction to permit the former alternative via the route of intervention. . .

That argument misconceives the legislative history and misconstrues the statute. A review of the legislative history shows that Congress made suit by the Secretary the exclusive post-election remedy for two principal reasons: (1) to protect unions from frivolous litigation and unnecessary judicial interference with their elections, and (2) to centralize in a single proceeding such litigations as might be warranted with respect to a single election. Title IV as enacted serves these purposes by referring all complaints to the Secretary so that he can screen out frivolous ones, and by consolidating all meritorious complaints in a single proceeding, the Secretary's suit in federal district court. The alternative proposals were rejected simply because they failed to accomplish these objectives. There is no evidence whatever that Congress was opposed to participation by union members in the litigation, so long as that participation did not interfere with the screening and centralizing functions of the Secretary. . . .

Intervention by union members in a pending enforcement suit, unlike initiation of a separate suit, subjects the union to relatively little additional burden. The principal intrusion on internal union affairs has already been acccomplished in that the union has already been summoned into court to defend the legality of its election. Intervention in the suit by union members will not subject the union to burdensome multiple litigation, nor will it compel the union to respond to a new and potentially groundless suit. Thus, at least insofar as petitioner seeks only to present evidence and argument in support of the Secretary's complaint, there is nothing in the language or the history of the LMRDA to prevent such intervention.

The question is closer with respect to petitioner's attempt to add to the Secretary's complaint two additional grounds for setting aside the union election. These claims the Secretary has presumably determined to be without merit. Hence, to require the union to respond to these claims would be to circumvent the screening function assigned by statute to the Secretary. We recognize that it is less burdensome for the union to respond to new claims in the context of the pending suit than it would be to respond to a new and independent complaint. Nevertheless, we think Congress intended to insulate the union from any complaint that did not appear meritorious to both a complaining member and the Secretary. Accordingly, we hold that in a post-election enforcement suit, Title IV imposes no bar to intervention by a union member, so long as that intervention is limited to the claims of illegality presented by the Secretary's complaint. . . .

The statute plainly imposes on the Secretary the duty to serve two distinct interests, which are related, but not identical. First, the statute gives the individual union members certain rights against their union and "the Secretary of Labor in effect becomes the union member's lawyer" for purposes of enforcing those rights. And second, the Secretary has an obligation to protect the "vital pubic interest in assuring free and democratic union elections that transcends the narrrower interest of the complaining union member." Both functions are important, and they may not always dictate precisely the same approach to the conduct of the litigations. Even if the Secretary is performing his duties, broadly conceived, as well as can be expected, the union member may have a valid complaint about the performance of "his lawyer." Such a complaint, filed by the member who initiated the entire enforcement proceeding, should be regarded as sufficient to warrant relief in the form of intervention.

Questions

1. What functions is the Secretary of Labor to perform under the LMRDA?
2. Why is "intervention" by a union member permissible but adding new charges of illegality to the complaint not permissible?

CONCLUSION

The essence of labor laws is the fostering of collective bargaining. The labor laws outline unfair labor practices that cannot be utilized by management or the union to modify the economic relationship of employer and employees. Having established the boundaries of unfair practices, the parties are left to their respective positions of economic power and political skill in negotiating a labor-management agreement. This collectively bargained contract becomes legally enforceable and establishes the rights and privileges enjoyed by both management and the union. Though not without critics, the labor laws appear to work reasonably well in reducing industrial strife.

CASE PROBLEMS

1. Within Easy-Heat, Inc., an "Employee's Council" was formed, composed only of employees. The firm's attorney spoke to the council to encourage the formation of an in-plant bargaining committee. The speech was made on company time. The company lawyer and facilities were made available for the council to discuss the transformation of the council into a more formally structured labor organization. Soon thereafter a management employee questioned a worker about whether a friend of that worker might want to organize an in-plant group. All of this occurred following an outside union's unsuccessful organizing campaign. The outside union has filed a charge of an 8(a)(2) violation. Decide.

2. After the union lost the election for the formation of a union, it filed a complaint against Florida Steel for alleged unfair labor practices in connection with the election.

   While the charge was pending, Florida Steel distributed a letter to all employees which read in part as follows:

   > . . . If you should want some legal counsel or just help in handling any of the situations described above, all you need to do is let your supervisor know. He will put you in touch with someone who can help you.

   By distributing this letter, did Florida Steel violate Section 8(a)(1)?

3. One election for the formation of a union within Clapper's Manufacturing resulted in a loss for the union, a result openly sought by the company. On the eve of a second such election, the company president questioned an employee about how he thought the election was going to go and how several of his fellow employees planned to vote. On the day of the election, a company supervisor questioned another employee about how the election would go and asked this employee "who he should talk to." The supervisor told a third employee that he planned to question employees in all of the plants about their feelings toward the union. The union lost the second election and initiated charges against the company for violations of 8(a)(1).

   In the circumstances given, were the company's actions lawful?

4. The Retail Store Employees Union fired one of its employees who then presented a wrongful discharge claim against the union to the NLRB. Anna P. was asked by the union president to testify at the resulting unfair labor practice hearing, to substantiate improprieties allegedly committed by the discharged employee. Although pressured to testify by the president who claimed she had knowledge of such misconduct, Anna P. refused and denied that she could substantiate the grounds for termination. Anna P. was not called as a witness, although she could have been subpoenaed.

   Thereafter, Anna P. was fired by the president by means of a letter in which the president detailed his reasons for letting her go, including that she "conveniently forgot" facts about the discharged employee, that she was disloyal, and that she had released a union mailing list to a man running for union office.

   Anna P. brought her own complaint to the NLRB, charging an unfair labor practice under 8(a)(4) LMRA, that the union fired her for her refusal to testify. Section 8(a)(4) prohibits discharge of or discrimination against an employee who has filed a charge or given testimony in an NLRB proceeding. What is the result?

chapter 20
FAIR AND SAFE EMPLOYMENT LAWS

FAIR EMPLOYMENT PRACTICES

There are four major federal laws which regulate fair and equal rights in employment. Title VII of the Civil Rights Act of 1964, as amended by the Equal Employment Opportunities Act of 1972, forbids union and employer discrimination based on race, color, religion, sex, or national origin. The Equal Pay Act of 1963 requires equal pay for men and women doing equal work. The Age Discrimination in Employment Act of 1967 prohibits discriminatory hiring practices against job applicants between the ages of 40 and 70. The Fair Labor Standards Act of 1938 has three broad objectives: (a) the establishment of minimum wages, reflecting concepts of a "rudimentary minimum standard of living"; (b) the encouragement of a ceiling on hours of labor which was to result in an increase in the scope of employment by increasing the cost of overtime work, defined as work in excess of 40 hours per week; and (c) the discouragement of "oppressive child labor." Several amendments have been made to the 1938 act, increasing the minimum hourly wage rate and enlarging the scope of the act by expanding its coverage.

EQUAL EMPLOYMENT OPPORTUNITY

One of the major purposes of Title VII of the Civil Rights Act of 1964 is to eliminate job discrimination based on race, color, religion, sex, or national origin. The act prevents employer or union discrimination for any of these reasons in regard to discharge, refusal to hire, compensation, or conditions of employment. The act is generally applicable to employers or labor unions with 15 or more employees and employment agencies of any size.

The Civil Rights Act of 1964 created the Equal Employment Opportunities Commission (EEOC) which is granted the authority to investigate and conciliate grievances under the act. The commission investigates complaints after giving a similar state agency an opportunity to handle the problem. If the commission is unable to satisfactorily resolve the dispute through conciliation, the EEOC may litigate the issues in federal court. If a "pattern and practice" of discrimination exists, the commission may bring a class action suit. The commission, through the issuance of standards, has put employers on notice about personnel policies that could lead to a charge of "pattern and practice" discrimination. The outlined six standards are as follows:

1. Employers who follow policies and practices that result in "low utilization" of available minorities and women despite the law's requirement that they recruit, hire, and promote such persons.
2. Employers who pay minorities and women less than other employers who use such workers for comparable work.
3. Companies that pay minorities and women less than other workers in comparable job categories.
4. Employers who follow personnel policies that have an "adverse impact" on those protected by federal antidiscrimination laws when such policies cannot be justified by "business necessity."
5. Employers whose discriminatory practices are likely to be emulated by other employers because of the company's size, influence in the community, or competitive position in the industry.
6. Employers who have an opportunity to hire and promote more minorities and women because of expansion or high turnover rates but neglect such workers in filling those positions.

Certain exemptions are provided in the act. It is not an unlawful employment practice for an employer to hire employees on the basis of his or her religion, sex, or national origin where these items have a bona fide occupational qualification reasonably necessary to the normal operation of the particular enterprise. However, it should be noted that there is no bona fide occupational qualification exemption for either race or color.

To prevent the Civil Rights Act of 1964 from violating the constitutional protection of free exercise of religion, a provision was inserted that states it is not unlawful for religious organizations to hire employees of a particular religion to perform work connected with carrying on its activities. Consequently, the Catholic Church could legally refuse to hire anyone other than members of the Catholic faith in carrying out its religious activities. However, secular employers have a statutory obligation to make reasonable accommodations for the religious observance or practice of its employees, if such accommodations are not an undue hardship on the employer. Consider the person whose religion regarded Saturday as the Sabbath and forbade work on the Sabbath. The union refused to allow any violations in the seniority system and the person had insufficient seniority to bid for a shift with Saturdays off. The company refused to permit the employee to work a four-day week or to replace the employee with another worker on the fifth day. Nevertheless, the employee's discharge did not violate the law because "accommodations" to the employee's beliefs would have caused an "undue hardship" on the employer.[1]

RACIAL DISCRIMINATION

Griggs v. Duke Power Co.
401 U.S. 424 (1971)
Supreme Court of the United States

Chief Justice Burger

We granted the writ in this case to resolve the question whether an employer is prohibited by the Civil Rights Act of 1964, Title VII, from requiring a high school education or passing of a standardized general intelligence test as a condition of employment in or transer of jobs when (a) neither standard is shown to be significantly related to successful job performance, (b) both requirements operate to disqualify Negroes at a substantially higher rate than white applicants, and (c) the jobs in question formerly had been filled only by white employees as part of a long-standing practice of giving preference to whites.

* * *

The objective of Congress in the enactment of Title VII is plain from the language of the statute. It was to achieve equality in employment opportunities and remove barriers that have operated in the past to favor an identifiable group of white employees over other employees. Under this Act, practices, procedures, or tests neutral on their face, and even neutral in terms of intent, cannot be maintained if they operate to "freeze" the status quo of prior discriminatory employment practices.

The Court of Appeals' opinion, and the partial dissent, agreed that, on the record in the present case, "whites fare far better on the Company's alternative requirements" than Negroes. This consequence would appear to be directly traceable to race. Basic intelligence must have the means of articulation to manifest itself fairly in a testing process. Because they are Negroes, petitioners have long received inferior education in segregated schools. . . . Congress did not intend by Title VII, however, to guarantee a job to every person regardless of qualifications. In short, the Act does not command that any person be hired simply because he was formerly the subject of discrimination, or because he is a member of a minority group. What is required by Congress is the removal of artificial, arbitrary, and unnecessary barriers to employment when the barriers operate invidiously to discriminate on the basis of racial or other impermissible classifications.

. . . The Act proscribes not only overt discrimination but also practices that are fair in form, but discriminatory in operation. The touchstone is business necessity. If an employment practice which operates to exclude Negroes cannot be shown to be related to job performance, the practice is prohibited.

On the record before us, neither the high school completion requirement not the general intelligence test is shown to bear a demonstrable relationship to successful performance of the jobs for which it was used. Both were adopted, as the Court of Appeals noted, without meaningful study of their relationship to job-performance ability. Rather, a vice president of the Company testified, the requirements were instituted on the Company's judgment that they generally would improve the overall quality of the work force.

The evidence, however, shows that employees who have not completed high school or taken the tests have continued to perform satisfactorily and make progress in departments for which the high school and test criteria are now used. The promotion record of present employees who would not be able to meet the new criteria thus suggests the possibility that the requirements may not be needed even for the limited purpose of preserving the avowed policy of advancement within the Company. . . .

The Court of Appeals held that the Company had adopted the diploma and test requirements without any "intention to discriminate against Negro employees." We do not suggest that either the District Court or the Court of Appeals erred in examining the employer's intent; but good intent or absence of discriminatory intent does not redeem employment procedures or testing mechanisms that operate as "built-in headwinds" for minority groups and are unrelated to measuring job capability. . . .

The facts of this case demonstrate the inadequacy of broad and general testing devices as well as the infirmity of using diplomas or degrees as fixed measures of capability. History is filled with examples of men and women who rendered highly effective performance without the conventional badges of accomplishment in terms of certificates, diplomas, or degrees. Diplomas and tests are useful servants, but Congress has mandated the common-sense proposition that they are not to become masters of reality.

The Company contends that its general intelligence tests are specifically permitted by §703(h) of the Act. That section authorizes the use of "any professionally developed ability test" that is not "designed, intended, *or used* to discriminate because of race. . . ." (Emphasis added.)

The Equal Employment Opportunity Commission, having enforcement responsibility, has issued guidelines interpreting §703(h) to permit only the use of job-related tests. The administrative interpretation of the Act by the enforcing agency is entitled to great deference. Since the Act and its legislative history support the Commission's construction, this affords good reason to treat the guidelines as expressing the will of Congress. . . .

Nothing in the Act precludes the use of testing or measuring procedures; obviously they are useful. What Congress has forbidden is giving these devices and mechanisms controlling force unless they are demonstrably a reasonable measure of job performance. Congress has not commanded that the less qualified be preferred over the better qualified simply because of minority origins. Far from disparaging job qualifications as such, Congress has made such qualifications the controlling factor, so that race, religion, nationality, and sex become irrelevant. What Congress has commanded is that any tests used must measure the person for the job and not the person in the abstract.

Questions

1. Must the employer "intend" to discriminate before the employment practice is unlawful?
2. Why did the intelligence test used by the Duke Power Company fail to be an acceptable exception to the Act of 1964?

Once it is shown that an employment practice (testing mechanisms) has a discriminatory impact, according to the Court in *Griggs,* the burden is on the employer to prove that any given requirement has a "manifest relationship" to the jobs in question and thereby represents a "business necessity." The justices also said that "Congress directed the thrust of the Act to the *consequences* of employment practices, not simply motivation."

For an employer to safely use a testing mechanism and satisfy the "job-relatedness" test of *Griggs,* the employer must comply with the 1978 Uniform Guidelines on Employee Selection Procedures prepared by federal enforcement agencies. One district court in interpreting the Guidelines ruled that an allegedly discriminatory promotion examination cannot be saved by a "job relatedness" study that fails to address alternative selection procedures. Such a study alone is unimpressive for providing the "business necessity" element to rebut a *prima facie* case of racial discrimination in violation of Title VII. Alternative selection procedures which would not have had the same racially discriminatory impact might be capable of being developed.

In the *Griggs* decision the seniority rights of the discrimination victims were "to be considered on a plant-wide, rather than a departmental, basis." The Court added that, "to apply a strict departmental seniority would result in the continuation of present effects of past discrimination." After the *Griggs* decision, most courts and employers operated on the principle that any seniority system that locked minorities or women into positions of previous discrimination was illegal. However, addressing the question in *U.S.* v. *Teamsters,* 431 U.S. 324 (1977), the Supreme Court said that a seniority system which perpetuated the effects of discrimination that took place before Title VII became law (July 1965) was legal. The Court refused to bar a departmental seniority system that was part of a *bona fide* labor contract when it was neutral and equally applied. The company seniority system can perpetuate past discrimination, but only if it is part of a *bona fide* labor contract and the original discrimination took place before July 1965. The Supreme Court dealt with this issue again in the following case.

American Tobacco Company v. Patterson

50 L.W. 4364 (1982)
Supreme Court of the United States

Justice White

Under *Griggs* v. *Duke Power Co.*, a *prima facie* violation of Title VII of the Civil Rights Act of 1964, "may be established by policies or practices that are neutral on their face and in intent but that nonetheless discriminate in effect against a particular group." A seniority system "would seem to fall under the *Griggs* rationale" if it were not for §703(h) of the Civil Rights Act. That section provides in pertinent part:

> Notwithstanding any other provision of this subchapter, it shall not be an unlawful employment practice for an employer to apply different standards of compensation, or different terms, conditions, or privileges of employment pursuant to a *bona fide* seniority or merit system, . . . provided that such differences are not the result of an intention to discriminate because of race, color, religion, sex, or national origin, nor shall it be an unlawful employment practice for an employer to give and to act upon the results of any professionally developed ability test provided that such test, its administration or action upon the results is not designated, intended, or used to discriminate because of race, color, religion, sex, or national origin. . . .

Under §703(h) the fact that a seniority system has a discriminatory impact is not alone sufficient to invalidate the system; actual intent to discriminate must be proved. The Court of Appeals in this case, however, held that §703(h) does not apply to seniority systems adopted after the effective date of the Civil Rights Act. We granted the petition for *certiorari* to address the validity of this construction of the section.

I

Petitioner American Tobacco Company operates two plants in Richmond, Virginia, one which manufactures cigarettes and one which manufactures pipe tobacco. Each plant is divided into a prefabrication department, which blends and prepares tobacco for further processing, and a fabrication department, which manufactures the final product. Petitioner Bakery, Confectionery & Tobacco Workers' International Union and its affiliate Local 182 are the exclusive collective bargaining agents for hourly-paid production workers at both plants.

It is uncontested that prior to 1963 the company and the union engaged in overt race discrimination. The union maintained two segregated locals, and black employees were assigned to jobs in the lower paying prefabrication departments. Higher paying jobs in the fabrication departments were largely reserved for white employees. An employee could transfer from one of the predominately black prefabrication departments to one of the predominantly white fabrication departments only by forfeiting his seniority.

In 1963, under pressure from government procurement agencies enforcing the antidiscrimination obligations of government contractors, the company abolished departmental seniority in favor of plant-wide seniority and the black union local was merged into the white local. However, promotions were no longer based solely on seniority but rather on seniority plus certain qualifications, and employees lost accumulated seniority in the event of a transfer between plants. Between 1963 and 1968, when this promotions policy was in force, virtually all vacancies in the fabrication departments were filled by white employees due to the discretion vested in supervisors to determine who was qualified.

In November 1968 the company proposed the establishment of 9 lines of progression, 6 of which are at issue in this case. The union accepted and ratified the lines of progression in 1969. Each line of progression generally consisted of two jobs. An employee was not eligible for the top job in the line until he had worked in a bottom job. Four of the six lines of progression at issue here consisted of nearly all-white top jobs from the fabrication departments linked with nearly all-white bottom jobs from the fabrication departments; the other two consisted of all-black top jobs from the prefabrication departments linked with all-black bottom jobs from the prefabrication departments. The top jobs in the white lines of progression were among the best-paying jobs in the plants.

On January 3, 1969, respondent Patterson and two other black employees filed charges with the Equal Employment Opportunity Commission alleging petitioners had discriminated against them on the basis of race. The EEOC found reasonable cause to believe that petitioners' seniority, wage, and job classification practices violated Title VII. After conciliation efforts failed, the employees filed a class action in District Court in 1973 charging petitioners with racial discrimination in violation of Title VII. Following trial, the District Court held that the petitioner's seniority, promotion, and job classification practices violated Title VII. The Court found that 6 of the 9 lines of progression were not justified by business necessity and "perpetuated past discrimination on the basis of . . . race." The Court enjoined the company and the union from further use of the 6 lines of progression. The Court of Appeals for the Fourth Circuit affirmed and remanded for further proceedings with respect to remedy.

On remand petitioners moved to vacate the District Court's 1974 orders and to dismiss the complaints on the basis of this Court's decision in *Teamsters* v. *United States,* which held that §703(h) insulates *bona fide* seniority systems from attack even though they may have discriminatory impact on minorities. The District Court denied the motions, holding that petitioners' seniority system "is not a *bona fide* system under *Teamsters* . . . because this system operated right up to the day of trial in a discriminatory manner. . . ."

The Court of Appeals . . . held that . . . "Congress intended the immunity accorded seniority systems by §703(h) to run only to those systems in existence at the time of title VII's effective date, and of course to routine post-Act application of such systems." We reverse.

II

Petitioners argue that the plain language of §703(h) applies to post-Act as well as pre-Act seniority systems. The respondent employees claim that the provision "provides a narrow exemption [from the ordinary discriminatory impact test] which was specifically designed to protect *bona fide* seniority systems which were in existence before the effective date of Title VII."

* * *

On its face §703(h) makes no distinction between pre- and post-Act seniority systems, just as it does not distinguish between pre- and post-Act merit systems or pre- and post-Act ability tests. . . .

III

Although the plain language of §703(h) makes no distinction between pre-Act and post-Act seniority systems, the court below found support for its distinction between the two in the legislative history. Such an interpretation misreads the legislative history.

We have not been informed of and have not found a single statement anywhere in the legislative history saying that §703(h) does not protect seniority systems adopted or modified after the effective date of Title VII. Nor does the legislative history reveal that Congress intended to distinguish between adoption and application of a *bona fide* seniority system. The most which can be said for the legislative history of §703(h) is that it is inconclusive with respect to the issue presented in the case.

* * *

Going behind the plain language of a statute in search of a possibly contrary Congressional intent is "a step to be taken cautiously" even under the best of circumstances. "[I]n light of its unusual legislative history and the absence of the usual legislative materials," we would in any event hesitate to give dispositive weight to the legislative history of §703(h). More importantly, however, the history of §703(h) does not support the far-reaching limitation on the terms of §703(h) announced by the court below and urged by respondents. The fragments of legislative history cited by respondent, regardless of how liberally they are construed, do not amount to a clearly expressed legislative intent contrary to the plain language of the statute.

IV

Our prior decisions have emphasized that "seniority systems are afforded special treatment under Title VII itself," and have refused to narrow §703(h) by reading into it limitations not contained in the statutory language. In *Teamsters* v. *United States,* we held that §703(h) exempts from Title VII the disparate impact of a *bona fide* seniority system even if the differential treatment is the result of pre-Act racially discriminatory employment practices. Similarly, by holding that "[a] discriminatory act which is not made the basis for a timely charge is the legal equivalent of a discriminatory act which occurred before the statute was passed," *United Air Lines, Inc.* v. *Evans,* 431 U.S. 553, 558 (1977), the Court interpreted §703(h) to immunize seniority systems which perpetuate post-Act discrimination. Thus taken together, *Teamsters* and *Evans* stand for the proposition stated in *Teamsters* that "[s]ection 703(h) on its face immunizes *all bona fide* seniority systems, and does not distinguish between the perpetuation of pre- and post-

Act" discriminatory impact. Section 703(h) makes no distinction between seniority systems adopted before its effective date and those adopted after its effective date. Consistent with our prior decisions, we decline petitioners' invitation to read such a distinction into the statute.

Seniority provisions are of "overriding importance" in collective bargaining, and they "are universally included in these contracts." The collective bargaining process "lies at the core of our national labor policy. . . ." Congress was well aware in 1964 that the overall purpose of Title VII, to eliminate discrimination in employment, inevitably would, on occasion, conflict with the policy favoring minimal supervision by courts and other governmental agencies over the substantive terms of collective bargaining agreements. Section 703(h) represents the balance Congress struck between the two policies, and it is not this Court's function to upset that balance.

Because a construction of §703(h) limiting its application to seniority systems in place prior to the effective date of the statute would be contrary to its plain language, inconsistent with our prior cases, and would run counter to the national labor policy, we vacate the judgment below and remand for further proceedings consistent with this opinion.

Questions

1. Under the *Griggs* decision, a practice may be neutral on its face and in intent but cause a disproportionate negative impact on a particular group, and thereby become illegal unless required by "business necessity." A seniority system may have a disproportionate impact on a particular group and fall under the *Griggs* rationale (ignoring "intent") if not exempted by Section 703(h). From the language of Section 703(h), is a seniority system with a disproportionate impact exempt from a violation of Title VII?
2. The respondent employees claimed that Section 703(h) contains a narrow exemption from the discriminatory impact rationale to protect *bona fide* seniority systems that were in existence *before* the effective date of Title VII. How does the Supreme Court respond to this argument?
3. What other legislative enactment of Congress suggests a policy contrary to Title VII and consistent with Section 703(h)?
4. When can a seniority system be illegal because of racial discrimination?

REVERSE DISCRIMINATION

United Steelworkers v. Weber
443 U.S. 193 (1979)
Supreme Court of the United States

Justice Brennan

In 1974 petitioner United Steelworkers of America (USWA) and petitioner Kaiser Aluminum & Chemical Corporation (Kaiser) entered into a master collective-bargaining agreement covering terms and conditions of employment at 15 Kaiser plants. The agreement contained an affirmative action plan designed to eliminate conspicuous racial imbalances in Kaiser's then almost exclusively white craft work forces. Black craft hiring goals were set for each Kaiser plant equal to the percentage of blacks in the respective local labor forces. To enable plants to meet these goals, on-the-job training programs were established to teach unskilled production workers—black and white—the skills necessary to become craft workers. The plan reserved for black employees 50% of the openings in these newly created in-plant training programs.

This case arose from the operation of the plan at Kaiser's plant in Gramercy, La. Until 1974 Kaiser hired as craft workers for that plant only persons who had had prior craft experience. Because blacks had long been excluded from craft unions, few were able to present such credentials. As a consequence, prior to 1974 only 1.83% (five out of 273) of the skilled craft workers at the Gramercy plant were black, even though the work force in the Gramercy area was approximately 39% black.

Pursuant to the national agreement Kaiser altered its craft hiring practice in the Gramercy plant. Rather than hiring already trained outsiders, Kaiser established a training program to train its production workers to fill craft openings. Selection of craft trainees was made on the basis of seniority, with the proviso that at least 50% of the new trainees were to be black until the percentage of black skilled craft workers in the Gramercy plant approximated the percentage of blacks in the local labor force.

During 1974, the first year of the operation of the Kaiser-USWA affirmative action plan, 13 craft trainees were selected from Gramercy's production work force. Of these, 7 were black and 6 white. The most junior black selected into the program had less seniority than several white production workers whose bids for admission were rejected. Thereafter one of those white production workers, respondent Brian Weber, instituted this class action in the United States District Court for the Eastern District of Louisiana.

The complaint alleged that the filling of craft trainee positions at the Gramercy plant pursuant to the affirmative action program had resulted in junior black employees receiving training in preference to more senior white employees, thus discriminating against respondent and other similarly situated white employees in violation of §§703 (a) and (d) of Title VII. . . .

We emphasize at the outset the narrowness of our inquiry. Since the Kaiser-USWA plan does not involve state action, this case does not present an alleged violation of the Equal Protection Clause of the Constitution. Further, since the Kaiser-USWA plan was adopted voluntarily, we are not concerned with what Title VII requires or with what a court might order to remedy a past proven violation of the Act. The only question before us is the narrow statutory issue of whether Title VII *forbids* private plans that accord racial preferences in the manner and for the purpose provided in the Kaiser-USWA plan. . . .

Respondent argues that Congress intended in Title VII to prohibit all race-conscious affirmative action plans. Respondent's argument rests upon a literal interpretation of §§703 (a) and (d) of the Act. Those sections make it unlawful to "discriminate . . . because of . . . race" in hiring and in the selection of apprentices for training programs. Since, the argument runs, . . . the Kaiser-USWA affirmative action plan operates to discriminate against white employees solely because they are white, it follows that the Kaiser-USWA plan violates Title VII.

Respondent's argument is not without force. But it overlooks the significance of the fact that the Kaiser-USWA plan is an affirmative action plan voluntarily adopted by private parties to eliminate traditional patterns of racial segregation. In this context respondent's reliance upon a literal construction of §703 (a) and (d) . . . is misplaced. It is a "familiar rule, that a thing may be within the letter of the statute and yet not within the statute, because not within its spirit, nor within the intention of its makers." The prohibition against racial discrimination in §703 (a) and (d) of Title VII must therefore be read against the background of the legislative history of Title VII and the historical context from which the act arose. . . .

Congress' primary concern in enacting the prohibition against racial discrimination in Title VII of the Civil Rights Act of 1964 was with "the plight of the Negro in our economy." Before 1964, blacks were largely relegated to "unskilled and semi-skilled jobs." As a consequence "the relative position of the Negro worker [was] steadily worsening. . . ."

Congress feared that the goals of the Civil Rights Act—the integration of blacks into the mainstream of American society—could not be achieved unless this trend were reversed. And Congress recognized that that would not be possible unless blacks were able to secure jobs "which have a future." . . . Accordingly, it was clear to Congress that "the crux of the problem [was] to open employment opportunities for Negroes in occupations which have been traditionally closed to them," and it was to this problem that Title VII's prohibition against racial discrimination in employment was primarily addressed.

It plainly appears from the House Report accompanying the Civil Rights Act that Congress did not intend wholly to prohibit private and voluntary affirmative action efforts as one method of solving this problem. The Report provides:

> No bill can or should lay claim to eliminating all the causes and consequences of racial and other types of discrimination against minorities. There is reason to believe, however, that national leadership provided by the enactment of Federal legislation dealing with the most troublesome problems *will create an atmosphere conducive to voluntary or local resolution of other forms of discrimination.* H. R. Rep. No. 914, 88th Cong., 1st Sess. (1963), at 18. (Emphasis supplied.)

Given this legislative history, we cannot agree with respondent that Congress intended to prohibit the private sector from taking effective steps to accomplish the goal that Congress designed Title VII to achieve. The very statutory words intended as a spur or catalyst to cause "employers and unions to self-examine and to self-evaluate their employment practices and to endeavor to eliminate, so far as possible, the last vestiges of an unfortunate and ignominious page in this country's history," cannot be interpreted as an absolute prohibition against all private, voluntary, race-conscious affirmative action efforts to hasten the elimination of such vestiges. It would be ironic indeed if a law triggered by a Nation's concern over centuries of racial injustice and intended to improve the lot of those who had "been excluded from the American dream for so long," constituted the first legislative prohibition of all voluntary, private, race-conscious efforts to abolish traditional patterns of racial segregation and hierarchy.

Our conclusion is further reinforced by examination of the language and legislative history of §703(j) of Title VII. Had Congress meant to prohibit all race-conscious affirmative action, as respondent urges, it easily could have provid[ed] that Title VII would not require or *permit* racially preferential integration efforts. But Congress did not choose such a course. Rather Congress added Section 703(j) which . . . provides that nothing contained in Title VII "shall be interpreted to *require* any employer . . . to grant preferential treatment . . . to any group because of the race . . . of such . . . group on account of" a *de facto* racial imbalance in the employer's work force. The section does *not* state that "nothing in Title VII shall be interpreted to *permit*" voluntary affirmative efforts to correct racial imbalances. The natural inference is that Congress chose not to forbid all voluntary race-conscious affirmative action.

. . . In view of this legislative history and in view of Congress' desire to avoid undue federal regulation of private businesses, use of the word "require" rather than the phrase "require or permit" in Section 703(j) fortifies the conclusion Congress did not intend to limit traditional business freedom to such a degree as to prohibit all voluntary, race-conscious affirmative action.

We therefore hold that Title VII's prohibition in Sections 703(a) and (d) against racial discrimination does not condemn all private, voluntary, race-conscious affirmative action plans. . . .

We conclude, therefore, that the adoption of the Kaiser-USWA plan for the Gramercy plant falls within the area of discretion left by Title VII to the private sector voluntarily to adopt affirmative action plans designed to eliminate conspicuous racial imbalance in traditionally segregated job categories. . . .

Questions

1. Why was the charge of "reverse discrimination" not within the purpose of Title VII?
2. Did Congress intend to prohibit all race-conscious affirmative action? What language could Congress have used if it intended to accomplish that goal?

SEXUAL HARASSMENT

Bundy v. Jackson
641 F. 2d 934 (1981)
U.S. Court of Appeals (D.C. Cir.)

In *Barnes* v. *Costle*, 561 F.2d 983 (D.C. Cir., 1977), we held an employer who abolished a female employee's job to retaliate against the employee's resistance of his sexual advances violated Title VII of the Civil Rights Act of 1964. The appellant in this case asks us to extend *Barnes* by holding that an employer violates Title VII merely by subjecting female employees to sexual harassment, even if the employee's resistance to that harassment does not cause the employer to deprive her of any tangible job benefits.

The District Court in this case made an express finding of fact that in appellant's agency "the making of improper sexual advances to female employees [was] standard operating procedure, a fact of life, a normal condition of employment," and that the director of the agency, to whom she complained of the harassment, failed to investigate her complaints or take them seriously. Nevertheless, the District Court refused to grant appellant any declaratory or injunctive relief, concluding that sexual harassment does not in itself represent discrimination "with respect to . . . terms, conditions, or privileges of employment" within the meaning of Title VII. . . .

* * *

[We] have held that Title VII places the same restrictions on federal and District of Columbia agencies as it does on private employers. . . .

We . . . made clear in *Barnes* that sex discrimination within the meaning of Title VII is not limited to disparate treatment founded solely or categorically on gender. Rather, discrimination is sex discrimination whenever sex is for no legitimate reason a substantial factor in the discrimination.

We thus have no difficulty inferring that [appellant] Bundy suffered discrimination on the basis of sex. Moreover, applying *Barnes*, we have no difficulty ascribing the harassment—the "standard operating procedure"—to Bundy's employer, the agency. Although Delbert Jackson himself appears not to have used his position as Director to harass Bundy, an employer is liable for discriminatory acts committed by supervisory personnel, and there is obviously no dispute that the men who harassed Bundy were her supervisors. *Barnes* did suggest that the employer might be relieved of liability if the supervisor committing the harassment did so in contravention of the employer's policy and without the employer's knowledge, and if the employer moved promptly and effectively to rectify the offense. Here, however, Delbert Jackson and other officials in the agency who had some control over employment and promotion decisions had full notice of harassment committed by agency supervisors and did virtually nothing to stop or even investigate the practice. And though there was ample evidence in this case that at least two other women in the agency suffered from this harassment, *Barnes* makes clear that the employer could be held liable even if Bundy were the only victim, since Congress intended Title VII to protect *individuals* against class-based prejudice.

We thus readily conclude that Bundy's employer discriminated against her on the basis of sex. What remains is the novel question whether the sexual harassment of the sort Bundy suffered amounted by itself to sex discrimination with respect to the "*terms, conditions, or privileges of employment*." Though no court has as yet so held, we believe that an affirmative answer follows ineluctably from numerous cases finding Title VII violations where an employer created or condoned a substantially discriminatory work *environment*, regardless of whether the complaining employees lost any tangible job benefits as a result of the discrimination.

Bundy's claim on this score is essentially that "conditions of employment" include the psychological and emotional work environment—that the sexually stereotyped insults and demeaning propositions to which she was indisputably subjected and which caused her anxiety and debilitation, illegally poisoned that environment. This claim invokes the Title VII principle enunciated by Judge Goldberg in *Rogers* v. *Equal Employment Opportunity Com'n*, 454 F.2d 234 (5th Cir. 1971). . . . Granting that the express language of Title VII did not mention this situation, Judge Goldberg stated:

> Congress chose neither to enumerate specific discriminatory practices, nor to elucidate *in extenso* the parameter of such nefarious activities. Rather, it pursued the path of wisdom by being unconstrictive, knowing that constant change is the order of our day and that the seemingly reasonable practices of the present can easily become the injustices of the morrow. . . .

The Fifth Circuit then concluded that the employer had indeed violated Title VII, Judge Goldberg explaining that "terms, conditions, or privileges of employment"

> is an expansive concept which sweeps within its protective ambit the practice of creating a work environment heavily charged with ethnic or racial discrimination as to destroy completely the emotional and psychological stability of minority group workers. . . .

. . . Racial or ethnic discrimination against a company's minority clients may reflect no intent to discriminate directly against the company's minority employees, but in poisoning the atmosphere of employment it violates Title VII. Sexual stereotyping through discriminatory dress requirements may be benign in intent, and may offend women only in a general, atmospheric manner, yet it violates Title VII. Racial slurs, though intentional and directed at individuals, may still be just verbal insults, yet they too may create Title VII liability. How then can sexual harassment, which injects the most demeaning sexual stereotypes into the general work environment and which always represents an intentional assault on an individual's innermost privacy, not be illegal?

* * *

Thus, unless we extend the *Barnes* holding, an employer could sexually harass a female employee with impunity by carefully stopping short of firing the employee or taking any other tangible actions against her in response to her resistance, thereby creating the impression—the one received by the District Court in this case—that the employer did not take the ritual of harassment and resistance "seriously."

Indeed, so long as women remain inferiors in the employment hierarchy, they may have little recourse against harassment beyond the legal recourse Bundy seeks in this case. The law may allow a woman to prove that her resistance to the harassment cost her her job or some economic benefit, but this will do her no good if the employer never takes such tangible actions against her.

And this, in turn, means that so long as the sexual situation is constructed with enough coerciveness, subtlety, suddenness, or onesidedness to negate the effectiveness of the woman's refusal, or so long as her refusals are simply ignored while her job is formally undisturbed, she is not considered to have been sexually harassed.

It may even be pointless to require the employee to prove that she "resisted" the harassment at all. So long as the employer never literally forces sexual relations on the employee, "resistance" may be a meaningless alternative for her. If the employer demands no response to his verbal or physical gestures other than good-natured tolerance, the woman has no means of communicating her rejection. She neither accepts nor rejects the advances; she simply endures them. She might be able to contrive proof of rejection by objecting to the employer's advances in some very visible and dramatic way, but she would do so only at the risk of making her life on the job even more miserable. It hardly helps that the remote prospect of legal relief under *Barnes* remains available if she objects so powerfully that she provokes the employer into firing her.

The employer can thus implicitly and effectively make the employee's endurance of sexual intimidation a "condition" of her employment. The woman then faces a "cruel trilemma." She can endure the harassment. She can attempt to oppose it, with little hope of success, either legal or practical, but with every prospect of making the job even less tolerable for her. Or she can leave her job, with little hope of legal relief and the likely prospect of another job where she will face harassment anew.

Bundy proved that she was the victim of a practice of sexual harassment and a discriminatory work environment permitted by her employer. Her rights under Title VII were therefore violated. We thus reverse the District Court's holding on this issue and remand it to that court so it can fashion appropriate injunctive relief.

The Final Guidelines on Sexual Harassment in the Workplace (Guidelines) issued by the Equal Employment Opportunity Commission on November 10, 1980, offer a useful basis for injunctive relief in this case. . . . The general goal of these Guidelines is *preventive*. An employer may negate liability by taking "immediate and appropriate corrective action" when it learns of any illegal harassment, but the employer should fashion rules within its firm or agency to ensure that such corrective action never becomes necessary.

Applying these Guidelines to the present case, we believe that the Director of the agency should be ordered to raise affirmatively the subject of sexual harassment with all his employees and inform all employees that sexual harrassment violates Title VII of the Civil Rights Act of 1964, the Guidelines of EEOC . . . and the policy of the agency itself. The Director should also establish and publicize a scheme whereby harassed employees may complain to the Director immediately and confidentially. The Director should promptly take all necessary steps to investigate and correct any harassment, including warnings and appropriate discipline directed at the offending party, and should generally develop other means of preventing harassment within the agency.

Perhaps the most important part of the preventive remedy will be a prompt and effective procedure for hearing, adjudicating, and remedying complaints of sexual harassment within the agency. . . .

Questions

1. Bundy's claim for lost wages due to the denial of a promotion because of the sexual discrimination was remanded to the District Court with the following instructions:

   To establish a *prima facie* case of illegal denial of promotion in retaliation against the plaintiff's refusal of sexual advances by her supervisors, the plaintiff must show (1) that she was a victim of a pattern or practice of sexual harassment attributable to her employer (Bundy has, of course, already shown this); and (2) that she applied for and was denied a promotion for which she was technically eligible and of which she has a reasonable expectation. If the *prima facie* case is made out, the employer then must bear the burden of showing, by clear and convincing evidence, that he had legitimate nondiscriminatory reasons for denying the claimant promotion. . . . [If] the employer successfully rebuts the *prima facie* case, the claimant should still have the opportunity to prove that the employer's purported reasons were mere pretexts.

   If Bundy was eligible for promotion and had reasonable expectation of the promotion, how could the employer show a "legitimate and nondiscriminatory" reason for denying the promotion?
2. How is an employer to avoid liability for sexual harassment by its supervisors and employees?

EQUAL PAY FOR EQUAL WORK

Wirtz, Secretary of Labor, v. Basic Inc.
256 F. Supp. 786 (1966)
U.S. District Court (Nev.)

. . . The case for the plaintiff was presented by a feminine attorney of the Department of Labor, resisted by a masculine attorney of the Nevada Bar, and considered by a Judge who, for the purposes of this case at least, must be sexless, a possibility not apparent when the oath of office was taken and one which may bespeak the appointment of older judges. . . .

The employees involved in the instant dispute are laboratory analysts Jo Ann Barredo, Ann Jones, and Byron O'Dell. Barredo was hired by Thompson, the then Chief Chemist, on September 1, 1959, and was trained under his supervision to perform the analytical tests required to determine the metallurgy of the various ores and compounds required to be analyzed. She had had no previous experience. Jones was hired by Thompson in 1953 and was trained by him. She had had no previous experience. O'Dell was hired by Thompson in March, 1962. He was trained by Thompson, with the assistance of Barredo and Jones, in the particular analytical procedures used at Basic. In his early life, he had been employed as a miner and mill superintendent and from 1949 until 1962, was employed by Standard Slag Co. at Gabbs, Nevada, as a laboratory analyst, using similar analytical procedures to those at Basic to determine the metallurgy of similar ores and products. . . .

The primary work of all three laboratory analysts is the running of relatively simple, standardized chemical tests on various materials performed strictly in accordance with the company's testing manual and directives. . . .

After the passage of the Equal Pay Act of 1963, the then Chief Chemist, Thompson, discussed with his superiors the necessity of either equalizing the pay of the laboratory analysts or setting up legal job classifications of jobs requiring different skill, effort, or responsibility or which were to be performed under different working conditions, but no final action was taken. Thompson resigned before September 1, 1964, and the present Chief Chemist, Lawson, succeeded him. . . .

The defendant's answer to the complaint, after denying any discrimination among employees on the basis of sex, affirmatively alleges:

> Any lesser pay received by Jo Ann Barredo and Ann Jones results from the fact that their work requires less skill, effort, and/or responsibility than the work of higher paid employees who work under similar conditions. . . .

The burden of proof in this case is upon the Secretary to show that the jobs under consideration require equal work, equal skill, equal effort, and equal responsibility and are performed under similar working conditions. The defendant has invoked none of the statutory exceptions permitting payment differentials made pursuant to a seniority system, a merit system, a system which measures earnings by quantity or quality of production or a differential based on any other factor other than sex, which are affirmative defenses the burden of proof of which would be borne by the employer.

The Secretary has promulgated comprehensive regulations interpreting the equal pay provisions. Such regulations are generally valid and binding . . . and our perusal of them persuades us that the Secretary has produced a helpful and reasonable aid to a correct interpretation of the law.

Fundamental in the application of the law is the premise that it establishes an objective standard requiring that a judgment with respect to alleged discrimination between sexes be based upon the requirements of the particular jobs being compared, rather than a comparison of the skill of individual employees, the effort of individual employees, or their previous training and experience. "Application of the equal pay standard is not dependent on job classifications or titles but depends rather on actual job requirements and performance." Equal does not mean identical and insubstantial differences in the skill, effort, and responsibility requirements of particular jobs should be ignored. The job requirements should be viewed as a whole.

The preponderance of the evidence clearly shows that the work performed by O'Dell, Barredo, and Jones is substantially equal and that their jobs as laboratory analysts require substantially equal skill, effort, and responsibility. The only requirement, as we see it, as to which there is room for a reasonable difference of opinion concerns the existence of similar working conditions.

We have no doubt that this defendant may, as it apparently has attempted to do, establish a position for a male analyst designated "Shift Analysts," if you will, where the working conditions are different from other analysts' jobs, provided the classification is made in good faith and there is no unreasonable discrimination on the basis of sex. The Secretary agrees. "However, in situations where some employees performing work . . . have working conditions substantially different from those required for the performance of other jobs the equal pay principle would not apply." The evidence shows that O'Dell's swing shift work every two weeks is performed under substantially different working conditions; the supervising chemists are absent after 5 p.m., the other analysts are absent after 5 p.m., and part of the work is at night.

The difficulty here is that what the defendant company has done belies any announced intention to differentiate between a day shift and a swing shift analyst on the basis of dissimilar working conditions. The facts are: Between June 11, 1964, the effective date of the Equal Pay Act, and September 1, 1964, O'Dell, Barredo, and Jones all worked the day shift, performed the same work, and received different wages; since September 1, 1964, O'Dell has worked a swing shift every alternate two-week period and has received an additional five cents per hour for such work; during the alternate two-week periods that O'Dell works the day shift, his job requires substantially the same skill, effort, and responsibility as those performed by Barredo and Jones, yet he receives a higher hourly rate of compensation. We think these facts compel the conclusion that the job classification "Swing Analyst" is a paper classification unrelated to the true working conditions, and that the five-cent pay differential for swing shift work is intended to compensate for the different working conditions.

Section 800.145 of the Regulations states:

> When applied without distinction to employees of both sexes, shift differentials, incentive payments, production bonuses, performance and longevity raises, and the like will not result in equal pay violations. For example, in an establishment where men and women are employed on a job, but only men work on the night shift for which a night shift differential is paid, such a differential would not be prohibited. However, the payment of a higher hourly rate to all men on that job for all hours worked because some of the men may occasionally work nights would result in a prohibited wage differential.

These provisions seem reasonable on their face and as applied to our situation. There could be no effective enforcement of the equal pay provisions if differentials between sexes were permitted for all hours worked because of the substantially different working conditions and responsibilities entailed in a specific part of the work performed at identifiable times and places. As a "Shift Analyst," O'Dell is entitled to a different rate of pay while he is working as a shift analyst, but not while working on the day shift. He and the company apparently have agreed that five cents per hour is a reasonable differential.

The Equal Pay Act of 1963, which, like other Congressional enactments concerning employment practices, was induced by social conditions and working conditions pertaining in metropolitan and industrial areas, presents unique headaches in application to an agrarian-mining-tourist economy such as Nevada's where employers of large numbers of employees are few and far between. Nevertheless, just as the interpretive opinions of the Act by industrially oriented courts in Michigan, New York, Ohio, California, and elsewhere will be persuasive authority for us in future cases, so should we interpret the law with deference to the expressed intention of Congress in the light of its nationwide application. Provincial differences in business practices and customs are not excepted by the law.

Anomalously, the compensation of two females, Barredo and Jones, will also be equalized by our decree. We see no escape from this result. The last proviso of 29 U.S.C. 206(d)(1) states:

> That an employer who is paying a wage rate differential in violation of this subsection shall not, in order to comply with the provisions of this subsection, reduce the wage rate of any employee.

We cannot adjust O'Dell's wage rate downward, and inasmuch as Barredo and Jones are doing equal work, must increase the wage rate of both their jobs to equal O'Dell's.

Questions

1. Must jobs be identical in all respects to require equal pay?
2. What justifications are allowed for differences in wage rates?

AGE DISCRIMINATON

The Age Discrimination in Employment Act of 1967 prohibits discriminatory hiring and firing practices against individuals between the ages of 40 and 70. In 1979, 3,097 complaints of age discrimination were filed with the EEOC. In 1980 the EEOC received 8,779 such complaints. Sixty days after registering their complaints with the EEOC, individuals may file suits on their own. Most experts agree that the explosive growth of these actions will continue, fueled by periodic weakening of the economy with its ensuing layoffs, by an aging workforce, and by the increasing propensity of employees to fight back when their companies fire them.

Coates v. National Cash Register Co.

433 F. Supp. 655 (1977)
U.S. District Court (WD. VA.)

Section 623(a)(1) of the Age Discrimination in Employment Act . . . states that it is unlawful for an employer to discharge or to discriminate against any individual "because of such individual's age." The phrase "because of such individual's age" is used several times throughout the prohibitory sections of ADEA and constitutes the standard by which to judge employment decisions. The problem with this standard for courts has been to interpret how much weight age must be given in the employment decision before the Act is violated. . . .

The court in *Laugesen* v. *Anaconda Co.*, 510 F.2d 307 (6th Cir. 1975) adopted a "determining factor" test and explained how the jury should judge the legality of the employment decision:

> [W]e believe that it was essential for the jury to understand from the instructions that there could be more than one factor in the decision to discharge him and that he was nevertheless entitled to recover if one such factor was his age and if in fact it made a difference in determining whether he was retained or discharged. This is so even though the need to reduce the employee force generally was also a strong, and perhaps even more compelling reason. . . .

NCR has several reasons for its reduction of the Danville field engineers staff, including deteriorating economic conditions in mid-1975. While the company can discharge its employees, it cannot base the decision about which employee to discharge on age or on factors created by age discrimination.

NCR's decision to discharge plaintiffs was not directly based on age, but it was based on the training of plaintiffs. The evidence clearly established that the relative training levels of NCR employees was directly related to the age of the employees. So by using the training level as the basis of the discharge decision, NCR indirectly discharged plaintiffs because of their age. Therefore this court holds that the training or lack of training, which ostensibly is an objective and valid criterion for employment decisions cannot form the basis of an employment decision when that lack of training is created by age discrimination. The age discrimination which invalidates an employment decision need not be direct or intentional. This court further holds that both plaintiffs were discharged "because of" their "age."

Damages

Besides asking for reinstatement, plaintiffs requested back wages from May 2, 1975, until reinstatement, liquidated damages and attorney's fees and costs. . . .

To summarize the measure of back pay, it is still the difference between the salary an employee would have received but for the violation of the Act and the salary actually received from other employment. The period of back pay is measured from the time of the loss of employment as a result of the violation to the time when the employee accepts or declines reinstatement at his former position or at a position of comparable status, salary, benefits, and potential for advancement. The back pay amount computed in this way must be reduced by severance pay received, unemployment compensation collected, and any amounts earnable with reasonable diligence. Finally, the back pay amount should be increased by the value of any pension benefits, health insurance, seniority, leave-time, or other fringe benefits which the employee would have accrued during the back pay period but for the violation of the Act.

* * *

Both plaintiffs also prayed for liquidated damages and attorney's fees and costs. Liquidated damages are only available for "willful violations" of ADEA.

In this case, the advisory jury was instructed that they should find that the discharges were willful violations of ADEA only if the acts were "done voluntarily and intentionally, and with the specific intent to do something which is forbidden by law." This court finds that neither discharge was a willful violation of the law; therefore, no liquidated damages are available to plaintiffs.

Finally, it is well settled that plaintiffs who are victims of age discrimination are entitled to reasonable attorney's fees and costs.

Questions

1. In what fashion did NCR discriminate on the basis of age?
2. Besides gaining reinstatement, what damages were ordered to be paid to the plaintiffs?
3. When the Supreme Court ruled in *McMann* v. *United Airlines* that retirement could be forced when an employee reached an age prescribed in a *bona fide* retirement pension plan, it suggested that if Congress wanted to change that rule, it should pass a law. As a result, Congress passed a law in 1978 which forbids the involuntary retirement of an employee at any age up to 70. The new rule was to be phased in with differing dates for differing types of employees, but generally applicable to all by the beginning of 1980. Can one expect that Congress will eventually eliminate all compulsory retirement ages?

UNEMPLOYMENT AND INJURY PROTECTION

Considerable state and federal legislation has been enacted to protect the employee from physical injury and loss of job. The principal statutes covering these risks are unemployment compensation laws, workers' compensation laws, and the Occupational Safety and Health Act of 1970.

UNEMPLOYMENT COMPENSATION

Unemployment compensation is usually administered jointly by the states and the federal government. It provides compensation to the unemployed. Although qualifications vary from state to state, the employee generally must be off the job for at least a week, remain ready for work in other jobs requiring similar training and experience, and must not have quit his or her previous employment without cause or been fired for misconduct. Generally, if the unemployment is the result of a labor dispute in which the employee is actively participating, the employee is disqualified. The following case involves an administrative officer's determination of whether the employee was qualified for unemployment compensation when unemployment resulted from a labor dispute.

Armstrong v. Prophet Foods Co.

287 N.E. 2d 286 (1972)
Common Pleas Court of Richland County

Denver Armstrong and some 19 other claimants have appealed from a decision of the Board of Review, Ohio Bureau of Employment Services dated June 30, 1971. . . which in effect disallowed claimants' claims for benefits on the basis that their unemployment was due to a labor dispute.

General Motors Corporation owned and operated one of its Fisher Body Plants near Mansfield and the production workers were members of a local union of United Auto Workers. A labor dispute developed between the union members and General Motors and this culminated in a strike by said local union . . . [P]icket lines were set up around the entrance to the plant.

Now there existed . . . at said plant, some two cafeterias and one dining room . . . [which] were provided for and used by the production workers and other workers for the General Motors Corporation. Prophet Foods Company handled the cafeterias [and] dining room . . . under an agreement with General Motors. . . .

When the picket lines were set up the Prophet Foods Company employees were thrown out of work. . . .

Now, Prophet Foods is a totally separate corporation from General Motors, and no one at General Motors either controls or has the right to control the activity of any employee of Prophet Foods. Prophet Foods had its own collective bargaining agreement with Prophet Foods employees, and this was in full force during all times involved herein. At none of the times involved herein was there any labor dispute between Prophet Foods and any of its employees. At no time was there any labor dispute between employees of Prophet Foods and General Motors or any other employer.

It was after the labor dispute started at General Motors that appellants were laid off by Prophet Foods, since there was no work available—no customers to serve.

. . . [T]he referee denied said claimed rights to receive unemployment compensation benefits because their unemployment was due to what he termed the dispute between the General Motors corporation and the United Auto Workers. . . .

The court notes that before an amendment to the law in 1963 the statutory disqualification in effect then provided:

"Lost his employment or has left his employment by reason of a labor dispute . . . *at* the factory, establishment, or other premises *at* which he was employed." (Emphasis by the court.)

It appears a dispute "at the factory, establishment or other premises" under the old law would have involved all employees of any employer. But the law was changed. This change was effective October 20, 1963. It will be noted that a word was stricken and the phrase now reads "owned or operated by the employer by which" he was employed. Under the present law, status of the employee takes on a new significance. If an employer in a labor dispute thus shuts down or reduces operations at another location it owns or operates, then its employees at such other location would be disqualified. If the employer is in a labor dispute resulting in a supplier receiving no orders and thus has to lay off people then those people are not disqualified. Their employer, the supplier, is not in the labor dispute. He is a separate employer. From the evidence in the instant case, the referee initially adopted the two-unit theory with relationship between Prophet Foods and General Motors. The plant was not viewed as a single unit. According to the theory adopted there are two distinct premises within the gates at General Motors, their manufacturing facility and the second which is the cafeteria operations by Prophet Foods.

It naturally follows under the theory adopted, it must be accepted that a labor dispute at the establishment or premises that is operated by General Motors is not a labor dispute at the establishment or premises that is operated by Prophet Foods. Under the statute appellants would be entitled to receive unemployment compensation unless their unemployment was due to a labor dispute at the premises operated by Prophet Foods. The referee expressly found that General Motors did not operate the premises used by Prophet and that the unemployment of appellants herein was due solely to the labor dispute at General Motors. There was no labor dispute at the food operation business of Prophet Foods. Further, the Unemployment Compensation Act must be liberally construed. A referee cannot broadly construe a proviso or exception which restricts the general scope of the Act. Such must be strictly construed.

The courts in other states have not disqualified claims where somebody else's employer has a labor dispute with his employees. . . .

Ordinarily an employee can't receive unemployment compensation if unemployment results from a labor dispute of the employer and the employees of the same company. If employees under such circumstances could rely on unemployment compensation, it would place the employers at a disadvantage. But in our case at hand these workers are mere victims of the circumstances, the type of situation prompting the adoption of unemployment compensation laws for relief.

The decision of the Board of Review denying appellants compensation as prayed for is unlawful, unreasonable and contrary to the manifest weight of the evidence and is hereby reversed.

WORKERS' COMPENSATION

In common law, if an employee was injured as the result of the negligence of the employer, the employee was entitled to recover money damages. However, the common law also provided the employer with three defenses known as (1) assumption of risk, (2) contributory negligence, and (3) the fellow servant rule. These defenses normally provided the employer with an escape from liability to the employee. For example, if an employer knowingly supplied a hazardous working tool for employees an employee injured in handling the equipment would be entitled to recover damages. However, if the employee had understood the hazards of the defective equipment and knowingly assumed the risk of this injury, the employee would be barred from recovery. In addition, the employee could not recover if he or she was in some way contributorially negligent in the manner in which the machine was handled. Finally, if a fellow servant was negligent and caused the injury to the employee, the employee was denied recovery under the fellow servant rule. Hence, at common law it was only in rare instances that an employee was able to gain a recovery against an employer because of an injury sustained in the working environment.

State workers' compensation statutes were enacted to provide a system to pay workers or their families if a worker was accidentally killed or injured while employed. In addition, occupational diseases which arise out of and in the course of employment are likewise covered. Under these acts, the negligence or fault of the employer in causing the employee injury is not an issue. Instead, the law affords the employee an assured recovery and in turn, limits the dollar amount of damages that the employer must pay to the injured employee. Normally, the employers pay monies into a state fund and an industrial commission decides which employees are entitled to recovery. Some states allow an employer to be self-insured or to purchase insurance for the protection of the employees.

The following case illustrates a typical workers' compensation situation.

Bunkley v. Republic Steel

30 Ohio Misc. 39 (1972)

Common Pleas Court of Cuyahoga County

. . . The Republic Steel Company, is a self insurer under the Workmen's Compensation Act of Ohio. It is the claim of the plaintiff that he ruptured himself when he, and two other workmen, were lifting, by hand, a heavy article called a "twyer" or "twill" which weighed approximately 175 to 200 pounds and inserting it into an opening in a Republic furnace at an elevation about five feet about the floor level of the defendant's mill. . . .

It is the contention of Republic that claimant is not entitled to have a judgment entered which would have the effect of requiring Republic to pay his surgical and hospital expenses incidental to the repairing of his hernia, compensation for temporary, total disability for the period when he was hospitalized for the surgery and subsequent convalescence and for such other allowances as he is entitled to receive as a result of his injury, including an award for attorney fees payable by Republic because of the necessity for bringing this lawsuit.

The bases for Republic's contention as to why plaintiff should not be entitled to the benefits of the Workmen's Compensation Act with reference to his rupture may be summarized as follows:

1. The incident in which claimant contends he was ruptured did not occur. The jury found, upon the basis of adequate testimony, that the incident did in fact occur.
2. The words used by the claimant in his description of the incident were not such as to describe the sustaining of an injury as required by R.C. 4123.01. . . .

There is no validity to any of these contentions of Republic.

R.C. 4123.01 provides as follows:

> (C) 'Injury' includes any injury, whether caused by external accidental means or accidental in character and result, received in the course of, and arising out of the injured employee's employment.

"Accident" is defined as follows:

> An event which takes place without one's foresight or expectation; or an unusual effect of a known cause and, therefore, not expected; an event which, under the circumstances, is unusual and not expected to the person to whom it happens.

Counsel for the defendant wasted considerable trial time in this action in attempting to elicit statements from the plaintiff to the effect that there was no unexpected, unusual, or fortuitous happening in connection with plaintiff's injury, other than the occurrence of the injury.

Testimony of such a happening was unnecessary in order to establish plaintiff's right to recovery even though his testimony did include such evidence.

Plaintiff testified that on the day of the injury, the twill in the furnace had burned out and that it became necessary for himself and two other workmen to replace it; that a twill is inserted into the furnace by lifting it up by hand to a point where there is an opening in the furnace at about his shoulder height—above five feet; that:

"You can't put it in straight. You have to put it in sideways in order to get it in and sometimes that quill [*sic*] will get stuck and you jerk on it and that is when I felt this pain (indicating in the groin area);" "I went over and sat down for awhile and the pain left;" "I went back to work. It wasn't long before it was time to quit anyway;" "Well, that pain kept coming but it never stayed. It come and go till I notice it begin to swell. I had swelled up. It would swell up and go back down and it starts having pains and that is when I went to this Dr. Oppenheim." He testified he was having the swelling in the same spot where he felt the pain; that he was operated on there; that he had never previously had any swelling over there. . . .

It was the contention of Republic that before a workman can participate in the Workmen's Compensation Fund as a result of an injury sustained while at work and engaged in the advancement of the work of the employer, that an unusual occurrence such as a slip, fall, jerk, jar, external force, unusual strain, pressure, etc., must be described as having brought about the injury, even though it was sustained when a workman was extending himself beyond his physical capabilities in order to further this business of his employer.

Beyond question, the plaintiff's description of the occurrence, even though in less than artful words, if believed by the jury, sufficiently complied with the . . . statutory requirements that are brought into question herein by Republic.

Questions

1. Was the employee's injury the result of an accident as defined in R.C. 4123.01?
2. How did Republic define an accident under R.C. 4123.01?

OCCUPATIONAL SAFETY AND HEALTH ACT

The Occupational Safety and Health Act of 1970 (OSHA) was the result of testimony and documentary evidence presented before Congress which pointed out that the American work site was a place of peril. More than 14,500 workers were killed annually in connection with their job, a mortality rate two and one half times greater than experienced by U.S. troops in Vietnam. More than 2,200,000 workers are disabled in America each year, and this represents a loss of about 250 million worker-days, which is in excess of lost work time due to strikes. Of course, these statistics do not measure the social and emotional cost to the individuals injured.

The act requires business organizations to be maintained free from recognized hazards. The duty placed on the employer is no more than the common law concept that a person must refrain from actions that will cause harm to others. Three federal agencies were created to develop and enforce occupational safety and health standards. The Occupational Safety and Health Administration is a component part of the Department of Labor with authority to promulgate standards, make inspections, and enforce the act. The National Institute for Occupational Safety and Health (NIOSH) is a component part of the Department of Health and Health Services. Its primary function is to conduct research on various safety and health problems and recommend standards for OSHA administrators to adopt. The Occupational Safety and Health Review Commission is an independent agency whose primary functions are to handle all appeals from actions taken by OSHA administrators and to assess penalties recommended by OSHA administrators.

Variances

Variances from promulgated standards may be petitioned for and granted under certain circumstances. A *permanent* variance may be permitted if the secretary of labor decides that employers have demonstrated that they are using or will use safety measures that are at least as effective as the OSHA standards from which the variance is sought. A *temporary* variance will be granted only if the company can establish that it lacks the material, personnel, equipment, or some other item to comply with the standard and that it is taking all available steps to protect the employees against the hazard contemplated by the standard. Moreover, the company must demonstrate that it has an effective program to bring about compliance in the future. However, cost of compliance is not a valid factor to be considered in application for a variance.

Inspections

OSHA compliance officers may enter and inspect all facilities of any establishment covered by OSHA, which includes any business "affecting commerce." The employer or a designated representative participates in an opening conference with the compliance officer and then accompanies the officer during inspection of the facilities. The officer may confer with employees if no employee representative accompanies the officer during inspection. In any case, the officer may question any employee in private.

OSHA inspectors are not permitted to make "partial" inspections. They must make a complete inspection which occurs without advance warning.

The OSHA representative must point out and discuss with the employees accompanying him or her any violation that the inspector discovers. However, the compliance officer does not suggest solutions or methods of correction to any violation discovered. After the inspection, the compliance officer will confer with the employer and advise the employer concerning any conditions and practices which may constitute safety or health violations.

Violations and Citations

When the inspector discovers an alleged violation, he or she issues the company a written citation which will describe the specific nature of that violation and the standard allegedly violated. The citation will also fix a time for abatement. All citations will be issued by the area director of OSHA and sent to the employer by certified mail. Thereafter, each citation must be prominently posted at or near the place where the violation occurred. There are four types of violations.

Imminent Danger. The act defines imminent danger as "any conditions or practices in any place of employment which are such that a danger exists which could reasonably be expected to cause death or serious physical harm immediately or before the imminence of such danger can be eliminated through the enforcement procedures otherwise provided by this Act." Consequently, when an inspection officer determines that an imminent danger exists, he or she will try to have the danger corrected immediately through voluntary compliance. The employer will be advised that such a danger exists and, if it threatens any employees, they will also be informed of the imminent danger. Such violations, of course, carry a penalty.

Serious Violation. A serious violation is defined under the act as one in which there is a "substantial probability" that the consequences of an accident would be death or serious physical harm unless the employer did not, and could not with the exercise of "reasonable diligence," know the hazard was present. In OSHA's initial enforcement, before a serious violation occurred, the inspector had to find "substantial probability" of both a violating condition *and* that death or serious harm would result. More recent OSHA policy states that there need only be exposure to a violating condition that *could* result in injury or illness *and* that it is "reasonably predictable" that the result would be death or serious physical harm. The consequence of this reinterpretation is that the OSHA inspector no longer needs to consider the degree of probability of whether an accident or illness will occur in classifying a violation as serious. If a serious violation is determined, a monetary penalty must be assessed.

Nonserious Violation. A nonserious violation occurs when the likely consequence of the violation is something less than death or serious physical harm, or if the employer did not know of the hazard. For example, a violation of housekeeping standards may result in a tripping hazard which could be classified as nonserious. Nonserious violations may or may not carry a monetary penalty.

De Minimis Violation. Instead of a citation, the officer will issue a notice for *de minimis* violations which have no direct relation to safety or health. An example of a *de minimis* violation is a lack of partitions in toilet facilities.

Other types of violations include (*a*) willful violations and (*b*) repeated violations.

A willful violation occurs when evidence shows either of the following:

1. The employer committed an intentional and knowing violation of the act.
2. Even though the employer did not consciously violate the act, he or she was aware that a hazardous condition existed and yet made no reasonable effort to eliminate it.

A repeated violation occurs when a second citation is issued for a violation. It differs from a failure to abate in that it is clear the employer has abated an earlier violation but a second violation of the same standard has occurred.

Record-Keeping Requirements

Every employer with more than seven employees is covered by the act and is required to keep occupational injury and illness records for each employee. The employer must keep records for each employee at each building or plant at which the employee reports for work. Each record must be kept and updated for a continuous five-year period and made available for inspection at any time in that period.

To aid in the enforcement of the act, employers are required to make reports of work-related injuries and diseases to OSHA. The administrators of OSHA summarize the data and make periodic reports to the President and Congress on the progress of their administration. Moreover, OSHA utilizes the data received from industry to promulgate rules of safety which must be followed by employers.

If an employee is killed in an industrial accident or if five or more employees are hospitalized by one accident, the Department of Labor must be notified within 48 hours. The company will be fined if OSHA is not so notified. Thereafter, a complete inspection of the premises on which the accident occurred is mandatory.

EMPLOYER'S DUTIES

Ace Sheeting & Repair v. Occup. S. & H. Review Commission
555 F.2d 439 (1977)
U.S. Court of Appeals (5th Cir.)

The facts are undisputed. Petitioner Ace Sheeting and Repair Company is a roof repair company. In September 1973 J. C. Ledger, the owner of Ace, and employee Stroud were replacing corrugated metal panels on the roof of a warehouse in Houston. The roof was pitched rather steeply and contained 60 skylight openings arranged in two rows running the length of the building. The skylights were covered with a translucent plastic material called coralux. There was no guard rail or cover around or over any of these skylights. While walking to another section of the roof to obtain additional materials Stroud stepped in the middle of one of the coralux sheets. The sheet gave way beneath his 175-pound weight, and Stroud fell 25 feet to his death.

A few days after this fatality the Secretary of Labor inspected the job site. On the basis of this inspection, Ace was served with a citation for violation of § 1926.500(b)(4). That section provides:

> Wherever there is danger of falling through a skylight opening, it shall be guarded by a fixed standard railing on all exposed sides or a cover capable of sustaining the weight of a 200-pound person.

This regulation was promulgated by the Secretary under the Act. Title 29 U.S.C.A. § 654 (a)(2) imposes on all employers covered by the Act the duty to comply with such regulations. The proposed penalty in the citation served on Ace was a $30 fine.

Ace challenged the citation, and a hearing was held before an administrative law judge. . . . The administrative law judge vacated the citation on the ground that the Secretary had failed to prove that compliance with the regulation was feasible under the circumstances. The Commission reversed by a two-to-one vote. Ace petitioned this Court for review of that decision. . . .

The outcome of this case turns on who has the burden of proof. Must the Secretary prove that compliance with the regulation is feasible, as thought by the administrative law judge; or is feasibility of compliance assumed unless the employer proves otherwise?

Title 29 U.S.C.A. § 654(a) creates two kinds of obligations requiring employers to take steps for the occupational safety and health of their employees:

Each employer—

(1) shall furnish to each of his employees employment and a place of employment which are free from recognized hazards that are causing or are likely to cause death or serious physical harm to his employees;

(2) shall comply with occupational safety and health standards promulgated under this chapter.

Paragraph (1) has come to be called the "general duty clause," while paragraph (2) is referred to as the "specific duty clause." This case involves a safety standard promulgated under the specific duty clause. The Act itself gives no guidance as to who must bear the burden of proving the feasibility of eliminating a particular hazard under either clause.

Ace relies on *National Realty & Construction Co., Inc.* v. *OSHRC,* 489 F.2d 1257 (1973), to show that this burden is properly placed on the Secretary. But *National Realty* dealt with the general duty clause. No regulation or standard guided the employer as to the way to eliminate the hazard there involved. The D.C. Circuit for that reason placed the burden on the Secretary of demonstrating in what manner the Company's conduct fell short of the statutory mandate. The court reasoned that "the Secretary must be constrained to specify the particular steps a cited employer should have taken to avoid citation, and to demonstrate the feasibility and likely utility of those measures."

Two circuits have extended the *National Realty* principle to "specific duty clause" situations. . . .

In both [of those cases] . . . however, there was no specific direction as to what the employer should do. The regulations involved did nothing more than create, in effect, a general duty of the employer to meet a safety standard, without stating what specific employer conduct was required for compliance.

Here, the regulation stated specific ways for the employer to eliminate the hazard. If the employer put up guard rails or covered the skylights, the safety standard would have been met. If for any reason guard rails or covers are not feasible, the employer knows this better than anyone else, and it is reasonable to require him to come forward with the evidence to prove it.

Regulations are promulgated only after industry-wide comment during which time general feasibility considerations can be voiced. If a regulation contains a proposed method of abating a safety hazard which employers consider to be infeasible in the ordinary case, they can directly challenge the regulation as factually unsupported. Furthermore, a particular employer who finds that he cannot comply with the safety measures required by the regulations can request a variance. . . . When the citation stage is reached, it is eminently reasonable for courts to cast upon the employer the burden of proving impossibility of compliance.

The standard prescribed the precise conduct required of the employer. It may be easily complied with in many shops. Others may have difficulty, but where compliance with either of two specific alternatives, a guard rail or cover, would eliminate the hazard with which the deceased employee in this case was confronted, the employer should prove why he cannot meet either of those alternatives. We therefore hold that where a specific duty standard contains the method by which the work hazard is to be abated, the burden of proof is on the employer to demonstrate that the remedy contained in the regulation is infeasible under the particular circumstances.

To state this rule is to decide the present case. The factual decisions of the Commission are to be sustained if supported by substantial evidence on the record as a whole. Ace argues that even if it did have the burden of showing infeasibility, that burden was carried by the testimony of the Secretary's witnesses. Ace itself presented no evidence as to why it could not use skylight covers on this particular roof. Although the Secretary's witnesses did express some concern that skylight covers might slide off the pitched roof, the possibility of using "some type of abrasive surface on the bottom of a covering to . . . prevent the covering from sliding off the roof" was also discussed. In any event, on the state of the record, it was not the Secretary's job to describe precisely how covers or guard rails could be placed on Ace's premises. There is therefore sufficient evidence in the record to support the Commission's finding that "[i]mpossibility has not been established in this case." That being so, the citation for violation of 29 C.F.R. § 1926.500(b)(4) was proper, and the Commission's decision enforcing the $30 penalty is affirmed.

Questions

1. What is the employer's "general duty" under the act?
2. What is the employer's responsibility under the "specific duty clause"?
3. When must the Secretary of Labor prove that compliance with the regulations of OSHA is feasible in order to sustain its citations and penalties? When does the violating employer have the burden of proof that feasibility of compliance was nonexistent?

DANGER—REFUSAL TO WORK

Whirlpool v. Marshall
445 U.S. 1 (1980)
Supreme Court of the United States

Justice Stewart

The Occupational Safety and Health Act of 1970 (Act) prohibits an employer from discharging or discriminating against any employee who exercises "any right afforded by" the Act. The Secretary of Labor (Secretary) has promulgated a regulation providing that, among the rights that the Act so protects, is the right of an employee to choose not to perform his assigned task because of a reasonable apprehension of death or serious injury coupled with a reasonable belief that no less drastic alternative is available. The question presented in the case before us is whether this regulation is consistent with the Act.

I

The petitioner company maintains a manufacturing plant in Marion, Ohio, for the production of household appliances. Overhead conveyors transport appliance components throughout the plant. To protect employees from objects that occasionally fall from these conveyors, the petitioner has installed a horizontal wire mesh guard screen approximately 20 feet above the plant floor. This mesh screen is welded to angle-iron frames suspended from the building's structural steel skeleton.

Maintenance employees of the petitioner spend several hours each week removing objects from the screen, replacing paper spread on the screen to catch grease drippings from the material on the conveyors, and performing occasional maintenance work on the conveyors themselves. To perform these duties, maintenance employees usually are able to stand on the iron frames, but sometimes find it necessary to step onto the steel mesh screen itself.

In 1973 the company began to install heavier wire in the screen because its safety had been drawn into question. Several employees had fallen partly through the old screen, and on one occasion an employee had fallen completely through to the plant floor below but had survived. . . .

On June 28, 1974, a maintenance employee fell to his death through the guard screen in an area where the newer, stronger mesh had not yet been installed. Following this incident, the petitioner effectuated some repairs and issued an order strictly forbidding maintenance employees from stepping on either the screens or the angle-iron supporting structure. . . .

On July 7, 1974, two of the petitioner's maintenance employees . . . reported for the night shift at 10:45 p.m. Their foreman, after himself walking on some of the angle-iron frames, directed the two men to perform their usual maintenance duties on a section of the old screen. Claiming that the screen was unsafe, they refused to carry out this directive. The foreman then sent them to the personnel office, where they were ordered to punch out without working or being paid for the remaining six hours of the shift. The two men subsequently received written reprimands, which were placed in their employment files.

A little over a month later, the Secretary filed suit alleging that the petitioner's actions against [the employees] constituted discrimination in violation of Section 11(c)(1) of the Act. As relief, the complainant prayed that the petitioner be ordered to expunge from its personnel files all references to the reprimands issued to the two employees, and for a permanent injunction requiring the petitioner to compensate the two employees for the six hours of pay they had lost by reason of their disciplinary suspensions.

. . . The District Court . . . denied relief, holding that the Secretary's regulation was inconsistent with the Act and therefore invalid.

The Court of Appeals for the Sixth Circuit reversed the District Court's judgment. . . .

The Act itself creates an express mechanism for protecting workers from employment conditions believed to pose an emergent threat of death or serious injury. Upon receipt of an employee inspection request stating reasonable grounds to believe that an imminent danger is present in a workplace, OSHA must conduct an inspection. In the event this inspection reveals workplace conditions or practices that "could reasonably be expected to cause death or serious physical harm immediately or before the imminence of such danger can be eliminated through the enforcement procedures otherwise provided by" the Act, the OSHA inspector must inform the affected employees and the employer of the danger and notify them that he is recommending to the Secretary that injunctive relief be sought. At this juncture, the Secretary can petition a federal court to restrain the conditions or practices giving rise to the imminent danger. By means of a temporary restraining order or preliminary injunction, the court may then require the employer to avoid, correct, or remove the danger or to prohibit employees from working in the area.

To ensure that this process functions effectively, the Act expressly accords to every employee several rights, the exercise of which may not subject him to discharge or discrimination. An employee is given the right to inform OSHA of an imminently dangerous workplace condition or practice and request that OSHA inspect that condition or practice. He is given a limited right to assist the OSHA inspector in inspecting the workplace, and the right to aid a court in determining whether or not a risk or imminent danger in fact exists. Finally, an affected employee is given the right to bring an action to compel the Secretary to seek injunctive relief if he believes the Secretary has wrongfully declined to do so.

In the light of this detailed statutory scheme, the Secretary is obviously correct when he acknowledges in his regulation that, "as a general matter, there is no right afforded by the Act which would entitle employees to walk off the job because of potential unsafe conditions at the workplace." By providing for prompt notice to the employer of an inspector's intention to seek an injunction against an imminently dangerous condition, the legislation obviously contemplates that the employer will normally respond by voluntarily and speedily eliminating the danger. And in the few instances where this does not occur, the legislative provisions authorizing prompt judicial action are designed to give employees full protection in most situations from the risk of injury or death resulting from an imminently dangerous condition at the worksite.

As this case illustrates, however, circumstances may sometimes exist in which the employee justifiably believes that the express statutory arrangement does not sufficiently protect him from death or serious injury. Such circumstances will probably not often occur, but such a situation may arise when (1) the employee is ordered by his employer to work under conditions that the employee reasonably believes pose an imminent risk of death or serious bodily injury, and (2) the employee has reason to believe that there is not sufficient time or opportunity either to seek effective redress from his employer or to apprise OSHA of the danger.

Nothing in the Act suggests that those few employees who have to face this dilemma must rely exclusively on the remedies expressly set forth in the Act at the risk of their own safety. But nothing in the Act explicitly provides otherwise. Against this background of legislative silence the Secretary has exercised his rulemaking power under [the law] and has determined that, when an employee in good faith finds himself in such a predicament, he may refuse to expose himself to the dangerous condition, without being subjected to "subsequent discrimination" by the employer.

* * *

The regulation clearly conforms to the fundamental objective of the Act—to prevent occupational deaths and serious injuries. The Act, in its preamble, declares that its purpose and policy is "to assure so far as possible every working man and woman in the Nation safe and healthful working conditions and to *preserve* our human resources . . ." 29 U.S.C. Section 651(b). (Emphasis added.)

To accomplish this basic purpose, the legislation's remedial orientation is prophylactic in nature. The Act does not wait for an employee to die or become injured. It authorizes the promulgation of health and safety standards and the issuance of citations in the hope that these will act to prevent deaths or injuries from ever occurring. It would seem anomalous to construe an act so directed and constructed as prohibiting an employee, with no other reasonable alternative, the freedom to withdraw from a workplace environment that he reasonably believes is highly dangerous.

Moreover, the Secretary's regulation can be viewed as an appropriate aid to the full effectuation of the Act's "general duty" clause. That clause provides that "[e]ach employer . . . shall furnish to each of his employees employment and a place of employment which are free fron recognized hazards that are causing or are likely to cause death or serious physical harm to his employees." As the legislative history of this provision reflects, it was intended itself to deter the occurrence of occupational deaths and serious injuries by placing on employers a mandatory obligation independent of the specific health and safety standards to be promulgated by the Secretary. Since OSHA inspectors cannot be present around the clock in every workplace, the Secretary's regulation ensured that employees will in all circumstances enjoy the rights afforded them by the "general duty" clause.

The regulation thus on its face appears to further the overriding purpose of the Act, and rationally to complement its remedial scheme. In the absence of some contrary indication in the legislative history, the Secretary's regulation must, therefore, be upheld, particularly when it is remembered that safety legislation is to be liberally construed to effectuate the congressional purpose.

Questions

1. What conditions must exist to justify the employee's refusal to work without reprimand?
2. Why did the Court feel the Secretary's regulation was lawful?

CONCLUSION

Title VII's purposes are to urge employers to adopt racially neutral and job-related criteria for employment and promotion. However, validation of such criteria to avoid liability for discrimination is expensive and imprecise. Moreover, there is no assurance that the EEOC or the courts will accept such validations. Therefore, employers avoid the cost of validation and, instead, make sure their "statistics" of new hirings and promotions reveal no "disproportionate impact." As a consequence, Title VII's purpose of neutral job criteria remains unfulfilled and preceptions of "reverse discrimination" brought about by statistic-improving decisions breed resentment. To avoid the statistic-oriented compliance policies, professional management must eschew the "easy road" and, instead develop the appropriate job-related criteria that are mandated by the law and suggested by professional business practices.

On the other hand, government needs to modify its regulatory techniques to comply with new social conditions and to consider a balancing of costs with benefits. For example, the Federal Labor Standards Act (minimum wages) was fashioned in times of economic crisis in thc 1930s. Modern problems of inflation and mass unemployment among youth suggest modification by government is needed. Also, overregulation, as was initially imposed by OSHA, reveals the necessity of government analysis of cost and benefits before regulations are imposed.

In summary, for a more efficient system, Congress, administrative agencies, and business firms must interact and cooperate with one another to achieve the desired social goals.

CASE PROBLEMS

1. Cariddi, a school principal's assistant, worked a summer job supervising ticket takers for the Kansas City Chiefs. Cariddi and one other of the six supervisors were Italian-Americans, and on Cariddi's recommendation, 18 Italian-Americans were hired by the stadium director as ticket takers. Cariddi's wife and daughter were also employed by the Kansas City Chiefs. The stadium director referred to Cariddi and other Italian-American employees as "dagos" or "the Mafia."

   Cariddi was fired and after he sued for discrimination on the basis of national origin, the trial court found that the firing was for insubordination and failure to comply with club policy with respect to the use of the press box on game days.

   What is your opinion of the discrimination in employment claim?

2. A savings and loan association enforced a dress code for its employees, under which female office employees wore a uniform consisting of slacks or a choice of three skirt styles, and a jacket or tunic or vest, and male office employees were to wear business suits or business-type sports jackets and pants and ties, or a leisure suit with suitable shirt and tie. The uniforms were all of one color and were provided by the employer savings association, but the value of the uniform was included in their income for tax purposes. On the last Tuesday of each month the women were permitted to wear clothing of their own

choosing while the uniforms were being cleaned, and the uniform requirement was suspended during the week between Christmas and New Year's.

A female employee sued the savings association, claiming a violation of the Civil Rights Act because female office employees were required to wear uniforms whereas comparable male office employees were not. The association believed that the uniform requirement was necessary to preserve a business atmosphere, because dress competition exists among women and current fashion might not promote a business atmosphere. Some women favored the uniform. Was the Civil Rights Act violated?

3. Alicia, a department store sales clerk, was embarrassed in public when she was verbally attacked by a co-worker accusing her of showing items not in Alicia's product line. When she left work that day, Alicia suffered a severe headache. One and a half days later, she was treated by a physician and one day thereafter received medication from a family doctor for nervous tension. Alicia returned to work that week still under medication, but collapsed and was hospitalized. She was diagnosed as having suffered a myocardial ischemia (a condition caused by a deficient blood supply to the heart, due to a functional constriction or an actual obstruction of blood vessels), and this condition was attributed to the humiliation caused by the verbal assault Alicia suffered.

   Alicia applied for workers' compensation but her claim was disallowed by the Ohio Industrial Commission because she had received no physical injury or trauma on the job but rather suffered only emotional stress which resulted in her heart condition.

   Should Alicia be entitled to workers' compensation for her disability?

4. Fernandez was employed by the Wynn Oil Company. During her employment, she held various positions, the last being administrative assistant to the vice-president of Wynn's International Operations Division. When Wynn failed to promote her to the director of international operations, she sued Wynn alleging sex discrimination. Wynn defended on the ground that male sex is a *bona fide* occupational qualification for a job performed in foreign countries where women are barred from business. Evaluate Wynn's defense.

END NOTE

1. *Trans World Airlines, Inc.* v. *Hardison,* 432 U.S. 73 (1977).

chapter 21

ENVIRONMENTAL PROTECTION LAWS

Most societies at some time in their development have expressed concern over the pollution of their natural environment. The task of defining what constitutes pollution is dependent upon society's choice in the use of its environment and resources. It is society's concept of "public interest," therefore, that becomes the controlling factor in defining pollution.

Under the common law, the environment was thought to be able to "cleanse itself." The discharge of waste into the environment became "unreasonable" when the environment's cleansing ability was exceeded. Consequently, business firms were allowed to discharge "reasonable" amounts of waste into the environment without legal liabilities. However, when discharges became unreasonable interferences with the use and enjoyment of a neighbor's land, the court labeled such activity a "nuisance" entitling the adjoining land owner to compensation for the harm caused to his or her property. If it could be shown that polluted air, for example, was injuring his or her house or crops, the plaintiff could secure judicial aid to prevent the injury and obtain compensation from the polluter. However, if the plaintiff could not establish that he or she sustained specific harm which was distinct from the harm that all members of the public at large sustained, the plaintiff could be denied standing to object to the polluter's behavior. Moreover, the crowding conditions of industrial and urban society had made it more difficult for the plaintiff to establish which polluter was the single cause of the harm. Without proof of causation, the plaintiff was not entitled to legal relief. Finally, the court would balance harm caused by the pollution against the benefits of the polluting activity to the community. If the court considered the "social value" of the business and its payroll (employment) to exceed the harm caused by the pollution, the pollution was considered reasonable, denying the plaintiff any right to relief. As a result, the tort system was not effective in eliminating the growing levels of pollution in industrial and urban society.

The growing crisis of environmental degradation caused society to redefine pollution. The federal environmental quality laws, therefore, have defined pollution in terms of its effects on the public health and welfare. However, efforts to clean the air often come in conflict with the other goals of society. The implementation and enforcement of environmental improvement laws have imposed extensive costs on society. Although some believe these costs are too high, others think the cost is simply necessary to prevent the continuing deterioration of our natural resources.

NATIONAL ENVIRONMENTAL POLICY ACT

The National Environmental Policy Act (NEPA) was enacted in 1970 as the culmination of efforts by Congress to recognize the need for establishing a federal policy on the environment. Various federal acts preceding NEPA dealt with narrow specific problems. The enactment of NEPA, however, represented the first federal government statement of its basic policy on environmental quality. The purposes of the act are as follows:

> . . . To declare a national policy which will encourage productive and enjoyable harmony between man and his environment; to promote efforts which will prevent or eliminate damage to the environment and biosphere and stimulate the health and welfare of man; to enrich the understanding of the ecological system and natural resources important to the Nation. (NEPA Sec. 2)

Besides declaring the national policy toward the environment, NEPA required appropriate action to achieve that policy and established the Council on Environmental Quality.

The Council on Environmental Quality, composed of "three members who shall be appointed by the President to serve at his pleasure," advises the president of growing environmental problems, and aids the president in formulating the administration's environmental policies.

ENVIRONMENTAL IMPACT STATEMENT

NEPA requires a "detailed statement" addressing particular environmental questions to be prepared by responsible federal agency officials whenever their decisions have an environmental impact. This detailed statement has come to be known as an Environmental Impact Statement (EIS). The majority of litigation under NEPA has centered on the EIS. Is an EIS required? Have the requirements of the act been met in the EIS? Has the agency, in preparation and use of the EIS, met the purpose and intent of NEPA?

Calvert Cliff's Coordinating Committee v.
United States Atomic Energy Commission

449 F. 2d 1109 (1971)
U.S. Court of Appeals (D.C. Cir.)

NEPA, like so much other reform legislation of the last 40 years, is cast in terms of a general mandate and broad delegation of authority to new and old administrative agencies. It takes the major step of requiring all federal agencies to consider values of environmental preservation in their spheres of activity, and it prescribes certain procedural measures to ensure that those values are in fact fully respected. . . .

We begin our analysis with an examination of NEPA's structure and approach and of the Atomic Energy Commission rules which are said to conflict with the requirements of the Act. The relevant portion of NEPA is Title I, consisting of five sections. Section 101 sets forth the Act's basic substantive policy: that the federal government "use all practicable means and measures" to protect environmental values. Congress did not establish environmental protection as an exclusive goal; rather, it desired a reordering of priorities, so that environmental costs and benefits will assume their proper place along with other considerations. In Section 101(b), imposing an explicit duty on federal officials, the Act provides that "it is the continuing responsibility of the Federal Government to use all practicable means, consistent with other essential considerations of national policy," to avoid environmental degradation, preserve "historic, cultural, and natural" resources, and promote "the widest range of beneficial uses of the environment without . . . undesirable and unintended consequences."

Thus the general substantive policy of the Act is a flexible one. It leaves room for a responsible exercise of discretion and may not require particular substantive results in particular problematic instances. However, the Act also contains very important "Procedural" provisions—provisions which are designed to see that all federal agencies do in fact exercise the substantive discretion given them. These provisions are not highly flexible. Indeed, they establish a strict standard of compliance.

NEPA, first of all, makes environmental protection a part of the mandate of every federal agency and department.

The sort of consideration of environmental values which NEPA compels is clarified in Section 102(2) (A) and (B). In general, all agencies must use a "systematic, interdisciplinary approach" to environmental planning and evaluation "in decisionmaking which may have an impact on man's environment." In order to include all possible environmental factors in the decisional equation, agencies must "identify and develop methods and procedures . . . which will insure that presently unquantified environmental amenities and values may be given appropriate consideration in decisionmaking along with economic and technical consideration." "Environmental amenities" will often be in conflict with "economic and technical consideration." To "consider" the former "along with" the latter must involve a balancing process. In some instances environmental costs may outweigh economic and technical benefits and in other instances they may not. But NEPA mandates a rather finely tuned and "systematic" balancing analysis in each instance.

To insure that the balancing analysis is carried out and given full effect, Section 102(2) (C) requires that responsible officials of all agencies prepare a "detailed statement" covering the impact of particular actions in the environment, the environmental costs which might be avoided, and alternative measures which might alter the cost-benefit equation. The apparent purpose of the "detailed statement" is to aid the agencies' own decision-making process and to advise other interested agencies and the public of the environmental consequences of planned federal action. Beyond the "detailed statement," Section 102(2) (D) requires all agencies specifically to "study, develop, and describe appropriate alternatives to recommend courses of action in any proposal which involves unresolved conflicts concerning alternative uses of available resources." This requirement, like the "detailed statement" requirement, seeks to ensure that each agency decision maker has before him and takes into proper account all possible approaches to a particular project (including total abandonment of the project) which would alter the environmental impact and the cost-benefit balance. Only in that fashion is it likely that the most intelligent, optimally beneficial decision will ultimately be made. Moreover, by compelling a formal "detailed statement" and a description of alternatives, NEPA provides evidence that the mandated decision-making process has in fact taken place and, most important, allows those removed from the initial process to evaluate and balance the factors on their own.

Of course, all of these Section 102 duties are qualified by the phrase "to the fullest extent possible." We must stress as forcefully as possible that this language does not provide an escape hatch for foot-dragging agencies; it does not make NEPA's procedural requirements somehow "discretionary." Congress did not intend the Act to be such a paper tiger. Indeed, the requirement of environmental consideration "to the fullest extent possible" sets a high standard for the agencies, a standard which must be rigorously enforced by the reviewing courts.

* * *

Thus the Section 102 duties are not inherently flexible. They must be complied with to the fullest extent, unless there is a clear conflict of statutory authority. Considerations of administrative difficulty, delay or economic cost will not suffice to strip the section of its fundamental importance.

We conclude, then, that Section 102 of NEPA mandates a particular sort of careful and informed decision-making process and creates judicially enforceable duties. The reviewing courts probably cannot reverse a substantive decision on its merits, under Section 101, unless it be shown that the actual balance of costs and benefits that was struck was arbitrary or clearly gave insufficient weight to environmental values. But if the decision was reached procedurally without individualized consideration and balancing of environmental factors—

conducted fully and in good faith—it is the responsibility of the courts to reverse. . . .

* * *

In the cases before us now, we do not have to review a particular decision by the Atomic Energy Commission granting a construction permit or an operating license. Rather, we must review the Commission's recently promulgated rules which govern consideration of environmental values in all such individual decisions. The rules were devised strictly in order to comply with the NEPA procedural requirements—but petitioners argue that they fall far short of the congressional mandate.

* * *

Petitioners . . . attack specific parts of the rules which, they say, violate the requirements of Section 102 of NEPA. . . . Although environmental factors must be considered by the agency's regulatory staff under the rules, such factors need not be considered by the hearing board conducting an independent review of staff recommendation, unless affirmatively raised by outside parties or staff members. . . .

* * *

The question here is whether the Commission is correct in thinking that its NEPA responsibilities may "be carried out in total outside the hearing process"—whether it is enough that environmental data and evaluations merely "accompany" an application through the review process, but receive no consideration whatever from the hearing board.

We believe that the Commission's crabbed interpretation of NEPA makes a mockery of the Act. What possible purpose could there be in the Section 102(2) (C) requirement (that the "detailed statement" accompany proposals through agency review processes) if "accompany" means no more than physical folders and paper, unopened, to reviewing officials along with other folders and papers? What possible purpose could there be in requiring the "detailed statement" to be before hearing boards, if the boards are free to ignore entirely the contents of the statement? NEPA was meant to do more than regulate the flow of papers in the federal bureaucracy. The word "accompany" in Section 102(2) (C) must not be read so narrowly as to make the Act ludicrous. It must, rather, be read to indicate a congressional intent that environmental factors, as compiled in the "detailed statement," be considered through agency review processes.

Beyond Section 102(2) (C), NEPA requires that agencies consider the environmental impact of their action "to the fullest extent possible." The Act is addressed to agencies as a whole, not only to their professional staffs. Compliance to the "fullest" possible extent would seem to demand that environmental issues be considered at every important stage in the decision-making process concerning a particular action—at every stage where an overall balancing of environmental and nonenvironmental factors is appropriate and where alterations might be made in the proposed action to minimize environmental cost. Of course, consideration which is entirely duplicative is not necessarily required. But independent review of staff proposals by hearing provides a crucial check on the staff's recommendations. The Commission's hearing boards automatically consider nonenvironmental factors, even though they have been previously studied by the staff. Clearly, the review process is an appropriate stage at which to balance conflicting factors against one another. And, just as clearly, it provides an important opportunity to reject or significantly modify the staff's recommended action. Environmental factors, therefore, should not be singled out and excluded, at this stage, from the proper balance of values envisioned by NEPA.

The Commission's regulations provide that in an uncontested proceeding the hearing board shall on its own "determine whether the application and the record of the proceeding contain sufficient information, and the review of the application by the Commission's regulatory staff has been adequate, to support affirmative findings on" various nonenvironmental factors. NEPA requires at least as much automatic consideration of environmental factors. In uncontested hearings, the board need not necessarily go over the same ground covered in the "detailed statement." But it must at least examine the statement carefully to determine whether "the review by the Commission's regulatory staff has been adequate." And it must independently consider the final balance among conflicting factors that is struck in the staff's recommendation.

* * *

It is, moreover, unrealistic to assume that there will always be an intervenor with the information, energy, and money required to challenge a staff recommendation which ignores environmental costs. NEPA establishes environmental protection as an integral part of the Atomic Energy Commission's basic mandate. The primary responsibility for fulfilling that mandate lies with the Commission. Its responsibility is not simply to sit back, like an umpire, and resolve adversary contentions at the hearing stage. Rather, it must itself take the initiative of considering environmental values at every distinctive and comprehensive stage of the process beyond the staff's evaluation and recommendation.

* * *

Questions

1. Must federal officials take environmental values into account in federal decision making?
2. What "approach" to environmental planning and evaluation is mandated by NEPA Sections 102(A) and (B)?
3. According to Section 102(2)(C), what must the "detailed statement" include? What does 102(2)(D) add as a requirement?
4. According to the court in *Calvert Cliff's,* what is the true value of EIS preparation? Does the review of environmental alternatives under the NEPA require that the least damaging alternative always be used? Or does the agency in fact have discretion in choosing an alternative?
5. When is a reviewing court to reverse the substantive environmental decision of an agency?
6. How were the rules of the Atomic Energy Commission in conflict with the NEPA?

ENFORCEMENT

All federal agencies are required to comply with NEPA requirements and complete an EIS when their actions significantly affect the natural environment. Although the act requires federal agencies to comply with its reporting requirements, enforcement of NEPA comes almost exclusively from the private sector. In most cases, the plaintiff in the NEPA case is a private citizen or conservation organization which has some interest in the environment about to be affected by the agency action. The primary remedy sought by private litigants is an injunction which prevents continuation of the project or activity until the agency complies with NEPA. Once the agency has met NEPA requirements and considered the environmental alternatives, it is free to exercise its discretion to choose the most appropriate alternative. Only where the agency has clearly abused its discretion, violated the Constitution, exceeded its statutory authority, or made its decision in disregard of the facts can it be prevented from going forward with its decision. However, not just anyone who objects to a proposed agency action can bring suit under NEPA. The concept of "standing to sue" requires the person bringing suit to allege that the challenged agency action has caused him "injury in fact" or he is about to be injured in fact. It seeks to ensure that only those persons with a legitimate interest in the litigatory issues be permitted to use the courts to resolve the issues.

ENVIRONMENTAL PROTECTION AGENCY

Many argued that the initial inadequacy of federal pollution controls resulted from the dispersal of power among too many federal agencies. A more centralized government agency was believed to be an improvement. Consequently, 15 pollution-control administrative functions from five different agencies were combined and merged with the creation of the Environmental Protection Agency (EPA). The EPA is responsible for the regulation of four basic types of environmental pollutants that are emitted by industry into the external environment. It is to control air pollution through the Clean Air Act, water pollution through the Clean Water Act, various kinds of land pollution through the Resource Conservation and Recovery Act, and pollutants derived from the use of products by consumers (see Exhibit 21-1).

AIR POLLUTION REGULATION

The involvement of the federal government in air pollution regulation developed slowly. The Air Pollution Control Act of 1955 empowered the Surgeon General to study the problem of air pollution and its control. The original Clean Air Act (CAA) of 1963 was administered by the Department of Health, Education, and Welfare (HEW) and contained such a cumbersome enforcement process that it was only used once. The Air Quality Act of 1967 amended the Clean

Exhibit 21-1
ENVIRONMENTAL POLLUTION REGULATIONS

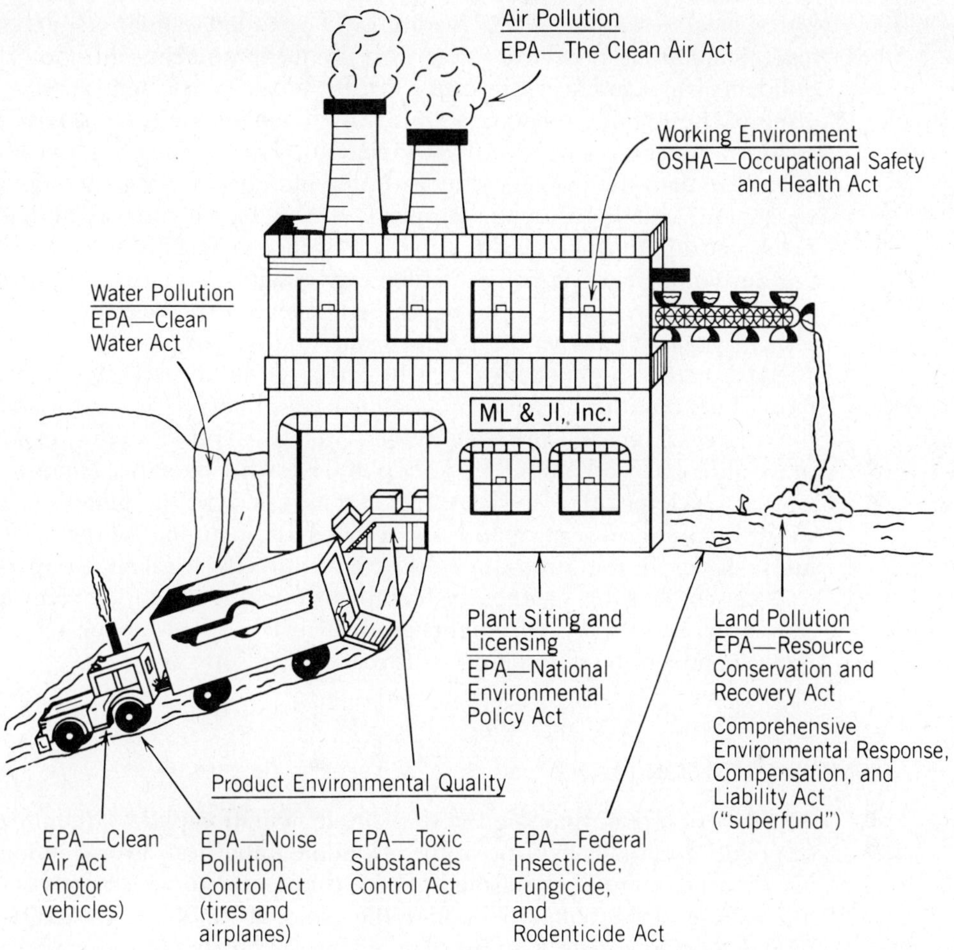

Air Act and strengthened the federal role in air pollution control by authorizing HEW to oversee the establishment of state ambient air quality standards and state implementation plans. Despite the increased federal role, the states retained such wide latitude in air quality standards and in time periods for compliance that by the beginning of 1970, no states had adopted complete standards or an implementation plan.

The Clean Air Act amendments of 1970 sharply expanded federal authority. It instructed the newly formed EPA to establish nationally uniform primary and secondary ambient air quality standards for air pollutants. The EPA was given nine months to establish these standards and each state was required to create an implementation plan to meet the federal standards within the state. The State Implementation Plan (SIP) had to be submitted to the EPA for approval, and deadlines were specified in the act.

The Clean Air Act required the EPA administrator to publish National Ambient Air Quality Standards (NAAQS) for six major pollutants: sulfur dioxides, particulates, carbon monoxide, photochemical oxidants, hydrocarbons, and nitrogen oxides. Later, the EPA administrator added standards for the pollutant lead. The *primary* standards prescribed the maximum concentration that an air pollutant is not to exceed in order to protect the public against adverse health effects. These standards were set with an "adequate margin of safety" to protect against a potential hazard not yet identified. The *secondary* standards are more restrictive than the primary standards and attempt to protect the environment, vegetation, visibility, climate, property, and personal comfort and well-being. Economic and technological feasibility were not to be considered by the EPA in the development of national ambient air quality standards. According to the act, the standards were to be developed solely on the basis of the adverse effects of the pollutant on the public health and welfare.

Mobile sources of pollution run by internal combustion engines account for most of the unnatural carbon monoxide in the atmosphere and for about half of the hydrocarbons and nitrogen oxides. Mobile sources also are responsible for most airborne lead pollution and photochemical oxidants (smog). *Stationary sources,* which include electric utilities and industrial plants, generate most of the sulfur dioxide and particulates and account for about half of the nitrogen dioxide pollution in the atmosphere. The EPA directly regulates the producers of internal combustion engines for compliance with national ambient air quality standards, and state governments are primarily responsible for achievement of federal ambient quality standards for stationary sources.

STATE IMPLEMENTATION PLANS

The first step in developing the state implementation plans is the measurement of pollution actually existing in the air. Some numerical "average of air quality" for each pollutant is established. Then, the degree to which the current levels exceed the permitted levels under the national standards (NAAQS) is determined. Finally, each state must decide how the burden of reducing emissions is to be allocated among its industrial sources. A least-cost abatement approach would allocate the degree of pollution reduction to those firms with the lowest cost of pollution reduction. However, businesses with lower costs of pollution reduction have opposed this approach as being unfair to them. Consequently, most states have adopted an equal percentage reduction for all industrial sources. Nevertheless, particular businesses may argue with the state that economic and technological infeasibility prohibit their compliance. In effect, they would prefer to have their "emission limitations" raised under the state plan. If the state is to concede to any industry's request for lower "emission limitations," it must require other polluters to further reduce their pollution levels so that the state can comply with national ambient air quality standards. Once the SIP has been adopted by the state and approved by the EPA, all industry sources have been assigned "emission limitations" to which they must comply. Failure to comply can result in the plant being shut down. Only good faith efforts at compliance and the presentation of a tight compliance schedule to accomplish its assigned emission limitations would protect a firm from being shut down if it did not comply within the appropriate time frame.

SIP's must require businesses to use "continuous emission controls" that either prevent pollutants from being generated or remove them from "waste air" on a continuous basis. "Dispersion" techniques (high smoke stacks) are permitted only if the state has already adopted regulations that require the maximum degree of continuous emission controls achievable.

The EPA has the power to accept or reject the SIP. If a plan was not submitted and accepted by July 1, 1979, or if an accepted plan is not being properly enforced by the state, the EPA is empowered to step in and assume the full burden of enforcement. Further, under certain conditions, a state's failure to develop or enforce its SIP could result in a complete halt to construction of major sources of pollution.

As of July 1, 1979, eight states had failed to submit implementation plans (Alaska, California, Colorado, Idaho, Indiana, Michigan, New York, and Ohio). The rest of the states had submitted either partial or complete plans, but only Wyoming had a fully accepted plan.

As of April 7, 1980, all but 10 states had submitted complete plans. The 10 remaining had submitted partial plans (Arizona, California, Idaho, Indiana, Kansas, Minnesota, Missouri, Ohio, Pennsylvania, and Tennessee). Final plans with all required revisions must be submitted by the end of 1982.

BUSINESS GROWTH?

The Clean Air Act required the EPA and the states to reduce air pollution to the national levels as quickly as possible. Those states in which the air was dirtier than the national standards could not permit new air-polluting businesses to be built. Also, those states in which the air was cleaner than national standards were required under the act to "protect and enhance" the existing quality of air. If a strict interpretation of the act were followed, new construction of any air pollution business would be prohibited everywhere.

To avoid the no-growth consequence, the EPA developed different policies for "dirty" and "clean" air regions. For dirty air areas, called "nonattainment" areas, the EPA adopted the Emissions Offset Policy. For clean air areas, or attainment areas, it adopted regulations to "prevent significant deterioration" of air quality.

DIRTY AIR AREAS

The Emissions Offset Policy for "nonattainment" areas delineates preconstruction requirements on major new or modified plants. First, the new plant has to install the greatest pollution control technology possible. Second, the plant owner has to certify that any other plants it owns are in compliance with any applicable state implementation plan (emission limitations) requirements. Third, new emissions from the proposed plant have to be offset by emission reductions of the same pollutant from other existing plants in the nonattainment area. The reductions in pollutants could be achieved by utilizing pollution control devices on other plants of the owner or by purchasing pollution control devices for other firms, if that is a less costly selection of the proposed plant owner. Finally, the emission offsets achieved have to be sufficient to create a "net air quality benefit" so as to assure that the area would be making "reasonable further progress" toward obtaining the national ambient air quality standards.

The 1977 amendments to the Clean Air Act approved of the EPA's Emissions Offset Policy and required each state to submit to the EPA a list identifying its nonattainment areas. The 1977 amendments also defined a "major emitting facility" as one that emits 100 tons of pollutants per year. Such a facility must obtain a permit before it can undertake construction or modification. The permit system contains the same basic requirements as that adopted by the EPA in its "emissions offset policy" and requires that the states' implementation plans be designed to achieve the national ambient air quality standards by the end of 1982.

Beginning in 1981 the EPA approved of the "bubble concept."[1] The bubble concept treats all the buildings and facilities of a firm's industrial complex as a single pollution source to be evaluated in the aggregate. The complex is considered under an imaginary bubble with a single stack emitting pollutants from the top of the bubble. Increases in emission from modifications or additions to the complex can occur as long as decreases in emissions from other components of the complex more than offset the new increase. The net effect of such changes would be a decrease in emissions from the imaginary smoke stack on the top of the bubble.

The bubble concept grants discretion to the owners of industrial complexes to apply whatever control measures they select from major emitting facilities. Owners can develop a mix of controls at the lowest possible costs.

From an economic point of view, both the Offset Policy and the "bubble concept" produce a more efficient allocation of resources. The EPA's adoption of the Offset Policy was a retreat from the strict regulatory scheme of the 1970 act and allowed owners to find the least expensive offsets available. However, the bubble concept is even more efficient because it allows owners to avoid the application of the expensive "lowest achievable emissions rate" technology requirement imposed by the Offset Policy.

States have been urged to revise their State Implementation Plans to allow existing industrial complexes to use the bubble concept.

CLEAN AIR AREAS

Initially the EPA imposed no requirement to control new sources of pollution in clean air areas. Hence, new plants were free to pollute in those areas up to the national ambient air quality standards. The Sierra Club sued the EPA, arguing that the Clean Air Act demanded the EPA to "protect and enhance" the air quality in clean air areas. Thus, the Sierra Club maintained, the EPA's approval of State Implementation Plans that did not attempt to prevent "significant deterioration" of the air was in violation of the act. The Supreme Court upheld the trial court's decision to enjoin the EPA from approving any SIP that did not set regulations to prevent significant deterioration in clean air areas.[2]

As a result of the Court's decision in *Sierra Club,* clean air areas were to be protected from "significant deterioration" even though the areas were already below the national ambient air quality standards. Therefore, the EPA developed regulations to prevent "significant deterioration" but also to allow for economic growth.

The "prevention of significant deterioration" (PDS) regulations divided clean air areas into three classes. Class I includes the cleanest areas, including wilderness areas and national parks. Class II and Class III areas are progressively less clean. Increased air pollution in each class is allowed, but limited to a *maximum allowable increase.* Maximum allowable increases vary in size with each class. Class I has the smallest maximum allowable increase and Class II and III are allowed progressively larger increases. Hence, new plants that emitted pollution up to the maximum allowable increase could be constructed. Beyond that point, plant construction would be prohibited.

The EPA created these classes and maximum allowable increases for two air pollutants: sulfur dioxide and particulate matter. The EPA contended that monitoring techniques were not adequate to measure significant deterioration from other pollutants. Only the largest facilities from a list of industries were required to obtain preconstruction review by the EPA. Owners of such new facilities had to use the best available control technology for minimizing particulate matter and sulfur dioxide and show that the proposed plant's emissions would not cause the maximum allowable increase in the area to be exceeded. Smaller plants and those not on the list of industries were not subject to the preconstruction review by the EPA.

Congress approved of the EPA's PSD regulations in 1977 amendments to the Clean Air Act, but reduced the maximum allowable increase in Class III areas. The maximum allowable increase in Class III areas now approximately equals one half of the national secondary standards. Congress also prohibited the EPA from reclassifying Class I areas.

Finally, the 1977 amendments defined new plants subject to the preconstruction permit process as any "major emitting facility" (emission of 100 tons of pollutants per year), if it is on the especially designated industries list. All stationary sources not on the designated industries list must also go through the preconstruction permit process if the source emits 250 tons per year of any air pollutant. Consequently, owners of these proposed facilities meeting these size requirements in clean air areas must install the best available control technology and show that their operation will not cause the "maximum allowable increase" to be exceeded.

HAZARDOUS AIR POLLUTANTS

A hazardous air pollutant is defined under the Clean Air Act as an "air pollutant which may result in an increase in mortality or in a very serious illness." The EPA is required under the act to determine which air pollutants are hazardous and to develop appropriate emission standards to protect public health. Any plant emitting hazardous air pollutants must use the best available technology to reduce such emissions to the appropriate standards, or plant closure may result.

The EPA has issued emissions standards for four hazardous pollutants: asbestos, beryllium, mercury, and vinyl chloride. Pressure from environmental groups is likely to induce the EPA to identify other hazardous air pollutants and establish appropriate emission standards in the future.

ENFORCEMENT

The CAA provides for enforcement by empowering the states, the federal government, and the private citizen to seek compliance by bringing action against violators.

The states, through their State Implementation Plans, have the primary responsibility for the day-to-day enforcement of their respective SIP's. The states may also be delegated certain federal enforcement powers upon meeting prescribed conditions.

A private citizen may bring a lawsuit on his or her own behalf against (1) anyone who is believed to be violating the emission standards of the CAA, (2) the administrator of the EPA if the administrator fails to act within the law in cases where he or she has no discretion, and (3) any person who violates clean air standards or standards restricting increases in emissions in nonattainment areas. The chief remedy sought by private citizens is an injunction, and as an incentive when it is in the "public interest" the CAA provides for payment of the costs of litigation, including attorney fees, by the polluter. However, if the citizen's action is obviously frivolous or harassing, the court may assess litigation costs to the citizen.

In passing the Clean Air Act, Congress made its intent clear that the CAA was to have its desired effect. Congress presented the EPA and the states in some instances with strong enforcement tools, designed to encourage compliance and to soundly penalize noncompliance. It then becomes the responsibility of the EPA and the states to utilize these tools to enforce the Clean Air Act (see Exhibit 21-2).

Exhibit 21-2
AIR POLLUTION REGULATIONS

EPA—National Ambient Air Quality Standards (NAAQS)

1. Primary Standards—maximum concentration allowed; set with adequate margin of safety to protect against adverse health effects.
2. Secondary Standards—more restrictive concentration standards to protect property and personal comfort.

Exhibit 21-2 (*continued*)

3. Standards are set for the following pollutants: (1) sulfur dioxide, (2) particulates, (3) ozone, (4) carbon monoxide, (5) hydrocarbons, (6) nitrogen dioxide, and (7) lead.

State Implementation Plans

1. Assigns "emission limitations" to all industry sources of pollutants so that EPA's National Standards (NAAQS) are obtained.
2. Identifies state's attainment and nonattainment regions and imposes appropriate regulations.

"Dirty Air" Regions

(Nonattainment areas—pollution above national standards)

Regulations: "emission offset policy."

Preconstruction requirements of "major emitting facility":

1. Use of best control technology possible—"lowest achievable emission rate" technology.
2. Certification that *all* other plants are in compliance with "emission limitations" of SIP.
3. New emissions being more than offset by emission reductions elsewhere in area. (Bubble concept—finds the least expensive offsets under "bubble" rather than force the utilization of expensive best technology.)

"Clean Air" Regions

(Attainment areas—pollution below national standards)

Regulations: "prevention of significant deterioration" (PSD)

Divide area into three classes and permit "maximum allowable increases" in sulfur dioxide and particulate matter for each class.

Preconstruction requirements review of "major emitting facilities" from a list of industries:

1. Use of best control technology.
2. "Maximum allowable increase" not to be exceeded.

Hazardous Air Pollutants: (1) asbestos, (2) beryllium, (3) mercury, and (4) vinyl chloride.

ECONOMIC OR TECHNOLOGICAL INFEASIBILITY

Enforcement of the Clean Air Act involves a difficult task of balancing many socioeconomic issues. The following case involves a challenge of the validity of emission limitations in the Missouri State Implementation Plan and addresses the process Congress adopted to deal with one part of the many socioeconomic issues involved in air quality regulation.

Union Electric Co. v. Environmental Protection Agency

427 U.S. 246 (1976)

Supreme Court of the United States

Justice Marshall

After the Administrator of the Environmental Protection Agency (EPA) approves a state implementation plan under the Clean Air Act (CAA), the plan may be challenged in a court of appeals within 30 days, or after 30 days have run if newly discovered or available information justifies subsequent review. We must decide whether the operator of a regulated emission source, in a petition for review of an EPA-approved state plan filed after the 30-day appeal period, can raise the claim that it is economically or technologically infeasible to comply with the plan. . . .

The heart of the [CAA] . . . is the requirement that each State formulate, subject to EPA approval, an implementation plan designed to achieve national primary ambient air quality standards—those necessary to protect the public health—"as expeditiously as practicable but . . . in no case later than three years from the date of approval of such plan." The plan must also provide for the attainment of national secondary ambient air quality standards—those necessary to protect the public welfare—within a "reasonable time." Each State is given wide discretion in formulating its plan, and the Act provides that the (EPA) Administrator "shall approve" the proposed plan if it has been adopted after public notice and hearing and if it meets eight specified criteria.

On April 30, 1971, the Administrator promulgated national primary and secondary standards for six air pollutants he found to have an adverse effect on the public health and welfare.

Included among them was sulfur dioxide, at issue here. After the promulgation of the national standards, the State of Missouri formulated its implementation plan and submitted it for approval. Since sulfur dioxide levels exceeded national primary standards in only one of the State's five air quality regions—the Metropolitan St. Louis Interstate region—the Missouri plan concentrated on a control strategy and regulations to lower emissions in that area. The plan's emission limitations were effective at once, but the State retained authority to grant variances to particular sources that could not immediately comply. The Administrator approved the plan on May 31, 1972.

Petitioner is an electric utility company servicing the St. Louis metropolitan area, large portions of Missouri, and parts of Illinois and Iowa. Its three coal-fired generating plants in the metropolitan St. Louis area are subject to the sulfur dioxide restrictions in the Missouri implementation plan. Petitioner did not seek review of the Administrator's approval of the plan within 30 days, as it was entitled to do under §307(b)(1) of the Act, but rather applied to the appropriate state and county agencies for variances from the emission limitations affecting its three plants. Petitioner received one-year variances, which could be extended upon reapplication. The variances on two of petitioner's three plants had expired and petitioner was applying for extensions when, on May 31, 1974, the Administrator notified the petitioner that sulfur dioxide emissions from its plants violated the emission limitations contained in the Missouri plan. Shortly thereafter, petitioner filed a petition in the Court of Appeals for the Eighth Circuit for review of the Administrator's 1972 approval of the Missouri implementation plan.

Section 307(b)(1) allows petitions for review to be filed in an appropriate court of appeals more than 30 days after the Administrator's approval of an implementation plan only if the petition is "based solely on grounds arising after such 30th day." Petitioner claimed to meet this requirement by asserting, that various economic and technological difficulties had arisen more than 30 days after the Administrator's approval and that these difficulties made compliance with the emission limitations impossible.

The Court of Appeals . . . [dismissed] the petition [and] . . . held that "only matters which, if known to the Administrator at the time of his action [in approving a state implementation plan], would justify setting aside that action are properly reviewable after the initial 30-day review period.

* * *

Since, in the court's view, claims of economic and technological infeasibility could not properly provide a basis for the Administrator's rejecting a plan, such claims could not serve—at any time—as the basis for a court's overturning an approved plan.

* * *

Since a reviewing court—regardless of when the petition for review is filed—may consider claims of economic and technological infeasibility only if the Administrator may consider such claims in approving or rejecting a state implementation plan, we must address ourselves to the scope of the Administrator's responsibility. . . . After surveying the relevant provisions of the Clean Air Amendments of 1970 and their legislative history, we [hold] that Congress intended claims of economic and technological infeasibility to be wholly foreign to the Administrator's consideration of a state implementation plan.

* * *

The Amendments place the primary responsibility for formulating pollution control strategies on the States, but nonetheless subject the States to strict minimum compliance requirements. These requirements are of a "technology-forcing character," and are expressly designed to force regulated sources to develop pollution control devices that might at the time appear to be economically or technologically infeasible.

* * *

Section 110(a)(2)(A)'s three-year deadline for achieving primary air quality standards is central to the Amendments' regulatory scheme and, as both the language and the legislative history of the requirement make clear, it leaves no room for claims of technological or economic infeasibility.

In sum, we have concluded that claims of economic or technological infeasibility may not be considered by the Administrator in evaluating a state requirement that primary ambient air quality standards be met in the mandatory three years. . . . Accordingly, a court of appeals reviewing an approved plan under Section 307(b)(1) cannot set it aside on those grounds, no matter when they are raised.

* * *

Perhaps the most important forum for consideration of claims of economic and technological infeasibility is before the state agency formulating the implementation plan. So long as the national standards are met, the State may select whatever mix of control devices it desires, and industries with particular economic or technological problems may seek special treatment in the plan itself.

* * *

While the State has virtually absolute power in allocating emission limitations so long as the national standards are met, if the state plan cannot meet the national standards, the EPA is implicated in any postponement procedure. There are two ways that a State can secure relief from the EPA for individual emission sources, or classes of sources, that cannot meet the national standards. First, if the Governor of the State so requests at the time the original implementation plan is submitted and if the State provides reasonable interim controls, the Administrator may allow a two-year extension of the three-year deadline for attainment of primary air quality standards if he finds, *inter alia,* that it is technologically infeasible for the source to comply. Second, again upon application of the Governor of the State, the Administrator may allow a one-year postponement of any compliance date in an implementation plan if he finds, *inter alia,* that compliance is technologically infeasible and that "the continued operation of [the emission source] is essential to national security or to the public health or welfare. . . ."

Even if the State does not intervene on behalf of an emission source, technological and economic factors may be considered in at least one other circumstance. When a source is found to be in violation of the state implementation plan, the Administrator may, after a conference with the operator, issue a compliance order rather than seek civil or criminal enforcement. Such an order must specify a "reasonable" time for compliance with the relevant standard, taking into account the seriousness of the violation and "any good faith efforts to comply with applicable requirements." Claims of technological or economic infeasibility, the Administrator agrees, are relevant to fashioning an appropriate compliance order. . . .

In short, the Amendments offer ample opportunity for consideration of claims of technological and economic infeasibility. Always, however, care is taken that consideration of such claims will not interfere substantially with the primary goal of prompt attainment of the national standards. . . . Technology forcing is a concept somewhat new to our national experience and it necessarily entails certain risks. But Congress considered those risks in passing the 1970 Amendments and decided that the dangers posed by uncontrolled air pollution made them worth taking. Petitioner's theory would render that considered legislative judgment a nullity, and that is a result we refuse to reach.

Questions

1. Who made the policy decision to remove economic and technological factors from consideration in setting deadlines for compliance with the Clean Air Act's "primary" standards?
2. What costs or benefits do you see from the "technological forcing" concept embodied in the Clean Air Act?
3. What procedures exist in the act for consideration of economic and technological aspects in its enforcement?

WATER POLLUTION REGULATION

ORIGIN OF WATER REGULATIONS

The role of the federal government in water quality regulations has developed through a series of federal legislative enactments. The Rivers and Harbors Appropriation Act of 1899 imposed regulation of specific source discharge into navigable waters, primarily seeking to avoid the blockage of navigation. The Water Pollution Control Act of 1958 authorized the surgeon general to investigate the nature of industrial and municipal waste and, thereafter, to inform and encourage the states to develop water pollution abatement programs. The Water Pollution Control Act amendments of 1956 provided grants for municipal sewage plants and created a cumbersome "enforcement conference" to prohibit water pollution in one state from endangering the health and welfare of the citizens of another state. The Water Quality Act of 1965 created the Federal Water Pollution Control Administration, later merged into the EPA, and required the states to establish water quality standards for waterways which had to be first "zoned" as to use. Thereafter, the states were to test water quality according to its "zoned" standards and, if it was poor, develop an implementation plan. However, barely over half of the states had developed standards by 1970.

In light of the poor performance of the states, Congress enacted the Federal Water Pollution Control Act of 1972, which established a comprehensive program for making waters safe for fishing and swimming by 1983 and eliminating pollutants from navigable waters by 1985. The act authorized the EPA to specify industrial and municipal effluent emission standards. The EPA was also authorized to specify the pollution control technology that was to be applied to each pollutant source. The act was amended in 1977, and its name was changed to the Clean Water Act (CWA).

NATIONAL UNIFORM EFFLUENT STANDARDS

Since water pollution comes from such a wide variety of sources, creating an impossible regulatory task to control all sources, the EPA concentrates on "point sources" which involve all industrial and municipal sources that discharge liquid waste. Agricultural and urban runoff (nonpoint sources) have to be ignored by the EPA for the present.

As to industrial sources, the EPA establishes national uniform effluent limitations on an industry-by-industry basis. Consequently, the pollution control standards for each industry are technology-based. Every firm in the industry utilizes the same technology to meet its effluent limitations. The 1972 act required industries to comply with EPA standards by July 1, 1977. The technology adopted by the EPA was the "best practicable control technology currently available."

The 1972 act contained a second-phase in which new standards incorporating the top-of-the-line water pollution control technology were to be instituted by July 1, 1983. However, the 1977 Clean Water Act amendments extended the deadline to 1984 and divided water pollutants into three types, with separate deadlines and control provisions.

Conventional (nontoxic) pollutants are to be controlled by the "best conventional pollutant control technology" by July 1, 1984. The EPA, in determining the appropriate technology, is required to consider the "reasonableness of the relationship between the costs of attaining a reduction in effluents and the effluent reduction benefits derived." New control technologies for conventional pollutants were not to be adopted unless justified by cost-benefit.

The EPA is also required to develop effluent standards to control *toxic* pollutants with the "best available control technology economically achievable" by July 1, 1984. More than 65 toxic pollutants must be controlled, but information on control strategies for toxic pollutants is sorely lacking. Development of toxic standards and control technology will be difficult and costly.

Nonconventional pollutants, such as thermal pollution, are to be controlled by the "best available control technology economically achievable" within three years after the EPA has designated the pollutant and the technology.

The Clean Water Act also requires the EPA to set "new source" effluent standards for 27 major water-polluting industries. Although the goal is no discharge of pollutants, the EPA is required to consider the costs in setting standards for the greatest degree of effluent reduction achievable.

PERMIT SYSTEM

The Clean Water Act provides that "the discharge of any pollutant is illegal" without a discharge permit. The EPA applies the uniform effluent standards to each permit application, and thereby defines the obligations of the applicant business. The permit spells out the water pollution control technology that must be utilized, the date of compliance, and the actual limits of pollution that the source may legally discharge. Also, the EPA may reserve the right to modify the permit should new information of toxic pollutants become available. The Clean Water Act requires the permit system to be designed so that states, if they choose, may insert stricter standards than those imposed by the federal standards. For heavily polluted waterways, the federal standards alone are probably insufficient.

VARIANCES

Businesses that are unable to comply with water pollution control specified by the EPA are forced to close down. However, the act provides for two exceptions. First, a business discharging nonconventional pollutants may seek a variance if adoption of the phase II compliance technology would be a significant economic hardship on a firm already implementing pollution control to its financial limits. Second, owners may apply for variance from state water quality limitations on thermal wastewaters. If other businesses along the waterway can absorb additional requirements and the variance would not interfere with public water supplies, the variance from the state water quality limitations may be granted. Finally, if a business within an industry utilizes different methods of productions for which the standard's technology is inappropriate for their wastewater characteristics, the EPA will develop an alternative set of limitations specifically for that business.

PENALTIES FOR VIOLATIONS

The enforcement provisions of the Clean Water Act are similar to those discussed under the Clean Air Act. The act authorizes the state authority or the EPA to bring civil actions against business violators to obtain compliance. When the EPA determines that a business is violating a law, it must first notify the appropriate state authority about the violation. Thirty days thereafter the EPA may bring action on its own to obtain compliance if the state has taken no action.

The CWA can be enforced through an administrative compliance order, civil action including injunction and civil penalties up to \$10,000 per day of violation, or criminal penalties of between \$2,500 and \$25,000 for each day of violation or imprisonment up to one year, or both. Additionally, knowingly making false statements in any required reports or knowingly tampering with monitoring devices carries fines of up to \$10,000 or imprisonment of up to six months, or both. It should be noted that the criminal penalties of imprisonment apply only to natural persons and include "responsible corporate officers" when corporations are involved.

Prior to the mid-1970s, the chief emphasis of enforcement of federal water pollution legislation was a combination of negotiation, public opinion, voluntary compliance, and appropriate civil action. The late 1970s witnessed a departure from that emphasis. The EPA began using the criminal sanctions provided in the CWA.

United States v. Frezzo Bros. Inc.

602 F. 2d 1123 (1979)
U.S. Court of Appeals (3rd Cir.)

I.

Frezzo Brothers, Inc., is a Pennsylvania corporation engaged in the mushroom farming business near Avondale, Pennsylvania. The business is family-operated with Guido and James Frezzo serving as the principal corporate officers. As a part of the mushroom farming business, Frezzo Brothers, Inc., produces compost to provide a growing base for the mushrooms. The compost is comprised mainly of hay and horse manure mixed with water and allowed to ferment outside on wharves.

The Frezzo's farm had a 114,000 gallon concrete holding tank designed to contain water run-off from the compost wharves and to recycle water back to them. The farm had a separate storm water run-off system that carried rain water through a pipe to a channel box located on an adjoining property owned by another mushroom farm. The channel box was connected by a pipe with an unnamed tributary of the East Branch of the White Clay Creek. The waters of the tributary flowed directly into the Creek.

Counts One through Four of the indictment charged the defendants with discharging pollutants into the East Branch of the White Clay Creek. . . . Richard Casson, a Chester County Health Department investigator, observed pollution in the tributary flowing into the Creek and collected samples of wastes flowing into the channel box. The wastes had the distinctive characteristics of manure and quantitative analysis of the samples revealed a concentration of pollutants in the water. The Government introduced meteorological evidence at trial showing that no rain had been recorded in the area on these four dates. Based on this evidence, the Government contended that the Frezzos had willfully discharged manure into the storm water run-off system that flowed into the channel box and into the stream.

Investigator Casson returned to the Frezzo farm on January 12, 1978, to inspect their existing water pollution abatement facilities. Guido and James Frezzo showed Casson both the holding tank designed to contain the waste water from the compost wharves, and the separate storm water run-off system. Casson returned to the farm on May 9, 1978, with a search warrant and several witnesses. This visit occurred after a morning rain had ended. The witnesses observed the holding tank overflowing into the storm water run-off system. The path of the wastes from the Frezzo holding tank to the channel box and into the stream was photographed. James Frezzo was present at the time and admitted to Casson that the holding tank could control the water only 95% of the time. Samples were again collected, subjected to quantitative analysis and a high concentration of pollutants was found to be present. This incident gave rise to Count Five of the indictment.

Additional samples were collected from the channel box on May 14, 1978, after a heavy rain. Again, a concentration of pollutants was found to be present. This evidence served as the basis for Count Six of the indictment. At trial, the Government introduced evidence of the rainfall on May 9 and May 14 along with expert hydrologic testimony regarding the holding capabilities of the Frezzos' tank. The Government theorized that the holding tank was too small to contain the compost wastes after a rainstorm and that the Frezzos had negligently discharged pollutants into the stream on the two dates in May.

The jury returned guilty verdicts on all six counts against the corporate defendant, Frezzo Brothers, Inc., and individual defendants, Guido and James Frezzo.

* * *

II.

The Frezzos first argue that the Administrator of the Environmental Protection Agency must either give them some notice of alleged violations of the Federal Water Pollution Control Act, or institute a civil action before pursuing criminal remedies under the Act. Judge Broderick, the trial judge, rejected this argument, relying primarily on *United States* v. *Phelps Dodge,* 391 F. Supp. 1181 (D. Ariz. 1975), which held that there were no civil prerequisites to the Government's maintenance of criminal proceedings under the Act. We agree.

. . . The criminal provision of the Act, Section 1319(c) provides in relevant part:

> (1) Any person who willfully or negligently violates Section 1311 . . . of this title . . . shall be punished by a fine of not less than $2,500 nor more than $25,000 per day of violation, or by imprisonment for not more than one year, or by both. . . .

. . . There is nothing in the text of Section 1319(c) that compels the conclusion that prior written notice, other administrative or civil remedies are prerequisite to criminal proceedings under the Act. The Senate acceded to the House in not making civil enforcement manatory upon the Administrator under Section 1319. Hence, we can only conclude that whatever support existed for the position urged by the Frezzos did not prevail in the enactment of the final Bill.

Further, we see no reason why the Government should be hampered by prerequisites to seeking criminal sanctions under the Act. The Frezzos urge that it can only be through prior notification, followed by continued polluting in the face of such notice, that willful violations of the Act can be established. We find this argument unconvincing. Although continued discharges after notification could be one way for the Government to prove scienter, it is certainly not the only way to establish willful violations. The Government could logically argue, as it did in this case, that the circumstances surrounding the alleged discharges manifested willful violations of the Act and that it had the power to pursue criminal rather than civil sanctions. Furthermore, in view of the broad responsibilities imposed upon the Administrator of the EPA, he should be entitled to exercise his sound discretion as to whether the facts of a particular case warrant civil or criminal sanctions. We therefore hold that the Administrator of the EPA is not required to pursue administrative or civil remedies, or give notice, before invoking criminal sanctions under the Act.

III.

The Frezzos next contend that the indictment should have been dismissed because the EPA had not promulgated any effluent standards applicable to the compost manufacturing business. The Frezzos argue that before a violation of Section 1311(a) can occur, the defendants must be shown to have not complied with existing effluent limitations under the Act. . . .

The core provision of the Act is found in Section 1311(a) which reads:

> Except as in compliance with this section and Sections 1312, 1316, 1317, 1318, 1342, and 1344 of this title, the discharge of any pollutants by any person shall be unlawful.

The Government argues, however, . . . and cites *American Frozen Food Institute* v. *Train,* 539 F.2d 107, 115 (1976) for the proposition that:

By 1972 Congress determined upon wholly a new approach. The basic concept of the Act [Section 1311(a)] we construe in this case is an ultimate flat prohibition upon all discharges of pollutants.

Indeed, the court specifically noted that "[t]his prohibition which is central to the entire Act is statutory and requires no promulgation."

. . . The Government contends in the instant case that the lack of effluent limitations is no defense to a violation of Section 1311(a). It argues that when no effluent limitations have been established for a particular business, the proper procedure is for the business to apply for a permit to discharge pollutants . . . , which allows the Administrator to establish interim operating conditions pending approval. [Other courts have] . . . explicitly rejected this argument as placing too harsh a burden on the defendant because it viewed the Act as not allowing any discharge pending approval of the permit. The Government contends in the present case, however, that the absence of effluent limitations should not be allowed to nullify the flat prohibition on discharges under Section 1311(a). We agree.

. . . The basic policy of the Act is to halt uncontrolled discharges of pollutants into the waters of the United States. In fact, the Act sets forth "the national goal that the discharge of [all] pollutants into the navigable waters be eliminated by 1985." We see nothing impermissible with allowing the Government to enforce the Act by invoking Section 1311(a), even if no effluent limitations have been promulgated for the particular business charged with polluting. Without this flexibility, numerous industries not yet considered as serious threats to the environment may escape administrative, civil, or criminal sanctions merely because the EPA has not established effluent limitations. Thus, dangerous pollutants could be continually injected into the water solely because the administrative process has not yet had the opportunity to fix specific effluent limitations. Such a result would be inconsistent with the policy of the Act.

We do not believe . . . that the permit procedure urged by the Government is unduly burdensome on business. If no effluent limitations have yet been applied to an industry, a potential transgressor should apply for a permit to discharge pollutants. . . . The Administrator may then set up operating conditions until permanent effluent limitations are promulgated by EPA. The pendency of a permit application, in appropriate cases, should shield the applicant from liability for discharge in the absence of a permit. EPA cannot be expected to have anticipated every form of water pollution through the establishment of effluent limitations. The permit procedure, coupled with broad enforcement under Section 1311(a) may, in fact, allow EPA to discover new sources of pollution for which permanent effluent standards are appropriate.

In the present case, it is undisputed that there was no pending permit to discharge pollutants; nor had Frezzo Brothers, Inc., ever applied for one. This case, therefore, appears to be particularly compelling for broad enforcement. . . . The Frezzos, under their interpretation of the statute, could conceivably have continued polluting until EPA promulgated effluent limitations for the compost operation. The Government's intervention by way of criminal indictments brought to a halt potentially serious damage to the stream in question, and has no doubt alerted EPA to pollution problems posed by compost production. We therefore hold that the promulgation of effluent limitation standards is not a prerequisite to the maintenance of a criminal proceeding based on violation of . . . the Act.

IV.

The Frezzos next contend that there was insufficient evidence to convict them of the charges in the indictment. They virtually concede that the Government presented sufficient evidence to sustain Count Five. However, defendants charge that the Government had failed to prove willful or negligent discharges of pollutants. We disagree because we are persuaded that substantial evidence in the record supports all six counts of the indictment.

The Government contended at trial that the discharges giving rise to Counts One through Four of the indictment were willful. To establish this claim, the Government relied on the samples collected on those four occasions, the absence of rain on the dates in question, and the elimination of other possible causes for the pollution. The Frezzos maintain that the Government on this evidence failed to establish a willful act. We disagree. The jury was entitled to infer from the totality of the circumstances surrounding the discharges that a willful act precipitated them. The Government did not have to present evidence of someone turning on a valve or diverting wastes in order to establish a willful violation of the Act.

The Government's theory on Counts Five and Six was that the discharges were negligently caused by the inadequate capacity of the holding tank. Count Five was amply supported by eyewitness testimony, samples of the pollutants, evidence of rainfall and expert hydrologic evidence of the holding tank's capacity. Count Six was similarly supported by evidence of rainfall, samples, expert testimony, and photographs of the holding tank three days before the incident, showing it to be near capacity. The jury could properly have concluded that the water pollution abatement facilities were negligently maintained by the Frezzos and were insufficient to prevent discharges of the wastes. We therefore conclude that there was sufficient evidence to sustain the verdict on all six counts.

Questions

1. As exhibited by the preceding case, the CWA provides for imposition of criminal sanctions for willful or negligent violation of the CWA. What must be established to show a willful violation? A negligent violation?
2. Is a willful violator more or less at fault than a negligent violator? Should the willful violator be subject to more stringent sanctions? The act does not provide for such differentiation. Is there a way that the courts can reflect the difference and still meet the act's mandate?
3. Would an application for a permit to pollute the waters have protected the corporation and the two brothers from criminal charges?

4. To what extent will the policies of the administration in office affect the choice of enforcement remedy? Should they?
5. If you were the administrator of the EPA, what policies would you establish to guide the selection of targets for criminal prosecution? What is your reaction to the EPA's choice of criminal sanction against this defendant as compared to sanctions against much larger, more notorious polluters?
6. Frezzo Brothers, Inc., was fined $50,000, and the individual defendants Guido and James Frezzo received jail sentences of 30 days each and fines aggregating $50,000. Do these penalties seem adequate or insufficient?

Case Note

The preceding case was denied *certiorari* by the United States Supreme Court. The courts, however, have not yet fully disposed of the matter. The defendants petitioned the trial court to vacate the sentences imposed. The trial court denied the petition and the defendant appealed (642 F.2d 59 [1981]). Upon the second review of the case, the circuit court of appeals remanded the case to the trial court telling the lower court that it had failed to properly consider whether the holding tank was the type of pollution source that came under the criminal sanction sections.

SOLID WASTE REGULATION

The first major attempt to regulate solid waste, the Solid Waste Disposal Act, was passed by Congress in 1965. This act encouraged states to make efficient and safe disposal of solid waste by providing federal assistance to state and local governments in developing solid waste disposal systems.

In 1976, Congress acted to strengthen federal authority in the solid waste disposal area. With air and water pollution laws being given new "teeth" by the amendments of the mid-1970s, it was only appropriate that Congress act in the same manner in the area of solid waste. Accordingly, the Resource Conservation and Recovery Act (RCRA) became the primary solid waste regulatory statute. It absorbed the Solid Waste Disposal Act and placed primary federal authority within the EPA. The act is patterned after the Clean Air and Clean Water Acts, giving the EPA overall national regulatory authority while placing the primary authority for day-to-day enforcement for nonhazardous solid waste disposal on the states.

The EPA's primary responsibility is to identify and issue national guidelines for *hazardous* solid waste. After identifying hazardous wastes, the RCRA authorizes the EPA to provide "cradle-to-grave" control over hazardous waste by utilizing two major control methods. First, the owner of a hazardous waste disposal site must obtain a permit from the EPA and comply with EPA performance standards in order to be considered an approved hazardous waste disposal facility.

The second control mechanism is the "manifest system" which records the movement of hazardous waste from the generator's premises to an approved disposal facility. Generators of hazardous wastes must properly package and label the substances and prepare a document, the "manifest," indicating the name of the generator, the name of the transporter, the name and address of the approved facility to which the wastes are being transported, a description of the waste, and the quantity. The generator must give copies of the manifest to the transporter who obtains the signature of the owner of the approved hazardous waste facility after delivery. The transporter must notify the EPA of any spill in transport and clean up the spill. The owner of the approved disposal facility must send a signed copy of the manifest to the generator so that the generator knows that the quantity of waste shipped was actually received.

The RCRA provides for both civil and criminal penalties. A civil fine of $25,000 per day of violation can be imposed through judicial action. Criminal violations of the act can result in fines up to $25,000 per day of violation or up to one year in prison, or both, for individuals found guilty. If an individual, which is defined to include business organizations and responsible natural persons, knowingly engages in the transportation, treatment, storing, or disposal of solid wastes without a permit, conviction can result in fines up to $50,000 per day of violation or up to two years in prison, or both. Cognizant of the potential for serious health problems developing from improper solid waste disposal, Congress provided for more severe criminal penalties under certain circumstances. If it is shown that there is a knowing violation of any part of the act, that the violator has knowledge that his or her acts place another person in imminent danger of death or serious injury, and that the action demonstrates an unjustified and inexcusable disregard for human life, the violator can be fined up to $250,000 or imprisoned for up to two years, or both. If, however, the violator manifests an extreme indifference for human life rather than an unjustified and inexcusable disregard to human life, then the violator can be fined up to $250,000 or imprisoned for up to five years, or both. Finally, if an organization is found guilty of such violations, it can be fined up to $1 million.

"SUPERFUND"

Since the RCRA did not deal with problems of cleaning up inactive dump sites or with the clean-up of hazardous waste spills, Congress enacted the Comprehensive Environmental Response, Compensation, and Liability Act in 1980. This act created the "Superfund," which is supported mostly by a system of taxes levied on the production of 42 hazardous chemicals and petroleum products. The act does not apply to oil spills, but it does provide the President with funds to clean up abandoned hazardous sites and to provide assistance in the case of a hazardous spill. However, the president's actions are limited to the expenditure of $1 million. The taxes to support the Superfund are set to terminate at the end of September 1985.

Owners of polluting facilities, whether production or disposal, are liable for all costs of remedial action. The owner's liability may be limited if he or she cooperates in the clean-up efforts and if the release of the pollutant was not from "willful negligence or misconduct." The act also requires businesses to obtain insurance to help pay for damages from the release of hazardous waste.

Private citizens injured by the release of a hazardous substance must litigate their claims in state courts. However, if the injury to the citizen is caused by waste at a dump site in which the owner is unknown, the injured party may make limited claims against the Superfund.

Finally, the act creates a special $200 million Post-Closure Tax and Trust Fund. This is supported by a tax on hazardous waste delivered to a disposal facility and it is to be used to pay for the monitoring and maintenance cost for "closed" hazardous waste sites that have been previously issued permits under RCRA.

ENVIRONMENTALLY HARMFUL PRODUCTS REGULATION

The EPA also enforces laws regulating the production of products that could have adverse affects on the environment. For example, the Clean Air Act requires the EPA to regulate pollution emissions from automobiles, the greatest contributor to the nation's air pollution. The EPA prescribes emission standards for motor vehicles, regulates fuel and fuel additives, and requires the industries to test and document the control devices developed to meet EPA's standards.

The Noise Control Act of 1972 empowers the EPA to develop noise emission standards "to protect the public health and welfare, taking into account the magnitude and conditions of the use of the product, the degree of noise reduction achievable through the use of the best available technology, and the cost of compliance." The EPA has issued noise emission standards for a variety of construction equipment, most transportation equipment, and some electric equipment, such as air conditioners and compressors. A manufacturer found selling a product not in compliance with the noise emission standards is subject to fines up to $25,000 per day, a jail term of not more than one year, or both.

The Federal Insecticide, Fungicide, and Rodenticide Act and the Federal Environmental Pesticide Control Act provide that pesticides must be registered with the EPA before they can be sold to consumers. Only pesticides that will not cause "unreasonable adverse affects in the environment" may be registered.

In 1976, Congress took steps to control the introduction of new chemical substances into the environment that are threatening to the environment and to human health. Under the Toxic Substances Control Act (TOSCA), the EPA is empowered to identify and regulate the use of new toxic substances or new uses of old toxic substances. TOSCA requires the testing of substances that may present "an unreasonable risk of injury to health or environment" so that the dangers of products can be known and prevented prior to the products' distribution.

TOSCA prohibits the manufacture of new substances or new uses of old substances unless the manufacturer or user files a notice with the EPA (together with the results of prescribed tests, a description of quality controls, the disposal characteristics, and other information) 90 days prior to the initiation of use of the substance. If the EPA determines that the proposed substance poses a danger to the environment or to human health, the administrator may issue a proposed order regulating or prohibiting manufacture or use of the substance. The proposed order is challengeable through the administrative process.

As might be imagined, utilization of this process can be long and drawn out. In order to give the administrator additional powers to act quickly where it is deemed necessary, TOSCA empowers the administrator to obtain federal court permission to seize the hazardous substance or to obtain an injunction, or both. Finally, TOSCA empowers the EPA to impose fines up to $25,000 for each violation of the law by way of administrative judicial proceeding. If TOSCA is knowingly or willfully violated, criminal penalties in the form of fines up to $25,000 for each day of violation or imprisonment up to one year, or both, are provided.

WILDLIFE PROTECTION REGULATION

Another example of federal regulation of the environment is the Endangered Species Act of 1966 as amended in 1973. This act was designed to identify and protect forms of life in danger of extinction.

The legislative proceedings in 1973 contain numerous expressions of concern over the risk that might lie in the loss of *any* endangered species. Typifying these sentiments is the following statement:

> From the most narrow possible point of view, *it is in the best interests of mankind to minimize the losses of genetic variations.* The reason is simple: they are potential resources. They are keys to puzzles which we cannot solve, and may provide answers to questions which we have not yet learned to ask.
>
> To take a homely, but apt, example: one of the critical chemicals in the regulation of ovulations in humans was found in a common plant. Once discovered, and analyzed, humans could duplicate it synthetically, but had it never existed—or had it been driven out of existence before we knew its potentialities—we would never have tried to synthesize it in the first place.
>
> Who knows, or can say, what potential cures for cancer or other scourges, present or future, may lie locked up in the structures of plants which may yet be undiscovered, much less analyzed? . . . Sheer self-interest impels us to be cautious.
>
> *The institutionalization of that caution* lies at the heart of . . . [the Endangered Species Act].[3]

Application of the act can best be exemplified by the now famous "snail darter" case, *Tennessee Valley Authority* v. *Hill* (1978).[4] In that case, the Tellico

Dam project was halted because it was determined that completion of the project would jeopardize the existence of the snail darter, a small fish on the endangered species list. After the United States Supreme Court had upheld the injunction prohibiting completion of the dam, Congress in 1979 passed legislation specifically exempting the Tellico Dam project from the Endangered Species Act. Congress weighed the social value of the dam (its electrical power while saving consumption of oil) over the value of the snail darter. Congress also noted that over 700 snail darters have been transplanted from the Little Tennessee to the Hiwassee River and seem to be thriving.

STATE REGULATION OF THE ENVIRONMENT

It should not be forgotten that state governments, in addition to participating in the federal scheme of environmental regulation, have the power of environmental regulation within their boundaries. In exercising their "police power," the states have long legislated in the areas of zoning, environmental planning, and regulation of specific uses of land. Recently, for example, all states, and over 500 municipalities, have enacted landmark preservation laws designed to preserve historic landmarks from destruction. In *Penn Central Transportation Co.* v. *City of New York,* 98 S.Ct. 2646 (1978), the U.S. Supreme Court upheld the validity of such laws as long as they did not unreasonably interfere with the reasonable use of such property. If unreasonable interference with the use of the property is embodied within the law, then such legislation is, in effect, held to be an exercise of the "eminent domain" power rather than the police power. Of course, the exercise of eminent domain requires the legislature to compensate the property owner for the state's unreasonable interference with the property.

The steps taken by local governments to improve the environment almost always involve increasing economic costs for private or public enterprises. To minimize pollution abatement costs, the polluters have tried many arguments to avoid the local laws. One argument often advanced is the notion that the Commerce Clause of U.S. Constitution requires uniformity of regulation which is not achieved by state and local ordinances of pollution control and, consequently, the local ordinances are said to be in violation of the U.S. Constitution. The court in the following case had to deal with this argument in relation to Oregon's new "bottle bill."

BOTTLE BILL

American Can Co. v. Oregon Liquor Control Commission
517 P. 2d 691 (1974)
Court of Appeals of Oregon

This is an appeal from a circuit court decree declaring that Oregon's so-called bottle bill, is valid and denying plaintiffs' . . . application for injunctive relief against the enforcement of the law. Plaintiffs are (a) manufacturers of cans . . . (b) brewers in California and Arizona . . . (c) out-of-state soft drink canners . . . (d) soft drink companies . . . and (e) the Oregon Soft Drink Association. . . .

The primary legislative purpose of the bottle bill is to cause bottlers of carbonated soft drinks and brewers to package their products for distribution in Oregon in returnable, multiple-use deposit bottles toward the goals of reducing litter and solid waste in Oregon and reducing the injuries to people and animals due to discarded "pull tops." . . .

Plaintiffs' most substantial challenge to the bottle bill is under the Commerce Clause of the United States Constitution.

The development of the one-way container provided a great technological opportunity for the beverage industry to turn logistical advantages into economic advantages. By obviating the expensive necessity of reshipping empty bottles back to the plant for refilling, the new containers enabled manufacturers to produce in a few centralized plants to serve more distant markets. The industry organized its manufacturing and distribution systems to capitalize maximally on the new technology.

The Oregon legislature was persuaded that the economic benefit to the beverage industry brought with it deleterious consequences to the environment and additional cost to the public. The aggravation of the problems of litter in public places and solid waste disposal and the attendant economic and esthetic burden to the public outweighed the narrower economic benefit to the industry. Thus the legislature enacted the bottle bill over the articulate opposition of the industries represented by plaintiffs.

As with every change of circumstance in the market place, there are gainers and there are losers. Just as there were gainers and losers, with plaintiffs apparently among the gainers, when the industry adapted to the development of nonreturnable containers, there will be new gainers and losers as they adapt to the ban. The economic losses complained of by plaintiffs in this case are essentially the consequences of readjustment of the beverage manufacturing and distribution systems to the older technology in order to compete in the Oregon market.

The purpose of the Commerce Clause . . . was to assure to the commercial enterprises in every state substantial equality of access to a free national market. It was not meant to usurp the police power of the states which was reserved under the Tenth Amendment. Therefore, although most exercises of the police power affect interstate commerce to some degree, not every such exercise is invalid under the Commerce Clause.

Plaintiffs acknowledge the authority of the state to act, but assert that the state exercise of its police power must yield to federal authority over interstate commerce because, they claim, the impact on interstate commerce in this case outweighs the putative benefit to the state and because alternative methods exist to achieve the state goal with a less deleterious impact on interstate commerce. . . .

Specifically upholding the authority of the states to enact environmental legislation affecting interstate commerce, the court held in *Huron Cement Co.* v. *Detroit,* 362 U.S. 440 (1960):

> . . . Legislation designed to free from pollution the very air that people breathe clearly falls within the exercise of even the most traditional concept of what is compendiously known as the police power. In the exercise of that power, the states and their instrumentalities may act, in many areas of interstate commerce and maritime activities, concurrently with the federal government.

The United States Supreme Court has also made clear that it will not only recognize the authority of the state to exercise the police power, but also its right to do so in such manner as it deems most appropriate to local conditions, free from the homogenizing constraints of federal dictation. . . .

The Oregon legislature is thus constitutionally authorized to enact laws which address the economic, esthetic and environmental consequences of the problems of litter in public places and solid waste disposal which suit the particular conditions of Oregon even though it may, in doing so, affect interstate commerce.

The enactment of the bottle bill is clearly a legislative act in harmony with federal law. Congress has directed that the states take primary responsibility for action in this field. By enacting the Federal Solid Waste Disposal Act (1970), Congress specifically recognized that the proliferation of new packages for consumer products has severely taxed our disposal resources and blighted our landscapes. It disclaimed federal preemption and assigned to local government the task of coping with the problem with limited federal fiscal assistance. . . .

While it is clear that the Oregon legislature was authorized to act in this area, plaintiffs assert that the means incorporated in the bottle bill are not effective to accomplish its intended purpose and that alternative means are available which will have a lesser impact upon interstate commerce. Particularly, they offered evidence to show: (1) that the deposit system is inadequate to motivate the consuming public to return containers, (2) that mechanical means are being developed for improved collection of highway litter; and (3) that public education, such as the "Pitch In To Clean Up America" campaign, is a desirable means of dealing with container litter.

Selection of a reasonable means to accomplish a state purpose is clearly a legislative, not a judicial, function. . . . In particular, the courts may not invalidate legislation upon the speculation that machines may be developed or because additional and complementary means of accomplishing the same goal may also exist. The legislature may look to its imagination rather than to traditional methods such as those which plaintiffs suggest, to develop suitable means of dealing with state problems, even though their methods may be unique. Each state is a laboratory for innovation and experimentation in a healthy federal system. What fails may be abandoned and what succeeds may be emulated by other states. The bottle bill is now unique; it may later be regarded as seminal.

We conclude, therefore, that the bottle bill was properly enacted within the police power of the state of Oregon and that it is imaginatively, but reasonably, calculated to cope with problems of legitimate state concern.

Questions

1. What scheme of regulation was developed by Oregon to reduce litter and solid waste?
2. Does the commerce clause of the U.S. Constitution usurp the police power of the state?
3. Does the state's police power include aesthetic values which may be protected by government?
4. Have federal laws indicated the proper role for states to take in dealing with environmental pollution?

CONCLUSION

Congress, in passing the recent pollution laws, clearly intended to achieve an improved environment. Although there has been a significant improvement in reducing environmental pollution, particularly in water, the continued improvement remains in doubt.

The laws themselves and their interpretation by the courts have not yet been fully clarified. And in some instances, control technologies have yet to be performed. Congress, the EPA, and industry, each for its own reasons, continue to grapple with the pollution control laws. Even now, there have been proposals for the relaxation of pollution laws, particularly the Clean Air Act, in Congress. Industry is bringing many cases to court seeking interpretation of many sections of the statutes. And the EPA itself, under the Reagan Administration, is reconsidering its enforcement policies in several areas. It is unclear what future environmental policies will develop from these political adjustments.

CASE PROBLEMS

1. Plaintiffs filed a "citizens suit" under Section 304 of the Clean Air Act requesting the court to declare the defendant, Potomac Electric Power Company (PEPCO), in violation of regulations establishing emissions standards and limitations promulgated under the act and to enjoin PEPCO to comply with all regulations under the act. The coal-fire stoker boilers at defendant's facility emit smoke with visible emissions. Clean Air Act regulations prohibit any visible emissions. However, PEPCO asserts the technological and economic infeasibility of the absolute prohibition on visible emissions constitutes a defense. The plaintiff argues that the act is meant to be "technology-forcing" and that the public health should be given absolute priority over continued operations by noncomplying polluters.

   What is the decision?

2. Georgia's State Implementation Plan (SIP) for achieving compliance with the National Ambient Air Quality Standards (NAAQS) of the Clean Air Act allows Georgia's power plants to construct tall smokestakes to disburse harmful pollutants over a wider area, thereby reducing the ground level concentration of pollutants in the immediate vicinity of the facility in order to comply with NAAQS. The Natural Resources Defense Council (NRDC) challenged the EPA approval of Georgia's SIP, arguing that the Clean Air Act's policy of "nondegradation" prohibits areas of clean air from being degraded, even though the degradation in issue will not reduce the quality of the air below the level specified by the NAAQS. NRDC argued the use of dispersion techniques is at odds with the nondegradation policy. The only techniques fully capable of guaranteeing nondegradation are "emission limitation" controls.

   Under what circumstances could Georgia adopt the "tall stack" strategy?

3. Widget Company desires to build a new plant that will emit 150 tons per year of sulfur dioxide. The area selected for the plant site is classified as a "nonattainment" area. What requirements does the Clean Air Act place on Widget Company before it can begin building the plant?

4. Kopy, Inc., discharges pollutants into the local river which is heavily polluted. The EPA permit requests Kopy to install pollution-control equipment to clean the discharged waters beyond the national standards. The state had requested the tougher standards and the EPA complied. Kopy seeks a court order to prohibit the EPA from imposing the tougher state standards.

   What is the result?

END NOTES

1. Bureau of National Affairs, *Environmental Reporter—Current Developments,* Vol. 12, p. 1143, Jan. 15, 1982.
2. *Sierra Club* v. *Ruckelshaus,* 412 U.S. 41 (1973).
3. *Tennessee Valley Authority* v. *Hill,* 98 S. Ct. 2279 (1978).
4. Bureau of National Affairs, *Environmental Reporter—Current Developments,* Vol. 11, p. 1761, Jan. 23, 1981.

epilogue chapter 22

BEYOND THE LAWS: SOCIAL RESPONSIBILITIES OF BUSINESS

Social systems, such as political and economic systems, are the results of the values held by society. The political and economic functions and relationships of institutions of society are determined by the aggregation of beliefs held by members of the society. As the social values of the people change, the social systems and institutions also change. Change in social values and social systems usually is a continuous process with one stage's development building on previous stages. Each successive step of social change usually retains portions of the older social values and adds new ones.

In trying to understand this process of social change, it is important to recognize the role of values and beliefs, otherwise called ideology. Ideology is a set of beliefs and ideas concerning what is and what should be. Without an ideology, there can be no coherent choice or purposeful action. Choice and action operate by reference to an ideological complex of ideas. Ideology provides a judgmental process; it has a choice-making, problem-solving capability.

The summation of individual beliefs forms a "prevailing ideology" for society. The prevailing ideology directs social policies and guides institutional behavior. It conveys legitimacy and status to those in power and supports social institutions. If ideology provides the blueprint for institutional organization and for social policy, it follows that a change in ideology that prevails or that dominates will bring about a change in all that constitutes the social system.

This chapter discusses the ideological beliefs of businesspersons concerning their role in society and illustrates how business philosophy has changed in recent years, focusing attention on the ideological dilemmas likely to be faced in the future. One can be sure that as long as the philosophies of business direct business practices to contribute positively to social goals, society will accept and support contemporary business practices. On the other hand, if business ideology gives rise to business practices that society believes are contrary to the common good, society will initiate and enforce restrictions against those practices.

THE IDEOLOGY OF FREE ENTERPRISE

Important to America's development was a body of social and economic philosophy shared by business and social leaders. The ideology of the free enterprise system provided direction and justification for both business and governmental affairs. It provided the key elements that make up *the* ideal way to organize economic life. Basic components of this free enterprise ideology are easy to identify. According to George Cabot Lodge, the traditional ideology consists of five great ideals which were expressed as "natural laws" by John Locke and Adam Smith.[1] These ideals fit well in the vast, underpopulated wilderness of America and have served for hundreds of years. The Lockean ideals are as follows:

Individualism. Individuals are to be free to promote and protect their own personal interests. In economic affairs, this means that individuals should be free to own property and enter into contracts with others whereby they sell their skills and products in the free marketplace. Free choice for the individual becomes a core concept of the ideology of "free enterprise."

Equality of Opportunity. Closely tied to individualism is the concept of equality, which means "equal opportunity." Because America was free of the European rigidities of social rank and class and because of a general shortage of labor in America to fill the jobs of the expanding economic system, opportunities seemed open for all people, and the notion of equal opportunity took firm root in early America. Everyone was felt to have an equal chance to engage in trade and commerce, to make one's own way, or to pull up stakes and move to the Western frontier if necessary for a new start. Although American Indians, freed slaves, European immigrants, and women found American society to offer less than its announced free opportunity for all, the philosophical ideal of equality of opportunity has developed into an enduring ideological principle of free enterprise.

Private Property Rights. The rights of private property are the legal mechanism for strengthening individualism and preserving free choice. The self-sufficiency afforded to citizens through the rights of private property forms the basis by which individuals are able to secure their personal liberties. Aristotle said a "moderate and sufficient property" for the great mass of people will maintain liberty. The ownership of property allows one to control one's own destiny rather than to have important decisions made by someone else.

Private property also becomes the basis for decentralization of political and economic power. The free enterprise system is founded on the right of private property and the decentralization of control over national economic resources. Society has delegated to individuals the right to own and use physical property for the production and distribution of goods and services to the public. The right to profit—that is, to increase one's holdings of private property—is dependent on the ability of businesspersons to discharge their production and service responsibilities to the public. Profit is a payment made to owners who use their property for productive purposes. Thus, profits become a powerful incentive for property owners to use their property in productive ways that contribute to their own personal welfare as well as to the well-being of society in general.

Competition. The notion of competition is an indispensable part of the free enterprise system. Individuals are to compete for economic rewards, such as good jobs, promotions and quality goods and services. A competitive system will reward the economically competent and punish those who are incompetent or have little ambition. Competition, therefore, is society's method of encouraging high levels of economic performance from all its citizens. Competition channels the interest of self-seeking individuals into productive enterprise which has socially valuable consequences. The competitive process also is felt to be a successful means of selecting those most fit for positions of leadership. And beyond these factors, competition keeps power from being concentrated exclusively in the hands of a few.

Limited Government. If people are to be free to dedicate their private property and energies to working hard and producing needed goods and services to promote their own self-interest, competition is necessary to regulate these individual efforts to maximize the well-being of the entire society also. Consequently, in a free market system with sufficient competition, there is no natural need for governmental interference. Moreover, if government laws and regulations stand in the way of individual initiative and general social welfare, they should be stripped away. Beyond protecting private property, enforcing contracts, and providing for the general security of the individual, the government has little to do. This philosophical ideal of limited government that follows a "hands-off" policy toward business is still a popular belief of the free enterprise ideology.

Specialization. Adam Smith argued that specialization of workers and capital was the method by which increased productivity could be obtained. He also argued for specialization among nations and free international trade to increase the general welfare of all nations. In effect, Smith believed that competition would provide sufficient coordination among the specialized parts to efficiently and effectively run the economic world.

PRESSURES ON TRADITIONAL IDEOLOGY

Over the years, and particularly since the Civil War, the free enterprise ideology has been tested for usefulness by the major social changes occurring in America. However, time and again Americans handled historic confrontations not so much by the ideological blueprint of free enterprise as through innovative institutional mechanisms which permitted decisions to be made as specific challenges arose. Americans did not intentionally abandon the ideals of free enterprise, but their piecemeal solutions to immediate needs and pressures of different groups added up to an erosion of the fundamental concepts of the free enterprise ideology.

The most important social changes that challenged the free enterprise ideology include the following:

- The growth of big business firms and the formulation of cartel arrangements brought about a reduction in competition and an increase in monopolistic practices. Populist movements to counteract these trends resulted in the antitrust laws and the beginning of the expansion of the power of government.
- The formulation of early interest groups signaled a retreat from the idea of limited government. Farmers sought price supports for farm commodities; workers demanded minimum wages; and small businesses sought protection from big business competition.
- The Great Depression of the 1930s further expanded government programs to offset unemployment and lagging business conditions. The depression seemed to eliminate the idea that unemployment was the result of laziness or lack of individual initiative. Instead, many persons believed the free enterprise *system* contained flaws which necessitated governmental efforts to support the economic level of operations and the individuals within the system who were not receiving a "fair share." In effect, the concept of *laissez-faire* became unacceptable policy to society.
- The size of government grew even larger as a result of World Wars I and II. The concept of a government limited in size seemed to be gone forever.
- The formulation of the organizational society challenged the ideological concepts of individualism and self-reliance. With the growth of big business came the demand for organized labor. Government welfare operations grew in size. Large-scale farming put tremendous pressure on the family farm, and educational institutions became massive. As a result, group membership became more important than property as a means to ensuring one's income, health, and other privileges granted through membership. The struggle to achieve one's livelihood through independence and self-reliance seemed to be superseded by the effort to organize and make group demands.
- The group demands of the 1960s and 1970s challenged traditional business ideology even more. Industrial pollution and resource depletion caused ecological concerns. Environmentalists pressed for a slowdown from America's unbounded economic expansion. Minorities and women demanded equality in employment and promotion rights because they feel true equality of opportunity never existed for them. The consumer movement pressed for more and truthful information about products; for safe

> products; and for more competition among firms as an effort to reduce prices. The elderly pressed for retirement security. All of these group concerns challenged the traditional ideological concepts of freedom, individual initiative, limited government, and the social effectiveness of competition and the market system itself.
>
> Big business has grown to accept and seek governmental policies which stabilize the economy and protect domestic firms from foreign competitors. Businesses have also long sought the aid of government in the form of subsidies, loans, or regulatory protection. Such governmental actions erode the concept of a *free* market.

It is hard for managers in either business or government to operate within an environment where old ideals no longer seem to work. It is even more difficult because new concepts or ideology are still unfamiliar and disruptive. There is a need to stand back in order to look at the whole array of problems and not merely at those questions which come one by one.

However, meeting the challenge is not easy. Old ideas die hard. They had glorious associations with the past. And the old ideology is often used to legitimize the seats of power and justify the status quo. Nobody likes to look at the weaknesses of the ideology that justifies his or her position and privilege. More often than not, arguments are made to "return to the ideas that made America great."

ARGUMENTS AGAINST CHANGE IN BUSINESS IDEOLOGY

Some business firms have embraced the idea of business involvement in accomplishing social goals. Others have expressed a difference of opinion concerning business' "social responsibilities." The opponents of business' social involvement argue for the preservation of the free enterprise system and its ideology.

LOSS OF ECONOMIC EFFICIENCY

Classical economists argued that business enhances public welfare when it reduces costs and improves efficiency in its effort to maximize profits. Even though businesspersons are selfishly motivated in their drive for profits, competition forces them to behave in the public interest in the long run by reducing costs and prices. Classical economists argued that businesspersons are more socially responsive when they adhere strictly to their economic interests and thereby achieve economic efficiency in the allocation of scarce economic resources. In contrast, if executives use resources for social purposes, they would have to rely on directives from sources other than the free market in allocating scarce resources to alternative uses. Without the discipline and direction of market stimuli in the allocation of social resources, businesspersons lack appropriate criteria for the direction of those resources. Since the function of business is economic, economic rather than social values should be the only criteria used to measure success and direct the use of resources. Use of social criteria will cause a loss of economic efficiency.

Some people feel that the public is being misled about who will pay the costs for such social activities by business. Sometimes the public thinks they are going to get these benefits "free." However, the public must bear the costs of businesses' social involvement. Businesses will pass these costs through the price structure. As the ancient economist has stated, "There is no free lunch." Moreover, society may well demand social programs by companies where the costs of the program exceed the benefits of the program. This obviously involves a misallocation of economic resources.

MANAGERIAL INCOMPETENCE

Since society's resources are limited, there is a need to set social priorities because not all social goals can be achieved at once. Sometimes unreasonable societal expectations do not allow for appropriate establishment of priorities among the social goals. In either case, there is a severe question concerning the right of private management to make decisions concerning social priorities in the allocation of social resources. Business managers may have no social competence in justifying and settling social issues. Placing the burden of nonmarket responsibilities on businesspersons forces them to abandon their professional competence in the pursuit of a set of skills and perceptions that they do not possess. Consequently, even if social concerns are brought within the purview of management without loss of economic efficiency, managers are not likely to correctly identify and effectively deal with social problems.

LOSS OF LEGITIMACY

The historical character of the business firm has been one of a private entity dealing with private property. When managers divert business property into any activity other than furthering the economic interests of the business owners, they are effectively depriving the owners of their property and thereby weakening the justification both for the manager's own authority and for the existence of the organization itself. Thus, any attempt to transform the business into a more public institution, one acting on some concept of the "public interest" and governed by political processes, only brings into question the basic legitimacy of the firm as a private entity.

Moreover, because the business firm is a private entity, it has no direct lines of accountability to the people. Consequently, many have argued that it is unwise to allow business activities in social areas where it is not accountable. Arguing against an expanded scope of social responsibility for business, Milton Friedman asked a series of questions: "Can self-selected private individuals decide what burden they are justified in placing on themselves and their stockholders to serve that social interest? Is it tolerable that these public functions . . . be exercised by the people who happen at the moment to be in charge of a particular enterprise, chosen for those posts by strictly private groups?"[2] The implication of Friedman's questions is that business leaders are illegitimate in the sense that they are not elected as public officials and that they are not held accountable to the public as long as they remain private entities. The obvious fear of the opponents of the social responsibility doctrine is that its adoption will inevitably lead to cries for the accountability of management and the evolution of a political government system within business organizations. Such an evolution would transform the business firm from a voluntary association into a potentially coercive political institution. For these reasons, Friedman referred to the expanded scope of social responsibility as "a fundamentally subversive doctrine."[3]

THREAT TO POLITICAL PLURALISM

Even if businesses are able to expand their scope of social responsibility without excessive loss of economic efficiency, without taking on tasks for which they are totally incompetent, and without undermining their status of legitimacy, opponents of the social responsibility doctrine insist that it constitutes a threat to social and political pluralism and freedom in America. They argue that if the market system no longer directs the activities of the business firm, political direction from the state will become increasingly necessary as businesses involve themselves in social causes. This will result in a gradual expansion of the political direction over business and an expansion of the centralization of control over society.

Frederick Hayek argued that the increasingly pervasive influence of business will give rise to increasing demand for governmental control:

> The more it comes to be accepted that corporations ought to be directed in the services of specific public interests, the more pervasive becomes the contention that, as government is the appointed guardian of public interest, government should also have the power to tell corporations what they must do.[4]

Theodore Levitt added the following:

> Welfare and society are not the corporation's business. Its business is making money, not sweet music. The same goes for unions. Their business is "bread and butter" and job rights. In a free enterprise system, welfare is supposed to be automatic; and where it is not, it becomes government's job. This is the concept of pluralism. Government's job is not business and business' job is not government. And unless these functions are resolutely separated in all respects, they are eventually combined in every respect. In the end, the danger is not that government will run business, or that business will run government,

but rather that the two of them will coalesce . . . into a single power, unopposed and unopposable.[5]

Finally, John K. Galbraith has written the following:

Given the deep dependence of the industrial system upon the state and . . . its identification with public goals and the adaptation of these to its needs, the industrial system will not long be regarded as something apart from government. . . . Increasingly, it will be recognized that the mature corporation, as it develops, becomes part of the larger administrative complex associated with the state. In time, the line between the two will disappear. Men will look back in amusement at the pretense that once caused people to refer to General Dynamics and North American Aviation and AT&T as *private* businesses.[6]

Besides the merging of business and government, Galbraith suggested that the corporation itself may become the principal government structure of society. He argued that not only will the elite of the managerial class, which he termed "the technostructure," control the business firms throughout society but the large business firms will develop interconnections so that the technostructure will gradually come to dominate society as a whole. However, in the process of taking over society, the technostructure itself will be influenced by society, so that the technostructure and society will tend to merge into a single decision-making system in which social goals are accomplished.

Whether it is government or business that comes to dominate society, political pluralism is threatened by the expansion of the scope of business involvement in social affairs.

ARGUMENTS FOR CHANGES IN BUSINESS IDEOLOGY

Arguments for an expanded scope of social involvement by business suggest that there are potential benefits for society and for business. They generally imply that business firms can be effective producers of economic values as well as effective socially minded citizens.

CHANGED SOCIETAL EXPECTATIONS

The major argument for business assumption of an expanded social involvement is the changing needs and expectations of society. Society has unquestionable authority to issue or retract grants of privilege, including the basic rights of private property and the decentalization of control over economic resources. The owners of economic resources, in order to maintain a "free" system, are obliged to provide goods and services of the quality and quantity needed by society. The right to profit is dependent on the ability of business organizations to discharge their service responsibilities to the public. To the extent that business is able to comply with this responsibility, it is not necessary for society to modify the rights and privileges of private property and the private management of economic resources. Therefore, if business wishes to remain successful in the long run, it must respond to society's needs and expectations.

Many argue that the basic economic needs of American citizens have been met by successes of the free enterprise system. However, it is precisely because business has been so successful in meeting these basic economic needs that society has increased its levels of expectation concerning social needs. In short, the production of goods and services alone is no longer sufficient to satisfy society. Society's concern for the "quality of life" requires that business concern itself with social goals as well as production goals.

It has been argued that businesspersons need to recognize that they are part of the complex and interdependent social system in which their decisions may affect the quality of life. Failure to recognize this interdependence may well lead to severe modifications of the business institution. Many argue that businesspersons will commit a grievous error if they perceive societal request for social involvement as a passing fad.[7]

DISCOURAGEMENT OF MORE GOVERNMENT REGULATION

Many argue that if business is socially responsive, this will reduce the need for additional regulation of the business system by government. With reduced regulation, businesses will be free to adopt different courses to solving problems and decision making itself will be decentralized in keeping with our political philosophy. Moreover, this would keep the decision making at the point where the operating problem occurs and allow a more appropriate remedy to be fashioned without bureaucratic entanglements.

Many social problems will not be solved through the normal processes of the market system. Society long ago recognized that if persons are excluded from the market by institutional barriers such as sex or race discrimination or by the simple fact of poverty, their preferences for the distribution of productive resources will not be registered in the market system. Such arbitrary exclusion of members of society from the economic decision-making process undermines the philosophical basis for pluralistic democracy. The allocation of resources by the market system under such conditions can be accepted at a social optimum only if the preferences of the excluded members of society are considered irrelevant. Failure of the business system to modify its discriminatory hiring and training progams resulted in governmental regulations attempting to integrate the excluded members. Other social goods such as environmental qualities are not achieved through the simple market system. Voluntary programs of social involvement in these and other areas were required. Failure to integrate these social goals in the decision-making process for business firms resulted in an enlargement of the governmental regulatory sphere. Business firms reap enlarged public appreciation and reduced governmental regulations when they voluntarily set up programs that achieve social goals expected by society.

INADEQUACY OF REGULATORY TECHNIQUES

If businesses are acting irresponsibly, people always turn to the government for more laws. But laws do not always seem to solve the problems. Christopher Stone argues that we have put the problem backwards.[8] As a society, since corporations will not be responsive on their own, we demand new laws. Stone argues that since law doesn't work, we need "social responsibility."

Stone argues law is not an adequate control of *institutional* behavior, because laws are designed to control individuals. Moreover, he maintains the inadequacy of present regulatory techniques preclude their adoption as the primary means of achieving responsible corporate behavior. He points out that the lawmaking process itself suffers from a time lag problem in identifying behavior that should be outlawed. The legal process also operates with an information gap because those in government seldom know as much as corporate officials. Moreover, legal forums are generally unsuitable for the resolution of complex business-social issues. Stone argues that society's "trust in the legal machinery as a means of keeping corporations in bounds is misplaced—and that, therefore, something more is needed." And the "something more," according to Stone, is voluntary moral judgments by responsible business people.

According to Stone, the role of the law should be limited to (1) ensuring a representative cross section of private and public members on the board of directors and (2) mandating the collection and reporting of pertinent corporation-social data to the board. This "reformed" board with adequate data of the current corporation-social affairs can be generally relied on to form voluntary moral judgments consistent with social expectations.

Laws set standards for general applicability which establishes minimum standards of behavior. American society has been reluctant to require "excellence" in legal standards. Laws that specify minimum standards of conduct (Thou shalt not steal) seem more legally enforceable than laws of "aspiration" which exhort individuals to realize their fullest potential (Thou shalt do justice). Consequently, law will never be a good mechanism for drawing out of a company the best of which it is capable. Therefore, voluntary efforts to become socially responsible are needed as a better alternative to the governmental directives for behavior.

Connected to the idea that law cannot control the social behavior of business is the notion that "prevention is better than cure." Business firms may well find it to their advantage to tackle social problems in their incipiency, rather than waiting for them to become full-blown social breakdowns requiring governmental intrusions into business practices. If business would aspire to higher levels of moral behavior through "preventive" efforts, proponents of social involvement argue that business could use its valuable resources in the design of solutions to social problems. Many have pointed to the managerial, technical, and financial resources that business has which could be utilized in innovative ways to deal with social problems. Indeed, many argue that government efforts have often failed in handling social problems and that business may well provide an organizational environment more conducive to achieving social goals. Such assets belie the argument that management lacks competence to deal with social issues. Business' neglect of social involvement on the grounds of incompetence is no more tolerable to society than its negligence to keep accounting records because its accountant is not fully trained. Business either develops the ability to handle these social tasks or it goes out of business.

SOCIAL INVOLVEMENT IN STOCKHOLDER'S INTEREST

Though the argument is not without critics, some individuals believe that if investors diversified their stock ownership, corporate activities that would not be worthwhile to stockholders in a single firm would become worthwhile to the diversified stockholders.[9] Responsible corporate behavior that would enrich the public sector as a whole would also operate to benefit holders of a diversified stock portfolio. For example, a corporation training program for poorly qualified employees could benefit the business community as a whole. Even if the employees left for another company, the benefit of their training would not be lost to more diversified investors. With more and more individual savings being held by financial institutions with diversified portfolios, this argument gains strength.

Firms have also discovered that the solution of certain social problems can result in a direct flow of profit. For example, some companies have found that their reclamation of industrial waste can be profitable. Others have noted that failure to become socially involved jeopardizes not only their profit but the very survival of the firm itself. Increasingly larger number of investors and financial institutions are restricting their funds to those socially minded firms who have forestalled the possibility of long-term problems occasioned by socially inept decision making.

THE SOCIALIZATION PROCESS

Gradual recognition of social responsibilities by business is an evolutionary process. The evolving patterns of new attitude and behavior are reflected in the pragmatic reaction of business to changing circumstances rather than in the adoption of a new coherent ideology. Groping for solutions that "succeed" often entails a compromise of ideological principles. Therefore, in spite of the historical dominance of the free enterprise ideology in American society, the actual practices of management often deviate from ideological norms. Increasingly, business firms are recognizing that social approbation does not flow from the achievement of profits alone. Economic and *social* criteria have become the basis for appraising the role of business in society today. The process by which new criteria for performance are formed has been identified by Preston and Post as involving three stages.[10]

The first stage in the socialization process involves the *recognition* of relevant publics affected by the firm's activities. In the second stage, the firm *acknowledges* "some responsibility to consider its impact upon such publics in the process of making decisions and conducting its activities." When "negative" impacts are identified, decisions ought to be modified to reduce such impact. The third stage in the socialization process involves the firm's *development of a positive stance* of its own whereby the goals of the "publics" become incorporated into the goals of the firm itself. In essence, the firm becomes further socialized, interacting with the relevant publics in the solution of common problems. As the socialization process proceeds, management develops a new rhetoric to explain its involvement in society. The changes in behavior and rhetoric during the last decades seem to clearly indicate that most businesses are already socially involved, especially larger firms that have a significant impact on society. Free enterprise thinking still dominates American consciousness; however, ideological shifts are evident.

THE AMERICAN BUSINESS CREED

Researchers in the 1950s analyzed the content of many speeches, articles, and books written by business executives.[11] The researchers sought to determine if business ideology had shifted as a result of the events of the Great Depression. They found that two distinct strains of thought among business people existed. The classical strain embodied the concepts of free enterprise. However, the managerial strain emphasized the importance of professional management. These socially minded managers saw themselves as public trustees directing their corporations not just for stockholders, but also to promote the public interest. Other researchers in the 1960s confirmed the existence of the managerial strain.[12]

A NEW IDEOLOGY?

The great social changes of the 20th century have led George Cabot Lodge to suggest the beginning contours of a new American ideology.[13] He argued that five new ideological contours seem to have replaced the old Lockean five of individualism, property rights, competition, limited state, and specialization. Lodge's five are the following.

Communitarianism. The imperative of individual involvement with social organizations today negates the opportunities for individuals to live in ways Locke or Emerson idealized.

In 1951, the editors of *Fortune* Magazine wrote:

> In our time, individualism has clashed with the whole industrial development, mass production, and the division of labor. The key to industrial development is not indepen-

dence, but interdependence. No individual is self-sufficient; each is involved with others in complicated relationships. Dominating all of this is the modern corporation, an organization of vast powers, which exacts of its managers purely impersonal decisions. It is little wonder that men have turned to the state in order to protect themselves in such a world.[14]

The communitarian organizational style of both corporations and unions fostered this evolution. Usually the changes have been initiated without consideration of the ideological significance of the change. For example, the teachings of the Protestant Ethic include the notion of individual fulfillment in the worker's secular "calling" or work. However, the traditional beliefs in individualism find little fulfillment on the assembly line or in the factory setting. Consequently, business' extolling of the virtues of hard work and obedience to authority is increasingly unacceptable to the community of workers as a means to self-fulfillment. Alternatively, a few workers sought gratification of their individualistic desires by joining absentee lists, by acting insubordinately toward management, or by finding individual fulfillment away from the job. However, most workers attained new identity and fulfillment in mutual associations. The result is an organizational style (management and union group) which seeks a "consensus" (a communitarianism ideal) rather than individualistically designed contracts of employment. In short, individuals achieve status through working with others rather than struggling alone. Rugged individualism and self-reliance are being replaced by new forms of consensus.

Another example of the evolving contours of communitarianism is the field of employment opportunity. In the past, individualism demanded no more than *equal opportunity* for workers when gaining employment or seeking promotions. However, if a prohibited type of discrimination has become institutionalized, as in the case of several large corporations, the remedies accepted by the parties involved an *equality of representation* of the minorities at all levels of employment. In the *AT&T* case, the company agreed to upgrade 50,000 women and 6,600 minority group workers and to hire 4,000 men to fill traditionally female jobs. Thus, the remedy sought is *equality of result,* not of opportunity. This communitarian idea seems to be supplanting the individualistic one. Since individuals are unequal in many respects, companies must redesign themselves to adapt to these inequalities and to ensure a measure of equality of results.

Membership Rights. A new right has come to supersede property rights in political and social importance. It is the right to enjoy membership in some component of the community. For example, U.S. citizens who have reached the age of 65 or who are blind or disabled have an absolute right to minimum income provided by the government. These rights derive not from the individual's effort or property. Instead, they are communitarian rights which society has judged to be consistent with a "good community." Other "rights," either from membership in the union or in the management team, confer privileges and entitlements associated with the group. These membership rights supersede the rights and privileges of owning property; indeed, they are often at the expense of property owners. Membership rights, rather than property rights, tend to guarantee a person's security and well-being.

In addition, the ethical teachings encouraging the individual to practice thrift and to delay gratification have been undermined by the marketing and credit extension policies of business. Coupled with the reality of individuals seeking security from group membership, this has produced in America a declining rate of savings for investment purposes. Individuals do not perceive the need to *accumulate* property to enjoy life or secure their old age.

In the process of social transformation, the utility of property as a legitimizing idea has been eroded also. Large public corporations are not private entities controlled by private owners (shareholders). The shareholders do not control or assume responsibility for company affairs. They are investors who receive an adequate return on their investments or they put their money elsewhere. Ralph Nader and his followers, who organized "Campaign GM" tried to force shareholders to behave like owners and thus legitimize corporations as property. GM managers labeled such stockholder agitation as radically designed by "an adversary culture . . . antagonistic to our American ideas of private property and individual responsibility." Of course, the reverse is true; GM was the radical. Nader was the conservative, attempting to realign and control the corporation according to its ideological line of authority.

Without the legitimacy of private owners directing the use of their property, corporations have become a "collective" of various interests and amenable to community control. The shareholders, workers, managers, and government claim some "legitimate" interest in corporate resources. Corporate managers become less agents for shareholder-owners and more arbiters of conflicting interests. Managers seek to fashion an agreeable consensus.

Community Needs. Lodge pointed out that the International Telephone and Telegraph (IT&T) Company in 1977 utilized the concept of "community needs" in its appeal to be freed from the requirements of the antitrust laws. Antitrust laws seek to preserve free trade and competition. However, IT&T argued that the public interest needs IT&T to be big and strong at home so that it can withstand the political fluctuations abroad. Antitrust policy should be balanced against other public policies, such as the desire for a favorable balance of payments. In effect, the company favored a government-business identification of "community need" over the uniform application of pro-competitive laws. This notion is radically different from the traditional idea that the public interest is obtained through free and vigorous competition among companies trying to satisfy community desires. Nevertheless, more and more business firms seem willing to set aside the old idea of domestic competition so that they can better organize to meet world competition. However, if we abandon competition, "other forces" will be needed to define and preserve the community interests. The process to define community needs will doubtlessly involve a larger role for the political authority.

The Active-Planning State. The role of the state is changing radically. It will become the arbiter of community needs. Without effective competition, it will take up the task of coordination, priority setting, and planning. It will decide the contours of the trade-offs which confront us, for example, between environmental purity and energy supplies or between more revenues for auto workers or for computer programmers.

However, the impact of the old ideology of the limited state precludes government from fashioning a coherent and directive plan. An obvious example of the failure of government planning is the "energy crisis." Instead of forthrightly planning, the government attempts to deal with problems through piecemeal solutions. Lodge argues that in the future citizens will come to recognize the planning function of the state and allocate the planning responsibilities between local, regional, centralized, and global authorities.

Systems-Wide Interdependence. The ideas of atomistic competition in economic affairs and of scientific specializations in formulating knowledge seem to have given way to a new consciousness of the interrelatedness of all things. Large business firms dominate industries and multidisciplinary studies are becoming imperative. Business firms must formulate holistic planning techniques in order to comply effectively with governmental regulations on ecology and human rights. These legal requirements must be integrated into traditional business planning which heretofore has limited its horizon to costs and revenues.

In proposing these five notions as the contours of an evolving new ideology, Lodge warns against the dangers of "wishing" communitarianism away or of relegating the accommodation of the communitarianism ideology to posterity. Instead, Lodge advocates forthright ideological analysis which will allow preservation of what is best from the old ideology while consciously adapting to the new communitarian norms.

EMERGING NEW IDEOLOGY*

Old Ideology	*Emerging Ideology*
Individualism	Communitarianism
Equal Opportunity	Equality of Result
Contract	Consensus
Property Rights	Rights of Membership
Competition	Cooperation-Community Need
Limited Government	Active-Planning Government
Atomistic	Holistic
Independence	Interdependence

THE REAGAN ADMINISTRATION

President Reagan has often referred to the "oppression of big government" which, in his view, has "swallowed up" the money, rights, and liberties of the people. His administration intends to reduce the scope of federal responsibility and to transfer federal functions as much as possible to the states. These ideals expressed by the president in this "new federalism" captured more than

*Adapted from George Cabot Lodge, "Managerial Implications of Ideological Change," *The Ethics of Corporate Conduct* (Englewood Cliffs, N.J.: Prentice-Hall, 1977), pp. 79–105.

sufficient votes to win his election and to oust an incumbent president. The success of the Reagan Administration in accomplishing its goals and pleasing the populace may reverse the historical movement toward the active-planning central government envisioned by Lodge.

The programs of Reagan's presidency could well be as pronounced a change in social philosophy as Roosevelt's New Deal. On the other hand, if Reagan's plans collapse, the country may revert to seeking federal government remedies for social problems.

One person who is skeptical of the "new federalism" is Arthur Schlesinger, Jr., who has pointed out that most government growth has occurred, not at the federal level, but at the state and local level. From 1949 to 1979, the percentage of federal government employees has actually declined from 13.9 to 12.7 percent for every 1,000 Americans. The federal payroll as a percentage of the gross national product (GNP) was actually smaller in 1979 than in 1950. Moreover, the federal budget in 1954 was 19.4 percent of the GNP. This percentage increased to only 21.3 percent in 1979. In contrast, the 4.2 million employees of state and local governments in 1950 soared to 13.1 million in 1979. This 212 percent increase dwarfs the 27 percent increase at the federal level. State and local purchases of goods and services in 1980 were nearly twice as great as the federal government's purchases. As recently as 1960, the federal government's purchases had exceeded state and local purchases. Armed with such data, Schlesinger argues that the overburdened states will not be able to assimilate the federal functions Reagan intends to transfer to state and local governments, Nor does Schlesinger believe that history supports the notion that state and local governments are less corruptable, more expert, or more competent than the federal government in handling human and constitutional rights. In short, Schlesinger predicts Reagan's policies will not reverse the historical tide of a vigorous national government.

Reagan economic policies favor market-directed solutions to economic ills. Regulatory reform to Reagan usually means the abolition of regulations and the freeing of the forces of the marketplace. The success or failure of these policies will also have profound impact on which ideological beliefs emerge to dominate policies in the future.

CONCLUSION

An ideology is a set of basic beliefs that define the "good life." Free enterprise ideology consists of the basic ideas of individualism, equality of opportunity, private property rights, competition, limited government, and specialization in economic and scientific affairs.

Major economic, political, and social changes have occurred since the initial formulation of the free enterprise ideology. These changes have challenged and modified the basic beliefs of the old ideology. The emerging ideology of the modern era seems to stress communitarianism, equality of results, rights of membership, community needs, activist government, and systems-wide thinking.

Today's business ideology seems to be a mixture of old ideas and new social conditions. Corporate managers have adopted new solutions outside the ideological contours of free enterprise. Under the modern era of responsive capitalism, professional business executives act more like trustees for the public interest than for the limited interest of stockholder owners. The new ideology seems to be gaining momentum in shaping social policies, although some cling nostalgically to the old ideology in the present era, with the hope of its revitalization.

Questions

1. The traditional "economic model" of business places primary emphasis on production, profit, exploitation of resources, market-based decisions, and limited government. How would a "socially responsible" model of business contrast with these attributes?
2. What are three basic arguments against business assumption of social responsibilities?
3. What are three basic arguments supporting business assumption of social responsibilities?
4. "We can choose either to understand and move with the tides of history, whatever they may be—or attempt to resist them." Which choice is business adoption of social responsibilities?
5. Compare your ideological beliefs about business with that of (a) your parents and (b) your boss. Can you explain the reasons for any differences or similarities?
6. Which ideal of the free enterprise ideology seems most crucial? Can you rank the other ideals of the free enterprise ideology?
7. Identify a change in American society that has challenged the free enterprise ideology and explain its modification.
8. Given the emergence of a new ideology as described by Lodge, what guidance does it provide for business decision making?
9. Are financial loans and guarantees provided to Chrysler Corporation a challenge to the free enterprise ideology?
10. What are the obligations of business under the traditional economic model when it closes a plant? Under a socioeconomic model, what are its obligations?

END NOTES

1. George Cabot Lodge, "Managerial Implications of Ideological Change," *The Ethics of Corporate Conduct* (Englewood Cliffs, N.J.: Prentice-Hall, 1977), pp. 84–86.
2. Milton Friedman, *Capitalism and Freedom* (Chicago: University of Chicago Press, 1963), pp. 133–134.
3. Ibid.
4. Frederick Hayek, "The Corporation in a Democratic Society," in *Management and*

Corporation, 1985., ed. Melvin Anshen and George Bach (New York: McGraw-Hill, 1960), p. 116.
5. Theodore Levitt, "The Dangers of Social Responsibility," *Harvard Business Review,* September–October 1958, p. 41.
6. John Kenneth Galbraith, *The New Industrial State* (Boston: Houghton Mifflin Co., 1967), p. 393.
7. Dow Votaw, "Genius Becomes Rare: A Comment on the Doctrine of Social Responsibility, Pt. II," *California Management Review,* Spring 1973, pp. 16–17.
8. Christopher D. Stone, *Where the Law Ends: The Social Control of Corporate Behavior* (New York: Harper & Row, 1975).
9. Henry C. Wallich and John J. McGowan, "Stockholder Interest and the Corporation's Role in Social Policy," in *A New Rationale for Public Policy,* ed. William J. Baumol et al., (New York: Committee for Economic Development, 1970), pp. 39–59.
10. Lee E. Preston and James E. Post, *Private Management and Public Policy* (Englewood Cliffs, N.J.: Prentice-Hall, 1975), pp. 46–47.
11. Francis X. Sutton et al., *The American Business Creed* (Cambridge, Mass.: Harvard University Press, 1956).
12. Robert F. Heilbroner, "The View from the Top," in *The Business Establishment,* ed. Earl F. Sheit, (New York: Wiley, 1964), pp. 1–36.
13. Lodge, *The Ethics of Corporate Conduct.*
14. *Fortune,* February 1951.

appendix

THE CONSTITUTION OF THE UNITED STATES OF AMERICA

We the People of the United States, in Order to form a more perfect Union, establish Justice, insure domestic Tranquility, provide for the common defence, promote the general Welfare, and secure the Blessings of Liberty to ourselves and our Posterity, do ordain and establish this Constitution for the United States of America.

Article I

SECTION 1. All legislative Powers herein granted shall be vested in a Congress of the United States, which shall consist of a Senate and House of Representatives.

SECTION 2. The House of Representatives shall be composed of Members chosen every second Year by the People of the several States, and the Electors in each State shall have the Qualifications requisite for Electors of the most numerous Branch of the State Legislature.

No Person shall be a Representative who shall not have attained to the Age of twenty five Years, and been seven Years a Citizen of the United States, and who shall not, when elected, be an Inhabitant of that State in which he shall be chosen.

Representatives and direct Taxes shall be apportioned among the several States which may be included within this Union, according to their respective Numbers, which shall be determined by adding to the whole Number of free Persons, including those bound to Service for a Term of Years, and excluding Indians not taxed, three fifths of all other Persons. The actual Enumeration shall be made within three Years after the first Meeting of the Congress of the United States, and within every subsequent Term of ten Years, in such Manner as they shall by Law direct. The Number of Representatives shall not exceed one for every thirty Thousand, but each State shall have at Least one Representative; and until such enumeration shall be made, the State of New Hampshire shall be entitled to chuse three, Massachusetts eight, Rhode Island and Providence Plantations one, Connecticut five, New-York six, New Jersey four, Pennsylvania eight, Delaware one, Maryland six, Virginia ten, North Carolina five, South Carolina five, and Georgia three.

When vacancies happen in the Representation from any State, the Executive Authority thereof shall issue Writs of Election to fill such Vacancies.

The House of Representatives shall chuse their Speaker and other Officers; and shall have the sole Power of Impeachment.

SECTION 3. The Senate of the United States shall be composed of two Senators from each State, chosen by the Legislature thereof, for six Years; and each Senator shall have one Vote.

Immediately after they shall be assembled in Consequence of the first Election, they shall be divided as equally as may be into three Classes. The Seats of the Senators of the first Class shall be vacated at the Expiration of the second Year, of the second Class at the Expiration of the fourth Year, and of the third Class at the Expiration of the sixth Year, so that one third may be chosen every second Year; and if Vacancies happen by Resignation, or otherwise, during the Recess of the Legislature of any State, the Executive thereof may make temporary Appointments until the next Meeting of the Legislature, which shall then fill such Vacancies.

No Person shall be a Senator who shall not have attained to the Age of thirty Years, and been nine Years a Citizen of the United States, and who shall not, when elected, be an Inhabitant of that State for which he shall be chosen.

The Vice President of the United States shall be President of the Senate, but shall have no Vote, unless they be equally divided.

The Senate shall chuse their other Officers, and also a President pro tempore, in the Absence of the Vice President, or when he shall exercise the Office of President of the United States.

The Senate shall have the sole Power to try all Impeachments. When sitting for that Purpose, they shall be on Oath or Affirmation. When the President of the United States is tried, the Chief Justice shall preside: And no Person shall be convicted without the Concurrence of two thirds of the Members present.

Judgment in Cases of Impeachment shall not extend further than to removal from Office, and disqualification to hold and enjoy any Office of honor, Trust or Profit under the United States: but the Party convicted shall nevertheless be liable and subject to Indictment, Trial, Judgment and Punishment, according to Law.

SECTION 4. The Times, Places and Manner of holding Elections for Senators and Representatives, shall be prescribed in each State by the Legislature thereof; but the Congress may at any time by Law make or alter such Regulations, except as to the Places of chusing Senators.

The Congress shall assemble at least once in every Year, and such Meeting shall be on the first Monday in December, unless they shall by Law appoint a different Day.

SECTION 5. Each House shall be the Judge of the Elections, Returns and Qualifications of its own Members, and a Majority of each shall constitute a Quorum to do Business; but a smaller Number may adjourn from day to day, and may be authorized to compel the Attendance of absent Members, in such Manner, and under such Penalties as each House may provide.

Each House may determine the Rules of its Proceedings, punish its Members for disorderly Behaviour, and, with the Concurrence of two thirds, expel a Member.

Each House shall keep a Journal of its Proceedings, and from time to time publish the same, excepting such Parts as may in their Judgment require Secrecy; and the Yeas and Nays of the Members of either House on any question shall, at the Desire of one fifth of those Present, be entered on the Journal.

Neither House, during the Session of Congress, shall, without the Consent of the other, adjourn for more than three days, nor to any other Place, than that in which the two Houses shall be sitting.

SECTION 6. The Senators and Representatives shall receive a Compensation for their Services, to be ascertained by Law, and paid out of the Treasury of the United States. They shall in all Cases, except Treason, Felony and Breach of the Peace, be privileged from Arrest during their Attendance at the Session of their respective Houses, and in going to and returning from the same; and for any Speech or Debate in either House, they shall not be questioned in any other Place.

No Senator or Representative shall, during the Time for which he was elected, be appointed to any civil Office under the Authority of the United States, which shall have been created, or the Emoluments whereof shall have been encreased during such time; and no Person holding any Office under the United States, shall be a Member of either House during his Continuance in Office.

SECTION 7. All Bills for raising Revenue shall originate in the House of Representatives; but the Senate may propose or concur with Amendments as on other Bills.

Every Bill which shall have passed the House of Representatives and the Senate, shall, before it become a Law, be presented to the President of the United States; If he approve he shall sign it, but if not he shall return it, with his Objections to that House in which it shall have originated, who shall enter the Objections at large on their Journal, and proceed to reconsider it. If after such Reconsideration two thirds of that House shall agree to pass the Bill, it shall be sent, together with the Objections, to the other House, by which it shall likewise be reconsidered, and if approved by two thirds of that House, it shall become a Law. But in all such Cases the Votes of both Houses shall be determined by Yeas and Nays, and the Names of the Persons voting for and against the Bill shall be entered on the Journal of each House respectively. If any Bill shall not be returned by the President within ten Days (Sundays excepted) after it shall have been presented to him, the Same shall be a Law, in like Manner as if he had signed it, unless the Congress by their Adjournment prevent its Return, in which Case it shall not be a Law.

Every Order, Resolution, or Vote to which the Concurrence of the Senate and House of Representatives may be necessary (except on a question of Adjournment) shall be presented to the President of the United States; and before the Same shall take Effect, shall be approved by him, or being disapproved by him, shall be repassed by two thirds of the Senate and House of Representatives, according to the Rules and Limitations prescribed in the Case of a Bill.

SECTION 8. The Congress shall have Power to lay and collect Taxes, Duties, Imposts and Excises, to pay the Debts and provide for the common Defence and general Welfare of the United States; but all Duties, Imposts and Excises shall be uniform throughout the United States;

To borrow Money on the credit of the United States;

To regulate Commerce with foreign Nations, and among the several States, and with the Indian Tribes;

To establish an uniform Rule of Naturalization, and uniform Laws on the subject of Bankruptcies throughout the United States;

To coin Money, regulate the Value thereof, and of foreign Coin, and fix the Standard of Weights and Measures;

To provide for the Punishment of counterfeiting the Securities and current Coin of the United States;

To establish Post Offices and post Roads;

To promote the Progress of Science and useful Arts, by securing for limited Times to Authors and Inventors the exclusive Right to their respective Writings and Discoveries;

To constitute Tribunals inferior to the supreme Court;

To define and punish Piracies and Felonies committed on the high Seas, and Offences against the Law of Nations;

To declare War, grant Letters of Marque and Reprisal, and make Rules concerning Captures on Land and Water;

To raise and support Armies, but no Appropriation of Money to that Use shall be for a longer Term than two Years;

To provide and maintain a Navy;

To make Rules for the Government and Regulation of the land and naval Forces;

To provide for calling forth the Militia to execute the Laws of the Union, suppress Insurrections and repel Invasions;

To provide for organizing, arming, and disciplining, the Militia, and for governing such Part of them as may be employed in the Service of the United States, reserving to the States respectively, the Appointment of the Officers, and the Authority of training the Militia according to the discipline prescribed by Congress;

To exercise exclusive Legislation in all Cases whatsoever, over such District (not exceeding ten Miles square) as may, by Cession of particular States, and the Acceptance of Congress, become the Seat of the Government of the United States, and to exercise like Authority over all Places purchased by the Consent of the Legislature of the State in which the Same shall be, for the Erection of Forts, Magazines, Arsenals, dock-Yards, and other needful Buildings;—And

To make all Laws which shall be necessary and proper for carrying into Execution the foregoing Powers, and all other Powers vested by this Constitution in the Government of the United States, or in any Department or Officer thereof.

SECTION 9. The Migration or Importation of such Persons as any of the States now existing shall think proper to admit, shall not be prohibited by the Congress prior to the Year one thousand eight hundred and eight, but a Tax or duty may be imposed on such Importation, not exceeding ten dollars for each Person.

The Privilege of the Writ of Habeas Corpus shall not be suspended, unless when in Cases of Rebellion or Invasion the public Safety may require it.

No Bill of Attainder or ex post facto Law shall be passed.

No Capitation, or other direct, Tax shall be laid, unless in Proportion to the Census or Enumeration herein before directed to be taken.

No Tax or Duty shall be laid on Articles exported from any State.

No Preference shall be given by any Regulation of Commerce or Revenue to the Ports of one State over those of another: nor shall Vessels bound to, or from, one State, be obliged to enter, clear, or pay Duties in another.

No Money shall be drawn from the Treasury, but in Consequence of Appropriations made by Law; and a regular Statement and Account of the Receipts and Expenditures of all public Money shall be published from time to time.

No Title of Nobility shall be granted by the United States: And no Person holding any Office of Profit or Trust under them, shall, without the Consent of the Congress, accept of any present, Emolument, Office, or Title, of any kind whatever, from any King, Prince, or foreign State.

SECTION 10. No State shall enter into any Treaty, Alliance, or Confederation; grant Letters of Marque and Reprisal; coin Money; emit Bills of Credit; make any Thing but gold and silver Coin a Tender in Payment of Debts; pass any Bill of Attainder, ex post facto Law, or Law impairing the Obligation of Contracts, or grant any Title of Nobility.

No State shall, without the Consent of the Congress, lay any Imposts or Duties on Imports or Exports, except what may be absolutely necessary for executing its inspection Laws: and the net Produce of all Duties and Imposts, laid by any State on Imports or Exports, shall be for the Use of the Treasury of the United States; and all such Laws shall be subject to the Revision and Controul of the Congress.

No State shall, without the Consent of Congress, lay any Duty of Tonnage, keep Troops, or Ships of War in time of Peace, enter into any Agreement or Compact with another State, or with a foreign Power, or engage in War, unless actually invaded, or in such imminent Danger as will not admit of delay.

Article II

SECTION 1. The executive Power shall be vested in a President of the United States of America. He shall hold his Office during the Term of four Years, and, together with the Vice President, chosen for the same Term, be elected, as follows.

Each State shall appoint, in such Manner as the Legislature thereof may direct, a Number of Electors, equal to the whole Number of Senators and Representatives to which the State may be entitled in the Congress: but no Senator or Representative, or Person holding an Office of Trust or Profit under the United States, shall be appointed an Elector.

The Electors shall meet in their respective States, and vote by Ballot for two Persons, of whom one at least shall not be an Inhabitant of the same State with themselves. And they shall make a List of all the Persons voted for, and of the Number of Votes for each; which List they shall sign and certify, and transmit sealed to the Seat of the Government of the United States, directed to the President of the Senate. The President of the Senate shall, in the Presence of the Senate and House of Representatives, open all the Certificates, and the Votes shall then be counted. The Person having the greatest Number of Votes shall be the President, if such Number be a Majority of the whole Number of Electors appointed; and if there be more than one who have such Majority, and have an equal Number of Votes, then the House of Representatives shall immediately chuse by Ballot one of them for President; and if no Person have a Majority, then from the five highest on the List the said House shall in like Manner chuse the President. But in chusing the President, the Votes shall be taken by States, the Representation from each State having one Vote; A quorum for this Purpose shall consist of a Member or Members from two thirds of the States, and a Majority of all the States shall be necessary to a Choice. In every Case, after the Choice of the President, the Person having the greatest Number of Votes of the Electors shall be the Vice President. But if there should remain two or more who have equal Votes, the Senate shall chuse from them by Ballot the Vice President.

The Congress may determine the Time of chusing the Electors, and the Day on which they shall give their Votes; which Day shall be the same throughout the United States.

No Person except a natural born Citizen, or a Citizen of the United States, at the time of the Adoption of this Constitution, shall be eligible to the Office of President; neither shall any Person be eligible to that Office who shall not have attained to the Age of thirty five Years, and been fourteen Years a Resident within the United States.

In Case of the Removal of the President from Office, or of his Death, Resignation, or Inability to discharge the Powers and Duties of the said Office, the Same shall devolve on the Vice President, and the Congress may by Law provide for the Case of Removal, Death, Resignation or Inability, both of the President and Vice President, declaring what Officer shall then act as President, and such Officer shall act accordingly, until the Disability be removed, or a President shall be elected.

The President shall, at stated Times, receive for his Services, a Compensation, which shall neither be encreased nor diminished during the Period for which he shall have been elected, and he shall not receive within that Period any other Emolument from the United States, or any of them.

Before he enter on the Execution of his Office, he shall take the following Oath or Affirmation:—"I do solemnly swear (or affirm) that I will faithfully execute the Office of President of the United States, and will to the best of my Ability, preserve, protect and defend the Constitution of the United States."

SECTION 2. The President shall be Commander in Chief of the Army and Navy of the United States, and of the Militia of the several States, when called into the actual Service of the United States; he may require the Opinion, in writing, of the principal Officer in each of the executive Departments, upon any subject relating to the Duties of their respective Offices, and he shall have Power to grant Reprieves and Pardons for Offences against the United States, except in Cases of Impeachment.

He shall have Power, by and with the Advice and Consent of the Senate, to make Treaties, providing two thirds of the Senators present concur; and he shall nominate, and by and with the Advice and Consent of the Senate, shall appoint Ambassadors, other public Ministers and Consuls, Judges of the supreme Court, and all other Officers of the United States, whose Appointments are not herein otherwise provided for, and which shall be established by Law: but the Congress may by Law vest the Appointment of such inferior Officers, as they think proper, in the President alone, in the Courts of Law, or in the Heads of Departments.

The President shall have Power to fill up all Vacancies that may happen during the Recess of the Senate, by granting Commissions which shall expire at the End of their next Session.

SECTION 3. He shall from time to time give to the Congress Information of the State of the Union, and recommend to their Consideration such Measures as he shall judge necessary and expedient; he may, on extraordinary Occasions, convene both Houses, or either of them, and in Case of Disagreement between them, with Respect to the Time of Adjournment, he may adjourn them to such Time as he shall think proper; he shall receive Ambassadors and other public Ministers; he shall take Care that the Laws be faithfully executed, and shall Commission all the Officers of the United States.

SECTION 4. The President, Vice President and all civil Officers of the United States, shall be removed from Office on Impeachment for, and Conviction of, Treason, Bribery, or other high Crimes and Misdemeanors.

Article III

SECTION 1. The judicial Power of the United States, shall be vested in one supreme Court, and in such inferior Courts as the Congress may from time to time ordain and establish. The Judges, both of the supreme and inferior Courts, shall hold their Offices during good Behaviour, and shall, at stated Times, receive for their Services, a Compensation, which shall not be diminished during their Continuance in Office.

SECTION 2. The judicial Power shall extend to all Cases, in Law and Equity, arising under this Constitution, the Laws of the United States, and Treaties made, or which shall be made, under their Authority;—to all Cases affecting Ambassadors, other public Ministers and Consuls;—to all Cases of admiralty and maritime Jurisdiction;—to Controversies to which the United States shall be a Party;—to Controversies between two or more States;—between a State and Citizens of another State;—between Citizens of different States;—between Citizens of the same state claiming Lands under Grants of different States, and between a State, or the Citizens thereof, and foreign States, Citizens or Subjects.

In all Cases affecting Ambassadors, other public Ministers and Consuls, and those in which a State shall be Party, the supreme Court shall have original Jurisdiction. In all the other Cases before mentioned, the supreme Court shall have appellate Jurisdiction, both as to Law and Fact, with such Exceptions, and under such Regulations as the Congress shall make.

The Trial of all Crimes, except in Cases of Impeachment, shall be by Jury; and such Trial shall be held in the State where the said Crimes shall have been committed; but when not committed within any State, the Trial shall be at such Place or Places as the Congress may by Law have directed.

SECTION 3. Treason against the United States, shall consist only in levying War against them, or in adhering to their Enemies, giving them Aid and Comfort. No Person shall be convicted of Treason unless on the Testimony of two Witnesses to the same overt Act, or on Confession in open Court.

The Congress shall have Power to declare the Punishment of Treason, but no Attainder of Treason shall work Corruption of Blood, or Forfeiture except during the Life of the Person attainted.

Article IV

SECTION 1. Full Faith and Credit shall be given in each State to the public Acts, Records, and judicial Proceedings of every other State. And the Congress may by general Laws prescribe the Manner in which such Acts, Records and Proceedings shall be proved, and the Effect thereof.

SECTION 2. The Citizens of each State shall be entitled to all Privileges and Immunities of Citizens in the several States.

A Person charged in any State with Treason, Felony, or other Crime, who shall flee from Justice, and be found in another State, shall on Demand of the executive Authority of the State from which he fled, be delivered up, to be removed to the State having Jurisdiction of the Crime.

No Person held to Service or Labour in one State, under the Laws thereof, escaping into another, shall, in Consequence of any Law or Regulation therein, be discharged from such Service or Labour, but shall be delivered up on Claim of the Party to whom such Service or Labour may be due.

SECTION 3. New States may be admitted by the Congress into this Union; but no new State shall be formed or erected within the Jurisdiction of any other State; nor any State be formed by the Junction of two or more States, or Parts of States, without the Consent of the Legislatures of the States concerned as well as of the Congress.

The Congress shall have Power to dispose of and make all needful Rules and Regulations respecting the Territory or other Property belonging to the United States; and nothing in this Constitution shall be so construed as to Prejudice any Claims of the United States, or of any particular State.

SECTION 4. The United States shall guarantee to every State in this Union a Republican Form of Government, and shall protect each of them against Invasion; and on Application of the Legislature, or of the Executive (when the Legislature cannot be convened) against domestic Violence.

Article V

The Congress, whenever two thirds of both Houses shall deem it necessary, shall propose Amendments to this Constitution, or, on the Application of the Legislatures of two thirds of the several States, shall call a Convention for proposing Amendments, which, in either Case, shall be valid to all Intents and Purposes, as Part of this Constitution, when ratified by the Legislatures of three fourths of the several States, or by Conventions in three fourths thereof, as the one or the other Mode of Ratification may be proposed by the Congress; Provided that no Amendment which may be made prior to the Year One thousand eight hundred and eight shall in any Manner affect the first and fourth Clauses in the Ninth Section of the first Article; and that no State, without its Consent, shall be deprived of its equal Suffrage in the Senate.

Article VI

All Debts contracted and Engagements entered into, before the Adoption of this Constitution, shall be as valid against the United States under this Constitution, as under the Confederation.

This Constitution, and the Laws of the United States which shall be made in Pursuance thereof; and all Treaties made, or which shall be made, under the Authority of the United States, shall be the supreme Law of the Land; and the Judges in every State shall be bound thereby, any Thing in the Constitution or Laws of any State to the Contrary notwithstanding.

The Senators and Representatives before-mentioned, and the members of the several State Legislatures, and all executive and judicial Officers, both of the United States and of the several States, shall be bound by Oath or Affirmation, to support this Constitution; but no religious Test shall ever be required as a Qualification to any Office or public Trust under the United States.

Article VII

The Ratification of the Conventions of nine States, shall be sufficient for the Establishment of this Constitution between the States so ratifying the Same.

AMENDMENTS TO THE CONSTITUTION OF THE UNITED STATES OF AMERICA

Amendment I [1791]

Congress shall make no law respecting an establishment of religion, or prohibiting the free exercise thereof; or abridging the freedom of speech, or of the press; or the right of the people peaceably to assemble, and to petition the Government for a redress of grievances.

Amendment II [1791]

A well regulated Militia, being necessary to the security of a free State, the right of the people to keep and bear Arms, shall not be infringed.

Amendment III [1791]

No Soldier shall, in time of peace be quartered in any house, without the consent of the Owner, nor in time of war, but in a manner to be prescribed by law.

Amendment IV [1791]

The right of the people to be secure in their persons, houses, papers, and effects, against unreasonable searches and seizures, shall not be violated, and no Warrants shall issue, but upon probable cause, supported by Oath or affirmation, and particularly describing the place to be searched, and the persons or things to be seized.

Amendment V [1791]

No person shall be held to answer for a capital, or otherwise infamous crime, unless on a presentment or indictment of a Grand Jury, except in cases arising in the land or naval forces, or in the Militia, when in actual service in time of War or public danger; nor shall any person be subject for the same offence to be twice put in jeopardy of life or limb; nor shall be compelled in any criminal case to be a witness against himself, nor be deprived of life, liberty, or property, without due process of law; nor shall private property be taken for public use, without just compensation.

Amendment VI [1791]

In all criminal prosecutions, the accused shall enjoy the right to a speedy and public trial, by an impartial jury of the State and district wherein the crime shall have been committed, which district shall have been previously ascertained by law, and to be informed of the nature and cause of the accusation; to be confronted with the Witnesses against him; to have compulsory process for obtaining witnesses in his favor, and to have the Assistance of Counsel for his defence.

Amendment VII [1791]

In Suits at common law, where the value in controversy shall exceed twenty dollars, the right of trial by jury shall be preserved, and no fact tried by a jury, shall be otherwise re-examined in any Court of the United States, than according to the rules of the common law.

Amendment VIII [1791]

Excessive bail shall not be required, nor excessive fines imposed, nor cruel and unusual punishments inflicted.

Amendment IX [1791]

The enumeration in the Constitution, of certain rights, shall not be construed to deny or disparage others retained by the people.

Amendment X [1791]

The powers not delegated to the United States by the Constitution, nor prohibited by it to the States, are reserved to the States respectively, or to the people.

Amendment XI [1798]

The Judicial power of the United States shall not be construed to extend to any suit in law or equity, commenced or prosecuted against one of the United States by Citizens of another State, or by Citizens or Subjects of any Foreign State.

Amendment XII [1804]

The Electors shall meet in their respective states and vote by ballot for President and Vice-President, one of whom, at least, shall not be an inhabitant of the same state with themselves; they shall name in their ballots the person voted for as President, and in distinct ballots the person voted for as Vice-President, and they shall make distinct lists of all persons voted for as President, and of all persons voted for as Vice-President, and of the number of votes for each, which lists they shall sign and certify, and transmit sealed to the seat of the government of the United States, directed to the President of the Senate;—The President of the Senate shall, in the presence of the Senate and House of Representatives, open all the certificates and the votes shall then be counted;—The person having the greatest number of votes for President, shall be the President, if such number be a majority of the whole number of Electors appointed; and if no person have such majority, then from the persons having the highest numbers not exceeding three on the list of those voted for as President, the House of Representatives shall choose immediately, by ballot, the President. But in choosing the President, the votes shall be taken by states, the representation from each state having one vote; a quorum for this purpose shall consist of a member or members from two-thirds of the states, and a majority of all the states shall be necessary to a choice. And if the House of Representatives shall not choose a President whenever the right of choice shall devolve upon them, before the fourth day of March next following, then the Vice-President shall act as President, as in the case of the death or other constitutional disability of the President. The person having the greatest number of votes as Vice-President, shall be the Vice-President, if such number be a majority of the whole number of Electors appointed, and if no person have a majority, then from the two highest numbers on the list, the Senate shall choose the Vice-President; a quorum for the purpose shall consist of two-thirds of the whole number of Senators, and a majority of the whole number shall be necessary to a choice. But no person constitutionally ineligible to the office of President shall be eligible to that of Vice-President of the United States.

Amendment XIII [1865]

SECTION 1. Neither slavery nor involuntary servitude, except as a punishment for crime whereof the party shall have been duly convicted, shall exist within the United States, or any place subject to their jurisdiction.

SECTION 2. Congress shall have power to enforce this article by appropriate legislation.

Amendment XIV [1868]

SECTION 1. All persons born or naturalized in the United States, and subject to the jurisdiction thereof, are citizens of the United States and of the State wherein they reside. No State shall make or enforce any law which shall abridge the privileges or immunities of citizens of the United States; nor shall any State deprive any person of life, liberty, or property, without due process of law; nor deny to any person within its jurisdiction the equal protection of the laws.

SECTION 2. Representatives shall be apportioned among the several States according to their respective numbers, counting the whole number of persons in each State, excluding Indians not taxed. But when the right to vote at any election for the choice of electors for President and Vice President of the United States, Representatives in Congress, the Executive and Judicial officers of a State, or the members of the Legislature thereof, is denied to any of the male inhabitants of such State, being twenty-one years of age, and citizens of the United States, or in any way abridged, except for participation in rebellion, or other crime, the basis of representation therein shall be reduced in the proportion which the number of such male citizens shall bear to the whole number of male citizens twenty-one years of age in such State.

SECTION 3. No person shall be a Senator or Representative in Congress, or elector of President and Vice President, or hold any office, civil or military, under the United States, or under any State, who, having previously taken an oath, as a member of Congress, or as an officer of the United States, or as a member of any State legislature, or as an executive or judicial officer of any State, to support the Constitution of the United States, shall have engaged in insurrection or rebellion against the same, or given aid or comfort to the enemies thereof. But Congress may by a vote of two-thirds of each House, remove such disability.

SECTION 4. The validity of the public debt of the United States, authorized by law, including debts incurred for payment of pensions and bounties for services in suppressing insurrection or rebellion, shall not be questioned. But neither the United States nor any State shall assume or pay any debt or obligation incurred in aid of insurrection or rebellion against the United States, or any claim for the loss or emancipation of any slave; but all such debts, obligations and claims shall be held illegal and void.

SECTION 5. The Congress shall have power to enforce, by appropriate legislation, the provisions of this article.

Amendment XV [1870]

SECTION 1. The right of citizens of the United States to vote shall not be denied or abridged by the United States or by any State on account of race, color, or previous condition of servitude.

SECTION 2. The Congress shall have power to enforce this article by appropriate legislation.

Amendment XVI [1913]

The Congress shall have power to lay and collect taxes on incomes, from whatever source derived, without apportionment among the several States, and without regard to any census or enumeration.

Amendment XVII [1913]

The Senate of the United States shall be composed of two Senators from each State, elected by the people thereof, for six years; and each Senator shall have one vote. The electors in each State shall have the qualifications requisite for electors of the most numerous branch of the State legislatures.

When vacancies happen in the representation of any State in the Senate, the executive authority of such State shall issue writs of election to fill such vacancies: *Provided,* That the legislature of any State may empower the executive thereof to make temporary appointments until the people fill the vacancies by election as the legislature may direct.

This amendment shall not be so construed as to affect the election or term of any Senator chosen before it becomes valid as part of the Constitution.

Amendment XVIII [1919]

SECTION 1. After one year from the ratification of this article the manufacture, sale, or transportation of intoxicating liquors within, the importation thereof into, or the exportation thereof from the United States and all territory subject to the jurisdiction thereof for beverage purposes is hereby prohibited.

SECTION 2. The Congress and the several States shall have concurrent power to enforce this article by appropriate legislation.

SECTION 3. This article shall be inoperative unless it shall have been ratified as an amendment to the Constitution by the legislatures of the several States, as provided in the Constitution, within seven years from the date of the submission hereof to the States by the Congress.

Amendment XIX [1920]

The right of citizens of the United States to vote shall not be denied or abridged by the United States or by any State on account of sex.

Congress shall have power to enforce this article by appropriate legislation.

Amendment XX [1933]

SECTION 1. The terms of the President and Vice President shall end at noon on the 20th day of January, and the terms of Senators and Representatives at noon on the 3d day of January, of the years in which such terms would have ended if this article had not been ratified; and the terms of their successors shall then begin.

SECTION 2. The Congress shall assemble at least once in every year, and such meeting shall begin at noon on the 3d day of January, unless they shall by law appoint a different day.

SECTION 3. If, at the time fixed for the beginning of the term of the President, the President elect shall have died, the Vice President elect shall become President. If a President shall not have been chosen before the time fixed for the beginning of his term, or if the President elect shall have failed to qualify, then the Vice President elect shall act as President until a President shall have qualified; and the Congress may by law provide for the case wherein neither a President elect nor a Vice President elect shall have qualified, declaring who shall then act as President, or the manner in which one who is to act shall be selected, and such person shall act accordingly until a President or Vice President shall have qualified.

SECTION 4. The Congress may by law provide for the case of the death of any of the persons from whom the House of Representatives may choose a President whenever the right of choice shall have devolved upon them, and for the case of the death of any of the persons from whom the Senate may choose a Vice President whenever the right of choice shall have devolved upon them.

SECTION 5. Sections 1 and 2 shall take effect on the 15th day of October following the ratification of this article.

SECTION 6. This article shall be inoperative unless it shall have been ratified as an amendment to the Constitution by the legislatures of three-fourths of the several States within seven years from the date of its submission.

Amendment XXI [1933]

SECTION 1. The eighteenth article of amendment to the Constitution of the United States is hereby repealed.

SECTION 2. The transportation or importation into any State, Territory, or possession of the United States for delivery or use therein of intoxicating liquors, in violation of the laws thereof, is hereby prohibited.

SECTION 3. This article shall be inoperative unless it shall have been ratified as an amendment to the Constitution by conventions in the several States, as provided in the Constitution, within seven years from the date of the submission hereof to the States by the Congress.

Amendment XXII [1951]

SECTION 1. No person shall be elected to the office of the President more than twice, and no person who has held the office of President, or acted as President, for more than two years of a term to which some other person was elected President shall be elected to the office of the President more than once. But this Article shall not apply to any person holding the office of President when this Article was proposed by the Congress, and shall not prevent any person who may be holding the office of President, or acting as President, during the term within which this Article becomes operative from holding the office of President or acting as President during the remainder of such term.

SECTION 2. This article shall be inoperative unless it shall have been ratified as an amendment to the Constitution by the legislatures of three-fourths of the several States within seven years from the date of its submission to the States by the Congress.

Amendment XXIII [1961]

SECTION 1. The District constituting the seat of Government of the United States shall appoint in such manner as the Congress may direct:

A number of electors of President and Vice President equal to the whole number of Senators and Representatives in Congress to which the District would be entitled if it were a State, but in no event more than the least populous State; they shall be in addition to those appointed by the States, but they shall be considered, for the purposes of the election of President and Vice President, to be electors appointed by a State; and they shall meet in the District and perform such duties as provided by the twelfth article of amendment.

SECTION 2. The Congress shall have power to enforce this article by appropriate legislation.

Amendment XXIV [1964]

SECTION 1. The right of citizens of the United States to vote in any primary or other election for President or Vice President, for electors for President or Vice President, or for Senator or Representative in Congress, shall not be denied or abridged by the United States or any State by reason of failure to pay any poll tax or other tax.

SECTION 2. The Congress shall have power to enforce this article by appropriate legislation.

Amendment XXV [1967]

SECTION 1. In case of the removal of the President from office or of his death or resignation, the Vice President shall become President.

SECTION 2. Whenever there is a vacancy in the office of the Vice President, the President shall nominate a Vice President who shall take office upon confirmation by a majority vote of both Houses of Congress.

SECTION 3. Whenever the President transmits to the President pro tempore of the Senate and the Speaker of the House of Representatives his written declaration that he is unable to discharge the powers and duties of his office, and until he transmits to them a written declaration to the contrary, such powers and duties shall be discharged by the Vice President as Acting President.

SECTION 4. Whenever the Vice President and a majority of either the principal officers of the executive departments or of such other body as Congress may by law provide, transmit to the President pro tempore of the Senate and the Speaker of the House of Representatives their written declaration that the President is unable to discharge the powers and duties of his office, the Vice President shall immediately assume the powers and duties of the office as Acting President.

Thereafter, when the President transmits to the President pro tempore of the Senate and the Speaker of the House of Representatives his written declaration that no inability exists, he shall resume the powers and duties of his office unless the Vice President and a majority of either the principal officers of the executive department or of such other body as Congress may by law provide, transmit within four days to the President pro tempore of the Senate and the Speaker of the House of Representatives their written declaration that the President is unable to discharge the powers and duties of his office. Thereupon Congress shall decide the issue, assembling within forty-eight hours for that purpose if not in session. If the Congress, within twenty-one days after receipt of the latter written declaration, or, if Congress is not in session, within twenty-one days after Congress is required to assemble, determines by two-thirds vote of both Houses that the President is unable to discharge the powers and duties of his office, the Vice President shall continue to discharge the same as Acting President; otherwise, the President shall resume the powers and duties of his office.

Amendment XXVI [1971]

SECTION 1. The right of citizens of the United States, who are eighteen years of age or older, to vote shall not be denied or abridged by the United States or by any State on account of age.

SECTION 2. The Congress shall have power to enforce this article by appropriate legislation.

glossary

Abandoned property. Property the title to which has been surrendered by owner.

Abate. To reduce or put a stop to a nuisance; to reduce or decrease a legacy because the estate is insufficient.

Ab initio. From the beginning. An agreement is said to be "void ab initio" if it at no time had any legal validity.

Abrogate. To annul, repeal.

Abstract. A history of the title to land, consisting of a summary of all transactions that may in any manner affect the land, or any estate or interest therein, together with a statement of all liens or liabilities to which the title may be subject.

Acceleration clause. A provision in a contract or another legal instrument that upon occurrence of a stated event, the time for performance shall be advanced.

Acceptance. The act by which one obligates oneself, or the inference that one intends to obligate oneself, to the terms of a contract offered. Also, the act by which the person on whom a draft is drawn assents to the request of the drawer to pay it or makes himself or herself liable to pay it when it falls due.

Accession. The acquisition of title to all property produced by, or united to, one's original property.

Accessory after the fact. One who, after a felony has been committed, knowingly assists the felon.

Accessory before the fact. One who was not present at the commission of a crime but nevertheless had some part in its commission.

Accommodation paper. A negotiable instrument to which the acceptor, drawer, or indorser has put his or her name, without consideration, for the purpose of benefiting or accommodating some other party who desires to raise money on it and who is to pay the instrument when it becomes due.

Accord and satisfaction. The substitution of a second agreement between contracting parties in satisfaction of a former one, and the execution of the latter agreement. Accord is the agreement to substitute; satisfaction is the performance of the accord.

Accretion. The acquisition of title to additional land when land already owned is built up by gradual deposits made by natural causes.

Acknowledgment. The act by which a party who has executed an instrument goes before a competent officer or court and affirms that its execution was a genuine and voluntary act on the party's part; certification by an authorized person on the face of an instrument that it has been acknowledged.

Action. A suit brought to enforce a right.

Act of God. Any injury or damage that happens by the direct and exclusive operation of natural forces, without human intervention, and that could not have been prevented or escaped from by any reasonable degree of care or diligence.

Adjudication. The giving or pronouncing of a judgment in a case; also the judgment given.

Ad litem. While an action is pending.

Administrator. A person appointed by the court to administer the estate of a deceased person.

Advisory opinion. An opinion rendered by the court when there is no actual controversy before it on a matter submitted to obtain the court's opinion.

Affiant. One who makes or attests to an affidavit.

Affidavit. A written declaration made voluntarily and confirmed by the oath of the party making it, taken before a person having authority to administer such an oath.

A fortiori. By a stronger reason.

Agency. A relationship created by an express or implied contract or by law whereby one party (the principal) delegates the transaction of some business to another person (the agent), who undertakes a commercial transaction for him or her.

Agent. One who represents and acts for another under an agency relationship.

Aleatory contract. A contract under which all risks without exception are assumed by the parties.

Alienability. Transferability.

Alienation. The transfer of property from one person to another.

Allegation. The statement of a party to an action, made in a pleading, setting forth the charges he or she expects to prove.

Allege. To state or charge, to make an allegation.

Allonge. A paper attached to a commercial paper that provides additional space for endorsements.

Alluvion. An addition made to land by accretion.

Alteration. Any material change of the terms of a written instrument.

Ambulatory. Not effective.

Amicus curiae. A friend of the court, a person appointed by the court to assist in litigation by offering his or her opinion on some important matter of law.

Amortize. To provide for the paying of a debt in installments.

Ancillary. Auxiliary.

Annexation. The attachment of personalty to real property in such a manner as to make it part of the realty.

Answer. In a pleading, the written statement made by the defendant setting forth his or her defense.

Antenuptial contract. A contract made prior to marriage between a prospective wife and her prospective husband.

Appeal. The removal of an adjudicated case from a trial court to a court of appellate jurisdiction for the purpose of obtaining a review or retrial.

Appearance. A coming into court as plaintiff or as defendant.

Appellant. A party who takes an appeal from one court to another.

Appellate jurisdiction. The power of a court to hear cases on appeal from another court or an administrative agency.

Appellee. The party in a legal action against whom an appeal is taken.

Appurtenance. An incidental adjunct to some thing that is considered the principal thing.

Arbitration. An agreement to submit a matter in dispute to selected persons and to accept their decision or award as a substitute for the decision of a court.

Arguendo. By way of argument.

Arrest of judgment. The act of staying a judgment or refusing to render judgment in an action at law after the verdict has been given, for some matter appearing on the face of the record that would render the judgment, if given, reversible.

Assault. A threat of an "offensive or injurious touch" to a person made by another person who is able to carry out the threat.

Assignment. The transfer of property or contract rights.

Assumpsit. A form of action brought to recover damages for the nonperformance of a contract.

Assurance. A conveyance whereby an estate being transferred is assured to the transferee with all controversies, doubts, and difficulties affecting his or her quiet enjoyment of the property either prevented or removed.

Attachment. Seizure of the property of a debtor by the service of process upon a third person who is in possession of the property.

Attest. To act as a witness to.

Attestation clause. A clause at the end of an instrument stating that the document has been properly witnessed as to its execution.

"Attractive nuisance." The courts hold a landowner liable for injuries sustained by small children while they were playing on his or her land if they were reasonably attracted there by something on the property.

Averment. A positive statement of fact.

Avulsion. A sudden addition to land by the action of water.

Bad faith. The intent to mislead, deceive, or take unfair advantage of another.

Bailment. The giving up of the possession of personal property to another for some purpose, upon the accomplishment of which the goods are to be redelivered to the owner.

Battery. An unlawful beating, wrongful physical violence, or "offensive touch" inflicted on another without his or her consent.

Bearer. The holder of a commercial paper.

Beneficiary. A person for whose benefit property is held by a trustee, administrator, or executor.

Bequeath. To give personal property to another by a will.

Bequest. A gift of personal property by will.

Bill. A formal, written declaration, complaint, or statement of fact.

Bill in equity. The complaint in an action in equity.

Bill of attainder. A legislative act which inflicts punishment without a judicial trial.

Bill of particulars. A written statement giving the details of the demand for which an action is brought, or of a defendant's counterclaim against such a demand, furnished by one of the parties to the other, either voluntarily or in compliance with a court order.

Bill of sale. Written evidence of the completion of a sale.

Blank indorsement. The signing of one's name to a commercial paper.

Blue-Sky laws. State laws regulating the sale of stocks and bonds to the general public.

Bona fide. In good faith.

Brief. A written statement of a party's case.

Burden of proof. The necessity of proving the facts at issue in court.

Case. A dispute to be resolved in a court of law or equity.

Case law. Legal principles evolved from case decisions.

Cause of action. Perhaps best defined as the fact or facts which give rise to a right of action; in other words, give to a person a right to judicial relief.

Caveat emptor. Let the buyer beware.

Caveat venditor. Let the seller beware.

Certificate of deposit. A writing that acknowledges that the person named has deposited in the issuing bank a specified sum of money and that the bank will repay the money to the named individual, or to his or her order, or to some other person named in the instrument as payee.

Cestui que trust. A person who is the beneficial owner, or beneficiary, of property held in trust.

Charter. A grant of authority to exist as a corporation, issued by a state.

Chattel. An article of personal property.

Chattel mortgage. An instrument of sale of personalty that conveys the title of the property to the mortgagee and specifies the terms of defeasance.

Check. A draft drawn on a deposit of funds in a bank directing the unconditional payment on demand of a sum certain in money to the person named on the instrument, or to his or her order, or to bearer.

Chose in action. A right to personal property that is not in the owner's possession, but to which the owner has a right of action for its possession.

Chose in possession. Personal property that is in the owner's possession and to which he or she has a right of possession.

Circumstantial evidence. Evidence relating to the circumstances of a case from which the jury may deduce what actually happened.

Civil rights. Private rights, protected by law, or members of society.

Class action. A legal action brought by a limited number of persons on behalf of a larger number of persons similarly situated.

Close. An area of land bounded by a visible enclosure.

Closed shop. Such shop exists where the worker must be a member of the union as condition precedent to employment.

Cloud on title. Evidence that a third person has a claim to property.

Codicil. An addition to a will, executed in the same manner as the will itself.

Cognovit. Admission by the defendant of the legitimacy of the plaintiff's claim.

Cognovit note. A promissory note which contains a provision authorizing any attorney, agent, or other representative to confess judgment on the instrument and direct entry of such judgment.

Collateral heirs. Persons descended from a common ancestor but in different lines; cousins, for example.

Collusion. An agreement between two or more persons to defraud, or a conspiracy for some other illegal purpose.

Color of title. Apparent title; the misleading appearance that someone owns something, when in fact legitimate title may lie elsewhere.

Commodatum. A loan of property to be returned in kind and without payment.

Common law. A body of unwritten law based on the customs, habits, and usages of society which is evidenced by the decisions of courts.

Complainant. The plaintiff in a legal or an equitable pleading.

Complaint. The first pleading on the part of the plaintiff in a civil action (corresponding to a declaration in common law). Also, a charge, preferred before a court in order to begin prosecution, that the person named (or a certain person whose name is unknown) has committed a certain offense, together with an offer to prove the facts alleged.

Composition. An agreement between an insolvent debtor and his or her creditors whereby the latter agree to accept an amount less than the whole of their claims, to be distributed pro rata, in discharge and satisfaction of the entire debt.

Compos mentis. Of sound mind.

Compounding a felony. The offense committed by a person who, after having been directly injured by a felony, makes an agreement with the felon that he or she will not prosecute the felon, on the condition that the latter will make reparation or will tender the person a bribe.

Concealment. The failure to volunteer relevant facts not apparent to the other party.

Conditional sale. A sale under the terms of which the passage of title depends on the performance of a stated act.

Condition precedent. The qualification to an agreement whereby an event must occur before a party becomes bound to the terms of the contract; failure of the event to occur releases the party from any contractual obligation.

Condition subsequent. The qualification to an agreement whereby a future event relieves a party from the duty to complete performance of a contract to which he or she is already bound.

Conditions concurrent. Performance by the parties to a contract is to occur "at the same time"; the requirements of the agreement are mutually contingent.

Confession of judgment. The act by which a debtor permits a judgment to be entered against him or her by his or her creditor without any legal proceedings having taken place.

Confusion. The mixing of goods of a similar nature belonging to different owners under such circumstances that the owner of one portion may become the owner of the entirety.

Connivance. Secret or indirect consent to, or permission for, the commission of an unlawful act.

Consanguinity. Blood relationship; the relationship that exists between persons descended from a common ancestor.

Consent order. A judicial decree rendered with the consent of the parties to an action which, in the absence of any fraud, binds the parties to the settlement.

Conservator. The court-appointed guardian of someone's property.

Consideration. The inducement to a contract; the thing of value which induces a contracting party to enter into a contract.

Consignee. One to whom a consignment is made; the person to whom goods are shipped for sale.

Consignor. One who sends or makes a consignment; a shipper of goods.

Conspiracy. An agreement between two or more persons to work together to commit an act; perhaps a criminal act.

Constructive. Inferred, legally interpreted to be so; construed by the courts to have a particular character or meaning other than or beyond what is actually expressed.

Contempt. Conduct that is disruptive of a legislative or judicial proceeding or disobedience of a lawful order of a legislative or judicial body.

Contract. An agreement enforceable in a court of law.

Contract of adhesion. A contract of one-sided bargaining whereby the terms are forced on the weaker party. Contracts of adhesion usually occur in industries that lack competition on the particular provisions of the contract, such as insurance.

Contribution. The sharing of a loss or a payment among several individuals; also reimbursement of a surety who has paid the entire debt by his or her co-sureties.

Contributory negligence. Negligence on the part of the plaintiff that contributes to his or her injury. At common law a person guilty of such negligence cannot recover damages.

Conversion. The unauthorized assumption of ownership of goods belonging to another.

Copyright. A grant to an author or publisher of an exclusive right to publish and sell literary work for a period of years, renewable for a second period.

Corporation. An artificial legal person, created by the state, which for some purposes may act as a natural person and be treated as such.

Corporeal property. Property that is discernible by the senses and may be seen and handled (as opposed to incorporeal property, which cannot be seen or handled and exists only in contemplation).

Corpus delicti. The body of the offense; evidence that a crime has been committed.

Costs. An allowance made to a successful party for his or her court costs in prosecuting or defending a suit. Costs rarely include attorney's fees.

Count. A division of a complaint, declaration, bill of petition wherein a separate cause of action is stated.

Counterclaim. A claim made by the defendant against the plaintiff; a cross-complaint.

"Court above"—"Court below." The "court above" is the court to which a case is removed for review; the "court below" is the court from which the case is removed.

Court of record. A court in which a permanent record is kept of proceedings.

Covenant. An agreement or promise of two or more parties, given in a written, signed delivered deed, by which one party promises the other that something either is done or shall be done, or by which one party stipulates the truth of certain facts. Also, a promise contained in such an agreement.

Covenants of title. Covenants made by the grantor of real property that guarantee such matters as the right to make the conveyance, ownership of the property, and the freedom of the property from encumbrances.

Covert. Covered, protected, sheltered, hidden, or secret.

Coverture. The condition or state of a married woman; her legal status.

Crime. A violation of the law punishable as an offense against the state.

Cross-complaint. A counterclaim made by the defendant against the plaintiff.

Cross-examination. The examination of a party's witness by the attorney for the other party.

Culpable. Evil or criminal.

Curtesy. The common-law right of a husband in the real property of his deceased wife, when there are surviving children who would also be capable of inheriting.

Cypres doctrine. As nearly as possible. When a trust cannot be carried out literally, an effort will be made to approximate the intent of the settler.

Damage. Loss or injury to one's person or property caused by the negligence or intentional actions of another.

Damages. Compensation claimed or awarded in a suit for damage suffered.

Deceit. A fraudulent misrepresentation made to one or more persons who are ignorant of the true facts, to their injury.

Declaration. The initial pleading filed by the plaintiff on beginning an action, also called the complaint or petition.

Deed. An instrument purporting to convey an interest in real property, delivered by the party who is to be bound thereby and accepted by the party to whom the contract is given.

De facto. In fact; actually.

Defalcation. Embezzlement.

Default. Failure to perform.

Defeasance clause. A term of a mortgage that enables the mortgagor to defeat a foreclosure claim of the mortgagee by paying off the amount of his or her obligation.

Defendant. The person against whom a declaration or complaint is filed and who is named therein.

Deficiency judgment. A judgment against a debtor for the amount that still remains due after a mortgage foreclosure that did not discharge the full amount of the debt.

De jure. Of right; legitimate, lawful.

Delictum. A tort, crime, or wrong.

Delivery. The physical or constructive transfer of an instrument or of goods from one person to another.

De minimus. Smallest, being of the smallest size.

Demise. (1) A conveyance of an estate to another for life, for a term of years, or at will; a lease. (2) Death of deceased.

Demonstrative evidence. Evidence that consists of physical objects.

Demurrer. A plea by the defendant that concedes the truth of the facts in the case but alleges that the plaintiff does not have a cause of action.

De novo. Anew, over again.

Deponent. One who takes an oath in writing that certain facts are true.

Deposition. The testimony of a witness in response to questioning not given in court, but taken for use in court.

Derivative action. Action brought by shareholders to enforce a corporate cause of action.

Descent. Hereditary succession.

Devise. A testamentary disposition of real property by the donor's will.

Dictum. A statement of law by a judge in an opinion that is not essential to the determination of that controversy.

Directed verdict. An instruction by the trial judge to the jury to return a verdict in favor of one of the parties to an action. The party requests the instruction.

Disparagement. The unscrupulous sales tactic of enticing a customer to purchase a more expensive item by degrading the quality or value of the item originally sought.

Domestic corporation. A corporation chartered by the state in which it is doing business.

Domicile. The home of a person; the state in which a corporation was incorporated.

Dominant tenement. The tract of land benefited by an easement to which another tract, the servient tenement, is subject.

Dower. An estate for life, to which a widow is entitled in that portion of her husband's estate to which she has not given up her right during the marriage.

Drawee. The person to whom a draft is addressed and who is requested to pay the sum of money therein named.

Drawer. The person drawing a draft and addressing it to the drawee.

Duces tecum. Literally, to bring (the documents) with you.

Due care. The degree of care that a reasonable person can be expected to exercise in order to prevent harm that, under given circumstances, is reasonably foreseeable should such care not be taken.

Duress. A use of force or threat of force that deprives the victim of free will.

Earnest. A payment of a part of the price of goods sold, or a delivery of part of such goods, in order to make a contract binding.

Easement. A right to use the land of another for a special purpose.

Ejectment. An action to determine the title to certain land.

Emancipation. The act by which all rights and obligations in regard to a child are given up by the parents.

Embezzlement. The fraudulent appropriation to one's own use or benefit of property or money entrusted to the appropriator by another.

Eminent domain. The right of the government to take private property for public use in the name of the people.

Encumbrance. A claim or lien that affects title to real property.

Endorsee. The person to whom draft, promissory note, or other commercial paper is assigned by endorsement and who therefore has cause of action if payment is not made.

Endorsement. The signature of a payee, a drawee, or accommodation endorser, or a holder of a negotiable instrument, written on the back of the instrument, in order to transfer it to another.

Endorser. One who makes an endorsement.

Entirety. The whole (as opposed to a part). When land is conveyed to a husband and wife jointly, both own the entirety.

Equitable. Just, fair, or right; existing in equity.

Equity. A field of jurisdiction different in its origin, theory, and methodology from the common law.

Equity of redemption. The right of the mortgagor of an estate to redeem it, after the estate has been forfeited by a breach of a condition of the mortgage, by paying the amount of the debt, the interest, and other costs of foreclosure.

Error. A mistaken judgment or incorrect belief of a trial court as to the existence or effect of matters of fact, or a false or mistaken conception or application of the law. (1) *Assignment of errors.* A statement of the errors upon which an appellant will reply, submitted to assist an appellate court in its examination of the transcript of a case under appeal. (2) *Harmless error.* An error committed during the progress of a trial that was not prejudicial to the rights of the party assigning it and for which therefore, an appellate court will not reverse a judgment. (3) *Reversible error.* An error in original proceedings for which an appellate court will reverse the judgment under review.

Escheat. The reversion of the property of a decedent to the government when there is no legal heir.

Escrow. A deed that is held by a third person until a specified condition is fulfilled.

Estate. An interest in land or in any other subject of property.

Estoppel. A rule of law designed to prevent a person from denying a fact that his or her conduct influenced others to believe was true.

Et ux. And his wife.

Eviction. The act of depriving a person of the possession of lands held by him or her, pursuant to a court order.

Evidence. Any type of proof legally presented at a trial through witnesses, records, documents, or physical objects, for the purpose of inducing belief in the mind of the court or the jury as to the truth or falsity of the facts at issue.

Exception. A formal objection to the action of the court raised during a trial, implying that the objecting party does not agree with the decision of the court and will seek a reversal of the judgment handed down.

Ex contractu. From or out of a contract. The term is usually used to refer to a cause of action arising from a contract.

Exculpatory. Tending or serving to exculpate or clear from alleged fault or guilt.

Ex delicto. From a tort or crime.

Executed. Completed; fully carried into effect.

Executor. A person appointed by a testator to carry out the directions and requests in his or her will and to dispose of the testator's property according to the testamentary provisions of the will.

Executory. Something that is yet to be executed or performed; that which is incomplete or dependent on a future performance or event.

Exemplary damages. Damages in excess of the amount needed to compensate the plaintiff for his or her injury, awarded to punish the defendant for malicious or willful conduct.

Exemption. A privilege allowed by law to a debtor by which he or she may hold a certain amount of property or certain classes of property free from all liability—free from seizure and sale by court order or from attachment by creditors.

Ex parte. On one side only; by one party; done for, or on behalf of, one party only.

Ex post facto law. A law which, in its operation, makes that criminal which was not so at the time of the act, or which increases the punishment, or, in short, which, in relation to the offense or its consequences, alters the situation of a party to his or her disadvantage.

Express. Set forth in direct and appropriate language (as opposed to that which is implied from conduct).

Ex rel (Ex relatione). On the relation or information.

Extant. Currently or actually existing.

Featherbedding. The requiring of an employer, usually under a union rule or safety statute, to pay more employees than are needed or to require payment without performing work.

Fee simple. The most complete form of ownership of real property.

Fee tail. A common-law form of inheritance under which property descends only to a certain class of heirs.

Felony. An offense punishable by confinement in prison or by death, or an offense that statute has expressly deemed a felony.

Fiction. An assumption of the law.

Finis opus coronat. A finish, a fine, the end work, labor, benefit.

Fisc. Fiscal, belonging to the public treasury or revenue.

Fixture. Personal property attached to real property in such a manner that it is considered part of the realty.

F.O.B. Free on board. A shipping term designating a seller's intention to deliver goods on board a car or ship at a designated place without charge to the buyer.

Forcible detainer. The offense of keeping possession of lands by force and without legal authority.

Forcible entry. The offense or a private wrong committed by taking possession of lands by force and without legal authority.

Foreclosure. A proceeding by which the rights of the mortgagee of real property are enforced against the mortgagor.

Foreign corporation. A corporation created by, or organized under, the laws of another state government.

Forgery. The fraudulent making of an instrument that, if genuine, would appear to create contractual liability in another.

Franchise. Any special privilege conferred by a governmental body on an individual or a corporation.

Fraud. A knowing and intentional misinterpretation of a material fact made in order to deprive another of his or her rights or to induce him or her to enter into a contract.

Fungible goods. Goods of a class in which any unit is the equivalent of any other unit.

Future estate. An estate that will not take effect until the termination of the present estate.

Garnishment. See ***Attachment.***

General creditor. A creditor who has an unsecured claim against a debtor.

General issue. A plea that denies every material allegation in the plaintiff's complaint.

General verdict. The ordinary form of verdict, either for the plaintiff or for the defendant, without answering special submitted questions.

Gift causa mortis. A gift made by the donor in contemplation of his or her supposedly imminent death.

Good faith. Honest intentions.

Grant. To convey a property interest to another.

Gratuitous bailment. A bailment without legal considerations.

Gravamen. The material part or gist of a charge.

Guaranty. A promise to be responsible for the performance of another.

Habeas corpus. A writ obtained to test whether a prisoner is being lawfully held.

Habendum clause. The clause in a deed describing the estate granted.

Hearsay. Evidence attested by a witness that is derived not from personal knowledge but from what others have told the witness.

Heirs. Persons entitled to receive an estate or a portion of an estate that a decedent has not effectively disposed of by will.

Hereditaments. Things capable of being inherited.

Holder. The person in possession of a negotiable instrument.

Holographic will. A will entirely handwritten by the testator.

Homestead. Real estate occupied as a home. It is exempt within certain limitations from attachment by creditors.

Hung jury. A jury that is unable to agree on a verdict.

Hypothecation. Deposit of stocks, bonds, or negotiable instruments with another to secure the repayment of a loan, and with the power to sell the same in case the debt is not paid to reimburse the person with the proceeds.

Illusory. Appears to be but is not.

Immunity. Freedom from legal duties and obligations.

Impanel. To make a list of those who have been selected for a jury.

Implied. Found from the circumstances of the case.

In camera. In chambers; secretly.

Inchoate. Not perfect, nor perfected.

Inculpatory. Incriminating.

Indemnify. To make good another's loss caused by a specified act or omission.

Indemnity. That which is given or granted to a person to prevent his or her suffering damage.

Indicia. A sign or indication.

Indictment. The formal written accusation of a crime, presented by a grand jury.

Indorsee. See endorsee.

Indorsement. See endorsement.

Indorser. See endorser.

Infant. A person under lawful age; a minor.

Information. In criminal law, an accusation by a public officer (as distinguished from a finding by a grand jury) that is made the basis of a prosecution of a crime.

Injunction. An order issued by a court of equity directing a person or a group to do, or to refrain from doing, a specified act.

Injury. Any wrong or damage to the person, rights, reputation, or property of another.

In pari delicto. In equal fault; equally guilty.

In personam. Against a specific person (as opposed to *In rem*).

In re. In the matter.

In rem. Against a thing; directed at specific property or at a specific right or status.

Insolvency. A state in which debts and liabilities exceed assets.

Interlocutory appeal. Incidence to a suit still pending; as an order or decree, made during the progress of a case, which does not amount to a final decision.

Interpleader. A form of action by which a third person who holds property or monies to which he or she has no claim and against whom conflicting claims are made may bring the complaining parties into court to settle their claims.

Inter alia. Among other things or matters.

Inter se. Between or among themselves.

Inter vivos. Any transaction that takes place among living persons.

Intestate. Without a will.

Intestate succession. A distribution, directed by statute, of property owned by a decedent and not effectively disposed of by will.

Ipso facto. By the fact itself.

Jeopardy. Danger, peril. A person is said to be in jeopardy when officially charged with a crime before a court of law.

Jointly. Acting together. When persons are jointly liable, they all must be sued or none can be sued.

Jointly and severally. Acting together and separately. Anyone so liable can sue (or be sued) with or without the others joining (or being joined) in the action.

Joint tenancy. An estate in entirety held by two or more persons with the right of survivorship.

Judgment. The final order of a court, entered upon the completion of an action.

Judgment note. A note authorizing a judgment to be entered against a debtor if the note is not paid when it falls due.

Judgment n.o.v. See ***Non obstante veredicto.***

Judgment on the pleadings. A judgment entered on the request of either party to an action after the pleadings have been filed, when it is apparent from the content of the pleadings that one party is entitled to a decision in his or her favor without proceeding further.

Judicial sale. A sale made under a court order by an officer appointed to make the sale.

Jurisdiction. The power and authority conferred on a court, either constitutionally or by statute.

Justiciable. Liable to trial in a court of justice.

Laches. An equitable principle that discourages delay in the enforcement of legal rights.

"Last clear chance." In accident cases, the courts hold that if the defendant had the last clear chance to avoid an accident, he or she is liable even though the plaintiff may have been guilty of contributory negligence.

Leading question. A question that suggests to the witness what the response should be.

Lease. A conveyance of lands or tenements to a person for life, for a term of years, or at will, in consideration of a return of rent or some other form of compensation.

Leasehold. An estate held under a lease; an estate for a fixed term of years.

Legacy. A bequest of personal property by will.

Legal tender. A medium of exchange that the law compels a creditor to accept in payment of a debt when it is legally offered to the creditor by the debtor.

Lessee. One to whom a lease is made.

Lessor. One who grants a lease.

Let. To demise, to lease.

Letters of administration. The formal instrument that appoints an administrator, issued by the court having jurisdiction over an estate. They empower him or her to enter upon the discharge of administratorial duties.

Letters testamentary. The formal instruction that appoints an executor, issued by the court having jurisdiction over a decedent's property. They empower the executor to enter upon the discharge of his or her duties as executor.

Levy. To exact, collect, gather, seize.

Lex loci. The law of the place where an accident occurred.

Lex loci contractus. The law of the place where a contract was made.

Lex loci fori. The law of the place where an action was brought.

License. A personal privilege on authority to do something which would otherwise be inoperative.

Lien. A claim against, or a right to, property.

Life estate. An estate the duration of which is limited to the life of the person named in the grant; a freehold estate that cannot be passed on to one's heirs.

Life tenant. One who holds an estate in lands for the period of his or her own life or that of another person named.

Limitation. Anything that defines or limits, either by words or by implication, the time during which an estate granted may be enjoyed.

Lineal heirs. Those directly descended from an ancestor; children or grandchildren, for example.

Liquidated. Determined, clarified, fixed.

Liquidated damages. A sum stipulated and agreed upon by the parties, at the time of entering into a contract, as being payable as compensation for loss suffered in the event of a breach.

Lis pendens. A suit pending; the filing of legal notice that there is a dispute about the title to property.

Maker. One who executes a legal instrument or promissory note.

Malfeasance. The performance of an unlawful act.

Malum in se. An act that is wrong in itself.

Malum prohibitum. An act that is prohibited by law.

Mandamus. A court order compelling an individual to fulfill an official duty.

Marshalling assets. The distributing of a partner's assets upon termination of a partnership so as to obtain the greatest benefit for creditors.

Maturity. The due date of an instrument.

Mechanic's lien. A claim created by statute for the benefit of persons supplying materials for the construction of a building, giving them a lien on the building.

Mens rea. The state of mind of the actor.

Merchantable. Of good quality; salable in the regular course of business or intended purpose.

Merger. A joining of two corporations whereby one company retains its original identity.

Mesne. Intermediate, intervening.

Metes and bounds. The boundary lines of land.

Minor. A person who is under the age of legal competence specified by statute; usually, a person under 21 years of age.

Misdemeanor. A crime that is neither a felony nor treason.

Misfeasance. The performing of a lawful act in an improper manner.

Misprision. Maladministration, concealing, embezzlement.

Misrepresentation. An intentionally false statement of fact.

Mitigation of damages. The duty of the plaintiff to avoid increasing his or her damages and to limit them where possible.

Moiety. One half.

Moot case. A hypothetical or nonexisting controversy.

Motion to dismiss. To dismiss the defendant from the suit for lack of good cause shown to retain.

Motion to quash. See ***motion to dismiss;*** usually only consider questions of law as apparent on the face of the record.

Mutuality. Reciprocation of understanding. Both parties to a contract must have a clear understanding of the legal obligations of their agreement.

Necessaries. That which is reasonably needed to maintain one's accustomed standard of living.

Negative covenant. An agreement in a deed to refrain from doing something.

Negligence. The failure to do something that a reasonable person would do or the commission of an act that a reasonable person would not commit, that results, in an ordinary and natural sequence, in damage to another.

Negotiable instrument. An instrument containing an obligation for the payment of a sum certain in money, the legal title to which may be transferred from one person to another by endorsement and delivery by the holder or by delivery only.

Nil debit. A plea that the defendant owes nothing.

Nisi prius. A trial court (as distinguished from an appellate court).

Nolo contendere. Not contesting the charge, it has the effect of a guilty plea in a criminal action.

Nominal damages. A token sum awarded to the plaintiff when he or she has suffered no actual damage.

Non compos mentis. Not sound of mind; insane.

Non est factum. A plea that a note sued on was never made or executed.

Nonfeasance. The neglect or failure to do something that one ought to do.

Non obstante veredicto. A judgment given that is contrary to the verdict of the jury.

Nonsuit. An abandonment of suit by the plaintiff.

Novation. Release by agreement from a contractual obligation by substitution of a third party for the original obligor.

Nudum pactum. An agreement or promise made without consideration and thus not legally enforceable under normal circumstances.

Nuisance. Improper personal conduct, or the unreasonable use by a person of his or her own property, that obstructs the rights of others or of the public and produces material inconvenience or hardship.

Nuncupative will. An oral will.

Obliteration. An erasure or crossing out that makes all or portions of a will impossible to read. Sections so altered and considered to be revoked when the changes were made by the testator for the purpose of revocation.

Occupation. Taking possession of property; a method of acquiring title to personal property that is in an ownerless state.

Operation of law. The automatic attaching of certain legal consequences to certain facts.

Opinion evidence. The conclusions that a witness draws from what he or she has observed (as opposed to the observation itself).

Option. A contract to hold an offer open for a fixed period of time.

Ordinance. A statutory enactment of the legislative branch of a municipal government.

Ostensible agency. An implied agency that exists when a supposed principal by his or her conduct induces another to believe that a third person is the principal's agent, although the principal never actually employed him or her.

Ostensible partner. A partner whose name is publicly made known (as opposed to a silent partner).

Parens patriae. The "father of the country" constituted in law by the state; in the capacity of legal guardian of persons not sui juris.

Parol. Oral, spoken.

Parol evidence rule. The construction that parol evidence is not considered by the courts to alter a written contract that is complete on its face.

Partition. A division of real property between co-owners.

Patent. The giving of a privilege or property by a government to one or more individuals. (1) The conveyance by which a government grants lands in the public domain to an individual. (2) The privilege given to an inventor allowing him or her the exclusive right to make and sell the invention for a definite period of time.

Pawn. A bailment of goods to a creditor as security for a debt; a pledge.

Payee. One to whom a negotiable instrument is made payable.

Payer, payor. One who pays a negotiable instrument.

Per curiam opinion. A written decision by the court which is not signed by the authoring judge or justice.

Perform. To do any action, other than making payment, in discharge of a contract.

Performance. The fulfillment of a contractual obligation according to the terms of the agreement.

Perpetual succession. The right of a corporation to carry on its corporate existence for an unlimited period of time.

Per se. By itself; standing alone; not related to other matters.

Personal jurisdiction. Court power to deal with the person by reason of proper service of process (summons).

Per stirpes. The distribution of a decedent's estate according to the number of families, as opposed to number of individuals.

Petition. The first pleading by the plaintiff in a civil case, also called the complaint.

Petty jury, petit jury. The jury in a trial court.

Plaintiff. One who brings an action.

Plaintiff in error. A party who bases an appeal on an error in a judgment rendered by a trial court.

Plead. To make, deliver, or file a pleading.

Pleadings. The papers filed by the parties in an action.

Pledge. A bailment of goods as security for a debt.

Pledgee. One to whom the goods are pledged.

Pledgor. The party delivering the goods in a pledge.

Police power. The power of the state to enact laws for the protection of the public health, safety, welfare, and morals.

Polling the jury. Asking each member of the jury in open court how he or she voted on the verdict.

Possessory lien. The right to retain property as security for a debt.

Postdate. To record a date later than the date of execution of an instrument.

Precatory. Indicate a desire or wish; opposite of command.

Preference. The payment of money or the transfer of property to one creditor in priority to other creditors.

Prescription. The acquisition of title to incorporeal hereditaments by virtue of having used or enjoyed them for a long period of time.

Presentment. The exhibition of a draft to the drawee for his or her acceptance or to the acceptor for payment; also, the exhibition of a promissory note to the maker, with a demand for payment.

Presumption. An inference of the truth or falsehood of a proposition or a fact, in the absence of actual certainty as to its truth or falsehood, by a process of probable reasoning.

Prima facie. At first sight, on first appearance; presumably.

Privileged communication. A communication concerning which a witness may refuse to testify in open court because of his or her relationship with the person from whom he or she received the information; a communication between a lawyer and client, for example.

Privity. An immediate relationship. A party to a contract is said to have "privity" with regard to the making of the contract.

Probate. The act or process of proving the validity of a will.

Process. A court order informing the defendant that he or she is required to appear in court.

Proffered evidence. Testimony or documentation presented to the trial court which is ruled inadmissible but is entered into the record for consideration on appeal.

Promissory note. A promise in writing to pay a specified sum within a certain time, on demand, or at sight, to a named person, to his or her order, or to bearer.

Promoters. The organizers of a corporation.

Prosecute. To bring suit and carry on an action against a person in court.

Pro tanto. For so much; as far as it goes.

Protest. A formal, written statement, made by a notary at the request of the holder of a commercial paper, that the draft or note was presented for payment (or acceptance) and that payment (or acceptance) was refused. The protest also states the reasons, if any, given for the dishonor.

Proximate cause. That act which is the effective cause of an injury; an act from which the injury could reasonably be expected to result.

Proximate damage. Damage that is a reasonably forseeable result of an action.

Prurient interest. To itch or crave wantonly and restlessly or to be lascivious (lewd, lustful), in thought or desire.

Punitive damages. Damages over and above the amount necessary to compensate an injured party. They are imposed to punish a wrongdoer.

Qualified acceptance. A conditional or modified acceptance of a draft that in some way changes the terms of the instrument.

Qualified endorsement. An endorsement containing the words "without recourse," or words of similar import, evidencing the endorser's intent not to be bound should the primary party fail to pay.

Quantum meruit. As much as he deserved.

Quasi. As if it were; having the characteristics of.

Quasi contract. A contract implied in law.

Quid pro quo. Something for something; this for that.

Quiet title. An action brought to settle claims against the title to a piece of property.

Quit-claim deed. A deed purporting to transfer whatever interest, if any, the grantor has in the property concerned.

Quorum. The minimum number of persons that must be present before business can be trasacted.

Quo warranto. An action compelling someone (usually a corporation) to show by whose authority he or she is transacting business.

Ratification. The acceptance of responsibility for, and the undertaking of the obligations incurred by, a previous act committed either by oneself or by one's agent.

Real property. A general term for land and everything attached to it.

Receipt. Acceptance of something delivered.

Receiver. A person appointed by the court to collect the rents and profits of land, or the growth of personal estates, or to transact other business that the court thinks not reasonable that either party should transact or that a party is incompetent to transact.

Recognizance. An obligation entered into before a court or magistrate to do a particular act—for example, to appear in court or to pay a debt.

Recoupment. The right of the defendant to obtain a reduction in the amount of the plaintiff's damages because the plaintiff, too, has failed to comply with certain obligations or conditions of the contract.

Recovery. The collection of a debt through an action at law. (See also ***Right of recovery.***)

Redemption. A buying back of property. A mortgage conveys the title to property to the morgagee, subject to a right of redemption of the mortgagor. The mortgagor has a right to defeat the conveyance of the title by paying the amount of the debt secured by the mortgage.

Reimbursement. A surety's right to be repaid by his or her principal for debts paid or the principal's behalf.

Release. The giving up of a right or privilege by the person in whom it existed to the person against whom it might have been demanded or enforced.

Remainder. An estate that takes effect and may be enjoyed only after another estate is determined.

Remand. To send a case back to a trial court for a new trial in accordance with the decision of an appellate court.

Remedial. Pertaining to a legal remedy, or to the form of procedural details of such a remedy, that is to be taken after a legal or an equitable wrong has been committed.

Remedy. The means by which the violation of a right is prevented or compensated for.

Replevin. A personal action brought to recover possession of goods taken from one unlawfully.

Rescission. Cancellation of a contract by one or both parties.

Residuary. Constituting the residue; entitled to the residue.

Residuary devisee. The person named in a will to take all the real property that remains after the specified devises have been granted.

Residuary estate. The part of a testator's estate and effects that remains after all particular devises and bequests have been made.

Residuary legatee. The person to whom a testator bequeaths the residue of his or her personal estate after the payment to all other legacies which are specifically mentioned in the will.

Respondeat superior. A legal maxim that a master is liable in certain cases for the wrongful acts of his servant, and a principal for those of his or her agent.

Respondent. One who makes an answer to or argues against an appeal.

Reversal. The decision of an appellate court to annul or vacate a judgment or decree of a trial court.

Revocation. The recall of some power, authority, or thing granted; also, the destruction or voiding of a legal document.

Right of entry. The right of taking or resuming possession of land by entering peaceably on it.

Right of recovery. A right of action deriving from a legal wrong committed in a given case.

Right to redeem. The right of a debtor whose property has been mortgaged, then sold to another to pay a debt, to repurchase the property.

"Right to work." Section 14(b) of the National Labor Relations Act leaves to the various states the power to enact laws limiting or prohibiting labor agreements which make union membership a condition of employment. Such state laws simply declare unlawful any agreement which conflicts with the policy that individuals have the right to work without abridgement on account of nonmembership in any labor organization.

Riparian. Relates to the bank of a river.

"Run with the land." Certain covenants in a deed to land are deemed to "run" or pass with the land in order that whoever owns the land is bound by or entitled to the benefit of the covenants, even though the agreements are not in the public record.

Sale or return. A sale in which, although title passes to the buyer at the time of the agreement, the buyer has the option of returning title to the seller.

Satisfaction. The act of discharging an obligation owed to a party by paying what is due or awarded to him or her by the judgment of a court.

Scienter. Knowingly.

Scintilla. A spark, a remaining particle; hence, the least evidence.

Scire facias. A judicial writ, founded upon some record, requiring the person against whom it is brought to show cause why the party bringing it should not be able to enforce or annul that record.

Seal. An impression on wax or some other substance used at common law to authenticate legal documents.

Seisin. Possession with the intention to claim a freehold interest.

Set-off. A counterclaim, a cross-demand.

Severable contract. A contract one part of which may be separated from the other parts and performed or enforced alone.

Severalty. The sole ownership of real property.

Severance. The separating of anything from the land.

Short sale. A sale of stock which the seller does not possess at the time, but which he or she expects to acquire subsequently for delivery under his or her contract.

(sic). So, thus, simply, in this manner. (Confirms a word that might be questioned.)

Silent partner. A partner whose name or connection with a firm is not known to the public (as opposed to an ostensible or acknowledged partner).

Simple contract. A contract based on consideration, not on any special formal document.

Slander. Oral defamation of character.

Slander per se. Words slanderous in themselves whether or not damage can be proven to result from them. To have a case, it is necessary merely to allege that they have been published.

Special agent. An agent authorized to conduct a specific transaction.

Special appearance. A person's appearance in court for a specific purpose, without his or her submitting to the jurisdiction of the court.

Special damages. Damages that are the actual and natural, although not the necessary, result of the proximate cause of an injury. They must be proven according to the special circumstances of a particular case.

Specific performance. An equitable remedy by which a contracting party is compelled to perform obligations under the terms of the contract.

Standing to sue. The assertion of a bona fide claim in a court of proper jurisdiction.

Stare decisis. To stand by that which has been decided. A case decision serves as a legal precedent in the deciding of subsequent similar cases.

State of the forum. The state in which the court sits or has its hearing or forum.

Statute of frauds. A statute that requires certain contracts to be in writing before they will be accepted as valid, enforceable contracts. It is designed to prevent contracts based on perjured testimony.

Statute of limitations. A statute that limits the period of time in which an enforceable cause of action may be brought.

Stipulation. An agreement between opposing counsel that they will accept certain things in evidence without the necessity of proof.

Stoppage in transitu. The right of an unpaid seller to stop goods before they arrive at the buyer's destination.

Sua sponte. On its own responsibility or motion, as an order "sua sponte" made by a court without prior motion by either party.

Subrogation. The substitution of one thing for another, or of one person in place of another, with respect to rights, claims, or securities.

Subscribe. To write one's name at the bottom or end of a writing.

Substantive law. That part of the law that creates, defines, and regulates rights (as opposed to procedural law, which prescribes methods enforcing rights or obtaining remedies for this invasion).

Sui generis. Of its own kind of class.

Sui juris. Of his own right; having legal capacity to manage his own affairs.

Summary. Immediate; rendering without a hearing.

Summary judgment. A judgment entered by a court when no substantial dispute of fact exists; consequently, there is no need for a trial.

Summary proceeding. A brief proceeding, usually conducted with less formality than a normal court proceeding.

Summons. A writ served on a defendant to secure his or her appearance in court.

Supra. Noted above or previously.

Surety. A person who makes himself or herself liable for the obligations of another.

Survivorship. The right of a surviving tenant (or tenants) to take the share (or shares) of a tenant who dies.

Tangible. Having physical qualities.

Tenancy at sufferance. An illegal staying-on by a tenant after a lease has expired.

Tenancy at will. The possession of land for an indefinite period of time that may be terminated at any time by either party without notice being given.

Tenancy for years. A tenancy for any fixed period of time. (The period may be less than a year.)

Tenancy from year to year. A tenancy that continues indefinitely from year to year (or any other period of time) until terminated.

Tenancy in common. The ownership of property by two or more persons.

Tenancy in partnership. The form of ownership of partnership property that was created by the Uniform Partnership Act.

Tender. An unconditional offer by a party who is able to complete an obligation.

Tenor. The true meaning or effect of an instrument.

Terminable fee. An estate that may be terminated upon the occurrence of some event.

Testamentary. To take effect at death.

Testamentary capacity. The capacity to make a will.

Testate. Having left a will.

Testate succession. The distribution of a testator's estate according to the terms of his or her will.

Testator, testatrix. One who makes a will.

Third-party beneficiary. A third person who is directly benefited by the making of a contract to which he or she is not a party.

Toll the statute. To stop the operation of the time period specified by the statute of limitations.

Tort. A wrong committed upon the person or property of another; an invasion of a private right.

Tort feasor. One who commits a tort.

Tortious. Wrongful.

Transcript. A copy of a writing; a court record.

Transitory action. An action brought against a defendant in any county where service of process may be obtained.

Trespass. (1) An injury to the person, property, or rights of another. (2) A common-law action for money damages for injury to one's person, property, or rights.

Trier of fact. Usually a jury.

Trover. An action against a person who has wrongfully converted another's goods to his or her own use. The action is for damages, not for the return of the goods.

Trust. An equitable right to land or other property, held for a beneficiary by another person, in whom the legal title rests.

Trust deed. An instrument that is substituted for and serves as a mortgage, by which the legal title to real property is placed in one or more trustees, to secure the repayment of a sum of money or the performance of other conditions.

Trustee. One appointed to execute a trust; a person in whom an estate interest, or power is vested under an agreement that he or she shall administer or exercise it for the benefit or use of another.

Ultra vires. Beyond the powers conferred on a corporation by its charter.

Undisclosed principal. A principal whose existence and identity are unknown to third parties.

Undue influence. Dominance of one person in a fiduciary relationship over another, sufficient to inhibit or destroy the weaker party's free will.

Unilateral contract. A contract consisting of a promise made by one party in return for an act to be done by the other.

Unincorporated association. A combination of two or more persons to achieve a common end.

Union shop. Such shop exists where the employer is permitted to employ a nonunion worker but such worker is required to join the union as a requisite to continuing employment.

Universal agent. An agent authorized to commit any act that the principal himself or herself might lawfully perform.

Usque ad coelum. As far as heaven—referring to a rule in law that the owner of land owns the air space above it indefinitely upward.

Usury. The charging of an illegally high interest rate.

Vacation of judgment. The setting aside of a judgment by a court.

Valid. Legally sufficient.

Vendee. A purchaser, a buyer.

Vendor. A seller.

Venire. To appear in court. A writ of venire is used to summon a jury.

Veracity. Truthfulness.

Verdict. The decision of a jury.

Vested. Accrued, settled, absolute; not contingent upon anything; having an immediate right to the enjoyment of property.

Void. Having no legal effect; not binding.

Voidable. Subject to being declared ineffectual. A contract is voidable when one party has grounds for refusing to perform his or her obligations.

Voidable preference. A preference given by a bankrupt person or firm to one creditor over others. It may be set aside by the trustee in bankruptcy.

Voir dire examination. An examination to determine the qualifications of a juror or witness.

Volenti non fit injuria. One who consents cannot be injured.

Voluntary nonsuit. A means available to the plaintiff for stopping a trial in a civil suit without prejudice to bring the suit again.

Waiver. The giving up of a legal right.

Ward. A person under the care of court.

Warrant. A guaranty that certain facts are true as represented.

Warranty of authority. An implied warranty that an agent possesses the authority that he or she represents himself or herself as possessing.

Waste. A reduction in value of property caused by the person in possession.

Watered stock. Stock recorded in the books of a corporation as being fully paid when in fact it is not because the property received by the corporation is valued less than the value of the stock issued.

Will. The legal expression of a person's wishes regarding the disposition of his or her property after death.

Witness. An individual who testifies under oath in a legal action.

Writ of certiorari. An order from an appellate court to a lower court requesting the record of a case that is to be reviewed by the appellate court.

Writ of entry. An action to recover the possession of real property.

Writ of error. The order of an appellate court authorizing a lower court to remit to it the official record of the proceedings in a case in which an error sufficient to invalidate the verdict is claimed.

index